Use the attached order cards to order your own or extra subscriptions to **SPECIAL EDUCATION AND THE HANDICAPPED** ... the monthly newsletter service reporting the very latest special education school law cases and late-breaking legislation.

Order an extra subscription for the Assistant Superintendent, the school Personnel Officer, a board member or the faculty lounge. The attached order cards may be removed from the book for your order.

Yes, please send me ______ subscriptions to **SPECIAL EDUCATION AND THE HANDICAPPED**... the monthly newsletter service reporting the very latest special education school law cases and late-breaking legislation.

☐ Send two years at $158.00 (your best price)

☐ Send one year at $88.00

Name ____________________

Title ____________________

Address ____________________

City ____________________ **State** ____ **Zip** ________

Purchase Order Number, if needed ____________________

Send order and check payable to: DATA RESEARCH, INC.,
P.O. Box 490, Rosemount, MN 55068

Yes, please send me ______ subscriptions to **SPECIAL EDUCATION AND THE HANDICAPPED**... the monthly newsletter service reporting the very latest special education school law cases and late-breaking legislation.

☐ Send two years at $158.00 (your best price)

☐ Send one year at $88.00

Name ____________________

Title ____________________

Address ____________________

City ____________________ **State** ____ **Zip** ________

Purchase Order Number, if needed ____________________

Send order and check payable to: DATA RESEARCH, INC.,
P.O. Box 490, Rosemount, MN 55068

OUR GUARANTEE: If you are not satisfied with **SPECIAL EDUCATION AND THE HANDICAPPED**, for any reason, we will refund the unused portion of your subscription payment.

HANDICAPPED STUDENTS AND SPECIAL EDUCATION

FIFTH EDITION

"This publication is designed to provide accurate and authoritative information in regard to the subject matter covered. It is sold with the understanding that the publisher is not engaged in rendering legal, accounting or other professional service. If legal advice or other expert assistance is required, the services of a competent professional person should be sought."—*from a Declaration of Principles jointly adopted by a Committee of the American Bar Association and a Committee of Publishers and Associations.*

Published by
Data Research, Inc.
P.O. Box 490
Rosemount, Minnesota 55068

OTHER TITLES PUBLISHED
BY DATA RESEARCH, INC.:

Deskbook Encyclopedia of American School Law
Private School Law in America

First edition published 1984

Printed in the United States of America

Library of Congress Cataloging-in-Publication Data

Handicapped students and special education.

Includes index.
1. Special education—Law and legislation—United States. 2. Handicapped children—Education—Law and legislation—United States. I. Data Research, Inc. (Rosemount, Minn.)
KF4210.H36 1988 344.73'0791 88-20267
ISBN 0-939675-08-0 347.304791
ISBN 0-939675-07-2 (pbk.)

PREFACE

Federal law requires that school districts provide each handicapped child with a free appropriate education. This volume, *Handicapped Students and Special Education,* has been published in response to the need of school administrators and others involved in providing special education services to have a reference available when confronted with any of the multitude of problems in the special education area. The textual development of this new and revised Fifth Edition is based upon examination of state and federal appellate court decisions in the field of special education. In addition, this volume contains the full text of the Education for All Handicapped Children Act of 1975, as amended through 1988, as well as the full text of the major federal regulations governing the education of handicapped children. This volume also contains the full text of the five landmark U.S. Supreme Court decisions dealing with special education. *School Board of Nassau County v. Arline*, has been included because of its impact on cases involving students and employees with AIDS. The full legal citation is given for each case reported, and all cases have been indexed and placed in a Table of Cases following the Table of Contents. A Subject Matter Table of Recent Law Review Articles is also included.

The intent of this volume is to provide professional educators and lawyers with access to important case, statutory and regulatory law in the field of special education and handicapped student rights.

EDITORIAL STAFF
DATA RESEARCH, INC.

INTRODUCTORY NOTE ON THE JUDICIAL SYSTEM

In order to allow the reader to determine the relative importance of a judicial decision, the cases included in ***Handicapped Students and Special Education, Fifth Edition,*** identify the particular court from which a decision has been issued. For example, a case decided by a state supreme court generally will be of greater significance than a state circuit court case. Hence, a basic knowledge of the structure of our judicial system is important to an understanding of school law.

The most common system, used by nearly all states and also the federal judiciary, is as follows: a legal action is commenced in **district court** (sometimes called a trial court, county court, common pleas court or superior court) where a decision is initially reached. The case may then be appealed to the **court of appeals** (or appellate court), and in turn this decision may be appealed to the **supreme court**.

Several states, however, do not have a court of appeals; lower court decisions are appealed directly to the state's supreme court. Additionally, some states have labeled their courts in a nonstandard fashion.

In Maryland, the highest court is called the Court of Appeals.

In the state of New York, the trial court is called the Supreme Court. Decisions of this court may be appealed to the Supreme Court, Appellate Division. The highest court in New York is the Court of Appeals.

Pennsylvania has perhaps the most complex court system. The lowest state court is the Court of Common Pleas. Depending on the circumstances of the case, appeals may be taken to either the Commonwealth Court or the Superior Court. In certain instances the Commonwealth Court functions as a trial court as well as an appellate court. The Superior Court, however, is strictly an intermediate appellate court. The highest court in Pennsylvania is the Supreme Court.

While supreme court decisions are generally regarded as the last word in legal matters, it is important to remember that trial court and appeals court decisions also create important legal precedents.

TABLE OF CONTENTS

Page

Page

Page

Page

TABLE OF CASES

TABLE OF CASES

TABLE OF CASES

TABLE OF CASES

CHAPTER ONE
RIGHT OF THE HANDICAPPED TO AN EDUCATION

I. THE EDUCATION FOR ALL HANDICAPPED CHILDREN ACT OF 1975.

The Education for All Handicapped Children Act (EAHCA)* was enacted by Congress to assist the states in providing handicapped children with a free public education appropriate to their needs. Local school districts and states may be sued by handicapped children, or their parents or guardians, if a free appropriate public education is not provided. A recent amendment to the EAHCA, the Handicapped Children's Protection Act of 1986 (HCPA), encourages the handicapped to bring such lawsuits by requiring the losing defendants in EAHCA cases to pay attorney's fees and/or money damages to handicapped children. The Education of the Handicapped Act Amendments of 1986 brought handicapped infants and preschool children within the EAHCA's coverage.

A. Background

The EAHCA establishes minimum requirements which must be complied with in order for states to be eligible to receive financial assistance. First, each state must have "in effect a policy that assures all handicapped children the right to a free appropriate public education" [20 U.S.C. § 1412(1)], and must develop a plan which details the policies and procedures which insure the provision of that right [§ 1412(2)]. Each state must also establish the requisite procedural safeguards [§ 1412(5)], and must insure that local educational agencies in this state will establish the individualized educational programs (IEP's) required by the Act [§ 1412(4)]. Individual states are responsible for establishing and maintaining education standards for the handicapped [§ 1412(6)]. The Act additionally requires that each state must formulate a plan for educating its handicapped children which must be sub-

*Sometimes referred to as the EHA (Education of the Handicapped Act).

mitted to and approved by the Secretary of Education before the state is entitled to federal assistance.

The EAHCA has remedied a situation whereby local school districts, prior to the Act, often excluded children whose handicaps prevented them from participating in regular school programs. Now, states receiving federal assistance under the EAHCA must prepare an IEP for each handicapped student and review the program at least annually. Both the preparation and review processes must be conducted with participation by the child's parents or guardian. The EAHCA and its accompanying regulations, the full text of which are reprinted in the appendix, also require that a participating state provide specified administrative procedures by which the child's parents or guardians may challenge any change in evaluation and education of the child.

B. Overview

"Special education means specially designed instruction, at no cost to parents or guardians, to meet the unique needs of a handicapped child, including classroom instruction, instruction in physical education, home instruction, and instruction in hospitals and institutions" [§ 1401(16)]. The term *handicapped children* is defined in the EAHCA as any children who are "mentally retarded, hard of hearing, deaf, speech impaired, visually handicapped, seriously emotionally disturbed, orthopedically impaired, or other health impaired children, or children with specific learning disabilities, who by reason thereof require special education and related services" [§ 1401(1)]. The public schools must provide all such children with a *free appropriate public education*, which means "special education and related services which (A) have been provided at public expense, under public supervision and direction, and without charge, (B) meet the standards of the State educational agency, (C) include an appropriate preschool, elementary, or secondary school education in the State involved, and (D) are provided in conformity with the individualized education program required under section 1414(a)(5) of this title" [§ 1401(18)].

The above-mentioned *related services* are in turn defined as "transportation, and such developmental, corrective, and other supportive services (including speech pathology and audiology, pyschological services, physical and occupational therapy, recreation, and medical and counseling services, except that such medical services shall be for diagnostic and evaluation purposes only) as may be required to assist a handicapped child to benefit from special education, and includes the early identification and assessment of handicapping conditions in children" [§ 1401(17)]. While medical services are excluded from the definition of related services, insofar as they may be needed by a child for diagnostic and evaluative purposes, medical services must also be provided free of charge.

Section 1401(17) states that psychological services are related services and thus are to be provided free of charge by school districts to handicapped students who require such services. While it is clear that not all services involving psychotherapy are related services, if the psychotherapy required by the child is of the type that could be provided by a social worker, school psychologist, nurse or counselor, it will be considered a related service. Where the required psychotherapy is of such a nature that it can only be competently administered by a licensed psychiatrist, then it will be considered a medical service and the school district will not be required to furnish it. Thus, a U.S. district court in New Jersey held that a school district was required to pay $25,200 for a child's stay at a day school which provided individualized psychotherapy, family therapy, group therapy, and individual and group counseling. The court held that the psychotherapy provided here was an integral part of the child's special education. See *T.G. v. Board of Education*, 576 F.Supp. 420 (D.N.J.1983). It is important to remember that under section 1401(17), even medical and psychiatric services must be provided free of charge if such services are required for evaluative or diagnostic purposes. See *Darlene L. v. Illinois State Bd. of Educ.*, 568 F.Supp. 1340 (N.D.Ill.1983).

Section 1415 of the EAHCA contains mandatory procedures designed to safeguard the rights of handicapped students. The safeguards emphasize, among other things, notice to parents and an opportunity for parental participation in the development of a child's special education program. Most important, the various subsections under § 1415 require that parents be informed of all available procedures and methods by which any grievances or dissatisfaction may be resolved. Written notice must be given to parents if a school proposes to change or refuses to initiate a change in a child's educational program, or if the school refuses to perform an initial evaluation and placement of the child [§ 1415(b)(1)(C)].

In case of any dispute over their child's IEP, § 1415 of the EAHCA states that parents have the right to an impartial hearing before a hearing officer who is neither an employee of the school district nor of the state education department [§ 1415(b)(2)]. If either the parents or the school are unhappy with the hearing officer's decision, appeal may be taken to the state education department [§ 1415(c)]. During pendency of a dispute over any aspect of a special education program, the child must remain in his or her "then current" program [§ 1415(e)(3)]. The Supreme Court has recently held that indefinite suspensions of handicapped students is a violation of this provision. See our discussion of *Honig v. Doe*, 108 S.Ct. 592 (1988), in Chapter 3. A lawsuit may be commenced in either state or federal court after a decision has been reached by the state education department [§ 1415(e)(2)]. If the parents or guardians are successful in a special education lawsuit, the defendant will be liable for their attorney's fees. However, parents or guardians who are unsuccessful will not be required to pay the school district's (or state's) attorney's fees [§ 1415(e)(4)(B)]. Money damages, in addition to tuition reimbursement, may be awarded on behalf of a handicapped child [§ 1415(f)].

II. STATE AND LOCAL RESPONSIBILITIES TO HANDICAPPED CHILDREN: *BOARD OF EDUCATION v. ROWLEY*

The U.S. Supreme Court case of *Board of Education v. Rowley* established the following standard for evaluating the appropriateness of a handi-

capped child's education: the child's program must be calculated to allow him or her to receive educational benefits.

Board of Education v. Rowley, 458 U.S. 176 (1982), arose when the parents of an eight-year-old child, deaf since birth, claimed the child was entitled to have a sign language interpreter in her classroom to enable her to have the same educational opportunity as her classmates. The district court held that the child was entitled to have a sign language interpreter in her classroom (483 F.Supp. 528). The case was appealed to the U.S. Court of Appeals, Second Circuit, which affirmed the district court (632 F.2d 945). The school board then made a final appeal to the U.S. Supreme Court, which reversed the two lower courts. The Supreme Court held that the EAHCA is satisfied when a school provides personalized instruction with sufficient support services to permit the handicapped child to *benefit educationally* from that instruction. The court went on to state that the IEP required by the EAHCA should be reasonably calculated to enable the child to achieve passing marks and to advance from grade to grade. The EAHCA does not require a school to provide a sign language interpreter as requested by a child's parents. The court stated that the EAHCA was not meant to guarantee a handicapped child a certain level of education but merely to open the door of education to handicapped children by means of special educational services. Under the EAHCA a school is not required to maximize the potential of each handicapped child, nor is it required to provide equal educational opportunity commensurate with the opportunity provided to nonhandicapped children. However, several states have education laws which surpass the EAHCA standards. In such cases the state standard is incorporated into the EAHCA and such states are required to meet the standard in educating handicapped students. See *Geis v. Board of Education of Parsippany-Troy Hills*, 774 F.2d 575 (3d.Cir.1885), in Chapter 2, Section III. (The *Board of Education v. Rowley* case is reprinted in the Appendix of U.S. Supreme Court Cases of this volume.)

Other cases elaborating upon state and local responsibilities to handicapped children follow.

In 1978, the state of New York agreed to pay the tuition costs of a schizophrenic boy who had been placed in a residential psychiatric hospital which operated an accredited academic high school. Behavioral problems prevented the boy from attending the high school, but he continued to reside at the hospital. His doctors hoped that the behavior problems could be overcome. The boy's parents, after petitioning state officials in vain, sought to compel the state to pay the cost of the boy's residential care at the hospital from the time of his placement, July, 1978, through June, 1983.

The state contended before a U.S. district court that as long as the child's behavioral problems prevented him from attending the high school at the institution, he was in effect uneducable and therefore the state had no responsibility for any of his expenses. The court ruled that once the state placed the boy at the psychiatric hospital, it became obligated to pay the entire expense of the placement. The state could not escape its responsibility for costs of the boy's residential care simply by stating that those costs did not directly address educational problems. As long as the boy could be educated (however little) through a residential placement, the state remained responsible for the cost of that placement. *Vander Malle v. Ambach*, 667 F.Supp. 1015 (S.D.N.Y. 1987).

At least one federal court has held that the protections extended to handicapped and other exceptional children are not applicable to gifted children. In this Pennsylvania case a student who had scored 121 on an I.Q. test sued her school district in U.S. district court claiming that her exclusion from a gifted student program violated her rights under the EAHCA. Pennsylvania law provides as follows:

> Persons shall be assigned to a program for the gifted when they have an IQ of 130 or higher. A limited number of persons with IQ scores lower than 130 *may* be admitted to gifted programs when other educational criteria in the profile of the person strongly indicates gifted ability. (22 Pa.Admin. Code § 341.1)

In addressing the student's arguments, the district court first observed that the "[p]laintiff's argument as to why the [EAHCA] applies to her exclusion from gifted education is, at best, extraordinarily convoluted, difficult to explain and tangled into a veritable legal rat's nest." First, the court held that although Pennsylvania law extends the same due process guarantees to gifted students as it does to handicapped students, the student was not entitled to the procedural protections of the EAHCA as a matter of federal law because the extent to which Pennsylvania chose to extend such benefits to gifted students was solely a matter of state law. Second, the court rejected the student's claim that she had been denied due process of law under the Fourteenth Amendment. Because she had not achieved an I.Q. score of 130 or higher, the student had no "property interest" in being admitted to the gifted student program. Although under Pennsylvania law a student with a I.Q. score of less than 130 "may" be admitted to a gifted student program, this did not mean that such a student was entitled to admittance. Third, the court rejected the argument that the student's equal protection rights had been violated by the school district. Because there is no fundamental right to an education under the U.S. Constitution, Pennsylvania's I.Q. regulations were only required to be "rationally related" to some legitimate state purpose. The court held that the state I.Q. regulations obviously were rationally related to the state's legitimate goal of identifying gifted students and controlling who would be admitted to gifted student programs. Accordingly, the district court ruled in favor of the school district. *Student Roe v. Commonwealth*, 638 F.Supp. 929 (E.D.Pa.1986).

An Indiana case demonstrates the proposition that although state education departments are, under the terms of the EAHCA, the primary parties responsible for special educational services, states may require local school districts to assume responsibility for such services and related expenses. Here, the parents of a mentally retarded boy sued their school board and the State Board of Education seeking reimbursement for the tuition and transportation costs involved in their son's placement in a private residential facility in Kansas. The boy was first identified in 1975 as being in need of special educational services, and in 1976 the school board concurred with the parents' decision to place the child in the Kansas facility. Pursuant to Indiana law the school board sought and was granted State Board approval for such placement. The school board therefore made transfer tuition payments to cover the cost of the boy's special education. State Board approval was similarly granted for the 1976-77 school year.

However, for the 1977-78 year the school board neglected to forward an application to the State Board but nevertheless assumed that it concurred in the school board's decision to continue the boy's placement at the Kansas school. When the school board forwarded its application for approval for the 1978-79 school year, the State Board rejected it and furthermore refused to meet with the parents' attorney to discuss its decision. The child's parents then sued the school board and the State Board contending that under state law they were entitled to tuition and transportation expenses. An Indiana trial court ruled that the school district was liable for the boy's transportation costs and that the State Board was liable for transfer tuition fees. On appeal, the Court of Appeals of Indiana reversed the trial court and held that under Indiana law the local school board is primarily liable for all special education expenses. The case was remanded to the trial court to determine whether the State Board was obligated to reimburse the school board for the excess transfer tuition. *Weesner v. Baker*, 477 N.E.2d 337 (Ind.App.2d Dist.1985).

Three school districts in Pennsylvania brought suit against the state's Department of Education challenging a change in the special education plan of an "intermediate unit" which had been educating handicapped children. The unit proposed to suspend operation of classes for the educable mentally retarded (EMR). The unit's decision placed responsibility for operation of all EMR classes on each individual school district, with the unit providing support services and supervision for the classes. The adopted changes affected four school districts, one of which acceded to the plan changes. The remaining three districts argued in the Commonwealth Court of Pennsylvania that the unit had an obligation to continue to operate EMR classes in their districts unless each district consented to the cessation of the classes.

The court disagreed stating "that the primary responsibility for identifying all exceptional children and developing appropriate educational programs to meet their needs is placed on the local school districts." Because the unit was not bound to continue EMR classes absent a showing that the districts could not "efficiently and effectively" provide appropriate educational programs for EMR children in the districts, the proposed changes were upheld. *Bermudian Springs School Dist. v. Dep't of Educ.*, 475 A.2d 943 (Pa.Cmwlth.1984).

The Human Rights Authority of the State of Illinois Guardianship and Advocacy Commission appealed an order of an Illinois district court denying the enforcement of a subpoena issued by the Commission. Acting on a complaint which alleged that a local school district was not providing occupational and physical therapy for its students, the Commission started an investigation and asked the district superintendent to produce the students' educational program records. The records were to be masked so as to delete any information by which students could be identified. When the school district failed to turn over the information, the Commission issued a subpoena for the masked records. Again, the school district refused to comply. The Commission then sought judicial enforcement of the subpoena.

A trial court ruled that the Commission had no right to examine the records because it did not satisfy the access requirements of Illinois state law regarding student records. On appeal to the Appellate Court of Illinois, the school district argued that the Commission was somehow usurping the role of the State Board of Education by investigating the special education program of the school district. According to the school district, the Commission's inquiry was "tantamount to the control and direction of special education which makes local school authorities accountable to the [Commission] rather than the State Board of Education as required by the School Code."

The Appellate Court disagreed. The statutory authority of the Commission to investigate complaints concerning violations of the rights of handicapped persons, including the right to special education programs, was not subordinate to that of the State Board of Education. Further, the Commission's investigation of the school district's overall special education program and not merely individual students was within the bounds of the Commission's statutory authority. *Human Rights Authority v. Miller*, 464 N.E.2d 833 (Ill.App.3d Dist.1984).

CHAPTER TWO
"FREE APPROPRIATE EDUCATION" UNDER THE EAHCA

I. FINANCIAL CONTRIBUTION TO SPECIAL EDUCATION

Under the EAHCA and the Act's implementing regulations, state educational agencies are charged with the responsibility to ensure that all eligible children within the state are provided with a free appropriate education. This duty is carried out by allocating federal funds to local educational agencies which in turn are to apportion the funds to educate handicapped children.

A. Financial Contribution by Relatives of Child

Courts will not allow schools to assess parents or other relatives for expenses incurred in educating a handicapped child, if such expenses were necessary in order to provide the child with an appropriate education. The following New Hampshire case shows that parents may be responsible for educational expenses when placement is for some reason other than a handicap even when the child is deemed handicapped.

The town of Henniker, New Hampshire, was not entitled to reimbursement from a local school district for the placement expenses of a handicapped child adjudged delinquent, according to the New Hampshire Supreme Court. When the boy entered the Henniker school system, he was diagnosed as educationally handicapped and an IEP was established for him. When he entered junior high school in the Hillsboro-Deering school district, the district found the boy was emotionally disturbed. It decided that his problem could be addressed within the school system under an IEP that provided for psychological counseling, parent consultations and academic monitoring. The student was later adjudicated a delinquent child by a New Hampshire district court. The court ordered that he be placed in a foster home and put him on probation. He violated probation and was placed by the court in the Chamberlain School. The town of Henniker was billed for the cost of the student's educational and residential fees at the Chamberlain School. The town sought reimbursement for these costs from the Hillsboro-Deering school district in state district court. The court found that the school district was liable for the educational portion of the expenses. The school district appealed the decision.

The Supreme Court of New Hampshire held that the district court had exceeded its authority. When a handicapped child is involved in delinquency proceedings a court can only order a review of the IEP by the school district; it has no authority to order a school district to assume financial responsibility for a placement not addressed or provided for in a child's IEP. Since the child's placement arose out of his delinquency adjudication, his residential and educational cost at Chamberlain had to be paid by the town in which he resided, with a right of reimbursement from the person legally responsible for the child's support. The school district was held not liable for the cost of the child's private residential school placement. *In re Todd P.*, 509 A.2d 140 (N.H.1986).

Two Virginia cases which were consolidated illustrate the principle of "cooperative federalism" in special education cases. Cooperative federalism is the distribution of authority between the national and state governments. Here, that distribution of authority was between the EAHCA and Virginia Code § 22.1-214(D). Both cases involved handicapped students whose parents asked their local school boards to reimburse them for the private school placements of the students. After hearing officers granted the parents' requests the school boards appealed to separate state circuit courts. In both cases, the parents removed the appeals to a U.S. district court believing that they had greater opportunity for grants of tuition reimbursement there.

The school boards opposed removing the cases from state court to federal court, arguing that since they were the ones appealing the cases, it was up to the school boards to choose the court system (state or federal) into which the appeal would go.

The U.S. district court agreed with the school boards and held that removal of the cases from the state courts was improper. The only circumstance in which the parents could have removed the cases into federal court would be if state law somehow fell short of the EAHCA's requirements. Here, there was no showing that Virginia courts, in applying § 22.1-214(D), would fail to protect the students' rights to the same extent as a federal court. The U.S. district court thus remanded the cases to the state circuit courts and upheld the school boards' choice of appealing the cases to the state rather than federal courts. *Amelia County School Bd. v. Virginia Bd. of Educ.*, 661 F.Supp. 889 (E.D.Va.1987).

Two Illinois cases illustrate the principle that any state statutory scheme which assesses parents or guardians or other relatives and requires reimbursement to the state for educating a handicapped child will not stand as valid law. This is due to the EAHCA's mandate of *free* appropriate public educations for handicapped children and the supremacy of federal law over state law.

In the first case the parents of a handicapped child appealed from an order of the Illinois Department of Mental Health and Developmental Disabilities assessing them a "responsible relative liability charge" for the care of their child. The department's decision was based upon its belief that this was mandated by the Illinois Mental Health and Developmental Disabilities Code. The Appellate Court of Illinois upheld a lower court decision reversing the department's order, ruling that the department's decision was in violation of the EAHCA.

The court observed that federal law requires maintenance by the state of "a policy that assures all handicapped children the right to a free appropriate public education." This education is to include both "special education" and "related services." The state's contention was that federal statute should not prevent the assessment of charges pursuant to state law. The court disagreed, observing that there is a strong insistence by federal law on the requirement that all expenditures of every kind for the education and welfare of the child are to be borne by the educational authorities of the state. The assessment was therefore prohibited. *Parks v. Illinois Dep't of Mental Health and Developmental Disabilities*, 441 N.E.2d 1209 (Ill.App.1st Dist.1982).

In the second case, a U.S. district court held that an Illinois statute requiring relatives to reimburse the state for payments made to support the residential placement of developmentally disabled children was contrary to the EAHCA and, therefore, invalid under the Supremacy Clause of the U.S. Constitution. The EAHCA requires that states provide handicapped children with a free appropriate public education, which includes both special educational and related services. The court characterized the Illinois scheme as a blatant violation of federal law. In overturning the "responsible relatives" statute, the court ordered that relatives who had paid prior assessments be reimbursed for the $100 monthly contribution fee they had paid (back to the year 1978) for the residential care of their developmentally disabled children.

On appeal by the state, the U.S. Court of Appeals, Seventh Circuit, affirmed the ruling that Illinois violated the EAHCA by requiring parents to pay any part of the living expenses of handicapped children who are placed in a private residential facility on the ground of developmental disability rather than of educational need. The court rejected the state's argument that the class of developmentally disabled children are placed in residential institutions for reasons other than education and, therefore, those children fall outside the protection of the EAHCA. It noted that "if the child is so far handicapped as to be unconscious, and is thus wholly uneducable, he falls outside the Act even though his handicap is more rather than less severe than that of the children protected by the Act." However, the court continued that "in light of the close connection between mental retardation and special educational need . . . developmental disability, far from being an exempted category, is an important subcategory of the handicaps covered by the Act." What Illinois had done, found the court, was to carve out a class of handicapped children and deny them the full reimbursement to which they were entitled under EAHCA.

The appellate court, however, reversed that portion of the district court's ruling which ordered the state to reimburse the parents for expenses they had paid back to the year 1978. The parents were only entitled to reimbursement necessary to clear outstanding bills, thus preventing the expulsion of children from their residential placements. *Parks v. Pavkovic*, 753 F.2d 1397 (7th Cir.1985).

Neglect proceedings involving a New Hampshire child resulted in the child's placement in a residential school and a court order requiring the child's father to reimburse the city in which the school was located for the costs of her educational placement. The father brought suit seeking to terminate his financial liability for his daughter's placement. He argued that he was not financially obligated because his daughter should have been placed as an educationally handicapped child at public expense under the EAHCA. In support of his argument he pointed out that the child's former school district had formulated a special education plan for her. The New Hampshire Supreme Court observed that the lower court which had ordered the child's neglect placement properly did so without considering the child's special education needs. The court then turned to the father's allegations that the state had violated the EAHCA by not placing the child in a special education setting. It held that the judiciary was not the proper forum to decide, in the first instance, whether the child was entitled to special education. The father's complaint was dismissed until such time as he completed the administrative appeals process. *In re Laurie B.*, 489 A.2d 567 (N.H.1984).

B. Financial Contribution by State Educational Agencies and Local School Districts

Parents or guardians of handicapped children sometimes assert that their children are not receiving a "free appropriate education" because of a state educational agency's or a local school district's failure to pay the educational and related expenses involved in educating the child. Generally, the school district of the child's residence is responsible for the educational expenses of a handicapped child. Disputes have arisen when a child is temporarily institu-

tionalized within the boundaries of one school district and the parents reside in another school district.

State educational agencies must allocate federal funds in timely fashion or risk forfeiture. Under the EAHCA states receive grants of federal funding which are then subgranted to qualified local educational authorities (LEA's) for use in providing educational services to handicapped children. Each LEA is entitled to a share of the state's grant based on its proportionate share of the state's population of handicapped children. If an LEA does not spend its subgrant in a timely fashion, the funds revert to the state. Also, if the state fails to obligate funds to LEA's by the end of the fiscal year (FY) succeeding the fiscal year for which the funds were appropriated, those funds have to be returned to the U.S. Department of Education.

Several LEA's returned unspent FY1979 funds to the state of Massachusetts on September 26th, 1980, four days before the deadline for state obligation of funds to LEA's. The state, however, directed these funds to LEA's which had received only partial subgrants for FY1979 after the obligation period had ended. Because these LEA's had been less than fully funded by FY1979 subgrants the state allowed them to apply the reallocated funds to expenditures that they had paid for themselves prior to the deadline. The U.S. Department of Education determined that Massachusetts had impermissibly retained and reallocated the funds and Massachusetts petitioned for review of this determination in the U.S. Court of Appeals, First Circuit.

Massachusetts argued before the court of appeals that because the LEA's spent their own funds before the September 30, 1980, deadline on programs deserving of EAHCA funding, the obligation of reallocated funds to the LEA's after the deadline was proper. The U.S. Department of Education, however, argued that reallocations had to be approved prior to the deadline. The court noted that the department's interpretation was reasonable and "entirely consistent" with the EAHCA plan for fund allotment. The court upheld the department's decision that Massachusetts had impermissibly retained and reallocated the funds. *Massachusetts Dept. of Educ. v. U.S. Dept. of Educ.*, 837 F.2d 536 (1st Cir.1988).

The parents of a boy with Down's syndrome placed the boy in a family home in Edmeston, New York. The parents' school district (the Bedford school district) paid for the boy's education but when his parents moved to Massachusetts, the Bedford school district claimed that the burden of paying for the boy's education was upon the Massachusetts district. After the Massachusetts district declined responsibility his parents sued the New York Commissioner of Education and the Edmeston school district. A U.S. district court held for the parents ruling that the boy was a resident of the Edmeston district and therefore his educational costs were the responsibility of the commissioner and the Edmeston school district. The commissioner and the Edmeston school district appealed to the U.S. Court of Appeals, Second Circuit.

The controversy centered on the commissioner's interpretation of New York Education Law § 3202(4)(b):

> Children cared for in free family homes and . . . family homes at board, when such family homes shall be the actual and only residence of such

> children and when such children are not supported and maintained at the expense of a social services district or of a state department or agency, shall be deemed residents of the school district in which the family home is located.

The commissioner claimed that a presumption arose that the child's residence was that of the child's natural parents. He further contended that the presumption could be overcome by showing that the parents neither exercised control over the child nor were financially responsible for the child. The parents argued that § 3202(4)(b) made no mention of the "presumption" or of the information necessary for rebuttal. Because the controlling issue concerned the interpretation of the term "actual and only residence," the court of appeals held that the district court should have abstained from deciding the issue (i.e., the state courts should decide it). The fact that the commissioner went beyond the terms of § 3202(4)(b) to further define "residence" indicated ambiguity, observed the court. The case was remanded to the district court pending a resolution on the state law issue. *Catlin v. Ambach*, 820 F.2d 588 (2d Cir.1987).

A California case illustrates the potential conflicts that may arise between states and local school districts in paying for special education. From 1977 to 1979 each school district was required to make annual payments to the department of education for each pupil from the district who attended a state-operated school. In July, 1979, the law was repealed and the state assumed the total cost of the state-operated schools. A new state law (article XIIIB) which expressly forbade the state from imposing a new program or higher level of service on any local government without reimbursement for cost to the local government became effective in July, 1980. In 1981, Education Code § 59300, which required local school districts to pay ten percent of the "excess annual cost" of educating any pupil attending a state-operated school whose parent or guardian lived within the district, became part of state education law. When the state's method of collection resulted in nonpayment of $1.2 million, it began to automatically deduct the amount owed by the school district from the district's principal apportionment funds. In 1984, a school district filed a test claim with a state agency seeking reimbursement for costs. The agency denied the school district's claim and the district sued the state Superintendent of Public Instruction in a California superior court. The superior court ruled for the superintendent and the school district appealed to the California Court of Appeal.

The school district argued that § 59300 created a "new program or higher level of service" within the meaning of article XIIIB. The court of appeal disagreed, commenting that § 59300 only shifted ten percent of the excess cost of attending a state-operated school to the local school district. It observed that because the program offered is the state-operated school it is not a new service. Further, a shift in funding of an existing program is not in itself a new program or higher level of service. Furthermore, article XIIIB required that the new program be mandated. If the program is optional, reasoned the court, reimbursement by a local government is not required. The court stated that the law did not require a school district to send a pupil to a state-operated school. There was nothing to indicate that a school district could not exercise the placement option given to it by law if it wished to do so. The lower court decision was affirmed and the local school district had to continue paying ten percent of the excess cost of its students attending a state-operated school. *Lucia Mar Unified School Dist. v. Honig*, 233 Cal.Rptr. 531 (App.2d Dist.1987).

In a New York case the New York Supreme Court, Appellate Division, has issued a ruling which interprets section 4004(2)(a) of that state's Education Law. This section declares that "[t]he school district in which a child resided at the time the social services district . . . assumed responsibility for the support and maintenance of the child . . . [shall] reimburse the state toward the state's expenditure on behalf of such child." The dispute in this case arose when custody of a handicapped child was surrendered by his mother to a county social services department. He was later returned to the custody of his mother. At that time he began to attend school in the Brentwood school district, his district of residence.

When the mother once again surrendered custody of her child to the county social services department, the state sought reimbursement from the Brentwood district. Brentwood refused, arguing that the school district where the child resided at the time of his first placement with the social services department was his school district of origin for the purpose of section 4004(2)(a). This interpretation would mean that any subsequent residence was irrelevant. The state Commissioner of Education had previously ruled that "when a child is returned to the custody of his parents and then subsequently replaced with the Department of Social Services, the financial burden of such care falls on the school district in which the child resided at the time of placement, regardless of his residence at the time of any earlier placement." The Appellate Division agreed with the Commissioner, holding that section 4004(2)(a) requires that whatever school district in which a child resides at the time of his placement in a social services program must bear the financial burden. The five-judge panel concluded that the Commissioner's ruling that Brentwood reimburse the state was practical because it "relieves a [former] school district of the responsibility for underwriting the expenses of a subsequently relocated child with whom the district may not have had any contact for years." *Brentwood Union Free School Dist. v. Ambach*, 495 N.Y.S.2d 513 (A.D.3d Dept.1985).

A Massachusetts town providing special educational services to a child brought suit challenging the burden imposed upon it to pay the child's expenses. The town sought reimbursement from another town in which the child's natural parent resided. However, the child was temporarily in the custody of the Department of Social Services (DSS) and the town from which reimbursement was sought argued that the DSS should assume the child's residential and educational expenses. The Supreme Judicial Court of Massachusetts found this argument without merit. The agency with custody, found the court, has the power to determine the child's place of abode, medical care and education. However, quoting Massachusetts law, the court stated that an acceptance of a child into DSS custody "shall entail no abrogation of parental rights or responsibilities, [rather, it is] a temporary delegation of certain rights and responsibilities necessary to provide foster care . . . agreed upon by both and terminable by either." The purpose of the child's transfer to DSS custody was only to aid him in obtaining appropriate residential care and educational services, not to place full legal responsibility in the agency. The DSS, therefore, was not a parent for purposes of Massachusetts law and thus was not liable for the child's expenses. *Town of Northbridge v. Town of Natick*, 474 N.E.2d 551 (Mass.1985).

In a Colorado case, a juvenile court terminated the parent-child relationship between an emotionally handicapped child and his parents and granted custody of the child to the Denver Department of Social Services (DDSS). The department then placed the child with a set of foster parents. The child was enrolled in a special education program for children with emotional disorders in the school district in which he resided with his foster parents. Because the child experienced great difficulty in school adjustment, the school district recommended that he be placed in a twenty-four hour residential child care facility. The foster parents objected to this proposal because they believed he was doing well living in their home and because they believed it would destroy the bonding which had developed between them and the child. The foster parents unilaterally enrolled the child in the Denver Academy, a private day school specializing in the treatment of children with learning disabilities. The child's guardian ad litem then filed a motion with the juvenile court seeking to compel the DDSS to pay the $5,400 annual tuition at the Denver Academy. The juvenile court held that it lacked authority to consider such matters and the guardian ad litem appealed.

The Colorado Court of Appeals affirmed the juvenile court's ruling. The child's guardian ad litem argued that since the juvenile court had placed the child in the custody of the department, the court had authority to review all aspects of the child's care, including his educational program. This argument was rejected on the ground that Colorado's Exceptional Children's Act provides that a student's school district of residence is completely responsible for providing and paying for special educational services. Thus, although the juvenile court had jurisdiction over the child's welfare, the responsibility for his special education lay with his school district. The DDSS was not the responsible party and could not be compelled to fund the child's education at the private academy. *A.C.B. v. Denver Dep't of Social Servs*, 725 P.2d 94 (Colo.App.1986).

In a New Hampshire case a declaratory judgment action was brought to determine which school district was liable for the special education expenses of an educationally handicapped child. The child had lived for nearly one year with a married couple who wished to adopt him. However, later the couple decided not to adopt him and the child then became a patient at a New Hampshire state hospital. He later lived at a group home and at a training center in Massachusetts. A New Hampshire trial court placed all responsibility for the child's educational expenses on the school district in which the child had lived with the couple who had wished to adopt him. The school district appealed to the Supreme Court of New Hampshire, which affirmed the trial court ruling, saying that a state statute which obligated "the district in which the child last resided" to pay his special education expenses referred to the place where a child actually lived outside of a facility. Because the evidence was sufficient to support a finding that the child's residence for nearly one year with the couple who had wished to adopt him was bona fide, that district was liable for his special education expenses incurred after his leaving the couple's home. *In re Gary B.*, 466 A.2d 929 (N.H.1983).

In a Pennsylvania case involving a dispute over who was to pay the educational expenses of a handicapped child, the Pennsylvania Secretary of Education declined to approve an exceptional child's special education program and placement at a private residential school located in a district other than that of the parents' residence. The secretary concluded that the child was a "low functioning educable retarded child who required a highly structured special education program," but rejected the private school placement because of a Pennsylvania statute requiring the school district in which a child was institutionalized to assume responsibility for a public education, regardless of whether the child was a legal resident of the district. The parents appealed the secretary's decision to the Commonwealth Court of Pennsylvania, which held that the school district had failed to meet its legal responsibility to provide an appropriate program of education and training for the child. The court based its ruling on the fact that the district, instead of making an initial recommendation, merely provided the parents with a list of "approved private schools" and took twenty-one months to make an official recommendation of appropriate educational placement. Further, the statute protecting the rights of institutionalized children did not preclude the secretary from recommending a private school as an appropriate placement, nor did it relieve the school district of the child's legal residence from responsibility in providing an appropriate education. *Pires v. Commonwealth*, 467 A.2d 79 (Pa.Cmwlth.1983).

A federal court has held that the Illinois State Board of Education was not relieved of its obligation to provide an education to a handicapped child by the possibility of financial assistance from another government or private agency. The mother of an exceptional child placed him in a residential school in Kansas after a hearing officer exonerated an Illinois school district from liability for all but "purely educational" expenses of the severely multiple handicapped child and determined that residential expenses should be borne by another agency. The mother then brought suit against state educational officials seeking an injunction to prohibit the district from adhering to its policy of distinguishing between "educational" and "noneducational" components of "related services" needed to enable handicapped children to perform adequately in school. The state argued that the Kansas placement was not "appropriate" because it was inordinately expensive. The court upheld the residential placement saying that the school district had the sole responsibility for providing a special education to the child and, further, that the allegedly inordinate cost of the placement did not preclude it from being the appropriate placement. *William S. v. Gill*, 572 F.Supp. 509 (N.D.Ill.1983).

II. EVALUATION OF HANDICAPPED STUDENTS

Section 1412(2)(C) of the EAHCA requires states to assure that all children residing in the state who are handicapped are identified, located and evaluated. Parents or guardians of handicapped children sometimes take issue with the procedures by which schools identify and classify handicapped children.

A. Identification and Classification of Handicapped Children

The problems surfacing in identification and classification cases involve methods of assessing the intellectual ability of mentally or emotionally handicapped children, determining whether cultural, social or economic deprivation or emotional disturbances constitute handicaps for purposes of the EAHCA, and determining whether proper classification procedures have been utilized.

In 1967, a student entered the Philadelphia public school system and was diagnosed by school officials as being educable mentally retarded (EMR). She was placed in an EMR classroom, and although she was reevaluated every other year she remained an EMR student until her departure in 1980. In 1981, she sued the Philadelphia school district alleging that it had negligently diagnosed her as EMR when, in fact, she was learning disabled (LD). A Pennsylvania common pleas court characterized the student's claims as an educational malpractice lawsuit. Stating that educational malpractice was not recognized in Pennsylvania, the court dismissed her suit.

On appeal before the Pennsylvania Commonwealth Court, the student attempted to characterize her lawsuit as one claiming negligence rather than educational malpractice. The commonwealth court, however, agreed with the lower court and held that the student was limited to the legal remedies provided in the Pennsylvania Public School Code, which did not recognize educational malpractice claims.

The commonwealth court further observed that school districts were not required by the school code to devise educational programs which made the best use of each student's abilities. They were only required to identify handicapped children and develop educational programs appropriate to their particular needs. Since the school code did not provide for any monetary damages remedy arising out of the breach of a school district's placement duties, the student's lawsuit was properly dismissed. *Agostine v. School Dist. of Philadelphia*, 527 A.2d 193 (Pa.Cmwlth.1987).

The parents of several handicapped students in New York filed a class action lawsuit against the New York State Department of Education, the local school board and other local defendants alleging that they had violated the EAHCA by failing to properly identify, evaluate and place handicapped students. The parents entered into a consent judgment with the local school board and the other local defendants which provided the parents with the relief they had sought in correcting the violations. The parents then sought attorney's fees, which were awarded by a U.S. district court. The local school district appealed this award of attorney's fees to the U.S. Court of Appeals, Second Circuit.

The court of appeals considered the local school district's argument that attorney's fees could not be awarded under the EAHCA because the parents in this case were not challenging a final decision of a state administrative agency relating to the evaluation or placement of a specific handicapped student. The court noted that the generalized procedural violations challenged by the parents "lend themselves well to class action treatment," and that administrative remedies need not be exhausted where they would not provide adequate relief. The court of appeals then noted that the consent judgment in this case provided substantial relief to the parents which could not have been obtained through administrative appeal processes. It therefore concluded that the parents were entitled to attorney's fees. *J. G. v. Rochester City School Dist. Bd. of Educ.*, 830 F.2d 444 (2d Cir.1987).

Two U.S. Court of Appeals decisions demonstrate the difficulties that exist in classifying and identifying handicapped students.

In the first case the U.S. Court of Appeals, Ninth Circuit, upheld a U.S. district court's issuance of an injunction against various California education officials prohibiting the use by any public school of standardized I.Q. tests to aid in placing students in EMR (educable mentally retarded) classrooms. The opinion of the court of appeals also upheld the district court's order that any California school district with a black EMR enrollment greater than one standard statistical deviation above its white student EMR enrollment must prepare a plan to rectify the racial imbalance. The case was filed as a class action suit in 1971 two years after the rapid implementation by California education officials of standardized I.Q. testing for EMR placement purposes. The district court found that the overrepresentation of black children in California EMR classrooms violated the EAHCA, Title VI of the Civil Rights Act of 1964 and other state and federal laws. The State Education Superintendent's arguments that the overrepresentation was due to a higher incidence of mental retardation in black children (due to their adverse socioeconomic positions) was discounted by the district court.

The case followed a tortuous procedural history and was eventually appealed to the U.S. Court of Appeals, Ninth Circuit, which held several hearings and rehearings and finally issued the present decision affirming the district court's judgment. The court of appeals agreed that the superintendent's explanation of the overrepresentation of black children in EMR classrooms was erroneous because extremely poor or culturally disadvantaged black children had the same level of EMR placement as black children generally. The court thus believed that the superintendent's logic was inconsistent, and it adopted the district court's conclusion that the standardized I.Q. testing mistakenly placed black children in EMR classes. It emphasized the evil inherent in disproportionate black student EMR placements and upheld the district court's order that standardized I.Q. testing for placement purposes be stopped. *Larry P. v. Riles*, 793 F.2d 969 (9th Cir.1984), as amended after denial of rehearing 6/25/86.

In the second case the court ruled that objective testing was necessary to placement decisions. Here a Washington state boy was found to be eligible for special educational service having scored 70 on an I.Q. test. The district developed an individualized educational plan (IEP) for him which recommended placement in an "educable handicapped classroom." After further testing the school district recommended continued placement in a special education class, but his parents chose to have him repeat first grade in a regular class during the 1976-77 school year. In May, 1979, another assessment by the district found the boy's I.Q. to be 69 and his academic performance less than half the expected grade level. The parents again refused the district's placement in an "educable handicapped classroom" for mildly retarded students and placed him in a private school. In the summer of 1981, a school district employee began tutoring the boy. When the parents placed the boy in a public school in the fall of 1981 they asked that the tutoring continue. After the tutor resigned, the district told the parents that a new tutor would instruct the boy. The parents alleged that this constituted a change of placement in violation of the "status quo" provision of the EAHCA. The parents chose to remove the boy from school three hours daily to be tutored by the original tutor at their own expense. Another test was then performed by the school district which revealed that the boy's I.Q. was 66 and that he was "mildly mentally retarded." After two hearings favored the school district's position the parents appealed to a U.S. district court which ruled in their favor. The school district appealed to the U.S. Court of Appeals, Ninth Circuit.

The school district challenged the district court's ruling that the boy had a learning disability and was not mentally retarded. In 1982, a neurologist had concluded that the boy was dyslexic, not mildly retarded. The court of appeals agreed with the school district noting that the trial record provided no support for the district court's conclusion that the boy had a learning disability, not mild retardation, according to state regulations. It refused to accept the neurologist's subjective conclusion that the boy could not benefit from placement in the school district's special education classes. State regulations required placement to be based upon objective criteria such as the I.Q. test. The boy's eligibility for special education was correctly based on "mild mental retardation." The district court's decision in favor of the parents was reversed. *Gregory K. v. Longview School Dist.*, 811 F.2d 1307 (9th Cir.1987).

In a Rhode Island case a federal court ruled that a school district, faced with a hostile set of parents, acted properly in attempting to provide a learning disabled boy with an appropriate special education. The parents had enrolled their child at the age of six in the Scituate, Rhode Island, public school system. He received remedial reading instruction during first grade. The following year his parents placed him in a private school, but eighteen months later they concluded that he was learning disabled and once again enrolled him in the Scituate public schools. Eighteen months after this the parents placed him in a private day school, and later at the Linden Hill School, which specializes in the education of learning disabled boys. The child never returned to the Scituate public school system.

Three years later, in April, 1981, the parents sought future financial assistance under the EAHCA for their son's placement at Linden Hill. In May, 1981, they met with the special education multi-disciplinary team (MDT) and expressed their dissatisfaction with Scituate's past education of their child. When the MDT said that due to flawed and dated prior tests, a new evaluation of the child would be required, the parents objected and withheld consent until June, 1981. A partial evaluation was then performed by the MDT, but due to parental resistance it was never completed. At a September, 1981, meeting with the MDT, the parents were advised that it would recommend placement in a Scituate self-contained classroom. Due to delays caused by the parents, an IEP meeting was not held until October 20, 1981. They attended this meeting with their attorney and later contested the resultant IEP (which provided for Scituate placement) at a due process hearing. The hearing officer ruled in favor of the school district, but a review officer reversed. The Scituate school district then appealed to a Rhode Island federal district court.

The court examined the parents' allegation that Scituate's letter notifying them of the October IEP meeting had failed to state who would be in attendance and that other individuals could attend. The court excused this failure due to the fact that the parents had attended one IEP meeting previously (in 1978) and thus were probably aware of their rights. No one was a surprise attendee, nor was anyone absent whom the parents expected to attend. Also, there was no evidence of bad faith on the part of Scituate. The parents' second allegation was also dismissed by the court. They had correctly pointed out that the EAHCA places great emphasis on parental involvement in the formulation of an IEP. They alleged that at the October 20 meeting, an IEP was presented to them which read "Independent Education Program," to be effective from "October 20, 1981 October 20, 1982." The parents argued that this was an attempt to steamroll them into accepting an already completed plan, which was subject only to their acceptance or rejection—not their participation. The court, however, held that the parents were aware of their right to offer input and make suggestions at the IEP meeting, noting that their attorney had written a letter to school officials after the meeting which stated: "they [the parents] will then inform the school what, if anything they feel must be added, eliminated, or changed. . . ."

Finding that Scituate was innocent of any procedural violations, the district court then proceeded to determine whether the proposed IEP was adequate. Rhode Island law requires that a school district "shall provide such type of education that will *best satisfy* the needs of a handicapped child" (emphasis added). This educational standard is incorporated into the federal EAHCA by reference. The district court held that this standard was identical to the federal standard set forth in *Rowley v. Board of Education*. The U.S. Supreme Court held in *Rowley* that, at a minimum, an IEP must be designed to allow a handicapped child to "benefit educationally" from his or her instruction. The district court based its ruling on the fact that the Rhode Island statute using the language "best satisfy" was decades old and could not correctly be interpreted to give handicapped children the right to the best possible education. All that was required was that a child derive educational benefits under the IEP. Examining all the evidence, the court concluded that Scituate's proposed IEP was adequate. Reimbursement for the child's placement at Linden Hills was therefore denied to the parents. *Scituate School Comm. v. Robert B.*, 620 F.Supp. 1224 (D.R.I.1985).

The New Jersey Superior Court, Appellate Division, struck down two regulations promulgated by that state's Department of Education as being contrary to the EAHCA. The first regulation defined a preschool handicapped child as one who possesses "a condition which seriously impairs a child's functioning and which has a high predictability of seriously impairing normal educational development." Children without a "serious" condition were excluded from receiving special education services by the plain and unambiguous language of this regulation. Noting that section 1412(2)(C) of the EAHCA requires that services be provided to all handicapped children "regardless of the severity of their handicap," the court struck down the regulation.

The second regulation, which defined the circumstances in which special educational services may be terminated for any child, read as follows: "The child study team, after parental notification, shall terminate a pupil's eligibility when sufficient written documentation is presented to indicate that the pupil no longer requires special educational and/or related services." The court held that "[t]he authority to terminate services when 'sufficient written documentation is presented' runs against the grain of every other enactment on the subject." Section 1415 of the EAHCA sets forth elaborate procedural safeguards as a precondition for the termination of special educational services. Although the Department of Education stated that the regulation in question was interpreted to reflect all federal requirements, the court held that it was invalid because its plain language was contrary to the EAHCA. *Matter of Repeal of N.J.A.C. 6:28*, 497 A.2d 1272 (N.J.Super.A.D.1985).

The Michigan Court of Appeals was asked to decide whether there was liability on the part of a school district for the alleged misdiagnosis of a handicapped child. In this case the parents of a handicapped child brought suit against their local school district alleging that the school had misdiagnosed the child's language impairment. The parents claimed the school had failed to use reasonable care in maintaining diagnostic procedures and had failed in its diagnosis of the child's language impairment. The school district's motion for summary judgment was granted on the ground that the school, in its operation of a speech therapy program, was involved in a governmental function and thus entitled to governmental immunity. In handing down its decision the court outlined the guidelines it used in deciding whether a particular function is entitled to immunity. The court stated that it examines the precise activity giving rise to the plaintiff's claim rather than overall department operations. In this situation the examination and diagnosis of students in a public school was "intended to promote the general public health and [was] exercised for the common good of all." The court held, therefore, that the school district was immune from liability in performing that function. *Brosnan v. Livonia Pub. Schools*, 333 N.W.2d 288 (Mich.App.1983).

A school district can be liable for failing to timely and properly classify a child as handicapped as the following case illustrates.

A father of six children in Louisiana sued a local school board for actions taken between the years 1976 and 1978 in which the board allegedly misclassified each of his six children as mentally retarded in violation of the Rehabilitation Act. The father alleged that one of his children who was not mentally retarded was placed in a class for mentally retarded students without parental consent; two who were tested as normal or having no exceptionality were also placed in such a class without parental consent; and the other three were so placed without testing or the consent of the parents. He brought suit in a U.S. district court seeking an injunction prohibiting the school board from placing any child in classes for the mentally retarded without parental consent, the correction of his children's school records and $15,000,000 in compensatory damages. The court dismissed the suit, saying that the Rehabilitation Act does not grant a private cause of action for money damages.

On appeal, the U.S. Court of Appeals, Fifth Circuit, affirmed the district court ruling but for different reasons. The Court of Appeals held that the Rehabilitation Act does afford a personal cause of action not only to persons who are excluded from federally funded programs because they are handicapped but also to those who are excluded because officials have incorrectly classified and treated them as being handicapped when they in fact were not. However, because the children no longer remained in classes for the mentally retarded and because the father failed to allege that they would likely be placed in such classes again in the future, the father was not entitled to injunctive relief under the Rehabilitation Act; the claim was moot. Further, the father was not entitled to recover damages where he failed to allege that the misplacement was a result of intentional discrimination. *Carter v. Orleans Parish Pub. Schools*, 725 F.2d 261 (5th Cir.1984).

Pennsylvania and New York courts have held that a school district and private school were not liable for the alleged failure to identify two children's disabilities.

The mother of a public school student in Pennsylvania alleged before the Commonwealth Court of Pennsylvania that her son suffered from a learning disability which was not identified by school officials who had a statutory duty to identify exceptional children and provide them with a proper education. The mother claimed damages for the alleged mental and emotional suffering and loss of earnings which she and her son had experienced as a result of the school district's failure to follow the statutory provisions of the Public School Code. The court held that the school district was not liable for money damages for failure to identify the boy's disability. The Pennsylvania School Code reflected the intent of Congress in enacting the EAHCA, i.e. to improve the educational opportunities of exceptional children. Since the EAHCA afforded no private cause of action for money damages, no such remedy could be inferred from the Pennsylvania Code. *Lindsay v. Thomas*, 465 A.2d 122 (Pa.Cmwlth.1983).

A private school in New York brought an action to recover tuition expenses from the mother of a student. The mother counterclaimed against the private school for breach of contract, fraudulent/negligent misrepresentation and negligent infliction of emotional distress. The private school moved to dismiss the mother's counterclaim for failure to state a claim for which relief could be granted.

The mother's counterclaim alleged that the private school's agents represented to her that they possessed a specialized faculty that could identify and individually treat children with learning disabilities. She claimed that these representations were fraudulently and/or negligently made, and that, to her detriment, she relied on the representations in entering into her agreement with the private school. She also claimed that the school did not provide the stated services and therefore breached their contract. Finally, the mother alleged that psychiatric intervention was necessary because her son received services which proved to be inappropriate and harmful when the school failed to diagnose or misdiagnosed his learning disability. This, she claimed, constituted negligent infliction of emotional distress.

The court granted a portion of the private school's motion and denied part of the motion. The court held that the mother's breach of contract claim alleging that the school agreed to detect her child's learning deficiencies and to provide the necessary tutorial and guidance services but failed to do so was permissible. However, the mother could make a claim for fraudulent misrepresentation only if she could show that the private school knowingly made the misrepresentations to her. Thus, she could only maintain an action based on intentional misrepresentation, not negligent misrepresentation.

Finally, the mother could not recover under her claim for negligent infliction of emotional distress. The court noted that it is well established that physical contact or injury is no longer necessary for such a claim. However, the courts have unanimously held that monetary damages for educational malpractice based on a negligence theory are not recoverable. Therefore, the mother could not sue for alleged mental distress caused by negligence in educational practices. *Village Comm. School v. Adler*, 478 N.Y.S.2d 546 (N.Y. City Civ.Ct.1984).

How schools evaluate children to determine whether they are handicapped is sometimes a source of litigation between schools and parents or guardians.

A U.S. district court in Ohio was asked to rule upon the alleged invalidity of one school's identification procedures. In this case the parents of an autistic and possibly mentally retarded child brought suit against an Ohio school district alleging that the procedures utilized by the school district to identify and classify their child were inadequate. Specifically, the parents claimed the district failed to provide a publicly-financed medical evaluation of the child, that the school district conducted some evaluations without obtaining parental permission, that the information provided to parents when parental permission was sought was inadequate, and that the use of standardized tests to evaluate an autistic child was improper. The parents claimed that had a medical evaluation been completed in 1974 prior to the child's placement in the school district's Severely and Multiply Impaired unit, as required, his allergic reaction to certain foods would have been discovered a year earlier and would have prevented a troubled first year in the program due to improper diet. The district court held that the school had not improperly failed to conduct a medical evaluation. The applicable standard in 1974 merely stated that "[a]ll children being considered shall be examined by a licensed physician for initial placement . . ." The court noted that the parents had to take their son to Chicago in order to obtain the allergy treatment outlined by the child's doctor. Thus, because the treatment was not available locally, the court was persuaded that a standard medical examination by a local physician would not have uncovered the child's condition.

As to the parents' allegation of lack of parental consent to conduct an evaluation of their child, the court found that the evaluations in question were conducted pursuant to the school's application for federal funding and did not involve placement decisions for any specific child, including the child in this case. Thus, the court found no legal necessity to obtain permission of the parents prior to conducting these assessments. Finally, the court held that the application for permission to do an evaluation submitted to the parents, although substantially in compliance, failed to give a "[g]eneral description of procedures and instruments that *will be used*" in evaluating the child, but instead provided merely a list of "possible" procedures and instruments. To this extent, the court found the application or permission to conduct an evaluation inadequate. To the parents' argument that standardized tests should not be used to evaluate their child, the court pointed to the testimony in the case that despite the problems associated with standardized tests, they can be used to gain certain information and insight into the capabilities of autistic children and, in addition, provide an objective criterion for comparison in the future. *Rettig v. Kent City School Dist.*, 539 F.Supp. 768 (N.D.Ohio 1981).

The following case addresses the issue of whether an emotional disturbance is a condition rendering a child "handicapped" under the EAHCA.

The Court of Appeal of California found that merely because a child's emotional disturbance is related to his home environment does not preclude a finding that a child is in need of special services. In defending its failure to formulate an individualized educational program (IEP) for the child, the school district submitted that since the child's emotional problems were not related to educational disabilities, but rather to his home environment, the child suffered from no such disability as would require an IEP. The district relied on a federal regulation [35 C.F.R. § 300.5 (b)] which states that the term "specific learning disability . . . does not include children who are having learning problems which are primarily the result of . . . environmental, cultural or economic disadvantage." The California appellate court, in overturning a lower court decision which had set aside an administrative determination that the child required a residential treatment program, said that substantial evidence supported the administrative hearing officer's determination that the child's emotional problems were so linked with his learning disability as to justify and require that he be provided with an IEP. The court was persuaded that the child's emotional problems adversely affected his ability to learn and thus interfered with his educational progress. *San Francisco Unified School Dist. v. State*, 182 Cal.Rptr. 525 (Cal.App.1st Dist.1982).

B. Post-Placement Evaluations

The appropriateness of evaluation procedures is an issue which has arisen in post-placement situations as well as in the initial stages, i.e., the identification and classification stages of placing handicapped children in suitable programs.

A boy entered a New York school district at the fifth grade level in 1985. His teacher requested that he be evaluated by the school psychologist for the presence of a learning disability because he demonstrated writing and attention problems. A school psychologist evaluated the boy and decided not to refer him to the local Commission on Special Education (CSE). The boy's parents were not notified of their procedural rights as required by New York regulations. The boy was subsequently evaluated at the Boston Children's Hospital, which concluded that he had a learning disability and recommended remedial help outside the classroom.

In September, 1986, the CSE held a hearing and found the boy to be learning disabled. An Individualized Educational Program (IEP) was then developed for the 1986-87 school year. The boy's parents, however, appealed this IEP and a hearing officer found that the school district had "violated nearly all of the parents' procedural rights under New York and federal law." The contested IEP was remanded to the CSE and revised. In January, 1987, the parents appealed the IEP again, alleging that it did not provide the boy with an appropriate education. The boy's status as a learning disabled child was not contested by the parents or the school district in this appeal. In considering the appeal, however, the Commissioner of the New York State Department of Education reclassified the boy as not handicapped under either state or federal law. The CSE, in turn, declared the boy ineligible for special educational services because of this reclassification.

The boy's parents sought a declaration from a U.S. district court that the Commissioner lacked authority to review the uncontested CSE finding that the boy was handicapped.

The court noted that the EAHCA provided that "[a] decision made in a hearing . . . shall be final, except that any party involved in such hearing may appeal such decision." It observed that the decision in *Antkowiak v. Ambach*, 638 F.Supp. 1564 (W.D.N.Y.1986) held that the decision of an impartial hearing, such as that held by the CSE in this case, was final as to issues not appealed.

The court disagreed with the Commissioner and the school district who argued that in considering an IEP the commissioner has discretion to review the "nature and existence of the handicap itself." The court declared that allowing the Commissioner to reconsider the handicap issue in an IEP appeal would "remove all the procedural safeguards from the process, which the EAHCA was enacted, in part, to provide. It would mean that the Commissioner could, as he did here, completely alter the outcome of the hearing." It would also mean, declared the court, that decisions by the CSE with respect to labeling a child handicapped would never become final, which was a violation of the finality requirement of the EAHCA. The court determined that the Commissioner lacked the power to reclassify the boy as not handicapped because the issue of the boy's handicap was not before him. It ruled in favor of the boy's parents. *Hiller v. Bd. of Educ.*, 674 F.Supp. 73 (N.D.N.Y.1987).

Due to its failure to follow proper post-placement evaluation procedures, a California school district was ordered to pay the tuition and related expenses for a learning disabled boy whose parents unilaterally placed him in an out-of-state private residential facility. In November, 1976, the boy's first individualized educational program (IEP) in which he was classified as suffering from a mild learning disability was formulated by school district officials. The boy progressed and by June, 1977, he had been partially integrated into regular classes. A new IEP was formulated at this time which provided that he continue in regular classes with minimal supplementary educational services. Three months later, in September, 1977, another IEP was developed which noted the boy's progress and recommended continued regular placement with some special education assistance. However, his performance and behavior suffered greatly during the 1977-78 school year. School officials observed increased anger, hostility and rebelliousness during this period.

The boy's parents were contacted in February, 1978, and a review session was held at which it was agreed that the September, 1977, IEP would remain in effect. At the close of the 1977-78 school year the boy was removed from school after slashing the tires on a teacher's car. He also ran away from home in August, 1978, and was made a ward of the juvenile court. His behavior was described as "self-destructive" with "poor impulse control." In the fall of 1978, the boy was enrolled in the local high school where school officials, with the concurrence of his parents, tentatively decided that his September,

1977, IEP would remain in effect. He was thereafter truant from school on numerous occasions and ran away from home again for a week in September, 1978, at which time he committed the offenses of joyriding and marijuana possession. He spent the remainder of the school year in juvenile hall and various youth residential facilities. The school district made no effort to re-evaluate the boy or develop a new IEP during this period.

Due to the school district's failure to properly evaluate their son the parents decided to enroll him in a private residential facility in Utah in March, 1979, and asked that the school district pay the cost of his placement. The district, however, stated that it would pay only educational expenses at the facility. The parents requested a due process hearing on the matter and the hearing panel found that because the parents had acted unilaterally in placing their son at the residential facility the school district was not liable for the cost of the placement. The parents appealed, and the California Court of Appeal held that the school district was liable under the EAHCA for the boy's educational and related expenses at the private, out-of-state residential facility. The court based its decision on the failure of the school district to develop an IEP for the boy annually as required by the EAHCA. The court rejected the school district's contention that because the boy had been truant and was frequently involved in the juvenile court system, it would have been difficult to properly evaluate him. The school district was therefore ordered to pay the cost of the private school placement. *In re John K.*, 216 Cal.Rptr. 557 (App.1st Dist.1985).

A New York case resulted in a ruling that handicapped children should be periodically reevaluated. The case arose in 1983, when the family court of Nassau County found that a young boy was handicapped within the meaning of state law and ordered the county of the boy's residence to pay the cost of tuition and maintenance for the boy at a summer camp for the handicapped. The $2,450 award was payable directly to the boy's mother. One year later the mother again petitioned the family court to order the county to pay the cost of the boy's stay at the camp during the summer of 1984. She contended that since all the facts were the same as in the previous year there was no need to hold a second trial. The county, however, believed that the boy's condition had changed and that he was no longer entitled to reimbursement for summer camp expenses under New York law. The family court disagreed and held in favor of the mother. On appeal by the county to the New York Supreme Court, Appellate Division, the decision in favor of the mother was reversed because of the possible changes in her son's condition as a handicapped child. The appeals court remanded the case to the family court for a full trial, where the question of whether the boy's condition had materially changed since the preceding summer could be answered. *Schwartz v. County of Nassau*, 489 N.Y.S.2d 274 (A.D.2d Dept.1985).

In another New York case, after a family court ordered a handicapped child referred to her school district's Committee on the Handicapped (COH) for re-evaluation, to ascertain if an originally diagnosed handicapping condition continued to exist, the child's parents and the COH were unable to agree on the method by which the child was to be tested. The COH sought to test the child by using standardized tests while the parents would only consent to a home visit by the school psychologist and the school speech therapist so that they could observe and evaluate the child. A hearing was held after which the hearing officer directed the COH to designate a licensed psychologist of their choice to perform an evaluation of the child's educational needs, status and progress. The hearing officer's determination also provided that the evaluation was to take place in the home setting, where the child was then receiving home instruction.

The COH appealed this ruling to the New York Commissioner of Education, who modified the hearing officer's decision by removing the hearing officer's restrictions on the scope of the proposed examination. The parents appealed to the New York Supreme Court, which found a "reasonable foundation in fact" for the Commissioner's determination. The parents then appealed to the New York Supreme Court, Appellate Division, to decide whether there was sufficient evidence to support the Commissioner's determination.

Two related issues presented to the court were whether there were grounds for requiring the child to submit to an evaluation to determine if she had a handicapping condition and, if so, what type of evaluation was appropriate. With respect to the first issue, the court held that the fact that neither the parents nor the COH appealed the family court order requiring evaluation of the child precluded them from now presenting the issue. The unappealed family court order unequivocally required the COH to re-evaluate the child.

Regarding the second issue, the COH maintained that since the child had subsequently been enrolled in a parochial school, the parents' appeal was moot. The court held that the child's attendance at a parochial school neither obviated the family court order nor discharged the COH's duty to comply with it. Turning to the main issue of the Commissioner's determination, the court held that it was incumbent upon the Commissioner to tailor an evaluation for the child which would respond to her special needs. The matter was therefore returned to the Commissioner for the purpose of tailoring an individualized evaluation program. *Healey v. Ambach*, 481 N.Y.S.2d 809 (A.D.3d Dept.1984).

C. Competency Testing of Handicapped Students

The right of handicapped children to a free appropriate education apparently does not include the right to receive a diploma. The inability of some handicapped children to pass minimum competency tests to qualify for graduation has not been viewed by the courts to constitute a violation of the rights of the handicapped.

After the Illinois State Superintendent of Education ordered that several handicapped children be given their diplomas, an Illinois school district appealed to a U.S. district court challenging the order. The school district argued that the superintendent had allowed the issuance of the diplomas despite the fact that the children failed to pass a minimum competency test as required by the local school board. The district court held that school boards have the right to develop reasonable means to determine the effectiveness of their educational programs with respect to all individual students to whom they issue diplomas and the use of the minimum competency tests is a reasonable means of measuring that effectiveness. The court held that nothing in the EAHCA or other federal or state law stands in the way of such testing.

The court did advise schools to modify tests in order to minimize the effect of physical capacity. To that end, the court suggested that a blind student not be given a competency test which was printed in a normal manner. However, the court stated that the test should not be modified to avoid measuring a student's mental capabilities since to do so would fail completely to measure the results of the educational process. *Brookhart v. Illinois State Bd. of Educ.*, 534 F.Supp. 725 (C.D.Ill.1982).

After the New York Commissioner of Education and a local board of education invalidated diplomas received by two handicapped students enrolled in public school, the students' guardian brought suit to enjoin the commissioner and the board of education from invalidating the diplomas. The guardian objected to the requirement of basic competency tests as a prerequisite to obtaining a high school diploma. The Court of Appeals of New York affirmed two lower court rulings in favor of the school. The court stated that the students had no reasonable expectation of receiving a high school diploma without passing the competency test. The competency testing program had been in effect for three years prior to the completion of the students' studies and, thus, the students were not denied adequate notice of the requirement. *Bd. of Educ. v. Ambach*, 457 N.E.2d 775 (N.Y.1983).

III. DUTY TO PROVIDE APPROPRIATE EDUCATION

Congress was not explicit in the EAHCA as to what exactly constitutes an "appropriate" education, and in practice, parents and schools do not always agree on what is "appropriate" to the education of a particular handicapped child. The *Rowley* case (see Chapter One) provides the standard to which courts are to look in determining whether an education is appropriate.

This case demonstrates that the nature of an appropriate education be specified in detail at each step of the placement process. After a Washington, D.C., child was identified as eligible for special education the District of Columbia Public Schools (DCPS) proposed placement at the Prospect Learning Center, a DCPS facility. The child's parents opposed the DCPS placement and requested placement at the Lab School, a private institution. DCPS placed the child at the Lab School pending a September, 1985, due process hearing. The hearing officer determined that the Lab School was the appropriate placement noting that placement at Prospect would have been appropriate if it had been proposed prior to the beginning of the school year. DCPS funded the child's education at the Lab School for the 1985-86 school year. In June, 1986, DCPS proposed (by letter) a placement for the child at the Lab School for the 1986-87 school year but later informed the parents that its letter was incorrect and that it was recommending placement at Prospect. The parents requested another due process hearing at which the hearing officer determined that the Prospect placement was appropriate. The parents appealed to a U.S. district court requesting that it prevent DCPS from removing the child from the Lab School.

The child's parents contended the Lab School was her current educational placement because she was placed there by mutual agreement. DCPS argued that the Lab School never was her current educational placement because her original placement there in September, 1985, "was an *interim* placement only and did not represent a determination that it was an appropriate placement." The court observed that "any limitation in placement should be spelled out in detail, otherwise, the Court will assume that the placement, whether decided upon by administrative determination or by agreement of the parties, constitutes the child's current educational placement." Because such a limitation was not included in the September, 1985, agreement the court concluded that the Lab School was the child's current educational placement, consistent with the EAHCA's "status quo" provision. The court ordered DCPS to fund the child's education at the Lab School during the pendency of the court proceedings. Additionally, it ordered DCPS to reimburse the child's parents for any funds they expended for tuition or related services during the 1986-87 school year. *Saleh v. Dist. of Columbia*, 660 F.Supp. 212 (D.D.C.1987).

A Maryland case illustrates that when a local school district fails to implement a hearing officer's decision, its inaction may result in a failure to provide an appropriate education. In October, 1984, a hearing officer found four procedural violations of the EAHCA by the Baltimore City Schools relating to an eighteen-year-old handicapped student. The hearing officer found that the student was a seriously emotionally disturbed adolescent who required a residential placement and ordered the Baltimore City Schools to permanently place the student in a residential setting by November 20, 1984. On December 5, 1984, the student and his mother sued the city in a U.S. district court because the student had not received any change in his educational program. The district court dismissed the student's claims and he appealed to the U.S. Court of Appeals, Fourth Circuit.

The student claimed that he was denied a free appropriate public education when the city school system failed to implement the decision by the hearing officer in a timely manner. The district court had dismissed the complaint, holding that the student failed to exhaust his administrative remedies under the EAHCA. The court of appeals disagreed, noting that the student had received a final administrative decision under the EAHCA and that the student had neither the responsibility nor the right to appeal the favorable decision by the local hearing officer since he was not an aggrieved party.

The court of appeals also concluded that since the EAHCA did not contain any provision for enforcing final administrative orders by a hearing officer, the student was entitled to a claim under § 1983 of the Civil Rights Act. When the Baltimore City Schools refused to enforce the hearing officer's decision to put the student in a residential placement the Baltimore City Schools had, under color of state law, violated the EAHCA. The district court was therefore wrong in dismissing the student's § 1983 claim. The student's § 1983 claim was remanded to the district court for further proceedings. *Robinson v. Pinderhughes*, 810 F.2d 1270 (4th Cir.1987).

A nine-year-old Florida boy who lived with his parents suffered from juvenile autism. For three years the boy was enrolled in the Hendry County School Class for the Trainable Mentally Handicapped. Because the boy had made limited progress toward the educational goals set for him during the three-year period, both the school and the boy's parents agreed that the boy needed a different individualized educational plan (IEP) for the 1985-86 school year. Subsequently the boy was labeled severely emotionally disturbed (SED) and found to be in need of a program for the severely handicapped. In

May, 1985, the school held a planning conference to develop a new IEP for the boy. As a result of the conference, which was attended by the boy's mother and her attorney, the school's director of exceptional student education approved a new IEP for the boy.

When the new IEP was issued the parents rejected it. They contended that the boy needed residential placement if he was to reach necessary educational goals. In June, 1985, the parents asked for a due process hearing to determine the appropriateness of the IEP. In July, 1985, the hearing officer issued his order, rejecting the school's proposal and ordering residential placement for the boy. The school appealed the hearing officer's decision to the Florida District Court of appeal.

The issue before the court was whether the IEP provided the boy with an appropriate education even though residential placement was not part of the plan. The court observed that for Florida to receive federal assistance under the EAHCA it must demonstrate that it had a policy in effect that guaranteed all handicapped children the right to a "free appropriate education." It also observed that the IEP is to be developed at a meeting between a qualified representative of the local educational agency, the child's teacher and his parents or guardian. Noting that the proper procedure was followed in this case, the court ruled that the school did not have to provide services designed to maximize each child's potential. A residential placement was not necessary for the boy to benefit from his instruction. Additionally, the court concluded that a hearing officer is limited to determining the appropriateness of an IEP. The hearing officer's decision was reversed and the case was remanded for further proceedings. *Hendry County School Bd. v. Kujawski*, 498 So.2d 566 (Fla.App.2d Dist.1986).

The parents of an Oklahoma youth brought suit in U.S. district court after their local school district refused to fund their son's placement at a residential facility. The youth, who was classified as "educable mentally handicapped," had been enrolled at the age of eighteen in his local school district's EMH program. An IEP was developed at this time with the approval of his parents. Although his educational program included both high school instruction and vocational instruction, he was soon expelled from the vo-tech program due to his emotional outbursts. When these outbursts continued at the high school, school officials notified his parents that an alternative to classroom placement was necessary. Homebound instruction was suggested, but the parents rejected the proposal.

For the next several months the parents considered residential placement; during this period the youth received no educational services. His parents also failed to bring him to school for testing to aid in the formulation of a new IEP, as requested by school officials. At the beginning of the next school year they appeared once again at the high school to enroll their son, and school officials, who had not expected the youth to enroll, requested a week to formulate an IEP. Several days later school officials attempted to arrange a meeting with the parents to discuss a new IEP for the youth, but the parents refused because a new teacher had not yet been hired to instruct him. This impasse caused the parents to unilaterally enroll their son in the out-of-state residential facility. A due process hearing resulted in approval of the school district's decision not to reimburse the parents for the cost of his placement, and the parents sought judicial review. The U.S. Court of Appeals, 1st Circuit, upheld the denial of tuition reimbursement and found that the district had taken all steps necessary to provide the child with a free appropriate public education. *Cain v. Yukon Pub. Schools, Dist. I-27*, 775 F.2d 15 (10th Cir.1985).

The parents of a child in Virginia who suffered severe head trauma when she was injured in an automobile accident and who became mentally impaired as a result, alleged that the child was denied a "free appropriate public education" as required by the EAHCA. The parents contended that their local school district's refusal to implement an educational program proposed by the parents and its decision to implement its own program in the public school system was in violation of the EAHCA. The parents brought suit in a U.S. district court, which found the parents' plan to be unreasonable and the school's plan appropriate, saying: "The State is not required to pay all of the expenses incurred by parents in educating a child, whether the child be handicapped or non-handicapped. The State is also not required to provide a perfect education to any child . . . Rather, the Court must ascertain in the light of educational theories over which experts often disagree if the education provided plaintiff was, under the law, 'appropriate.' " The court relied on the standard for an appropriate education enunciated in *Board of Education v. Rowley,* which held that an "appropriate" education is not necessarily one that enables a child to achieve his or her full potential. The court concluded that "An appropriate education is not synonymous with the best possible education. [P]arents [do not] have the right under the law to write a prescription for an ideal education for their child and to have the prescription filled at public expense." *Bales v. Clarke*, 523 F.Supp. 1366 (E.D.Va.1981).

The following two cases demonstrate that states may establish higher standards for special educations than the EAHCA's "appropriate" standard. In the first, the U.S. Court of Appeals, Third Circuit, affirmed a district court decision which held that handicapped children in New Jersey are entitled to the "best" available special education placement, as opposed to merely an appropriate one. The Court of Appeals observed that the administrative code of New Jersey's State Board of Education required that handicapped students be provided a special education "according to how the pupil can best achieve success in learning." This provision indicated that the state of New Jersey had chosen to exceed the EAHCA's minimum requirement of an "appropriate" special education. *Geis v. Bd. of Educ. of Parsippany-Troy Hills*, 774 F.2d 575 (3d Cir.1985).

In the second case, the parents of a seventeen-year-old child with Down's syndrome became dissatisfied with their child's IEP because they felt it did not adequately address his sexual misbehavior. They believed that the child required a twenty-four-hour residential program. A U.S. district court found that the child was entitled to twenty-four-hour residential school placement to attempt to correct his sexual misbehavior. The court noted that under Massachusetts law a special educational program must "assure the maximum possible development of a child with special needs." Accordingly, the child was entitled to the more comprehensive behavior therapy available in a residential program, especially in light of the degree of his sexual maladjustment. On appeal by the school district, the U.S. Court of Appeals, First Circuit, upheld the district court's decision. The appellate court held that where state law sets a minimum educational standard for handicapped children, those standards are incorporated by reference into the federal EAHCA. The U.S. Supreme Court declined to review the decision. *David D. v. Dartmouth School Comm.*, 775 F.2d 411 (1st Cir.1985). *Cert. denied*, 106 S.Ct. 1790(1986).

A U.S. district court in Illinois found that handicapped children in Illinois were not receiving an appropriate education by reason of delays of the Illinois Superintendent of Education in resolving placement appeals. The case arose after a severely emotionally disturbed twelve-year-old child was recommended for placement by his school district in a self-contained classroom for behavior disordered students. His mother objected to the recommendation and said that she had been advised by experts that a highly structured residential program would be an appropriate placement for the child. The mother appealed the decision but after five months the superintendent had made no decision. The mother claimed that the superintendent was obligated to decide within thirty days. She alleged that the long delay and inappropriate educational setting had caused the deterioration of the child's condition to the extent that the child had to be placed in a mental hospital.

The mother then brought suit against the superintendent on behalf of her child and all handicapped school children in Illinois. The superintendent sought to dismiss the suit on the basis that the EAHCA creates no substantive rights for handicapped children. The U.S. district court disagreed saying that the EAHCA is the source of a federal statutory right to a free appropriate education in every state electing to receive financial assistance, and that is more than merely a "funding statute." The passage of time, said the court, caused the deprivation of a child's substantive right to an appropriate education. *John A. by and through Valerie A. v. Gill*, 565 F.Supp. 372 (N.D.Ill.1983).

The mother of the handicapped child, once again brought suit against her school district. She claimed that the district's policy of disclaiming any obligation to finance "related services" that primarily serve the handicapped student's noneducational needs, even when such services are also critical to his or her ability to benefit from an education, deprived her child of equal protection and a free appropriate education under the EAHCA. In a separate action the school district asked the U.S. district court which had decided the prior case to rule that the mother's action should be dismissed. The court dismissed the mother's claims.

The court held that the school district's policy of distinguishing between the educational and noneducational components of a special education with regard to related services did not deny equal protection to the child. It stated that the inability to look only to the school district for all needs and the occasional delay caused by the complexity of assessing noneducational needs and allocating the cost of these services to other agencies was amply justified by the state's interest in limiting the authority of local school districts to their area of expertise. The child had not proven that he was absolutely denied an education; he had merely shown that he must pursue noneducational placements from a variety of state agencies rather than obtaining financing and services from a single source, i.e., his local school district. *William S. v. Gill*, 591 F.Supp. 422 (N.D.Ill.1984).

A U.S. district court in Texas also found a public school education offered to a mentally handicapped child inappropriate for the child's needs. In ordering a Texas school district to provide a highly structured educational program, specifically designed to meet the child's particular and unique needs, the court analyzed its own role in assessing what an "appropriate" education is. The main factor to be taken into consideration by a district court in evaluating whether a child is receiving an appropriate education is the competing interests of the state which receives limited funding to educate handicapped children and the special and unique needs of the individual handicapped child. Nevertheless, the court found that a residential placement was warranted for the child in this case. Taking into account the limited funding provided to Texas schools, the court said that the EAHCA expressly authorizes residential placement of a handicapped child if such a program is necessary to provide an education to the child. *Stacey G. v. Pasadena Indep. School Dist.*, 547 F.Supp. 61 (S.D.Tex.1982).

IV. INDIVIDUALIZED EDUCATIONAL PROGRAMS

An individualized education program (IEP) under the EAHCA is a statement of a handicapped child's present education level, future educational goals for the child, future educational services to be provided, and the extent to which he or she will be able to participate in regular educational programs [§ 1401(19)]. At the heart of the EAHCA's "individualized educational program" provision is the idea that each handicapped child's particular needs are unique and thus require an educational program specifically tailored to a child's particular handicap. Courts have viewed the failure to provide a program specifically designed to meet the unique needs of a child as a failure to provide a free appropriate education.

Pursuant to his IEP a ten-year-old autistic boy attended the Cooperative Behavior Center, a facility operated by the Garland, Texas, Independent School District (GISD). He attended school during regular school hours and spent the remainder of his time at home. Dissatisfied with the placement, his mother supplemented his IEP by unilaterally obtaining after school and summer educational services for him. She also appealed GISD's IEP to a hearing officer who ordered residential placement. GISD appealed to a U.S. district court which overturned the hearing officer's decision because the family had moved out of the school district. The U.S. Court of Appeals, Fifth Circuit, vacated this decision and remanded the case to the district court.

Whether the mother was entitled to reimbursement for expenses she incurred by unilaterally obtaining supplementary care for her son was the issue before the court. GISD argued that it was not liable for such reimbursement for two reasons: 1) the mother's unilateral action, without consulting GISD and without specifically requesting after school care at the due process hearing, foreclosed reimbursement, and 2) the mother failed to exhaust administrative remedies regarding the expenses for which she sought reimbursement. The court observed that generally, a parent's unilateral action in obtaining supplemental education for a handicapped child, in lieu of that provided by the school district, did not constitute a waiver of the right to reimbursement. The court noted that the EAHCA permits reimbursement if a court determines that such placement, rather than the IEP, is appropriate under the EAHCA. Here, the evidence clearly indicated that the boy had made little or no progress under the IEP developed by GISD. The mother was entitled to reimbursement for the supplementary after school education since the IEP developed by GISD was not "reasonably calculated to enable the child to receive educational benefits." *Garland Indep. School Dist. v. Wilkes*, 657 F.Supp. 1163 (N.D.Tex.1987).

During the 1983-84 school year the teacher of a first grade student referred him to a psychologist for testing in order to determine if the student was in need of special education. In January, 1984, a psychologist for the Roanoke (Virginia) County Schools (RCS) tested the student and informed his mother that he did not require testing for a learning disability (LD). On March 1, 1984, RCS conducted an eligibility meeting to determine if the student was handicapped and to discuss an appropriate educational placement for him. A private school psychologist, who had evaluated the student on the mother's behalf, testified that the student should be placed in an LD classroom. However, RCS placed him in a "behavioral adjustment" (BA) classroom. The student's mother then removed him to a private school for learning disabled children.

Prior to the student's second grade year (1984-85) RCS held another eligibility meeting. RCS recommended a dual placement IEP in which the student would spend a part of each day in a BA classroom, an LD classroom and a regular classroom. The mother sued RCS seeking tuition reimbursement for the student's private school placement. After a U.S. district court concluded that she was entitled to reimbursement for the last three months (beginning March 1) of the 1983-84 school year only, she appealed to the U.S. Court of Appeals, Fourth Circuit.

The court of appeals agreed with the district court that the mother was entitled to tuition reimbursement for the last three months of 1983-84 but not the 1984-85 year. It reasoned that the 1984-85 dual placement was a reasonable judgment by RCS. It agreed with the district court's conclusion that the 1984-85 IEP enabled the student to "benefit" (as required under the EAHCA) from the IEP. The mother was also entitled to reimbursement for the costs of the evaluation by the private school's psychologist. *Hudson v. Wilson*, 828 F.2d 1059 (4th Cir.1987).

A U.S. district court in New York held that school districts must consider expert testimony in developing an IEP. In this case a boy was born with severe multiple handicaps including mental retardation, cerebral palsy and seizure disorders. Because his parents live in Maryland they placed him in the voluntary custody of the Eleanor Roosevelt Developmental Services (ERDS) when he was thirteen months old. The boy had the same ERDS employee as his care provider since 1979. The boy began receiving special education and related services from the Cerebral Palsy Center for the Disabled (CP Center) in 1982 as directed by ERDS.

In February, 1984, the boy's local school district's committee on the handicapped (COH) recommended that his placement be changed from the CP Center to a Board of Cooperative Educational Services (BOCES) school. The board of education approved the recommendation. In December, 1984, although the change was opposed by his parents, care provider, and the ERDS, a hearing officer upheld the COH recommendation. The parents appealed to the New York Commissioner of Education who held that the boy's IEP lacked specificity and was incomplete. He remanded the matter to the COH to develop an appropriate IEP for the 1985-86 school year. The IEP was revised, and the COH again recommended that the boy's placement be changed from the CP Center to the BOCES school. The parents appealed again, and when the commissioner sustained all aspects of the IEP in favor of the school district, they sued the school district in a U.S. district court. The district court applied the two-pronged inquiry used by the Supreme Court in *Board of Education v. Rowley*, 458 U.S. 176 (1982): First, had the state complied with EAHCA procedures? Second, did the IEP developed through EAHCA procedures enable the child to receive educational benefits?

The court concluded that the school district gave very little consideration to those professionals closest to the boy when it developed the IEP. Professionals who had worked with the boy at the CP Center testified that he needed constant occupational therapy, medical integration, and a functional curriculum, all of which would enable him to learn basic skills that would help him survive in the real world. The clear consensus of these professionals, observed the court, was that the BOCES placement would be totally inappropriate for the boy.

The IEP developed for the boy was not reasonably calculated to enable him to receive minimum educational benefits. The court found that because the COH had failed to consider the testimony of the professionals, it had failed to comply with the procedural requirements of the EAHCA. The court concluded by holding that an appropriate education for the boy could best be had at the CP Center. *Taylor v. Bd. of Educ.*, 649 F.Supp. 1253 (N.D.N.Y.1986).

A U.S. district court in Massachusetts ruled that noncustodial parents must be consulted in developing an IEP. Here, a twelve year old boy's parents were divorced in September, 1973. The divorce decree granted the boy's mother sole legal custody but his father retained responsibility for his son's educational expenses. In 1977, the boy was voluntarily admitted to the McLean Hospital, a private psychiatric hospital. The boy's mother contacted the Brookline public schools which conducted evaluations and began tutoring the boy in January, 1978. Shortly thereafter the boy left the hospital on the advice of his father (a clinical psychologist). He ceased medication but his condition worsened and in April, 1978, he was admitted to another hospital. Two weeks later he was back at McLean which conducted two IEP meetings in the fall of 1978. The boy's father was not notified about either meeting. In July, 1980, the father rejected two IEP's prepared by Brookline and initiated proceedings to recover $113,518. This sum represented the father's total costs for services rendered to the son from November, 1977 to November, 1979. The Bureau of Special Education Appeals (BSEA) dismissed the suit because a noncustodial parent had no legal authority to accept or reject an IEP according to Massachusetts law. The father appealed the decision to a U.S. district court.

The court noted that applicable special education law does not provide a direct answer to questions involving noncustodial parents. However, a parent's right to be involved in his child's educational planning and progress is basic. The EAHCA mandates extensive parental involvement, even in the event of divorce. According to the divorce decree the father had a continual financial responsibility for his son's educational expenses thus having a right to be consulted in the decisions regarding the boy's education. The father was improperly excluded from the IEP meetings, and the Brookline school department was ordered to reimburse the father for psychotherapy costs incurred at McLean. The father was not entitled to room and board costs since McLean was not a state approved facility. *Doe v. Anrig*, 651 F.Supp. 424 (D.Mass.1987).

In a Georgia case, the parents of a handicapped girl challenged the appropriateness of her IEP. The IEP had been developed in 1981 with the approval of the parents; however, they now contended that changes in circumstances had rendered the 1981 IEP inappropriate. After a state administrative determination that the IEP was appropriate, the parents sued the school district in U.S. district court seeking relief under the EAHCA. The court issued a ruling prior to trial which stated that in cases where parents seek to overturn a state administrative decision regarding the propriety of an IEP, the burden of proof is upon the parents. The court's ruling followed the general rule that the factual and legal conclusions reached by state administrative agencies must be afforded a proper amount of respect by reviewing courts. The case was set for trial and the parents were thus required to overcome the presumption that their daughter's IEP was appropriate. *Tracey T. v. McDaniel*, 610 F.Supp. 947 (N.D.Ga.1985).

A U.S. district court in Texas faced the difficult task of determining the appropriate IEP for a child exhibiting maladaptive behavior, which the parents of the child contended was autistic behavior and the child's school district asserted was the result of severe mental retardation. When the child reached fifteen years of age and the parents and the school district still could not agree on the nature of the child's handicap, and consequently could not agree on an IEP for the child, the parents brought suit against the school district to compel it to formulate an IEP designed for a child suffering from autism. The federal district court declined to rule on the child's particular disability, but rather concentrated its efforts on the question, "What is the appropriate educational placement for [the child] at the present time in light of her unique needs?" Based on testimony presented by expert witnesses during the trial, the court held that the school district was required to formulate an IEP for the child which provided a highly structured educational program with input from an autistic treatment center which had conducted an evaluation of the child. The court stated that "In formulating the IEP . . ., the district and those involved with the development of the IEP should bear in mind that one of the aims of educational . . . programming is to achieve the highest level of self-sufficiency possible; the ultimate goal of education programming for [the child] is, of course, the complete avoidance of institutionalization." *Stacey G. v. Pasadena Indep. School Dist.*, 547 F.Supp. 61 (S.D. Tex.1982).

The U.S. Court of Appeals, Ninth Circuit, has held that a homebound program for a handicapped child was not an inappropriate IEP. A girl in

Hawaii who suffered from cystic fibrosis and tracheomalacia, which caused her windpipes to be floppy instead of rigid, wore a tracheostomey tube which allowed her to breathe and expel mucus from her lungs two or three times a day. However, her ability to attend school was contingent upon her mother's presence in the school. The child's mother, also a teacher in the private school which the child was attending, suctioned the tube when necessary during the school day.

After the child was certified by the Hawaii Department of Education as eligible for special education services under the EAHCA, the child's school district proposed a homebound program because of the unavailability in the public schools of medical services which the child required. The child's parents rejected this IEP and the child remained in the private school. The school district then proposed for the following year a public school program whereby it would train its staff to see to the child's medical needs. The parents also rejected this IEP, enrolled their child in the private school for the following year, and brought suit against the school district to compel it to pay for the child's private education. A U.S. district court in Hawaii held in favor of the parents, and the school district appealed.

The U.S. Court of Appeals, Ninth Circuit, held that the proposed homebound program was decidedly inappropriate for the child's needs. Because the school district was unable to offer an appropriate public school program, it was liable for the child's tuition expenses for the year the proposed IEP was to be implemented. However, the alternative program offered by the school district wherein it would train its staff to take care of the child's medical needs was appropriate. Thus, the parents were not entitled to tuition reimbursement for the following year. *Dep't of Educ. v. Katherine D.*, 727 F.2d 809 (9th Cir.1983).

The parents of a twelve-year-old hearing impaired child sought review of a Kentucky Department of Education decision regarding the educational program for their child. The child's IEP required that he be taught using the "oral/aural" method of instruction. His school district sought to place him in a classroom where, along with several other oral/aural children, another child was being taught using the "total" method of instruction. The difference between these two methods of instruction is that the oral/aural method avoids the use of sign language and focuses on speech communication skills, while the total method relies upon sign language, residual hearing, and lip reading. The child's parents contended that the mixing of methods would result in him picking up sign language and neglecting his speech communication skills. A U.S. district court rejected the parents' claims, and they appealed to the U.S. Court of Appeals, Sixth Circuit. Agreeing with the lower court, the appeals court refused to overturn the school district's decision to mix the methods of instruction in one classroom. All other children in the child's classroom were making satisfactory educational progress and none of the children being taught using the oral method had begun picking up the total skills. *Age v. Bullitt County Pub. Schools*, 673 F.2d 141 (6th Cir.1982).

When a school district wishes to conduct an evaluation of a child for the purpose of developing an IEP, under the EAHCA the district must notify the parents of the child of its intention to conduct the evaluation and the type of evaluation to be administered.

A Rhode Island case dealt with the issue of whether, once an IEP has been formulated, parental consent is required for a re-evaluation of the child. A mother of a handicapped child sought to prevent the child's school district from making a second educational assessment of her child. The school district had based the boy's IEP on an evaluation conducted by a private school formerly attended by the child. The mother maintained that the assessment sought by the school district would constitute an original evaluation and, therefore, the school was barred from conducting it without her cooperation. The school district contended that its assessment would be a re-evaluation and under the law, a parent's consent was unnecessary. It further stated that any change in placement resulting from the re-evaluation would be subject to challenge by the parent in a statutorily mandated hearing. A U.S. district court agreed with the school district's position, stating that the private school assessment on which the IEP was based did not legitimately constitute an original pre-placement evaluation. Thus, the court held in favor of the school district and the case was dismissed. *Carroll v. Capalbo*, 563 F.Supp. 1053 (D.R.I.1983).

V. PLACEMENT OF HANDICAPPED CHILDREN

A. Mainstreaming

An additional component of an "appropriate" education is the requirement that each handicapped child be educated in the "least restrictive environment." Section 1412(5)(B) of the EAHCA requires that states provide procedures to ensure that handicapped children are educated "to the maximum extent appropriate" with nonhandicapped children in regular classes. Impediments to the learning process and to the normal functioning of handicapped children in their regular school environment, where possible, are to be overcome by the provision of special aids and other support services rather than by separate schooling for the handicapped. Thus, courts prefer to uphold a "mainstreaming" decision where a child's educational needs can be met in the regular classroom.

A Virginia student was identified as handicapped with a primary handicapping condition of autism. His local school district placed him in a special education program with other handicapped students. However, his mother preferred that he be educated in his neighborhood public school with nonhandicapped children. She challenged the student's placement through appropriate administrative hearings. Both the local hearing officer and the state appeals reviewing officer affirmed the school district's placement. The mother sued the school district in a U.S. district court seeking review of the placement. During the pendency of the lawsuit the student was transferred to a second special education program by the school district.

The court observed that the administrative proceedings involved deciding whether it was more appropriate to place the student in the original special education program or in the regular program for nonhandicapped students. There was no administrative record concerning whether the student's placement in the second special education program, as compared to the regular school program, would be appropriate. The mother argued that pursuing the administrative process regarding the student's second special education placement would consume additional time while the school district's decision remained in effect.

The court dismissed the mother's lawsuit. The EAHCA clearly required that state administrative hearings be held concerning the current placement of a handicapped student before a lawsuit could be brought in a federal district court. The EAHCA was designed to require the participation of parents and the school district in resolving problems associated with the proper placement of a student. Had administrative hearings taken place concerning the student's second special education placement a favorable decision for the matter may have resulted. The mother had opportunity to seek administrative review of the second special education placement at the time it occurred. Little delay, if any, would have resulted had the results of the administrative hearings not been in her favor. The mother was required to pursue the administrative process in seeking to have the student mainstreamed. *Devries v. Fairfax County School Bd.*, 674 F.Supp. 1219 (E.D.Va.1987).

A handicapped child who was born in September, 1980, was placed in Handicare, Inc., a private nonprofit daycare center for children ages one through six, in October, 1981. The daycare center's educational program was designed to promote relationships between handicapped and nonhandicapped children. In 1982, after the child was referred to the Grant Wood Area Education Agency (Grant Wood), Grant Wood agreed to place the child at Handicare again. However, in June of 1983, the child was reevaluated by Grant Wood which recommended that she be placed in a preschool development class in a public elementary school in the local district. The child's parents objected, believing that the child's placement at the private daycare center was more appropriate due to its commitment to the integration of handicapped and nonhandicapped children. A hearing officer of the Iowa Department of Public Instruction affirmed Grant Wood's placement decision and the parents appealed to a U.S. district court. The district court upheld the decision and the parents appealed to the U.S. Court of Appeals, Eighth Circuit.

The issue before the court was whether the decision to place the child in a public educational program teaching handicapped children only, rather than in a private program serving both nonhandicapped and handicapped children, violated the EAHCA's mainstreaming requirement. The EAHCA requires that states are to educationally integrate handicapped and nonhandicapped children "to the maximum extent appropriate." The child's parents alleged that the mainstreaming requirement was violated when she was placed in a program for handicapped students only. The district court, however, rejected the idea that mainstreaming requirements are met only when the handicapped child is educated in the same classroom as nonhandicapped children. It observed that the child could be educated in the same school as other handicapped children, and that this did not necessarily violate the "maximum extent appropriate" requirement. The court further observed that while the private facility may have offered the best educational opportunity for the child, the EAHCA does not require states to provide parents with the best possible option. *Mark A. v. Grant Wood Area Educ. Agency*, 795 F.2d 52 (8th Cir.1986).

A learning disabled child who attended New York City's public schools through the fourth grade (the 1979-80 school year) received resource room assistance and language therapy to augment his mainstream educational placement. When the city's COH recommended the same placement for the 1980-81 school year his parents disagreed and unilaterally enrolled their child in the Churchill School, a private school for disabled children. A hearing officer upheld the COH's recommendation. For the 1981-82 school year the COH made the same placement recommendation, but this time a hearing officer ruled that it was inappropriate and awarded the parents reimbursement for the child's tuition at the Churchill School for 1981-82. For subsequent school years the COH included a regular program of speech and language therapy in its public school mainstreaming recommendation for the child. The parents, however, kept him at Churchill and continued to contest the appropriateness of the COH's public school mainstreaming recommendations. A hearing officer found that despite the addition by the COH of speech and language therapy, its proposals were still inadequate and she awarded tuition reimbursement to the parents. The New York City Board of Education appealed to the State Education Commissioner, who reversed the hearing officer's decision. The parents sought review in federal district court.

The EAHCA's § 1412(5)(B), noted the district court, encourages the mainstreaming of handicapped children with nonhandicapped children to the maximum extent possible. This preference for mainstreaming, combined with the district court's view that the dispute in this case was essentially over two appropriate educational placements, induced the court to uphold the State Education Commissioner's decision in favor of the COH. The witnesses for the COH had testified credibly that the COH's educational proposals were calculated to allow the child to receive "educational benefits," and the parents' witnesses testified conversely that the COH's proposals would be "disastrous" to the child. Stating that the federal courts "must be careful to avoid imposing their view of preferable education methods upon the states," and that the primary responsibility for designing the handicapped child's education is left to state and local agencies along with the child's parents or guardians, the district court deferred to the State Education Commissioner's judgment. Tuition reimbursement was denied. *Manuel R. v. Ambach*, 635 F.Supp. 791 (E.D.N.Y.1986).

In May, 1980, the parents of a Missouri boy with Down's syndrome attempted to enroll him in a public elementary school. The public school recommended that he be placed at a private institution and referred him to the Missouri Department of Elementary and Secondary Education for evaluation and services. The department concluded that the boy was severely handicapped and was eligible for placement in State School No. 2, a school exclusively attended by and designed for handicapped children. Questioning his "severely handicapped" classification, the parents requested a due process hearing. The hearing panel concluded that it was inappropriate to place the boy in State School No. 2, and ruled that an appropriate educational program would include interaction with nonhandicapped peers. The parents appealed to the state board of education which agreed with the department's "severely handicapped" label. It ruled that the boy should be placed in State School No. 2 and the parents appealed to a U.S. district court, which decided against them. The parents then appealed to the U.S. Court of Appeals, Eighth Circuit.

The parents took issue with the district court's interpretation of the mainstreaming provisions of the EAHCA. They argued that the court was wrong in considering the cost of a mainstreaming placement to the school district. The court of appeals observed that the most important provision of the EAHCA, for its purposes, was § 1412(5), which provides that "to the maximum extent appropriate, handicapped children . . . are to be educated with children who are not handicapped, and that . . . removal of handicapped children from the regular educational program [should occur] only when the nature . . . of the handicap is such that education in regular classes . . . cannot be achieved satisfactorily." It also noted that the EAHCA revealed a strong congressional preference for mainstreaming of handicapped students. However, this preference is not absolute since Congress also recognized that regular classrooms would not be suitable for many handicapped children, and since the EAHCA itself provides for the education of some handicapped children in separate or institutional settings.

The question before the court of appeals was whether the IEP developed through the EAHCA's procedures was reasonably calculated to enable the child to receive educational benefits. It held that the district court was correct in concluding that the marginal benefit of the boy's mainstreaming was outweighed by the deprivation of benefit to other handicapped children. The boy's placement at the public elementary school would have required the hiring of at least one special education teacher, thus diminishing funds available to other students. The district court decision was affirmed and the school district was not required to mainstream the boy. *A. W. v. Northwest R-1 School Dist.*, 813 F.2d 158 (8th Cir.1987).

In a New Jersey case, the parents of a hearing impaired girl with an I.Q. of 120 brought suit under the EAHCA to prevent their daughter from being assigned to a program for hearing impaired children. The girl, whose hearing loss was profound in the left ear and severe in the right, had attended her local school district's hearing impaired preschool program. Her parents, however, believed that she should be educated with her nonhandicapped peers. The superintendent of schools decided to accommodate the parents and he temporarily assigned their daughter to a regular kindergarten class. Later the school district child study team (CST) disagreed with the decision to mainstream the child. The CST formulated an IEP for the child which proposed that she be placed in a hearing impaired special education class.

The girl's parents brought suit in U.S. district court and successfully blocked her removal from the regular classroom. The court noted that due to the EAHCA's "status quo" provision, the girl had remained in the regular class through kindergarten and first grade. She had made excellent progress socially and the other children in the class had helped her cope with her hearing impairment. In fact, the court felt that the girl's presence in the regular class benefited both her and her classmates. Furthermore, she "ended up making enormous progress in kindergarten, notwithstanding the dire forecasts of the CST to the contrary. . . . First grade also proved to be a success in certain respects." Also, the CST's evaluation methods were "woefully inadequate" because they had employed only one procedure: teacher evaluations. The court held that the girl should be placed in the regular classroom for homeroom, gym, art, music, lunch and free period, with part-time one-to-one instruction in a learning disabilities resource room. *Bonadonna v. Cooperman*, 619 F.Supp. 401 (D.N.J.1985).

The Hawaii case discussed in the preceding section illustrates the strong judicial preference for mainstreaming. In that case, the school district had initially proposed a "homebound" IEP for an eight-year-old girl. The school district claimed that it lacked qualified, medically trained personnel to care for the girl, who suffered from cystic fibrosis and required that her lungs be suctioned several times per day through her tracheostomy tube. The parents objected to the homebound IEP and sued in U.S. district court, which awarded them the cost of placing their daughter in a private school. On appeal, the decision was affirmed. The U.S. Court of Appeals, Ninth Circuit, held that the homebound program was not a "free appropriate education." However, the school district had in the meantime developed a satisfactory IEP that would place the child in the public school and provide medically trained staff. This plan would meet the test of "least restrictive environment;" therefore the appeals court stated that the parents would receive no future compensation if they chose to continue their daughter's education at the private school. *Dep't of Educ. v. Katherine D.*, 727 F.2d 809 (9th Cir.1983).

The Appellate Court of Illinois considered the question of what is the appropriate educational placement of a trainable mentally handicapped child with Down's syndrome who is also a carrier of an infectious disease, Hepatitis Type B. Local school officials contended that because of the risk of the child transmitting the disease to other children, the appropriate placement for her was in a "homebound" setting. The child maintained that the risk of transmission of the disease was remote and therefore not a sufficient reason to exclude her from classroom participation.

A hearing officer, the State Superintendent of Education and a lower court agreed with the child. So did the Appellate Court of Illinois. The question on appeal was whether the child's homebound placement was mandated by the school district's health and safety obligations to its students so that she was being educated in the least restrictive environment as required by Illinois law and the EAHCA. The court held it was not. Using the *Rowley* case as its guide, the court first noted that the trial court gave due deference to the state agency's determination of educational policy under the present circumstances.

Next, the court noted that there is a strong congressional preference in favor of mainstreaming wherever possible. A major goal of the educational process is the socialization process that takes place in the regular classroom, with the resulting capacity to interact in a social way with one's peers. The Superintendent of Education recognized this and determined that the risk of transmission of the disease did not outweigh the injury to the child if she remained isolated from her peers. After a thorough examination of the testimony of expert witnesses, the court concluded that the trial court's decision was not against the manifest weight of the evidence and thus the child could be integrated into the classroom if appropriate sanitary procedures were followed. *Comm. High School Dist. 155 v. Denz*, 463 N.E.2d 998 (Ill. App.1984).

A case arising in North Carolina involved a school district which placed a hearing-impaired child in a regular sixth grade class over the objections of the parents. The parents preferred an out-of-state residential institution. The disagreement reached the state's Court of Appeals after the parents unsuccessfully challenged the proposed placement in the administrative appeals process and then in a North Carolina trial court, which affirmed the final administrative decision. The Court of Appeals found that the school district had offered an appropriate educational program to the child.

The court was not persuaded by the parents' argument that the school system had made a decision to mainstream the child and had then proceeded to develop an IEP to suit mainstreaming. In effect, the parents' argument was that the placement offered to the child was not responsive and appropriate to the child's needs, but rather what the school system could most conveniently provide. The record from the administrative proceedings indicated that an extensive evaluation was performed prior to a determination of what placement was appropriate. Based on that information the school district determined that the child could be served by enrollment in a regular sixth grade class with support services. The court found this to be consistent with policies established in federal and state regulations that handicapped children be educated along with the nonhandicapped to the maximum extent possible. *Harrel v. Wilson County Schools*, 293 S.E.2d 687 (N.C.App.1982).

The proper standard of review in examining a mainstreaming issue was the question presented to the U.S. Court of Appeals, Sixth Circuit, where the mother of a nine-year-old severely mentally retarded boy brought suit against a local school district challenging his placement under the EAHCA.

An evaluation of the child by a private facility had led to the conclusion that the child would benefit from contact with nonhandicapped children. However, the local school district determined to place the child in a county school exclusively for mentally retarded children. The parents requested a hearing and a hearing officer ordered that the child be placed in an ordinary school setting. The school appealed to the State Board of Education which ordered him placed in the county school but with provision for contact with nonhandicapped children. The mother then filed suit.

The Court of Appeals vacated and remanded the case for further action. It held that the lower court erred in reviewing the school district's placement decision under an "abuse of discretion" standard. The proper standard of review to be used is that set forth in the U.S. Supreme Court case of *Board of Education v. Rowley*.

First, inquiry must be made as to whether the school or the state has complied with the Act's procedural requirements. Here the requirements were clearly satisfied. The second inquiry was whether the "individualized educational program developed through the Act's procedures [is] reasonably calculated to enable the child to receive educational benefits." Because the district court employed an improper standard of review, the appellate court ordered a new trial to allow reexamination of the mainstreaming issue in light of the proper standard of review. *Roncker v. Walter*, 700 F.2d 1058 (6th Cir.1983).

In the following cases mainstreaming was found to be inappropriate for students whose needs could only be met in special educational settings.

A Florida high school student who was handicapped by a special learning disability brought suit against a local school district under the EAHCA and the Rehabilitation Act, alleging that her involuntary transfer from high school to an alternative learning center violated her right to a publicly financed appropriate special education. The student requested a preliminary injunction to allow her to attend high school during pendency of the proceedings.

A U.S. district court denied the student's request and she appealed to the U.S. Court of Appeals, Eleventh Circuit. She argued that the hearing officer who upheld the decision to transfer her denied her the right to lay representation in the administrative proceedings. The student also contended that the record of the administrative proceedings contained uncontested evidence that the school district violated her procedural right to remain in the high school during the pendency of the action as guaranteed by the EAHCA. Finally, she claimed that neither the hearing officer nor the district judge determined whether the alternative learning center was the least restrictive environment in which she could be educated.

The court of appeals held that the Rehabilitation Act was not the appropriate provision under which to bring suit since the EAHCA provides the exclusive avenue for asserting rights to a publicly financed special education. Further, the student had no right under the EAHCA to lay representation in the administrative proceedings. The hearing officer's examination of the student's chosen representative revealed his almost complete ignorance of state administrative procedure. Thus, the hearing officer did not violate the EAHCA in limiting his role to offering advice. The uncontradicted evidence left no doubt that the student's behavior at the high school posed a threat to both students and school officials. Thus, the court found that the school district properly exercised its authority to transfer the student to the alternative learning center and the district did not violate her right to remain in the high school during the pendency of the action. Finally, the court held that because the student introduced no evidence that the proposed placement was inappropriate or that a less restrictive environment existed in which she could receive the special education she needed the proposed placement was appropriate. *Victoria L. By Carol A. v. Dist. School Bd. of Lee County, Florida*, 741 F.2d 369 (11th Cir.1984).

The parents of a handicapped child in Arizona brought suit against their local school district because of the district's proposed plan to relocate the child at a school which could provide assistance from an instructor specially qualified to train her. The child suffered from cerebral palsy and physical handicaps but possessed normal intelligence. However, because of her handicaps she had difficulty in learning to read and write. For this reason the child's school believed the child could best be served in a school which had teachers certified in physical disabilities. The parents objected to the move because they feared that moving the child from her neighborhood and friends would create emotional problems and would stigmatize her as "handicapped."

The U.S. Court of Appeals, Ninth Circuit, held that the school district's decision was reasonable under the circumstances. In affirming a U.S. district court decision, the Court of Appeals stated that the importance of mainstreaming a handicapped child must be balanced with the primary objective of providing handicapped children with an "appropriate education." The court found that the objective of mainstreaming would not be "thwarted" by requiring the child to be instructed for a period of time by a physical disabilities teacher at another school. At issue here, said the court, is a school district's ability, after determining that a handicapped student is not making satisfactory progress, to transfer that student to a school which can provide assistance from an instructor especially qualified to train a student with that particular disability. The court found that the school district's proposal complemented state and federal law by "providing the child with a teacher particularly suited to deal with her learning problems," and held that the transfer should be allowed. *Wilson v. Marana Unified School Dist. No. 6 of Pima County*, 735 F.2d 1178 (9th Cir.1984).

A parents' association in Missouri brought suit against Missouri education officials on behalf of a group of handicapped children challenging the state's alleged policy of labeling certain handicapped children "severely handicapped" and automatically educating them in schools separate from nonhandicapped children. The parents claimed that this practice violated the EAHCA, the Rehabilitation Act, the Equal Protection and Due Process clauses of the U.S. Constitution and Missouri law.

The specific allegations with respect to the EAHCA were that: 1) the policy did not treat the "severely handicapped" on an individual basis; 2) the placement of handicapped children in separate settings violated the least restrictive environment concept embodied in the EAHCA and 3) the policy was inherently unable to provide appropriate educational programs to handicapped children in separate schools.

A U.S. district court in Missouri held that the policy was consistent with the EAHCA. The court found evidence of an elaborate system for formulating IEP's and making a placement decision for each handicapped child on an individualized basis. It noted that if it were to order the wholesale transfer of all the children in separate schools to regular schools it would be committing the same wrong as the plaintiffs were alleging, which was not treating each child as a unique individual.

The court also found that the complained-of educational policy was consistent with the EAHCA's "least restrictive environment" requirement. The court held that it is possible to provide an appropriate educational environment to children attending a separate educational facility. The court was not persuaded by testimony from the plaintiffs' witnesses that a separate setting was inadequate because it could not provide sufficient interaction opportunities with nonhandicapped peers and that the quality of instruction was not as high in a separate school.

The plaintiffs also asserted no valid Rehabilitation Act claim in their argument that placing the profoundly handicapped in separate schools excluded them from the benefits of regular public school placement. The court stated that the availability of organized school activities is meaningless when the evidence indicated that most, if not all, of the handicapped children in separate schools had severe problems preventing them from participating in these activities anyway. Resources are too scarce, said the court, to provide the handicapped with activities or personnel from which they cannot benefit. Finally, the court found no violations of equal protection or due process and concluded that the plaintiffs' claims were without merit. *St. Louis Develop-*

mental Disabilities Treatment Center Parents Ass'n v. Mallory, 591 F.Supp. 1416 (W.D.Mo.1984).

The parents of a fifteen-yearold trainable mentally retarded child with a neurological impairment brought suit against a New Jersey school district, challenging the district's determination to remove the child from a residential school and place him in his home and local schools. A hearing officer had found that the child required a structured specialized program with major assistance in the development of communication skills and that such a program could be provided in the local public schools. It had not been established, found the hearing officer, that the child required a twenty-four hour residential placement in order to learn.

A U.S. district court in New Jersey disagreed. The court found both the program offered in the public school system and the residential program to be excellent. However, it concluded that the residential program was best for this particular child. The court found that continued attendance at the residential school would enable the child to best achieve success in learning and that placing him in his home and in local schools would have an adverse effect on his ability to learn and develop to the maximum possible extent. Accordingly, the hearing officer's determination was overturned. *Geis v. Bd. of Educ. of Parsippany-Troy Hills*, 589 F.Supp. 269 (D.N.J.1984).

B. Placement in Public School Programs

Placements of handicapped children in special education programs provided by public schools are generally upheld if the educational program offered by the school is appropriate and responsive to the particular child's needs.

Courts have generally held that students with AIDS are handicapped and must be admitted to public school programs if their enrollment is not a health threat to the school community (see Chapter Four, Section V D). In a recent Florida case a U.S. district court held that three brothers who were hemophiliacs and who had tested positive for the HIV virus could not be excluded from public school classes. The school district contended that although no actual physical harm had been done to their classmates or teachers due to the brothers' class attendance, there was the possibility of future harm. This future harm allegedly included transmission of the HIV virus (which is AIDS-related) in the classroom setting and liability of the school district for allowing the brothers to attend the classes.

The court granted the parents' request for a preliminary injunction against the continued exclusion of the brothers from public school classes for three reasons. First, the brothers would continue to suffer irreparable injury by the exclusion. Second, the ongoing injury to the brothers clearly outweighed the potential harm to others since the school district had failed to prove that the HIV virus could be transmitted in the school setting. Third, the individual rights of the brothers outweighed the public interest which was characterized by community fear, parental pressure and the possibility of lawsuits.

The court also cited the Supreme Court's decision in *School Board of Nassau County v. Arline*, 107 S.Ct. 1123 (1987). In *Arline*, the Supreme Court held that tuberculosis was a handicap under § 504 of the Rehabilitation Act of 1973. The district court in the present case held that the HIV virus was also a handicap within the meaning of § 504. Because § 504 prohibits recipients of federal funds from discriminating against the handicapped solely because of their handicap, the school district could not exclude the three brothers from class. *Ray v. School Dist. of Desoto County*, 666 F.Supp. 1524 (N.D.Fla.1987).

A recent New Jersey case indicates that cases involving children with AIDS contain complicated issues regarding public school placement. A handicapped girl attended a public preschool program, but the school board requested that she be withdrawn from class upon learning that she had AIDS. Although two physicians advised the school board that the girl did not pose a threat to others, the board refused to let the girl into the classroom. A child study team appointed by the school board recommended that she be given a special education because she was neurologically impaired. The school board rejected the recommendation and voted to keep the girl in a home study program. On the same day as the school board vote, the New Jersey Commissioner of Education promulgated regulations on AIDS which allowed a student with AIDS to attend school if he or she was toilet trained, did not drool excessively and was not aggressive toward others. After a lawsuit was filed on the girl's behalf, the commissioner and a medical panel reviewed the case and found that the girl should be admitted to school.

The school board appealed the commissioner's decision to a state superior court, which upheld the decision to admit the girl. An appellate court then reversed that decision. It held that the commissioner's AIDS policy was invalid because comment from school boards had not been allowed before the policy was issued. The appellate court also held that due process had been violated because no hearing was held providing either side the opportunity to be heard or to present or cross-examine witnesses before the girl was admitted to class. On further appeal, the New Jersey Supreme Court rejected the school board's argument that the power to exclude students for health reasons was held solely by local school boards. The commissioner's AIDS policy was valid, but "the right to call witnesses with the attendant right of cross-examination must be provided automatically upon request of the parties." However, because the burden of proof fell on the local school board seeking to exclude the child, the child should be admitted pending a final decision to exclude. The decision of the appellate court was affirmed as modified. *Bd. of Educ. v. Cooperman*, 523 A.2d 655 (N.J.1987).

In a California case, the proposed IEP for a nine-year-old boy was challenged by his parents in federal district court. The boy was severely handicapped in three major categories: he had deficiencies in cognitive abilities; he had difficulties in language and communication; and he had severe physical problems resulting in his being very small and fragile for his age and making it difficult for him to walk. The boy functioned at the overall level of a child three to four years of age.

Previously, the child's parents and their local school district had provided for the boy's special educational and physical needs, and until 1983 the boy had been placed in the district's severe disorders of language (SDL) program. At that time all parties agreed that SDL was no longer appropriate, and a new IEP was formulated by the district which proposed to place the child in the district's program for the trainable mentally retarded (TMR). However, the parents objected to this placement on the grounds that the TMR program would not serve their child's physical or language needs. They contended that private school placement was required because the district maintained only SDL and TMR programs.

After a state hearing officer ruled that the district's proposed IEP was appropriate the parents brought suit in U.S. district court seeking review of the hearing officer's decision as provided by the EAHCA. The court found that the TMR program would be an inappropriate placement because the child would be endangered by the presence of physically larger children with Down's syndrome, and that since the program was mainly directed to children with cognitive deficiencies the child would also receive inadequate language assistance. The court reversed the hearing officer's determination that the TMR program was appropriate and ordered that the district provide a program that addressed all three of the child's areas of deficiency, or alternatively, that the district comply with the parents' request for funding of the private school placement. *Russell v. Jefferson School Dist.*, 609 F.Supp. 605 (N.D.Cal.1985).

A learning disabled child who also suffered from emotional problems had been educated in private day schools for over nine years. The local school district, the District of Columbia Public Schools (DCPS), had found that his placement at these private day schools was appropriate and funded his education. However, when the child reached the age of fourteen, officials at the private school determined that due to his increasing emotional problems the child required a full-time residential educational placement. Accordingly, at the close of the school year the private school notified DCPS that the child had completed his program of instruction and that he needed a new educational placement. On July 15, 1982, a review session was conducted by DCPS which resulted in a revised IEP for the child.

Under the new IEP, which called for placement in a public high school learning disabilities program, the child was to spend no time in regular classes but would receive twenty-five percent of his instruction in regular education. The parents rejected this proposed IEP on the grounds that their child required residential placement, and they requested a due process hearing. Prior to the hearing the parents unilaterally enrolled the child in a private residential school. On September 28, 1982, a hearing officer concluded that due to the child's status as a multihandicapped individual (i.e., emotional and learning disabilities), a change in placement from a private day school to a public high school would be detrimental to the child. The hearing officer noted that the child had never been enrolled in a public school program. He ordered DCPS to propose an appropriate placement by November 3, 1982. DCPS took no action with regard to the child's placement but instead it filed suit on January 7, 1983, to vacate the hearing officer's order. A federal court ruled against DCPS, and appeal was taken to the U.S. Court of Appeals for the District of Columbia Circuit.

The appellate court held that the hearing officer's recommendation of residential placement was correct, noting that the alternative proposal by DCPS was clearly unacceptable. The "unique needs" of the child were not adequately considered by DCPS, which had made its recommendations on preprinted forms using "boilerplate language." The court ordered that DCPS fund the child's placement at the residential school and reimburse the parents for the costs incurred in their unilateral placement decision. The lower court's award of attorney's fees to the parents was, however, reversed. *McKenzie v. Smith*, 771 F.2d 1527 (D.C.Cir.1985).

The parents of a handicapped child in Delaware challenged a local school district's decision denying tuition funding for residential placement of their child. The parents argued that a free appropriate education would not meet their child's needs unless it were a twenty-four hour residential program. A U.S. district court in Delaware disagreed with the parents and held that the educational program offered by the public school system could provide an adequate free appropriate public education within the meaning of the EAHCA.

The court found that although the child was better off emotionally because of her attendance at a private facility, the school district offered a free appropriate program which could confer educational benefits. The court also held that delays in the administrative and due process hearings did not violate the parents' rights to due process and that there was no due process violation in the school district's unilateral appointment of a hearing officer and the seating of educators as hearing officers.

In addition, the ex parte contact between the attorney for the school district and the hearing officer presiding at the hearing did not violate due process as the contact was in the nature of a letter supplying the hearing officer with requested information relevant to the hearing. Further, the school district mailed the parents a copy of the letter and the parents made no request to respond. The court held in favor of the school district. *Ahren v. Keene*, 593 F.Supp. 902 (D.Del.1984).

A U.S. district court in Tennessee addressed the issue of whether a school board recommendation to place a seriously emotionally disturbed eighteen-year-old child in a state program satisfied the requirement that a "free appropriate public education" be provided to the child within the meaning of the EAHCA. The boy's mother objected to the placement recommendation and preferred placement at a private school in Texas or alternatively a private school located in Pennsylvania. After a series of unsuccessful appeals the mother requested the district court to reverse the placement recommendation and order placement at one of the two suggested private schools. The court affirmed the school's placement recommendation saying that because the Tennessee public mental health facility provided programs which included an academic and psychiatric therapy component as well as a social interaction component, the requirements of the EAHCA were met. *Clevenger v. Oak Ridge School Bd.*, 573 F.Supp. 349 (E.D.Tenn.1983).

The U.S. Court of Appeals, Fourth Circuit, held that a Maryland school district was under no duty to consider private school placement where an appropriate public education could be provided. In this case, a handicapped student and her parents brought suit seeking tuition reimbursement when the parents placed their child in a private school, which they deemed a more appropriate placement than that offered by their county board of education. They contended that the county board improperly failed to consider placing their child in a private school when formulating a special education program for her.

The court noted that, while state law permits placement of handicapped students in an appropriate nonpublic educational program, such a placement is limited to those instances in which public educational services appropriate for the handicapped child are not available. Thus, under federal regulations pertaining to the EAHCA the duty of a state to pay for nonpublic schooling does not attach "if the handicapped child has available a free appropriate public education and the parents choose to place the child in a private school or facility. . . ." Of course, parents retain the right to challenge the placement. In this case such a challenge resulted in the state board of education upholding the public school placement. *Hessler v. State Bd. of Educ. of Maryland*, 700 F.2d 134 (4th Cir.1983).

C. Private School and Residential Placement

Private school and residential placements are made when public schools are unable or unwilling to offer a program responsive and appropriate to a handicapped child's unique needs, or where a child's ability to learn and develop is contingent upon his or her placement in a residential setting.

A sixteen-year-old child in Georgia had a combination of infantile autism and mental retardation. The child could not speak and communicated primarily with limited sign language or by pointing to objects. He had difficulty coping with changes in his routine and environment and needed constant care. Special education was provided to the child by a local public school district in a classroom for the severely retarded or emotionally disturbed. In 1984, the local school district looked for a "foster-type" home in which the child could be placed. When none was found it suggested that an in-home trainer be provided. When this approach failed the school district placed the child on a thirty day trial basis in a residential treatment facility for the mentally retarded. A doctor who evaluated the child at the facility recommended that he be placed in a residential center which concentrated on the instruction of autistic children. The doctor felt that this type of placement was appropriate because it could provide a "sameness" of environment which is often necessary for autistic children.

In the fall of 1985, the child's parents placed him in a residential placement facility which treated autistic children, located in Tokyo, Japan. The following year the Tokyo school started a sister school in Boston. The child then started attending the Boston school. The child's mother noted that he had made significant progress since being enrolled in the Tokyo and Boston schools. The parents filed a lawsuit against the local school district asserting that it had failed to provide the child with a free appropriate public education as required by the EAHCA. The parents sought placement for the child in a residential treatment facility for autistic children, reimbursement for the costs of placing the child in the Tokyo and Boston schools and attorney's fees.

A U.S. district court considered the question of whether the local school district's failure to provide the child with residential placement denied him a free appropriate education through which he could achieve some educational benefit. Evidence showed that although the child made some progress while in public school, that progress did not carry over to his home life. Experts testified that autistic children find it difficult to transfer skills from one environment to another. They pointed out that "sameness" is an important element in an autistic child's ability to progress. The court concluded that the school district had deprived the child of a free appropriate public education by not placing him in a residential treatment facility. It therefore ordered that the child be placed in such a facility at no cost to his parents.

The court also determined that reimbursement of costs and payment of attorney's fees were proper. However, it stopped short of approving reimbursement of the entire cost of placing the child 8,000 miles from home in the Tokyo school. The court requested that the parents submit itemized statements of the costs they incurred in placing the child so that a proper reimbursement amount could be determined. *Drew P. v. Clarke County School Dist.*, 676 F.Supp. 1559 (M.D.Ga.1987).

A Florida state court held that a free appropriate education does not always require residential placement. A nine-year-old Florida boy who lived with his parents suffered from juvenile autism. He had severe thought and behavioral difficulties which could not be controlled with medication. For three years the boy was enrolled in the Hendry County School Class for the Trainable Mentally Handicapped. Because the boy had made limited progress toward the educational goals set for him during the three-year period, both the school and the boy's parents agreed that the boy needed a different IEP for the 1985-86 school year. Subsequently the boy was labeled severely emotionally disturbed (SED) and in need of a program for the severely handicapped. In May, 1985, the school held a planning conference to develop a new IEP for the boy. As a result of the conference, which was attended by the boy's mother and her attorney, the school's director of exceptional student education approved a new IEP for the boy.

When the new IEP was issued the parents rejected it. They contended that the boy needed residential placement if he was to reach necessary educational goals. In June, 1985, the parents asked for a due process hearing to determine the appropriateness of the IEP. In July, 1985, the hearing officer issued his order, rejecting the school's proposal and ordering residential placement for the boy. The school appealed the hearing officer's decision to the Florida District Court of Appeal.

The issue before the court was whether the IEP provided the boy with an appropriate education even though residential placement was not part of the plan. The court observed that for Florida to receive federal assistance under the EAHCA it had to demonstrate that it had a policy in effect that guaranteed all handicapped children the right to a "free appropriate education." It also observed that the IEP had to be developed at a meeting between a qualified representative of the local educational agency, the child's teacher and his parents or guardian. Noting that the proper procedure was followed in this case, the court ruled that the school did not have to provide services designed to maximize each child's potential. In this case, the school provided the boy with personalized instruction and enough support services to permit the boy to benefit from the instruction. The court ruled that a residential placement was not necessary. *Hendry County School Bd. v. Kujawski*, 498 So.2d 566 (Fla.App.2d Dist.1986).

In a similar case, a Virginia court reached the same conclusion. The case involved an adopted emotionally handicapped boy. According to his parents, the boy had been physically abused by his natural father and foster parents. The boy suffered serious emotional disabilities such as lack of self-esteem and an inability to check his aggressive impulses or accept responsibility for his actions. His performance on various tests placed him in the low-average range of intelligence. School reports and tests indicated that the boy performed well in reading but was learning disabled in math. After a circuit court reversed an administrative decision which suggested residential placement for him, his parents appealed to the state court of appeals.

The controversy in the case involved the school board's obligation to educate the boy according to the EAHCA. The EAHCA requires placement in residential programs only when local school districts are unable to educate handicapped children in either regular or special education classes. The Virginia special education statute further mandates that local school boards pay for reasonable tuition costs and other costs that result from residential care.

In December, 1983, the boy's parents had requested that the local school board place the boy in a residential setting with special education services. In March, 1984, the local school proposed an IEP of segregated emotionally disturbed instruction in one of the local schools. The boy's parents rejected the proposal and requested a due process hearing. The hearing officer ruled that the local school's proposed placement was deficient and suggested that the boy be placed in a residential setting. On appeal the court of appeals ruled that the hearing officer's concern, well-intended as it was, improperly focused on the total social and behavioral needs of the boy. The local school was not required to address social and psychological problems. By offering the boy a placement in a self-contained classroom for emotionally disturbed students, the school district had met its obligations under both the EAHCA and Virginia law. The court of appeals affirmed the circuit court decision. *Martin v. School Bd. of Prince George County*, 348 S.E.2d 857 (Va.App.1986).

Parents are generally responsible for educational costs of a student if the parents place the student in a nonapproved private institution. In an Illinois case, the parents of an emotionally handicapped student challenged their school district's recommendation that their son be placed in a day-only special education program. The parents based their challenge on the findings of a private psychologist who recommended twenty-four hour residential placement for the boy. They were granted a due process hearing at which the hearing officer found the school district's proposed placement of the boy in the day program to be adequately supported by a case study done on the student. Also, the hearing officer found that the day program met the student's educational and psychological needs.

Prior to the hearing the parents had placed their son at the Grove School, a private facility in Madison, Connecticut. The Grove School was not approved by either the Illinois Governor's Purchase Review Board or the State Board of Education. The parents appealed the hearing officer's decision and requested reimbursement for the cost of placing their son at the Grove School. The State Superintendent denied the request because the Grove School was not approved by the state of Illinois. The parents appealed the

State Superintendent's decision to an Illinois circuit court, which ruled for the parents.

The school district appealed the circuit court's decision to the Appellate Court of Illinois, claiming that the parents were not entitled to tuition reimbursement for the child's Grove School placement. The parents claimed that their son's needs constituted an "exceptional circumstance" upon which the circuit court had correctly based its decision. However, the appellate court held that a parent cannot be reimbursed for tuition at a nonapproved school even if there were exceptional circumstances. Regardless of the right of tuition reimbursement under section 1415(e)(2) of the EAHCA, the appellate court observed that the Illinois School Code prohibits the placement of a student in a nonapproved institution. Since the school district did not have the authority to place students in nonapproved facilities, the court reasoned that the district could not be responsible for such placements when made by parents. *Taglianetti v. Cronin*, 493 N.E.2d 29 (Ill.App.1st Dist.1986).

In Massachusetts, the parents of a seventeen-year-old child with Down's syndrome became dissatisfied with their child's IEP because they felt it did not adequately address his sexual misbehavior. The child, who had been receiving special educational services from his public school system in a highly structured day school program, exhibited no significant behavioral problems during the school day. However, after school he appeared preoccupied with sex, touching young girls in an inappropriate manner and attempting to sexually abuse animals. The boy's parents believed that in order to correct this misbehavior and instill in the child proper attitudes toward sex, thus enabling him to enter into private employment as an adult, the child required a twenty-four-hour residential program.

School officials rejected this proposal, stating that the child was progressing satisfactorily at school and that his sexual misbehavior after school did not mandate his placement in a residential facility. They agreed to address the parents' concerns only by adding individual therapy and family counseling to the child's IEP. After a hearing officer ruled in favor of the school district the parents brought suit in U.S. district court.

Reversing the hearing officer's decision, the court found that under the EAHCA, the child was entitled to twenty-four-hour residential school placement to attempt to correct his sexual misbehavior. The court noted that under Massachusetts law a special educational program must "assure the maximum possible development of a child with special needs." Accordingly, the child was entitled to the more comprehensive behavior therapy available in a residential program, especially in light of the degree of his sexual maladjustment.

The school district appealed to the U.S. Court of Appeals, First Circuit, contending that the district court had erroneously applied the requirements of Massachusetts state law to the case. This argument was rejected by the court of appeals. Where state law sets a minimum educational standard for handicapped children, those standards are incorporated by reference into the federal EAHCA. Thus a Massachusetts child suing a school district will be able to hold it to the same educational standards regardless of whether the suit is brought in state or federal court. The Court of Appeals approved the federal district court's application of Massachusetts law, and the residential placement was upheld. *David D. v. Dartmouth School Comm.*, 775 F.2d 411 (1st Cir.1985), *cert. denied*, 106 S. Ct.1790 (1986).

In a case involving placement in a residential facility, the U.S. Court of Appeals, Third Circuit, affirmed a district court decision which held that handicapped children in New Jersey are entitled to the "best available" special education placement, as opposed to merely an appropriate one. This case arose in 1981 when the child study team of a New Jersey school district decided to change a handicapped child's IEP, which had provided for his placement at a private residential school since 1974. The child study team recommended a new IEP which would remove the child from the residential school and place him in the local school district's trainable mentally retarded (TMR) program. The child's parents objected and requested a due process hearing. The hearing officer upheld the child study team's recommendation.

On appeal by the school district, the federal district court reversed the hearing officer's decision and ordered continued residential placement. The Court of Appeals agreed with the district court. The administrative code of New Jersey's State Board of Education requires that handicapped students be provided a special education "according to how the pupil can best achieve success in learning." This provision indicated that the state of New Jersey had chosen to exceed the EAHCA's minimum requirement of an "appropriate" education. As such, all handicapped children in New Jersey are entitled to the "best" special education placement suitable to their needs. The district court's determination was upheld. *Geis v. Bd. of Educ. of Parsippany-Troy Hills*, 774 F.2d 575 (3d Cir.1985).

In another New Jersey case, the U.S. Court of Appeals, Third Circuit, upheld a district court decision favoring a residential placement. A New Jersey boy was born in 1971 with several congenital physical impairments. His local school board placed him in the Midland School, a private school for disabled children. However, in 1980, Midland School notified the parents that it was unable to provide an appropriate education for the boy. Because the school board failed to act the parents removed the boy to a Rhode Island private school in June, 1981. Although the boy was making remarkable progress at the Rhode Island school his parents were forced to place him in the Mercer Special Services School district because the school board refused to reimburse the parents for the private school program.

After the boy's condition deteriorated the parents requested another due process hearing in which the hearing officer directed the school board to place the boy in a residential program and to reimburse his parents for all his residential placement expenses. The school board appealed to a U.S. district court seeking an order to place the boy in Mercer and a denial of reimbursement for the boy's residential placement. The district court ruled for the parents. On appeal to the U.S. Court of Appeals, Third Circuit, the school board contended that the district court was wrong in determining that a residential placement was appropriate for the boy and in ordering reimbursement to the parents. However, a psychologist who had observed the boy in the nonresidetial setting at Midland testified that the boy's program required a high degree of one-to-one instruction, and that he required "behavior modification involving administration of consequences for at least [ninety percent] of targeted behavior." The court of appeals ruled that the district court was correct in concluding that the Mercer program was inappropriate for the boy's needs.

Both courts rejected the school board's argument that it was obligated by law to provide no more than an education that would be "of benefit" to the boy. Under the EAHCA, the school district was required to provide a "free appropriate education'' to the boy. His program must be tailored to his individual needs by using an IEP. Only a residential program such as the one found at the Rhode Island private school would provide this "appropriate'' education for the boy. The court of appeals also upheld the district court's decision ordering tuition reimbursement. The school district was also ordered to redraft the boy's IEP. (See also Chapter Four, Section VIII.) *Bd. of Educ. v. Diamond*, 808 F.2d 987 (3d Cir.1986).

The parents of a handicapped child challenged a local school district's decision denying tuition funding for residential placement of their child. The parents argued that a free appropriate education would not meet their child's needs unless it were a twenty-four-hour residential program. A U.S. district court in Delaware disagreed with the parents and held that the educational program offered by the public school system could provide an adequate free appropriate public education within the meaning of the EAHCA.

The court found that although the child was better off emotionally because of her attendance at a private facility, the school district offered a free appropriate program which could confer educational benefits. The court also held that delays in the administrative and due process hearings did not violate the parents' right to due process and that there was no due process violation in the school district's unilateral appointment of a hearing officer and the seating of educators as hearing officers. The court held in favor of the school district. *Ahren v. Keene*, 593 F.Supp. 902 (D.Del.1984).

In a Rhode Island case a U.S. district court found that a proposed public school placement of two learning disabled children violated the children's right to a free appropriate education under the EAHCA. The proposed placement involved pupil/teacher ratios possibly as high as ten to one and provided for some mainstreaming. The children's father brought suit against the school district which had made the placement decision seeking a permanent injunction compelling the district to fund the children's placement at a private residential school.

The district court, persuaded by evidence that the children were severely learning disabled and that both children had significant accompanying emotional problems, found that the district's proposal to educate the children in a "self-contained" classroom for learning disabled children would not serve the children's needs and that only a residential placement would provide the children with the type of education anticipated by the EAHCA. The school district appealed the case to the U.S. Court of Appeals, First Circuit, which upheld the district court ruling. *Colin K. by John K. v. Schmidt*, 715 F.2d 1 (1st Cir.1983).

A California court also found that a residential placement was necessary to serve the needs of an emotionally handicapped child. The school district charged with placing the child in a special education program disputed that the child was entitled to a special education under the EAHCA. The school asserted that the child's emotional disturbance was linked exclusively with his home environment and, therefore, did not qualify as a "handicap" under the EAHCA.

The California Court of Appeal disagreed with the district's characterization of the child's problem saying that merely because his emotional disturbance may have stemmed from his home environment, this did not preclude a finding that the child was entitled to special education services. Further, only a program calling for a residential placement was appropriate for this particular child's needs. A residential setting would remove the child from his turbulent home environment and provide consistency which would not otherwise be possible. The court found that without removal from his home situation the child would be unable to learn. The school district was ordered to fund a residential placement. *San Francisco Unified School Dist. v. State*, 182 Cal.Rptr. 525 (Cal.App.1st Dist.1982).

In a similar case, the parents of a multiply handicapped child brought suit against a Texas school district over a dispute involving the district's proposed placement of the child. The district formulated an IEP which called for a six-hour-day program to be augmented by home support. The parents claimed this did not constitute a "free appropriate public education" as required by the EAHCA. Complicating the situation was a dispute between the child's parents and the school district as to the nature of the child's handicap. The parents maintained she suffered from organic childhood schizophrenia and the district contended that its evaluation of the child showed she suffered from severe mental retardation. A U.S. district court held in favor of the parents. The court deemed the dispute over whether the child was schizophrenic or mentally retarded to be irrelevant. What mattered, said the court, was whether the child was receiving an education suited to her unique needs. Finding the proposed public school placement inadequate to meet the child's needs, the court said residential placement is required under the EAHCA when necessary for educational purposes. Here, residential placement was required where the child's social, emotional, medical, and education problems were so intertwined that it was impossible to separate them. *Gladys J. v. Pearland Indep. School Dist.*, 520 F.Supp. 869 (S.D.Tex.1981).

The U.S. Court of Appeals, First Circuit, has affirmed a U.S. district court decision which upheld the right to a residential education program where an alternative public school program failed to meet a handicapped child's particular needs. The parents of a severely retarded child in Massachusetts brought suit under the EAHCA challenging the school district's placement of their child in a day school training program. The parents sought residential placement as well as a day educational program. When the parents' proposal was rejected, they appealed to the Massachusetts Bureau of Special Education Appeals. It found that the day school training would provide an appropriate education and that, while the child required residential care, such needs were not "educational" under the EAHCA, and thus not the responsibility of the school board.

The Court of Appeals disagreed, saying that the only way this child would make any educational progress would be through a combined day school and residential program. The court noted that under regulations promulgated pursuant to the EAHCA, if a public or private residential program, including nonmedical care and room and board, is necessary in order to provide services to a handicapped child, such services must be provided at no cost to the parents of the child. Here, the lower court properly concluded that not only would the child fail to make educational progress without a residential program, he would very likely regress without one. The combined day school-residential placement was upheld. *Abrahamson v. Hershman*, 701 F.2d 223 (1st Cir.1983).

The allegedly inordinate cost of residential placement, according to a U.S. district court in Illinois, did not preclude it from being the appropriate placement. This case arose after a hearing officer exonerated an Illinois school district from liability for all but "purely educational" expenses of a severely multiply handicapped child and determined that residential expenses should be borne by another agency. The child's mother responded to this determination by placing the child in a residential school in Kansas. She then brought suit against state educational officials seeking an injunction to prohibit the district from adhering to its policy of distinguishing between "educational" and "noneducational" components of "related services" needed to enable handicapped children to perform adequately in school. The court, finding that the child could be best served by placement in a residential facility, ordered the school district to fund the child's placement at the school in Kansas. *William S. v. Gill*, 572 F.Supp. 509 (E.D.Ill. 1983).

Where a state elects to provide state-subsidized residential care for handicapped children, the U.S. Court of Appeals, Second Circuit, has held that the state may require the parents of the children to transfer temporary custody of the children to the state. The parents in this case claimed that the temporary custody transfer requirement violated their right to privacy and family integrity without sufficient justification and that it discriminated against handicapped children solely on the basis of their handicaps.

The Court of Appeals, in upholding New York's custody transfer requirement, placed great emphasis on the voluntary nature of New York's benefits program and stressed that the state, while under no constitutional obligation to provide residential treatment for handicapped children, elected to do so. Consequently when the state provided voluntary social services, it could administer the program without having to consult and satisfy the individual concerns of each of the recipients.

The court dealt with the handicap discrimination issue by saying that "*all* parents whose children need state-subsidized home substitutes must transfer custody to the state, regardless of whether the child is or is not handicapped." Therefore, New York's foster care scheme discriminated between children only as to the type of assistance needed and not solely on the basis of their handicaps. The court upheld the constitutionality of the New York law. *Joyner By Lowry v. Dumpson*, 712 F.2d 770 (2d Cir.1983).

A private day school education was ordered for a child by a U.S. district court in Massachusetts after that court found a learning disabled child's IEP offered by a public school system to have fallen "far short of meeting his unique needs." The parents of the child had brought suit against the school district responsible for the child's education alleging that the IEP proposed by the district was inadequate. The district court agreed. The court found that the school district, which was aware of the child's inability to work independently and also aware that the child had to be placed in an environment with few distractions, nevertheless failed to structure a program designed only to improve his basic skills.

Although it was well known in the school that the child's poor self-image and "defeatist" attitude were obstacles to his learning progress, no program was structured whereby the child might realize some success in his weaker subjects. In contrast, the program offered at the private school was specifically designed to provide children having severe learning disabilities and problems of low self-esteem with sufficient skills to return to a normalized educational program. The court ordered the school district to fund a private residential education for the child. *Norris v. Massachusetts Dep't of Educ.*, 529 F.Supp. 759 (D.Mass.1981).

Residential placement was held to be inappropriate for a profoundly handicapped child in the following Virginia case. The child's parents asked the U.S. Court of Appeals, Fourth Circuit, to reverse certain administrative decisions made by a local school district and to issue both a preliminary and permanent injunction requiring the state of Virginia and county school officials to provide a twenty-four-hour residential placement for their son. The child had been placed in a residential program but local school officials later recommended that the child be placed in a day education program and live at home. The parents rejected this decision and applied for tuition assistance for the residential school. Tuition assistance was denied by a county special education committee on the ground that the day program could meet the child's needs.

The parents appealed to the Superintendent of Public Education of the Commonwealth of Virginia, who concurred in the committee's decision. After exhausting their administrative remedies, the parents brought suit in a U.S. district court, which released the school district from its obligation to provide twenty-four-hour residential care and education for the child.

The child and his parents appealed to the U.S. Court of Appeals, which upheld the district court ruling. The court of appeals was persuaded by testimony which indicated that the child had reached the point in his education at which a continuation of the residential program would at best yield only marginal results and probably none at all. Testimony by the school district's witnesses also indicated that basic living skills could easily be taught at home by teaching the child's family the cues the child had developed for implementing such skills. *Matthews v. Davis*, 742 F.2d 825 (4th Cir.1984).

D. AIDS

In *School Board of Nassau County v. Arline*, 107 S.Ct. 1123 (1987), the U.S. Supreme Court ruled that tuberculosis (and any other contagious disease, such as AIDS) is a "handicap" under § 504 of the Rehabilitation Act so long as the individual suffers some physical impairment from the disease. The Court refused to accept the school board's argument that the teacher was not protected by § 504 because her tuberculosis was contagious and therefore dangerous to her students. The Court remanded the case to the U.S. district court to determine if the teacher was "otherwise qualified" for her job (see Chapter 6, Section I B, for a full discussion of the case). In light of *Arline*, students with AIDS should be considered handicapped under § 504 and cannot "solely by reason of [their] handicap, be excluded from participation in any program receiving federal financial assistance." In order for a student with AIDS to be excluded from the classroom (without penalty to the school) the school will have to demonstrate that the student is not "otherwise qualified," i.e., is a danger to students, faculty or staff.

A girl born with respiratory distress received 39 blood transfusions during the first four months of her life and was diagnosed as having AIDS-Related Complex (ARC) at the age of three. The girl was evaluated as having significant neurological impairment. It was not known how much damage was due to ARC, an AIDS precursor. The girl had attended schools for the handicapped prior to the ARC diagnosis and spent parts of two years in health care facilities. She was classified as trainable mentally handicapped (TMH). At the age of six the girl had a mental age of between one and one-half years in expressive language and three and one-half years in perceptual motor skills. The girl was incontinent and was observed by doctors to drool and suck her thumb continually. In the past the girl had developed skin lesions. When these occurred, her mother kept her home.

When the girl approached school age her mother attempted to enroll her in a Florida public school. The school district operated two schools which each maintained classes for TMH children. However, the school district excluded the girl from public schools based upon her incontinence. The school district recommended that the girl be educated in its homebound program.

The girl appealed to the Florida State Division of Administrative Hearings. The school district prevailed after an evidentiary hearing. After the hearing was held, but before the decision was announced, the girl began treatment with azidothymidine and showed significant progress in her developmental and neurological skills. An evaluating physician reported that her progress would be enhanced by social interaction and that her development could not be enhanced in isolation. A specialized educational setting such as the public school TMH program would be the appropriate supportive environment for further development. Other physicians testified that the girl's presence in an integrated classroom presented only a "remote theoretical possibility" of transmitting the AIDS virus.

The administrative decision was appealed to a federal district court which held in favor of the school district. The court stated that to grant an order to enroll the girl in public school it would have to find that she was likely to prevail on the merits of her claim, that her claimed injuries were irreparable and that others attending the school would not be harmed. The court ruled that potential harm to others clearly outweighed the girl's interest in attending classes. This conclusion was primarily due to conflicting expert testimony before the district court. The court also relied upon publications by the Center for Disease Control and other sources which indicated that students who lack control of body secretions increase the risk to others attending school. *Martinez v. School Bd. of Hillsborough County, Florida*, 675 F.Supp. 1574 (M.D.Fla.1987).

After a kindergarten boy, who was infected with the AIDS virus, bit a fellow student's pant leg, his California school district instructed the boy's parents to keep him at home until the school district considered "whether [his] potential for again biting another student posed any danger to the health of others in the class." Following an examination a psychologist determined that the boy would behave aggressively in a kindergarten setting. The school district then recommended that the boy be kept out of class and in home tutoring for the rest of the academic year. The boy's parents sued the school district in a U.S. district court seeking an order allowing the boy to attend his kindergarten class.

The court observed that the boy was "handicapped" within the meaning of § 504 of the Rehabilitation Act of 1973. It also noted that the school district had failed to demonstrate that the boy was not "otherwise qualified" to attend kindergarten. Specifically, the school district had failed to prove that the AIDS virus could be transmitted in the classroom setting through biting or otherwise. Therefore, it could not exclude the boy from his kindergarten class on the ground that he posed a risk of transmission of the AIDS virus to his classmates or teachers. The court also observed that the boy had been subjected to discrimination and had been excluded from class solely because of his handicap. Section 504 triggered statutory protection for the boy. The court ordered the school district to allow him to attend his regular kindergarten class once again. *Thomas v. Atascadero Unified School Dist.*, 662 F.Supp. 376 (C.D.Cal.1987).

The Superior Court of New Jersey held that a neurologically impaired student who was afflicted with AIDS could be refused admittance to school until proper state guidelines on AIDS were developed and the school board could hold a hearing on the child's case. It noted that children should receive a regular classroom education where possible but held that classmates, faculty and staff have an equally important interest in being free from a communicable disease in the public school system.

When she was an infant, the girl had received a blood transfusion containing the AIDS virus. She had attended a public preschool program, but the school requested that she be withdrawn from class upon learning that she had AIDS. Two leading physicians specializing in children afflicted with AIDS advised the board that the girl did not pose a threat to others. The board, however, still refused to accept the girl into the school system. A child study team then evaluated the girl and recommended that she be given a special education designed for a neurologically impaired student. According to the report, the appropriate placement would be in a "Pre-K-Handicapped Program." The school board rejected the recommendation and voted to keep her in a home study program.

On the same day as the school board vote, the New Jersey Commissioner of Education promulgated regulations on AIDS. The regulations allowed a student with AIDS admittance to school if he or she was toilet trained, did not drool excessively and was not aggressive toward others. A suit filed on the girl's behalf claimed she was being denied an appropriate education. The commissioner and a medical panel reviewed the case and found that the girl should be admitted to school. The commissioner cautioned the board not to use the educationally handicapped classification as a means of denying her a regular classroom environment.

The school board appealed the decision to a state Chancery Division judge who upheld the decision to admit the girl. The Superior Court of New Jersey reversed that decision. It held that the AIDS regulations were improper because the commissioner had not allowed comment from school boards and others before promulgating the regulations. Also, the court held that a school board should be allowed to conduct a hearing before admitting a student having AIDS. Until the rules governing students afflicted with AIDS were properly made and a new hearing conducted, the court held that the girl should remain in a home study program.

On further appeal, the New Jersey Supreme Court rejected the school board's argument that the power to exclude students for health reasons was held solely by local school boards. The commissioner's AIDS policy was valid, but "the right to call witnesses with the attendant right of cross-examination must be provided automatically upon request of the parties." However, because the burden of proof fell on the local school board seeking to exclude the child, the child should be admitted pending a final decision to exclude. The decision of the appellate court was affirmed as modified. *Bd. of Educ. v. Cooperman*, 523 A.2d 655 (N.J.1987).

Another case involving AIDS arose when two public school boards in New York City sought to prohibit a child thought to have AIDS from attending class. Although the child was later found to have HTLV-III/LAV rather than AIDS, the New York Supreme Court nonetheless addressed the issues because of the likelihood of their recurrence and the desirability of resolving the issues. The court ruled that neither the New York City Commissioner of Health nor the Chancellor of the Board of Education, nor any other city or state education officials, were required by law to exclude children afflicted with AIDS, AIDS-related complex (ARC) or HTLV-III/LAV from public school classrooms. The court reasoned that since neither city nor state health or education codes had defined AIDS and its related afflictions as "communicable diseases," provisions in the laws requiring exclusion of children with communicable diseases did not apply. The court cited expert testimony regarding Centers for Disease Control (CDC) studies showing that the risk of infection from AIDS is "apparently nonexistent" in the classroom setting. CDC studies have also shown that only about ten percent of adults infected with HTLV-III/LAV have progressed to ARC, and that approximately thirty percent of ARC patients thereafter developed AIDS. The court also held that the proposal in this case to exclude only children with AIDS from the classroom and not those afflicted with ARC or HTLV-III/LAV would be a denial of equal protection of the laws, because all three groups are carriers of the same virus. Although public education is not a "fundamental right" granted to individuals by the U.S. Constitution, "the right to an education must be made available to all on equal terms." The proposal, stated the court, would also violate the rights of AIDS-infected children under § 504 of the Rehabilitation Act for the same reasons. *Dist. 27 Comm. School Bd. v. Bd. of Educ. of City of New York*, 502 N.Y.S.2d 325 (Sup.Ct.1986).

VI. "RELATED SERVICES" UNDER THE EAHCA

A. Psychological Services

Psychological services are included in the definition of "related services" in the EAHCA. However, the Act does not define psychological services, which has left to the courts the responsibility to determine what services are and are not psychological services for purposes of the EAHCA.

During the 1983-84 school year the teacher of a first grade student referred him to a psychologist for testing in order to determine if the student was in need of special education. In January, 1984, a psychologist for the Roanoke (Virginia) County Schools (RCS) tested the student and informed his mother that he did not require testing for a learning disability (LD). On March 1, 1984, RCS conducted an eligibility meeting to determine if the student was handicapped and to discuss an appropriate educational placement for him. A private school psychologist, who had evaluated the student on the mother's behalf, testified that the student should be placed in an LD classroom. However, RCS placed him in a "behavioral adjustment" (BA) classroom. The student's mother then removed him to a private school for learning disabled children.

Prior to the student's second grade year (1984-84) RCS held another eligibility meeting. RCS recommended a dual placement IEP in which the student would spend a part of each day in a BA classroom, an LD classroom and a regular classroom. The mother sued RCS seeking tuition reimbursement for the student's private school placement. After a U.S. district court concluded that she was entitled to reimbursement for the last three months (beginning March 1) of the 1983-84 school year only, she appealed to the U.S. Court of Appeals, Fourth Circuit.

The court of appeals agreed with the district court that the mother was entitled to tuition reimbursement for the last three months of 1983-84 but not the 1984-85 year. It reasoned that the 1984-85 dual placement was a reasonable judgment by RCS. It agreed with the district court's conclusion that the 1984-85 IEP enabled the student to "benefit" (as required under the EAHCA) from the IEP. The mother was also entitled to reimbursement for the costs of the evaluation by the private school's psychologist. *Hudson v. Wilson*, 828 F.2d 1059 (4th Cir.1987).

A federal district court awarded $8,855 to the parents of an emotionally impaired youth as reimbursement for psychological services which their school district admittedly had failed to provide. The court's decision reverses an earlier denial of relief to the parents. The court was able to reconsider its earlier ruling because it had not yet finally disposed of the case. After the U.S. Supreme Court's ruling in *Burlington School Committee v. Department of Education*, 105 S.Ct. 1996 (1985) (see Chapter Four, Section II), the parents asked the district court for a new ruling. The district court observed that its earlier ruling that the parents could not be reimbursed for their child's psychotherapy unless the school district had denied it in bad faith, was wrong in light of *Burlington*. In that case the U.S. Supreme Court stated that where a school district fails to provide a handicapped child with a service essential to his special education, the child's parents will be entitled to reimbursement for their efforts to provide their child with the service. Since the parents had spent $8,850 on psychotherapy, the court ordered the school district to pay the parents this amount. Since the school district failed to provide evidence that it could have supplied the psychotherapy for less than the psychiatrist selected by the parents had charged, the parents were entitled to the full $8,855. *Max M. v. Illinois State Bd. of Educ.*, 629 F.Supp. 1504 (N.D.Ill.1986).

A Tennessee child who suffered from a learning disability, impaired vision and seizures was being provided with a special education under the EAHCA by his local school district. In the fall of the 1983-84 school year, school personnel noticed that the child's behavior and performance appeared to have worsened since the previous spring. They suspected that the child had suffered several grand mal seizures during the summer and that the child had not recently been examined by a physician. After the school district's multidisciplinary team ("M Team") made a recommendation to his parents that he be medically evaluated by a physician, the parents had the child examined by a pediatrician, a neurologist and a psychologist. Although the M Team utilized the results of these neurological and psychological evaluations, they did not result in any change in the child's IEP.

A dispute later arose over whether the school district was required under the EAHCA to pay the costs of these evaluations. The parents' insurance company had paid $79 of the $265 bill for the neurological evaluation, and $99 of the $247 psychological evaluation. A hearing officer ordered the school district to pay the difference between the amount paid by the parents' insurance company and the total cost of the evaluations. The parents filed suit in U.S. district court, seeking an order that the school district reimburse them for the amount the insurer had paid to the neurologist. The parents argued that because their insurance policy provided a maximum of $30,000 lifetime coverage for psychological expenses, the $99 payment made by their insurer resulted in their coverage being reduced to $29,901. This, they alleged, was contrary to the EAHCA's requirement that "related services," i.e., psychological and neurological evaluations, be provided free of charge.

The district court agreed that the parents were entitled to reimbursement for the $99 which their insurer had paid for the psychological evaluation. However, because there was no comparable policy limit for neurological expenses, the parents had incurred no cost as a result of their insurer's payment of $79 for the neurological evaluation. The school district was thus ordered to reimburse the parents for all sums which they had paid to the neurologist and psychologist, minus the $79 paid to the neurologist pursuant to their insurance policy. The court concluded by ordering the district to pay the parents $99 to compensate for the reduction of the amount of coverage available for psychological expenses. *Seals v. Loftis*, 614 F.Supp. 302 (E.D.Tenn.1985).

The parents of an emotionally disturbed eleven-year-old boy sued a New Jersey school board seeking to have the board pay the cost of psychotherapy services allegedly provided for the boy as part of an individualized education plan developed by the board. Both the child's parents and the board agreed that the child should be placed in a therapeutic environment. Thereafter, he was placed in a special education day school for the emotionally disturbed. The school provided an integrated program of individual child psychotherapy, family therapy with the parents, a therapeutic activity group, individual and group counseling and behavior modification, as well as special education on a daily basis in self-contained and departmentalized classes.

Due to the success of the program, the child was able to return to his local school approximately two years later. The parents were informed by the school that the cost of the psychotherapy provided to the child as part of the program would be assessed to them. At the time of the child's discharge the charges had grown to a total of $25,200. The parents sought to have the school board pay the cost of the psychotherapy, which the board refused to do.

The board gave three reasons for its decision. First, it argued that psychotherapy was not part of the IEP agreed to by both the board and the parents. Second, it noted that the New Jersey Department of Education had issued a policy statement to the effect that "psychotherapy," other than that necessary for diagnostic and evaluative purposes, was not a "related service'' for which a local school district would be responsible under the mandate of the EAHCA. Finally, the board took the position that nothing else in the EAHCA or its implementing regulations required it to pay for this service.

A U.S. district court in New Jersey held that psychotherapy provided to an emotionally disturbed child as an integral part of that child's special education is a "related service'' within the meaning of the EAHCA. Further, the definitions contained in the EAHCA superseded inconsistent New Jersey regulations and "policy statements." Thus, while no explicit reference to psychotherapy is made in the EAHCA, the definitions of "related services" which are provided are indicative of a congressional intent to include it where appropriate among those services which are to be provided at no cost to the parents under the Act. The court concluded that the psychotherapy services should be paid for by the board of education. *T.G. v. Bd. of Educ.*, 576 F.Supp. 420 (D.N.J.1983).

An emotionally disturbed student in Connecticut sought an injunction requiring the state to pay the full cost of her attendance at a private school, including psychotherapy. The student's school district had denied such services on the ground that the psychotherapy was not a "related service'' under the EAHCA because the definition of related service excludes medical services that are not diagnostic or evaluative. A. U.S. district court disagreed with the school district's characterization of related services. The plain meaning of the EAHCA distinguishes between "medical services" and other supportive services, including speech pathology and audiology, physical therapy and recreation, as well as psychological services. Only medical services are singled out as limited to services for diagnostic and evaluative purposes. Thus, the court concluded that psychological services required to assist the student to benefit from her special education were related services required to be provided by the state, without cost to the student or her parents. *Papacoda v. State of Connecticut*, 528 F.Supp. 68 (D.Conn.1981).

B. Medical Services

Generally, medical services are excluded from "related services" under the EAHCA unless the services are for diagnostic or evaluative purposes. However, the U.S. Supreme Court held in *Irving Independent School District v. Tatro,* 104 S.Ct. 3371 (1984) (reprinted in the Appendix of U.S. Supreme Court cases in this volume), that clean intermittent catheterization is a related service.

In the *Tatro* case, the U.S. Supreme Court ruled that clean intermittent catheterization (CIC) is a related service not subject to the "medical service'' exclusion of the EAHCA. The parents of an eight-year-old daughter born with spina bifida brought suit against a local Texas school district after the district refused to provide catheterization for the child while she attended school. The parents pursued administrative and judicial avenues to force the district to train staff to perform the simple procedure.

After a U.S. district court held against the parents they appealed to the U.S. Court of Appeals, Fifth Circuit, which reversed the district court ruling. The school district then appealed to the U.S. Supreme Court.

The Supreme Court affirmed that portion of the Court of Appeals decision which held that CIC is a "supportive service," not a "medical service" excluded from the EAHCA. The court was not persuaded by the school district's argument that catheterization is a medical service because it is provided in accordance with a physician's prescription and under a physician's supervision, even though it may be administered by a nurse or trained layperson. The court listed four criteria to determine a school's obligation to provide services that relate to both the health and education of a child.

First, to be entitled to related services, a child must be handicapped so as to require special education. Second, only those services necessary to aid a handicapped child to benefit from special education must be provided, regardless of how easily a school nurse or layperson could furnish them. Third, regulations under the EAHCA state that school nursing services must be performed by a nurse or other qualified person, not by a physician. Fourth, the child's parents in this case were seeking only the *services* of a qualified person at the school, they were not asking the school to provide *equipment*. The court reversed those portions of the Court of Appeals ruling which held the school district liable under the Rehabilitation Act and which held that the parents were entitled to attorney's fees. *Irving Indep. School Dist. v. Tatro*, 104 S.Ct. 3371 (1984).

In Pennsylvania, a severely handicapped child was admitted to a classroom for handicapped children on the condition that her parents would pay the cost of nursing services and related equipment required by the child. The child was profoundly mentally retarded and legally blind. She breathed through a tracheostomy tube and was fed and medicated through a gastrostomy tube. A nurse administered a constant oxygen supply to the child, administered chest physical therapy each day, suctioned mucus from the child's lungs and supervised her positioning for physical and occupational therapy. The child required the constant presence of a nurse to clear her tracheostomy tube in the event that it became plugged by mucus. When this occurred, several times a day, the tube had to be cleared within thirty seconds to prevent injury to the child.

The child's parents and the school district both agreed that the program to which the child was admitted was the most appropriate and least restrictive for the child. When the parents requested that the school district assume the costs of the nursing services as "related services" under the EAHCA, the school district refused. A hearing officer ruled in favor of the parents, but that ruling was reversed by the Pennsylvania Secretary of Education. The parents appealed to a U.S. district court.

The court began by noting that the purpose of the EAHCA was to provide a "free appropriate education" to all handicapped children. A free appropriate education is defined as "special education and related services." "Related services" are defined in the EAHCA to exclude medical services provided for other than diagnostic or evaluation purposes. Regulations implementing the EAHCA define "medical services" to include only "services provided by a licensed physician."

The court then addressed the parents' argument that the services required by the child could not be excluded as medical services because they were not provided by a physician. It looked to previous decisions which, instead of looking solely to whether the provider of a service was a physician, considered the reasonableness of providing a service to determine whether it was a covered "related service." The court concluded that the nursing services required by the child in this case were so extensive that placing the burden of providing them on the school district did not "appear to be consistent with the spirit" of the EAHCA and its regulations. The court concluded that "the nursing services required are so varied, intensive and costly, and more in the nature of 'medical services' that they are not properly includable as 'related services.'" *Bevin H. v. Wright*, 666 F.Supp. 71 (W.D.Pa.1987).

A U.S. district court in New York has ruled that school districts are not required to pay for in-school nursing care. The mother of a severely handicapped seven-year-old student requested that her local school district provide in-school nursing care for her daughter. After the school district denied her request she asked for an impartial hearing and the hearing officer found that because the nursing care constituted "related services" under the EAHCA, the local school district was required to provide and pay for the special nursing services. The school district appealed the decision and the New York State Commissioner of Education reversed the hearing officer's order. The commissioner determined that the in-school nursing care was not a related service. The mother appealed to a U.S. district court.

The district court observed that the EAHCA mandates a "free appropriate public education," including "related services," and requires that an individualized education program (IEP) be developed for each handicapped child providing for his or her specific educational needs. The issue before the district court was the extent to which school health support services are mandated by the EAHCA. The mother contended that the extensive medical attention required by her daughter qualified as a related service under the EAHCA. The school physician testified that the services required by the daughter would require the expertise of a licensed practical nurse or a registered nurse. The school district argued that the medical care required did not constitute related services because the EAHCA excludes from the definition of "related services" medical services required for purposes other than diagnosis or evaluation. It asked that the court consider the type of related services required by the EAHCA as the crucial element in deciding whether the district was required to provide for the medical services. The mother, however, focused on the qualifications of the person performing the services, contending that because the necessary services were to be performed by a qualified person other than a physician, they fell within the description of "school health services," which are not excluded by the EAHCA. The court concluded that the child's daily medical needs did not qualify as related services and that the EAHCA does not require that school districts provide a severely physically handicapped child with constant, in-school nursing care. The mother's request for relief in the form of payment for the daily nursing care of her child was denied.

The mother appealed to the U.S. Court of Appeals, Second Circuit. The mother contended that the district court gave "insufficient deference" to the decision in *Department of Education v. Katherine D.*, 727 F.2d 809 (9th Cir.1983). Although the student in that Hawaii case needed special care, she only required the intermittent services of a lay person. Here, the handicapped daughter needed a full-time person with special training, and thus the decision of the district court was affirmed. *Detsel v. Bd. of Educ.*, 820 F.2d 587 (2d Cir.1987).

Courts will generally not order a school district to pay the medical expenses of a handicapped child where the services are not diagnostic or evaluative, and are not aimed at allowing the child to benefit from his education. The following case illustrates.

A public school system in the District of Columbia appealed an order compelling it to pay a profoundly schizophrenic child's medical expenses during her stay at a private psychiatric hospital as a "related service" under the EAHCA. The child's mother requested special education placement at the private hospital. Treatment at the hospital involved intensive psychotherapy and a drug program. A U.S. district court held that the school system did not have to subsidize the child's medical expenses. The court reasoned that under the EAHCA, a child who is placed in a residential treatment program must have been placed there to render him educable, not for medical reasons only. Here, the placement in the residential treatment program was primarily for medical reasons and not educational reasons. The stay in the hospital was not related to the child's education but was, rather, for treatment of her condition. Therefore, the public school system, although obligated to provide the child with a "free and appropriate public education" under the EAHCA, was not obligated to finance the medical expenses. *McKenzie v. Jefferson*, 566 F.Supp. 404 (D.D.C.1983).

C. Integrated Treatment Programs

Other services, such as occupational therapy, family counseling and extracurricular activities are sometimes requested by parents or guardians of handicapped children. Whether a court will order a school district to provide such services seems to depend upon the particular facts of the case.

A thirteen-year-old girl suffering from anorexia nervosa and various other emotional problems was placed at a Pennsylvania treatment center by her father. This placement occurred after the local school district committee on the handicapped (COH) had determined that the girl could be categorized as an "emotionally disturbed" child with medical problems. The father placed the girl at the Pennsylvania center because of placement delays by the COH. After being denied tuition reimbursement by the New York Commissioner of Education, the father sued in U.S. district court. The court denied reimbursement because the father had failed to comply with EAHCA procedures. The father then sought and received a ruling by a hearing officer that his daughter was emotionally handicapped. However, the commissioner refused to provide tuition reimbursement because the Pennsylvania treatment center was approved by the commissioner only for children age fourteen or older. The father once again sought review in the same U.S. district court.

The district court held that the decisions of the hearing officer that the girl was emotionally handicapped, and that she required placement at the Pennsylvania center, were not reviewable by the commissioner. The court also observed that the girl had applied to nine in-state approved institutions, and had been rejected by all nine, indicating that the father had been reasonable in attempting to place her at a school acceptable to the commissioner. The commissioner claimed that under the EAHCA, the state was required to provide special education and related services which are a part of a "free public education" but that other services, such as medical services, are not provided for in the EAHCA. The district court ordered a trial to determine what portion of the girl's expenses at the Pennsylvania treatment center were related services to be paid by the state of New York. After trial, the district court concluded that counseling, psychological services and periodic psychiatric evaluations for medication purposes were "related services when provided by a psychologist, social worker, or other professional." The father was entitled to reimbursement for both these expenses and tuition, according to the court.

The commissioner appealed to the U.S. Court of Appeals, Second Circuit. Although the court of appeals did not dispute that the tasks performed for the girl's benefit were related services under the EAHCA, it reversed the district court decision. It concluded that the court and the hearing officer wrongly placed the girl at the Pennsylvania treatment center without the commissioner's prior approval (see Chapter Three, Section IV A). *Antkowiak v. Ambach*, 838 F.2d 635 (2d Cir.1988).

A child in California suffered from mental retardation and infantile autism. The Regional Center for the East Bay (RCEB) was a nonprofit community agency created under the California Welfare and Institutions Code. The child was eligible for the services RCEB provided. RCEB placed the child at the Behavior Research Institute of California (BRI). BRI was licensed as a community care facility by the California Department of Social Services. RCEB funded the child's residential program at BRI and a school district paid his educational costs.

In October, 1987, RCEB terminated the child's placement and funding at BRI due to his self-abusive behavior. RCEB claimed that the California Administrative Code permitted it to remove the child when his health or safety was threatened.

The child's parents asked a U.S. district court for a temporary order to prevent RCEB from terminating their child's placement and funding at BRI pending a hearing. The court denied their request. The parents then requested a preliminary injunction against the change in placement.

At the court hearing RCEB contended that the court had no authority over it because RCEB was not an educational agency, did not receive EAHCA funding and had no control over the child's educational program. The parents argued that the EAHCA's procedural safeguards applied since RCEB was providing "related services" under the EAHCA.

The court noted that it had authority over noneducational state agencies that provide related services under the EAHCA. Residential placements qualify as "related services" under the EAHCA if they are made for educational purposes. Here, the child's residential placement at BRI was not a related service under the EAHCA. It was an independent residential placement made pursuant to state law. There was no evidence that the child's placement at BRI was made for educational purposes. Because RCEB's placement of the child at BRI was not protected by EAHCA safeguards the parents' request for a preliminary injunction was denied. *Corbett v. Regional Center for the East Bay*, 676 F.Supp. 964 (N.D.Cal.1988).

The U.S. Court of Appeals, Sixth Circuit, has affirmed a district court ruling that the EAHCA did not obligate school districts to provide continuous occupational therapy to a handicapped student in Ohio. The Court of Appeals also held that the inclusion of nonacademic extracurricular activities once per week was not automatically required. The court observed that the EAHCA, in and of itself, does not require that states maximize the potential of handicapped children commensurate with the opportunity provided to other children. These programs, the court found, were not necessary to permit the child to benefit from his instruction. *Punikaia v. Clark*, 720 F.2d 463 (9th Cir.1983).

D. Transportation

The provision of transportation services to handicapped children has been viewed by the courts to be part of a free appropriate education.

A deaf girl in Ohio was provided with special education and transportation at no cost by a school district for three years. The child's parents then unilaterally enrolled the child in a private school for the deaf for the 1985-86 school year. Both the parents and the school district agreed that the child had been provided a free appropriate education in public school as required by the EAHCA. The parents nevertheless requested that the school district pay for the child's transportation to and from the private school and reimburse them for transportation costs that they had already paid. They asserted that the transportation was a related service for which the school district was liable under the EAHCA. The school district refused to pay and this refusal was upheld by the state education agency. The child's parents appealed.

A U.S. district court declared that "'special education' means the educational program established and monitored by the state, financed with authorized state and federal funds as expressly mandated by the [EAHCA] to appropriately educate the handicapped." Required related services therefore "are those required to be provided to the handicapped child with regard to the child's 'special education' program." The court determined that the EAHCA required the state to provide related services only for programs that the state has designed and offered as "special education." Because the parents unilaterally chose to place the child in private school for their own reasons, that placement was not "special education" within the meaning and intent of the EAHCA. The court concluded that "Congress did not intend the public to bear the additional expense of a private education for handicapped children where those children have already been provided a free, appropriate special education program and services related to that program by the state." It ruled that the school district did not have to pay for the child's transportation to and from the private school. *McNair v. Cardimone*, 676 F.Supp. 1361 (S.D.Ohio 1987).

The mother of a multi-handicapped girl requested special education and related services for the girl in March, 1986. However, the District of Columbia Public Schools (DCPS) did not propose an educational program for the girl until August, 1986. The mother unilaterally placed the girl in the Lab School (a private special education day school) claiming that because DCPS failed to timely propose an appropriate placement for the girl she was forced to seek an appropriate program on her own. The mother then sought a U.S. district court order that DCPS provide the girl with transportation from home to the Lab School.

The mother argued that a federal regulation implemented pursuant to the EAHCA [34 CFR § 300.451(a)] required DCPS to provide transportation to the Lab School as a related service even though the girl had been unilaterally placed. DCPS argued that the federal regulation cited by the mother to support her claim only applied to cases where a child was placed in a private school by his or her parents and required a particular program that was not offered by the public school. The district court observed that 34 CFR § 300.451(a) had to be construed in light of § 300.403. The latter section made it clear that when the public agency (DCPS) provided a free appropriate education and the mother chose to place the girl in a private school nevertheless, "the regulations relating to payment for a private school are not involved and therefore the public agency is not required . . . to pay for the child's education at the private school." Section 300.451(a) merely clarified that DCPS was not relieved of *all* responsibility for the girl. The court concluded that neither the EAHCA nor the implementing regulation required DCPS to provide transportation for the girl to attend the Lab School. *Work v. McKenzie*, 661 F.Supp. 225 (D.D.C.1987).

The individualized education program (IEP) developed for an orthopedically handicapped child recommended that he be educated in a regular class because he was functioning at or above his grade level in all of his academic subjects. It also provided that a special vehicle was needed for his transportation in order to meet his special physical needs. Though the child's local school district offered an appropriate education in and transportation to a public school, his father voluntarily placed him in a private school. After two hearing officers determined that the school district only had to pay $406 per year (considerably less than the actual cost) for the child's transportation to the private school, his father sued the New Jersey Department of Education seeking the actual cost.

The issue before the Superior Court of New Jersey, Appellate Division, was whether the child was entitled to transportation as a "related service" under the EAHCA even though his IEP did not indicate the need for special education. The court held that the child was not entitled to transportation as a "related service." It reasoned that, although the child had a handicap, he did not have a handicap that required special education. Therefore, stated the court, related services auxiliary to special education were not mandated by the EAHCA. The court accepted the school district's argument that under New Jersey law, if a school district provided transportation for students to and from public schools, it was also required to do so for private school students. Since the child was being transported as a private school student and not as a handicapped student, he was held to be entitled only to the fixed amount of $406 under New Jersey law. *A.A. v. Cooperman*, 526 A.2d 1103 (N.J.Super.A.D.1987).

The West Virginia Supreme Court of Appeals held that under state law, two handicapped children were entitled to transportation to school. In this case, two families lived on a dirt road, located in rural West Virginia, known as Dry Monday Branch. The road, which was often traversable only by four-wheel drive vehicle, was owned by a timber company which never objected to its use by the two families. The families had, respectively, a seven-year-old boy and a six-year-old girl who were both afflicted with spina bifida. Both children wore orthopedic braces from waist to feet and were unable to walk to the established school bus stop, which was located on a regular road one-half to nine-tenths of a mile from the children's homes. The county school board refused to send a school bus up Dry Monday Branch because of the road's poor condition, and the children's parents did not own a reliable vehicle in which to transport them to the established bus stop. As a result, the children were unable to attend school during the 1984-85 school year.

Throughout the summer of 1985 the children's parents attempted to persuade school officials to provide transportation for their children. Finally the superintendent sent them a letter informing them that because Dry Monday Branch was a privately owned road, was poorly maintained and was unsafe for a school bus, the parents would have to provide transportation themselves.

Because the laws of West Virginia [W.Va.Code 18-5-13(6)(a)] require that county boards of education provide "adequate" transportation to any student living more than two miles from school, the parents sought an order that the board provide their children with transportation down Dry Monday Branch. The West Virginia Supreme Court of Appeals agreed and issued a writ of mandamus directing the county school board to provide proper transportation. The court held that poor road conditions could not excuse the board from providing adequate transportation to all students. Since neither child was able to walk to the established school bus stop, the board's arrangements were inadequate as a matter of law. As further justification for its decision, the court noted that the timber company which owned Dry Monday Branch regarded it as a public road. *Kennedy v. Bd. of Educ., McDowell County*, 337 S.E.2d 905 (W.Va.1985).

VII. SPECIAL EDUCATION FOR PRESCHOOL CHILDREN AND CHILDREN OVER EIGHTEEN YEARS OF AGE

The EAHCA requires that states provide a free appropriate education to children between the ages of three and twenty-one. However, section 1412(B) of the Act states that with respect to handicapped children aged three to five and eighteen to twenty-one, the requirement to provide an education shall not apply if to do so would conflict with state law regarding public education for such age groups.

Additionally, a 1986 amendment to the EAHCA established a new federal discretionary funding program encouraging states to develop "early intervention services" for handicapped children from birth until their third birthday. The 1986 amendment also established a new preschool grant program which

created incentives for states to ensure that all handicapped children ages three to five receive special education services.

In 1978, the state of New York agreed to pay the tuition costs of a schizophrenic boy who had been placed in a residential psychiatric hospital which operated an accredited academic high school. Behavioral problems prevented the boy from attending the high school, but he continued to reside at the hospital. His doctors hoped that the behavior problems could be overcome. The boy's parents, after petitioning state officials in vain, sought to compel the state to pay the cost of the boy's residential care at the hospital from the time of his placement, July, 1978, through June, 1983, when the boy turned twenty-one years old.

The state contended before a U.S. district court that as long as the child's behavioral problems prevented him from attending the high school at the institution, he was in effect uneducable and therefore the state had no responsibility for any of his expenses. The court ruled that once the state placed the boy at the psychiatric hospital, it became obligated to pay the entire expense of the placement. The state could not escape its responsibility for costs of the boy's residential care simply by stating that those costs did not directly address educational problems. As long as the boy could be educated (however little) through a residential placement, the state remained responsible for the cost of that placement until the boy became twenty-one. *Vander Malle v. Ambach*, 667 F.Supp. 1015 (S.D.N.Y. 1987).

The U.S. Court of Appeals ruled that a twenty-three year old man had no EAHCA claims. The case involved a Michigan man, born in 1954, who was able to communicate only through limited use of sign language. He was enrolled in three different special education programs from 1973 until he reached the age of twenty-five in 1979. The man was never excluded from attending any of the schools or from participating in special education programs, and he was never enrolled in a program that received federal financial assistance. He sued the three school districts in a U.S. district court alleging that the school districts had deprived him of a meaningful education. Specifically, the man claimed that his due process and equal protection rights under the Fourteenth Amendment had been violated. He also claimed that the school districts had failed to afford him a free appropriate education according to the EAHCA and the Rehabilitation Act. The district court ruled against the man and he appealed to the U.S. Court of Appeals, Sixth Circuit.

At the time, the EAHCA was the exclusive avenue through which a person could assert an equal protection claim to a publicly financed special education. The court had to determine whether the EAHCA had been available to the young man. The man claimed that the EAHCA became effective in 1975 but the court found that the EAHCA's requirement to make a free appropriate public education available did not become effective until 1977. It also noted that when the man entered one of the school district's programs in the fall of 1977 he was twenty-three years old. The EAHCA only requires an appropriate public education for handicapped children between ages three and twenty-one. The man thus had no legitimate equal protection claims under the EAHCA.

The court of appeals stated that in order to establish a deprivation of an interest protected by the due process clause, the man had to show that he was excluded from the school districts' special education programs. He argued that he was in effect excluded from the districts' programs because he had no communicative skills and sat in classrooms where he was unaware of what was happening. In ruling for the school district, the court noted that other courts have repeatedly rejected the idea that the due process clause secures a right to the "most appropriate" education. Even though the man was limited in what he gained from the special education classes he was not excluded from those classes and did receive an appropriate education. Thus, the school district did not infringe upon the man's due process rights.

The court also denied the man's Rehabilitation Act claim since none of the programs that he participated in received federal financial assistance. It was not enough to show that the schools that the man attended were federally financed because the most common standard applied is whether the specific program was federally financed. The EAHCA and Rehabilitation Act claims were inapplicable and the court found no constitutional violations. The district court decision against the man was upheld. *Gallagher v. Pontiac School Dist.*, 807 F.2d 75 (6th Cir.1986).

A handicapped child in Oklahoma who was about to be graduated by her school district brought suit against the school district alleging that she was in the tenth, not the twelfth, grade and was therefore entitled to two additional years of special education. The school district argued that any notations in the student's individual education program (IEP) or her report card indicating that she was in the tenth grade were a mistake and that the child was in the twelfth grade and thus eligible for graduation. The district further argued that Oklahoma state law did not obligate school districts to provide education to handicapped students from eighteen through twenty-one years of age nor did the EAHCA impose such a requirement. A U.S. district court in Oklahoma held in the child's favor and the school district appealed.

The U.S. Court of Appeals, Tenth Circuit, affirmed the district court ruling finding that since nonhandicapped children in the eighteen to twenty-one age group may be entitled to additional years of education when one or more grades are failed, handicapped children within this age group are similarly entitled to continue their education.

The court found evidence of the school district's different methods used to determine when handicapped and nonhandicapped children are in the twelfth grade and found that certain standards for the evaluation of handicapped children, as with nonhandicapped children must be met before a handicapped child can be deemed to have advanced a grade. A nonhandicapped student's performance was evaluated by standardized course content whereas a handicapped student's progress was measured by whether the goals in his or her IEP were met. The court found that the EAHCA contemplates that a handicapped child's progress in school should be measured by objective, if not standardized, criteria. It would make a farce of the clear intent of Congress to interpret the EAHCA as allowing a handicapped child to fail to meet his or her IEP objectives and yet advance a grade level. Here, the court found a failure on the part of the school district to adequately measure the child's progress. A notation in the child's IEP and in her report card indicating that she was in tenth grade prompted the court to rule that the child was entitled to two additional years of special education. *Helms v. Indep. School Dist. No. 3*, 750 F.2d 820 (10th Cir.1985).

VIII. LENGTH OF SCHOOL YEAR FOR THE HANDICAPPED

The majority of cases hold that handicapped children are entitled to a summer program to prevent regression of progress made during the regular school year.

A middle school student was placed in a treatment program at a residential school after she exhibited bizarre behavior. The student was diagnosed as being schizophrenic and an individualized educational program was developed for her. Although she performed satisfactorily in her academic fields, she made little progress in emotional and social areas and had serious problems readjusting after vacations spent at home. Authorities at the residential school requested that the school district declare her eligible for an extended school year program so that she could live at the residential school during the summer. This request was denied. Her parents enrolled her in the summer program anyway.

The parents then contested the district's determination that the student was ineligible for the summer residential program. A hearing officer decided that because her classroom performance had been satisfactory, she was ineligible. On appeal, the Pennsylvania secretary of education reversed the hearing officer's determination, reasoning that a child's emotional, behavioral and social problems must also be considered. Because the student suffered regression following breaks in her educational program, the secretary ordered the district to reimburse the parents for the cost of the summer program. The school district appealed this order to the Commonwealth Court of Pennsylvania.

The court cited a previous decision which recognized the following standard:

> A handicapped student is entitled to an educational program in excess of 180 days per year if regression caused by an interruption in educational programming, together with the student's limited recoupment capacity, renders it impossible or unlikely that the student will attain the level of self-sufficiency and independence from caretakers that the student would otherwise have [been] expected to reach in view of his/her handicapping condition.

Another cited decision recognized that "for emotionally disturbed children, their regression need not be in the academic area." Since the student's emotional and social regression was well established in this case the court affirmed the determination of the secretary of education that the school district had to reimburse the parents for the cost of the summer residential program. *Bucks County Pub. Schools v. Commonwealth*, 529 A.2d 1201 (Pa.Cmwlth.1987).

A Texas school district appealed to the U.S. Court of Appeals, Fifth Circuit, seeking reversal of a U.S. district court's order that it was required to provide out-of-district transportation and a full summer program for a handicapped child. The court of appeals rejected the school district's arguments and held that the school was required to provide the summer program to the child, with transportation after school to a babysitter's home one mile outside the school district. The child suffered from physical deformities in his hands and face, had an unusual laxity in his joints, uncoordinated vision, a significant lack of muscle tone and he could walk only with assistance.

After he had completed the first grade, his mother requested that the district provide a summer program. However, the lack of available transportation and the class schedule made it impossible for the boy to attend. Instead, he stayed with a babysitter who was not trained in special education; consequently he suffered regression in his ability to stand and feed himself. The next year his mother requested a summer program with transportation, but her request was refused. The mother appealed the denial to the Texas Education Agency, and a hearing examiner ruled for the mother. The school district then filed suit seeking review in U.S. district court.

The district court found that the student had suffered substantial regression of the knowledge gained and skills learned during the school year without the summer program. The court of appeals, agreeing with the district court's decision, held that if a handicapped child experiences severe or substantial regression during the summer months in the absence of a summer school program, the child is entitled to year-round services. The court of appeals also found that the request for transportation was reasonable because the mother worked full-time and because it did not create an undue burden on the school district. *Alamo Heights Indep. School Dist. v. State Bd. of Educ.*, 790 F.2d 1153 (5th Cir.1986).

Several young handicapped children in New York were denied summer education programs to which they believed they were entitled under the EAHCA. Following the inception of a lawsuit seeking injunctive relief the children were placed in adequate summer schools. However, the lawsuit was pursued because of the plaintiff's contention that there was a reasonable expectation that the same problems were likely to occur again in the immediate future. The defendants in the case, a local school board and the state of New York, sought a dismissal of the complaint contending that because the children had been placed there was then no case or controversy to be decided. Additionally, the defendants maintained that the complaint failed to state a claim upon which relief could be granted since they had not refused to provide or arrange for special educational services for the plaintiffs on a twelve-month basis and since the statutes upon which the children relied did not require the provision of a twelve-month program for all handicapped children.

A U.S. district court in New York denied the motion to dismiss. It stated that the children were definitely suffering from severe handicaps and there was no indication in the record that the problems encountered by them would not persist. In fact, all indications were to the contrary. The court felt it had good reason to believe, therefore, that the challenged conduct would continue. In light of those circumstances, the court found that the plaintiffs had presented a justiciable controversy over which the court could exercise its jurisdiction.

The court also held that the children stated a claim under the provisions of the EAHCA. It was noted that the EAHCA provides federal funding to state and local educational agencies in order to insure provision of special education services to handicapped children. Along with the funding, however, the act also imposes an obligation upon those state and local agencies to develop for each child an "individualized education program." Here the defendants acknowledged that the children and all other members of that particular class require twelve-month schooling. However, they failed to provide for or arrange for the provision of special educational services for the summer months for these children. The motion to dismiss was denied and the case went forward for trial. *Stanton v. Bd. of Educ. of Norwich Cent. School Dist.*, 581 F.Supp. 190 (N.D.N.Y.1983).

In this case the Georgia Association of Retarded Citizens brought suit against the state of Georgia and a local school board, seeking a change in school policies and practices which refused to consider the needs of mentally retarded children for schooling beyond the traditional 180 days. The court, relying heavily on the Pennsylvania decision, decided in favor of the retarded children. It noted that federal law places the responsibility on state educational agencies to make sure that local agencies provide adequate educational services to handicapped children or directly provide such services themselves. It was pointed out that many future problems, such as financial limitations and the possibility of overburdening available school personnel, lie ahead, but those problems would have to be dealt with by a court or some other appropriate body at a future date.

This case was appealed to the U.S. Court of Appeals, Eleventh Circuit, which affirmed the district court's ruling, saying that a blanket refusal to extend the 180-day school year violated the EAHCA and the U.S. Supreme Court decision *Board of Education v. Rowley*, which imposes an obligation upon schools to consider *individual* educational needs of handicapped children. The court held that because the state of Georgia failed to follow the procedures set forth in EAHCA it also failed to develop adequate individualized educational programs for the children, which might have included an extension of the school year beyond 180 days. *Georgia Ass'n of Retarded Citizens v. McDaniel*, 716 F.2d 1565 (11th Cir.1983).

Other cases have held that handicapped children are entitled to a year-round education.

The U.S. Court of Appeals, Fifth Circuit, has also held that a local school district was required to provide an education for handicapped children beyond the regular nine-month school year. The court struck down a Mississippi rule limiting the length of the school year for all school children to 180 days, saying that rigid rules such as 180-day limitations violate the EAHCA's procedural command that each child receives individual consideration, and also the substantive requirement that each child receives some benefit from his education. *Crawford v. Pittman*, 708 F.2d 1028 (5th Cir.1983).

The parents of a severely handicapped child in Missouri brought suit against a local special school district and the Missouri Department of Education alleging that the school district's refusal to provide for severely handicapped children programs extending beyond the regular nine month school year violated the EAHCA and the Rehabilitation Act. The parents claimed that such programs were provided in the summer to nonhandicapped children.

A U.S. district court issued an injunction prohibiting the Department of Education from discrimination against handicapped children. The district court found that the state's policy which did not provide for more than 180 days of education per school year for the severely handicapped denied those children "free appropriate education" in violation of the EAHCA. It quoted language from the U.S. Supreme Court case of *Board of Education v. Rowley* (see this volume's Appendix of U.S. Supreme Court cases): "access to specialized instruction and related services which are individually designed to provide educational benefit to the handicapped child" is the responsibility of the state educational agency.

The parents, dissatisfied with this ruling, appealed to the U.S. Court of Appeals, Eighth Circuit. The Court of Appeals agreed with the district court that under the EAHCA and *Rowley*, the state educational agency is exclusively responsible for providing an "appropriate" education to handicapped children. Thus, it was beyond the court's power to compel the school district to do something which was, strictly speaking, not the district's responsibility. Moreover, the special school district was not in a position to discriminate against the handicapped in the form of providing services to the nonhandicapped which it had failed to provide to the handicapped. The district's funds were used exclusively for the education of the handicapped. Since the primary responsibility to extend the school year for the severely handicapped children lay at the state level, the court affirmed the district court ruling. *Yaris v. Special School Dist. of St. Louis County*, 728 F.2d 1055 (8th Cir.1984).

Year-round schooling was not mandated in a Virginia case which arose when the parents of a handicapped child brought suit against a local school district attacking the quality of the district's program which was provided to their child. Here, in ruling that the educational program afforded to the child was more than adequate to meet the child's needs, the court stated that the child was not entitled to year-round schooling without showing an irreparable loss of progress during summer months. *Bales v. Clarke*, 523 F.Supp. 1366 (E.D.Va.1981).

IX. SPECIAL EDUCATION FOR INCARCERATED CHILDREN

Incarcerated children are entitled to a free appropriate education if otherwise eligible.

A handicapped child was confined to a juvenile detention center in Florida. He sued a local school board in a U.S. district court under § 504 of the Rehabilitation Act and the EAHCA. He alleged that the detention center was overcrowded, unsanitary, lacked adequate staffing and was deficient in special education opportunities. The school board moved for dismissal. It contended that the child's claims under § 504 were invalid because the EAHCA provided all the remedies and procedures which Congress afforded handicapped children. It also claimed that the child's lawsuit should be dismissed because he failed to exhaust administrative remedies. The child contended that exhaustion of administrative remedies would be futile.

The court held for the child with respect to his § 504 claim. Under the Handicapped Children's Protection Act the child could assert claims under both § 504 and the EAHCA. However, the court held for the school board regarding its exhaustion of administrative remedies argument. The child failed to show that exhaustion of administrative remedies would be futile or cause him irreparable harm. The school board's motion to dismiss the child's claim was granted. *G.C. v. Coler*, 673 F.Supp. 1093 (S.D.Fla.1987).

A twenty-one-year-old prison inmate in Massachusetts sued state education officials on behalf of himself and other inmates alleging that the failure to provide special education services to inmates who were under age twenty-two, and who had not already received a high school diploma, was a denial of a free appropriate education as required under state and federal law. A U.S. district court held that the incarcerated status of the plaintiffs did not preclude their entitlement to a free and appropriate special education under the EAHCA and state law. Accordingly, the court issued an injunction enjoining the education officials from failing to provide special education services to the plaintiffs. *Green v. Johnson*, 513 F.Supp. 965 (D.Mass.1981).

CHAPTER THREE
PROCEDURAL SAFEGUARDS OF THE EAHCA

The procedural safeguards of the EAHCA are designed to ensure that parents and children are able to enforce their rights under the Act. The safeguards include the right to an "impartial due process hearing" when parents or guardians are dissatisfied with their child's IEP [section 1415(b)(2)]. These hearings are to be conducted by the state or local educational agency responsible for providing services. However, no employee of an agency involved in the education or care of the child may conduct the hearing; the hearing must be conducted by an impartial hearing officer. The initial due process hearing may be provided at the state or local educational agency level. If the initial hearing is held at the local level, either party may appeal "to the State educational agency which shall conduct an impartial review of such hearing" [section 1415(c)]. The decision of the initial hearing officer is final unless appealed; the decision of the state officer is likewise final unless either party brings an action in state court or federal district court [section 1415(e)(1)].

I. ROLE OF THE HEARING OFFICER

The role of the hearing officer at the initial hearing is to make an impartial decision on the appropriateness of a school's individualized educational program for a particular child. If the initial hearing decision is appealed, the reviewing officer "shall conduct an impartial review of such hearing" and "shall make an independent decision upon completion of such review" [section 1415(c)].

This case illustrates that the role of the hearing officer is limited by the provisions of the EAHCA and state law. A New York father placed his thirteen-year-old daughter who suffered from anorexia nervosa at a Pennsylvania residential treatment facility. He placed her there due to several placement delays by a school district's committee on the handicapped (COH). A U.S. district court denied his request for tuition reimbursement because he had failed to exhaust administrative remedies. He then sought an administrative hearing and the hearing officer ordered placement at the Pennsylvania center. However, the New York Commissioner of Education refused to provide tuition reimbursement because the Pennsylvania center was approved only for fourteen-year-olds and older. The father appealed to the same U.S. district court. It upheld the placement and ordered a trial to determine what portion of the daughter's expenses were to be reimbursed by the state of New York.

The district court ruled that the father was entitled to total reimbursement for his daughter's education and related services at the Pennsylvania center. The daughter received all of the benefits and rights at the Pennsylvania center that she would have received at a New York school even though it was not approved for her age. The court also directed the commissioner to develop an IEP for the daughter which would provide for placement at the Pennsylvania center. The commissioner then appealed to the U.S. Court of Appeals, Second Circuit.

On appeal, the commissioner contended that the district court exceeded its authority by ordering the placement. The court of appeals agreed with the commissioner. EAHCA § 1401(18)(B) required that the daughter receive special education and related services which met the state educational agency standards. Section 1413(a)(4)(B)(ii) of the EAHCA provided that the state determine whether private facilities like the Pennsylvania center met those standards. Thus, the EAHCA incorporated state educational standards. It was the state of New York's obligation (through the commissioner) to ensure that private facilities met applicable state educational standards. The hearing officer and the district court wrongly placed the daughter at the Pennsylvania center without the commissioner's approval. The court of appeal observed that "[t]he hearing officer had no jurisdiction to compel either the school or the state to violate federal law, and thus her decision was void to the extent that it ordered . . ." the daughter's placement at the Pennsylvania center without the commissioner's approval. The district court decision was reversed and the father was denied reimbursement. *Antkowiak v. Ambach*, 838 F.2d 635 (2d Cir.1988).

The Michigan Court of Appeals reversed on procedural grounds a state review officer's decision in favor of the parents of a handicapped child, citing a lack of impartiality on the part of the review officer. The court's opinion also indicated that it was displeased with the review officer's disregard of financial burdens on school districts. In this case a girl suffered a stroke at the age of ten which left her with a full scale I.Q. of forty-seven and a potential I.Q. of sixty-four (using the WISC-R schedule). When her parents approached their local school district requesting a free appropriate public education for their daughter, the district evaluated her and proposed placement in a classroom for the "educable mentally impaired." The parents disagreed and a due process hearing was held. The hearing officer, rejecting the parents' claim that the girl required a two-to-one student-teacher ratio, approved the school district's proposed EMI placement. The parents appealed to the state review officer, who exercised his statutory power to allow neither the school nor the parents to file written briefs or present oral arguments. After examining the evidence which had been presented to the hearing officer, the review officer ruled that the girl was entitled to a student-teacher ratio of not more than three to one, and the school district appealed.

The state court of appeals held that because the parents had written arguments attacking the hearing officer's decision on the appeal form they filed with the review officer, the review officer had, in effect, allowed the parents to file a written brief. The review officer had therefore been obligated to allow the school district to present its position as well. Since the review officer had improperly allowed only one side to file a brief, his decision was vacated and the case was remanded to the review officer with instructions that oral arguments be allowed.

Although the court cautioned that "[w]e do not pass on the merits as to which side should prevail," it went on to observe that the hearing officer had acted impartially and without bias. Further, although Michigan law requires that handicapped children be provided with a special education designed to maximize their potential, "[w]e believe that there is some limitation on what kind of program is required. When two competing educational programs which meet the child's requirements are evaluated, the needs of the handicapped child should be balanced with the needs of the state to allocate scarce funds among as many handicapped children as possible. . . . [A]ssuming in this case, that funds are available for two proposed educational programs, each suitable to enable the child to reach her maximum potential, it would appear reasonable to adopt the program requiring less expenditure." Having made these judicial comments, the appeals court remanded the case to the state review officer for reconsideration. *Nelson v. Southfield Pub. Schools*, 384 N.W.2d 423 (Mich.App.1986).

A nine-year-old Florida boy who lived with his parents suffered from juvenile autism. For three years the boy was enrolled in the Hendry County School Class for the Trainable Mentally Handicapped. Because the boy had made limited educational progress both the school and the boy's parents agreed that the boy needed a different IEP for the 1985-86 school year. Subsequently the boy was labeled severely emotionally disturbed (SED) and in need of a program for the severely handicapped. In May, 1985, the school held a planning conference to develop a new IEP for the boy. As a result of the conference the school's director of exceptional student education approved a new IEP for the boy. It provided for a profoundly handicapped class program, a mainstreaming opportunity with first grade students, an aide to accompany the student to music class, and an SED class placement in a varying exceptionalities class.

When the new IEP was issued the parents rejected it contending that the boy needed residential placement if he was to reach necessary educational goals. In June, 1985, the parents asked for a due process hearing to determine the appropriateness of the IEP. In July, 1985, the hearing officer issued his order, rejecting the school's proposal and ordering residential placement for the boy. The school appealed the hearing officer's decision to the Florida District Court of appeal.

The court concluded that a hearing officer is limited to determining the appropriateness of an IEP. Here the hearing officer overstepped his authority when he ordered a residential placement for the boy. The most the hearing officer could do was to remand the matter to the school district for further deliberation with an attached recommendation for residential placement. The court held that the school's proposed program met the needs of the boy and that a residential placement was not necessary for the boy to receive an appropriate public education. The hearing officer's decision was reversed and the case was remanded for further proceedings. *Hendry County School Bd. v. Kujawski*, 498 So.2d 566 (Fla.App.2d Dist.1986).

Where state law regarding the role of a hearing officer contradicts the EAHCA, the EAHCA prevails as this case illustrates. In the fall of 1983, following the private evaluations of their two children, the children's parents informed the principal of the public school in which the children were enrolled that the children were being placed in a private educational facility for half of each school day. Subsequently, the parents asked that the board of education provide the children with an IEP comparable to that of the private institution or, alternatively, that the board provide transportation and tuition for the children to continue at the private facility for the 1984-85 school year. They asked to be reimbursed for expenses incurred by them resulting from the children's private school placement during the 1983-84 year. The board of education denied their request and the parents requested a due process hearing. The hearing officer determined that he had no authority under North Carolina state law to grant an award of reimbursement and no hearing was held. When the state board of education denied a request by the parents that the hearing officer be granted such authority, the parents appealed to a U.S. district court.

The parents claimed that the board of education, through the appointed administrative hearing officer, deprived them of their procedural rights secured by the EAHCA. They also contended that the state board of education refused to interpret or amend state regulations to be consistent with the EAHCA. The state board argued that reimbursement costs were monetary penalties that could only be imposed by the courts.

The district court noted that the EAHCA contained a detailed procedural component with which local and state boards were required to comply. It concluded that to allow a state hearing officer to conduct a hearing on the issue of reimbursement and to enter findings of fact based on that hearing, but to refuse to order reimbursement even when appropriate, made the EAHCA less than complete. To the extent North Carolina's interpretation of the authority of a hearing officer contradicted the EAHCA, the terms of the EAHCA must control. The local board of education was ordered to conduct another hearing and order reimbursement costs if appropriate. *S-1 v. Spangler*, 650 F.Supp. 1427 (M.D.N.C.1986).

Two handicapped children in Alabama, dissatisfied with the educational plans that had been prescribed for them, sought and were afforded due process hearings. Prior to the hearings, the children, through their parents, filed written objections to the method used by the state for selecting due process hearing officers. They alleged that the selection of hearing officers who are officers or employees of local school systems in which the children were enrolled or who were university personnel involved in the formulation of state policies concerning special education violated the EAHCA and its implementing regulations. Despite these objections, due process hearings were conducted and in each case a determination adverse to the children was reached. The children's claims were then evaluated by a review panel which was selected by the same method as the due process panel. Prior to the second hearing the children filed a second set of written objections to the method of selecting hearing officers. The review panel affirmed the adverse ruling of the due process panel and the children brought suit in federal court.

A U.S. district court enjoined the local school superintendent from selecting, as due process hearing officers under the EAHCA, individuals who are officers or employees of local school systems which the children attended, or university personnel who have been or are involved in the formulation of state policies on educating handicapped children.

The school district appealed to the U.S. Court of Appeals, Eleventh Circuit, which affirmed the district court ruling. The court of appeals found that officers and employees of local school boards in Alabama are employees of agencies "involved in the education and care of the child" with a personal or professional interest in the type of educational assistance extended to handicapped children, and thus are not eligible to serve on due process hearing panels under the EAHCA. Further, university personnel involved in the formulation of state policies for the education of the handicapped are not sufficiently impartial to serve as due process hearing officers under the EAHCA. *Mayson v. Teague*, 749 F.2d 652 (11th Cir.1984).

A U.S. district court in Connecticut has dealt with the procedural problem of whether testimony of a hearing officer regarding her mental processes while making a decision can be allowed in a case involving an administrative determination that a minor's placement in a private residential facility was not necessary for educational reasons. The case arose on appeal of a state administrative determination to the district court. The defendant school board was excused from any financial obligation in excess of tuition costs by the administrative determination and the minor, through his parents, appealed.

At the appeal stage the state listed as its sole witness the hearing officer whose decision was being appealed. The minor's motion to preclude her testimony at trial was granted. The court noted that in reviewing a decision of an administrative agency, it is not the proper function of the court to probe the mental processes of the agency or its members, particularly if the agency makes a considered decision upon a full administrative record. Such probing should ordinarily be avoided and there must be a strong showing of bad faith or improper behavior before such inquiry may be made.

In this case, the state based its opposition to the motion on the premise that the mental processes rule has little or no application in a case where the officer is testifying voluntarily and the purpose of the testimony is not to contradict or impeach the record which has already been established.

The court stated that this proposition was supported neither by logic nor authority. The objectivity and independence of the hearing officer in her role as administrative adjudicator would likely be undermined by her being offered by the state as a probative witness in support of its case. Cross examination and the court's assessment of the testimony would involve, necessarily, a review of the mental processes of the adjudicative officer. Such an examination of a judge would be destructive of judicial responsibility. Just as a judge's mind should not be subjected to scrutiny, so the integrity of the administrative process must be equally respected. The court, therefore, granted the motion to exclude the hearing officer's testimony. *Feller v. Bd. of Educ. of State of Connecticut*, 583 F.Supp. 1526 (D.Conn.1984).

A hearing officer is not charged with the responsibility of choosing between an educational program offered by a school district and counterproposals submitted by parents. To give the hearing officer such powers would be to diminish the role of the school districts in selecting the best possible educational program appropriate to the needs of handicapped children. This ruling was handed down by a federal district court in the District of Columbia in a case in which the parents of a handicapped child challenged District of Columbia hearing procedures. The court observed that the EAHCA calls for a due process hearing if the parents of a handicapped child object to the placement of their child in a program they deem inappropriate to the child's needs.

Here, the parents were dissatisfied with the program offered by the school district. They asked the court to order the hearing officer to weigh the proposals of both the school district and the parents and then to determine which of the two proposals was most appropriate for their child. The court refused to grant such powers to the hearing officer. Instead the court reiterated the duties of the hearing officer in such cases—the officer is required to hear the school district's proposal. If the parents are dissatisfied with that proposal they may offer alternative suggestions to the school district. If, after hearing the proposal and the counterproposals, the hearing officer deems the school district's proposal to be inadequate, the hearing officer must remand the district's proposal to the district with instructions to submit a new proposal within 20 days. The parents were not allowed to alter the meaning of the EAHCA. *Davis v. Dist. of Columbia Bd. of Educ.*, 530 F.Supp. 1215 (D.D.C.1982).

A hearing officer in Rhode Island ordered a school district to fund the special education of two learning disabled children at a private school in Massachusetts. A U.S. district court upheld the hearing officer's order. The school district appealed claiming that because the hearing officer was an employee of the Department of Education, the hearing did not satisfy the requirement of the EAHCA that it not "be conducted by an employee of [the local or state educational] agency . . . involved in the education or care of the child." The U.S. Court of Appeals, First Circuit, upheld the district court ruling saying that the school district was not within the "protected class" of handicapped children and their parents that Congress envisioned when it prohibited employees of a state educational agency from acting as review officers. *Colin K. v. Schmidt*, 715 F.2d 1 (1st Cir.1983).

The parents of a developmentally disabled child in California requested and received a hearing after both a county educational agency and a California health services organization had denied occupational therapy services to their child. The hearing officer ruled in favor of the child and his parents finding that he exhibited a lack of motor skills and required the related services of OT in order to benefit from his education. The hearing officer ordered the county to provide therapy.

The county appealed to a California superior court which denied its request to challenge the administrative decision. The county then sought relief from the California Court of Appeal. It argued that the hearing was procedurally inadequate because it was conducted by one hearing officer instead of a panel of three officers in violation of California administrative regulations. The court held that the California Education Code requirement that a hearing be conducted "by a person knowledgeable in the laws governing special education" superseded the inconsistent administrative regulation requiring a panel of three persons. *Nevada County Office of Educ. v. Superintendent of Pub. Instruction*, 197 Cal.Rptr. 152 (Cal.App.3d Dist.1983).

One court has held that a state agency does not have the right to appeal an unfavorable decision by an administrative hearing officer. In this case the Hawaii Department of Education appealed from a Hawaii trial court order dismissing its appeal of a hearing officer's decision. The appeal was prompted by the decision and order of an administrative hearing officer in favor of the parents of a handicapped student who had complained that the Department had not provided him with a free appropriate public education as required by the EAHCA.

The Supreme Court of Hawaii held that under the EAHCA the Department was not entitled to appeal from the administrative decision. Section 1415(e)(2) of the Act provides only that "any party aggrieved by the findings and decision made pursuant to the hearing process may bring a separate civil action in a state or federal district court." The court noted that the standard of review in such an action "is very different" from the standard of review in an appeal. This was discussed in the case of *Board of Education v. Rowley*, where the U.S. Supreme Court stated that in an appeal, the court's inquiry into suits brought under the EAHCA is twofold. First, how has the State complied with the procedures set forth in the Act? Second, is the IEP developed through the Act's procedures reasonably calculated to enable the child to receive educational benefits? If these requirements are met, the State has complied with the obligations imposed by Congress and the courts can require no more. In a separate civil action the state court or federal district court "shall receive the records of the administrative proceedings, shall hear additional evidence at the request of a party and, basing its decision on the preponderance of the evidence, shall grant such relief as the court determines appropriate." The court concluded that the EAHCA did not confer the right of appeal upon state agencies. The district court's dismissal of the appeal was reversed, however, on the ground that a claim for relief in a separate civil action was presented, even though misdesignated on appeal. *Matter of Eric G.*, 649 P.2d 1140 (Hawaii 1982).

The California Court of Appeal was asked to decide whether a school district should have sought review of a hearing officer's decision pursuant to the EAHCA or by way of state administrative remedies. In this case involving a hearing officer's determination that a handicapped child should be placed in a full-time residential environment, the school district pursued the less expensive state administrative appeal procedures rather than bringing a separate civil action under the EAHCA in a state or federal court.

The school district then asked a California trial court to review the hearing officer's decision and issue an order commanding the state department of education to set it aside. The court granted the district's request but later ordered the school district to place the child at the residential school requested by the mother or in "any other appropriate twenty-four hour residential program selected by the [district]." The child refused placement in a residential school other than the one requested. Both the mother of the child and the California State Department of Education appealed arguing that the school district pursued the incorrect procedures to challenge the hearing officer's final decision.

The Court of Appeal found it unnecessary to decide which method of appeal was proper for two reasons. First, the child was not a party "aggrieved" by the administrative decision and therefore could not, under the express language of section 1415(e)(2) of the EAHCA bring a civil action. Also, he never objected to the district's use of the state administrative procedure at the trial, and thereby waived any right to complain of it on appeal.

Second, the Department was neither an "aggrieved party" under the Act, nor did it suffer prejudice from the use of that method of review. However, the court expressed a clear preference for the use of the appeal procedures set out in section 1415(e)(2) of the EAHCA, particularly where state review procedures, as in California, provide lesser protection or a more limited scope of review to the party aggrieved. Using the "substantial evidence'' test as required by California state administrative procedure, rather than the "preponderance of the evidence'' test as outlined in the EAHCA, the court concluded that substantial evidence warranted the child's placement in a full-time residential setting. *San Francisco Unified School Dist. v. State*, 182 Cal.Rptr. 525 (Cal.App.1st Dist.1982).

II. CHANGE IN PLACEMENT

Recognizing that a school district's unfettered discretion to change a handicapped child's placement could result in a denial of a free appropriate education to the child, section 1415(b)(1)(C) of the EAHCA requires that prior written notice of any proposed change in the educational placement of a child be afforded to the parents or guardians of the child. A hearing must also be granted to parents wishing to contest a change in placement of their child. In *Honig v. Doe*, 108 S.Ct. 592 (1988) (see next section for a complete discussion), the U.S. Supreme Court held that suspensions of handicapped children which exceed ten days constitute a change in placement under the EAHCA.

The District of Columbia Public Schools (DCPS) found a child to be eligible for special education and placed him at the Brent Public Elementary School. His parents were dissatisfied with the placement and asked for a due process hearing. The hearing officer concluded that the Brent placement was inappropriate and gave DCPS a deadline of November 25, 1985, to provide a new placement. On November 27, 1985, DCPS proposed a placement at the Prospect Learning Center. However, the parents were also dissatisfied with the Prospect placement and requested a second due process hearing. In the meantime, they unilaterally placed the child in the Lab School, a private special education facility.

The second hearing officer determined on March 24, 1986, that both Prospect and the Lab School were appropriate and that DCPS was responsible for the child's placement at the Lab School for the 1985-86 school year until April 7, 1986, because it missed the November 25, 1985, deadline. The hearing officer also determined that the child should be placed at Prospect after

April 7, 1986. The parents sued DCPS seeking a court order that DCPS place the child at the Lab School retroactive from April 7, 1986, during the pendency of the court proceedings. They argued that the Lab School was his current educational placement and that DCPS was required to maintain this "status quo" under the EAHCA. DCPS contended that only after April 7, 1986, was Prospect his placement.

The U.S. district court concluded that there was substantial evidence that the Lab School was his current educational placement during the court proceedings. First, the child never had a true placement in the public school system. The Brent placement was aborted after one day and the first hearing officer found that DCPS could not prove that the Brent placement was appropriate. Second, the second hearing officer found that DCPS did not have an appropriate program in place for the child until November 27, 1985, and therefore he concluded that DCPS was responsible for the Lab School placement from the beginning of the 1985-86 school year until April 7, 1986. Based upon the above facts, the court held that the parents were justified in unilaterally placing the child at the Lab School. It declined to order DCPS to fund the child's Lab School placement from April 7, 1986, to May 1, 1987, since a later court could find that the Lab School was not the child's current educational placement for that period. However, the court held that effective May 1, 1987, DCPS had to fund the child's education during the pendency of the court proceedings. *Cochran v. Dist. of Columbia*, 660 F.Supp. 314 (D.D.C.1987).

In January, 1976, a Washington state boy was found to be eligible for special educational service having scored 70 on an I.Q. test. The district developed an IEP for him which recommended placement in an "educable handicapped classroom." After further testing the school district recommended continued placement in a special education class, but his parents chose to have him repeat first grade in a regular class during the 1976-77 school year. In May, 1979, another assessment by the district found the boy's I.Q. to be 69 and his academic performance less than half the expected grade level. The parents again refused the district's placement in an "educable handicapped classroom" for mildly retarded students and placed him in a private school.

In the summer of 1981, a school district employee began tutoring the boy. When the parents placed the boy in a public school in the fall of 1981 they asked that the tutoring continue. After the tutor resigned, the district told the parents that a new tutor would instruct the boy. The parents alleged that this constituted a change of placement in violation of the "status quo" provision of the EAHCA. The parents chose to remove the boy from school three hours daily to be tutored by the original tutor at their own expense. Another test was then performed by the school district which revealed that the boy's I.Q. was 66 and that he was "mildly mentally retarded." After two hearings favored the school district's position the parents appealed to a U.S. district court which ruled in their favor. The school district appealed to the U.S. Court of Appeals, Ninth Circuit.

The school district challenged the district court's ruling that the boy had a leaning disability and was not mentally retarded. In 1982, a neurologist had concluded that the boy was dyslexic, not mildly retarded. The court of appeals agreed with the school district noting that the trial record provided no support for the district court's conclusion that the boy had a learning disability, not mild retardation, according to state regulations. It refused to accept the neurologist's subjective conclusion that the boy could not benefit from placement in the school district's special education classes. State regulations required placement to the based upon objective criteria such as the I.Q. test. The boy's eligibility for special education was correctly based on "mild mental retardation." The district court decision was reversed. *Gregory K. V. Longview School Dist.*, 811 F.2d 1307 (9th Cir.1987).

A U.S. district court in Ohio issued a preliminary injunction ordering that two violently disruptive students, ages twelve and fifteen, be allowed to return to their classrooms. Both boys, wards of the state, had been evaluated as severely behaviorally handicapped (SBH) and were placed in a residential facility. The local school district conducted classes at the facility to provide the students with an appropriate education under the EAHCA. During the 1983-84 school year the boys were involved in several episodes of destructive and violent classroom behavior at the residential facility.

The school district decided that for the 1984-85 school year it would conduct the SBH classes at a regular school building. During the first week of classes the fifteen-year-old boy violently attacked another student and began throwing books and a ruler around his classroom; the twelve-year-old boy, after telling his teacher, "I'm going to kick your ass," picked up a plastic baseball bat and generally destroyed the classroom. The school district removed the students from the SBH classes and instead provided the boys with one hour per day of personalized tutoring at the residential facility. The school district then caused the boys to be prosecuted for their misbehavior and each was adjudged delinquent under Ohio law.

The boys sued the school district in federal court claiming that the school district had violated the provisions of the EAHCA by changing their placement. The EAHCA provides that whenever a school district proposes to change a child's educational placement there must be a hearing before an impartial hearing officer and, most importantly, that during the pendency of these proceedings the child must remain in his then current educational placement unless the child or his guardian agrees to a change in placement. The school district argued that because of their behavior the boys presented a danger to themselves and others, and that their education could not be safely continued even in an SBH class.

The district court rejected this reasoning and granted a preliminary injunction allowing the students to return to the SBH classroom. The court was disturbed that the school district had not used its normal disciplinary procedures, which included a one to two week suspension or expulsion, before it decided to prosecute the boys and change their educational placements. It further held that although the students must be allowed to return to their classroom, and thus to their "then current" educational placements as required by the EAHCA, the school district would not be precluded from using normal disciplinary procedures to deal with any future disruptive conduct by the students. *Lamont X v. Quisenberry*, 606 F.Supp. 809 (S.D.Ohio 1984).

A U.S. district court has ruled that the party who proposes to change the placement of a handicapped child bears the burden of proof in demonstrating the propriety of such a change. This case arose when a Georgia school district proposed to change a child's residential school placement to placement in a self-contained learning disabilities classroom in the county school district. The district had placed the boy in a residential facility under his IEP and had paid all costs associated with his attendance there since 1979. However, in June 1982, the district reevaluated the boy and recommended a change from residential placement to special class placement in a regular school system. The child's parents objected to this change and two administrative hearings were held. The parents then brought suit in U.S. district court challenging the standard of proof used in the hearings. While stating that it would not address the results of the administrative hearings, the court agreed to order that the school district should bear the burden of proof in the administrative hearings because it was the party seeking to change the boy's placement. The residential placement, which had been previously agreed to by both the school and the boy's parents, was therefore presumed to be the child's appropriate placement under the EAHCA until the school district was able to prove otherwise. *Burger v. Murray County School Dist.*, 612 F.Supp. 434 (N.D.Ga.1984).

The parents of a handicapped child brought a complaint against their Massachusetts school district after a privately-run after-school day care program refused to continue accepting their child. The parents alleged that the school district had deprived them of due process by failing to notify them in advance of this so-called change in placement. After the Massachusetts Bureau of Special Education Appeals ruled in favor of the parents, the school district appealed to the federal district court arguing that it had not changed the child's placement. Here, the child's IEP had included two afternoons per week at a BASS program, and three afternoons per week at a private day care center located at Driscoll Public School. Unfortunately, the following fall the day care center decided that the child was too old to attend. The parents then requested of school officials that he be allowed to attend the BASS program five days per week. The school responded by proposing that the child attend the BASS program three days per week and spend the remaining two days at an individualized public school program at the Driscoll Public School. The one-on-one aides for the child while at the Driscoll public school program would be the same persons who were involved in Driscoll's private program.

The district court ruled that such a minor alteration in the child's program (the change from two days at BASS and three days at Driscoll to three days at BASS and two days at Driscoll) was not a "change in educational placement" under section 1415(e)(2) of the EAHCA. This was especially true where the private day care group, which was composed of parents at the Driscoll school, was the entity responsible for the change in the child's schedule. Because no change in placement had occurred, the school district had no duty to notify the parents. The court reversed the Bureau of Special Education Appeals and ruled in the school's favor. *Brookline School Comm. v. Golden*, 628 F.Supp. 113 (D.Mass.1986).

A Florida high school student who was handicapped by a special learning disability sued a local school district under the EAHCA and the Rehabilitation Act alleging that her involuntary transfer from high school to an alternative learning center violated her right to a publicly financed appropriate special education. The student requested a preliminary injunction to allow her to attend high school during pendency of the proceedings. A U.S. district court denied the student's request and she appealed to the U.S. Court of Appeals, Eleventh Circuit, arguing that 1) the hearing officer who upheld the decision to transfer her denied her the right to direct lay representation in the administrative proceedings by refusing to allow the student's friend, a legal and educational layman, to present her case and examine witnesses; 2) that the record of the administrative proceedings contained uncontested evidence that the school district violated her procedural right to remain in the high school during the pendency of the action as guaranteed by the EAHCA; and 3) that neither the hearing officer nor the district judge determined whether the alternative learning center was the least restrictive environment in which she could be educated.

The Court of Appeals held that the Rehabilitation Act was not the appropriate provision under which to bring suit since the EAHCA provides the exclusive avenue for asserting rights to a publicly financed special education. Further, the student had no right to direct lay representation in the administrative proceedings. The EAHCA creates no such right. The EAHCA states that a complainant has a right "to be accompanied and advised by counsel and by individuals with special knowledge or training with respect to the problems of handicapped children." The hearing officer's examination of the student's chosen representative revealed his almost complete ignorance of state administrative procedure. Thus, the hearing officer did not violate the EAHCA in limiting his role to offering advice.

Further, the uncontradicted evidence left no doubt that the student's behavior at the high school posed a threat to both students and school officials. Thus, the court found that the school district properly exercised its authority to transfer the student to the alternative learning center and the district did not violate her procedural right to remain in the high school during the pendency of the action. Finally, the court held that because the student introduced no evidence that the proposed placement was inappropriate or that a less restrictive environment existed in which she could receive the special education she needed, the proposed placement was deemed appropriate. *Victoria L. v. Dist. School Bd. of Lee County, Florida*, 741 F.2d 369 (11th Cir.1984).

Two other cases have addressed the issue of whether changes in the individualized educational program of handicapped children constituted a "change in educational placement" triggering the procedural safeguards of the EAHCA.

In the first case the U.S. Court of Appeals, Third Circuit, held that a change in the method of transportation of a severely handicapped child to and from school did not constitute a "change in educational placement." A Pennsylvania school district changed the method of transportation from a system whereby the child's parents were reimbursed for their expenses in driving the child to school to a "combined run" involving other children and a small increase in travel time. The parents objected to the combined run on the ground that the increase in transportation time would be detrimental to the child's education. The school district denied the parents a due process hearing because it did not consider the change in transportation to be a "change in educational placement."

The Court of Appeals agreed, finding that the change in the method of transporting the child did not constitute a "change in educational placement" under the EAHCA and thus could be implemented without a prior due process hearing. It is clear, said the court, that the "stay put" provision under the EAHCA does not entitle parents to demand a hearing when minor administrative decisions alter the school day of their children. The question is whether the school district's decision is likely to affect in some significant way a child's learning experience. Here, the parents' objections were merely speculative. *DeLeon v. Susquehanna Comm. School Dist.*, 747 F.2d 149 (3d Cir.1984).

In the second case, the U.S. Court of Appeals, District of Columbia Circuit, held that a change in the feeding program that a profoundly handicapped child would receive as a result of a transfer from a private hospital to a government-run institution did not constitute a "change in educational placement" within the meaning of the notice and hearing provisions of the EAHCA. The child's guardian sued the District of Columbia Board of Education alleging that the change in residence from the private hospital at which the child had been placed to a government-run institution where the child would live but continue to receive a day education at the private hospital, constituted a "change in educational placement" triggering the requirement of a due process hearing. The guardian specifically alleged that differences in the feeding programs of the private hospital and the public institution constituted a sufficient change in the child's individual education program to warrant the child's retention in the private hospital until resolution of the matter.

The Court of Appeals disagreed, finding that an individual voicing objections to a handicapped child's educational program must identify, at a minimum, a fundamental change in, or the elimination of, a basic element of the education program in order for the change to qualify as a change in educational placement. Here, although the child's transfer from one facility to another was decidedly a "change in placement," it was not alone sufficient to constitute a change in educational placement requiring the board of education to keep the child at the private hospital or a comparable facility until the hearings were completed. A move from a "mainstream" program to one consisting only of handicapped students, said the court, would constitute a change in educational placement; a move from one mainstream program to another, with the elimination, for instance, of a theater arts class, would not be such a change. Here, the board of education, using the residential services of the public institution and the out-patient education program of the private hospital, had fulfilled its obligation under the EAHCA to maintain the child's educational placement pending the resolution of any complaint proceedings brought on the child's behalf. Thus, the Court of Appeals held that the child could be discharged from the private hospital prior to his guardian's consent and prior to a hearing. *Lunceford v. Dist. of Columbia Bd. of Educ.*, 745 F.2d 1577 (D.C.Cir.1984).

In Massachusetts, parents of an eleven-year-old boy who suffered from acquired encephalopathy challenged in U.S. district court a proposed change in their son's educational placement. For seven years the child had attended a special education center for brain-injured children. This center offered special teaching techniques which would not be available to the child at the new location. The parents argued that the transfer of their child from the center to the new program would halt his progress and cause him to regress. In deciding whether the placement change was appropriate, the court relied on language set forth by the U.S. Supreme Court in *Board of Education v. Rowley.* That case held that handicapped children are to be provided a "basic floor of opportunity" and that educational services must be sufficient to confer some educational benefit upon them. Here, the court stated that the relative validity of the differing techniques used by the two institutes was a matter of dispute among special education experts. In light of the court's unwillingness to make educational policy and insufficient evidence that the child would regress at the new institute, the court refused to hold that the change of placement would be inappropriate. Judgment was rendered in favor of the school district. *Doe v. Lawson*, 579 F.Supp. 1314 (D.Mass.1984).

In a Rhode Island case, the mother of a handicapped child, enrolled in public school in accordance with an IEP, sued the school district to prevent it from making a second educational assessment of her child. The school district had based the boy's IEP on an evaluation conducted by a private school formerly attended by the child. The mother maintained that the assessment sought by the school district would constitute an original evaluation and, therefore, the school was barred from conducting it without her cooperation. The school district contended that its assessment would be a re-evaluation and under the law, a parent's consent was unnecessary. It further stated that any such change in placement resulting from the re-evaluation would be subject to challenge by the parent in a statutorily mandated hearing. The court agreed with the school district's position, stating that the private school assessment on which the IEP was based did legitimately constitute an original pre-placement evaluation. The case was dismissed. *Carroll v. Capalbo*, 563 F.Supp. 1053 (D.R.I.1983).

A dispute in Michigan resulted in a U.S. district court determination that the proposed transfer of an eleven-year-old girl with cerebral palsy from a traditional elementary school to an elementary school specially designed to meet the needs of handicapped children did not violate the EAHCA. The mother sued the school district which proposed the transfer alleging that her daughter was denied a free appropriate education in the least restrictive environment without due process of law. The court was persuaded that the child could not receive a satisfactory education in the traditional school, even with the use of supplementary aids and services to the maximum extent possible. Further, the mother had exhausted all of the administrative remedies available to her. Thus, the mother's due process claim was without merit because she had been afforded and had availed herself of every procedural safeguard of the EAHCA. In addition, the court held that the mother's equal protection claim asserted on behalf of her child was unfounded, because there was no showing that the child was treated any differently from other handicapped children who were being evaluated by procedures mandated by state and federal law. *Johnston v. Ann Arbor Pub. Schools*, 569 F.Supp. 1502 (E.D.Mich.1983).

The Supreme Judicial Court of Massachusetts held that the decision to graduate a child with special education needs is a "change in placement," triggering mandatory procedural safeguards included in the EAHCA. In this case a twenty-one-year-old male suffering from multiple cognitive and motor disabilities, emotional and behavioral difficulties, and also confined to a wheelchair, brought suit against a Massachusetts school district alleging that his graduation, which terminated his right to special education services, violated the procedural provisions of the EAHCA.

In the fall of 1980, the boy's teachers had met to formulate his IEP for the 1980-81 school year. The teachers agreed that the child was to graduate at the end of the school year, although his IEP did not state this. Neither the student nor his parents were invited to the meeting at which this decision was made. The student signed the IEP but the parents did not. At no time were the parents provided formal, written notice of their right to challenge the IEP or of the procedural avenues open to them to make that challenge. Neither were they told that graduation would terminate their son's eligibility for special education services. In June, 1981, the boy was presented with a high school diploma; his eligibility for special education services was thereby terminated. In the time between the student's graduation and the commencement of this lawsuit, no special education services were afforded to the boy. Evidence showed that he failed to adapt either to sheltered workshops or independent living settings. Furthermore, at the time of the lawsuit, the boy was hospitalized in a chronic care unit.

The Massachusetts Supreme Judicial Court reversed a lower court decision in favor of the school district, holding that the failure to provide to the parents a formal, written notice concerning the decision to graduate the student, the failure to provide notice regarding the rights of the parents to involvement in that decision and the failure to notify them of their rights to a hearing and administrative review violated state and federal statutory law. This was true even though the parents had actual notice of the student's graduation and had participated to a limited extent in the transitional planning surrounding the graduation, and even though the student signed the IEP. *Stock v. Massachusetts Hospital School*, 467 N.E.2d 448 (Mass.1984).

Does a school closing constitute a "change in placement" for purposes of the EAHCA? This was the question before the New York Supreme Court after a local school district and concerned parents of handicapped students objected to the New York City Board of Education's refusal to renew its contract with a special school on the ground of claimed financial mismanagement. The board had conducted an audit of the school and discovered that large sums of money were being misspent and that serious educational deficiencies existed in the programs offered. Upon termination of the contract with the school, the Board of Education offered an alternative "location" for the majority of the students and was seeking placement for the balance. The school district and the parents argued that the placement of the handicapped children from one school to another involved a change in educational placement which triggered the requirement of a court order preventing the immediate closing of the school.

The court disagreed, holding that a change of school is not *per se* a change in educational placement of a handicapped student. Further, for the court to order a temporary stay of the school closing, the students must show irreparable injury resulting from the closing. This could be shown by demonstrating the educational uniqueness of the school or by showing that another school would not similarly aid such students. No such potential injury was shown. Thus, although it is conceivable that the placement of a child from one school to another may involve a change in educational placement within the meaning of the EAHCA which would then trigger the requirement of an order preventing the immediate closing of a school, no sufficient proof of the required irreparable injury to the student was shown. *Cohen v. Bd. of Educ. of City of New York*, 454 N.Y.S.2d 630 (Sup.Ct.1982).

III. SUSPENSION AND EXPULSION OF HANDICAPPED STUDENTS

Whether suspension or expulsion of handicapped students from school constitutes a "change in placement" for purposes of the EAHCA is an issue which has been presented before the courts. The U.S. Supreme Court has clarified the issue in *Honig v. Doe*, 108 S.Ct. 592 (1988) (reprinted in the Appendix of U.S. Supreme Court Cases in this volume). Indefinite suspensions violate the "stay put" provisions of the EAHCA. Suspensions up to ten days do not constitute a change in placement. The Court seemed to leave intact the principle that where a student's misbehavior is caused by his or her handicap, any attempt to expel the student from school will be turned aside.

Honig v. Doe involved two emotionally disturbed children in California who were given five day suspensions from school for misbehavior which included destroying school property and assaulting and making sexual comments to other students. Pursuant to state law, the suspensions were continued indefinitely during the pendency of expulsion proceedings. The students sued the school district in U.S. district court contesting the extended suspensions on the ground that they violated the "stay put" provision of the EAHCA, which provides that a student must be kept in his or her "then current" educational placement during the pendency of proceedings which contemplate a change in placement. The district court issued an injunction preventing the expulsion of any handicapped student for misbehavior which arises from the student's handicap and the school district appealed.

The U.S. Court of Appeals, Ninth Circuit, determined that the indefinite suspensions constituted a prohibited "change in placement" under the EAHCA and that no "dangerousness" exception existed in the EAHCA's "stay put" provision. It ruled that indefinite suspensions or expulsions of disabled children for misconduct arising out of their disabilities violated the EAHCA. The court of appeals also ruled, however, that fixed suspensions of up to thirty school days did not constitute a "change in placement." It determined that a state must provide services directly to a disabled child when a local school district fails to do so. The California Superintendent of Public Instruction filed for a review by the U.S. Supreme Court on the issues of whether a dangerousness exception existed to the "stay put" provision and whether the state had to provide services directly when a local school district failed to do so.

The Supreme Court declared that the intended purpose of the "stay put" provision was to prevent schools from changing a child's educational placement over his or her parents' objection until all review proceedings were completed. While the EAHCA provided for interim placements where parents and school officials were able to agree on one, no emergency exception for dangerous students was included. The Court concluded that it was "not at liberty to engraft onto the [EAHCA] an exception Congress chose not to create." The Court went on to say that where a disabled student poses an immediate threat to the safety of others, school officials may temporarily suspend him or her for up to ten school days. The court held that this authority insured 1) that school officials can protect the safety of others by removing dangerous students, 2) that school officials can seek a review of the student's placement and try to persuade the student's parents to agree to an interim placement, and 3) that school officials can seek court rulings to exclude students whose parents "adamantly refuse to permit any change in placement." School officials could seek such a court order without exhausting the EAHCA's administrative remedies "only by showing that maintaining the child in his or her current placement is substantially likely to result in injury either to himself or herself, or to others."

The Court therefore affirmed the court of appeals' decision that indefinite suspensions violated the "stay put" provision of the EAHCA. It modified that court's decision on fixed suspensions by holding that suspensions up to ten rather than up to thirty days did not constitute a change in placement. The Court also upheld the court of appeals' decision that states could be required to provide services directly to disabled students where a local school district fails to do so. *Honig v. Doe*, 108 S.Ct. 592 (1988).

The following cases were decided prior to the *Honig v. Doe* ruling. How they will be affected by *Honig* depends upon the particular fact situation.

On January 9, 1986, after a severe temper tantrum at school, an eight-year-old boy was suspended for thirty-five days until a February 13, school board meeting. The boy was readmitted on January 13, but was suspended again after another disruptive incident on January 15. A January 20, examination by a psychologist found that the boy suffered from a learning disability. The school board was notified of the child's learning disability and the school psychologist began testing him on February 3. His parents requested on two occasions that in light of his learning disability he be readmitted to school. The school board suggested both times that they allow their child to receive homebound instruction and refused to lift the suspension until February 13. On February 4, the parents sued the school board seeking a temporary restraining order ordering the boy's readmission and a hearing. A U.S. district court ordered the school board to provide the boy with an appropriate educational program after which the board began devising an appropriate IEP for him. The school board then moved to dismiss the parents' lawsuit.

The parents argued that leaving the boy under disciplinary suspensions for twenty-nine days with no educational services constituted irreparable harm. The court observed that the facts of the case required a two-part examination: first, the child's due process rights had to be considered as those of a nonhandicapped child facing a twenty-nine day disciplinary suspension since the school officials did not at first perceive him to be handicapped. Second, once school officials were notified of the child's learning disability, his due process rights had to be considered in light of the EAHCA. The court ruled that both examinations revealed that the boy had due process rights. The U.S. Supreme Court held in *Goss v. Lopez* that a disciplinary suspension for even a nonhandicapped child gives rise to due process rights. *Goss* stated that notice of suspension proceedings must be sent to a student's parents and a hearing held with the student present "as soon as practicable." The district court ruled that under *Goss* a due process hearing twenty-nine days after an incident would not be adequate. Such a time lapse would result in irreparable harm to the boy which justified the initiation of the civil lawsuit before February 13.

Section 1415(e)(3) of the EAHCA provides that district courts have authority to grant appropriate relief prior to exhaustion of state remedies if pursuing those remedies would be inadequate or futile. The school board argued that the district court did not have jurisdiction to hear the boy's claims since the school board had begun to comply with the EAHCA and therefore the boy's claims had not been futile. However, the court ruled that the futility doctrine should be appealed here. It observed that, while a continuing disciplinary suspension may be proper in some EAHCA cases, here the school board did not even attempt to demonstrate that the suspension of the boy was of educational benefit. The school board wrongly relied upon the "stay-put" doctrine of the EAHCA which provides that a child shall remain in his current educational placement "[d]uring the pendency of any proceedings . . ." (i.e. enrolled in school but under suspension). Having learned of the boy's learning disability, the school board was required to abide by the EAHCA and its refusal to reinstate the boy (but in a more restrictive setting) triggered the full procedural remedies of the EAHCA. Since his civil rights were violated he was entitled to relief under § 1983 including an award of attorney's fees. Because the school board was in the process of devising a proper IEP, other measures of relief requested by the boy were denied. The boy was entitled to summary judgment in his favor. *Doe v. Rockingham County School Bd.*, 658 F.Supp. 403 (W.D.Va.1987).

A fourteen-year-old Virginia boy who had been identified by his school district as having a serious learning disability was suspended from school in March, 1983. The boy had acted as a middleman for two nonhandicapped girls who desired to buy "speed" from another student. He made no money doing this and took no drugs himself. The boy was suspended, but during his suspension the school district's committee on the handicapped held proceedings which culminated in the determination that the boy's handicap was not the cause of his involvement with drugs. The school board then voted to expel the boy for the remainder of the school year. One month later the parents requested and received a due process hearing pursuant to the EAHCA at which the hearing examiner ordered the expulsion reversed because he found that the boy's misbehavior was related to his learning disability. A state reviewing officer affirmed this decision.

The school board then filed suit in U.S. district court contending that in situations like this, the EAHCA allows expulsions without review. The district court dismissed the school board's complaint and the U.S. Court of Appeals, Fourth Circuit, affirmed. The appeals court noted that it is settled law that any expulsion of a handicapped student is a "change in placement" for EAHCA purposes, triggering the Act's procedural safeguards. Also, the district court's determination that the boy's involvement in drug sales was caused by his handicap would not be overturned on appeal unless it was "clearly erroneous." The dismissal of the school board's complaint was therefore affirmed. *School Bd. of Prince County v. Malone*, 762 F.2d 1210 (4th Cir.1985).

In 1978, a handicapped girl obtained a preliminary injunction from a federal district court in Connecticut which prevented her school board from expelling her from high school. The board was also ordered to conduct an immediate review of her IEP under the EAHCA. The girl's class action suit continued in district court for the next five years, with the girl seeking a declaratory judgment that the school board "was bound by the procedural requirements of the EAHCA if it desired to exclude a handicapped student from class attendance for longer than a ten day period." In 1984, the class action suit was dismissed because the girl graduated and was no longer a member of the class she purported to represent. She then petitioned the district court for an award of attorney's fees pursuant to section 1988 of the Civil Rights Act.

The court, while noting that attorney's fees are rarely justified in cases involving the EAHCA, ordered the school board and state department of education to pay the full amount of the girl's attorneys' fees ($57,631). Although plaintiffs in EAHCA cases often allege violations of the Civil Rights Act, the U.S. Supreme Court held in *Smith v. Robinson*, 104 S.Ct. 3457 (1984), that substantive claims made under the EAHCA will not justify the use of section 1988 as a basis for attorneys' fees. The Supreme Court held however, that where a plaintiff is successful in proving that a school board or other state entity has deprived the plaintiff of procedural protections, attorney's fees may be awarded. In the present case, the girl proved that the board, by excluding her from class attendance for longer than a ten day period, had failed to provide her with the procedural safeguards mandated by the EAHCA. These procedural violations gave rise to an award of attorneys' fees under section 1988 of the Civil Rights Act, and the court ordered that the school board, as the primary party at fault, pay 80% of the award and that the state department of education pay 20%. *Stuart v. Nappi*, 610 F.Supp. 90 (D.Conn.1985).

In a Mississippi case, a student's sexual misconduct prevented his return to the classroom. Here a behaviorally handicapped student admitted to school officials that while in a special education class he had unbuttoned a girl's blouse and touched her breast. As a result, the school suspended him for three days and he was sent before the County Youth Court. Because this was the boy's third instance of school-related sexual misconduct, the Youth Court sent him to a state hospital for one month of treatment. After he lived at home for seven months following his hospitalization, the boy's mother sought to re-enroll him at his school under his former IEP program. However, school officials claimed that the old IEP was inapplicable in light of the boy's continuing sexual misconduct and proposed that he be placed in a closely supervised group home.

The boy's mother then brought suit in U.S. district court seeking a preliminary injunction to compel school officials to allow her son to attend class under his former IEP. The court ruled in favor of the school district, noting that in order to grant a preliminary injunction there must be an immediate threat of irreparable harm to the plaintiff. However, in this case the boy's mother had delayed for seven months before seeking to once again enroll her son in the school. Also, school officials had evidenced a genuine concern for the boy's welfare by offering to provide home tutoring during the time in which a new appropriate IEP could be formulated. The court held that because the boy had neither a current IEP nor a current educational placement, and because of the danger that he presented to others, there were insufficient grounds to order that he be returned to the classroom.

On appeal by the boy's mother, the U.S. Court of Appeals, Fifth Circuit, affirmed the district court, holding that when a handicapped student presents a substantial danger to himself or others, immediate removal from the classroom may be justified. The school's decision to provide the boy with home tutoring was upheld. *Jackson v. Franklin County School Bd.*, 765 F.2d 535 (5th Cir.1985).

The boy and his mother appealed again to the court of appeals. They argued that the district court was wrong in not finding that the boy's due process rights were violated by being excluded from school during the spring of 1984 and the first two months of the 1984-85 school year.

The court of appeals held that when the school failed to convene an IEP conference in the spring of 1984 it violated the EAHCA. The EAHCA specifically required that "written prior notice to the parents or guardian" be provided whenever a school "proposes to initiate or change . . . the identification, evaluation, or educational placement of the child or the provision of a free appropriate public education to the child." The court observed that the U.S. Supreme Court has held that even a short suspension of up to ten days required notice of charges and some type of informal hearing. It stated that a failure on the part of the school to follow the procedural requirements of the EAHCA amounted to a failure by the school to provide a free appropriate education for the boy. The court concluded that, under the EAHCA, the burden rested on the school or agency to safeguard handicapped children's rights by informing the parents or guardians of those rights. It also noted that the writers of the EAHCA intended that students and parents should participate as much as possible in outlining the educational program of the handicapped student. Both the EAHCA and the Fourteenth Amendment required the school to provide the boy with notice and a hearing regarding his continued exclusion from school.

The case was remanded to the district court to determine the extent of the boy's loss caused by the school's failure to provide notice and a hearing in April and August, 1984. The court of appeals also instructed the district court to determine what damages, either monetary or in remedial educational services, would be appropriate for the boy. *Jackson v. Franklin County School Bd.*, 806 F.2d 623 (5th Cir.1986).

In an Illinois case when a seventeen-year-old "exceptional" child told his teacher, "I'm not serving your fucking detention. Fuck you," he was promptly suspended for five days. His parents contested the suspension and he was given a hearing at which an impartial hearing officer upheld the suspension. On appeal to the Department of Education, the State Superintendent of Education overturned the suspension saying that the child's emotional outburst was evidence that the system had misplaced this child in a class setting too advanced. The school district appealed to a U.S. district court, which reversed the State Superintendent's decision. The court stated that if the seventeen-year-old had managed to complete eleven years of education and had advanced to the point where he was placed in a mainstream educational course, it was nonsense to suggest that his shameful outburst was somehow the fault of the system. The child knew, or should have known, that his behavior was unacceptable. Further, the court pointed to the U.S. Supreme Court decision *Goss v. Lopez*, 419 U.S. 565 (1975), which held that "suspension is considered not only to be a necessary tool to maintain order but a valuable educational device." The court concluded by noting that a five-day suspension should not be equated to expulsion or termination, and that federal law permits the enforcement of ordinary classroom discipline through such suspensions. *Bd. of Educ. of the City of Peoria, School Dist. 150 v. Illinois State Bd. of Educ.*, 531 F.Supp. 148 (C.D.Ill.1982).

The following case illustrates that a suspension can constitute a "change in placement" if it is to last for an indefinite period. Here a school for the blind in New York suspended a deaf, blind and emotionally disturbed residential student who engaged in persistent self-abusive behavior. The reason for the suspension was that the school lacked the staff to supervise the fourteen-year-old girl, who needed to be watched continually. Without the proper supervisory staff the girl was a danger to herself. In fact, at one time during her enrollment at the school the girl had to be hospitalized because of self-inflicted injuries. The suspension was to last "until such time it appeared to be in the best interests of the child and the school to revoke the suspension." The student's mother brought suit against the school to compel it to reinstate her daughter as a residential student and to force it to provide a hearing in compliance with the EAHCA. Shortly after the suit was commenced the girl was reinstated in the school and the school argued that the mother's claim was then moot.

The U.S. district court disagreed with the school's claim, saying that the actions of the school were unlawful. The court observed that the time during which the child had been hospitalized as a result of self-inflicted injuries stemming from her self-abusive behavior did not constitute a "change in placement" triggering procedural safeguards. However, the indefinite suspension period which was to last until such time as "it appeared to be in the best interests of the child and the school to revoke the suspension" was unlawful within the meaning of the EAHCA. The indefinite suspension constituted a "change in placement" within the meaning of the EAHCA and thus required a hearing. *Sherry v. New York State Educ. Dep't*, 479 F.Supp. 1328 (W.D.N.Y.1979).

The following cases illustrate that expulsions are not viewed in the same light as suspensions. Expulsions trigger the procedural safeguards of the EAHCA and require a showing that the behavior leading to the expulsion was not the result of an expelled child's handicap.

A learning disabled Mississippi high school student was found with marijuana cigarettes and knives at school. A local school district recommended that he be expelled for the remainder of the school year and that he receive no academic credit for the year. It also offered the student homebound instruction during the expulsion period. A hearing officer concluded that the expulsion was impermissible because the student did not present an immediate danger to himself or other students, and the school district appealed.

The Mississippi Supreme Court held that a handicapped student could be expelled based upon a reasonable conclusion that the student would otherwise disrupt the educational process of other students. The school district, however, would have to provide quality educational services to the handicapped student during the expulsion period. The test in expelling a student, stated the court, was whether the behavior for which the student was expelled was caused in some way by his handicap. It held that school districts could expel handicapped students so long as less harsh forms of discipline are considered and proper procedures are followed under the EAHCA. *Bd. of Trustees v. Doe*, 508 So.2d 1081 (Miss.1987).

A Kentucky case arose after a fifteen-year-old ninth grade student, identified and evaluated since kindergarten as a handicapped or exceptional child, defied the authority of his teacher. He refused to do assigned work, destroyed a worksheet, destroyed a coffee cup, and pushed and kicked the teacher while leaving the classroom. The following day the child was suspended. A hearing regarding the suspension was held by the school board which did not convene nor consult the Administrative Admissions and Release Committee (AARC), a multi-disciplined group which, in Kentucky, is the organization responsible for reviewing challenged placement decisions. In addition, the board did not address the relationship, if any, between the child's handicap and his disruptive behavior. Expulsion followed. The child, through his parents, then sought legal help in the federal courts.

The U.S. Court of Appeals, Sixth Circuit, affirmed a U.S. district court decision which held than an expulsion from school is a "change of placement" within the meaning of the EAHCA, thus requiring certain procedural protections prior to expulsion. The Court of Appeals also determined that an expulsion must be accompanied by a determination as to whether the handicapped student's misconduct bears a relationship to his handicap. The lower court injunction requiring the expungment of expulsion records from the board minutes and school attendance records was upheld. *Kaelin v. Grubbs*, 682 F.2d 595 (6th Cir.1982).

The Nebraska Supreme Court has held that the expulsion of a disruptive handicapped student violated the EAHCA. In this case a student expelled for disruptive behavior from a school for the trainable mentally retarded was found by the court to have been denied a free appropriate education. After the expulsion the student, who suffered from autism, mental retardation and epilepsy, was placed in regional institutions by his parents. While in the institutions, many of the skills the child previously learned were lost, but the school district made no attempt to relocate the student. The Nebraska Supreme Court held that the expulsion constituted a change in placement which was subject to the procedural protections of the EAHCA. It further stated that under the Act, local school officials are prohibited from expelling students whose handicaps are the cause for their disruptive behavior. The school's only course of action in such circumstances is to transfer the disruptive student to an appropriate, more restrictive environment. The court ordered that the school district reimburse the parents for the cost incurred in the institutionalization of their child. *Adams Cent. School Dist. No. 690 v. Deist*, 334 N.W.2d 775 (Neb.1983).

In a similar case arising in Indiana, the mother of a handicapped child sued a local school district challenging the child's expulsion from school. The child had been expelled for disciplinary reasons. The mother sued the school district in U.S. district court which held that the school was prohibited from expelling students whose handicaps caused them to be disruptive, but was allowed to transfer the disruptive student to an appropriate, more restrictive environment.

The court noted that the EAHCA does not prohibit all expulsions of disruptive handicapped children. It only prohibits the expulsion of handicapped children who are disruptive because of their handicap. The distinction between a handicapped child and any other child is that, unlike any other disruptive child, before a disruptive handicapped child can be expelled, it must be determined whether the handicap is the cause of the child's disruptiveness. This must be determined through the change of placement procedures required by the EAHCA. In this case the school district was found to have violated the due process provisions of EAHCA when it expelled the student without first determining whether his propensity to disrupt was the result of his inappropriate placement. *Doe v. Koger*, 480 F.Supp. 225 (N.D.Ind.1979).

A U.S. district court in Florida granted a preliminary injunction against state and local school officials preventing them from enforcing the expulsion of nine handicapped students. The students, expelled for alleged misconduct, were all classified as "educable mentally retarded," "mildly mentally retarded," or "EMR/dull normal." The Florida school district which had expelled the students did so on the ground that the students knew right from wrong.

The students sued the school district alleging they were denied a free appropriate education under the EAHCA as a result of their expulsions. The district court agreed with the students finding that under § 504 of the Rehabilitation Act and the EAHCA, no handicapped student could be expelled for misconduct related to the handicap. The court found that no determination was made as to the relationship between the students' handicaps and their behavioral problems. The court also found that an expulsion is a change in educational placement. The students' request for an injunction was granted.

The school district appealed to the U.S. Court of Appeals, Fifth Circuit, which affirmed the district court ruling. The court of appeals held that the determination that a handicapped student knows the difference between right and wrong is not sufficient to support a determination that his misconduct was or was not a manifestation of his handicap. Only a trained, knowledgeable group of persons should determine whether a student's misconduct bears a relationship to his handicapping condition. Because no such determination was made in this case, the court found the expulsion of the nine students to have constituted a change in placement invoking the procedural protections of the EAHCA and section 504 of the Rehabilitation Act. *S-1 v. Turlington*, 635 F.2d 342 (5th Cir.1981).

IV. EXHAUSTION OF ADMINISTRATIVE REMEDIES

The doctrine of exhaustion of remedies provides that "no one is entitled to judicial relief for a supposed or threatened injury until the prescribed administrative remedy has been exhausted." This was pointed out by the U.S. Supreme Court in the case of *Myers v. Bethlehem Shipbuilding Corp.,* 303 U.S. 41 (1938). The reasons supporting the exhaustion of remedies doctrine were advanced in a later Supreme Court case, *McKart v. U.S.*, 395 U.S. 185(1968). Among the reasons given were the development of an accurate factual record, thus allowing more informed judicial review, encouraging "expeditious decision making," and furthering Congressional intent.

A. Operation of the Exhaustion Doctrine

Section 1415 of the EAHCA provides for an initial independent review of a contested IEP at the agency level. Section 1415(e)(2) provides that an "aggrieved party" may bring a separate civil action in state or federal court to challenge the final decision of a state educational agency. Normally the parents or guardians of a handicapped child have the duty to exhaust all administrative channels before resorting to a state or federal court. However, some courts have excused the "exhaustion" requirement under certain exceptional circumstances.

The father of a handicapped student in Virginia sued the county school board in a U.S. district court alleging that it had failed to develop a proper IEP for his son. He argued that because the school board had violated federal and state law in its failure to provide appropriate educational services for his son, he did not need to exhaust administrative remedies under the EAHCA prior to commencing court proceedings. The school board asked the court to dismiss the father's lawsuit, claiming that he had failed to first seek all of his remedies at the administrative level.

The court observed that according to § 3 of the Handicapped Children's Protection Act, administrative remedies must be exhausted prior to a court proceeding under the EAHCA, other statutes, the U.S. Constitution or any combination thereof. Further, although the EAHCA no longer limits the applicability of other civil rights laws to handicapped children, when the father sought to bring suit under other laws he was required to exhaust administrative remedies provided for by the EAHCA to the same extent that this exhaustion would be required if the suit had been brought under the EAHCA. This exhaustion doctrine, observed the court, serves the "interest of accuracy, efficiency, agency autonomy, and judicial economy." Here, although the father disagreed with the IEP developed for his son by the school board, he had made no attempt to invoke the administrative procedures available to him. Further, he had not shown that the exhaustion of administrative remedies would be futile. The court granted the school board's motion for dismissal and ruled that the father could seek relief in federal court if he was still dissatisfied with the IEP after he had fully exhausted his administrative remedies. *Davenport v. Rockbridge County School Bd.*, 658 F.Supp. 132 (W.D.Va.1987).

In a New York case, an eleven-year-old handicapped student who was transferred by his school district to a special school for disabled students objected to the transfer because it separated him from his classmates and friends. The student claimed that the school district could have made his original school accessible and, through reasonable accommodation, could have permitted him to attend that school. The student asked a New York supreme court to issue an injunction compelling the school district to reverse its transfer decision and return the child to his original school. The school district argued that the student had not exhausted his administrative remedies, a prerequisite to requesting judicial relief. The court agreed, finding that the injunction requested by the student was not proper until the administrative remedies provided by the EAHCA were fully pursued.

In its ruling the court stated: "Congress intended that the complaints of . . . handicapped students should be handled expeditiously by administrative law procedure and the educational agency is to keep the student in the facility where he was when the complaint was made." Congress wanted such complaints to be resolved in a matter of weeks; otherwise, students such as the plaintiff would be in high school before the controversy was resolved by the courts. The court dismissed the student's complaint until completion of administrative proceedings. *Robideau v. South Colonie Cent. School Dist.*, 487 N.Y.S. 2d 696 (Sup.Ct.1985).

A New York father placed his thirteen-year-old daughter who suffered from anorexia nervosa at the Hedges Treatment Center, a Pennsylvania residential treatment facility. He placed her at Hedges due to several placement delays by a school district's committee on the handicapped (COH). A U.S. district court denied his request for tuition reimbursement because he had failed to exhaust administrative remedies. He then sought an administrative hearing and the hearing officer ordered placement at Hedges. However, the New York Commissioner of Education refused to provide tuition reimbursement because Hedges was approved only for fourteen-year-olds and older. The father appealed to the same U.S. district court. It upheld the placement and ordered a trial to determine what portion of the daughter's expenses were to be reimbursed by the state of New York.

The district court ruled that the father was entitled to total reimbursement for his daughter's education and related services at Hedges. The commissioner then appealed to the U.S. Court of Appeals, Second Circuit. The commissioner contended that the district court exceeded its authority by ordering the placement. The court of appeals agreed with the commissioner. EAHCA § 1401(18)(B) required that the daughter receive special education and related services which met the state educational agency standards. Section 1413(a)(4)(B)(ii) of the EAHCA provided that the state determine whether private facilities like Hedges met those standards. No court or agency could approve a placement at a private facility consistent with the EAHCA unless the commissioner approved the facility prior to the placement. *Antkowiak v. Ambach*, 838 F.2d 635 (2d Cir.1988).

In the course of locating an alternative placement for a handicapped child, the District of Columbia Public Schools (DCPS) wrote the child's mother of progress being made and stated "[w]e appreciate the effort you have extended thus far to assist us in locating an appropriate placement for your son, and we solicit your continuing efforts to secure a speedy placement for him. . . ." The following day, DCPS requested a due process hearing on the grounds that the mother had failed to cooperate with DCPS placement efforts. A hearing was held in which testimony was presented on behalf of the mother which focused on the need for residential placement. The hearing officer, believing that it was beyond her power to order residential placement, remanded the case to DCPS with the direction that it was to submit the matter to the Residential Review Committee and propose a placement. Subsequently, the mother received a letter advising her that the Committee had declined to recommend residential placement and that the child was to be placed at a day school. The mother filed suit in federal district court and unilaterally placed the child in a school.

DCPS argued before the U.S. district court that because the mother had not been "aggrieved" by a final determination of a hearing officer and because she had failed to exhaust her administrative remedies, she should be precluded from bringing suit in federal court. The court found that the mother was "aggrieved" as that term is used in the EAHCA and thus her claims were properly before the court. The argument that the mother had failed to exhaust her administrative remedies was also rejected. Resorting to the administrative process would have been futile in light of DCPS's blanket rejection of residential placement without setting forth the criteria upon which it based its decision. The court held that DCPS should place and fund the child at the residential school.

Further, the court rejected the argument that the Residential Review Committee had official status and that parents seeking to have their children considered for residential placement must satisfy criteria established by the Committee. Finally, the mother's claim for compensatory and punitive damages was denied since Congress intended the EAHCA to be the exclusive avenue through which a plaintiff may assert a claim to publicly financed special education. However, the court granted the mother's claim for attorney's fees because of bad faith on the part of the school district, which had commended her for her cooperation and then the following day initiated a hostile due process hearing. *Diamond v. McKenzie*, 602 F.Supp. 632 (D.D.C.1985).

A fourteen-year-old emotionally disturbed and mentally handicapped student and his parents sued in U.S. district court in Wisconsin, arguing that the child's school district had failed to provide a free appropriate public education in violation of the EAHCA; had failed to properly evaluate and identify the severity of the child's handicap; had failed to provide special education and related services to enable the child to meaningfully benefit from his education; had failed to provide a full continuum of services, including therapy and residential placement; and had failed to consider independent educational evaluations obtained by the child's parents at their expense.

The dispute arose after the school district determined that it could provide a free appropriate public education to the child and the parents believed that only a residential treatment facility could provide the child with an appropriate education. After the school district's recommendation of public school placement, the parents unilaterally placed their child in a private treatment facility. The school district denied the parents' request for reimbursement for their expenses in sending their child to the private school. The parents requested a due process hearing. However, they later withdrew that request and brought suit in federal court.

The U.S. district court held that the failure of the parents to exhaust their state administrative remedies precluded a federal suit under the EAHCA. A federal court lawsuit can be brought only if state administrative remedies have been exhausted or if to pursue such remedies would be futile. Here, the parents had not shown that pursuing state remedies would have been futile. In addition, the parents' allegation of procedural inconsistencies between the EAHCA and Wisconsin's use of county boards to make decisions related to handicapped education conflicted with the EAHCA's requirement that local agencies make all such decisions. The court found that the parents misread the EAHCA since the Act clearly applies to both local educational agencies "or an intermediate educational unit."

The parents' argument that the Secretary of Education should withhold EAHCA funds from Wisconsin based on the alleged procedural inconsistencies was also rejected. Not only were the alleged procedural inconsistencies nonexistent, found the court, but the plaintiffs had no standing to request the enjoining of fund disbursement to the state. State funds may be withheld only if the U.S. Secretary of Education, after notice and hearing, determines that there has been no substantial compliance with the EAHCA. Thus, the Wisconsin Department of Public Instruction's motion to dismiss the parents' claims was granted. *Brandon v. Wisconsin Dep't of Pub. Instruction*, 595 F.Supp. 740 (E.D.Wis.1984).

In another Wisconsin case, a severely handicapped child, through her parents, brought suit in U.S. district court against the local school district and its special education director, alleging that her right to an appropriate special education and other constitutional rights had been violated by the school district. The child's IEP called for one-to-one instruction which the parents claimed was suspended without notice to them. The school district responded that this action was an "experiment" designed to determine whether the child would benefit by a program change. The parents appealed the child's IEP to the state superintendent of instruction.

Pending the result of the appeal the parents, dissatisfied with the child's instruction, had her independently evaluated and enrolled her at a special rehabilitation facility. When the superintendent finally ruled on the parents' claim, he concluded that the child was entitled to a full-day educational program. The case was tried and the court held that the parents' suit would be dismissed for their failure to exhaust state administrative remedies. The parents were not entitled to reimbursement for the expenses they incurred in having their child independently evaluated and for unilaterally enrolling their child in a special facility. This, said the court, was "self help" activity precluding reimbursement.

The court also found that the parents were not denied due process of law with regard to the change in the child's IEP without notification to the parents. The court stated that although the imposition of a change in an IEP without parental consent may deprive them of "liberty with finality," it was apparent in this case that the alleged damage as a result of the change was minimal. The parents' claim that their equal protection rights under the U.S. Constitution had been violated was without merit because the child had never been totally excluded from any program offered by the school district. The court noted that the parents' argument that exhaustion of remedies should be excused on the ground that the superintendent had failed to reach a final decision within thirty days as required by law was also without merit. This, the court said, would not excuse the parents' failure to exhaust their administrative remedies. The case was dismissed. *Williams v. Overturf*, 580 F.Supp. 1365 (W.D.Wis.1984).

A Virginia case illustrates the rule that the exhaustion of administrative remedies doctrine cannot be waived absent a clear showing of futility. Here the mother of an emotionally disturbed child sued Virginia education officials, alleging that her son had been denied a free appropriate education. Specifically, the mother claimed that local school officials had wilfully withheld educational opportunities from her child. To support her argument the mother noted that the child, at the time suit was brought, was at home receiving no educational services whatsoever.

A U.S. district court held that the mother's claims should be dismissed because of her failure to exhaust available administrative remedies prior to bringing suit in federal court. The child was receiving a homebound education and the school district had formulated an IEP. The IEP called for placement at a private residential school. The problem was that shortly after this proposal was made no openings were available in the selected school. The court stated that had the facts conclusively shown that the child was not receiving any education whatsoever and that the defendent school district had not taken any steps to provide him with an appropriate education, the school district's violation of the EAHCA would be clear. Under such circumstances, prior resort to administrative remedies would not be a prerequisite to bringing suit in federal court because "administrative remedies need not be pursued when to do so would be futile." Here, however, the mother was required to exhaust the available administrative remedies prior to bringing suit. *Harris v. Campbell*, 472 F.Supp. 51 (E.D.Va.1979).

A U.S. district court in Louisiana held that the parents of handicapped and exceptional children were not entitled to bring suit in federal district court because of their failure to seek administrative review provided for in EAHCA. The parents claimed that a local school district had in effect a policy which constituted a failure to provide a meaningful, appropriate education to their handicapped children. The parents alleged that there was no division of the students based on age or handicap. The court held that the parents must have exhausted their administrative remedies prior to bringing suit in federal court. The court next had to determine whether to dismiss the case or "stay" the case pending exhaustion of administrative remedies. The court decided to dismiss the case, noting that courts will retain jurisdiction where not to do so would cause irreparable harm to the plaintiffs. Here, the court found no such potential irreparable harm. *Sessions v. Livingston Parish School Bd.*, 501 F.Supp. 251 (M.D.La.1980).

In an action brought in Puerto Rico, the U.S. Court of Appeals, First Circuit, has held that the mother of a handicapped child was required to exhaust the administrative process prior to bringing suit in federal court, despite the fact that a state agency initially failed to provide the mother with an internal remedy. The child, severely learning disabled, was placed by her parents in a residential private school in Vermont although the parents resided in Puerto Rico. They then sought funding for the child's education from the Puerto Rico Department of Education. The parents' request was denied because the department was conducting an assessment of the child for purposes of making a placement recommendation. The parents then brought suit in a U.S. district court, which dismissed the case because of the parents' failure to exhaust administrative remedies. The parents appealed, arguing that the department had taken an excessive amount of time to make a placement recommendation. The U.S. Court of Appeals, First Circuit, affirmed the district court ruling and held that despite delays in the placement process, the parents were obligated to pursue administrative channels before bringing suit in federal court. The court noted that courts are free to use their discretion in applying the doctrine. In this case, however, the various interests served by the doctrine weighed heavily in its favor. *Ezratty v. Commonwealth of Puerto Rico*, 648 F.2d 770 (1st Cir.1981).

The exhaustion doctrine was also applied in a New York case which involved a blanket decision by the New York Commissioner of Education that learning disabled children were not eligible for residential placement unless their learning disability was accompanied by an additional problem, such as an emotional disturbance. Eighteen learning disabled children who were denied residential placement sued the commissioner in a U.S. district court without first requesting a hearing. The court enjoined the commissioner from adhering to the policy and did not require the parents of the children to exhaust administrative remedies. The commissioner appealed to the U.S. Court of Appeals, Second Circuit, which reversed the district court ruling.

The Court of Appeals held that the district court acted too hastily, and should have required that the children exhaust state administrative remedies before bringing suit in federal court. The court was not persuaded by the parents' argument that exhaustion might prove "futile." There was, according to the court, always the possibility that, during the hearing process, the commissioner might reverse himself in a compelling case if he were proved wrong and a residential placement was shown to be necessary for a learning disabled child. The court stated that exhaustion may well have afforded relief to the children. Accordingly, the parents were not entitled to judicial relief when administrative relief might be available. *Riley v. Ambach*, 668 F.2d 635 (2d Cir.1981).

A Nebraska case involved a mentally retarded child who also suffered from muscular dystrophy. The child, who eventually became confined to a wheelchair, was unable to continue his then current educational placement because of the school's inability to accommodate handicapped students in wheelchairs. The child's parents, dissatisfied with the alternate placement provided, brought suit in federal district court challenging the appropriateness of the placemnt decision. The boy and his parents never requested a due process hearing prior to bringing suit.

At the time the suit was commenced there existed inconsistencies between state and federal administrative procedures. At that time, therefore, the student was under no duty to exhaust administrative remedies. However, at the time the case went to trial the inconsistencies had been resolved. The court held that because the inconsistencies had been rectified there was no longer any justification for permitting the child to circumvent the exhaustion requirement. The court observed that a state hearing officer is in the best position to make an initial determination on a child's placement. Here, there was no reason to believe that the state would not proceed in an expeditious manner if the parents opted for a due process hearing. The parents appealed to the U.S. Court of Appeals, Eighth Circuit. The court of appeals agreed with the district court ruling. No relief could be provided by a federal court where the child's father had failed to exhaust administrative remedies. The boy and his father never invoked the impartial hearing process provided by state law. *Monahan v. State of Nebraska*, 687 F.2d 1164 (8th Cir.1982).

An epileptic child in Kansas brought suit in the state of Kansas contending that Kansas educational practices violated his right to a free appropriate public education. He did not object to the state's overall special education program, but claimed that the plan was insufficiently enforced against local school districts as to its identification, screening and evaluation requirements. The Kansas Commissioner of Education maintained that, at all times, the plan had been in conformity with the requirements of the EAHCA and was enforced against local school districts.

A U.S. district court denied the child's request for an injunction on the ground that he had failed to exhaust his administrative remedies. In fact, the court found that the available administrative review under the EAHCA had not even begun. While the exhaustion requirement is generally excused if the exhaustion would be futile, this was not established in this case. Accordingly, the child was not entitled to relief in federal court. *Akers v. Bolton*, 531 F.Supp. 300 (D.Kan.1981).

The U.S. Court of Appeals, Fourth Circuit, has denied relief to a handicapped child and her parents in Virginia where the child and her parents had not attacked a local school district's special educational policies administratively prior to bringing suit in federal court. In this case the parents alleged that the school district had failed to provide their child with adequate educational services and procedures under the EAHCA. The Court of Appeals affirmed a U.S. district court ruling dismissing the parents' complaint. *McGovern v. Sullins*, 676 F.2d 98 (4th Cir.1982).

In a New York case the mother of a handicapped child, concerned about her son's lack of progress in his second year of kindergarten, asked that he be evaluated by a psychologist. The mother claimed that a school representative who came to her home with a parental permission form put a check mark on the form in the box indicating that she denied the district permission to conduct an evaluation of her child. The mother later brought suit in a U.S. district court claiming that as a result of being denied the special education to which he was entitled, her son suffered damages to his intellect, emotional capacity and personality, and was impeded in acquiring necessary training. In addition, she alleged that she moved to a different school district to obtain the services her child needed and that she herself had suffered emotional distress. The court held in favor of the mother and the school district appealed. The U.S. Court of Appeals, Second Circuit, held that because the mother had not availed herself of her administrative remedies under the EAHCA, she was deprived of her means of relief under the Act. However, the court did find that the mother had a claim under the Civil Rights Act. *Quakenbush v. Johnson City School Dist.*, 716 F.2d 141 (2d Cir.1983).

Two Massachusetts cases addressed the issue of exhaustion of remedies under Massachusetts state law and the EAHCA. The first case arose after the parents of a child with special educational needs, dissatisfied with the individualized educational program proposed by a school committee, challenged the IEP before the Massachusetts Bureau of Special Education Appeals (BSEA). A hearing officer found that the education plan proposed by the school committee was "the least restrictive, adequate and appropriate education plan to meet his special needs." On a printed form notifying the parents of the BSEA's decision, the following sentence appeared: "I understand that this rejection automatically constitutes an appeal to the State Advisory Commission (SAC) without my having to separately note such an appeal." The parents returned the form with that sentence stricken and the following sentence substituted: "I will appeal directly to the U.S. District Court." The parents then filed a complaint in U.S. district court.

The school district argued that the parents should not be allowed to bring suit in federal court because of their alleged failure to exhaust their administrative remedies. Specifically, the parents had failed to appeal the decision of the BSEA to the SAC. Under Massachusetts state law, the school district argued, the decision of the BSEA did not constitute a "final decision of a state educational agency" as required by both state law and the federal EAHCA. The parents argued that any alleged failure to exhaust administrative remedies should be excused on the ground that the school failed to advise them of their due process rights.

The district court held that it lacked jurisdiction to hear the parents' complaint as to the first academic year in which the plan was to be implemented. The court found that the U.S. Department of Education was the primary "state" agency responsible for the administration of the EAHCA in Massachusetts. Because the department had not participated in the administrative process, no final decision had been made by a state agency as required by the EAHCA.

For the years following the first year during which the plan was to be implemented, the court held that it would retain jurisdiction to hear the case after participation by the department. Under the circumstances, the court felt it particularly appropriate to seek the review of the department as the agency primarily responsible for the EAHCA's administration and enforcement. Finding that the parties would not suffer irreparable injury due to any delay resulting from the ruling, the parties were instructed to review the matter and make changes where necessary prior to resumption of the case. *Doe v. Anrig*, 500 F.Supp. 802 (D.Mass.1980).

The second case involved a town in Massachusetts which appealed a decision of the SAC which had determined that an IEP proposed by the town for a severely handicapped child was inadequate and inappropriate. The parents of the child had rejected and appealed the proposed IEP. The BSEA sustained the town's proposed IEP and the SAC, the next review body, tentatively affirmed the IEP. However, upon review of additional material the SAC reversed and remanded the matter to the BSEA for further hearings to determine "in light of this *final decision*" what would be the least restrictive and appropriate program and placement for the child. Misled by the SAC's incorrect reference to its "final decision," the town sought judicial review of the SAC's determination without exhausting further administrative remedies. A Massachusetts trial court dismissed the suit on the ground that the town failed to exhaust its administrative remedies, and the town appealed. The Appeals Court of Massachusetts held that the trial court properly dismissed the action because the SAC's decision was not a final administrative decision, even though designated a "final decision" by the SAC. *Town of East Longmeadow v. State Advisory Comm.*, 457 N.E.2d 636 (Mass.App.1983).

The New Hampshire Supreme Court decided a case in which a fourteen-year-old girl, who suffered from a severe learning disability coupled with speech and language disorders, was placed in a private residential school in Massachusetts. The reason for this placement was the inability of the girl's New Hampshire school district to provide an appropriate educational program for her. During the summer, after the child's second year at the school in Massachusetts, the local school district in New Hampshire formulated an IEP for the child which utilized public resources. The girl's mother appealed the school district's decision to place the child in a public program, which resulted in a determination that the public program offered was both "free and appropriate," and that the school district would no longer be obliged to pay for the child's education at the school in Massachusetts or any other private facility. The determination also denied tuition reimbursement to the mother for the four month period following the proposed IEP. (The mother had enrolled the child for a third year at the private school pending the resolution of the appeals process.) The mother then asked the New Hampshire Supreme Court to order the school district to pay the expenses incurred for the four months.

The court declined to rule on the matter since the child's mother had not appealed the final administrative decision to a state trial court or federal district court, as required by the EAHCA. Petitioning the supreme court of a state is not the appropriate method for seeking review of a decision of a state board of education. Although the court declined to hear the merits of the mother's complaint, it noted that if a school district can provide satisfactory assurance that its programs meet the EAHCA's standards for "free appropriate public education" of handicapped children, it will only be liable for the costs resulting from the placement of handicapped children in its own public programs and not for the cost incurred in private placements. *Petition of Darlene W.*, 469 A.2d 1307 (N.H.1983).

A profoundly mentally handicapped student in Indiana and her parents sued a local school district alleging that the district failed to provide a sufficient educational program for the child under the EAHCA. The girl, since infancy, had lived in a nursing home. At age eighteen she was diagnosed as having a mental age that ranged from two to twenty-one months. She had been receiving one one-hour educational session daily but at an annual conference to develop an IEP, the girl's mother requested that the child be placed in a full-day instructional program in the hope that the increased attention would lessen her persistent self-abuse. The school district refused to do this on the ground that the self-abuse would increase if the child was placed in a full-day program.

The mother filed objections to the proposed IEP and a hearing officer found that the child should be placed in a full-day instruction program. The school board appealed this finding to the State Board of Education, which remanded the case for a professional evaluation on the issue of the correlation between increased activity and self-abuse. Before a report could be made on the issue the parents filed suit in a U.S. district court which dismissed the parents' suit. The parents appealed. The U.S. Court of Appeals, Seventh Circuit, affirmed the district court's ruling, saying that not only had the parents failed to exhaust their administrative remedies, but the child was over eighteen years of age and therefore past the age at which the state was required to provide an education. *Timms v. Metropolitan School Dist. of Wabash County, Indiana*, 722 F.2d 1310 (7th Cir.1983).

B. Exceptions to the Exhaustion Doctrine

The following cases illustrate that exhaustion of administrative remedies is not required when it is clear that the purpose of the administrative remedies would be futile. There are cases in which courts deem state administrative remedies inadequate and thus not subject to the exhaustion requirement. Such things as delay by an agency in making a decision, or the fact that the agency may not be empowered to grant relief, will excuse the "exhaustion" requirement. The unavailability of a state or local remedy or a predetermined result by an agency will also excuse the requirement.

The mother of a six-year-old boy who had been diagnosed as having hemophilia and AIDS intended to enroll the boy in the first grade in a new Illinois school district for the 1987-88 school year. When the school board learned that the boy had AIDS, it formulated a "Policy Regarding Children With Chronic Communicable Diseases," to serve as a basis for placing the boy. Following the guidelines set forth in the policy, the school board met with the boy's mother and her attorney and thereafter unanimously decided to exclude the boy from the normal classroom and to provide him with a tutor in his home. The boy and his mother filed a lawsuit under the Rehabilitation Act of 1973, claiming that the boy had been discriminated against.

The school board argued before a U.S. district court that the boy's lawsuit should be dismissed since he failed to exhaust his state law administrative remedies as required by the EAHCA. The boy asserted that he was not "handicapped," as that term is defined in the EAHCA, and that because his lawsuit did not arise under the EAHCA, he was not required to exhaust his administrative remedies. Exhaustion of remedies was not required under the Rehabilitation Act.

The court applied the definition of "handicapped children" under the EAHCA to determine whether the boy's diagnosis of AIDS qualified. The court concluded that three tests had to be met before the EAHCA could be applied to the boy: 1) the boy's strength, vitality, or alertness had to be limited due to chronic or acute health problems, 2) those problems had to adversely affect his educational performance, and 3) the problems had to cause the boy to require special education and related services. The court also quoted a Department of Education opinion which stated, "[c]hildren with AIDS could be eligible for special education programs . . . if they have chronic or acute health problems which adversely affect their educational performance." The court determined that because the boy's educational performance had not been adversely affected, the EAHCA did not apply and the boy was therefore not required to exhaust administrative remedies before filing his discrimination lawsuit. The court denied the school board's motion to dismiss the case. *Doe v. Belleville Pub. School Dist.*, 672 F.Supp. 342 (S.D.Ill.1987).

In 1978, the state of New York agreed to pay the tuition costs of a schizophrenic boy who had been placed in a residential psychiatric hospital which operated an accredited academic high school. Behavioral problems prevented the boy from attending the high school, but he continued to reside at the hospital. His doctors hoped that the behavior problems could be overcome. The boy's parents, after petitioning state officials in vain, sought to compel the state to pay the cost of the boy's residential care at the hospital from the time of his placement, July, 1978, through June, 1983, when the boy turned twenty-one years old.

The state contended before a U.S. district court that the parents had failed to exhaust their administrative remedies prior to the lawsuit and that the statute of limitations barred their claim. The court held that exhaustion of administrative remedies was not required since it would have been futile. This was due to the fact that although the parents had, through informal petitions and requests, presented the state with details of their situation, the state had refused to pay for the boy's residential care. *Vander Malle v. Ambach*, 667 F.Supp. 1015 (S.D.N.Y. 1987).

The parents of several handicapped students in New York filed a class action lawsuit against the New York State Department of Education, the local school board and other local defendants alleging that they had violated the EAHCA by failing to properly identify, evaluate and place handicapped students. The parents entered into a consent judgment with the local school board and the other local defendants which provided the parents with the relief they had sought in correcting the violations. The parents then sought attorney's fees, which were awarded by a U.S. district court. The local school district appealed this award of attorney's fees to the U.S. Court of Appeals, Second Circuit.

The court of appeals considered the local school district's argument that attorney's fees could not be awarded under the EAHCA because the parents in this case were not challenging a final decision of a state administrative agency relating to the evaluation or placement of a specific handicapped student. The court noted that the generalized procedural violations challenged by the parents "lend themselves well to class action treatment," and that administrative remedies need not be exhausted where they would not provide adequate relief. The court of appeals then noted that the consent judgment in this case provided substantial relief to the parents which could not have been obtained through administrative appeal processes. It therefore concluded that the parents were entitled to attorney's fees. It decided that since the parents had sought relief under §§ 1983 and 1988 of the Civil Rights Act as well as under the EAHCA, the award of attorney's fees would be made under § 1988. The court of appeals also ruled that the award of attorney's fees should be reduced by the amount of such fees which were spent by the parents in suing the state since the state had not participated in the consent judgment. *J. G. v. Rochester City School Dist. Bd. of Educ.*, 830 F.2d 444 (2d Cir.1987).

In October, 1984, a hearing officer found four procedural violations of the EAHCA by the Baltimore City Schools relating to an eighteen-year-old handicapped student. The hearing officer found that the student was a seriously emotionally disturbed adolescent who required a residential placement and ordered the city to permanently place the student in a residential setting by November 20, 1984. On December 5, 1984, the student sued the city in a U.S. district court because the student had not received any change in his educational program. The district court dismissed the student's claims and he appealed to the U.S. Court of Appeals, Fourth Circuit.

The student claimed that he was denied a free appropriate public education when the city school system failed to implement the decision by the hearing officer in a timely manner. The district court had dismissed the complaint, holding that the student failed to exhaust his administrative remedies under the EAHCA. The court of appeals disagreed, noting that the student had received a final administrative decision under the EAHCA and that he had neither the responsibility nor the right to appeal the favorable decision by the local hearing officer since he was not an aggrieved party. The student had exhausted all administrative remedies available to him under the EAHCA and, when the city did not appeal the hearing officer's decision, it became the final administrative decision of the state.

The court of appeals also concluded that since the EAHCA did not contain any provision for enforcing final administrative orders by a hearing officer, the student was entitled to a § 1983 claim. When the city refused to enforce the hearing officer's decision to put the student in a residential placement the city had, under color of state law, violated the EAHCA. The district court was therefore wrong in dismissing the student's § 1983 claim. His § 1983 claim was remanded to the district court for further proceedings. *Robinson v. Pinderhughes*, 810 F.2d 1270 (4th Cir.1987).

A case arising in New York has held that the exhaustion doctrine did not apply to a situation involving the suspension of a multiply handicapped student from a school for the blind. In this case, the parents of the child brought suit against the New York State Education Department and the school for the blind seeking an injunction to reinstate the student at the school. The parents brought suit without first having exhausted the available administrative remedies. This was done, claimed the parents, because of a denial of procedural safeguards when the parents wished to contest their child's suspension. The parents alleged that the state had failed to provide for an impartial hearing officer and that there was no provision requiring the agency to allow the child to remain in the school pending resolution of their complaint. The school argued that it had "substantially complied" with the procedural requirements of the EAHCA. However, the court disagreed stating that a "person who claims that the state defendants have not even provided the impartial hearing as required by federal law *a fortiori* asserts a claim over which [the] court has jurisdiction." Finding the parents and the child in that position, the court denied the school's motion to dismiss the case. *Sherry v. New York State Educ. Dep't*, 479 F.Supp. 1328 (W.D.N.Y.1979).

The exhaustion doctrine was also inapplicable in a case in Pennsylvania. Here, the parents of an emotionally disturbed son sought special education placement for him after he had been diagnosed as emotionally disturbed. The parents then activated the due process hearing system, but the responsible officials in the child's school district reached no decision in time to place the boy at a special school before the beginning of the following academic year. The parents then found what they believed to be an appropriate school in New York and began paying tuition. A hearing was held after the first year of the child's enrollment in the school chosen by the parents, which resulted in a determination that the placement chosen by the parents was appropriate. The parents raised the matter of tuition reimbursement but this was never resolved.

Believing they had received a favorable ruling from the hearing officer, the parents did not appeal the decision but their attempts to secure reimbursement proved unsuccessful. They claimed that there simply was no reimbursement procedure in Pennsylvania. The parents eventually brought suit in a U.S. district court against the school district, which argued that they were not entitled to do so on the ground that the reimbursement issue was never litigated at the hearing level and thus the parents had failed to exhaust their administrative remedies. The court concluded that the "exhaustion" doctrine was irrelevant where no administrative remedy had ever been available. *Hark v. School Dist. of Philadelphia*, 505 F.Supp. 727 (E.D.Pa.1980).

The parents of a handicapped child in Illinois challenged the failure of various state agencies to assume the full cost of the child's placement at a private residential facility. After being assessed by the state as "responsible relatives," the parents were told they must contribute $100 per month toward their son's placement. The state's reason for excluding this amount from the child's placement at the school was that it was attributable to "clothing, medical supplies and purchased services." An outstanding bill at the school in the amount of $2,154.53 resulted in the issue of a discharge notice to the child which was to become effective prior to the resolution of the parents' appeal of the decision to assess them as "responsible relatives." The parents, without waiting for resolution of the appeal, filed suit in U.S. district court. The state sought to have the case dismissed for failure to exhaust administrative remedies.

The district court excused the exhaustion requirement because the parents had no practical opportunity to obtain the appeal decision. They had done everything possible to obtain speedy administrative review, but were unable to do so through no fault of their own. Because of the state's failure to decide the parents' administrative appeal within the time specified by federal law, the purpose of the exhaustion requirement was undermined; the parents would have been unable to obtain the decision before the time that the school intended to discharge the child. The court stated that "when the press of time makes exhaustion impractical, it is not required by the EHA." The court also found that the parents had no "real administrative remedy" in this case. It was doubtful, said the court, that administrative review could provide the parents with the relief they sought. It appeared that the agency decision had been made pursuant to state law. Thus, by adopting the responsible relatives policy, the agency had already predetermined the result it would reach in the child's case. *Parks v. Pavkovic*, 536 F.Supp. 296 (N.D.Ill.1982).

In another Illinois case, a group of emotionally disturbed children brought suit in a U.S. district court against Illinois state education officials, challenging a rule excluding counseling and therapeutic services from being considered special education or related services. The children admittedly did not exhaust their administrative remedies but argued that an exhaustion attempt would be futile. They claimed that the Illinois State Board of Education was not the "appropriate forum" to address the issues relating to the Illinois Governor's Purchased Care Review Board determinations of allowable cost for related services. Noting that none of the children had attempted to exhaust the administrative remedies prescribed by § 1415 of the EAHCA and that, ordinarily, this would require dismissal, the court excused the exhaustion requirement in this case. The court concluded that Illinois had not established a meaningful process of administrative review. *Gary B. v. Cronin*, 542 F.Supp. 102 (N.D.Ill.1980).

The U.S. Court of Appeals, Second Circuit, reversed a district court's decision to dismiss a case because of the plaintiff's failure to exhaust her administrative remedies. The controversy originally centered on whether a school district was liable, under the EAHCA, for the transportation cost of the plaintiff's son. The school district declined to provide transportation reimbursement, because the tests necessary to determine whether the child was in fact handicapped were never made due to the parent's rejection of the school district's psychologists. A final administrative decision then was rendered in favor of the school district. When the case was appealed to a U.S. district court, the judge held that the plaintiff had not exhausted her administrative remedies because the testing data had not been provided. The Court of Appeals reversed the lower court, stating that the absence of the testing data did not mean that the proper administrative route was not followed by the plaintiff. The court concluded that if a final administrative decision has been rendered, it is to be reviewed on its merits. The case was remanded for further proceedings. *Dubois v. Connecticut State Bd. of Educ.*, 727 F.2d 44 (2d Cir.1983).

V. STATUTE OF LIMITATIONS

"Statute of limitations" refers to the time in which a person may file suit or an "aggrieved party" may appeal a decision after an alleged injury has occurred. The EAHCA does not specify a time limitation in which parties may bring suit in state or federal court after exhausting administrative remedies or appeal an adverse administrative decision. Administrative procedures are generally governed by state laws which usually specify a thirty-day limitation on appeals. However, state laws for other types of actions usually set a longer time limitation. Conflicts arise when one party files a lawsuit or appeals a decision outside what the other party perceives to be the applicable statute of limitations.

A mother placed her autistic son in a private school in California from February, 1974, through February, 1975. Her son entered his local school district's program in September, 1977, but was suspended in December, 1978, for disciplinary reasons. Without obtaining her consent the school district notified the mother that her son would be taught at home pending evaluation. However, the school district delayed his evaluation until May, 1979, and failed to hold an IEP meeting until June, 1979. The IEP recommended a special day school for her son but a teachers' strike delayed the school's opening until October, 1979.

Her son continued in the day school until 1985 when he was notified that he was no longer eligible for public education because he was twenty-two years of age. The mother requested a hearing to contest the decision to terminate his education. She alleged that the school district had violated § 504 of the Rehabilitation Act in 1974-75 by excluding her son from the public school. She requested total reimbursement for all private school expenses or a compensatory education. She also contended that the school district violated the EAHCA in 1979 by not timely providing her son with an appropriate education. After the hearing officer ruled for the school district the mother appealed to a U.S. district court, which upheld the hearing officer's decision. She then appealed to the U.S. Court of Appeals, Ninth Circuit.

Because § 504 contains no statute of limitations, the court borrowed the statute of limitations governing similar disputes under California law, which provided for a three-year limitation. Because the statute of limitations began to run when the mother knew or had reason to know of the injury she was too late in filing her claim. Her EAHCA claim was also barred because she waited six years to assert it. The district court's decision in favor of the school district was affirmed. *Alexopulos v. San Francisco Unified School Dist.*, 817 F.2d 551 (9th Cir.1987).

A handicapped nine-year-old New York boy who suffered from speech and motor difficulties was evaluated by his school district's committee on the handicapped (COH). The COH then made a recommendation for an educational placement of the boy which his parents believed to be inappropriate. They appealed the placement decision to the New York Commissioner of Education, who ruled in favor of the parents. However, the Commissioner declined to order that the parents be reimbursed for the boy's educational expenses incurred as a result of the parents' decision to unilaterally place their child in a private school. The private school had provided an appropriate education for the boy during the ten-month period from the time of the initial, incorrect COH evaluation to the time the Commissioner's decision was rendered.

Fifteen months after the Commissioner's decision denying reimbursement, the parents sued in U.S. district court seeking reimbursement for the private school tuition. The district court held that the suit was barred by the statute of limitations, a decision upheld by the U.S. Court of Appeals, Second Circuit. While noting that the EAHCA contains no statute of limitations, the appeals court stated that the applicable state statute of limitations will be used in lawsuits brought pursuant to the EAHCA. In this case there was a conflict between a New York statute governing educational proceedings in state courts which called for a four-month limit, and a more general New York statute providing for a three-year limit on any suit "to recover upon a liability . . . created or imposed by statute."

The district court had relied upon the law providing for a four-month limit because it was the one most closely analogous to the present cause of action had it arisen under state law. The Court of Appeals sanctioned this approach, noting that to allow the longer three-year statute of limitations to govern lawsuits seeking reimbursement for educational expenses would conflict with the EAHCA requirement that a child remain in his current educational placement during the pendency of any proceedings to review the appropriateness of a child's placement. Said the court, "this 'status quo' provision hardly contemplates a period of three years plus pendency of the proceedings. After all, it is a child's education we are talking about." The court therefore refused to allow the three-year general statute of limitations to govern the case and stated that because the parents had failed to appeal the Commissioner's decision within four months, their suit had been properly dismissed. *Adler v. Education Department of State of New York*, 760 F.2d 454 (2d Cir.1985). A New York federal district court has upheld the decision. The statute of limitations for New York EAHCA cases is four months, based upon state Article 78 proceedings, rather than three years as provided by the state's limitations period for federal civil rights cases. *Gerasimou v. Ambach*, 636 F.Supp. 1504 (E.D.N.Y.1986).

The mother of a twenty-year-old mentally handicapped, speech impaired and emotionally disturbed girl filed suit in U.S. district court against the Board of Education of Wood County, West Virginia. Since 1969, the girl had been enrolled at the Institute of Logopedics, a private school in Wichita, Kansas. For several years the mother paid the entire cost of this education. After Congress enacted the EAHCA, the Board of Education assumed responsibility for the bulk of her educational and residential costs at the Institute. However, when the girl reached the age of eighteen the board concluded that she could be appropriately educated in the Wood County public school system. The mother was told that the board would no longer pay the cost of her private school education.

The mother objected and requested a due process hearing. The hearing officer agreed with the Board of Education that the girl should be transferred from the private school to the Wood County public school. The mother appealed the hearing officer's decision to the West Virginia State Board of Education which agreed with Wood County's decision to place the girl in the public school system. The mother filed suit in U.S. district court nearly one year after the State Board's decision and the school board asked that the suit be dismissed because it had been filed more than 120 days after the State Board's decision.

The district court observed that the EAHCA does not specify a time limit within which claims must be brought. State law must be looked to in determining the time within which a party must bring a claim. The state does this by searching for an "analogous" state cause of action and using the applicable statute of limitations.

The school board argued that the 120-day limit imposed upon petitions for review by the West Virginia Supreme Court was the most analogous state cause of action. The district court agreed, holding that since parents in EAHCA cases are essentially appealing an administrative decision to the court system, the cause of action is analogous to a petition for review by a higher court. Here the parents were appealing the administrative decisions made by the school board and the State Board of Education.

The mother urged the court not to apply the 120-day limit in this case. She pointed out that after the State Board hearing her attorney had suffered a heart attack. Once the attorney returned to work, he cut down his practice and told the mother that he would find a different attorney to take the case. The district court refused to recognize the attorney's illness as a ground for not applying the 120-day limitations period. However, the court did not apply the limit to the present case because it decided the issue after the mother filed her suit. It held that it would be unfair to impose the newly decided 120-day limit on the mother because she and her attorney had no way of knowing that the new limit would be established. The 120-day limitation would be applied only to West Virginia special education cases filed after the present decision. *Thomas v. Staats*, 633 F.Supp. 797 (S.D.W.Va.1985).

A twelve-year-old handicapped boy was enrolled at the Achievement Center, a private school for the learning disabled in the Roanoke, Virginia, area. Previously, he had been enrolled in the Roanoke County public schools in which he had only taken special education classes in one area, mathematics. His parents were unhappy with a single math class being the only special education class provided. During the 1983-84 school year, the child's academic and social problems became severe and his parents filed a complaint against the superintendent for failure to develop a sufficient IEP.

A hearing officer held that the IEP was adequate and the parents were denied tuition reimbursement. The state review board affirmed the hearing officer's decision. Seventy-six days after the state board's decision, the parents filed a complaint under the EAHCA against the school superintendent claiming that the school district was denying their son an appropriate education. The school moved for dismissal on the ground that the complaint had been filed too late.

The U.S. district court noted that because the EAHCA does not specify a time limit in which to bring a lawsuit, the courts must determine the time limit based on the "most analogous" state cause of action. It found the Virginia Supreme Court Rules 2A:2 and 2A:4 analogous to EAHCA proceedings, but held that the thirty-day limit contained in the Rules was not in keeping with EAHCA policy. Instead, the court found that the one-year statute of limitations provided for tort actions under a state statute (Va.Code secs. 8.01-248) was the appropriate time limit. Congress' policy in EAHCA cases was that placement disputes be given as fair and complete a hearing as possible. Finding that the one-year statute of limitations for tort cases was more conducive to fairness, the court denied the school's motion to dismiss the complaint. *Kirchgessner v. Davis*, 632 F.Supp. 616 (W.D.Va.1986).

Two Pennsylvania cases have held that a thirty-day Pennsylvania statute of limitations governing appeals of administrative agency decisions did not apply to actions brought by handicapped students and their parents. The first case involved a suit brought by the parents of a handicapped child against the state and a local school district. The parents sought reimbursement of expenses they incurred in placing their child in a private residential school which was eventually determined to be the appropriate school for the child. The defendants claimed that a state thirty-day statute of limitations precluded the suit. A federal district court disagreed, saying that the action was not time barred since the parents were not appealing a "decision." In fact, the parents appealed to the federal court because of the state's excessive delay in reaching a decision as to the parents' request for reimbursement. *Hark v. School Dist. of Philadelphia*, 505 F.Supp. 727 (E.D.Penn.1980).

The second case arising in Pennsylvania held that a thirty-day statute of limitations period did not bar a suit brought against the Pennsylvania Department of Education and a local school district. A handicapped student requiring clean intermittent catheterization to enable her to attend school challenged a school district policy which denied such services. The U.S. Court of Appeals, Third Circuit, affirmed a district court ruling in favor of the child. The court of appeals agreed with the district court's decision to apply either a two-year or a six-year statute of limitations period to the child's claim under the EAHCA. Finding that the thirty-day limitations period was incompatible with the objective of the EAHCA, the court held that it did not apply. The court of appeals decided that the two-year state statute of limitations which applied to actions to recover damages for injuries caused by the wrongful act or negligence of another, and controlled in medical malpractice cases, was the most analogous statute. Because the child's claim was brought within the two-year period, her action was not barred. *Tokarcik v. Forest Hills School Dist.*, 665 F.2d 443 (3d Cir.1981).

The U.S. Court of Appeals, Sixth Circuit, has disagreed with the foregoing decisions ruling that the statute of limitations for EAHCA tuition reimbursement claims should be three years. In so ruling the court stated its belief that a one-year limitations period would simply be "too short."

Here, the Knox County, Tennessee, school system became aware that one of its male students was emotionally disturbed due to "multiple drug ingestion." On the recommendation of a psychologist the boy's parents sent him to the Brown School, a residential school in Texas, where the boy stayed for nearly three years. After receiving a high school equivalency diploma in April, 1981, the boy permanently left school.

In February, 1985, his parents filed suit under the EAHCA in U.S. district court seeking reimbursement for their son's tuition at the Brown School. They alleged bad faith on the part of the Knox County School System and claimed that it had failed to advise them of their EAHCA rights. The parents did not seek a due process hearing prior to filing suit because they believed it would be futile. Knox County moved for dismissal on various grounds, including the Tennessee statute of limitations. The district court granted Knox County's motion and the parents appealed.

The court of appeals agreed with the district court's adoption of the three-year statute of limitations provided by Tennessee law for "services performed but not paid for" [T.C.A. § 28-3-105(3)]. The one-year limitations period provided by Tennessee law for personal injury lawsuits was found to be inadequate, as was the state's sixty-day limitation on appeals for administrative agency rulings. Section 28-3-105(3), which applied to money owed for services rendered, was deemed to be the most analogous statute of limitations consistent with the EAHCA. Since the parents became aware of their right to tuition reimbursement in May, 1981, and did not file suit until February, 1985, their claims were barred by the Tennessee statute of limitations. The court of appeals upheld the dismissal of the parents' claims. *Janzen v. Knox County Bd. of Educ.*, 790 F.2d 484 (6th Cir.1986).

In a Texas case, a handicapped child was placed by her school district in a public facility which was equipped to treat children with emotional disturbances and autism. She made progress during her first year there. However, during the second year she regressed significantly. The parents removed her from the facility and placed her in another institute. After tuition expenses were denied by the child's school district, the parents sought relief in a U.S. district court which held that because the parents had brought suit nine months after the denial, their claim was barred by a thirty-day statute of limitations. In addition, said the court, the parents forfeited all rights to recover tuition for the private residential facility by unilaterally withdrawing the child from the school district's program. The parents appealed this decision to the U.S. Court of Appeals, Fifth Circuit, which agreed with the district court ruling that the parents were not entitled to reimbursement, but reversed the thirty-day statute of limitations ruling, saying that the limitation was inconsistent with the EAHCA's policy of investing parents with discretion to take action regarding their children's education. *Scokin v. State of Texas*, 723 F.2d 432 (5th Cir.1984).

In Hawaii, a thirty-day statute of limitations period did apply to a suit brought outside that period by the Hawaii Department of Education. The Department had filed two suits in federal court challenging adverse hearing officer decisions on the issue of responsibility for the costs of educating two handicapped children. The U.S. Court of Appeals, Ninth Circuit, held that the Department's suit was barred by its failure to appeal the hearing officer's decision within the thirty-day limitation period set by the Hawaii Administrative Procedures Act. The court found the APA to provide a more comprehensive standard of review than the EAHCA. Further, the need to avoid delays in resolving disputes over education plans for handicapped children supported the application of a thirty-day statute of limitations period for a state agency to appeal an adverse decision. The court affirmed a U.S. district court decision to dismiss the cases. However, the court noted that it was not being asked to decide whether the same thirty-day rule would apply to parents or guardians seeking judicial review of a handicapped child's placement. The thirty-day rule may not apply in those cases. *Dep't of Educ., State of Hawaii v. Carl D.*, 695 F.2d 1154 (9th Cir.1983).

VI. FAILURE TO COMPLY WITH EAHCA PROVISIONS

Due process of law is contingent upon a school district's adherence to the procedural safeguards of the EAHCA. The failure to adhere to the provisions of the EAHCA will generally result in a favorable ruling for the parents or guardians of handicapped students.

A Pennsylvania father filed a lawsuit under the EAHCA against his local school district and the Pennsylvania Secretary of Education. The father asserted that his child, who was learning disabled and had emotional problems, had been denied a free appropriate education and that Pennsylvania's procedures violated rights guaranteed by the EAHCA and its implementing regulations. A U.S. district court ruled in favor of the father and the school district and state appealed.

The U.S. Court of Appeals, Third Circuit, first determined that the father's placement of a child at a private school had been reasonable and that he should be reimbursed for the out-of-pocket expense of that placement. It then considered the argument put forth by the school district and the state that reimbursement of the father's expenses was barred by the Eleventh Amendment to the U.S. Constitution. The court pointed out that the Eleventh Amendment generally precludes lawsuits in federal court against a state by the state's citizens. It noted that Congress can set aside the immunity from federal lawsuits that states enjoy under the Eleventh Amendment if it makes its intentions clear. The court then observed that the EAHCA expressly gives handicapped children and their parents the right to enforce their EAHCA rights in federal or state courts. Furthermore, the Handicapped Children's Protection Act of 1986 mentioned that lawsuits in federal or state courts under the EAHCA would have to be filed against a "State or local educational agency." The court concluded that the EAHCA authorized lawsuits against states in federal court. It ruled in favor of the father and sustained the district court's order that he be reimbursed for the out-of-pocket expense of the child's placement. *Muth v. Central Bucks School Dist.*, 839 F.2d 113 (3d Cir.1988).

The father of a handicapped child allowed a Texas state agency to become the child's managing conservator in order to facilitate her placement at a psychiatric hospital. Subsequently, he sued a local school district claiming that the EAHCA required it to place the child in a residential psychiatric hospital with an in-house education program. He took this action because he wanted the school district to take responsibility for providing a residential education program for the child after she became eighteen years old when she would be ineligible for continuation of the managing conservatorship. A U.S. district court dismissed his lawsuit and the U.S. Court of Appeals, Fifth Circuit, affirmed the dismissal. It concluded that under Texas law, only the state agency, as the child's managing conservator, had authority to bring a lawsuit on her behalf. The court of appeals observed that the father could seek appointment as the child's "next friend" if he believed the state agency's interest to be in conflict with those of the child. Because the father was not the child's legal guardian or "next friend" the court of appeals held that he lacked legal standing to sue the school district. *Susan R.M. v. Northeast Indep. School Dist.*, 818 F.2d 455 (5th Cir.1987).

The U.S. Court of Appeals, Fourth Circuit, ruled that a school district's failure to fully advise the parents of a dyslexic child of their procedural rights under the EAHCA justified unilateral private school placement by the parents. In this North Carolina case, the child, who had been enrolled in his local public elementary school, had extreme difficulty in reading. Although he was required to repeat second grade, the child was thereafter advanced from grade to grade due to the school district's practice of making "social promotions." When the child reached the third grade, an IEP was developed which identified him as having reading deficiencies only and called for placement in a regular classroom ninety percent of the time, and placement in a learning disabilities resource room for the remainder of the time. When the child reached the fifth grade he still could not read. In desperation, his parents enrolled him in a private residential facility. At this time a private evaluation of the child was performed which finally disclosed that although he was of above average intelligence, the child suffered from dyslexia. The parents also discovered for the first time that under federal law their school district might be obligated to pay for their child's placement at the private school. The parents filed suit and a U.S. district court ruled in their favor.

On appeal, the U.S. Court of Appeals upheld the district court's ruling, ordering that the school district pay the cost of the child's placement at the private school. The child had made no educational progress while in the public schools and the IEP developed by public school officials was utterly inadequate, said the court. The school district's contention that the child had achieved educational benefits because he had advanced from grade to grade was dismissed by the appellate court, due to the school's policy of making social promotions. Furthermore, the school district's failure to fully inform the parents of their rights under the EAHCA constituted a *per se* breach of its statutory duties. The appellate court also noted that the child had finally begun to make educational progress after his placement at the private residential school. The child's parents were thus entitled to recover the costs of his placement from the school district. *Hall v. Vance County Bd. of Educ.*, 774 F.2d 629 (4th Cir.1985).

The parents of a learning disabled boy claimed that the Mississippi Board of Education violated provisions of the EAHCA by not having an impartial state review team decide whether to reimburse them for their son's tuition at a private school during the 1984-85 school year and to provide a private education for the next school year.

The parents had become dissatisfied with the IEP developed for their son, a learning disabled handicapped child. They sought an administrative hearing concerning the child's proper placement and reimbursement for the tuition they had paid at a private school. The hearing officer ruled that the parents should be reimbursed for the 1984-85 school year, but that the child should return to the public school system. On appeal, however, the state review board ruled that the parents should not receive tuition reimbursement and that the boy should return to public school.

The parents filed suit in federal district court, requesting a new hearing before the state review board. The district court granted the request because it found that the State Board of Education had violated the EAHCA. The court held that officers of local school boards and personnel active in state policy for the education of handicapped children should not serve on the state review panel. These individuals were too closely involved with the State Board of Education and could not provide the parents with an impartial hearing. Also, the court ruled that a state review team must make specific findings of fact in support of their conclusions under the EAHCA. *Kotowicz v. Mississippi State Bd. of Educ.*, 630 F.Supp. 925 (S.D.Miss.1986).

In a Rhode Island case, a federal court ruled that a school district, faced with a hostile set of parents, acted properly in attempting to provide a learning disabled boy with an appropriate special education. The parents had enrolled their child at the age of six in the Scituate, Rhode Island, public school system. He received remedial reading instruction during first grade. The following year his parents placed him in a private Catholic school, but eighteen months later they concluded that he was learning disabled and once again enrolled him in the Scituate public schools. Eighteen months after this the parents placed him at a private day school, and later at the Linden Hill School in Northfield, Massachusetts, which specializes in the education of learning disabled boys. The child never returned to the Scituate public school system.

Three years later, in April, 1981, the parents sought future financial assistance under the EAHCA for their son's placement at Linden Hill. In May, 1981, they met with Scituate's special education multi-disciplinary team (MDT) and expressed their dissatisfaction with the district's past education of their child. When the MDT said that due to flawed and dated prior tests, a new evaluation of the child would be required, the parents objected and withheld consent until June, 1981. A partial evaluation was then performed by the MDT, but due to parental resistance it was never completed. At a September, 1981, meeting with the MDT, the parents were advised that the MDT would recommend placement in a Scituate self-contained classroom. Due to delays caused by the parents, an IEP meeting was not held until October 20, 1981. They attended this meeting with their attorney and later contested the resultant IEP (which provided for Scituate placement) at a due process hearing.

The hearing officer ruled in favor of the school district, but the parents appealed and a review officer reversed. The Scituate school district appealed to a Rhode Island federal district court. The court examined the issues presented by the case, beginning with the parents' allegation that Scituate's letter notifying them of the October IEP meeting had failed to state who would be in attendance and that other individuals could attend. The court excused this failure due to the fact that the parents had attended one IEP meeting previously (in 1978) and thus were probably aware of their rights. Also, the individuals present on October 20, 1981, were the same individuals who had attended the September meeting. No one was a surprise attendee, nor was anyone absent whom the parents expected to attend. Also, there was no evidence of bad faith on the part of Scituate.

The parents' second allegation was also dismissed by the court. They had correctly pointed out that the EAHCA places great emphasis on parental involvement in the formulation of an IEP. They alleged that at the October 20 meeting, an IEP was presented to them which read "Independent Education Program," to be effective from "October 20, 1981 - October 20, 1982." The parents argued that this was an attempt to steamroll them into accepting an "immutable, unchangeable, completed plan," which was subject only to their acceptance or rejection—not their participation. The court, however, held that the parents were aware of their right to offer input and make suggestions at the IEP meeting, noting that their attorney had written a letter to school officials after the meeting which stated: "they [the parents] will then inform the school what, if anything, they feel must be added, eliminated, or changed. . . ."

Finding that Scituate was innocent of any procedural violations, the district court then proceeded to determine whether the proposed IEP was adequate. Rhode Island law requires that a school district "shall provide such type of education that will *best satisfy* the needs of a handicapped child" (emphasis added). This educational standard is incorporated into the federal EAHCA by reference. The district court, ruling on an issue of first impression, held that this standard was identical to the federal standard set forth in *Board of Education v. Rowley.* The U.S. Supreme Court held in *Rowley* that, at a minimum, an IEP must be designed to allow a handicapped child to "benefit educationally" from his or her instruction. The district court based its ruling on the fact that the Rhode Island statute using the language "best satisfy" was decades old and could not correctly be interpreted to give handicapped children the right to the best possible education. All that was required under Rhode Island law was that a child derive educational benefits under the IEP. Examining all the evidence, the court concluded that Scituate's proposed IEP was adequate.

The testimony of the parents' expert witness, Dr. Edwin M. Cole, a renowned language disability expert, was discounted by the court. It was the court's opinion that he was insufficiently familiar with the case, having met with the child for only one forty-minute period. At trial, Dr. Cole was unable to say whether the child wore glasses. These factors caused the district judge to give greater weight to the opinions of Scituate personnel, who were more familiar with the child. Finally, the court noted that the desirability of mainstreaming also supported placement in the Scituate public classroom. Reimbursement for the child's placement at Linden Hills was therefore denied to the parents. *Scituate School Comm. v. Robert B.*, 620 F.Supp. 1224 (D.R.I.1985).

The parents of an emotionally handicapped, learning disabled child with severe behavioral problems brought suit against an Oregon school district alleging that an appropriate education program was not being made available to their child and that the school district violated statutes and regulations it was legally bound to follow. They requested and received a complaint hearing before the state Department of Education (DOE). The DOE found that the school district had violated applicable state and federal laws and awarded the parents partial reimbursement of tuition costs they had incurred by enrolling their son in a private school. However, it denied the parents' request for attorney's fees.

Both the parents and the school district appealed to the Court of Appeals of Oregon which defined four issues: 1) whether the allegations that the district denied the child a "free appropriate public education" and otherwise violated state and federal laws were properly before the DOE; 2) whether the DOE, after finding that such violations had occurred, had the authority to require the district to reimburse the parents, in part, for expenses they had incurred; 3) whether the DOE was empowered to award the parents attorney's fees; and 4) whether the DOE's findings of fact were supported by substantial evidence.

The court held that the DOE was the correct forum in which to bring the complaint. Had the parents' complaint alleged only that they disagreed with the district's IEP or educational placement for their child, the proper forum for resolution of that matter would have been a due process hearing. However, it alleged that an appropriate educational program was not made available to the child and also that the district violated various other federal statutes and regulations. Accordingly, the correct forum was a "complaint hearing." Such a hearing is governed by Oregon state law, which requires that local school districts comply with the EAHCA, that school districts have complaint procedures available for alleged violations and that sanctions be imposed against noncomplying districts.

However, the DOE, after finding violations, did not have the authority to require the school district to reimburse the parents' expenses. The district had a duty, said the court, to provide the child with a free appropriate education and, its having failed in that duty, the DOE only had the authority to withhold funds from it. The court went on to hold that the DOE had the power to award attorney's fees even though it had not done so in this case, and that the DOE's findings of fact were supported by substantial evidence. *Laughlin v. School Dist. No. 1*, 686 P.2d 385 (Or.App.1984).

A Missouri case involved the proposed transfer of two handicapped children from an elementary school district to a state school for the severely handicapped. The parents of the children sued the school district alleging that the children were denied due process of law in violation of the EAHCA. A federal district court agreed with the parents. The court found that the referral of the children to the State Department of Education for placement was without prior notice to the parents. In addition, the first level hearing was defective because a three-member panel failed to review the facts and make a decision as required by the EAHCA. Instead, the State Department of Education decided to withdraw the proposed assignment of the children and to conduct further proceedings before making a final determination as to an appropriate educational placement. The court found that the state was thus bound to comply with federal procedural safeguards which became effective as of the date of the hearing. The actions taken by the Department were in violation of the procedural safeguards of the EAHCA which require a determination of the facts and a decision. Finally, the court found that the state level hearing was not conducted by an impartial hearing officer. This hearing was conducted by the Missouri State Board of Education which was an "agency or unit involved in the education or care of the child" within the meaning of the EAHCA. The Act also requires that the impartial individual who conducts a due process hearing at the state level may not be an employee of the State Department of Education or "of any local or intermediate unit thereof." Here, the parents were entitled to, but did not receive, an impartial hearing officer. *Vogel v. School Bd. of Montrose R-14 School Dist.*, 491 F.Supp. 989 (W.D.Mo.1980).

Another school district was found to have violated the procedural safeguards of the EAHCA by the failure to provide an impartial hearing officer. This case arose in Iowa and involved a challenge to a local school district's decision to place a child in special education classes. The child's guardian brought suit against the Iowa State Superintendent of Public Instruction alleging that the superintendent violated the "impartial hearing officer" provision of the EAHCA by presiding over the due process hearing which the child had received. A U.S. district court held that the superintendent violated the EAHCA provision barring employees of agencies involved in the education of a child from serving as hearing officers in due process hearings required by the Act. The district court remanded the case for a new hearing which was to be presided over by an outside hearing officer and the superintendent appealed to the U.S. Court of Appeals, Eighth Circuit.

The Court of Appeals was asked to decide whether the superintendent, as Superintendent of Public Instruction and an employee of the State Board of Public Instruction, was employed by a direct provider of educational services, the local school board, or whether he merely exercised supervisory authority over the direct provider. The court affirmed the district court ruling, declaring the superintendent to be statutorily disqualified from serving as a hearing officer. The EAHCA's clear language and history indicate that "no hearing may be conducted by an employee of the State or local educational agency involved in the education or care of the child." *Robert M. v. Benton*, 634 F.2d 1139 (8th Cir.1980).

The parents of an eleven-year-old learning disabled child in the District of Columbia, dissatisfied with a local school district's placement of the child, expressed their concern to the school staff. A meeting with school staff followed in which the parents again reiterated the concerns they had expressed earlier concerning the appropriateness of the child's education. After the meeting the school sent the parents a "Notice of Continuing Special Education Services," which stated that the child was to continue in the current program at the school. The notice did not inform the parents of the need to file any form, not did it state any way by which a dissatisfied parent could challenge the school's decision. A hearing was scheduled, but it was later canceled by the school. A letter to the parents' attorney stated that "since the [school was] 'unaware' of the [parents'] desire to change [the child's] program, no formal evaluation procedure had been initiated for the child." Accordingly, the letter continued, "the public schools will not be ready, nor are they required to participate at a hearing until they are given an opportunity to complete the formal evaluation/placement process."

The parents then brought suit against the school in federal court requesting the court to order the school to provide a due process hearing in which their objections to their child's continued placement at the school would be "fully ventilated." Without the hearing, claimed the parents, they were being denied due process guarantees mandated by the EAHCA and the Act's regulations which require that the parents or guardian of a child be afforded a hearing whenever they have a complaint about a school district's proposal to change or refusal to change a child's educational placement or any matter concerning the child's placement.

The school also argued that the parents had failed to submit a "Form 205" request which would have given the school notice of their objections. Noting that a school must be afforded reasonable notice of any parent's desire for a change of placement before the school is required to act upon the request, the court nevertheless found that the notice of placement to the parents did not inform them that filing "Form 205" was the proper procedure for objecting to their child's placement. Accordingly, the court denied the school's motion to dismiss the case and ordered that a hearing be held within five days of the court's order to address the parents' complaints about their child's IEP. *Pastel v. Dist. of Columbia Bd. of Educ.*, 522 F.Supp. 535 (D.D.C.1981).

A handicapped child and his mother brought suit on behalf of themselves and all handicapped children not receiving an appropriate education by reason of delays of the Illinois Superintendent of Education in resolving placement appeals. A severely emotionally disturbed twelve-year-old child was recommended for placement by his school district in a self-contained classroom for behavior disorder students. His mother objected to the recommendation and said that she had been advised by experts that a highly structured residential program would be appropriate placement for the child. The mother appealed the decision but after five months the superintendent had made no decision. The mother claimed that the superintendent was obligated to decide within thirty days. She alleged that the long delay and inappropriate educational setting had caused the deterioration of the child's condition to the extent that he had to be placed in a mental hospital. The superintendent sought to dismiss the suit on the basis that the EAHCA creates no substantive rights for handicapped children.

A U.S. district court in Illinois disagreed, saying that the EAHCA is the source of a federal statutory right to a free appropriate education in every state electing to receive financial assistance, and that it is more than merely a "funding statute." The court then applied due process analysis and said that the passage of time caused the deprivation of the child's substantive right to an appropriate education and timeliness of review is an essential element of due process. The superintendent's motion to dismiss was denied. *John A. v. Gill*, 565 F.Supp. 372 (N.D.Ill.1983).

A Pennsylvania case resulted in a determination that a local school district failed to meet its legal responsibility to provide an appropriate program of education in training for an exceptional child. The court based its ruling on the fact that the district, instead of making an initial placement recommendation, merely provided the parents with a list of "approved private schools" and took twenty-one months to make an official recommendation of appropriate educational placement. *Pires v. Commonwealth of Pennsylvania, Dep't of Educ.*, 467 A.2d 79 (Pa.Cmwlth.1983).

Parents are also required to comply with EAHCA provisions if they expect a favorable ruling. A fourth grade boy displayed signs of disruptive behavior and his teacher suggested that he receive psychological help. To avoid having such information on his school records, his parents enrolled him in a private school outside of the district. After he was expelled from the private school and had attended a series of public schools unsuccessfully, his grandmother contacted the Seattle school district to ask if the district could help with the costs of his private school enrollment. She was told the school district would have to do a "complete workup" to find out what his needs were and what could be done. The district psychologist contacted the boy's mother and told her that based on his limited information, he could not find the boy eligible for special education services but that the school district would evaluate his needs should he return to the area. The mother requested a hearing and in March, 1983, a due process hearing decision granted an award of tuition for the 1982-83 school year. The Seattle superintendent of public instruction reversed the decision and in September, 1983, the mother initiated a lawsuit asking for a judicial review.

The Court of Appeals of Washington stated that the issue was whether a school district must reimburse a parent for tuition costs when the parent unilaterally places a child in an out-of-state private school before the school district has had opportunity to assess the child's needs and make a recommendation. The EAHCA authorizes tuition reimbursement, in appropriate cases, when the parents and the district disagree as to which educational placement is appropriate for the child. In this case, however, such disagreement was absent. The mother's unilateral placement of her son in the private school without the district's assessment prevented recovery of her expenses for his private school education. *Hunter v. Seattle School Dist. No. 1*, 731 P.2d 19 (Wash.App.1987).

CHAPTER FOUR
REMEDIES UNDER THE EAHCA

The type of relief sought by parents or guardians of handicapped children for alleged wrongdoing on the part of local school districts or state education officials varies with the particular circumstances of the case.

I. INJUNCTIVE RELIEF

Injunctive relief is sought when handicapped children, through their parents or guardians, wish to compel education officials to comply with the provisions of the EAHCA. An injunction is a court order directing a person (or any legal entity) to perform a certain act, or refrain from doing an act. If the injunction is violated, the violator may be found to be in contempt of court and a fine or imprisonment may result.

Preliminary injunctions are temporary in nature and are issued prior to trial. They are issued only where (a) the plaintiff makes a showing that he or she will suffer irreparable harm if the preliminary injunction is not issued, and (b) the plaintiff is able to show there is a reasonable likelihood that he or she will succeed at trial and be awarded a permanent injunction.

A plaintiff will be awarded a permanent injunction if, after receiving all relevant evidence, the court determines that injunctive relief is necessary to protect a handicapped child's rights under the EAHCA, or to force education officials to abide by federal or state law.

After a Washington, D.C., child was identified as eligible for special education the District of Columbia Public Schools (DCPS) proposed placement at the Prospect Learning Center, a DCPS facility. The child's parents opposed the DCPS placement and requested placement at the Lab School, a private institution. DCPS placed the child at the Lab School pending a September, 1985, due process hearing. The hearing officer determined that the Lab School was the appropriate placement noting that placement at Prospect would have been appropriate if it had been proposed prior to the beginning of the school year. DCPS funded the child's education at the Lab School for the 1985-86 school year. In June, 1986, DCPS proposed (by letter) a placement for the child at the Lab School for the 1986-87 school year but later informed the parents that its letter was incorrect and that it was recommending placement at Prospect. The parents requested another due process hearing at which the hearing officer determined that the Prospect placement was appropriate. The parents appealed to a U.S. district court seeking a preliminary injunction to prevent DCPS from removing the child from the Lab School.

The child's parents contended that the Lab School was her current educational placement because she was placed there by mutual agreement. DCPS argued that the Lab School never was her current educational placement because her original placement there in September, 1985, "was an *interim* placement only and did not represent a determination that it was an appropriate placement." The court observed that "any limitation in placement should be spelled out in detail, otherwise, the Court will assume that the placement, whether decided upon by administrative determination or by agreement of the parties, constitutes the child's current educational placement." Because such a limitation was not included in the September, 1985, agreement the court concluded that the Lab School was the child's current educational placement, consistent with the EAHCA's "status quo" provision. The preliminary injunction was granted. The court ordered DCPS to fund the child's education at the Lab School during the pendency of the court proceedings. Additionally, it ordered DCPS to reimburse the child's parents for any funds they expended for tuition or related services during the 1986-87 school year. *Saleh v. Dist. of Columbia*, 660 F.Supp. 212 (D.D.C.1987).

In the fall of 1983, following the private evaluations of their two children, the children's parents informed the principal of the public school in which the children were enrolled that the children were being placed in a private educational facility for half of each school day. Subsequently, the parents asked that the board of education provide the children with an IEP comparable to that of the private institution or, alternatively, that the board provide transportation and tuition for the children to continue at the private facility for the 1984-85 school year. The parents also asked to be reimbursed for expenses incurred by them resulting from the children's private school placement during the 1983-84 year. The board of education denied their request and the parents requested a due process hearing. The hearing officer determined that he had no authority under North Carolina state law to grant an award of reimbursement and no hearing was held. When the state board of education denied a request by the parents that the hearing officer be granted such authority, the parents appealed to a U.S. district court.

The district court noted that the EAHCA contains a detailed procedural component with which local and state boards are required to comply. To allow a state hearing officer to conduct a hearing on the issue of reimbursement and to enter findings of fact based on that hearing, but to refuse to order reimbursement even when appropriate, would make the EAHCA less than complete. To the extent North Carolina's interpretation of the authority of a hearing officer is in contradiction with the EAHCA, the terms of the EAHCA must control. The court ruled that reimbursement costs were not monetary penalties (as the school board claimed) since they were costs the school board should have born in the first place. The local board of education was ordered to conduct another hearing and order reimbursement costs if appropriate. *S-1 v. Spangler*, 650 F.Supp. 1427 (M.D.N.C.1986).

The U.S. Court of Appeals, Fifth Circuit, affirmed a U.S. district court decision in favor of nine Florida handicapped students who had been expelled from school for disciplinary reasons. The court granted their request for an injunction because expulsion may have caused irreparable harm to the students. *S-1 v. Turlington*, 635 F.2d 342 (5th Cir.1981).

A U.S. district court in the District of Columbia also issued a preliminary injunction, this time on behalf of a multiply handicapped student. The student was a sixteen-year-old boy who was emotionally disturbed and learning disabled. The child's school district refused to fund a residential private school education for him which included necessary psychiatric and other services on the ground that the boy was not the school district's responsibility. The court disagreed and issued a preliminary injunction restraining the District of Columbia Board of Education from further denying the child a free appropriate education in violation of the EAHCA. The court issued the injunction to prevent irreparable injury to the boy.

The district court observed that in the absence of such an injunction, the boy would be required to participate in neglect proceedings involving his parents. This, the court said, would have a devastating impact on the boy. Because he demonstrated a likelihood of success on the merits of his claim and the potential injury to him far outweighed any injury to the school district by the issuance of the injunction, the court ordered the Board of Education to place the child in a residential academic program with the necessary related services. *North v. Dist. of Columbia Bd. of Educ.*, 471 F.Supp 136 (D.D.C.1979).

In another District of Columbia case, the parents of two handicapped children were granted a preliminary injunction requiring the Department of Defense (DOD) to place, at its expense, the children at two specific private schools in the United States. The children's father was a civilian employee of the U.S. government on loan to the North Atlantic Treaty Organization and the family lived in Europe. A U.S. district court held that if the DOD was unable to provide educational services to the children in American-run schools in Europe, it was required to fund private residential educations in the U.S. The court was persuaded by the testimony of witnesses who stated that the children could not "emotionally survive" the environment proposed by the DOD. In granting the parents' request for an injunction, the court stated that "absent extraordinary relief . . . in the nature of a preliminary injunction to prevent the defendants from interfering with the free educational rights [that the plaintiffs], and all children, enjoy and deserve, irreparable harm . . ." would result. *Cox v. Brown*, 498 F.Supp. 823 (D.D.C.1980).

A group of handicapped children in Wisconsin brought suit on behalf of themselves and all similarly situated handicapped students in the state. The children, who were students placed in day treatment facilities, sought a preliminary injunction enjoining Milwaukee public school officials from terminating their current placements until the completion of a full and impartial evaluation of their educational needs and handicapping conditions. As part of their request for injunctive relief, the children also sought an order from the court requiring extended school year programs continuing into the summer months. Finally, the children requested a court order to the school officials to force them to expedite the impartial evaluation process without delay.

The U.S. district court granted the children's request for the injunction. The court held that the injury to a handicapped child who is deprived of special education facilities required to be provided under the EAHCA constituted "irreparable harm" for purposes of the preliminary injunction. The court noted that a preliminary injunction may only be granted if it is found that: (1) the plaintiffs have no adequate remedy "at law" (i.e., money damages would be inadequate) and they will be irreparably harmed if the injunction does not issue; (2) the threatened injury to the plaintiffs outweighs the threatened harm the injunction may inflict on the defendant; (3) the plaintiffs have at least a reasonable likelihood of success on the merits; and (4) the granting of a preliminary injunction will not disserve the public interests. Finding all of the tests met in this case, the court granted the injunction. *M.R. v. Milwaukee Pub. Schools*, 495 F.Supp. 864 (E.D.Wis.1980). See also *M.R. v. Milwaukee Pub. Schools*, 584 F.Supp. 767 (E.D.Wis.1984), for another Wisconsin case dealing with similar issues.

An injunction was granted to a handicapped child in Texas who required clean intermittent catheterization which would enable her to attend school. The child's interest in attending public school outweighed the school's burden to provide this medical service to the child. *Tatro v. State of Texas*, 516 F.Supp. 968 (N.D.Tex.1981), *affirmed*, 104 S.Ct. 3371 (1984).

A seventeen-year-old handicapped boy in Illinois who suffered from autism, moderate mental retardation, severe emotional disturbances, speech and language impairments, and behavorial disorders was granted a preliminary injunction by a federal district court in Illinois. The child was about to be expelled from a private residential school he was attending for nonpayment of tuition. The child's parents sought an injunction ordering state agencies and the Illinois Superintendent of Education to pay the balance of the child's tuition expenses to prevent his discharge from the school. This was requested prior to the outcome of the parents' lawsuit challenging the agencies' and the superintendent's refusal to pay the child's tuition expenses in full. The district court granted the parents' request for an injunction requiring the state and local agencies to pay the child's outstanding bill at the school or to provide the facility with sufficient assurances of payment so that he would not be discharged from the facility prior to the trial on the merits of his claim. *Parks v. Pavkovic*, 536 F.Supp. 296 (N.D.Ill.1982).

Two "school closing" cases illustrate that requests for preliminary injunctions on behalf of handicapped students are not always granted. In the first case, a handicapped student in New York challenged a decision of New York City's Board of Education to close a special education school on the ground of financial mismanagement. The New York Supreme Court held that the students were not entitled to a preliminary injunction prohibiting the school closing because there was insufficient proof of the required irreparable injury to warrant such an injunction. The children had been placed in alternate school settings and had not shown that these placements were inappropriate. *Cohen v. Bd. of Educ. of New York*, 454 N.Y.S.2d 630 (Sup.Ct. 1982).

The second case also allowed the closing of a school for handicapped children. When a treatment facility in Kentucky providing a program for emotionally handicapped children was closed for budgetary reasons by the governing school district, parents of the attending children filed suit in U.S. district court seeking a preliminary injunction to compel the school district to continue operation of the facility. The court denied the motion. The parents appealed to the U.S. Court of Appeals, Sixth Circuit, maintaining that under the EAHCA the closing of the treatment facility constituted a change of placement and that, pursuant to the Act, the state was precluded from instituting the change during the pendency of proceedings contesting the action.

The court agreed that the closing of the facility constituted a change in placement, but affirmed the lower court's denial of a motion for a preliminary injunction. Stating the need for fiscal decisions to remain in the hands of school authorities, the court held that "authorities do not, by electing to receive funds under the EAHCA, abdicate their control of the fiscal decisions of their school systems." The court feared that if it granted such an injunction a school district would be compelled to finance a program it had determined to be unaffordable simply because of allegations of deficiency in substitute programs raised by one special group. The court also observed that maintaining an expensive program for some handicapped children reduced the amount of funds available for all handicapped children. *Shaffer v. Block*, 705 F.2d 805 (6th Cir.1983).

Other special education cases have also held that a preliminary injunction was not warranted.

In a New York case, a child with minimal brain dysfunction sought a preliminary injunction to prevent his transfer from a school for the handicapped to a public school program for the handicapped. A U.S. district court denied the child's request for an injunction. The court found that a "preponderance of the evidence" showed that the decision to place the child in a public school program for the handicapped was well supported. *ZVI D. v. Ambach*, 520 F.Supp. 196 (E.D.N.Y.1981).

In a second New York case, a group of autistic children, their parents and a private school attended by the children sought judicial help in preventing New York officials from reducing the rate, set by the state, at which local school districts should reimburse the private school for providing the autistic children with a free appropriate public education, pursuant to the EAHCA. The reduction in the tuition rate was made following an audit of the school's financial statement. State officials determined that the rate charged to parents of autistic children was greater than it should have been in relationship to the rate charged to the parents of normal children.

A U.S. district court refused to grant the requested injunction. The court determined that there was no showing of irreparable harm, nor a showing that the school had failed to establish a serious question going to the merits. Further, there was no showing of a denial of either due process or equal protection. This decision was appealed to the U.S. Court of Appeals, Second Circuit, which affirmed. The Court of Appeals stated that Congress did not intend the EAHCA to authorize wholesale challenges to state fiscal determinations. *Fallis v. Ambach*, 710 F.2d 49 (2d Cir.1983).

II. REIMBURSEMENT FOR TUITION EXPENSES: "STATUS QUO" REQUIREMENT OF THE EAHCA

Section 1415(e)(3) of the EAHCA requires that "during the pendency of any proceedings conducted pursuant to this section, unless the State or local educational agency and the parents or guardian otherwise agree, the child shall remain in the then current educational placement of such child . . . until all such proceedings have been completed." This provision is designed to preserve the "status quo" pending resolution of judicial or administrative proceedings held under the Act. The primary justification for the status quo provision is to maintain stability in handicapped children's educational programs while the resolution of disputes is carried out. See Chapter Three for a discussion of *Honig v. Doe*. There, the Supreme Court held that indefinite suspensions or suspensions of more than ten days violated the "status quo" requirement.

Parents or guardians of handicapped children who unilaterally change the placement of their child during the pendency of any review proceedings often seek reimbursement from their school district for tuition expenses. In *Burlington School Committee v. Department of Education of Massachusetts* (reprinted in the Appendix of U.S. Supreme Court Cases in this volume), the Supreme Court ruled that parents who violate the status quo provision may nevertheless receive tuition reimbursement from the school district, if the IEP proposed by the school is later found to be inappropriate. However, if the proposed IEP is found to be appropriate, the parents will not be entitled to reimbursement for expenses incurred in unilaterally changing their child's placement.

In the *Burlington* case, the father of a learning disabled third grade boy became dissatisfied with his son's lack of progress in the Burlington, Massachusetts, public school system. A new IEP was developed for the child which called for placement in a different public school. The father, however, followed the advice of specialists at Massachusetts General Hospital and unilaterally withdrew his son from the Burlington school system, placing him instead at the Carroll School, a state-approved private facility in Lincoln, Massachusetts. He then sought reimbursement for tuition and transportation expenses from the Burlington School Committee, contending that the IEP which proposed a public school placement was inappropriate.

The state Board of Special Education Appeals (BSEA) ruled that the proposed IEP was inappropriate and that, therefore, the father had been justified in placing his son at the Carroll School. The BSEA ordered the Burlington School Committee to reimburse the father for tuition and transportation expenses, and the School committee appealed to the federal courts. A U.S. district court held that the parents had violated the status quo provision of the EAHCA by enrolling their child in the private school without the agreement of public school officials. Thus, they were not entitled to reimbursement. The U.S. Court of Appeals, First Circuit, reversed the district court's ruling, and the Burlington School Committee appealed to the U.S. Supreme Court.

In upholding the court of appeals, the Supreme Court ruled that parents who place a handicapped child in a private educational facility are entitled to reimbursement for the child's tuition and living expenses, *if* a court later determines that the school district had proposed an inappropriate IEP. The Court stated that reimbursement could not be ordered if the school district's proposed IEP was later found to be appropriate. The Supreme Court observed that to bar reimbursement claims under all circumstances would be contrary to the EAHCA, which favors proper interim placements for handicapped children.

In addition, under the School Committee's reading of the EAHCA status quo provision, parents would be forced to leave their child in what might later be determined to be an inappropriate educational placement, or would obtain the appropriate placement only by sacrificing any claim for reimbursement. This result, found the Court, was not intended by Congress. However, the Court noted that "[t]his is not to say that [this provision] has no effect on parents." Parents who unilaterally change their children's placement during the pendency of proceedings do so at their own financial risk. If the courts ultimately determine that a child's proposed IEP was appropriate, the parents are barred from obtaining reimbursement for an unauthorized private school placement. *Burlington School Comm. v. Dep't of Educ. of Massachusetts*, 105 S.Ct. 1996 (1985).

The District of Columbia Public Schools (DCPS) found a child to be eligible for special education and placed him at the Brent Public Elementary School. His parents were dissatisfied with the placement and asked for a due process hearing. The hearing officer concluded that the Brent placement was inappropriate and gave DCPS a deadline of November 25, 1985, to provide a new placement. On November 27, 1985, DCPS proposed a placement at the Prospect Learning Center. However, the parents were also dissatisfied with the Prospect placement and requested a second due process hearing. In the meantime, they unilaterally placed the child in the Lab School, a private special education facility. The second hearing officer determined on March 24, 1986, that both Prospect and the Lab School were appropriate and that DCPS was responsible for the child's placement at the Lab School for the 1985-86 school year until April 7, 1986, because it missed the November 25,

1985, deadline. The hearing officer also determined that the child should be placed at Prospect after April 7, 1986. The parents sued DCPS seeking a court order that DCPS place the child at the Lab School retroactive from April 7, 1986, during the pendency of the court proceedings. They argued that the Lab School was his current educational placement and that DCPS was required to maintain this "status quo" under the EAHCA. DCPS contended that only after April 7, 1986, was Prospect his placement.

The U.S. district court concluded that there was substantial evidence that the Lab School was his current educational placement during the court proceedings. First, the child never had a true placement in the public school system. The Brent placement was aborted after one day and the first hearing officer found that DCPS could not prove that the Brent placement was appropriate. Second, the second hearing officer found that DCPS did not have an appropriate program in place for the child until November 27, 1985, and therefore he concluded that DCPS was responsible for the Lab School placement from the beginning of the 1985-86 school year until April 7, 1986. Based upon the above facts, the court held that the parents were justified in unilaterally placing the child at the Lab School. It declined to order DCPS to fund the child's Lab School placement from April 7, 1986, to May 1, 1987, since a later court could find that the Lab School was not the child's current educational placement for that period. However, the court held that effective May 1, 1987, DCPS had to fund the child's education during the pendency of the court proceedings. *Cochran v. Dist. of Columbia*, 660 F.Supp. 314 (D.D.C.1987).

The parents of learning disabled children in Florida who unilaterally placed their children in a private school sued the state Department of Health and Rehabilitative Services seeking reimbursement for the private school tuition. Although the district court granted injunctive relief to the parents it denied them tuition reimbursement and they appealed to the U.S. Court of Appeals, Eleventh Circuit.

The court of appeals observed that the district court had incorrectly held that reimbursement is appropriate only in exceptional circumstances, "*i.e.*, (1) where the school district's placement of the child would endanger the child's physical health, and (2) when the school district acted in bad faith in failing to comply with the [EAHCA's] procedural provision in an egregious fashion." It noted that the Supreme Court has rejected the characterization of reimbursement as "damages." "[R]eimbursement merely requires the [defendant] to belatedly pay expenses that it should have paid all along and would have borne in the first instance had it developed a proper [individualized educational program]," ruled the Supreme Court. The district court's decision was based on too restrictive a test and its decision was vacated. The case was remanded to the district court to make a decision consistent with the Supreme Court's standard. *Jenkins v. State of Florida*, 815 F.2d 629 (11th Cir.1987).

A New York U.S. district court recently applied the principles of *Burlington*. A child entered kindergarten in the Great Neck Union Free School District. It soon became apparent that he had difficulty learning in a normal classroom setting. The school district diagnosed the child as neurologically impaired and placed him in a nonmainstream special education program, where he remained for several years.

The child was placed for the first time in mainstream education classes during the 1980-81 school year. He spent approximately sixty percent of his time in special education classes and forty percent with regular education students. His parents concluded that the mainstreaming was exacerbating their son's emotional problems and they requested 1) that the school district Committee on the Handicapped (COH) reevaluate their son's educational placement and 2) that the district provide a summer program (for the summer of 1981) to compensate for his lack of achievement in the preceding school year. The COH responded by changing his classification from neurologically impaired to emotionally disturbed, leaving the child in his former educational placement by default. When the parents complained, the COH chairwoman said that an evaluation meeting could not be held until the fall of 1981.

During the summer of 1981 the parents had their son evaluated at the Hillsdale Center, which recommended placement at the Lowell School, a state-approved private school. In September, 1981, the Great Neck school district's COH met to reconsider the child's case, and the parents presented it with Hillsdale's recommendations. The COH reclassified the child as neurologically impaired and, while recognizing that the mainstreaming had "traumatized" him, proposed continued placement in the public school with "special support" during mainstreaming. Two days later the parents responded to the COH's new proposal by placing their son at the Lowell School, where he remained during the 1981-84 school years. A hearing officer ruled in January, 1983, that the Lowell School placement was appropriate, and the COH agreed to fund the placement beginning with the 1983-84 school year. The parents brought suit in U.S. district court to obtain reimbursement for the 1981-82 and 1982-83 school years.

On appeal, a U.S. district court observed that both an impartial hearing officer and the New York State Education Commissioner had concluded that the school district had offered an inappropriate educational placement for the child and that the Lowell School placement was appropriate. Citing the U.S. Supreme Court's unanimous ruling in *Burlington School Committee v. Department of Education of Massachusetts*, 105 S.Ct. 1996 (1985) (opinion by Justice Rehnquist), it ruled that the parents were entitled to reimbursement for all the years their child spent at the Lowell School. Any alleged delays by the parents were irrelevant because under *Burlington*, the crucial inquiry is whether the school district has proposed an appropriate educational program for the child. Because the school district had not, and because the Lowell School placement *was* appropriate, *Burlington* required that the parents receive full reimbursement for all tuition and related expenses at the Lowell School. The court ordered Great Neck to reimburse the parents. *Eugene B. Jr. v. Great Neck Union Free School Dist.*, 635 F.Supp. 753 (E.D. N.Y.1986).

In a Virginia case, lack of state approval of a private school prevented parental reimbursement for tuition and related expenses. After being declared eligible for special education services, the fourteen-year-old boy involved in this case was placed by the Fairfax County public schools in the Lab School in Washington, D.C. Later, Fairfax County determined that the Lab

School no longer met the boy's special needs and proposed a placement at the Little Keswick School, Inc., a Virginia residential school for handicapped children. This private facility is approved by the Virginia Department of Education.

Upon receiving Fairfax County's offer of placement at Little Keswick, the boy's mother wrote to Fairfax rejecting the proposal. She instead suggested that Fairfax fund her son's placement at the East Hill Farm and School in Andover, Vermont. Fairfax refused, stating that East Hill was not on the Virginia Department of Education's list of approved schools. The mother nonetheless placed her son at East Hill and requested a due process hearing to resolve the question of reimbursement for tuition and living expenses. The hearing officer provided by Fairfax County conducted a full and open evidentiary hearing, after which he concluded that Little Keswick was an appropriate placement. The boy's parents appealed; the review officer affirmed. The parents then brought an action in federal district court seeking further review.

The district court reviewed the evidence and concluded that Fairfax County was not obligated to fund the East Hill placement. Two grounds were specified for the court's decision. First, the Little Keswick School was approved by the Virginia Department of Education. The EAHCA's section 1413(a)(4)(B)(ii) allows states to establish minimum educational standards as a precondition to state approval of any school. This power of approval is expressly permitted by the EAHCA. Little Keswick was therefore an appropriate placement, said the court.

Second, East Hill was not on Virginia's list of approved schools. Indeed, it was not even on Vermont's list of schools certified for special education. Only one of East Hill's ten staff members was a certified teacher. In the court's view, lack of approval by the Virginia Department of Education precluded reimbursement. "Parents of handicapped students may not, because of personal desires, select a private institution of their choice and have the school system pay for the tuition," declared the court. "While the desires of the parents may be well motivated in that they seek the best for their child, the placement decision must be made by the school system in accordance with approved standards." The court affirmed the denial of reimbursement to the mother for the costs incurred in placing their child at the East Hill School. She then appealed to the U.S. Court of Appeals, Fourth Circuit.

The court of appeals affirmed the district court's decision to deny tuition reimbursement to the mother for the East Hill education. When a handicapped child is educated at a private school under the EAHCA, the state or local school district has an obligation to ensure that that school meets applicable state educational standards. Here, East Hill was not approved by Virginia to offer special education. Therefore, Fairfax County could not fund the boy's education at East Hill without violating the EAHCA's requirement that handicapped children be educated at public expense only in those private schools that met state educational standards. Therefore, the EAHCA did not require Fairfax County to place the handicapped boy at East Hill. *Schimmel v. Spillane*, 819 F.2d 477 (4th Cir.1987).

A New Jersey boy was born in 1971 with a neurological impairment which hindered his ability to walk and communicate. His local school board placed him in the Midland School, a private school for disabled children. However, in 1980, Midland School notified the parents that it was unable to provide an appropriate education for the boy. Because the school board allowed the Midland placement to continue and failed to act on a request for a hearing, the parents removed the boy to a Rhode Island private school in June, 1981. Although the boy was making remarkable progress at the Rhode Island school his parents were forced to place him in the Mercer Special Services School District because the school board refused to reimburse the parents for the private school program. In Mercer (a New Jersey nonresidential program) the boy's condition deteriorated because the program only provided one to one and one-half hours of home instruction per day.

The parents requested another due process hearing in which the hearing officer directed the school board to place the boy in a residential program and to reimburse his parents for all his residential placement expenses. The school board appealed to a U.S. district court which ruled for the parents, but denied the parents' request for money damages and attorney's fees.

On appeal to the U.S. Court of Appeals, Third Circuit, the school board contended that the district court was wrong in determining that a residential placement was appropriate for the boy and in ordering reimbursement to the parents. However, a psychologist who had observed the boy in the nonresidential setting at Midland testified that the boy's program required a high degree of one-to-one instruction, and that he required behavior modification involving administration of consequences for at least ninety percent of targeted behavior. The court of appeals ruled that the district court was correct in concluding that the Mercer program was inappropriate for the boy's needs.

Both courts rejected the school board's argument that it was obligated by law to provide no more than an education that would be "of benefit" to the boy. The court of appeals observed that under the EAHCA, the school district was required to provide a "free appropriate education" to the boy which must be tailored to his individual needs by using an IEP. Only a residential program such as the Rhode Island private school program would provide this "appropriate" education for the boy.

The court of appeals also upheld the district court's decision ordering tuition reimbursement. Reimbursement for private school tuition and related expenses incurred pending resolution over a dispute about placement is appropriate relief under the EAHCA. The matter of money damages was remanded to the district court for further proceedings. The school board was required to reimburse the parents for the boy's past, present and future residential placement. The school district was also ordered to redraft the boy's IEP. *Bd. of Educ. v. Diamond*, 808 F.2d 987 (3d Cir.1986).

A California school district was ordered to pay the tuition and related expenses for a learning disabled boy whose parents had unilaterally placed him in an out-of-state private residential facility. In November, 1976, the boy's first IEP, in which he was classified as suffering from a mild learning disability, was formulated by school district officials. The boy progressed and by June, 1977, he had successfully been partially integrated into regular classes. A new IEP was formulated at this time which provided that he continue in regular classes with minimal supplementary educational services. Three months later, in September, 1977, another IEP was developed which noted the boy's progress and recommended continued regular placement with some special education assistance. However, his performance and behavior suffered greatly during the ensuing 1977-78 school year. School officials observed increased anger, hostility and rebelliousness during this period. The boy's parents were contacted in February, 1978, and a review session was held at which it was agreed that the September, 1977 IEP would remain in effect.

At the close of the 1977-78 school year, the boy was removed from school after slashing the tires on a teacher's car. He also ran away from home in August, 1978, and was consequently made a ward of the juvenile court. His behavior was described as "self-destructive" with "poor impulse control." In the fall of 1978 the boy was enrolled in the local high school where school officials, with the concurrence of his parents, tentatively decided that his September, 1977, IEP would remain in effect. He was thereafter truant from school on numerous occasions and ran away from home again for a week in September, 1978, at which time he committed the offenses of joyriding and marijuana possession. He spent the remainder of the school year in juvenile hall and various youth residential facilities. The school district made no effort to reevaluate the boy or develop a new IEP during this period.

Due to the school district's failure to properly evaluate their son, the parents decided to enroll him in a private residential facility in Utah in March, 1979, and asked that the school district pay the cost of his placement. The district, however, stated that it would pay only educational expenses at the facility. The parents requested a due process hearing on the matter and the hearing panel found that because the parents had acted unilaterally in placing their son at the residential facility, thereby breaching the "status quo" provision of the EAHCA, the school district was not liable for the cost of the placement. The parents appealed and the California Court of Appeal held that the school district was liable under the EAHCA for the boy's educational and related expenses at the private, out-of-state residential facility.

The court based its decision on the failure of the school district to develop an IEP for the boy annually, as required by the EAHCA. An IEP had been formulated in September, 1977, but as of April, 1979, a new IEP had not been developed. The court rejected the school district's contention that because the boy had been truant and was frequently involved in the juvenile court system, it would have been difficult to properly evaluate him. The boy's status in the juvenile court system was well known to school officials and their failure to update the "manifestly inappropriate" September, 1977, IEP was characterized by the court as evidence of bad faith. The school district was therefore ordered to pay the cost of the private school placement. *In Re John K.*, 216 Cal.Rptr. 557 (Cal.App.1st Dist.1985).

A special education dispute of fourteen years' duration was settled by the U.S. Court of Appeals, Third Circuit. The court of appeals upheld a U.S. district court's ruling that the Westfield, New Jersey, board of education was not liable for the cost of nine years of private school placement. The child in this case was first identified as handicapped in 1968. At that time the Westfield Board of Education placed the child at the Midland School, a private facility. In 1972, further testing was performed by outside experts as well as Westfield's child study team. The child was thereafter labeled "mentally retarded-educable" by the child study team, and an IEP was formulated which called for placement at a different institution, the Tamaques School. Objecting to the label "mentally retarded-educable" (the parents felt their child was neurologically impaired), as well as the change in placement, the parents kept him at Midland and paid the tuition themselves.

In 1975, the parents filed a petition with the New Jersey Department of Education seeking review of Westfield's 1972 reclassification decision. The parents contended that during the pendency of all review proceedings, Westfield was obligated to pay for their child's tuition at Midland, since section 1415(e)(3) of the EAHCA requires that a child remain in his or her "then current" placement until review is completed. Due to the department's failure to comply with the procedural requirements of the EAHCA, a proper hearing on the merits of the parents' claim was not held until June 9, 1983.

During the period between the filing of the petition in 1975 and the 1983 hearing officer's decision, the child was evaluated many times by Westfield's child study team as well as the parents' outside experts. In 1976, the child study team changed its classification from mentally retarded-educable to "Multiply Handicapped: Primary—Mentally Retarded-Educable; Secondary—Neurologically Impaired." The child study team, however, did not change its recommendation of placement at the Tamaques School. Adhering to their view that the child study team's classifications were erroneous, the parents continued their child at the Midland School.

In 1980, the parents placed their child at the Maplebrook School. One year later, the Westfield child study team reclassified the child as "Neurologically or Perceptually Impaired: Perceptually Impaired" and agreed to fund the Maplebrook placement. An IEP was developed and agreed to, and pursuant to this IEP the child graduated from Maplebrook in the spring of 1982. The Westfield Board of Education granted a diploma to the child and contended that its responsibility for his education had terminated. The parents disagreed and enrolled him in the Summit Collegiate Studies Center in Jerusalem, Israel.

At the due process hearing in 1983, the parents claimed that they were entitled to tuition reimbursement for their child's education at the Midland school from 1972 to 1981, since they were entitled to leave their child at Midland during all review proceedings. They also claimed that the Westfield board of education was liable for the period their child attended school in Jerusalem. The hearing officer denied the parents' claims and they filed an action in U.S. district court, seeking review, but the court upheld the hearing officer's decision. The parents appealed their case to the U.S. Court of Appeals, Third Circuit, which similarly agreed with the hearing officer. The appeals court stated that since section 1415(e)(3) had not become effective until 1977, the Westfield Board of Education was relieved of responsibility for its 1972 decision to change the child's educational placement from Midland to Tamaques. Thus, the parents' decision to keep their child at Midland was not protected by section 1415(e)(3). The appeals court ruled that the parents should have placed the child at Tamaques in accordance with Westfield's 1972 recommendation.

The court also held that under section 1412(2)(B), the Westfield Board of Education would be responsible for the post-graduation education of the child only if the board made it a regular practice to educate children even after they had graduated. Since the board did not, and since the child had already graduated when his parents sent him to the school in Jerusalem, the board was not liable for those expenses. Noting that all the classifications and placements proposed by Westfield's child study team were appropriate under the EAHCA, the court of appeals affirmed the prior rulings against the parents. *Wexler v. Westfield Bd. of Educ.*, 784 F.2d 176 (3d Cir.1986).

Relying on the EAHCA's status quo provision, a U.S. district court ordered the New York City Board of Education to fund a handicapped child's placement at a private educational facility. The city's school system, explained the court, had been operating since 1972 under a federal court order which mandates that an offer of a public school placement must be made by the school system within sixty days of a child's identification as a handicapped individual. Under the court order, if the child is not offered such a placement within sixty days the parents have the right to place the child in a private facility at the board's expense.

The present case arose when a child was unilaterally enrolled by his parents in the Hebrew Academy for Special Children as provided by the order described above. The board agreed to pay for the placement at the academy, but at the beginning of the following school year it once again recommended public school placement. The parents, however, desired to keep their child at the academy, and he remained there during the due process hearings which ensued. The hearings culminated in an order by the state education commissioner that the board was required to fund the child's education at the academy, and the board appealed to the U.S. district court.

Ruling that the Hebrew Academy had become the child's "then current" educational placement under the EAHCA, the court upheld the commissioner's order. By initially failing to offer a placement within the required sixty days, the board had given the parents the unqualified right to place the child in a private facility at the board's expense. That placement then became the status quo, which could not be altered by the board until such time as they offered an acceptable placement. Under the EAHCA, the board then became unconditionally liable for the resulting tuition and related expenses. The court affirmed the commissioner's order of reimbursement for the parents' cost of placing the child at the Hebrew Academy. *Bd. of Educ. v. Ambach*, 628 F.Supp. 972 (E.D.N.Y.1986).

Another New York case, which also relied on New York City's sixty-day placement order, resulted in an award of tuition for private school placement. The parents of an emotionally handicapped student had sought to enroll their son in the New York City public school system in 1982. However, due to enormous delays by the Board of Education's Committee on the Handicapped (COH), the parents placed their son in a private facility. This was done pursuant to the 1982 court order, which attempted to prod New York's COH into action by granting parents of handicapped children in New York City the right to choose private school placement if the board's COH did not recommend an appropriate placement within sixty days of proposed entry of a child into the public school system. After the parents in this case enrolled their child in the private facility, the COH evaluated him and recommended public school placement. The parents disagreed with this recommendation and requested a hearing.

This hearing, which took place in March, 1983, resulted in a determination that the COH had not followed proper procedures, rendering its recommendation null and void. In May, 1983, the COH once again evaluated the child and again proposed a public school placement. The parents requested a hearing and this time an impartial hearing officer found that the COH's recommendation was proper. Appeal was taken to the state commissioner of education, who issued a decision in April, 1984, upholding the COH recommendation of public school placement. The commissioner also found that the board of education was liable for the child's private school tuition up until the date of the commissioner's decision. The board appealed to a U.S. district court, seeking a reversal of the award of tuition costs. The court stated that the EAHCA's status quo provision should govern, and hence upheld the award.

The court noted that the parents had placed their child in the private school pursuant to a court order intended to eliminate delay by New York's COH. This placement therefore became the child's "then current" educational placement, and the child was entitled to remain there until all review proceedings were completed. The fact that the COH later formulated an acceptable public school placement program for the child did not relieve the board of its duty to fund the child's private school placement until the COH's proposal was approved. The court then proceeded to award the parents the cost of the private school tuition, but only through April, 1984, the date of the commissioner's approval of the COH's public school placement recommendation. *Bd. of Educ. v. Ambach*, 612 F.Supp. 230 (E.D.N.Y.1985).

Reimbursement was denied to the parents of an Oklahoma youth, who brought suit in U.S. district court after their local school district refused to fund their son's placement at a residential facility. The youth, who was classified as "educable mentally handicapped" and who had serious emotional and behavioral problems, had been enrolled at the age of eighteen in his local school district's EMH program. An IEP was developed at this time with the approval of his parents, in which it was agreed that if the boy became "unmanageable'' he would be suspended for three-day intervals. Although his educational program included both high school instruction and vocational instruction, he was soon expelled from the vo-tech program due to his emotional outbursts. When these outbursts continued at the high school, school officials notified his parents that an alternative to classroom placement was necessary. Homebound instruction was suggested, but the parents rejected the proposal. For the next several months the parents considered residential placement; during this period the youth received no educational services. His parents also failed to bring him to school for testing to aid in the formulation of a new IEP, as requested by school officials.

The parents then requested funding for their child's placement at an out-of-state residential facility. When their school district refused they requested a due process hearing under the EAHCA. The parents, after discovering the name of the hearing officer, believed that he would find in favor of the school district and withdrew their request for a hearing. At the beginning of the next school year they appeared once again at the high school to enroll their son, and school officials, who had not expected the youth to enroll, requested a week to formulate an IEP. Several days later school officials attempted to arrange a meeting with the parents to discuss a new IEP for the youth, but the parents refused because a new teacher had not yet been hired to instruct him. The school officials explained that a new teacher would not be hired unless the parents approved the new IEP and assured them that they would enroll their son. This impasse caused the parents to unilaterally enroll their son in the out-of-state residential facility.

A due process hearing resulted in approval of the school district's decision not to reimburse the parents for the cost of his placement, and the parents sought judicial review. The U.S. Court of Appeals, First Circuit, upheld the denial of tuition reimbursement and found that the district had taken all steps necessary to provide the child with a free appropriate public education. The appeals court stated that "[a]lthough the [residential facility] undoubtedly offered . . . a superior educational program, an education which maximizes a child's potential is not required by the EAHCA." *Cain v. Yukon Pub. Schools, Dist. I-27*, 775 F.2d 15 (10th Cir.1985).

In a District of Columbia case, decided prior to *Burlington*, the parents of a handicapped student brought suit under the EAHCA, alleging that a District of Columbia public school had failed to provide their child with a free appropriate public education. The child, eleven years old, had been diagnosed as severely learning disabled with severe emotional problems. She had been attending special education classes four days a week at a learning center and regular classes one day a week at public school. Both schools were operated by the public school system. During this time the child's parents became very concerned about her schooling. They made arrangements to have the child evaluated at a private children's hospital and thereafter requested that she be placed there for the following school year. Public school officials proposed that the child continue her public school placement with increased mainstreaming. The parents then requested a due process hearing.

A hearing officer found that the child was handicapped, that she required special education and that her IEP failed to "address the emotional component associated with [the child's] deficiencies." The hearing officer went on to find that although mainstreaming is desirable and a "valid component in a special education program," mainstreaming attempts with the child had not proven successful and in fact had been harmful to her, perhaps even intensifying her emotional and academic difficulties. Finally, the hearing officer directed that the public school system must produce an alternative proposal with respect to mainstreaming the child. From that time on the parents claimed they were never contacted by the public school district, even though they wrote to school officials in early September of the following school year and were assured that their child would "be taken care of."

A second due process hearing was held in April of the school year in question, at which the parents stated that they had placed their child in a private school for that school year because she had no other appropriate placement, and that they were concerned that the public school district was not going to act. The hearing officer, the same individual who had presided over the first hearing, again found that the school district's proposed IEP was inappropriate to meet the child's needs but believed that the public schools could serve her educational needs.

The parents filed suit in a U.S. district court to obtain reimbursement of their expenses incurred in sending their child to the private school. The court held that the parents were entitled to reimbursement on the ground that there was a danger that the child's health would have been adversely affected but for the parents' placing her in the private school, and that the failure of the public schools to follow the determination of the hearing officer amounted to bad faith. Thus, the District of Columbia was required to reimburse the parents in the amount of the payments they were required to make to place the child in the private school. *Parker v. Dist. of Columbia*, 588 F.Supp. 518 (D.D.C.1983).

The U.S. Court of Appeals, Fifth Circuit, reversed a district court ruling which granted a preliminary injunction to the parents of a handicapped child who had placed the child in a private school of their choice pending the outcome of the parents' action against a local Texas school district. The parents of the child had requested the district court to issue the injunction ordering the school district to pay, pending resolution of the case, the costs of the private school in which they had placed their child. The Court of Appeals held that under federal law, maintenance of the present placement of a handicapped child (or the "status quo") during the pendency of proceedings demands only that school districts and state educational agencies maintain financial commitments to continue to fund an educational placement that it already funded prior to commencement of proceedings. Nothing requires a school district to pay the costs of parent-chosen private schooling pending judicial review of placement procedures and decisions by a state agency. *Stacey G. v. Pasadena Indep. School Dist.*, 695 F.2d 949 (5th Cir.1983).

The parents of a handicapped Massachusetts child were denied reimbursement for past tuition expenses at a private school which their child attended by the choice of the parents, and the local school district was also absolved from having to pay for any future tuition. The child had attended local public schools through the third grade but the following year, at the suggestion of a learning disabilities specialist, his parents enrolled him in a remedial program at a private school. The student remained there for several years. At approximately the same time as the child began his private schooling, the public school devised an IEP for him. However, the parents rejected the plan, preferring to place the child in the private school. Following an administrative determination, disputed by both the parents and the school district, a lawsuit was brought. A lower court entered judgment dismissing the parents' action for reimbursement and declaring that the school was not responsible for tuition at the private school.

On appeal to the Court of Appeals of Massachusetts, the lower court's determinations were affirmed. After resolving a number of procedural problems the court went on to say that "private placements are authorized only when the appropriate special education program . . . is not available within the public school system. . . . The private placement provisions of [the statute] only apply to a child who seeks services in the public school system and who is then identified as requiring special services which the school system either cannot, or chooses not to, provide." It was noted that parents who undertake a private placement unilaterally assume a financial risk because school authorities very possibly could recommend a different placement.

The court also commented on both federal and state laws which encourage a mainstreaming policy. It stated that the common objective of these laws is the prompt provision of needed services to learning-handicapped children through the free local public school system except where the resources of those schools cannot appropriately meet the childrens' needs. In this case, following that policy required a public school program for the child if one could be developed which would meet his special needs. Here the parents took the position that he would be better served by a private school education. This, of course, was their right but, subject to the limited exceptions, no public obligation to pay for this private education could arise unless a school authority determined that the public school system could not meet the child's special needs. Thus, the parents were obligated to pay their child's tuition costs. *School Comm. of Franklin v. Comm'r of Educ.*, 462 N.E.2d 338 (Mass.App.1984).

An emotionally handicapped New York child and his parents sued their local school district and various state officials under the EAHCA to recover tuition and costs incurred during the year and one-half the child spent at a private school in Maine. The child had been placed in a private school in New York by his school district but was expelled. He then returned home where he received four months of home tutoring. Then, concluding that no good faith effort was being made to place the child, the parents sent him to the Maine school from which he graduated. Because the out-of-state school was not on New York's list of approved facilities the parents were denied reimbursement for expenses for this placement. Suit was then brought, but a U.S. district court in New York granted the defendants' motion to dismiss. The court said that parents are generally entitled to an impartial due process hearing if they disagree with a local placement recommendation. However, this procedure is not available to review the state Commissioner of Education's refusal to contract with an out-of-state facility. *Smrcka v. Ambach*, 555 F.Supp. 1227 (E.D.N.Y.1983).

The parents of a seventeen-year-old boy with a learning disability brought suit on behalf of their son in a U.S. district court in New York. They sought a preliminary injunction directing their local board to implement a decision of the state commissioner of education, which required the board to identify their son as handicapped and to provide special education instruction for him in a learning disability resource room. The board declined to implement the order even after a hearing officer concurred in the commissioner's decision. Suit was brought after the board stated that it would not implement the commissioner's order until all proceedings had been completed, a process which would take months.

At trial, the school board maintained that the finding of the commissioner and the hearing officer had placed too much emphasis on individual testing and had ignored the assessment of teachers who had worked with the student for several years. The board also pointed to the fact that the boy was passing his subjects and advancing through the grades at a normal pace. The court stated that a child should remain in his current educational placement until proceedings are completed unless an agreement is reached between the state or local education agency and the parents regarding an alternative program. The fact that the commissioner and the parents both wanted the boy to be placed in a special education program constituted such an agreement. The court also relied on the U.S. Supreme Court decision of *Board of Education v. Rowley*, which held that the court should maintain a hands-off rule in cases where a commissioner has chosen an appropriate educational program for a student. The preliminary injunction was granted. *Blazejewski v. Bd. of Educ. of Allegany Cent. School Dist.*, 560 F.Supp. 701 (W.D.N.Y.1983).

In a District of Columbia case, a seventeen-year-old learning disabled boy had spent one year in a private special education boarding school. His parents were notified by the school board that it would not continue financial support of their son's placement at that school during the next year. The school board also informed the parents that it had decided on an alternative school for their boy's placement. The parents became very confused when, a few days after receiving the first notification, a second notice arrived recommending that their son attend yet another school. Letters written by the parents seeking an explanation for the conflicting recommendation went unanswered. When the next school year started, the parents reenrolled their son in the private boarding school. They then sued in the U.S. District Court for the District of Columbia, where they sought to have the school board held financially responsible for the boarding school placement.

The parents contended that since the school board had approved the boarding school during the previous year the provisions of the EAHCA dictated that the boy must remain at that school pending all administrative or judicial proceedings and until another appropriate placement was finally determined. The school board maintained that the boy's parents had purposefully delayed the proceedings and frustrated its attempts to find a new placement. The court held that while it was true that the parents had delayed the due process hearing, they did so out of confusion over the conflicting placement recommendations. Further, the notifications sent by the school board did not comply with the requirements set forth in the EAHCA. The court agreed with the parents' contention that the boarding school was the boy's current placement, and due to the procedural failures of the school board he must remain there pending further appeals. Summary judgment was granted in favor of the parents. *Jacobsen v. Dist. of Columbia Bd. of Educ.*, 564 F.Supp. 166 (D.D.C.1983).

In an Illinois case, the mother of an emotionally handicapped child brought an action on behalf of her child. The mother, because of dissatisfaction with her school district's recommendation for educational placement of the child, unilaterally transferred him to a private school of her choosing. Thereafter, the Illinois Office of Education determined the local school district could provide an appropriate education for the child. The mother appealed this decision to the Illinois courts which reversed and ordered reimbursement for educational expenses. Employing a pre-*Burlington* legal standard, the Appellate Court of Illinois held that there generally are two circumstances where a parent should be able to be reimbursed for expenses relating to unilateral placement in a private school without undergoing lengthy administrative processes. One is where a child's physical health is endangered. The other is where a school has acted in bad faith in refusing to assign a child to a special school. Here the court stated that both circumstances could arguably have existed. Therefore, the placement of the child at the special school was proper and the mother was entitled to reimbursement from the child's district of residence. *Walker v. Cronin*, 438 N.E.2d 582 (Ill.App.1982).

A Massachusetts case involved a Down's syndrome child who, almost since birth, had been living at a private special education school at his parents' expense. When the parents sought an IEP the initial response was to place the child in a nonresidential public school. The parents objected and a long series of hearings and appeals ensued. Pursuant to the provisions of the EAHCA the boy remained at the private school at his parents' expense pending the outcome of the proceedings. The district court finally settled the placement question by ruling that the private school was indeed the proper IEP for the child. The district court, however, declined to reimburse the parents for their private school expenditures while the proceedings were taking place.

When the reimbursement question was appealed to the U.S. Court of Appeals, First Circuit, it held that the EAHCA made provisions for reimbursement only under circumstances not met by this case (a pre-*Burlington* decision). It noted, however, that Massachusetts law did provide for reimbursement in some situations and remanded the case to the district court to decide this question. The district court held that the parents were entitled to reimbursement under Massachusetts law. *Doe v. Anrig*, 561 F.Supp. 121 (D.Mass.1983).

III. REIMBURSEMENT FOR OTHER EXPENSES

In addition to tuition reimbursement expenses, parents sometimes request reimbursement for other related expenses.

A New York boy was born with severe multiple handicaps. Because his parents live in Maryland they placed him in the voluntary custody of the Eleanor Roosevelt Developmental Services (ERDS) when he was thirteen months old. The boy began receiving special education and related services from the Cerebral Palsy Center for the Disabled (CP Center) in 1982 as directed by ERDS. When a recommendation by the school district's committee on the handicapped to place the boy in a Board of Cooperative Educational Services school was upheld by the commissioner of education the parents sued the school district in a U.S. district court.

Among other things, the district court ruled that the boy should remain at the CP Center and that his family care provider (employed by ERDS) should be reimbursed for transportation expenses which were adequately documented. *Taylor v. Bd. of Educ.*, 649 F.Supp. 1253 (N.D.N.Y.1986).

The outcome in a District of Columbia case was different. The mother of a multi-handicapped girl requested special education and related services for the girl in March, 1986. However, the District of Columbia Public Schools (DCPS) did not propose an educational program for the girl until August, 1986. The mother unilaterally placed the girl in the Lab School (a private special education day school) claiming that because DCPS failed to timely propose an appropriate placement for the girl she was forced to seek an appropriate program on her own. The mother then sought a U.S. district court order that DCPS provide the girl with transportation from home to the Lab School.

The mother argued that a federal regulation implemented pursuant to the EAHCA [34 CFR § 300.451(a)] required DCPS to provide transportation to the Lab School as a related service even though the girl had been unilaterally placed. DCPS argued that the federal regulation cited by the mother to support her claim only applied to cases where a child was placed in a private school by his or her parents and required a particular program that was not offered by the public school. The district court observed that 34 CFR § 300.451(a) had to be construed in light of § 300.403. The latter section made it clear that when the public agency (DCPS) provided a free appropriate education and the mother chose to place the girl in a private school nevertheless, "the regulations relating to payment for a private school are not involved and therefore the public agency is not required . . . to pay for the child's education at the private school." Section 300.451(a) merely clarified that DCPS was not relieved of *all* responsibility for the girl. The court concluded that neither the EAHCA nor the implementing regulation required DCPS to provide transportation for the girl to attend the Lab School. *Work v. McKenzie*, 661 F.Supp. 225 (D.D.C.1987).

A Tennessee child who suffered from a learning disability, impaired vision and seizures was being provided with a special education under the EAHCA by his local school district. In the fall of the 1983-84 school year, school personnel noticed that the child's behavior and performance appeared to have worsened since the previous spring. They suspected that the child had suffered several grand mal seizures during the summer and that the child had not recently been examined by a physician. After the school district's multidisciplinary team ("M Team") made a recommendation to his parents that he be medically evaluated by a physician, the parents had the child examined by a pediatrician, a neurologist and a psychologist. Although the M Team utilized the results of these neurological and psychological evaluations, they did not result in any change in the child's IEP. A dispute arose over whether the school district was required under the EAHCA to pay the costs of these evaluations. The parents' insurance company had paid $79 of the $265 bill for the neurological evaluation, and $99 of the $247 psychological evaluation. A hearing officer ordered the school district to pay the difference between the amount paid by the parents' insurance company and the total cost of the evaluations.

The parents filed suit in U.S. district court seeking an order that the school district reimburse them for the amount the insurer had paid to the neurologist. The parents argued that because their insurance policy provided a maximum of $30,000 lifetime coverage for psychological expenses, the $99 payment made by their insurer resulted in their coverage being reduced to $29,901. This, they said, was contrary to the EAHCA's requirement that "related services," i.e., psychological and neurological evaluations, be provided free of charge. The district court agreed that the parents were entitled to reimbursement for the $99 which their insurer had paid for the psychological evaluation. However, because there was no comparable policy limit for neurological expenses, the parents had incurred no cost as a result of their insurer's payment of $79 for the neurological evaluation. The school district was thus ordered to reimburse the parents for all sums which they had paid to the neurologist and psychologist, minus the $79 paid to the neurologist pursuant to their insurance policy. The court concluded by ordering the district to pay the parents $99 to compensate for the reduction of the amount of coverage available for psychological expenses. *Seals v. Loftis*, 614 F.Supp. 302 (E.D.Tenn.1985).

In a another Virginia case, a handicapped child brought suit against a school district alleging that the district failed to provide her with an appropriate education. The child, through her parents, requested reimbursement for the cost of summer programs which the child had attended as well as placement at a private school of the parents' choice. In addition, the child's parents requested reimbursement for their travel expenses incurred while the child was a patient and student at a home for crippled children in Pennsylvania. The U.S. district court held that neither state law nor the EAHCA required the state to pay all of the expenses incurred by parents in educating a child, whether the child is handicapped or nonhandicapped. Thus, the parents were not entitled to reimbursement for their travel expenses. *Bales v. Clarke*, 523 F.Supp. 1366 (E.D.Va.1981). See also *Helms v. Indep. School District No. 3*, 750 F.2d 820 (10th Cir.1984), a similar Florida case in which the parents of a handicapped child enrolled in a Georgia residential school were denied reimbursement for their travel expenses incurred as a result of visits to their son in Georgia.

IV. STATUTORY CEILINGS ON REIMBURSEMENT

A statutory ceiling on reimbursement for tuition expenses is not allowed.

Florida statutory law imposed a limit on the amount of tuition a school district in that state could spend on private school education of the handicapped. The Florida Supreme Court, however, struck down the application of the statutory ceiling where the ceiling itself imposed a denial of a handicapped child's right to a free public education appropriate to his needs. *Scavella v. School Bd. of Dade County*, 363 So.2d 1095 (Fla.1978).

V. MONETARY DAMAGES

In *Smith v. Robinson*, the U.S. Supreme Court ruled that money damages were generally not available to handicapped students (see § VII). However, the Handicapped Children's Protection Act of 1986 changes this result and provides that in proper cases a handicapped child may be awarded money damages, in addition to tuition reimbursement, for violations of the EAHCA.

In January, 1984, a handicapped Mississippi boy was suspended from school for unbuttoning a girl's blouse and he was sent to a state hospital for evaluation and treatment with his mother's consent. After the boy returned home he was refused admission to school but his mother was not informed officially of the refusal. The boy was refused admission again in September, 1984, and the mother filed complaints with local and state education authorities but received no satisfaction. She sued the school board in U.S. district court alleging that the boy's due process rights were violated. She also sought a court order to readmit her son to school.

The district court held a due process hearing in December, 1984, in which it upheld an October, 1984, school board IEP determination that the boy should be placed in a residential setting. The U.S. Court of Appeals, Fifth Circuit, upheld the decision and after further proceedings in the district court the mother appealed again to the court of appeals. She contended that the boy's due process rights were violated when he was excluded from school in the winter and fall of 1984.

The court of appeals held that when the school board failed to convene an IEP conference in the spring of 1984 it violated the EAHCA. The EAHCA specifically required that "written prior notice to the parents" be provided whenever the school proposes to initiate or change . . . the . . . educational placement of the child. . . ." The U.S. Supreme Court has held that even a short suspension of ten days requires notice and some type of formal hearing. Also, both the EAHCA and the Fourteenth Amendment require the school to provide the boy with notice and a hearing regarding his continued exclusion from school. The court held that this procedural violation gave rise to a claim by the boy for compensatory damages under the "due process" exception to *Smith v. Robinson*. It also observed that the Handicapped Children's Protection Act of 1986 provides for compensatory damages. The case was remanded to the district court to determine the extent of the boy's loss caused by the school's failure to provide notice and a hearing in April and August, 1984. The court of appeals also instructed the district court to determine what damages, either monetary or in remedial educational services, would be appropriate for the boy. *Jackson v. Franklin County School Bd.*, 806 F.2d 623 (5th Cir.1986).

In 1979, the parents of a handicapped girl sued the state of Missouri alleging that several state and local government agencies denied their daughter the educational services she desired. Two U.S. district court orders dismissed the parents' complaint and they appealed to the U.S. Court of Appeals, Eighth Circuit, seeking a compensatory education for their daughter (who was then twenty-four years of age).

On appeal the parents claimed that an earlier Eighth Circuit decision dismissing their claim was wrong since the compensatory educational services they sought were not damages as the court had earlier concluded. The court of appeals observed that the U.S. Supreme Court's ruling in *Burlington School Committee v. Department of Education of Massachusetts* had altered its understanding of what are "damages" under the EAHCA. The parents were seeking to recover educational services (which they could not afford to provide) that their daughter would have received during the three years she was in the Youth Center of the St. Louis State Hospital. The court of appeals stated that ". . . Congress did not intend the child's entitlement to a *free* education to turn upon her parent's ability to 'front' its costs." The parents were seeking the recovery of compensatory educational services in order to remedy denial of the benefit Congress sought to protect through the EAHCA (a free appropriate public education). It held that the parents would be entitled to recover compensatory educational services for their daughter (which would mean an actual education) if they prevailed on their claim that the state denied their daughter a free appropriate education in violation of the EAHCA. The compensatory education issue was remanded to the district court for further proceedings. *Miener v. State of Missouri*, 800 F.2d 749 (8th Cir.1986).

A Connecticut case demonstrates other circumstances where monetary damages are allowed under pre-1986 law. It involved a multi-handicapped boy who required a highly structured but flexible school program. A June, 1982, study found that the boy was making no academic progress in the Trumbull, Connecticut Public School program and recommended placement in the Foundation School. The parents unilaterally placed the boy in the Foundation School in December, 1982. When Trumbull proposed a new program for the boy for the 1983-84 school year, which was modeled after Foundation's program, a hearing officer found it to be appropriate but the parents insisted on leaving him at Foundation. They sued Trumbull seeking a court order requiring the school board to pay reasonable costs of tuition and transportation for the boy's attendance at Foundation. They also requested that the board be required to maintain the boy in his Foundation School placement during the pendency of the court proceedings. They sought damages of $10 million and costs incurred by the exhaustion of their EAHCA remedies. The board moved for a dismissal before a hearing officer who denied the motion, and the board then appealed to a U.S. district court.

The issue before the court was whether the parents were entitled to money damages under § 1983 of the federal Civil Rights Act and § 504 of the Rehabilitation Act of 1973. The court noted that prior to passage of the Handicapped Children's Protection Act of 1986, (Pub.L. No. 99-372, 100 Stat. 796) the exclusive remedy of the parents was the EAHCA, but that is no longer true. The court therefore had to determine whether the 1986 legislation should be given retroactive application in this case. Applying the law in effect at the time it rendered its decision would be appropriate, held the court, unless doing so would result in injustice or if there was statutory direction or legislative history to the contrary. All three exceptions were operative here. Congress did not intend to give retroactive effect to § 3 of the Handicapped Children's Protection Act of 1986 which provides that plaintiffs must exhaust all administrative procedures before seeking resolution in a civil action. The parents had to rely on prior law for relief. The motion to dismiss with respect to the parents' § 3 claim was granted to Trumbull.

The court noted that under pre-1986 law, monetary damages are generally denied but are allowed under two exceptional circumstances: (1) "where the child's physical health would have been endangered if the parents had not made alternative arrangements; and (2) where defendants acted in bad faith by failing, in an egregious fashion, to comply with the procedural provisions of the [EAHCA]." The court reasoned that the parents may qualify for the "bad faith" exception and accordingly it refused to dismiss this portion of the parents' lawsuit. *Silano v. Tirozzi*, 651 F.Supp. 1021 (D.Conn.1987).

Another case involved a fifteen-year-old learning disabled student in Connecticut who sued his school board pursuant to provisions of the EAHCA seeking a court order requiring board members to implement an individualized course of instruction designed to meet this student's educational needs. In addition, the complaint sought $1,000,000 in monetary damages for the alleged negligence of the board members in failing to implement an appropriate educational program earlier in the student's school career. Subsequent to the filing of the lawsuit the parties agreed to an appropriate educational program for this student. Thus, the question remaining was whether damages could be recovered for alleged negligence in failing to provide proper special education under federal law. A U.S. district court held that there was no implied private remedy for damages under the Act. The legislative history is devoid, said the court, of even the slightest suggestion that Congress intended it to serve as a vehicle through which to initiate a private cause of action for damages. The court dismissed the lawsuit against the board members. *Loughran v. Flanders*, 470 F.Supp. 110 (D.Conn.1979).

A U.S. district court in New York also held that money damages were not intended by Congress as a remedy for failure of a school board to place a handicapped child in an appropriate educational program. The question arose when parents of an emotionally handicapped student sued their school board seeking money damages as punishment for the board's failure to properly place their child in an appropriate educational program. The court noted that Congress passed the EAHCA in order to assist states in educating their handicapped. The legislation provides procedural safeguards to ensure appropriate placement while recognizing that diagnosis of special education problems is difficult and that errors can be made. The court also noted that the field of special education was new and undeveloped, and in need of flexibility for testing of new methods of educating handicapped children. Thus, if school officials were held to monetary liability for incorrect placement of a handicapped child, they would hesitate to implement innovative programs, which in turn would cause the education of handicapped children to suffer. For these reasons, the court held that money damages were not appropriate within the meaning of the EAHCA. *Davis v. Maine Endwell Cent. School Dist.*, 542 F.Supp. 1257 (N.D.N.Y.1982).

In a Georgia case, a young child, through his parents, brought an action against his school district, board of education and certain of its administrators seeking declaratory, injunctive and monetary relief for alleged violations of the EAHCA. When the child started school he was tested and it was determined by school authorities that he should be assigned to a self-contained learning disability classroom. The parents agreed to this placement. Approximately one year later the child's progress was reviewed and placement was changed to "research learning disability" which gave him part-time assistance. Again, the parents approved. Shortly thereafter, the parents insisted that their child be placed in a regular first grade class without resource assistance. This request was denied by the school board.

A hearing was later held at which the hearing officer determined that assistance was unnecessary, thus clearing the way for regular classroom placement. The school rejected this decision, prompting an automatic appeal to the state board of education. That board determined that the current school board placement was appropriate. Suit was then filed in federal court by the child and his parents. During pendency of the suit, the child was placed in a regular classroom setting. The trial court entered summary judgment for the local school board, a decision appealed to the U.S. Court of Appeals, Eleventh Circuit. The primary issue before the appellate court was whether the parents' monetary claims under the EAHCA were "moot" due to the child's removal from all special education during pendency of the action. The court said yes. The parents were entitled to no damages because, as a general rule, compensatory damages are not available under the EAHCA. *Powell v. Defore*, 699 F.2d 1078 (11th Cir.1983).

The parents of a high school freshman in Illinois sued a local school district seeking relief for their child who had been placed in a special education program. The child was referred to the district's Department of Special Education which recommended outside intensive psychotherapy. An IEP which did not include psychotherapy, was developed without participation by the child's parents. The child's condition worsened; nonetheless, the school district later issued the child a diploma. The parents brought suit seeking a revocation of the diploma, a court order directing remedial education for their child in a private residential facility, reimbursement for costs expended in providing services to their child under his independently prepared IEP, and $1,000,000 in general damages for alleged violations of the EAHCA.

In ruling against the parents, a U.S. district court cited Illinois law which requires that the state provide tuition-free education, but held that that did not require the state to provide psychotherapy. Further, general money damages are not available under the EAHCA. The attempt to have the diploma revoked was likewise dismissed since it would make no sense to revoke the diploma if the state was not required to provide the educational placement the parents sought. *Max M. v. Thompson*, 566 F.Supp. 1330 (N.D.Ill.1983). The case was appealed to the U.S. Court of Appeals, Seventh Circuit, which affirmed the district court ruling. The district court, however, was asked to reconsider its prior holding dismissing the child's claim for a compensatory education, and the case was remanded.

The Court of Appeals pointed out to the district court that shortly after it had rendered its opinion dismissing the child's claim for compensatory services, *Timms v. Metropolitan School District of Wabash County*, 722 F.2d 1310 (7th Cir.1983), was decided. That case denied a handicapped student's claim for a compensatory education on the ground that her parents failed to exhaust their administrative remedies prior to bringing suit. However, the court of appeals in *Timms* stated that an obligation placed upon the state to correct the effects of past eductional shortcomings would not "fall afoul" of the Eleventh Amendment, which serves to bar lawsuits against public officials (see Chapter 6, § II). Further, because compensatory services in *Timms* were recharacterized as prospective, they were allowable under the EAHCA. The district court, hearing the case for a second time, held that the *Timms* decision was controlling and reinstated the student's claim for compensatory services. *Max M. v. Thompson*, 585 F.Supp. 317 (N.D.Ill.1984).

The mother of a handicapped student in Pennsylvania brought suit claiming money damages for the alleged mental and emotional suffering and loss of earnings which she and her son had experienced as a result of a local school district's failure to follow the provisions of the Pennsylvania Public School Code. Specifically, the mother claimed that her son suffered from a learning disability which was not identified by school officials, who had a statutory duty to identify exceptional children and provide them with a proper education. The Commonwealth Court of Pennsylvania held that the Pennsylvania Code reflected the intent of Congress in enacting the EAHCA, i.e., to improve the educational opportunity of exceptional children. Since the EAHCA afforded no private cause of action for money damages, no such remedy could be inferred from Pennsylvania law. *Lindsay v. Thomas*, 465 A.2d 122 (Pa.Cmwlth.1983).

Money damages were allowed in a case in New York. The parents of a seventeen-year-old deaf child brought suit in a U.S. district court, seeking to compel their local school district and the New York State Commissioner of

Education to pay for their child's education since 1973-1974 at a special school for the deaf in Massachusetts. The suit was brought under the EAHCA with the parents claiming that the defendants' failure to bear such costs deprived their child of a free appropriate public education in violation of the Act. Up to the time of the suit the parents paid the expenses of sending the child to the school. The defendants claimed that adequate schools existed in New York, that the Massachusetts school was not approved by the Commissioner and that money damages may not be awarded in an action under the Act.

The court disagreed and held that money damages may be awarded under the Act, "at least to the extent of reimbursement for tuition and expenses related to providing an appropriate educational placement for the handicapped child. The statute's language authorizing the court to fashion such relief as it determines to be 'appropriate' grants a substantial amount of discretion to the court." However, the court did state that such damages could be awarded against the school district only and not against the Commissioner. The mere fact that the school was not approved by the commissioner did not necessarily preclude the plaintiffs from maintaining the present action but they were told by the court that they could not maintain an action for school years for which they had not made prior request that the school district pay. The net result of the lawsuit was that a motion by the defendants to dismiss was denied but the parents were required to undergo additional administrative proceedings to further clarify the issues involved. In the meantime, court action was stayed. *Matthews v. Ambach*, 552 F.Supp. 1273 (W.D.N.Y.1982).

VI. COMPENSATORY EDUCATION

Although compensatory education is not usually awarded under the EAHCA, it may be awarded where benefits which Congess intended to protect under the EAHCA were not granted.

In 1979, the parents of a handicapped girl sued the state of Missouri alleging that several state and local government agencies denied their daughter the educational services she desired. Two U.S. district court orders dismissed the parents' complaint and they appealed to the U.S. Court of Appeals, Eighth Circuit, seeking a compensatory education for their daughter (who was then twenty-four years of age).

On appeal the parents claimed that an earlier Eighth Circuit decision dismissing their claim was wrong since the compensatory educational services they sought were not damages as the court had earlier concluded. The court of appeals observed that the U.S. Supreme Court's ruling in *Burlington School Committee v. Department of Education of Massachusetts* had altered its understanding of what are "damages" under the EAHCA. The parents were seeking to recover educational services (which they could not afford to provide) that their daughter would have received during the three years she was in the Youth Center of the St. Louis State Hospital. The court of appeals stated that ". . . Congress did not intend the child's entitlement to a *free* education to turn upon her parent's ability to 'front' its costs." The parents were seeking the recovery of compensatory educational services in order to remedy denial of the benefit Congress sought to protect through the EAHCA (a free appropriate public education). It held that the parents would be entitled to recover compensatory educational services for their daughter (which would mean an actual education) if they prevailed on their claim that the state denied their daughter a free appropriate education in violation of the EAHCA. The compensatory education issue was remanded to the district court for further proceedings. *Miener v. State of Missouri*, 800 F.2d 749 (8th Cir.1986).

In November, 1985, a mildly retarded young adult sued his local school district and the state of Connecticut. He claimed that he was being denied his right to an education under the EAHCA. The case was settled through a consent decree which was signed by both the state and local defendants. The consent decree granted the young adult two years of compensatory education at the state's expense.

After passage of the Handicapped Children's Protection Act of 1986 (HCPA), the young adult sued both the school district and the state seeking the attorney's fees he incurred in the earlier lawsuit ($2,633). The school district argued that because the state had to pay the expense of the young adult's compensatory education he had "prevailed" only against the state and not against the school district. According to the district, this meant that the state was solely liable for the young adult's attorney's fees.

The court rejected the school district's arguments. It observed that the young adult did obtain limited success against the school district at the administrative level. Before filing the lawsuit, he had sought a compensatory education through the EAHCA's due process hearing procedures. The school district was involved in that administrative process. Even though a hearing officer denied the young adult's request for a compensatory education, that denial resulted in the lawsuit which in turn produced the consent decree favorable to him. Therefore, the young adult was deemed to have "prevailed" in the administrative process. The court ruled that the school district should pay twenty percent, and the state eighty percent, of the young adult's attorney's fees. *Counsel v. Dow*, 666 F.Supp. 366 (D.Conn.1987).

A twenty-five-year-old California man with Down's syndrome brought suit against the California education commissioner on the grounds that he had been excluded from the educational system prior to 1973. The lawsuit alleged that for several years his mother had unsuccessfully tried to enroll him in a San Francisco public school special education class. In 1973, at the age of twelve, he was finally allowed to enroll in the special education program. When he reached the age of twenty-one, his school district sought to terminate his placement in the special education program as provided by section 1415(b)(2) of the EAHCA. He claimed, however, that he should be allowed to stay in the program to compensate for the seven years he was wrongfully denied a special education prior to 1973. A federal district court denied his request, and he appealed to the U.S. Court of Appeals, Ninth Circuit, which affirmed the district court's decision.

The appeals court ruled that even though the man had been denied access to a special education prior to the enactment of the EAHCA in 1975, he was barred from bringing suit under any other statute, including the Rehabilitation Act. The court cited the U.S. Supreme Court's 1984 decision of *Smith v. Robinson*, 104 S.Ct. 3457 (1984), which stated that all special education lawsuits must be brought under the EAHCA. In *Smith* the Supreme Court held that Congress, having passed the EAHCA, had removed all other Acts as possible bases for special education lawsuits. Extending this doctrine to lawsuits which arose even before 1975, the court of appeals held that the man could make no claim under any Act but the EAHCA. Since the EAHCA contains no provision authorizing "compensatory educations" for pre-1975 denials of special educational services, and explicitly states that persons over the age of twenty-one are not entitled to such services, the man's lawsuit was dismissed. *Alexopulos v. Riles*, 784 F.2d 1408 (9th Cir.1986).

The parents of a profoundly mentally handicapped twenty-year-old girl in Indiana who had received one and one-half hours of educational instruction from 1976 to 1980 requested, in 1979, that their daughter be placed in a full-day instructional program in the hope that she would respond to increased attention. The school district denied the request because of a belief that there was a correlation between the girl's self-abusive behavior and increased attention. After exhausting their administrative remedies the parents brought suit in a U.S. district court, which held in favor of the school district. On appeal to the U.S. Court of Appeals, Seventh Circuit, the parents sought an injunction to prohibit the school district from excluding their daughter from a full school day and, in addition, asking for one full year of day-long instruction to compensate for the 1979-80 school year during which she received one and one-half hours of instruction. The Court of Appeals held that the request for an injunction was moot because the girl was past the age at which the school district was required to provide educational services. The court also denied a compensatory education on the ground that since neither the EAHCA nor the Rehabilitation Act provide for general money damages for an alleged inadequate IEP, except in cases of bad faith refusal to abide by the procedures set out in those acts, the remedy of a compensatory education also could not be implied. *Timms v. Metropolitan School Dist. of Wabash County*, 718 F.2d 212 (7th Cir.1983).

The parents of a handicapped student in Georgia sought in federal court a compensatory education for their child, whom they claimed was inappropriately placed. The child had been attending a special education program which had been recommended by his school district. The parents insisted that he be placed in a regular classroom. A series of administrative appeals resulted in a determination that a special education environment would be best for the child. However, the parents disagreed and filed suit in a U.S. district court, which entered summary judgment for the local school board. The parents appealed to the U.S. Court of Appeals, Eleventh Circuit, arguing that their child was entitled to a compensatory education so he could catch up to his age group, having fallen behind his nonhandicapped peers because of a year spent in the special education program. The court ruled against the parents, stating that there is nothing in the EAHCA requiring a school board to remediate a previously handicapped child. *Powell v. Defore*, 699 F.2d 1078 (11th Cir.1983).

The governor of Illinois and state education officials appealed a court order reinstating the parents' claim for a compensatory education for their child. The officials alleged that the order should be amended on four grounds: 1) the parents' failure to assert the compensatory educational claim at the state level administrative hearing; 2) the requested relief was moot because the child had turned twenty-one and was no longer eligible for special education services; 3) the parents failed to allege sufficient wrongdoing on the part of the school district, i.e., that the school district had acted in bad faith; and 4) state educational officials should not be held legally responsible for the acts of a local educational agency.

A U.S. district court held that the record of the administrative proceedings revealed that the parents did raise the compensatory education issue at the state level hearing. Second, the issue was not moot because Congress did not intend to prevent compensatory educational relief in cases where a child may have passed the age where he is legally entitled to special education services. A contrary holding, said the court, could result in school districts intentionally delaying services until the districts are no longer responsible for the child's education. Third, the state's argument that the plaintiffs had failed to allege sufficient wrongdoing on the part of the state was invalid. The court held that the pre-*Burlington* "exceptional circumstances" test, where parents are entitled to reimbursement only when a school district has acted in bad faith or somehow endangered or threatened the health and safety of the child, did not apply. Here, the parents were asking for prospective relief, and the exceptional circumstances test applied only when retroactive relief is requested.

Finally, the court did not absolve the state defendants from liability for the local school district's actions. The court noted that Congress intended that responsibility for the implementation of all services under the EAHCA be at the state level. However, the plaintiffs could only sue the state defendants in their official, not individual, capacity. The court held that there was no basis for holding the governor liable. The state's motion to amend the previous order was thus granted in part and denied in part. *Max M. v. Thompson*, 592 F.Supp. 1450 (N.D.Ill.1984). See also *Max M. v. Thompson*, 592 F.Supp. 1437 (N.D.Ill.1984).

VII. AVAILABILITY OF CIVIL RIGHTS REMEDIES

Section 1983 of the federal Civil Rights Act and the Rehabilitation Act of 1973 are sometimes invoked by plaintiffs as a remedy where the EAHCA fails to provide one. Both Acts prohibit unfair discrimination against handicapped individuals. The 1984 U.S. Supreme Court case *Smith v. Robinson* (see § VIII) barred recourse to the Rehabilitation Act in cases where the relief sought is available under the EAHCA. Additionally, *Smith v. Robinson* held that the Civil Rights Act may not be resorted to in special education cases, unless the child has been denied the benefits of the procedures outlined in the EAHCA. The Handicapped Children's Protection Act of 1986 reversed *Smith v. Robinson* by amending the EAHCA to state that the other federal civil rights laws may be relied upon by handicapped children.

After passage of the Handicapped Children's Protection Act of 1986 (HCPA) three handicapped children in New Hampshire asked a U.S. district court to reinstate their civil rights claims. The court held that since § 3 of the HCPA (which made § 1983 civil rights lawsuits and money damages available to handicapped students) was not expressly made retroactive, their civil rights claims could not be reinstated. On reconsideration, the district court found that § 3 of the HCPA was to be applied to cases that were pending as of the HCPA's effective date (August 5, 1986). It observed that "while section 3 is not to be applied retroactively, section 3 is to be applied to cases pending at the time of its enactment." It also noted that "a court is to apply the law in effect at the time it renders its decision, unless doing so would result in manifest injustice or there is statutory direction or legislative history to the contrary." Since no manifest injustice would occur if the handicapped children were allowed to reinstate their civil rights claims under § 1983, the court vacated its earlier decision not to reinstate the claims. It held that the children could bring a civil rights lawsuit against the local school officials. *Edward B. v. Brunelle*, 662 F.Supp. 1025 (D.N.H.1986).

In *Robinson v. Pinderhughes*, the U.S. court of appeals held that because the Baltimore City Schools failed to implement a hearing officer's decision in a timely manner (and had not appealed the decision) it had violated the EAHCA. The court of appeals also concluded that since the EAHCA did not contain any provision for enforcing final administrative orders by a hearing officer, the student was entitled to a § 1983 claim. When the Baltimore City Schools refused to enforce the hearing officer's decision to put him in a residential placement the Baltimore City Schools had, under color of state law, violated the EAHCA. The district court was therefore wrong in dismissing the student's § 1983 claim. His § 1983 claim was remanded to the district court for further proceedings. *Robinson v. Pinderhughes*, 810 F.2d 1270 (4th Cir.1987).

The U.S. Court of Appeals, Eleventh Circuit, held that where a school district deprives a handicapped child of a due process hearing under the EAHCA a lawsuit may be brought under § 1983 of the Civil Rights Act. This case involved an emotionally and physically impaired high school girl in Florida who was placed in a county special education school pursuant to her IEP. Although the girl made excellent progress at school she fought incessantly with her family. As a result her mother decided that placement at an out-of-state residential facility was warranted, and she requested a due process hearing on this matter. The school district special education director forwarded the mother's request for a due process hearing to the school district attorney, but no hearing was provided within the Act's forty-five day limit.

The child's parents then unilaterally placed the girl in the private facility and filed suit against the school district seeking to recover their tuition costs and attorney's fees. The parents' lawsuit was based upon the EAHCA, the Rehabilitation Act and § 1983. A U.S. district court held that 1) the EAHCA cannot provide the basis for an award of compensatory damages; 2) the Rehabilitation Act provides no private cause of action for money damages; and 3) § 1983 is inapplicable to special education cases because Congress intended that the EAHCA be the exclusive remedy.

The parents appealed to the U.S. Court of Appeals, Eleventh Circuit, which reversed in part and affirmed in part. The court held that section 1983 may provide the basis for a lawsuit in special education cases where, as here, the plaintiff has been denied the procedural protections of the EAHCA. This was significant because of the relative ease of obtaining money damages and attorney's fees under section 1983. The appeals court affirmed the district court ruling with regard to the claim under the Rehabilitation Act and remanded the case to the district court for a determination of money damages. *Manecke v. School Bd. of Pinellas County, Florida*, 762 F.2d 912 (11th Cir.1985).

The U.S. Court of Appeals, Sixth Circuit, affirmed a U.S. district court decision which dismissed claims under the Rehabilitation Act and Civil Rights Act. The Court of Appeals based its decision on *Smith v. Robinson*, which held that the Rehabilitation Act is inapplicable when relief is available under the EAHCA to remedy a denial of education services, and which also disposed of the issue of whether a plaintiff can base a claim under the Civil Rights Act when a handicapped child has been denied equal protection of the law due to the failure of school authorities to provide a free appropriate public education. *Smith* concluded that Congress intended the EAHCA to be the "exclusive avenue through which a plaintiff may assert an equal protection claim to a publicly financed special education," observed the court of appeals.

The court of appeals also denied the parents' contention that the alleged mistreatment of their child by school authorities constituted an independent constitutional claim. The parents asserted that allegations of mistreatment, e.g., isolation, corporal punishment, withholding of the child's coat, and exclusion from a school field trip were violations actionable under the Civil Rights Act, independent of their claim that the child was not provided a free and appropriate public education in accordance with the EAHCA. The court of appeals found that the parents' civil rights claim did not identify an independent claim, but rather alleged that education officials violated the Civil Rights Act by failing to obey commands of the EAHCA. The parents could not circumvent the procedural requirements of the EAHCA by basing their claim upon the Civil Rights Act. *Austin v. Brown Local School Dist.*, 746 F.2d 1161 (6th Cir.1984).

A U.S. district court in Wisconsin rejected the claims of two handicapped children who contended that they had valid claims under the Rehabilitation Act even if they were precluded from recovering under the EAHCA. The court stated that a plaintiff cannot proceed with a claim under the latter statute—whether it is based on a substantive or a procedural challenge to state and local agency action—without having exhausted administrative remedies under the EAHCA. Although the plaintiffs asserted that their claim under the one statute was independent of the one under the other statute, the court disagreed, stating that since both claims came from the same set of facts, they must at least be considered parallel. A further assertion by the plaintiffs was that they had an independent right of action for violation of constitutional rights under federal civil rights statutes. This contention was also rejected by the court, which noted that "a number of courts have addressed this issue and have concluded that exhaustion of the EAHCA's [administrative] procedures should be required before constitutional claims that parallel EAHCA claims can be pursued in federal court." The court concluded by granting the defendants' motion for summary judgment and dismissing both federal and state law claims. *M.R. v. Milwaukee Pub. Schools*, 584 F.Supp. 767 (E.D.Wis.1984).

The mother of a handicapped child in New York claimed that she and her son suffered damages as a result of a local school district's failure to evaluate the child and provide him the special education to which he was entitled. The child allegedly suffered damages to his intellect, emotional capacity and personality, and was impeded in acquiring necessary training. In addition, the mother alleged that she moved to a different school district to obtain the services her child needed and that she herself suffered emotional distress. A U.S. district court held in favor of the mother and child, and the school district appealed.

The U.S. Court of Appeals, Second Circuit, held that because the mother had not availed herself of her administrative remedies under the EAHCA, she was deprived of her means of relief under that Act. However, the court found it unthinkable that Congress would have intended that a parent in this situation, where the district had refused to evaluate the child, should be left without any remedy. Accordingly, the court permitted the Civil Rights Act to supply the remedy for the mother who had been denied procedural safeguards under the EAHCA. The court viewed the absence of any prescribed remedy in the EAHCA as a "gap" to be filled by § 1983 of the Civil Rights Act. The case was remanded to determine the amount of damages. *Quakenbush v. Johnson City School Dist.*, 716 F.2d 141 (2d Cir.1983).

The New Mexico Association for Retarded Citizens and others commenced a class action against the state of New Mexico, seeking declaratory and injunctive relief on behalf of handicapped children allegedly denied certain federally guaranteed special education services. The case, decided by the U.S. Court of Appeals, Tenth Circuit, involved the interpretation of § 504 of the Rehabilitation Act. Section 504 provides that "no otherwise qualified handicapped individual in the United States . . . shall, solely by reason of his handicap, be excluded from participation in, be denied the benefits of, or be subjected to discrimination under any program or activity receiving federal financial assistance." Under the regulations to this act schools are required to provide "free appropriate public education" to all handicapped students within their territorial jurisdiction.

The court of appeals observed that the U.S. Supreme Court has held, in interpreting § 504, that its purpose is to prohibit discrimination against the handicapped rather than mandate affirmative relief for them. This is distinguished from the affirmative duties required under the EAHCA, which makes the receipt of federal money contingent on a state's performing affirmative duties with respect to the education of the handicapped. The state of New Mexico had chosen not to participate in the EAHCA program. Against this legislative and regulatory backdrop, citizens in New Mexico contended that the state's entire program in dealing with the special needs of handicapped children was deficient. The court, while recognizing that discrimination against handicapped children could require the fashioning of a judicial remedy, remanded the case to a lower court, stating that § 504 violations must be evaluated in light of the Supreme Court's decision that the statute and its regulations are designed to prohibit discrimination rather than to require action. *New Mexico Ass'n for Retarded Citizens v. State of New Mexico*, 678 F.2d 847 (10th Cir.1982).

A fifteen-year-old New York girl, three and one-half feet tall with a partially amputated right arm, a functionally impaired left arm and hand, and legs of approximately one foot in length, asked for and received from her school district a special van to transport her to school and the help of an aide during the school day. The school sponsored a Spanish class trip to Spain for which this student was academically qualified. The trip involved tours of historical sites which required the students to walk many miles. The school denied this student permission to go on the trip on the ground that she would endanger herself by attending. She sued the school seeking to enjoin it from enforcing its ban on her attendance. She argued that because the school was receiving federal funding for this trip she could not be barred from going simply on the ground that she was handicapped.

A U.S. district court in New York noted that the Rehabilitation Act of 1973 specifically states that a handicapped student may not be excluded from participation in a program receiving federal funding solely on the basis of his or her handicap if that student is otherwise qualified. However, in this case, after the court itself witnessed the difficulty this child had even climbing onto the witness stand, it held that she was not otherwise qualified since she could not fulfill the physical requirements of the trip. Her complaint against the school district was dismissed. *Wolff v. South Colonie School Dist.*, 534 F.Supp. 758 (N.D.N.Y.1982).

In ruling that Rhode Island school officials failed to provide two learning disabled children an appropriate education, the U.S. Court of Appeals, First Circuit, nevertheless ruled that the children were not entitled to damages under the Rehabilitation Act for their alleged time, expense, inconvenience and suffering resulting from a local school district's failure to provide the children the appropriate education. The court said that because the EAHCA provided no remedy for damages, recourse to the more general provisions of the Rehabilitation Act could not be taken. *Colin K. v. Schmidt*, 715 F.2d 1 (1st Cir.1983).

The mother of an eleven-year-old girl with cerebral palsy, who challenged the proposed transfer of her child from a traditional elementary school to an elementary school specially designed to meet the needs of handicapped children, was denied relief under the EAHCA and the Rehabilitation Act. In holding that the child could not receive a satisfactory education in a traditional school, even with the use of supplementary aids and services to the maximum extent possible, a U.S. District Court in Michigan stated that there was no valid claim under the Rehabilitation Act because, under this Act, there must be an intentional, bad faith denial of education resources, or a grossly negligent placement decision. This was not the case here. Thus, the transfer decision was upheld. *Johnston v. Ann Arbor Pub. Schools*, 569 F.Supp. 1502 (E.D.Mich.1983).

VIII. ATTORNEY'S FEES

Prior to 1986 there was no provision in the EAHCA for attorney's fees. Accordingly, the U.S. Supreme Court held in *Smith v. Robinson* (reprinted in the Appendix of U.S. Supreme Court cases in this volume) that attorney's fees were not recoverable for special education claims made under the

EAHCA. It also held that attorney's fees were no longer recoverable under § 1983 or the Rehabilitation Act. With the passage of the Handicapped Children's Protection Act of 1986 Congress expressly provided for attorney's fees to a prevailing parent or guardian in cases that were pending on or after July 4, 1984.

A. Court Proceedings

An orthopedically handicapped student at the Louisiana Special Education Center (LSEC) was transferred to a hospital in March, 1985, to be treated for respiratory problems. When he attempted to return to the LSEC, it refused to admit him, arguing that it was not equipped to deal with his medical problems. The student subsequently sued the LSEC under the EAHCA. A federal district court ordered the school to admit the student who subsequently sought attorney's fees. The district court denied attorney's fees on the basis of *Smith v. Robinson*, in which the Supreme Court declared attorney's fees unavailable in EAHCA cases. He appealed but before the appeal reached court, Congress passed the Handicapped Children's Protection Act of 1986 which overruled the *Smith* decision by expressly providing for attorney's fees in EAHCA cases. The U.S. Court of Appeals, Fifth Circuit, ruled that he was entitled to attorney's fees and remanded the case to the district court. The district court awarded attorney's fees to the student in the amount of $9,300 and the LSEC appealed. He requested additional attorney's fees on appeal.

The court of appeals first determined that the LSEC could not avoid paying the attorney's fees on the ground that it had acted in good faith when it refused to admit the student. It also rejected the LSEC's argument that he could not sue for attorney's fees because the EAHCA allows payment of such fees only to "the parents or guardian of a handicapped child or youth." The student in this case was eighteen years or older while the suit was in progress and he therefore sought attorney's fees in his own name. The court declared that the legislative history of the EAHCA indicated that handicapped children can seek attorney's fees on their own behalf if they are old enough and are otherwise competent to bring suit. Because the district court had not abused its discretion in awarding attorney's fees, the award was proper. The court of appeals ruled in the student's favor and remanded the case to the district court for a determination of the amount of additional attorney's fees that he should receive for the appeal. *Fontenot v. Louisiana Bd. of Elementary & Secondary Educ.*, 835 F.2d 117 (5th Cir.1988).

In another Louisiana case a group of handicapped children sued the state of Louisiana in a U.S. district court seeking statewide extended year programs for handicapped students. The parties entered into a consent decree authorized by the court which provided for the extended year programs. Therefore, the handicapped children were prevailing parties under the EAHCA. The handicapped children then asked the court for an award of attorney's fees. They claimed that they were entitled to fees under § 1415(e) of the EAHCA. The state contended that the U.S. Constitution's Eleventh Amendment barred recovery of attorney's fees because the state did not expressly waive its immunity from a federal lawsuit. The district court held for the handicapped children. The state had consented to the court's jurisdiction by entering into the consent decree thus waiving its Eleventh Amendment immunity. The court ordered the state to pay the handicapped childrens' attorney's fees under § 1415(e). *Laura I. v. Clausen*, 676 F.Supp. 717 (M.D.La.1988).

In 1980, a U.S. district court held that the District of Columbia Board of Education's IEP for an autistic child was inadequate and ordered the board to place the child at a residential school in West Virginia. It also awarded attorney's fees to the child's parents under § 504 of the Rehabilitation Act. In 1984, however, the fee award was vacated in response to the U.S. Supreme Court's ruling in *Smith v. Robinson*. After the Handicapped Children's Protection Act (HCPA) was passed in 1986, the parents asked the district court to reinstate the attorney's fee award.

The court noted that the HCPA provides that courts may award attorney's fees to prevailing children or parents in EAHCA "actions or proceedings brought . . . after July 3, 1984, and actions or proceedings brought prior to July 4, 1984, . . . which were pending on July 4, 1984." The parents argued that since their earlier attorney's fee award had not been vacated until August 17, 1984, their action had still been "pending" on July 4, 1984. The district court agreed with the parents' interpretation. It rejected the board's arguments that the HCPA was unconstitutional retroactive legislation and ordered that the parents were entitled to $8,420, the amount of the previous fee award. *Capello v. Dist. of Columbia Bd. of Educ.*, 669 F.Supp. 14 (D.D.C.1987).

In 1983, a U.S. district court held that Missouri's policy precluding educational programs for handicapped children in excess of the nine-month school year was discriminatory against the handicapped and was unenforceable. However, under the authority of *Smith v. Robinson*, 104 S.Ct. 3457 (1984), the district court later denied a request by a handicapped student's parents for attorney's fees. After passage of the Handicapped Children's Protection Act of 1986 (HCPA) the parents sued their school district in U.S. district court. Once again they asked for attorney's fees. The school district argued that because the attorney's fees issue had already been finalized in its favor, it could not be held liable for attorney's fees now.

The court held that the parents could recover attorney's fees. It observed that federal court rules provided that parties could be relieved of final judgments against them when exceptional circumstances were present. The court reasoned that by authorizing attorney's fees in the HCPA and making such authorizations retroactive, Congress intended to reverse the affects of *Smith*. This reversal, stated the court, presented exceptional circumstances which favored the parents' case. The court rejected the school district's argument that a change in the law was not sufficient to provide relief when the judgment was final. It noted that although changes in court decisions cannot affect a final judgment, changes in statutory law (as in this case) can. The court reasoned that expressly retroactive changes in statutory law created new claims for parties seeking relief from previous judgments. This meant that the parents here had a new and viable claim for attorney's fees since the HCPA expressly provided for attorney's fees retroactive to cases pending on July 4, 1984.

The court also rejected the school district's argument that the Eleventh Amendment to the U.S. Constitution, which limits the power of federal courts in lawsuits against individual states, barred a retroactive award of attorney's fees against the state. It concluded that monetary awards against states were allowed when authorized by Congress in order to enforce the Fourteenth Amendment, which provides in part that states cannot infringe upon the privileges of its citizens. The court therefore awarded attorney's fees to the parents, payable by the state of Missouri. *Yaris v. Special School Dist.*, 661 F.Supp. 996 (E.D.Mo.1987).

In 1981, a group of handicapped students in Rochester, New York, sued the city board of education and the state department of education in a U.S. district court. They alleged that they were being denied an appropriate public education and sought relief under the EAHCA. The case was resolved in a consent decree between the students and the city board of education in August, 1983. In July, 1986, a U.S. district court judge granted a motion to dismiss requested by the students but denied their request for an award of attorney's fees since the consent decree was relief under the EAHCA which did not provide for the award of attorney's fees. When the HCPA was signed into law, the students withdrew an appeal and moved for reconsideration.

The motion focused on a clause in the new law which provides for attorney's fees to a "prevailing party." The district court ruled that the students were the prevailing party since the consent decree brought significant system-wide relief to the students. However, they only "prevailed" against the city board of education because the state department of education refused to enter into the consent decree. The court referred to the new law's language which says that "fee awards . . . shall be based on rates prevailing in the community . . . and the kind and quality of services furnished. . . ."

In awarding $204,748 to the students' three public interest attorneys, the court observed that the legislative history of the new law suggested that the intent of Congress was to allow non-profit law firms to recover attorney's fees at the same hourly rate as conventional law firms. It awarded the students' attorney's fees for the time spent monitoring the consent decree during the 1986-87 school year since the decree provided for such monitoring. The city board of education alone was ordered to pay the attorney's fees award on behalf of the students. *J.G. v. Bd. of Educ. of Rochester City School Dist.*, 648 F.Supp. 1452 (W.D.N.Y.1986).

B. Administrative Proceedings

1. Attorneys

After the father of a handicapped child disagreed with a local school district concerning an IEP for his child, he sought a due process hearing under the EAHCA. The hearing officer granted the IEP provisions he sought and the school district complied. However, the school district refused to pay the father for the attorney's fees he incurred in obtaining the IEP provisions. The father sued the school district in U.S. district court. The school district moved for dismissal claiming that the EAHCA did not authorize a parent who prevailed in a due process hearing to initiate a lawsuit in a federal court for the sole purpose of obtaining attorney's fees. The father contended that the legislative history of the EAHCA indicated that it did authorize such lawsuits.

The court held that such lawsuits were authorized by the EAHCA due to passage of the Handicapped Children's Protection Act (HCPA). It observed that, although the language of the EAHCA was inconclusive as to whether a parent could recover attorney's fees in such cases, it was reasonable to read "action or proceeding" in § 1415(e)(4)(B) of the EAHCA (which authorizes the recovery of attorney's fees) as referring to both judicial actions and due process hearings. It also looked to the language of the legislative history of § 1415(e)(4)(B) and concluded that the legislative history clearly indicated that separate lawsuits for attorney's fees were permissible. The court dismissed the school district's motion and held that the father could sue in a federal court for attorney's fees incurred in the due process hearing. *Prescott v. Palos Verdes Peninsula Unified School Dist.*, 659 F.Supp. 921 (C.D.Cal.1987).

In another case a U.S. district court in Texas looked to the reasoning in *Prescott*. The case involved the parents of a handicapped child who were dissatisfied with the child's IEP. A hearing officer granted two of the parents' five requests and omitted a ruling on two others. They sued their school district seeking attorney's fees contending that they prevailed in the due process hearing. The school district moved to dismiss their request arguing that the court lacked authority to grant attorney's fees because the parents had not first sued the school district in the U.S. district court on the case itself. The school district also claimed that the parents were not entitled to attorney's fees because they were not prevailing parties.

The district court held that the parents were entitled to attorney's fees. It observed that several district courts have found that an award of attorney's fees for work done with regard to due process hearings was proper where the case never reached the district court level. It accepted *Prescott*'s reasoning that the legislative history of § 1415(e)(4)(B) compelled a conclusion that such awards were intended by Congress. It also reasoned that the parents were prevailing parties because they acquired substantive changes in their child's IEP at the due process hearing. The court dismissed the school district's motion and held that the parents were entitled to attorney's fees. *Kristi W. v. Graham Indep. School Dist.*, 663 F.Supp. 86 (N.D.Tex.1987).

A lawsuit to recover attorney's fees under the EAHCA was instituted in a U.S. district court in the District of Columbia. The plaintiffs had successfully pursued an administrative action and sought the fees pursuant to the Handicapped Children's Protection Act of 1986 (HCPA). The HCPA effectively overturned the U.S. Supreme Court's holding in *Smith v. Robinson* that attorney's fees were not available to the prevailing party in special education cases.

The defendants in this case, the District of Columbia and others, argued 1) that the HCPA should not have been applied retroactively by Congress and 2) that attorney's fees should not be available for EAHCA administrative proceedings. The court stated that neither of these arguments had merit and therefore ruled in favor of the plaintiffs.

As to the retroactivity argument, the court stated that it is within the authority of Congress to pass retroactive legislation, especially where, as here, the legislators are attempting to explicate what they intended in an earlier version of the law. By the later, retroactive Act, Congress was expressing its explicit approval of attorney's fee awards after the Supreme Court had denied the award of such fees. This type of retroactive clarification is clearly within congressional authority and does not offend the U.S. Constitution.

As to the second argument regarding attorney's fees for parents who prevail at an administrative level, the court said that Congress has manifested its intention in the clear words of the HCPA that attorney's fees be recoverable for administrative proceedings. New section 1415(e)(4)(B) of the EAHCA reads, "in any action or proceeding brought under this subsection, the court, in its discretion, may award reasonable attorneys' fees. . . ." Thus, stated the court, the words of the statute support the plaintiffs' position that fees are recoverable for administrative proceedings. *Moore v. Dist. of Columbia*, 666 F.Supp. 263 (D.D.C.1987).

After the Cambridge, Massachusetts, School Department proposed an individualized education program (IEP) for a handicapped boy that his mother deemed in appropriate she appealed to the state Bureau of Special Education Appeals (BSEA). The BSEA ruled for her and ordered the school department to provide residential special education for her son. After passage of the Handicapped Children's Protection Act of 1986 (HCPA) the mother and her son sued the school department seeking attorney's fees due to their status as prevailing parties at the due process hearing. A U.S. district court held that parents who prevailed at a due process hearing under the EAHCA may later bring a lawsuit solely to obtain an award of attorney's fees.

The court looked to the language of the HCPA, which amended § 1415(e)(4) of the EAHCA. The new language provides that "in any action or proceeding brought under this subsection" a court may award attorney's fees. It held that "proceeding" referred to both judicial and administrative proceedings, rather than only judicial proceedings as the school department argued. The court concluded that a "close reading of [§ 1415(e)] indicates that it contemplates the award of attorney's fees for parties who prevail at the administrative hearing level."

The court also noted that § 1415(e)(4)(D) provided that parents may not obtain attorney's fees if "the court or administrative officer finds that the relief finally obtained by the parent" was less than any rejected settlement offer. This provision contemplated that fees could be awarded for administrative level hearings. The court also noted that the legislative history of the HCPA supported its decision. A Senate Committee Report stated that the HCPA allows "the award of reasonable attorney's fees to prevailing parents in [EAHCA] civil actions and in administrative proceedings to parents in certain specified circumstances." Thus, the court held that the parent in this case was entitled to a fee award. *Michael F. v. Cambridge School Dep't*, Civ. No. 86-2532-C (D.Mass.3/5/87).

Parents of a handicapped child filed a complaint with the Division of Community Programs of the Wyoming Department of Health and Social Services alleging that a county children's center had failed to properly develop an Individualized Educational Plan (IEP) for their child. After an administrative hearing, the hearing officer issued a final decision in favor of the parents and ordered that a teacher trained to teach deaf students be employed on a regular basis by the children's center to serve as a consultant. The parents then petitioned the Division for an award of attorney's fees incurred in the administrative hearing process. The Division's administrator denied the request on the ground that they could only be awarded by a court. The parents filed a lawsuit in a U.S. district court seeking attorney's fees.

The district court noted that the lawsuit was not an appeal from the Division administrator's decision. It was instead an independent action for attorney's fees following the administrator's determination that he was not empowered to award them. The issue, therefore, was not whether the administrator had decided wrongly, but whether the parents could recover attorney's fees despite the fact that the IEP dispute was resolved at the administrative level rather than in court. Also at issue was whether the separate lawsuit for attorney's fees was proper.

The court of appeals noted that the EAHCA, as amended by HCPA provides the following:

> In any action or proceeding brought under [the EAHCA], the court, in its discretion, may award reasonable attorneys' fees as part of the costs to the parents or guardian of a handicapped child or youth who is the prevailing party.

The court determined that this provision placed the decision of whether to award attorney's fees at the discretion of the federal district courts. This interpretation was supported by the legislative history of the HCPA.

The court of appeals also determined that Congress did not intend that EAHCA lawsuits would have to be decided in federal court as a prerequisite to an award of attorney's fees. The EAHCA allows an award of reasonable attorney's fees to parents if they are successful in "any action or proceeding" under the EAHCA. This language indicated that awards of attorney's fees are allowed when favorable results are achieved in lawsuits or administrative proceedings. The court awarded $3,000 to the parents as reasonable attorney's fees. *Mathern v. Campbell County Children's Center*, 674 F.Supp. 816 (D.Wyo.1987).

In 1985, the U.S. Court of Appeals, Fourth Circuit, held that a school board wrongly expelled a student for behavior which resulted from his handicap. After the passage of the Handicapped Children's Protection Act of 1986 (HCPA) his parents asked the court of appeals for an award of attorney's fees. The HCPA provides that a court may award reasonable attorney's fees to parents of handicapped children who are prevailing parties under § 1415(e)(4)(B)-(D) of the Education for All Handicapped Children Act (EAHCA). The court of appeals remanded the question to a U.S. district court in Virginia.

The school board resisted the application of the HCPA on several theories. It contended that a violation of the separation of powers doctrine would occur if the HCPA's retroactive application formed the basis of a decision in a pending case. It also argued that retroactive application of the HCPA to award attorney's fees to the parents would exceed the spending power of Congress. Specifically, it argued that Congress' power to impose liabilities on recipients of federal aid was limited since attorney's fees had not been available to parents when the board accepted EAHCA funds. It also claimed that the parents were too late in filing their request for attorney's fees. Finally, it contended that the HCPA only provided for an award of attorney's fees to parties who prevailed in court proceedings as opposed those who prevailed in due process hearings.

Concerning the school board's separation of powers argument, the court observed that here the law was changed only generally. Although the change had broad application, it only affected this case incidentally (i.e. attorney's fees, not the decision itself). The court held that the only limitation on Congress' power to impose liabilities on federal aid recipients was that Congress must do so unambiguously as it did here. The court also concluded that the parents had requested attorney's fees three months after passage of the HCPA which was not an unreasonable period of time. Finally, the court held that the HCPA only clearly prohibited an award of attorney's fees when court-obtained relief was less than any settlement offer. It also noted that the HCPA provided for fee awards in "any action or proceeding," implying the possibility of fee recovery for due process hearings. The court therefore ordered that the parents recover attorney's fees. *School Bd. v. Malone*, 662 F.Supp. 999 (E.D.Va.1987).

The parents of two handicapped children in New Hampshire were successful in securing relief for their children in administrative due process hearings. After passage of the HCPA they requested payment of attorney's fees from the Manchester School District (MSD). MSD refused and the parents sued MSD in U.S. district court. MSD moved for dismissal. The court observed that although the Supreme Court held in *Smith v. Robinson* that the EAHCA was the exclusive source of rights and remedies in special education cases, Congress has altered the effect of *Smith v. Robinson* by passing the HCPA. It held that the HCPA permits a court to award attorney's fees for success at either the administrative or judicial level. MSD's motion to dismiss was denied, and the court held that it was liable for attorney's fees. *Burpee v. Manchester School Dist.*, 661 F.Supp. 731 (D.N.H.1987).

After the parents of four handicapped children were successful in challenging a decision by the New York Commissioner of Education to terminate their children's placement under the EAHCA, they moved in a New York Supreme Court for an order awarding attorney's fees under § 1415(e)(4)(B) of the EAHCA. This subsection is part of the Handicapped Children's Protection Act of 1986. The commissioner contended that § 1415 did not authorize any fees in this case since the original lawsuit was not brought under it. Specifically, he claimed that the administrative action attacked in the original lawsuit did not involve a determination made by the commissioner after an appeal to him, but rather dealt with a claim that the commissioner's wrong interpretation of New York law was denying the students the placement they deserved under the EAHCA. Such a distinction required the denial of attorney's fees according to the commissioner.

The court disagreed, concluding that, because the commissioner had recognized from the outset of the original lawsuit (according to statements made by his attorney) that the theory behind the lawsuit was a violation of the EAHCA, he was therefore liable for attorney's fees. The court also ruled that the EAHCA should be broadly construed to "effect its purpose of providing appropriate free public education for handicapped students" and that any remedy (including attorney's fees) which encouraged parents to protect the child's interests should be "viewed expansively." The supreme court awarded attorney's fees to the parents. *Esther C. by Ephraim C. v. Ambach*, 515 N.Y.S.2d 997 (Sup.1987).

At least one federal court has held that attorney's fees are not recoverable for those who prevail at the administrative level. A U.S. district court held that the Delaware State Board of Education was liable for attorney's fees to the parents of a handicapped child whose private school placement had been wrongly changed to a public school. It also ruled that the local board of education was not liable for attorney's fees since the parents had not prevailed against it in a court proceeding. The parents moved for reargument contending that in enacting the HCPA, Congress intended to permit attorney's fees for plaintiffs who prevailed in due process hearings. Specifically, the parents argued that legislative history and case law mandated that plaintiffs who prevailed in due process hearings under the EAHCA may bring a lawsuit for the sole purpose of recovering attorney's fees.

The district court disagreed citing two reasons for its decision. First, it noted that in cases involving other federal civil rights laws, the U.S. Supreme Court has held that plaintiffs may not recover fees for prevailing in administrative hearings. Second, the parents in the present case had not succeeded on any significant issue in the due process hearings. Nothing in the record suggested that the parents had sought or had benefited from the prospective change in procedures ordered by the due process hearing officer or that any attorney time was spent on that issue. The district court denied the parents' motion for reargument. *Rollison v. Biggs*, 660 F.Supp. 875 (D.Del.1987).

2. Lay Advocates

A New Jersey special education lay advocate sued the New Jersey State Board of Education in a U.S. district court. She sought compensation for her services. The court held that she was not entitled to compensation for her services as a lay advocate in due process hearings under the EAHCA. She then appealed to the U.S. Court of Appeals, Third Circuit.

On appeal she contended that the EAHCA preempted a New Jersey Court Rule which required that lay advocates represent the handicapped free of charge. The no-fee provision was preempted because it hindered the fulfillment of the goals set out by Congress in the EAHCA. The advocate argued that because the EAHCA gave parents the right to representation by lay advocates, Congress intended that lay advocates charge fees. She also claimed that the no-fee provision violated her rights under the Equal Protection Clause of the U.S. Constitution.

The court of appeals upheld the district court decision. The EAHCA did not support the advocate's contention that Congress intended no distinction between lay advocates and attorneys. The EAHCA, which permitted a prevailing party to recover attorney's fees, contained no express provision granting fees to lay advocates.

The advocate's equal protection argument failed because the court found the New Jersey no-fee provision rationally related to New Jersey's interest in maintaining high ethical and fiduciary standards among attorneys. According to the court, permitting lay advocates to charge fees for their representation would likely encourage an abundance of unlicensed legal practitioners to the detriment of the public. *Arons v. New Jersey State Bd. of Educ.*, 842 F.2d 58 (3d Cir.1988).

C. Pre-Handicapped Children's Protection Act Proceedings

In *Smith* the U.S. Supreme Court ruled that attorney's fees are not available under the EAHCA, the Civil Rights Act, or the Rehabilitation Act. This case involved a child in Rhode Island who suffered from cerebral palsy and other physical and emotional handicaps. The child's parents had prevailed in their claim against their local school district and the district was obligated to maintain the child in his then current residential school placement while a dispute involving who was to pay for the placement was resolved. After the parents collected their child's tuition costs from the school district, they sought attorney's fees. The federal district court granted them under the Civil Rights Act and the Rehabilitation Act, both of which contained provisions authorizing an award of attorney's fees to a successful plaintiff. The U.S. Court of Appeals, First Circuit, reversed and denied attorney's fees, and the U.S. Supreme Court upheld the reversal.

The Supreme Court undertook a three-step analysis. First, under the common law, attorney's fees are not available unless a specific statutory provision authorizes them. Second, the EAHCA contains no attorney's fees provision. Third, by enacting the EAHCA, Congress intended to make it the exclusive remedy for handicapped public school students, thereby preventing them from relying on either the Civil Rights Act or the Rehabilitation Act. The comprehensiveness of the EAHCA's "carefully tailored scheme," assuring that school districts will educate handicapped children, convinced the Supreme Court that when Congress gave handicapped children the rights contained in the EAHCA, it removed any other Act as a basis for special education lawsuits. Hence, a special education plaintiff could not use the Civil Rights Act or the Rehabilitation Act as the basis for an award of attorney's fees.

An exception was made, however, for cases in which a school district deprives a handicapped student of his or her procedural rights under the EAHCA. If a student proves that a school district denied him or her the procedural rights to which every handicapped child is entitled, then an attorney's fees award under the Civil Rights Act would be justified. This is because the EAHCA places great emphasis on following certain procedures. If the district denies a student due process of law, then a due process challenge under the Civil Rights Act is a legitimate remedy. In the present case, however, there was no evidence that the school district had violated the EAHCA's procedural safeguards, and attorney's fees were denied. *Smith v. Robinson*, 104 S.Ct. 3457 (1984).

A U.S. district court in Texas awarded attorney's fees to the mother of a handicapped child who successfully challenged denial of a free appropriate education under the EAHCA, the Equal Protection Clause and the Civil Rights Act. The defendant school district in that case appealed the award of attorney's fees to the U.S. Court of Appeals, Fifth Circuit, which deferred its decision until the U.S. Supreme Court case *Smith v. Robinson* was decided. The Court of Appeals held that under *Smith*, that portion of the award of attorney's fees compensating the attorneys for their efforts in securing relief which alternatively could have been provided by resort to the administrative avenues of the EAHCA was erroneous and should be reversed. In addition, any portion of the award of attorney's fees for Rehabilitation Act claims cognizable under either the EAHCA or on the equal protection theory must be reversed. Since the EAHCA itself can be employed to require the school district to grant appropriate relief from this violation, resort to the Rehabilitation Act or an equal protection theory was unnecessary, and a grant of fees inappropriate.

The court observed that *Smith* made it clear that where the Rehabilitation Act gives no more to a plaintiff's substantive claim than does the EAHCA, a plaintiff may not employ the Rehabilitation Act to circumvent the EAHCA's administrative procedures as a means to collect attorney's fees. The mother's due process claim based on the district's failure to involve her in the development of individualized education plans, found the court, precluded an award of attorney's fees because these fees may be appropriate in EAHCA cases where procedural due process claims are involved. Because the mother's right to privacy claim did not overlap or interfere with the EAHCA, it was also not precluded by the *Smith* case. Other constitutional challenges in the mother's claim which did not rest on the EAHCA also did not preclude attorney's fees. Finally, the court held that the district court, on remand, must, pursuant to *Smith*, only award attorney's fees to the extent that the plaintiffs actually prevailed on their constitutional claims. Any additional fees based on mere allegations of constitutional violations should be vacated. Accordingly, the case was remanded to the district court for a redetermination of attorney's fees. *Teresa Diane P. v. Alief Indep. School Dist.*, 744 F.2d 484 (5th Cir.1984).

After a U.S. district court in New Hampshire declared a state institution providing educational services to the mentally retarded an "educational wasteland" and awarded the residents of the institution attorney's fees in their lawsuit against state officials, both parties appealed. The residents claimed that the award was too low and that they should have been awarded fees against nine local school districts whose attempt to intervene in the lawsuit was aborted. The residents also claimed that they were entitled to interest on the award due to alleged delays in the district court's decision. The state officials challenged on appeal the inclusion of several items in the award to the plaintiffs and the fact that an award was made to the plaintiffs' at all when some of the plaintiffs' claims had been unsuccessful.

The U.S. Court of Appeals, First Circuit, held that the plaintiffs' overall success in "overhauling" the practices of the institution entitled them to a general award of attorney's fees without regard to whether some of the claims had been unsuccessful. However, the appellate court agreed with the defendants' arguments that no grounds to support attorney's fees connected with EAHCA claims. The U.S. Supreme Court made it clear in *Smith v. Robinson* that the EAHCA is the "exclusive avenue through which a [handicapped] plaintiff may assert an equal protection claim to a publicly financed special education." The Supreme Court similarly ruled out reliance upon the fees provision of the Rehabilitation Act, on the ground that the Rehabilitation Act does "not require affirmative action on behalf of handicapped persons, but only the absence of discrimination against those persons." In light of the

Smith case, the Court of Appeals reversed that portion of the attorney's fees award allocable to EAHCA claims.

The court upheld the portion of the award attributable to post-judgment monitoring fees, which were incurred in the process of making certain that the district court's orders were carried out, finding that such services necessary for reasonable monitoring of a court order are compensable. The court also upheld a twenty percent "bonus" awarded to two of the plaintiffs' counsel. The rule governing such bonuses requires that the legal representation rendered by the recipients of the bonuses be "unusually good and exceptional results obtained." The court, noting that such bonuses are only awarded on rare occasions, observed that exceptional results were indeed obtained in this case. Turning, then, to the residents' claim for interest on the fee award, the court held that because the district court, in its discretion, chose not to award interest on the award, the appellate court would not disturb the district court's ruling on this issue. Likewise, the appellate court rejected the residents' claim against the nine would-be intervenors, i.e., the school districts, on the ground that the only claims against the districts were EAHCA claims. *Garrity v. Sununu*, 752 F.2d 727 (1st Cir.1984).

In January, 1980, the New York State Education Department notified its County Boards of Cooperative Education Services (BOCES) that under current law, state funding for the education of learning disabled children by BOCES would no longer be available. The education department stated that funding would henceforth be available only for school district-run learning disabled programs. BOCES therefore notified its school districts that it would discontinue its learning disabled programs. On April 3, 1980, the state legislature amended its education code to allow continued funding of the BOCES programs. Despite this action on the part of the state to guarantee the ongoing provision of special educational services to children in BOCES-run programs, several parents of children in these programs brought a class action suit in U.S. district court against the commissioner of education. The lawsuit sought an injunction against the termination of learning disabled programs, to which the children were entitled under the Education for All Handicapped Children Act (EAHCA), and asked for an award of attorney's fees under the Civil Rights Act. The parents claimed that attorney's fees were justified in this case because, due to the former proposal that BOCES funding would be discontinued, their children had been in danger of being deprived of an appropriate education without benefit of a hearing. The district court awarded attorney's fees in the amount of $8,818 and the commissioner of education appealed.

The U.S. Court of Appeals, Second Circuit, reversed the award, holding that the children had never been in any danger of being deprived of appropriate educations. At the time the lawsuit was commenced, the legislature had already acted to assure continued funding for the BOCES programs. Thus the parents could hardly claim to have been successful in their lawsuit. In order for the Civil Rights Act to provide a basis for attorney's fees in EAHCA cases, the plaintiffs must be successful in their claims, and they must prove a violation of the EAHCA's procedural safeguards. As neither of these factors were present in this case, the court of appeals reversed the award of attorney's fees. Furthermore, in light of the parents' decision to bring suit after the state had already acted to assure the continued education of their children, the appeals court remanded the case to the district court for a determination of whether the commissioner of education was entitled to attorney's fees from the parents. *Bonar v. Ambach*, 771 F.2d 14 (2d Cir.1985).

The U.S. Court of Appeals, Eleventh Circuit, was asked by the U.S. Supreme Court to revise one of its prior holdings in light of *Smith v. Robinson.* In the original case, the Court of Appeals affirmed the judgment of a trial court granting an injunction against a Georgia school district's continuing policy of not considering or providing more than 180 days of education for profoundly mentally retarded children. The subsequent U.S. Supreme Court decision caused the court of appeals to reconsider its earlier opinion. Although the issue of attorney's fees was not presented in the earlier court of appeals case, the court of appeals did expressly state that recovery could be had under the Rehabilitation Act. The court of appeals, in light of the *Smith* decision, now found this to be incorrect. The court therefore modified its previous opinion by deleting certain references in its original opinion to the Rehabilitation Act. The court affirmed a U.S. district court ruling in favor of the plaintiffs in the prior case to the extent that it granted relief under the EAHCA, and reversed those portions of the ruling which held that the plaintiffs were entitled to relief under the Rehabilitation Act. *Georgia Ass'n of Retarded Citizens v. McDaniel*, 740 F.2d 902 (11th Cir.1984). See also *Hayward v. Thompson*, 593 F.Supp. 57 (N.D.Ill.1984), an Illinois case wherein relief under the Rehabilitation Act was denied on similar grounds.

The U.S. Court of Appeals, Seventh Circuit, was asked to decide whether the prevailing party in a lower court action was entitled to attorneys fees in an action brought under the EAHCA. The parents of a handicapped girl brought suit against state and local education and health officials in Indiana, alleging that their daughter had been denied the free, appropriate public education to which she was entitled under the EAHCA. A U.S. district court held that 1) the EAHCA did not provide a private cause of action for damages; 2) the parents had failed to comply with the EAHCA's statutory requirements by removing their daughter from her current educational placement before completing the administrative remedies available under the Act; 3) the parents had not exhausted available administrative procedures; and 4) the parents' claim was barred by a prior controlling court decision which had disposed of this issue. The school and health officials then filed a motion in U.S. district court for attorney's fees arguing that because the parents' claim for damages was brought in bad faith, the court should award fees. The district court held that the parents had litigated in bad faith, but denied attorney's fees to the school officials on the ground that the case of *Anderson v. Thompson*, 658 F.2d 1205 (7th Cir.1981), barred attorney's fees to a prevailing defendant even when the plaintiff litigated in bad faith.

The U.S. Court of Appeals affirmed the holding of the district court, but on different grounds. It disagreed with the district court that *Anderson* barred an award of attorney's fees. *Anderson* (decided prior to the Supreme Court's ruling in *Burlington School Committee v. Department of Education of Massachusetts*) held that, absent special circumstances, damages were not an appropriate remedy under the EAHCA. Two special circumstances may exist: 1) if the child's physical health was endangered by the current placement, or 2) if the defendant acted in bad faith. *Anderson*, therefore, did not present a complete bar to the parents' claim, as there was evidence that the school officials acted in bad faith in their dealings with the parents. Thus, the district court's conclusion that the parents litigated in bad faith was erroneous, but its ruling was upheld. Attorney's fees were denied. *Benner v. Negley*, 725 F.2d 446 (7th Cir.1984).

At issue before the Court of Appeal of California was whether a handicapped child, who had prevailed in a court action against a local school district for the district's failure to provide an appropriate special education for him, was entitled to have his attorney's fees paid by the school district. The Court of Appeal affirmed a California trial court decision which held that the student was not entitled to attorney's fees. The court noted that section 1988 of the federal Civil Rights Act provides for an award of attorney's fees to the prevailing part in an action to enforce a provision of the Civil Rights Act. However, the court held that the student, in an action under the EAHCA, could not invoke this provision to recover attorney's fees. The court relied upon other cases which have held that, although the violation of a federal statute can be the basis of a civil rights action, violation of the EAHCA may not be the basis of such an action. The EAHCA already provides for a comprehensive scheme of state administrative proceedings, and an action under section 1983 would, therefore, serve "no purpose other than that of a conduit for attorney's fees."

The court also held that there was no valid claim under the Rehabilitation Act for attorney's fees. The court stated that the student would be required to allege something more than mere failure to provide a "free appropriate education'' required by the EAHCA. The severely language-handicapped student failed to allege a substantial claim under the Rehabilitation Act and thus was not entitled to attorney's fees under that Act. Finally, Government Code section 800 could not be relied upon to provide attorney's fees. To recover under this provision the plaintiff must show that the hearing officer at the administrative level acted arbitrarily and capriciously, and no such showing was made. Attorney's fees were denied. *Byrnes v. Capistrano Unified School Dist.*, 204 Cal.Rptr. 100 (Cal.App.4th Dist.1984).

The parents of a handicapped child in Oregon brought a complaint before the Oregon Department of Education (DOE) alleging that the school district had violated various state and federal statutes and administrative rules concerning the education of their child. The DOE agreed and awarded the parents partial reimbursement of tuition and costs, but denied their request for attorney's fees. The Oregon Court of Appeals, in a prior holding, had reversed the DOE's ruling, stating that the department had the power to award attorney's fees. The school district sought reconsideration of this holding in light of the intervening U.S. Supreme Court decision of *Smith v. Robinson*.

The Court of Appeals held that because *Smith* does not specifically address situations where the EAHCA is not available, or situations where the right claimed is not provided by the EAHCA with more clarity and precision than the right provided by the Rehabilitation Act, the prior holding would not be disturbed. It was not apparent from the record of the prior proceedings that the parents relied solely on the Rehabilitation Act for an award of attorney's fees, or that the rights the parents claimed under the Rehabilitation

Act were more clearly and precisely guaranteed by the EAHCA. The court concluded that the case should be remanded to the DOE for specific consideration of the parents' Rehabilitation Act claims before *Smith* could effectively bar the parents' claim for attorney's fees. *Laughlin v. School Dist. No. 1*, 689 P.2d 334 (Or.App.1984).

The rationale behind the general rule against attorney's fees was set forth by the U.S. Court of Appeals, First Circuit, in its opinion in the *Smith v. Robinson* case. In this case the Cumberland, Rhode Island, school district successfully appealed an award of attorney's fees to a child handicapped by cerebral palsy. The child had been enrolled in a private program which all parties agreed provided him with an appropriate education. The school district paid tuition for a period of time, then discontinued such payments under the belief that the Rhode Island Department of Mental Health, Retardation and Hospitals was the responsible agency. Following a lawsuit by the student and his parents, judgment was rendered in their favor. The plaintiffs then sought attorney's fees, which were awarded by a U.S. district court. The U.S. Court of Appeals, First Circuit, reversed. The court stated that "under what is labeled the American Rule, attorney's fees are only available as a general matter when statutory authority so provides." Here the action fell within the parameter of the EAHCA, a federal law which contains no provisions for attorney's fees. The court said no right to attorney's fees could be created when it appeared that Congress, perhaps recognizing the shortness of school funds, made no effort to include such a provision in the law. *Smith v. Cumberland School Comm.*, 703 F.2d 4 (1st Cir.1983); affirmed, 104 S.Ct. 3457 (1984).

CHAPTER FIVE
STUDENTS

I. INJURIES

Courts have generally held schools and their agents liable for injuries received by handicapped children during the course of the regular school day which resulted from the schools' or their agents' failure to provide a reasonably safe environment, failure to warn participants of known hazards or to remove known dangers where possible, failure to properly instruct participants in an activity, or failure to provide supervision adequate for the type of activity, the ages of the participants involved and their physical and mental capabilities. However, the doctrine of governmental immunity, which has been eliminated in many states by legislation or judicial decision, may provide an absolute shield against liability for schools and their agents in the states where the doctrine still exists.

A. Liability Found

In December, 1984, the employee of a not-for-profit school for the handicapped accompanied a resident from a classroom building to the skilled nursing facility. The employee was with the resident for twenty minutes during which time the resident repeatedly fell down and resisted being lifted to her feet. After struggling with the resident for twenty minutes in subfreezing temperatures, the employee could no longer lift her and proceeded to drag the resident along the concrete sidewalk for a distance of ten feet. A nurse later found two abrasions on the resident's back. The school reported the incident to the Illinois Department of Public Health and was subsequently notified that the Department considered the incident an occurrence of abuse. The school requested a hearing but none was held for approximately nine months. After the hearing was held, the hearing officer recommended that the incident be classified as a "type B" violation of § 390.3240 of the Illinois Administrative Code which provides that employees of a facility "shall not abuse or neglect a resident." The Code defines "abuse" as "a physical or mental injury . . . inflicted on a resident other than by accident . . . ." A type B violation was defined as "a condition or occurrence . . . directly threatening to the health, safety or welfare of a resident."

The school appealed the Department's decision on the grounds that 1) evidence did not support the Department's finding of abuse, and 2) the finding was void because no hearing was held within 30 days of the school's request in violation of the Illinois Nursing Home Care Reform Act which provides that "[t]he Department shall commence a hearing within 30 days of the receipt of the request for a hearing . . . ."

The Illinois Appellate Court declared that sufficient evidence was presented to support the Department's finding of abuse despite the school's assertion that its employee's actions were reasonable under the circumstances and that the resulting injuries were accidental. The court noted that the resident's injuries could not be considered accidental because they were the likely result of being pulled on a concrete surface.

The court then determined that because the purpose of the Nursing Home Care Reform Act was to protect nursing home residents from acts of abuse rather than to protect schools, the 30 day hearing requirement was directory rather than mandatory. The Department's failure to abide by the requirement did not void its finding of abuse on the part of the school's employee. The court upheld the Department's finding that the school had committed abuse. *Grove School v. Dep't of Pub. Health*, 513 N.E.2d 973 (Ill.App.1st Dist.1987).

An emotionally handicapped male student at a Florida public school was mixed with regular students in a shop class as part of the federal mainstreaming requirement. On a day when a substitute teacher was entrusted with supervision of the shop class the student was sexually assaulted in class by another student. The assailant was a youth who was known by school officials to be prone to sexually assaultive behavior. The handicapped student was forced into performing oral sex on the assailant for ten minutes at the rear of the classroom. The substitute teacher claimed that he was unaware of this incident but that he had been diligently monitoring the classroom at the time of the assault. The assaulted student sued the school district in state court contending that the district had breached its duty of reasonable care owed to him. The jury found in favor of the student. However, the trial judge threw out the verdict and the student appealed. The Florida District Court of Appeal reversed the trial judge and reinstated the jury verdict in favor of the student. Only when there is no evidence upon which a jury could properly rely should its verdict be set aside. The case was remanded to the trial court with orders to reinstate the jury verdict and to act on other post-trial motions. *Collins v. School Bd. of Broward County,* 471 So.2d 560 (Fla.App.4th Dist.1985).

A U.S. district court in Missouri ruled that a school district may be sued under § 1983 of the federal Civil Rights Act for a bus driver's alleged beating and sexual molestation of handicapped children on his school bus. Handicapped students and their parents sued a school district alleging that while their school bus sat waiting at a transfer point the bus driver repeatedly assaulted the students on the bus. These assaults, which took place over a sixteen-month period, consisted of the bus driver fondling, stroking and pinching the students' genitals and buttocks. The bus driver also allegedly masturbated in front of the students. In addition, the plainiffs alleged that the bus driver struck several students, confined them to the bus for over one hour at the end of the bus route one day, made obscene gestures and uttered obscenities in the presence of the students and habitually started and stopped the bus so violently that students were thrown helplessly about the bus. The students alleged that despite complaints from parents, teachers and other school employees, the school district 1) failed to investigate the situation and even covered up the bus driver's actions, 2) failed to develop a program to screen employees to detect abusive propensities and 3) failed to fulfill its legally imposed duty to report the bus driver's conduct to the appropriate law enforcement agency. The students alleged that due to the school district's inaction they suffered serious physical and mental trauma. Their parents alleged that they suffered mental anguish and loss of their children's companionship. The students and parents sought compensatory and punitive damages from the school district in excess of $100 million.

The district court rejected the school district's motion to dismiss the lawsuit, observing that the plaintiffs were justified in invoking § 1983 of the Civil Rights Act because the bus driver had been acting "under color of state law." This conclusion was based on the fact that the school district was obligated by state law to provide transportation to handicapped children. Additionally, the school district had enacted rules and regulations (also pursuant to state law) necessary to the provision of transportation. The court also held that a violation of the students' constitutional rights, which is a prerequisite to a civil rights lawsuit, had been sufficiently established. The students possessed a right under the Due Process Clause of the Fourteenth Amendment to "bodily security," and the Civil Rights Act protected this right. However, the court dismissed the parents' claims under the Due Process Clause. Although parents have a constitutionally protected right to the care, custody and companionship of their children, they had not shown that they had been deprived of this right. At most they alleged that the bus driver had detained the students in the bus after school for one hour on one occasion, thus depriving them of one hour of companionship. The court held that such a minimal deprivation could not support the parents' civil rights claim.

Finally, the court held that the portion of the plaintiffs' lawsuit that was based upon state tort law was barred. First, the school district could not be held liable for failure to investigate the bus driver's conduct or for their failure to report the matter to the police. Under Missouri law such actions were discretionary administrative functions and thus were protected by official immunity. Second, the school district was protected by sovereign immunity under state law from any state tort law claims. The statutory exception to sovereign immunity which provided that school districts could be sued for injuries "resulting directly from the operation of motor vehicles" was deemed inapplicable by the court. The students' injuries resulted not from the operation of the bus but from the bus driver's wrongful conduct. Thus, while the parents' claims and all state law claims were dismissed by the court, the children were allowed to proceed with their federal civil rights claims against the school district. *Doe "A" v. Special School Dist. of St. Louis County,* 637 F.Supp. 1138 (E.D.Mo.1986).

A fourteen-year-old deaf girl contracted rheumatic fever while attending a summer camp operated by the National Council of Beth Jacob Schools. Due to the camp's negligence, the girl's disease was neither detected nor treated until she returned home at the end of the summer. Due to the disease she developed polyarthritis, an enlarged heart, a heart murmur and a leakage of her aortic valve. The girl was forced to miss two and one-half months of school. At the time the case went to trial (three years after she caught the disease) the girl tired easily and had a susceptibility to heart problems. Her medical expenses totaled $2,900. A New York trial court, sitting without a jury, awarded the girl $30,000 in damages and her mother $2,000. The girl's mother appealed, contending that the trial court's award of damages was insufficient. The New York Supreme Court, Appellate Division, noted that under state law, nonjury damage awards are freely reviewable by an appellate court. It agreed with the mother's contentions and modified the award to $50,000 for the child and $5,000 for the mother. The appellate court reasoned that the trial court's award was inadequate because the child, who already had been afflicted with one handicap, now had to deal with a heart condition that showed no signs of improving. *Berman v. Nat'l Council of Beth Jacob Schools, Inc.*, 501 N.Y.S.2d 413 (A.D.2d Dept.1986).

A twelve-year-old student enrolled in a school for trainable mentally retarded children was discovered during recess lying face down at the foot of a set of steps leading back into the school's classrooms. As a result of his probable fall, the student suffered extensive head injuries. He sued the New York board of education and his teacher, whom he alleged negligently failed to supervise the children in her care. The teacher testified before the trial court that she was aware of the student's perceptual motor difficulties and poor eye-hand coordination. She also testified that the student and another boy with whom he had been running on the day of the accident often played a chasing game called "monster" during recess. An expert witness testified that purposeless, "freestyle" running during school hours was dangerous and should never be permitted for any child, and was especially hazardous where mentally retarded children were concerned. She further testified that the proper procedure for a teacher to follow under the circumstances would have been to stop the children either by word or physical act. The trial court held that the school board was liable for damages for personal injuries the child suffered. The school board appealed to the New York Supreme Court, Appellate Division, which held that the student had established a *prima facie* case of negligence on the part of the teacher for failing to supervise her students. The trial court ruling was affirmed. *Rodriguez v. Bd. of Educ., City of New York*, 480 N.Y.S.2d 901 (A.D.2d Dept.1984).

In a case arising in the state of Washington, a mentally handicapped high school student was seriously burned during metal shop class. The eighteen-year-old student's shirt had ignited while he stood with his back to the forge. He sued the school district and shop instructor for his injuries, claiming negligent supervision. At trial, the evidence established that the student had a mental age of eleven. He sought a jury instruction that he should only be held to the standard of care of a child. The trial judge instead instructed the jury that the student should be held to the standard of care of any reasonable person. The jury reached a verdict in favor of the student, awarding him $50,000 in damages for his injuries. However, based upon the "reasonable person" standard of care, the jury also found that the student had been seventy percent contributorily negligent, which reduced his damages to $15,000. The student appealed, seeking a new trial on the issue of damages.

The Washington Court of Appeals ruled against the student, stating that the trial judge's instruction to the jury was correct and hence the reduction of the damage award was proper. Although he had a mental age of eleven, holding him to the reduced standard of care of a child would have been improper in light of the following Washington statute: "Except as otherwise provided by law, all persons should be deemed and taken to be of full age for all purposes at the age of eighteen years." Because the student had already reached the chronological age of eighteen, he was not entitled to a jury instruction imposing only the standard of care of a child. The reduction of the damage award to $15,000 due to the student's contributory negligence was affirmed. *Higgins v. East Valley School Dist.*, 704 P.2d 630 (Wash.App. 1985).

B. Liability Not Found

In a Pennsylvania case, the mother of a nine-year-old diabetic fifth grade girl met with the nurse at her daughter's elementary school. She explained the nature of her daughter's medical condition to the school nurse, and she and the nurse distributed written materials to school personnel describing the special care she needed. One day approximately three months later, while attending reading class, the student had a hypoglycemic reaction. She informed her reading class teacher that she needed to see the school nurse. The teacher refused to allow her to leave the room until class was over nearly forty-five minutes later.

By the time the student reached the nurses' office, she was having difficulty maintaining consciousness and was unable to inform the nurse that she needed her medication. She received no medical care for nearly two hours. Eventually school officials contacted her grandmother, who instructed them to take the girl to a hospital. She was in the hospital for six days.

The student sued the school district, the elementary school's principal, the nurse and the reading class teacher in U.S. district court under § 1983 of the federal Civil Rights Act. She claimed that the defendants had deprived her of needed medical attention in violation of the Fourteenth Amendment's Equal Protection and Due Process clauses, as well as the EAHCA. The defendants asked the court to dismiss the student's claims.

First, the court held that because the school officials had not been acting pursuant to any established school district policy on the day of the incident, the school district itself could not be held liable under § 1983.

Second, the girl's Equal Protection Clause claim was dismissed because, with regard to handicapped students, all equal protection claims are subsumed within the EAHCA.

Third, the court dismissed the student's due process claim. It held that even though she had a constitutional right to be free of interference by school officials in seeking needed medical attention, § 1983 was of no help to her. This was because imposing "additional administrative safeguards as a constitutional requirement would significantly intrude into the area of educational responsibility that lies primarily with public school authorities." The court stated that rather than attempting to prove a violation of her constitutional rights, the student should have relied upon traditional state common-law negligence principles.

Finally, the court dismissed her EAHCA claims, pointing out that she had proceeded directly to federal court and had bypassed the administrative remedies set forth in the EAHCA. Concluding that this was impermissible, the court dismissed the entire lawsuit. *DeFalco v. Deer Lake School Dist.*, 663 F.Supp. 1108 (W.D.Pa.1987).

Six mentally handicapped children enrolled in an Alabama middle school sued their school board claiming that the board had negligently failed to stop numerous incidents of physical, mental and sexual abuse at the school. After a state circuit court ruled in favor of the school board the children appealed to the Alabama Supreme Court. The children alleged that the board and school officials were negligent because they knew of the abuse but failed to take any steps to stop it. The students sought money damages and a court order requiring the promulgation of "rules and regulations designed to insure the protection of physical and mental abuse of mentally retarded students" in the schools. The supreme court ruled that school boards are immune from tort lawsuits, noting that the lawsuit filed in the circuit court charged the school officials with negligent, wanton, and intentional misconduct. The scope of "discretionary function" immunity for governmental bodies had been expanded in Alabama to include immunity from allegations of wanton conduct against state officials when there is no evidence of bad faith on their part. Because the handicapped students did not allege any fraud or bad faith on the part of the school officials, their claim was barred since it related to the performance of the school officials' statutory duties which are immune from tort claims. The lower court's decision was affirmed. *Hill v. Allen,* 495 So.2d 32 (Ala.1986).

A quadriplegic student at the Southwest Louisiana State School brought a negligence lawsuit against the school after suffering a spiral-type fracture of his right femur. On the morning of the injury the student's mother bathed him, fed him and strapped him into his wheelchair. She then gave him his usual dosage of phenobarbital. The school bus arrived and he was wheeled out to meet it without apparent incident. The bus driver testified that the student was in his usual good spirits as he transported him to the State School. He said that he strapped the student's wheelchair down securely that morning. Upon his arrival at the State School, the student, who weighed only thirty-two pounds, was wheeled into class where two of his instructors noticed that he was "crying and fussing." They sought to alleviate his discomfort by placing him on a mat. When this proved unsuccessful, one instructor lifted him off the mat and placed him on a table. She testified that as she did so, she heard a loud "pop." The student was immediately taken to a doctor, and the spiral fracture was diagnosed. He was hospitalized for three weeks and he recovered completely. Believing that the State School and its employees had somehow been negligent, causing the student's injury, his parents brought a lawsuit in state district court. They pointed to a statement one of the teachers had made immediately after taking the student to the doctor. She had said that she did not understand how the student's leg could have broken unless she had accidently knelt on it.

However, evidence was also presented of an incident which occurred one year after the original fracture. The student, while strapped in his wheelchair at home, became excited and pushed his leg until it became caught in the chair, then twisted it, causing the same type of spiral fracture as had occurred the previous year. He was using the same wheelchair at the time of this later incident. In light of this evidence, the district court ruled in favor of the State School and its employees, stating that a number of other explanations existed for the student's injury besides negligence on the part of a State School employee. On appeal by the parents, the Louisiana Court of Appeal upheld this ruling. Stated the court: "The mere fact that an accident occurred does not necessarily mean that someone was negligent." The court held that the parents had failed to meet their burden of proving by a preponderance of the evidence that a State School employee had caused their son's injury. *Henry v. State*, 482 So.2d 962 (La.App.3d Cir.1986).

In a Maryland case, as part of a handicapped female student's new IEP she was placed in a regular eighth grade physical education class, with no restrictions placed upon her participation. Her parents failed to express any dissatisfaction or challenge this new IEP. Midway through the school year she was seriously injured while maneuvering on a "Swedish Box." Her parents filed suit in state court against the school board and the physical education teacher, claiming that they had been negligent in placing the student in a regular physical education class without adequate safeguards. The parent's complaint did not allege negligent supervision, but negligent placement in the class.

The circuit court ruled that the parents could not base their lawsuit on negligent placement. The parents had not contested the revised IEP when it was initially implemented, and thus they were barred from contesting it now in a civil lawsuit. The court's ruling was based on the elaborate state procedural system through which disputes over special education placements could be contested. The parents had not availed themselves of this system and the circuit court refused to allow the parents to do in a civil lawsuit what they should have done through established procedures. This ruling effectively destroyed the parents' case since they would now have to prove that the teacher failed to use "reasonable care" in supervising the student. The circuit court therefore rendered a decision in favor of the school board and teacher.

The parents appealed to the Maryland Court of Special Appeals, which affirmed the circuit court decision. When the parents failed to contest the IEP which placed the student in the regular physical education class, they placed her in the same legal position as any other student in the class and no suit for "negligent placement" would be possible. Because the parents were unable to prove that the teacher had failed to exercise reasonable care in the supervision of the student the appeals court upheld the lower court's ruling against the parents. *Alban v. Bd. of Educ. of Harford County*, 494 A.2d 745 (Md.App.1985).

In a New York case, a severely disabled individual sustained serious injuries after being placed in a residential facility. Suit was brought on his behalf, alleging negligence on the part of the facility's employees. The suit alleged that employees at the residential facility had allowed the individual to participate in a normalization program designed to allow familiarization with tasks of daily living. During the program he accidently overturned a covered pot of hot water used to demonstrate the preparation of tea and coffee, causing him to be severely burned.

Reversing a lower court, the New York Court of Appeals dismissed the claim that employees had negligently placed him in the therapy program, stating that the decision to place him in the program involved medical judgment for which no liability could be imposed. The lower court's ruling that the use of a covered pot of hot water to instruct severely disabled persons was so negligent that a trial was not even necessary was reversed by the Court of Appeals, which stated that while a residential facility owes a duty of reasonable care to severely disabled persons, it is not required to maintain constant surveillance of each individual. After noting that "there are certain risks inherent in any therapeutic program, especially, as in this case, one which is designed to provide a normal homelike setting," the Court of Appeals remanded the case to the lower court for reconsideration of whether the lawsuit should be allowed to proceed. *Killen v. State*, 498 N.Y.S.2d 358 (1985).

The Supreme Court of Montana affirmed the dismissal of a lawsuit for wrongful placement in a special education program. The suit was brought in 1980 by a student against her school board and various state and local officials, alleging that she had suffered irreparable emotional harm as a result of her placement in 1973 in a special education program. The evidence showed that she was required to repeat a year of school, was called a "retard" and was taunted about flunking. When the trial court dismissed the case the student appealed. The Supreme Court of Montana upheld the trial court's decision, stating that insufficient evidence had been presented to prove that the student had suffered compensable emotional damage. In a suit for wrongful placement, expert testimony was necessary to prove that emotional harm had occurred. Because the only evidence offered to the trial court was the testimony of the student and her mother, the suit was properly dismissed. *Berger v. State*, 698 P.2d 399 (Mont.1985).

The mother of a blind, deaf and mute student in the District of Columbia, who had been sexually assaulted by the coordinator of a program for blind and deaf students, sued the coordinator and the District of Columbia. She contended that the district was liable for damages arising from the assault on her daughter due to the district's negligence in hiring or failing to supervise the coordinator. The District of Columbia Court of Appeals affirmed a trial court ruling in favor of the school district. The court of appeals found that although an employer may be held liable for the acts of employees committed within the scope of their employment, there was no showing that the coordinator's assault of the child was within that scope.

The court rejected the mother's argument that the assault was a direct result of the coordinator's job assignment since his employment necessarily included some physical contact with the child. The mother argued that a deaf, blind and mute child can be taught only through the sense of touch and, therefore, the fact that physical touching was necessarily a part of the teacher-student relationship made it foreseeable that sexual assaults would occur. The court found that a sexual assault cannot be deemed a direct result of a school official's authorization to take a student by the hand or arm in guiding her past obstacles in the building. Here, the attack was "unprovoked," had not arisen from the coordinator's instructions or job assignment and was not an integral part of the school's activities, interests or objectives. The coordinator's acts could not be viewed as being within the scope of his employment, and thus the school district was not liable. *Boykin v. Dist. of Columbia*, 484 A.2d 560 (D.C.App.1984).

II. HANDICAPPED STUDENTS IN SCHOOL ATHLETICS

Handicapped students may not be excluded from any athletic activity conducted by a school receiving federal financial assistance as long as the student is "otherwise qualified" to participate. "Otherwise qualified" means that the student is qualified to participate in spite of his or her handicap.

The Michigan Court of Appeals held that a placement decision made when a handicapped student was in fourth grade barred the student from playing varsity basketball. The student suffered from a severe hearing impairment and attended special education classes in his local school district. In 1976 he was placed in a regular education class as part of his school district's commitment to mainstreaming. However, when the student was mainstreamed he was placed in a regular education classroom one grade level below what his age would normally require. This mainstreaming decision presented no difficulties until it was discovered that the student would turn nineteen just before the beginning of his senior year, the 1984-85 academic year. He was declared ineligible to play varsity basketball during his senior year due to an age rule established by the Michigan High School Athletic Association (MHSAA). The rule prohibited students who reach their nineteenth birthday before September 1 of the academic year in question from participating in interscholastic athletics. The student sued his school district in a state circuit court, claiming that the enforcement of the age rule violated his Fourteenth Amendment right to due process and equal protection of the laws. Shortly after the beginning of the student's senior year the circuit court entered a ruling in favor of the school district and the student appealed.

In upholding the circuit court's decision, the Michigan Court of Appeals rejected each of the student's three constitutional claims. First, the student argued that he had been denied due process of law because no hearing had been held at the time he was mainstreamed. Under Michigan law the student and his parents could have requested a hearing to contest the student's placement in a grade level below the grade in which he would normally be placed. However, they had not sought a hearing. The court held that the failure to request a hearing at the time of the mainstreaming decision precluded a subsequent due process claim. The student's second contention was that he was denied equal protection by the MHSAA's refusal to grant him an exception to its age rule. The MHSAA's rules provide that it will consider waiving the age rule if a school district requests a waiver on behalf of a student. The court held that because the student never asked his school district to request a waiver from the MHSAA, his equal protection claim was barred. Finally, the student claimed that the age rule was discriminatory, arbitrary and capricious. This claim was also rejected by the court which observed that the rule was applied equally to all students regardless of sex, race, national origin or handicap. The rule also prevented the "red shirting" (holding back) of students for athletic purposes and reduced the opportunity for mismatches between older and younger athletes. Furthermore, if the September 1 age cutoff date was declared arbitrary and a new date such as August 1 established, then students turning nineteen on July 30 would seek to have the new date declared arbitrary as well. The September 1 cutoff date was a reasonable exercise of school authority. The circuit court's ruling against the student was upheld. *Nichols v. Farmington Pub. Schools,* 389 N.W.2d 480 (Mich.App.1986).

A New York school district attempted to prevent a junior high school girl from participating in contact sports by reason of her visual impairment, which resulted from a congenital cataract. New York law provides that upon a school district's determination that a student shall not be permitted to participate in an athletic program by reason of physical impairment, the student may commence a special proceeding to enjoin the school district from prohibiting such participation. Further, if the court finds that it is in the best interests of the student to participate in the athletic program and that it is reasonably safe to do so, the court shall grant permission to participate. The law further protects a school district from liability for any injury sustained by a student participating pursuant to such a court determination.

In this case, the lower court determined that with protective eyewear it would be reasonably safe for this student to participate in the athletic program, but denied her application on the grounds that it would not be in her best interests to participate, because of the immunity from liability granted to the school district should an injury occur. The New York Supreme Court, Appellate Division, rejected this lower court finding and granted the student permission to participate. Whatever immunity from liability is enjoyed by a school district is not to be weighed by the court in considering the best interests of the student. Here, ample evidence suggested that with protective eyewear it would be in the best interests of this student to participate in the athletic program. *Kampmeier v. Harris*, 411 N.Y.S.2d 744 (A.D.4th Dept.1978).

A high school athletic regulatory agency in Texas barred a male high school student from participating in high school football because he had moved to another district to live with his grandparents. The student had suffered emotional problems and was handicapped within the meaning of the Rehabilitation Act. The student sued alleging that there were compelling medical reasons why he should be permitted to participate in the football program. The U.S. district court issued a preliminary injunction restraining the athletic regulatory agency from enforcing its rule. The court said that the purpose of the rule was to prevent recruiting abuses and to prevent an athlete from irresponsibly shopping around for a school or coach. These evils were not present here. To deny the student the opportunity to play football would violate his rights as a handicapped individual. *Doe v. Marshall*, 459 F.Supp. 1190 (S.D.Tex.1978).

A student in New Jersey who was born with one kidney sued a local board of education seeking compensatory damages for the board's denial of his right to participate in his high school's interscholastic athletic program due to his handicap. In holding that the student could not be denied the right to participate in the program, the U.S. district court, stated that the federal Rehabilitation Act prohibits such discrimination against otherwise qualified handicapped individuals in federally funded programs solely on the basis of their handicap. Summary judgment was granted in favor of the student. *Poole v. South Plainfield Bd. of Educ.*, 490 F.Supp. 948 (D.N.J.1980).

A nineteen-year-old neurologically impaired high school senior challenged a New York Department of Education regulation prohibiting students over eighteen years of age from participating in interscholastic athletics. The boy had entered the public school system at the ninth grade level after leaving a private school, where he had failed the ninth grade. His participation in wrestling from the ninth grade until his senior year appeared to have significantly improved his self image. The boy brought suit in U.S. district court, alleging he had been discriminated against on the basis of his handicap and had been unlawfully denied the opportunity to participate in interscholastic wrestling in violation of the equal protection provisions of the U.S. Constitution and the Rehabilitation Act. The court held that because the student had reached the age of nineteen and had not been treated any differently than any other nonphysically handicapped nineteen-year-old student, there was no violation of equal protection, nor was there unfair discrimination. *Cavallaro v. Ambach*, 575 F.Supp. 171 (W.D.N.Y.1983).

III. STUDENT RECORDS

Generally, access to handicapped students' records will not be allowed when the privacy interest of the students outweighs the asserted need for inspection of the records.

A human rights advocacy committee in Florida petitioned for access to confidential school records which it considered pertinent to its investigation of the alleged abuse of four developmentally disabled students by public school personnel. A Florida trial court denied the committee's request and appeal was taken to the District Court of Appeal of Florida. The court affirmed the trial court rulings, saying that the committee was not entitled to access to the confidential school records of the students because a state statute limited the committee's area of jurisdiction, for the purpose of obtaining client records, to matters occurring solely within a program or facility operated, funded or regulated by the Department of Health and Rehabilitative Services. The court also based its decision on a school code provision protecting the privacy interests of every student with regard to his or her educational records. *Human Rights Advocacy Comm. v. Lee County School Bd.*, 457 So.2d 522 (Fla.App.2d Dist.1984).

The Human Rights Authority of the State of Illinois Guardianship and Advocacy Commission appealed an order of an Illinois district court denying the enforcement of a subpoena issued by the commission. Acting on a complaint which alleged that a local school district was not providing occupational and physical therapy for its students, the commission began an investigation and asked the district superintendent to produce the students' educational program records. The records were to be masked so as to delete any information by which students could be identified. When the school district failed to turn over the information, the commission issued a subpoena for the masked records. Again, the school district refused to comply. The commission then sought judicial enforcement of the subpoena.

The district court ruled that the commission had no right to examine the records because it did not satisfy the access requirements of Illinois state law regarding student records. After the commission appealed to the Appellate Court of Illinois, the school district argued that, along with the access provisions of the Student Records Act, the commission had no authority to investigate or review special education programs, and that the commission's right to investigate did not apply to all of the handicapped students in a school district, but was limited to individual cases. The thrust of the school district's first argument was that the commission was somehow usurping the role of the State Board of Education by investigating the special education program of the school district. The commission's inquiry was "tantamount to the control and direction of special education which makes local school authorities accountable to the [Commission] rather than the State Board of Education as required by the School Code."

The appellate court disagreed. The statutory authority of the commission to investigate complaints concerning violations of the rights of handicapped persons, including the right to special education programs, was not subordinate to that of the State Board of Education. Further, the commission's investigation of the school district's overall special education program, and not merely individual students, was within the bounds of the commission's statutory authority. *Human Rights Authority of the State of Illinois Guardianship Comm. v. Miller*, 464 N.E.2d 833 (Ill.App.3d Dist.1984).

CHAPTER SIX
SCHOOLS AND SCHOOL DISTRICTS

Page

Many of the problems public and private schools encounter in connection with operating special education programs are typical of problems encountered in other facets of school operations. Some problems, such as a private school's eligibility to educate handicapped children, a private school's contract to perform special educational services, or a public school's training of personnel employed in the special education area or the parents of handicapped children, are unique to the field of special education.

I. EMPLOYEES

The following cases address issues involving special education employees. Employee misconduct, discrimination, teachers' constitutional privacy rights, hiring practices, salary, termination, seniority, tenure, and unemployment compensation benefits represent the range of special education employee-related concerns which have been before the courts.

A. Dismissals for Cause

The following cases involve dismissals of special education employees "for cause," i.e., due to misconduct or incompetence.

A woman taught in a Missouri school district for thirty-six years. In the 1983-84 academic year she taught remedial math in an elementary school during which there were in effect board of education regulations, which included a provision regarding corporal punishment of students. Teachers were only to administer corporal punishment by blows to the child's "fleshy posterior" in the presence of the principal or a principal's designee. The provision also stated that a teacher should never hit a child on the head. These regulations were placed in the teacher's lounge and/or library of each school building in the district.

In the fall of 1983, the principal received a report from a mother that the teacher had slapped her ten-year-old son. The principal also received at least one other complaint from a parent who stated that the teacher had struck her son in the back with her hand. In March, 1984, the district superintendent sent a letter to the teacher alleging that she had violated the board's corporal punishment regulations by striking children without the presence of the principal and by hitting students about the head. It further stated that if any of the shortcomings still existed by May 1, 1984, the teacher's contract would be terminated. After receiving another similar letter from the superintendent the teacher requested a school board hearing on the matter. The board found that the teacher had persistently violated the corporal punishment regulations and her teaching contract was terminated as of October 30, 1984. The teacher appealed the decision to a Missouri circuit court, which ruled for the school board. She appealed this decision to the Missouri Court of Appeals.

The teacher argued that because the warning letter did not meet the requirements of Missouri law and because all the actions charged occurred before the warning letter was sent, she was denied the opportunity to avoid firing through the improvement of her performance. The court of appeals rejected this argument observing that a warning letter is not necessary in order to terminate a teaching contract on the grounds of wilful or persistent violation of regulations.

The teacher also argued that her contract should not be terminated since the principal promulgated corporal punishment policies that contradicted the board of education regulations posted in the teacher's lounge. The principal allegedly told his teachers that if any of them had a disciplinary problem with children to "bop them in the mouth." The principal had also prepared and distributed to the teachers a handbook that sanctioned spanking in front of another teacher which was in conflict with the board of education regulation. The court reasoned that even though the principal's statement and handbook were inconsistent with the board regulation, the teacher's testimony clearly indicated that she had not relied on the principal's statement because she denied hitting the children at all. The board's decision to terminate the teacher's contract was valid. The lower court decision was upheld. *Shepard v. South Harrison R-II School Dist.*, 718 S.W.2d 195 (Mo.App.1986).

The Orange County, Florida, school board operated the Woodlands School for learning disabled, physically handicapped and multi-handicapped children. The school was located on the campus of the Sunland State Hospital and was a tenant of the hospital. Due to the Woodland School's location on the grounds of the State Hospital, work-release prisoners sometimes were present at Woodlands. Hospital rules expressly prohibited any fraternization by employees with work-release prisoners.

Beginning in 1979, a woman was employed by the school board as a noncertified special education teacher's aide at Woodlands on a series of ten-month contracts. In March, 1982, her principal recommended that her contract for the following year not be renewed due to numerous minor problems: excessive absenteeism, reading magazines on the job, wearing inappropriate shoes, failure to require her guests to check in when visiting her, and inability to get along with other teacher's aides. The superintendent and the school board concurred. After the teacher's aide was informed of the decision not to renew, she was reprimanded for fraternizing on the job with work-release prisoners. She began harassing the teacher who reported her infractions of the no-fraternization rule, and on one occasion chased the teacher to her home in her car. The board immediately relieved the teacher's aide with pay for the remaining two weeks of her contract. She then brought suit alleging that a number of her constitutional rights had been violated, but a federal district court ruled against her on all counts.

First, the court rejected her due process claim because she had not achieved tenure; she had been employed under a fixed-term contract. Also, the board had not deprived her of her right to a good reputation because she had admitted to fraternizing with the prisoners while at work. Second, her First Amendment right to freedom of association did not include a right to engage in social contact with prisoners while on the job in violation of official written policy. The court's decision was made easier by the fact that the teacher's aide admitted that her contact with prisoners was purely social in nature, because political association is more vigorously protected by the First Amendment. In any event, she had failed to prove that the board's decision not to renew her teacher's aide contract was based upon her fraternization with prisoners. Finding no constitutional violation, the court dismissed the suit. *Brew v. School Bd. of Orange County*, 626 F.Supp. 709 (M.D.Fla. 1985).

After the New York City Board of Education caused the A.C.J. Transportation Corp., a private contractor providing private bus transportation to handicapped children on behalf of the board, to terminate the contract of a male bus driver following complaints of sexual misconduct, a federal court jury awarded him $15,000 in damages plus attorney's fees. The U.S. Court of Appeals, Second Circuit, has reversed the damage award and sent the case back to the district court with instructions to award only nominal damages to the bus driver.

The case arose when the Board of Education's Bureau of Pupil Transportation began to receive anonymous phone calls that a school bus driver for handicapped students had fondled himself while on the job. The bureau told A.C.J. to investigate, and A.C.J. soon reported to the bureau that one of its bus attendants reported that the bus driver had exposed himself on the bus; the bureau promptly told A.C.J. not to allow the driver to drive on any Board of Education routes "until a hearing could be held." The next day A.C.J. sent the bureau additional reports by several female bus attendants that the driver had made sexual advances toward them, that he had brought women "who looked very much like prostitutes" on the bus, and that he had once asked a bus attendant to buy marijuana for him.

The bureau decided to conduct a hearing. It sent a notice of hearing to A.C.J. and requested that a copy be given to the bus driver. However, A.C.J. failed to do so. All the bus driver received was a handwritten note from his A.C.J. supervisor to appear at the bureau office on April 12, 1982. He appeared at the hearing with a union representative, and both were shown the accusatory letters from the bus attendants. Bureau officials allowed the bus driver to present letters attesting to his good character. The next day the bus driver was informed that due to his lack of good moral character he was forever barred from Board of Education routes. A.C.J. fired him, an action later upheld by an arbitrator.

The bus driver brought suit in federal district court alleging that because he had never received adequate or fair notice of the bureau hearing, he had been denied his federal due process rights. The district court ruled that the bus driver had been entitled to due process from the bureau before it caused A.C.J. to fire him. Finding that the unintentionally defective hearing notice given by the bureau to the bus driver did not meet due process requirements, the district court jury awarded him $15,000 in compensatory damages for the lost salary plus attorney's fees. The New York City Board of Education appealed.

The U.S. Court of Appeals upheld the determination that the bus driver had been deprived of due process, but reversed the award of damages. The district court had acted improperly when it failed to consider that even if the bureau had afforded due process to the handicapped student bus driver, he probably would have been fired anyway. Thus, the compensation for lost salary may have been erroneous. The court of appeals remanded the case for further proceedings with instructions that if the district court concluded that the bus driver would have been fired even if a proper hearing notice had been given to him, the court could award him nominal damages only. *Stein v. Bd. of Educ. of City of New York*, 792 F.2d 13 (2d Cir.1986).

In an Arkansas case, the state's supreme court refused to set aside a tenured special education teacher's dismissal, where her attorney did not adequately prove the case in the lower court. Here a special education teacher had been employed in a school district for thirteen years. She had never received an unsatisfactory evaluation and in the past had been used as a model for new teachers. However, soon after a new principal arrived at her school he informed her that her performance was inadequate. He recommended dismissal, and her employment was terminated by the school board shortly thereafter. The teacher sued in county court seeking reinstatement to her position on the ground that her dismissal had been politically motivated. Evidence was presented that the teacher's husband had been a former school employee and had twice engaged in disputes with the superintendent. Also, her husband had twice (unsuccessfully) run for the school board, and a board member had once stated that he wanted to "get a shot" at the teacher. The county court, however, found that the school board had acted out of dissatisfaction with the special education teacher's classroom performance, and she appealed.

The Arkansas Supreme Court upheld the county court. Although admitting that the teacher's attorney had presented strong evidence of political reasons for her dismissal, he had not sufficiently explored during trial the bases for her principal's unsatisfactory evaluations. Without proof that the principal had possessed political motives, the school board was entitled to rely upon his recommendation of dismissal. The Supreme Court declined to intervene. *Kirtley v. Dardanelle Pub. Schools*, 702 S.W.2d 25 (Ark.1986).

A Pennsylvania school board's decision to dismiss a school psychologist because of incompetency has been upheld by the Commonwealth Court of

Pennsylvania. The psychologist argued that her dismissal should have been based on provisions contained in the Public School Code which states that, in evaluating school personnel, due consideration shall be given to "personality, preparation, technique and pupil reaction." She maintained that her dismissal did not relate to these concerns. The court, in rejecting that argument, stated that the fact that consideration should be given to the qualities mentioned in the statute does not mean that other matters, such as lack of judgment or simple ability, may not also be considered. The school board's dismissal order was affirmed. *Grant v. Bd. of School Directors of the Centennial School Dist.*, 471 A.2d 1292 (Pa.Cmwlth.1984).

A Lutheran school for the deaf in New York hired a female art teacher in March, 1979. She possessed permanent certification as an art teacher, but was not certified as a teacher for the deaf as required by state law. At the time she was hired, she was told that in order to waive the certification requirement she would have to pursue courses toward deaf education certification. At the close of the 1980-81 academic year, however, the teacher had taken only two courses toward certification. In November, 1981, she left to have a baby and began her child-rearing leave in January, 1982. In March, 1982, school officials wrote to the woman and again informed her that in order to waive certification she must pursue at least six semester hours of study per year. She then met with the school superintendent, assuring him that she would continue to work toward certification. She was also granted an additional year of child-rearing leave.

In March, 1983, the superintendent asked the woman if she intended to return to her position in the fall. He refused to extend her child-rearing leave but told her that if she became pregnant again she would have "no trouble" in receiving additional pregnancy leave. At this time the woman told the superintendent that she had taken only three semester hours of courses toward certification in the past year. One month later she told the principal that she was pregnant. This prompted him to offer her a woodworking teacher position instead of art because when she would be forced to leave again in the fall a woodworking teacher's sudden absence would be less disruptive to the learning process. The woman refused this offer and one month later she was dismissed.

She sued in U.S. district court, alleging unlawful discrimination due to pregnancy. The court disagreed with her claims, holding that the school had proven that the decision to terminate her employment was based upon her lack of deaf education certification. It was entirely proper for school officials to show concern for the continuity and quality of instruction at the school in the face of the woman's lack of certification and lengthy child-rearing leaves. The court noted that while pregnancy leaves are protected by the Civil Rights Act, child-rearing leaves are not. Because no unlawful discrimination was proven, the court dismissed the woman's complaint. *Record v. Mill Neck Manor Lutheran School for the Deaf*, 611 F.Supp. 905 (E.D.N.Y.1985).

In a Maryland case, reinstatement was ordered for a teacher who was also a Catholic priest. The teacher, who had taught in Japan for over twenty years, took employment teaching groundskeeping and home maintenance to severely retarded males of secondary school age at a center for the mentally handicapped. His teaching objective was to train students to enter the employment market as handymen or custodial workers. The teaching program consisted of working with a small group of students in the classroom for several days a week, and at various outdoor worksites on the remaining school days.

One day, without authorization, the teacher left four of his six students under a teaching aide's supervision at a recreational center, where they were to clean the building and the adjacent grounds. He took the two remaining students with him to work on other groundskeeping projects. When it began to snow the teacher took the boys to a work shed located behind his home and directed them to work on a project at this site. One of the boys became disruptive and began throwing glass bottles and mishandling the saw he was using. The teacher ordered him to stop his disruptive behavior but to no avail. At this point, the teacher decided that the boy needed to be "timed out," a behavior modification technique used by some special education teachers whereby a misbehaving student is isolated and kept still, in order to calm him and to cause him to reflect on his misbehavior. The teacher ordered the boy to leave the shed and kneel outside on two wooden blocks under a plastic-covered picnic table for an extended period in below-freezing snowy weather. Throughout the incident, the other boy remained inside the shed shivering and shaking from the cold. A neighbor who witnessed the episode called the police, who found the boy sobbing and crying.

The County Board of Education terminated the teacher's employment and the teacher appealed to the State Board of Education, which modified the disciplinary sanction from dismissal to suspension. The County Board appealed and the case finally reached the Court of Appeals of Maryland, which held that the dismissal was not warranted and that the State Board did not exceed its statutory power in imposing a lengthy suspension instead of dismissal. The court took note of the teacher's excellent teaching record and stated that the teacher's action, although improper, was motivated by and intended to modify the behavior of a student whom he could not reach by verbal direction. *Bd. of Educ. of Prince George's County v. Waeldner*, 470 A.2d 332 (Md.1984).

B. Racial, Sexual, and Handicap Discrimination

Under Title VII of the Civil Rights Act of 1964 (42 U.S.C. § 2000e *et seq.*), a plaintiff has the initial burden to establish that he or she was not hired or promoted due to racial or sexual discrimination by the employer. The plaintiff must show that he or she 1) is a member of a protected minority class; 2) applied and was qualified for the position sought; 3) was not hired or promoted; and 4) that a non-minority was hired or promoted to the position the plaintiff was seeking. Once the plaintiff makes this initial showing, the burden shifts to the employer to articulate a legitimate, nondiscriminatory reason for not hiring the plaintiff. If the employer is able to do so, then the courts will rule in favor of the employer.

Discrimination on the basis of handicap by employers receiving federal financial assistance is prohibited by § 504 of the Rehabilitation Act. Such employers must "reasonably accommodate" handicapped individuals who are "otherwise qualified" for employment.

The U.S. Supreme Court ruled that tuberculosis is a handicap under § 504 of the Rehabilitation Act. Federal law defines a handicapped individual as "any person who (i) has a physical or mental impairment which substantially limits one or more of such person's major life activities, (ii) has a record of such impairment or (iii) is regarded as having such an impairment." It defines "physical impairment" as disorders affecting, among other things, the respiratory system and defines "major life activities" as "functions such as caring for one's self . . . and working."

The case involved a Florida elementary school teacher who was discharged because of the continued recurrence of tuberculosis. The teacher sued the school board under § 504 but a U.S. district court dismissed her claims. However, the U.S. Court of Appeals, Eleventh Circuit, reversed the district court's decision and held that persons with contagious diseases fall within § 504's coverage. The school board appealed to the U.S. Supreme Court.

The Supreme Court ruled that tuberculosis was a handicap under § 504 because it affected the respiratory system and affected her ability to work. The school board contended that in defining a handicapped individual under § 504, the contagious effects of a disease can be distinguished from the disease's physical effects. However, the Court reasoned that the teacher's contagion and her physical impairment both resulted from the same condition: tuberculosis. It would be unfair to allow an employer to distinguish between a disease's potential effect on others and its effect on the afflicted employee in order to justify discriminatory treatment. Allowing discrimination based on the contagious effects of a physical impairment would be inconsistent with the underlying purpose of § 504. That purpose is to ensure that handicapped persons are not denied jobs because of prejudice or ignorance. It noted that society's myths and fears about disability and disease are as handicapping as the physical limitations that result from physical impairment, and concluded that contagion cannot remove a person from § 504 coverage. The Supreme Court remanded the case to the district court to determine whether the teacher was "otherwise qualified" for her job and whether the school board could reasonably accommodate her as an employee. *School Bd. of Nassau County v. Arline*, 107 S.Ct. 1123 (1987). (Reprinted in Appendix C.)

The U.S. Court of Appeals, Ninth Circuit, applied *Arline* in a recent case. A teacher of hearing-impaired children was relegated to an administrative position when the school district discovered that he had AIDS. The teacher sued the school board asserting that it had violated his rights under the Rehabilitation Act of 1973 by removing him from the classroom. The teacher's request for a preliminary injunction which would have allowed him to teach until the court could hold a trial and issue a ruling was denied by a U.S. district court. The U.S. Court of Appeals, Ninth Circuit, reversed and issued the preliminary injunction. The court of appeals later issued a decision which sets out the reasons for the issuance of the preliminary injunction.

The court noted that to acquire the preliminary injunction the teacher had to demonstrate a combination of probable success at trial and a possibility of irreparable injury. Under the Rehabilitation Act the teacher could not be dismissed because of his handicapping condition (AIDS) if he was otherwise qualified to teach. The court then applied a test devised by the U.S. Supreme Court in *Arline*. The test provided that "[a] person who poses a significant risk of communicating an infectious disease to others in the workplace will not be otherwise qualified for his or her job if reasonable accommodations will not eliminate that risk." The court then pointed out the district court's finding that transmission of AIDS was unlikely to occur in the classroom. The court held that the teacher was otherwise qualified for his position because his presence in the classroom would not pose "a significant risk of communicating an infectious disease to others." This finding meant that the teacher would probably succeed at trial.

The court then noted that although the teacher's salary was not reduced when he was transferred to the administrative position, the transfer removed him from a job for which he had developed special skills and from which he derived "tremendous personal satisfaction and joy." The administrative position, on the other hand, involved no student contact and did not utilize the teacher's skills, training or experience. The court also observed that the teacher's ability to work would surely be affected in time by AIDS which has proved fatal in all reported cases. The court concluded that any delay in returning the teacher to the classroom caused an irretrievable loss of the teacher's productive time. This established the possibility of irreparable injury if the preliminary injunction was not awarded.

Because the teacher had shown 1) that he would probably succeed at trial, and 2) that the denial of a preliminary injunction in his favor could cause him irreparable injury the court awarded the preliminary injunction. The teacher was returned to the classroom. *Chalk v. U.S. Dist. Court*, 840 F.2d 701 (9th Cir.1988).

The Pulaski County, Arkansas, Special School District decided to have a "head teacher" serve as a liaison to represent the needs of special education students. Two teachers from the special education staff applied for the position: a black male and a white female. When the white female was awarded the head teacher position after being recommended by a two-person selection committee, the black male sued the school district in a U.S. district court claiming racial discrimination. After the district court ruled for the school district the man appealed to the U.S. Court of Appeals, Eighth Circuit.

The court of appeals observed that the district court had determined that the school district selected the white female teacher for legitimate, nondiscriminatory reasons. The school district relied on her prior experiences as a head teacher, the higher evaluations of her overall teaching skills, her flexibility and superior grasp of the fundamentals of developing individualized educational plans. The appellate court observed that the district court's choice to believe an employer's account of its motivations is a factual finding which may be overturned on appeal only if that decision was "clearly erroneous." The court was convinced that the district court carefully considered all the testimony and exhibits and that its findings had ample support in the trial court record. In ruling that the district court's decision was not clearly erroneous the court of appeals stated that "[a] factfinder's choice between two permissible views of the evidence cannot be clearly erroneous."

The man also argued that the district court was wrong in ruling that the ultimate burden of proving intentional discrimination remained with him. He said that in light of the school district's past history of racial discrimination, the district court should have shifted the burden to the district to prove by clear and convincing evidence that the reasons were nondiscriminatory for its selection of the white female. The court of appeals refused to apply the higher standard.

A further argument presented by the man was that the district court mistakenly admitted into evidence teacher evaluations of the two teachers made *after* the selection of the white female as head teacher. The court of appeals ruled, however, that even if it was a mistake to admit the postdecision evaluations into evidence, the district court did not consider them in making its findings. Instead, it relied on the testimony of the selection committee members concerning the areas in which they felt the white female was superior. The decision of the district court denying the man's racial discrimination claim was upheld. *Nelson v. Pulaski County Special School Dist.*, 803 F.2d 961 (8th Cir.1986).

An Alabama sex and race discrimination case concluded with a federal judge's dismissal of the case. The plaintiff, a black female teacher at a school for handicapped children, applied for the position of principal. The selection committee interviewed a total of twenty individuals for the principal position, including sixteen white males, one black female, one oriental female and two white females. The committee selected a white male for the job, citing his superior academic credentials, his experience in securing government grants, his extensive managerial experience and his experience with multi-handicapped children. The black female applicant brought suit in U.S. district court under Title VII of the Civil Rights Act, claiming sex and race discrimination. The court disagreed with her contentions. Although the selection committee was dominated by white males, the two black females on the committee had ranked the white male applicant higher than the plaintiff. The evidence established that he was clearly better qualified for the position than the plaintiff. The court also took notice of evidence that the plaintiff's attitudes were "too rigid." This put her at a disadvantage in seeking promotion to a position where she would be required to deal continuously with handicapped children and "their justifiably distressed parents." The case was dismissed due to the lack of evidence of any discrimination in the principal selection process. *Love v. Alabama Institute for the Deaf and Blind*, 613 F.Supp. 436 (N.D.Ala.1984).

A black woman who was employed by a Missouri school board as an assistant special education teacher sued the board in U.S. district court alleging that the board had failed to promote her to the position of teacher because of her race. The court ruled in favor of the school board holding that the board had articulated legitimate, nondiscriminatory reasons for not hiring the woman as a full teacher. Her superiors, including one other black woman, had conducted periodic evaluations of her abilities and had interviewed her. The evaluations revealed that she was unable to speak clearly and correctly and that her writing style was grammatically incorrect. The court agreed that these alone were grave deficiencies in an applicant for the position of special education teacher. Furthermore, the woman's interviews revealed that she had never given any diagnostic tests while she was employed as an assistant teacher, and she could not tell the interviewers how any of these tests were used. The court held that these deficiencies constituted sufficient grounds for the school board to refuse to promote her to the position of teacher. Judgment was rendered for the school board in all respects. *Love v. Special School Dist. of St. Louis County*, 606 F.Supp. 1320 (E.D.Mo.1985).

Since 1975, a Louisiana school board had employed a woman as special education supervisor. In 1982, after becoming dissatisfied with her performance, the board obtained an opinion from the Louisiana Attorney General which stated that because the supervisor was not certified for the position, she was not tenured under the state's tenure laws. The board then notified her that her contract would not be renewed for the following year. No dismissal hearing was held. She sued the board in state court, contending that she was tenured, and the court ordered that the board hold a dismissal hearing. When tis was done the board once again voted to dismiss, but failed to follow proper procedures. Once again the supervisor successfully sued the board, winning reinstatement and back pay. She then commenced the present lawsuit in federal court, claiming that her federal civil rights had been violated by the board's failure to adhere to state notice and hearing requirements. In essence, she claimed that this failure had deprived her of her federal due process rights.

The U.S. Court of Appeals, Fifth Circuit, disagreed with her claims. The fact that the state courts had forced the board to hold a dismissal hearing completely satisfied all federal due process requirements. Under the U.S. Constitution, due process requires only compliance with minimal notice and hearing requirements; the fact that state law provided greater protection was irrelevant. The court stated: "There is not a violation of due process every time a . . . government entity violates its own rules. Such action may constitute a breach of contract or violation of state law, but unless the conduct trespasses on federal constitutional safeguards, there is no constitutional deprivation." The dismissal of the special education supervisor's federal claims was thus affirmed. *Franceski v. Plaquemines Parish School Bd.*, 772 F.2d 197 (5th Cir.1985).

An applicant for a special education teaching position in Iowa sued a local education agency under the federal Rehabilitation Act and Iowa law alleging that the agency refused to hire him due to his physical disability. The teacher, a resident of Vermont, suffered from several severe handicaps but was able to walk without assistance and to lift children and drive. The teacher applied to the Iowa agency for a job, and was scheduled for an interview in Iowa at his own expense, with possible reimbursement if he were hired.

After arranging the interview, the teacher became concerned that he had not disclosed his handicaps. Because of limited financial resources, he did not wish to fly to Iowa only to be rejected because of his handicaps. He called the Iowa school, explained his handicaps and was told that the job involved transporting children which, in turn, required a bus driver's permit that the teacher probably could not get because of his handicaps. The agency suggested a trip to Iowa would probably be futile.

The teacher then sued in a U.S. district court, which found in his favor. The test of proof for a discrimination claim under the Rehabilitation Act is: 1) that the plaintiff is a handicapped individual under the terms of the Act; 2) that the plaintiff is otherwise qualified to participate in the program or activity at issue; 3) that the plaintiff was excluded from the program or activity solely by reason of her or his handicap; and 4) that the program or activity receives federal financial assistance.

Here, there was no dispute that the plaintiff was a handicapped individual within the meaning of the Rehabilitation Act. The court also had little difficulty in finding that the plaintiff was otherwise qualified for the position, because of his superior credentials. The court also found that the plaintiff had satisfied the third and fourth prongs of the test, in that the defendant agency was a recipient of federal financial assistance, including funds received pursuant to the EAHCA and that, with a minimum of accommodation, the school district could have arranged an alternative situation whereby the teacher would not have had to transport children. The court awarded the teacher $1,000 damages for mental anguish, and $5,150 for loss of earnings. *Fitzgerald v. Green Valley Educ. Agency*, 589 F.Supp. 1130 (S.D.Iowa 1984).

C. Right to Privacy

Special education teachers, like most other government employees, possess a right to privacy guaranteed by the U.S. Constitution. The government, as an employer, may not infringe upon this right absent a compelling reason.

A U.S. district court in Washington, D.C., declared that school bus attendants may not be subjected to mandatory urine testing unless there is probable cause to suspect that the attendant has engaged in drug use. In this case, a school bus attendant for handicapped children was forced to give a urine sample as part of a program instituted by the Washington school district to ferret out drug use by its transportation employees. When the bus attendant's urine tested positive, her employment was terminated. She sued in U.S. district court, contending that the school district's urinalysis program violated her Fourth Amendment rights.

The court first ruled that the test results were flawed. Although the manufacturers of the urinalysis test used, the EMIT Cannabinoid Assay Test, recommended that the test results be verified through an alternate testing method, the school district had not obtained such verification. After the bus attendant's first urinalysis test, effected by computer, showed that THC metabolites (indicative of marijuana use) were present in her urine, the school district ran the same test manually to verify that result. No alternative test was performed. Having disregarded the instructions of the manufacturers of the EMIT test, the school district could not use the results as a ground for termination.

Next, the court held that urinalysis testing could not be required without probable cause to suspect the bus attendant of drug use. Unlike school bus drivers or mechanics, who expect that their privacy rights will be limited by public safety considerations, school bus attendants legitimately expect a zone of personal privacy. Urine testing imposes upon this expectation of privacy. Therefore, the court stated, urine testing of school bus attendants is a "search" under the Fourth Amendment to the U.S. Constitution and requires probable cause. Since the school district had no probable cause to suspect that the bus attendant had ever used drugs, the board's decision to terminate her employment was reversed. Full back pay and reinstatement were ordered. *Jones v. McKenzie*, 628 F.Supp. 1500 (D.D.C.1986).

A Massachusetts public school teacher was suspended for two days and involuntarily transferred from her teaching position after being found guilty of insubordination and conduct unbecoming a teacher. The teacher had disagreed with her principal regarding the treatment of a handicapped boy. She wrote a case study paper for a night class that she was taking, which described the boy's situation and which was highly critical of the principal. Shortly thereafter, at a meeting held to evaluate the boy's progress, the teacher gave her paper to the special education supervisor at her school. She did not tell him that her case study paper contained confidential material. The supervisor never read her paper and returned it to the teacher the same day.

On the following day the principal requested that the teacher turn over a copy of the paper, claiming that it was part of the boy's official file which the principal had a duty to examine. The teacher refused and the principal informed her that she was being insubordinate. Two weeks later she turned over a copy of the paper, but the principal left the question of disciplinary action open until a later date. Several months later, on Parent's Night, the teacher posted copies of her correspondence with the principal concerning the allegedly insubordinate refusal to immediately turn over her case study paper. A parent later complained to school officials regarding the teacher's public display of this correspondence. The teacher was then suspended for two days and involuntarily transferred from her teaching post as a result of her insubordination in refusing to promptly furnish the principal with a copy of her paper, and for engaging in conduct unbecoming a teacher by posting the letters on Parents' Night.

Concluding that her constitutional rights had been violated, the teacher sued her school district in U.S. district court. The court held in favor of the school district and the U.S. Court of Appeals, First Circuit, affirmed. The appeals court held that the teacher had no Fourth Amendment privacy interest in her paper because she had given it to the special education supervisor. Therefore, when the principal demanded the paper she could not assert her right to privacy. The court further held that her act of posting the principal's letters to her concerning the paper were unprotected as well since the matter was primarily an employment dispute, and not a matter of public interest. The disciplinary sanctions against the teacher were, therefore, held not to violate the teacher's constitutional rights. *Alinovi v. Worcester School Comm.*, 777 F.2d 776 (1st Cir.1985).

D. Collective Bargaining

After a collective bargaining agreement between a teachers' union and a school district expired, a series of selective teacher strikes was called by the union. The school district asked for a preliminary injunction prohibiting further strikes which was granted by a Pennsylvania common pleas court. The union appealed to the Commonwealth Court of Pennsylvania, which ruled that the common pleas court was wrong in holding that the strike activity posed a threat to the health, safety or welfare of the public. The school district had argued that the strike infringed upon the right to an education guaranteed to all handicapped children under the EAHCA. Although the selective strikes did not violate the rights of handicapped students in this case, the commonwealth court conceded that the same facts could become aggravated by "some unexpected circumstances or [if] continued for such a period of time" so as to violate the rights of handicapped students. Such circumstances, however, were not yet present, and the lower court decision favoring the school district was reversed. *Wilkes-Barre Area Educ. Ass'n v. Wilkes-Barre Area School Dist.*, 523 A.2d 1183 (Pa.Cmwlth.1987).

In 1984, five Indiana school corporations entered into an agreement creating the Grant County Special Education Cooperative. The agreement was made for the express purpose of providing administration services and programs for handicapped children. The agreement derived its authority from state law, which provides for joint programs among school corporations. The Marion Community School Corp. was identified in the agreement as the administrative and fiscal agent of the cooperative. Special education teachers were employed by the individual school corporations in which they teach with the only joint employee of the cooperative being the director of special education. A local teachers' union sued the cooperative in an Indiana superior court alleging that the cooperative agreement was invalid because it failed to comply with state law. When the superior court ruled for the cooperative, the teachers' union appealed to the Indiana Court of Appeals.

The Indiana law cited by the teachers' union (I.C. § 20-5-11-1(c)) stated that a "'[j]oint program' shall be the joint employment of personnel, . . . by two or more school corporations, for a particular program or purpose. Such joint action shall include, but not be limited to, the joint investment of money . . . and special education." The teachers' union contended that the use of "shall" in the agreement required the cooperative to employ special education teachers. The appellate court disagreed, noting that although "shall" is used in the code, it did not interpret this as mandating the cooperative's employment of special education teachers. It ruled that the cooperative could choose not to employ special education teachers as a legitimate option within the code. The court stated that if it read "shall" as mandating all of the activities listed in the statute, a cooperative would be required to jointly employ personnel and purchase supplies and equipment. This clearly was not the legislative intent. The court reasoned that the cooperative was within state law when it chose to hire only one person, the director of special education, to administer the participating schools' special education program.

The court further stated that the teachers' union was correct in asserting that the school corporations cannot violate the continuing and indefinite contract rights of teachers by reorganizing the manner in which they provide educational services. However, there was no allegation by the union that any of the teachers' rights were violated by the joint program. The trial court was not wrong in concluding that the cooperative was entitled to a favorable judgment as a matter of law. The lower court decision was affirmed. *Marion Teachers Ass'n v. Grant County Special Educ. Coop.*, 500 N.E.2d 229 (Ind.App.1st Dist.1986).

In 1978, the Leonard Kirtz Mahoning County School for the Retarded hired a woman as a special education teacher. She was assigned to Developmental Classroom I, which consisted of students who were the least fortunate in terms of educational potential. After three years she discovered that three teachers for students with the most potential were leaving the school. She made a request to both the superintendent and the principal that she be transferred to one of the vacant positions. However, the county board denied her request and immediately transferred two other teachers, neither of whom had requested reassignment, and hired one new teacher, in order to fill the three vacancies.

The Ohio Supreme Court rebuked the county board for its blatant disregard of its own collective bargaining agreement. Reversing an errant lower court, the Supreme Court reinstated an arbitrator's ruling that because the agreement required the county board to respect a teacher's transfer requests, the board was bound to transfer her. Held the court: "The board argues, and the court of appeals decided, that collective bargaining agreements are not as binding upon public employers as they are upon private employers. It is time to put an end to that notion and categorically reject the argument. Today's decision gives notices that negotiated collective bargaining agreements are just as binding upon public employers as they are upon private employers." The county board was ordered to honor its contractual obligation to the teacher. *Mahoning County Bd. of Mental Retardation and Developmental Disabilities v. Mahoning County TMR Educ. Ass'n*, 488 N.E.2d 872 (Ohio 1986).

The Supreme Judicial Court of Massachusetts vacated a preliminary injunction entered by a three-judge panel of the Superior Court, which had enjoined a strike by bus drivers for special needs children. The case arose when several bus companies, with whom the Boston School Committee had contracted, and their bus drivers, failed to negotiate a mutually acceptable collective bargaining agreement. The bus drivers, who are affiliated with the AFL-CIO, declined to work without a contract. Parents of handicapped children were left to make their own arrangements for their children's transportation to and from school. As a result, the parents commenced a class action suit and asked the Superior Court for an injunction ordering the striking school bus drivers back to work, which was granted. On appeal by the school bus drivers' union, the Supreme Judicial Court reversed and held that under Massachusetts law [M.G.L.A. ch. 150E, sec. 9A(b)] the parents could not sue to enjoin the strike because the bus drivers, although ostensibly employed by private bus companies, were public employees. As such, only the public employer could petition the court to enjoin the strike. The court also noted that although state law clearly outlaws any strike by public employees, it just as clearly forbids anyone but the relevant public employer from seeking a back-to-work order. The Superior Court's injunction was therefore vacated. *Allen v. School Comm. of Boston*, 487 N.E.2d 529 (Mass.1986).

The Board of Trustees of the Florida School for the Deaf and the Blind entered into a three-year collective bargaining agreement with its teachers' union, effective July 1, 1983, to June 30, 1986. The agreement contained annual reopeners on salary, insurance benefits and any other two articles chosen by each. Less than one year after the contract had been in effect, the Board of Trustees and the teachers' union reached an impasse over the number of hours teachers were to work each day. A special master was consulted in an attempt to work out a solution, but the board rejected his report. Under Florida law, the board was required to submit the dispute to its legislative body for resolution [F.S.A. sec. 447.403(4)]. The term "legislative body" is defined as the state legislature, any county board of commissioners, any district school board, or the governing body of any municipality. The term also includes any body having authority to make appropriations of public funds [447.203(10)]. The Board of Trustees informed the teachers' union that in its opinion the board itself was a legislative body. The board claimed that since it transferred monies between categories of appropriations, it was a body that appropriates public funds. Therefore the Board of Trustees unilaterally changed the working hours of its special education teachers from seven to seven and one-half hours per day.

The teachers' union filed a complaint with the Public Employees' Relations Commission and received a ruling that the board had committed an unfair labor practice by unilaterally increasing the working hours of its special education teachers. On appeal, this ruling was affirmed. The court stated that just because the Board of Trustees transferred monies into different categories did not mean it was a legislative body. The board only acted pursuant to statutory authority; it was the legislature itself which did the actual appropriating. Since it was not a "legislative body," the Board of Trustees was without authority to unilaterally modify the collective bargaining agreement with the special education teachers' union. The court upheld the Commission's award of penalties and attorney's fees against the board. *Florida School for the Deaf and the Blind v. Florida School for the Deaf and the Blind, Teachers United, FTP-NEA*, 483 So.2d 58 (Fla.App.1st Dist.1986).

E. Tenure, Seniority, Salary and Benefits

When an Arkansas school district delayed and hindered the implementation of a special education program, the principal of a school and several teachers discussed these problems with the administrator of the program, then with school district administrators and the school board. When these efforts proved fruitless, the principal and teachers sent a letter to the state department of education. The letter enumerated instances of failure to follow established procedures relating to the education of handicapped students. The department of education conducted an investigation which resulted in a conclusion that the school district had not followed proper procedures in the placement of handicapped students.

Afterward, several of the teachers' contracts were not renewed and the principal and one teacher resigned under pressure by the school district. The principal and teachers sued the school district and various administrators seeking money damages for the retaliation they suffered in response to the letter. They claimed the retaliation was a violation of their First Amendment right of free speech on a matter of public concern in their community. When a U.S. district court ruled in favor of the principal and teachers, the school district and administrators appealed.

The U.S. Court of Appeals, Eighth Circuit, determined that the letter concerned the quality of education in the community and the school district's observance of federal policy as prescribed by Congress for the welfare of handicapped children. The letter therefore involved a matter of public concern and was protected by the First Amendment. The lower court's ruling was upheld. *Southside Pub. Schools v. Hill*, 827 F.2d 270 (8th Cir.1987).

In 1970, a woman began teaching physical education at the Regional Day School for hearing impaired children in Millburn, New Jersey. The teacher's employment was terminated along with that of four other teachers in July, 1982, when the state's Commissioner of Education determined that cutbacks were required in the school's operating budget. The teacher challenged the termination before the State Board of Education. The board affirmed the commissioner's decision and the teacher appealed to the New Jersey Superior Court, Appellate Division.

She argued that her tenure and seniority rights were not limited to the institution in which she was employed. She also contended that her dismissal was arbitrary and capricious. New Jersey state law provides that reducing the number of teachers is valid when student population naturally declines. The court ruled that the termination decision was an economic decision based upon a real reduction in students at Millburn and was neither arbitrary nor capricious. It also held that the law did not specify whether tenure rights attained can apply to more than one institution because the legislature intended that each educational institution be autonomous in its hiring practices. The court also observed that when she refused a teaching position at another school shortly after her dismissal, she had voluntarily relinquished her tenure and reemployment rights. The commissioner's decision against the teacher was upheld by the court. *O'Toole v. Forestal*, 511 A.2d 1236 (N.J. Super.A.D.1986).

A learning disabilities consultant was hired in March, 1980 by the Trenton, New Jersey, Board of Education. At the time of hiring he was placed at step eleven of the learning consultants' salary guide. Beginning in the fall of 1980, and for each academic year thereafter, the consultant was moved up one step on the salary guide. By 1983 he was at step 15, was being paid an annual salary of $27,227 and was scheduled for an increase to $28,569.

The school board and the teacher's association, however, had negotiated an agreement before the learning disabilities consultant was hired which provided that any employee hired after February 1 of any year would remain at his or her step on the salary guide during the following academic year. The school district, which had erroneously advanced the consultant on the salary guide in the fall of 1980 even though he had been hired after February 1, did not realize its error for three years; it then reduced the teacher to step fourteen and made a reduction in his salary from $28,569 to $27,751 a year. When the consultant received his first reduced check he contacted the personnel office immediately. His check was not corrected. On January 30, 1984, he informed the Board of Education that he had retained an attorney and requested back pay and reinstatement to his proper salary level. On February 8, 1984, the board sent him a letter refusing his request.

The consultant filed a complaint with the New Jersey Commissioner of Education. The case was heard by an administrative law judge (ALJ), who ruled that the complaint had not been filed within the required ninety days of the date the consultant first received notice of his salary reduction. The ALJ held that notice of the salary reduction had been accomplished by the consultant's receipt of his paycheck. The State Board of Education affirmed the ALJ's decision, and the consultant appealed to the New Jersey Superior Court, Appellate Division.

The court found that under the New Jersey Teacher Tenure Act the consultant had a vested right in his salary. Therefore, it held that the unilateral decision by the school district to reduce his salary violated his rights under the Act. It said that the fact that the consultant's paycheck was less than what he expected did not constitute proper notice that his salary was being reduced. It was not until the school board's letter of February 8, 1984, denying his requests for back pay and reinstatement to his proper salary that he was put on notice that a "dispute" existed. The court remanded the case to the Commissioner of Education for resolution of the dispute on the merits. *Stockton v. Bd. of Educ. of City of Trenton*, 509 A.2d 264 (N.J.Super. A.D.1986).

In the following case, state tenure laws were deemed inapplicable to special education teachers. Here an eighteen-year veteran at the Arizona State School for the Deaf and the Blind (ASDB) was suspended, with pay, pending investigation of reports of his actions with regard to certain students. Ten days later he was dismissed from employment at the school, effective immediately without further pay. He commenced a special legal action in superior court to contest his dismissal, arguing that the ASDB had not followed its own policies concerning suspension and dismissal from employment and that he had been denied due process of law. He contended that he should have been paid full salary until such time as a dismissal hearing was held. The superior court ruled in favor of the ASDB, and the teacher appealed to the Arizona Court of Appeals.

In upholding the lower court's decision, the Court of Appeals first disposed of the teacher's contention that the school had failed to follow proper procedures. An Arizona statute provided that any teacher at the ASDB may be discharged for cause. Under this statute, held the court, the superintendent of the ASDB had no choice but to discontinue the dismissed teacher's salary. If the teacher had been employed by a public school district, then the tenure statutes would apply, but this was not the case. Under the statutes regulating the ASDB, the teacher could not be paid any salary after dismissal even if the school had purported to adopt a policy to the contrary, because school policies cannot supersede state law.

The appellate court also rejected the teacher's argument that by dismissing him and then discontinuing his salary prior to a termination hearing, the school had deprived him of due process of law. The court stated that due process would be satisfied by a post-termination hearing. If the hearing resulted in a determination that the teacher had been improperly dismissed, then full back pay could be awarded. If on the other hand after the hearing an opposite conclusion was reached, the teacher would not be entitled to receive any pay. Stated the court: "Why should public funds be paid to an employee who has been discharged for cause and is no longer working, and who can recover the lost wages if vindicated? . . . Not only is wage continuation not mandated by due process, it might constitute wasteful expenditure of public funds." The superior court's rejection of the teacher's claims was thus upheld. *Bower v. Arizona State School for the Deaf and the Blind*, 704 P.2d 809 (Ariz.App.1984).

Special education employees in New York challenged the infringement of their seniority rights in the following two cases. In the first, two tenured teachers employed by the New York Board of Cooperative Educational Services (BOCES) in the special education area brought suit alleging that after two school districts for which BOCES provided special education services established their own special education programs, no longer utilizing the BOCES program, BOCES improperly dismissed them. The teachers were hired as of the date of their dismissal by the respective school districts as teachers in their programs. The teachers sought to have themselves reinstated to their former positions as tenured BOCES teachers. The court held that because BOCES retained teachers in the special education tenure area having less seniority that the dismissed teachers, the abolition of the teachers' positions may have violated teacher tenure law. The New York Supreme Court, Appellate Division, reversed a lower court ruling dismissing the teachers' complaint and remanded the case to the lower court, which was to reinstate the teachers if it found that teachers with less seniority than the dismissed teachers were retained by BOCES, in violation of New York tenure law. BOCES would then be directed to follow an appropriate procedure for correctly determining the teachers with less seniority to be made eligible for hiring by the school districts which had established their own special education program. *Koch v. Putnam-Northern Westchester Bd. of Coop. Educ. Serv.*, 470 N.Y.S.2d 651 (A.D.2d Dept.1984).

In a later case, a dispute arose after a school district and four other component districts took over part of a learning achievement program which had formerly been operated by BOCES. Two special education teachers who had been employed by BOCES sought to fill the new positions created but their applications were rejected. They brought suit against the school district claiming that they had a right, at their option, to claim such positions under a statute defining teachers' rights as a result of a school district taking over a program formerly operated by BOCES. The New York Supreme Court, Appellate Division, disagreed, saying that absent a showing that the teachers had been "excessed," the school district was not required by statute to hire them. *Buenzow v. Lewiston-Porter Cent. School Dist.*, 474 N.Y.S.2d 161 (A.D.4th Dept.1984).

The Director of Special Education Services for a local school district in South Dakota alleged that the board of education acted illegally in not finding him another position in the district after his position was eliminated due to economic necessity. The director argued before the state Supreme Court that the board was obligated to follow the state's staff reduction policy. Under the statute, he argued, he was classified as a "teacher" and thus was protected from termination under the circumstances. The board insisted that despite the fact that the director held a teaching certificate and was employed under a "Teaching Contract," only certain provisions of the statute were applicable to him because his employment was administrative in nature. The director, continued the board, was an "other administrative employee" under the statute. The director's other certifications, claimed the board, were not taken into account. The court held in the director's favor. The board acted illegally in not following the staff reduction procedures applicable to continuing contract teachers. Though the director may have been classed as an "other administrative employee" under the statute, the statute also provided that such persons were "teachers" for purposes of tenure. *Burke v. Lead-Deadwood School Dist. No. 40-1*, 347 N.W.2d 343 (S.D.1984).

A different result was reached by the Supreme Court of Iowa in a case involving a teacher who had filled a special education teaching vacancy for one year. The teacher was not special education-certified but was given special permission by the State Department of Public Instruction to teach a special education class, because of the school district's inability to find a replacement for a special education teacher who had resigned. At the close of the school year, the "substitute" teacher expressed an interest in returning the following year either in the same capacity or as a regular classroom teacher. He also offered to receive special education training over the summer months. However, he was not reemployed. The state Supreme Court affirmed a lower court ruling in the district's favor, finding that the teacher was a "temporary substitute" and therefore did not have probationary teaching status. The statutory tenure provisions thus did not apply to the teacher and his termination was upheld. *Fitzgerald v. Saydel Consol. School Dist.*, 345 N.W.2d 101 (Iowa 1984).

The following case illustrates that, for purposes of tenure, a transfer from a position not related to special education to one involving special education responsibilities is not a lateral transfer. After an "excessed" elementary school principal in New York was assigned to a position as assistant to the director of special education he filed suit against the school district claiming that his tenure rights had been violated. Following dismissal of his case by a lower court, he appealed to the Supreme Court, Appellate Division. The major issue before the appellate court was whether the new assignment, which would have required the principal to serve a 3-year probationary term, was outside the area in which he was granted tenure. The school district argued that the two positions were essentially the same because both included implementation of the curriculum and supervision of the teachers. The court rejected this argument, pointing to the unique responsibilities in special education and the need to focus on the remedial needs of certain groups of students in accordance with federal and state law. The court ordered the plaintiff appointed to a suitable position. *Cowan v. Bd. of Educ. of Brentwood Union*, 472 N.Y.S.2d 429 (A.D.2d Dept.1984).

Salary errors were alleged in a Louisiana case, where two special education teachers brought suit against their school board alleging that the board had wrongly calculated their salary supplements. Under a former statute, special education teachers were to be paid ten percent of their base salary. That statute was later amended, making the ten percent supplement discretionary, but mandating that no teacher currently receiving the supplement shall suffer a loss in pay. The lower court granted summary judgment to the board, stating that after passage of the amendment the plaintiffs had suffered no loss in pay. The Louisiana Court of Appeal overturned the lower court's judgment, stating that the amendment had no bearing on the factual issue of whether the plaintiffs' salaries were miscalculated. The case was remanded for further factual development. *Wattigney v. Jefferson Parish School Bd.*, 445 So.2d 1318 (La.App.5th Cir.1984).

In a case arising in the state of Washington, unemployment compensation benefits were claimed by employees of a state school for the deaf and blind. The noninstructional employees appealed a decision of the Washington Commissioner of the Department of Employment Security who denied them unemployment benefits during the summer closure of the schools. Washington Unemployment Compensation law prescribes that to deny unemployment benefits to an employee off work during the summer months, written notices to the employee must state that he or she will perform services at the end of the summer months. The civil service employees claimed that written notices they received advising them of the summer closure of the schools, informing them that they were being placed on "leave without pay," and stating that they would be expected to resume their positions at a time to be specified later, were ineffective when applied to civil service employees to exempt them from the unemployment compensation statute. The schools argued that the employees were noninstructional employees rendering services for an educational institution, thus making them ineligible for unemployment benefits while not working during summer recess. The Court of Appeals of Washington was persuaded by the schools' argument and found that the employees were not entitled to unemployment benefits. The written notices the employees received satisfied the unemployment compensation statute's exemption requirement by being "reasonable assurances" of reemployment and were consistent with civil service law. *Alexander v. Employment Security Dep't of the State of Washington*, 688 P.2d 516 (Wash.App.1984).

II. GOVERNMENTAL IMMUNITY

Broadly speaking, governmental immunity is a doctrine which prohibits a lawsuit against any governmental entity or its officials. The doctrine, which has its roots deep in Anglo-American common law, has suffered a great decline in the last century. While some states retain the doctrine in full force, others have partially or completely eliminated it by legislative or judicial decision. Congress has at least partially authorized lawsuits against the U.S. Government through passage of the Federal Tort Claims Act.

Where a lawsuit is brought against state education officials in state court, the type of relief available depends upon that state's view of governmental immunity. In some states, while a state agency such as an education department may not be sued by a private citizen, a lawsuit can usually be brought against a local political subdivision such as a city or school district. Nearly all states permit local political subdivisions to be sued by private citizens.

Where a lawsuit is brought against state officials in *federal* court, the Eleventh Amendment to the U.S. Constitution comes into play. Generally, a private citizen is barred by the Eleventh Amendment from seeking in federal court an award of money damages against a state or against state officials in their official capacities. However, the federal courts may issue injunctions ordering states and state officials to conform their future conduct to the dictates of federal law; this is known as "prospective relief" and is not barred by the Eleventh Amendment.

Local political subdivisions, unlike states and official state departments, are fully subject to lawsuits brought by private citizens in federal court because they are not considered "states" under the Eleventh Amendment. Further, the Eleventh Amendment is inapplicable to suits brought by the federal

government against a state, and is inapplicable to any lawsuit brought in state court.

A Texas elementary school student who suffered from cerebral palsy was pushed into a stack of chairs and sustained a head injury while a group of students were left unsupervised. The student had mild convulsions, developed cold sweats and became dazed and incoherent, but the teacher did not call for help or send her to the school nurse. When the student was later taken to the nurse by an occupational therapist, the nurse told her to stay in school. On the way to her daycare center on a school bus at the end of the day the student suffered severe convulsions. The bus driver contacted his supervisor requesting that a school nurse be provided at the next stop, but he was told to take the student to the daycare center, where she finally received medical treatment. The student's mother filed a lawsuit against the school district and school employees alleging that their grossly negligent failure to provide adequate care decreased the student's life expectancy. After the lawsuit was dismissed before trial the mother appealed.

The Texas Supreme Court considered whether the lawsuit was barred by the Texas Tort Claims Act. The court noted that the act provides an exception from immunity for professional school employees when in "disciplining a student the employee uses excessive force or negligence which results in bodily injury to the student." The mother argued that under this exception school employees could be held liable both for using excessive force when disciplining a student *and* for any "negligence which results in bodily injury to the student." Although the language of the exception was ambiguous because negligence isn't "used," the court observed that it has been interpreted by Texas courts to apply only when a student's bodily injury is a result of some form of punishment. Because the student in this case was not being punished when she incurred her injuries, the court determined that the exception did not apply.

The court next turned to the mother's assertion that the student's injuries fell within another exception to sovereign immunity for damages arising from the "use or operation of a motor vehicle." The court concluded that this exception did not apply because although the girl suffered convulsions on the school bus, those convulsions were not "the proximate result of the use or operation of the school bus." The supreme court affirmed the dismissal of the case. *Hopkins v. Spring Indep. School Dist.*, 736 S.W.2d 617 (Tex.1987).

Six mentally handicapped children enrolled in an Alabama middle school sued their school board and the superintendent claiming that they had negligently failed to stop numerous incidents of physical, mental and sexual abuse at the school. After a state circuit court ruled in favor of the school board and superintendent the children appealed to the Alabama Supreme Court. The children alleged that the school officials were negligent when they knew of the abuse but failed to take any steps to stop it. They sought money damages and a court order requiring the promulgation of regulations designed to insure the safety of mentally retarded students in the schools.

The supreme court ruled that school boards are immune from tort lawsuits, noting that the lawsuit filed in the circuit court charged the school officials with negligent, wanton, and intentional misconduct. It concluded that the scope of "discretionary function" immunity for governmental bodies had been expanded in Alabama to include immunity from allegations of wanton conduct against state officials when there is no evidence of bad faith on their part. It ruled that because the handicapped students did not allege any fraud or bad faith on the part of the school officials, their claim was barred since it related to the performance of the school officials' statutory duties which are immune from tort claims. The lower court's decision was affirmed. *Hill v. Allen*, 495 So.2d 32 (Ala.1986).

In a New Hampshire case, the parents of a handicapped child brought suit in federal court under the EAHCA seeking reimbursement for the cost of maintaining their child in a private residential facility. The federal judge certified two questions to the Supreme Court of New Hampshire: first, has that state waived its defense of sovereign immunity in cases involving tuition reimbursement for handicapped children, and second, has the state waived its privileges under the Eleventh Amendment to the U.S. Constitution, thus consenting to be sued in federal court? A unanimous supreme court answered both questions in the negative. As to the first question, the state of New Hampshire had implemented a program under the EAHCA by which its local school districts shouldered financial responsibility for the education of handicapped children. Thus, although a lawsuit against a school district could be brought in state or federal court, the state itself could not be named as a defendant.

As to the second question, the supreme court held that the state also could not be sued under the EAHCA in federal court. Parents could bring a proceeding in federal court to review a state agency or court decision, however. The court explained that while New Hampshire had received federal funds under the EAHCA, the state had left the actual provision of special educational services to the local school districts. Therefore, the supreme court held that the state of New Hampshire had not become involved in the provision of special educational services to such an extent as to waive its immunity from suit in federal court. The case was sent back to the U.S. district court with both certified questions answered in the negative.

The U.S. district court however, decided to disregard the state supreme court's legal conclusions. Instead, it made the following observations. The parents' claim involved an alleged state violation of the EAHCA made under the authority of New Hampshire law. Congress has stated that the EAHCA's purpose was to assist states in providing appropriate educations to handicapped children. Congress then allowed a citizen to sue a state for violation of the EAHCA. Thus, the court ruled that because a citizen is allowed to file a suit against the state under the EAHCA, the citizen should also be allowed to file a claim under a state law passed to carry out the EAHCA's purposes. The federal district court ruled that the state was not immune from suit. *John H. v. Brunelle*, 631 F.Supp. 208 (D.N.H.1986).

After the mother of a fourteen-year-old handicapped child brought suit against the Board of Education of the District of Columbia, the board sought to dismiss the case on several grounds. First, claimed the board, the mother improperly brought suit in her own name to enforce her rights and the rights of her child under the EAHCA. Second, the Board of Education may not be sued. Third, as government officers, the individual defendants were not properly included in the lawsuit. Fourth, the mother failed to state a claim for which relief could be granted under the Rehabilitation Act and the Civil Rights Act.

The U.S. district court held that the child's mother could maintain an action in her own name to enforce her rights and the rights of her child under the EAHCA. The court found that the EAHCA gives parents of handicapped children certain limited rights and that parents may sue to enforce those rights consistent with the purposes of the EAHCA. The court further held that the District of Columbia Board of Education was not subject to a lawsuit. Thus, the court dismissed the action against the Board of Education.

However, the individual defendants who were named in the mother's complaint, found the district court, were properly included since she sought injunctive relief against the individual defendants in their official, as opposed to their individual, capacities. Thus, the board's motion to dismiss the individual defendants was denied. Finally, the court held that the mother's claims under the Rehabilitation Act and Civil Rights Act were not properly before the court in light of the U.S. Supreme Court's ruling in *Smith v. Robinson*, which held that the EAHCA is the exclusive avenue of relief for claims involving the right to a special education. The mother's Rehabilitation Act and Civil Rights Act claims were therefore dismissed. *Tschanneral v. Dist. of Columbia Bd. of Educ.*, 594 F.Supp. 407 (D.D.C.1984).

A group of handicapped children and their parents brought suit against Oregon state and local education officials to enjoin their school district from discontinuing an educational program provided to handicapped children. A U.S. district court held in favor of the children and their parents, ruling that 1) the state defendants and, in particular, the Oregon Department of Education, were in violation of the EAHCA for failure to ensure that the plaintiffs would receive free appropriate public educations, and 2) the defendant school districts were not in violation of the EAHCA because they had no legal responsibility under Oregon law to provide the plaintiffs with free appropriate public educations under the EAHCA. The court also stated that in deference to the Oregon legislature, which has the responsibility and the expertise to resolve the problem, it would decline at that time to consider the remedy of injunctive relief, but it did enter a temporary, ninety-day injunction pursuant to the consent of all parties. The court further stated that during that ninety-day period the parties should meet and attempt to agree upon a plan to resolve the dispute. It then said that at the end of ninety days, if the matter had not been resolved, it would make a further determination as to what steps and procedures should then be taken.

Because no agreement was reached between the parties at the end of ninety days, a supplemental opinion was then issued by the court, which addressed the Eleventh Amendment issue and forced action upon the parties. The Eleventh Amendment issue was raised by the state of Oregon, which claimed absolute immunity from suit under that amendment. However, the court observed that the EAHCA had been enacted pursuant to § 5 of the Fourteenth Amendment, and thus constituted a congressional abrogation of Oregon's immunity from suit in federal court. Since the Eleventh Amendment did not bar suit and in light of the court's earlier ruling, the court held that the state of Oregon's receipt of federal funds for assistance in educating the plaintiffs required the state to comply with its part of the bargain—namely, to provide sufficient funds to cover the full cost of their educations. Budgetary constraints could not excuse the state from the obligations arising from the acceptance of federal funds. In other words, the Oregon legislature could not refuse or neglect to enact a legislative program—in whatever manner it should deem to be appropriate—to provide funding for the full cost of the plaintiffs' educations. The court ordered the parties to act in accordance with its decision. *Kerr Center Parents Ass'n v. Charles*, 581 F.Supp. 166 (D.Or.1983).

In an Illinois case, a handicapped student and his parents brought suit against the governor of Illinois and state and local educational officials, charging violations of the officials' legal duties created by the child's condition as a handicapped child. The officials moved for partial dismissal of the parents' complaint on four grounds. First, argued the officials, there was no basis for joining the governor as a defendant. Nothing the governor does, continued the argument, is asserted to have caused the alleged harm suffered by the parents and the child. Second, the parents should not be allowed to assert a Rehabilitation Act claim, as this Act was not a predicate for the relief sought. Third, the parents should not be allowed to assert their state law claim under an Illinois statute governing identification, evaluation and placement of handicapped children in special education in light of the U.S. Supreme Court's recent decision interpreting the Eleventh Amendment, *Pennhurst State School & Hospital v. Halderman*, 104 S.Ct. 900 (1984). Fourth, the officials claimed that once the Rehabilitation Act claim was gone, their request for attorney's fees should vanish with it because the EAHCA does not embody such relief. A U.S. district court in Illinois agreed with the officials' arguments and granted all four of their requests. Thus, the parents were allowed to proceed with their complaint only as narrowed. *Hayward v. Thompson*, 593 F.Supp, 57 (N.D.Ill.1984).

A U.S. district court in Wisconsin applied the doctrine of Eleventh Amendment governmental immunity in a claim against the Milwaukee public school system. A handicapped child brought suit in federal court against the school system on behalf of himself and all other similarly situated children in Milwaukee who were placed in day treatment facilities. After the state proposed termination of the day service placements, the parents of the children alleged that their children were being denied educational facilities in violation of the EAHCA. The court held that the parents' claim for damages against the Wisconsin state superintendent of public instruction was essentially a claim against state funds, and that no congressional authorization existed to abrogate the state's Eleventh Amendment immunity from retroactive monetary claims payable from the state treasury. However, the court did grant an injunction to the children against the superintendent of public instruction in her official capacity. The injunction restrained the Milwaukee public schools from terminating the current placement of the children and removing the children from those schools until completion of a full and impartial evaluation of their education needs. The injunction, said the court, was prospective in nature and thus was not barred by governmental immunity. *M.R. v. Milwaukee Public Schools*, 495 F.Supp. 864 (E.D.Wis.1980).

Georgia hearing procedures were successfully attacked by a handicapped child who, through her father, sued the Georgia Superintendent of the Georgia State Board of Education alleging that the procedures were in violation of the EAHCA. Specifically, the child alleged that in Georgia, the decision of a state educational agency, which should have been treated as final, was subject to "veto" by the state board of education. The U.S. Court of Appeals, Fifth Circuit, held that Eleventh Amendment immunity does not bar a federal court from enjoining state officials to conform their future conduct to the requirements of federal law. Accordingly, the state of Georgia was ordered to alter its procedures to conform to the provisions of the EAHCA, which provide that the decision of a state education agency is final. *Helms v. McDaniel*, 657 F.2d 800 (5th Cir.1981).

In a Michigan case, the parents of a handicapped child brought suit against a local school district alleging that the district had misdiagnosed their child's language impairment. The school district's motion for summary judgment was granted by the court on the ground that the school, in its operation of a speech therapy program, was involved in a government program and thus entitled to governmental immunity. In handing down its decision, the court outlined the guidelines it used in deciding whether a particular function is entitled to immunity. The court stated that it examines the precise activity giving rise to the plaintiff's claim, rather than the overall department operations. In this situation the examination and diagnosis of students in a public school was "intended to promote the general public health and [is] exercised for the common good of all." The court held, therefore, that the school district was immune from liability in performing the function. *Brosnan v. Livonia Pub. Schools*, 333 N.W.2d 288 (Mich.App.1983).

III. PRIVATE SCHOOLS

States receiving federal funding under the EAHCA are required to maintain a list of approved private schools to educate handicapped children where no public school program is available or appropriate.

A. Eligibility to Educate Handicapped Children

Disputes sometimes arise between states and private schools or states and students when a private school is excluded, for a particular reason or reasons, from the state's list of approved private schools.

A Pennsylvania father filed a lawsuit under the EAHCA against his local school district and the Pennsylvania Secretary of Education. The father asserted that his child, who was learning disabled and had emotional problems, had been denied a free appropriate education and that Pennsylvania's procedures violated rights guaranteed by the EAHCA and its implementing regulations. A U.S. district court ruled in favor of the father and the school district and state appealed.

The U.S. Court of Appeals, Third Circuit, first determined that the father's placement of a child at a private school had been reasonable and that he should be reimbursed for the out-of-pocket expense of that placement. It then considered the argument put forth by the school district and the state that reimbursement of the father's expenses was barred by the Eleventh Amendment to the U.S. Constitution. The court pointed out that the Eleventh Amendment generally precludes lawsuits in federal court against a state by the state's citizens. It noted that Congress can set aside the immunity from federal lawsuits that states enjoy under the Eleventh Amendment if it makes its intentions clear. The court then observed that the EAHCA expressly gives handicapped children and their parents the right to enforce their EAHCA rights in federal or state courts. Furthermore, the HCPA mentioned that lawsuits in federal or state courts under the EAHCA would have to be filed against a "State or local educational agency." The court concluded that the EAHCA authorized lawsuits against states in federal court. It ruled in favor of the father and sustained the district court's order that he be reimbursed for the out-of-pocket expense of the child's placement. *Muth v. Central Bucks School Dist.*, 839 F.2d 113 (3d Cir.1988).

The mother of a handicapped Fairfax, Virginia, boy unilaterally placed him in the East Hill Farm and School in Vermont. She then requested a due process hearing to resolve the questions of tuition reimbursement and living expenses. Two due process hearings found that the Fairfax County Public Schools' (FCPS) recommendation of placement at the Little Keswick School, Inc., was appropriate and the mother appealed to a U.S. district court. The district court ruled in favor of FCPS and the mother appealed to the U.S. Court of Appeals, Fourth Circuit.

The court of appeals affirmed the district court's decision to deny tuition reimbursement to the mother for the East Hill education. It noted that when a handicapped child is educated at a private school under the EAHCA, the state or local school district has an obligation to ensure that that school meets applicable state educational standards. Here, East Hill was not approved by Virginia to offer special education. Therefore, FCPS could not place the boy and fund his education at East Hill without violating the EAHCA's requirement that handicapped children be educated at public expense only in those private schools that met state educational standards. The court of appeals observed that "[w]hen a handicapped child is educated at a private school under the [EAHCA], the State has an obligation to ensure that the school meets applicable State educational standards." Therefore, the EAHCA did not require FCPS to place the handicapped boy in the unapproved Vermont school. The district court decision was affirmed. *Schimmel v. Spillane*, 819 F.2d 477 (4th Cir.1987).

The U.S. Supreme Court ruled unanimously on the issue of state aid to handicapped students at private religious schools. The Court held that the First Amendment to the U.S. Constitution does not prevent a state from providing financial assistance to a handicapped individual attending a Christian college. The plaintiff in this case, a blind person, sought vocational rehabilitative services from the state of Washington's Commission for the Blind pursuant to state law [Wash.Rev.Code sec. 74.16.181 (1981)]. The law provided that visually handicapped persons were eligible for educational assistance to enable them to "overcome vocational handicaps and to obtain the maximum degree of self-support and self-care." However, because the plaintiff was a private school student intending to pursue a career of service in the church, the Commission for the Blind denied him assistance. The Washington Supreme Court upheld this decision on the ground that the First Amendment to the U.S. Constitution prohibited state funding of a student's education at a religious college.

The U.S. Supreme Court took a different, much less restrictive view of the First Amendment and reversed the Washington court. The operation of Washington's program was such that the commission paid money directly to the student, who would then attend the school of his or her choice. The fact that the student in this case chose to attend a religious college did not constitute state support of religion, because "the decision to support religious education is made by the individual, not the state." The First Amendment was therefore not offended. *Witters v. Washington Dep't of Servs. for the Blind*, 106 S.Ct. 748 (1986).

A Virginia case resulted in a ruling that that state will not fund the education of handicapped students at out-of-state religious institutions. Here, a twenty-year-old handicapped citizen of Vietnam who was a permanent resident alien of the United States graduated from a Virginia high school in 1984. He applied to and was accepted for admission to St. Andrews Presbyterian College, a nonprofit liberal arts college affiliated with the Presbyterian Synod of North Carolina. Its primary purpose is to provide collegiate or graduate education and not to provide religious training through a theological education. The student and his foster father sought financial assistance from the state of Virginia under its program of financial aid to the handicapped, which is 80% federally financed and 20% Virginia financed. Virginia denied financial aid to the student to attend St. Andrews solely because it was a church-affiliated school located outside Virginia.

Until 1969 Virginia could not provide assistance to any church-affiliated schools through tuition grants to students. In 1969, the Virginia Constitution was amended to provide for loans to students attending in-state church-affiliated schools so long as the primary purpose of those schools was to provide collegiate or graduate education. The student sued the state of Virginia in a U.S. district court claiming that the denial of financial aid violated the Establishment Clause of the First Amendment to the U.S. Constitution. He also contended that even if tuition aid was properly denied, he should still receive payments for incidental expenses to attend St. Andrews. The district court ruled for the state and the student appealed to the U.S. Court of Appeals, Fourth Circuit. For a state law to be consistent with the Establishment Clause its primary effect must neither advance nor hinder religion. The student contended that distinguishing out-of-state schools on the basis of religious affiliation violated the primary effect standard because it disfavored church-affiliated schools. The appeals court disagreed, noting that the U.S. Supreme Court has recognized that a decision to fund religious studies, along with other postsecondary education, lies within a permissible zone of accommodation of religion but is not mandatory.

The student also claimed that the Virginia policy infringed upon his right to the free exercise of religion since it forced him to forfeit attendance at an out-of-state religious institution in order to receive tuition aid. The court dismissed this allegation, observing that Virginia was not obligated to provide the student with an ideal learning situation. The state was only prohibited from forcing him to give up essential beliefs and practices in order to obtain tuition aid. The student's free exercise of religion needs and physical needs could be met in Virginia schools.

Further, the court of appeals noted that the Virginia Constitution did not prohibit the student's reimbursement for incidental expenses (books, transportation costs, living expenses, etc.) should he still choose to attend St. Andrews. Such subsidies would be to the student and not to a disqualified school. The appeals court remanded the case to the district court to determine how the state determines the primary purpose of in-state church-affiliated schools and how it provides for their monitoring so as to insure that Virginia is not advancing religion. *Phan v. Commonwealth of Virginia*, 806 F.2d 516 (4th Cir.1986).

In a New York case the U.S. Court of Appeals, Second Circuit, held that a plan to provide remedial education classes on public school property for private parochial school students violates the Establishment Clause. Chapter One of the Education Consolidation and Improvement Act established a federally funded program to provide remedial instruction and related support services to elementary and secondary school children who were "educationally deprived" and who lived in an area having a high concentration of low income families. The purpose of the program was to meet the remedial educational needs of students that could not otherwise be met by the schools they attended. States receiving Chapter One funding were required to provide such remedial services to private as well as public school students.

In order to comply with a 1985 U.S. Supreme Court decision which held that sending federally supported public school teachers to teach in private religious schools violated the Establishment of Religion Clause of the First Amendment [*Aguilar v. Felton*, 105 S.Ct. 3232 (1985)], the city of New York adopted a new plan. One aspect of the plan called for the city to conduct remedial education classes for girls from a Hasidic Jewish school on public school premises. Specifically, the plan provided for a section of the public school to be completely closed off for use by the Hasidic girls by constructing a wall in a previously open corridor. It also provided for the girls to be taught only by women (in accordance with Hasidic tradition) who spoke Yiddish. Before the plan was implemented, a local parents' association sued the New York City School District in a U.S. district court seeking a preliminary injunction against the plan. When the injunction was denied, the parents appealed to the U.S. Court of Appeals.

The parents contended that the city's plan had the primary effect of promoting religion and excessively entangled the state in religious matters. The city argued that the injunction was properly denied because the plan did not have those effects and was only a reasonable effort to encourage the Hasidic Jews to send their children to the remedial classes conducted in the public school. The court of appeals observed that the U.S. Supreme Court has developed a three-part test for determining whether a given state law is one that "establishes" religion. First, the statute must have a secular legislative purpose; second, its primary effect must be one that neither advances nor hinders religion; third, the statute must not promote an excessive government entanglement with religion. The court of appeals stated that the issue was whether the city's plan had the primary effect of advancing the religious tenets of the Hasidic Jews and whether it fostered an excessive entanglement of the city with religion. The court of appeals observed that the city's plan seemed "plainly to create a symbolic link between the state and the Hasidic sect that [was] likely to have a magnified negative impact on the minds of the youngsters attending P.S. 16."

It also disagreed with the district court's observation that an injunction against the plan would hinder the free exercise of religion on the part of the Jewish girls. "The Free Exercise Clause of the First Amendment . . . does not prohibit a government from forcing a choice between receipt of a public benefit and a pursuit of a religious belief if it can show a compelling reason for doing so." Avoiding a violation of the Establishment Clause that would otherwise result from an apparent endorsement of the tenets of a particular faith was ample reason for compelling that choice. The court of appeals reversed the lower court decision and held that the parents were entitled to preliminary injunctive relief on the ground that the city plan had the primary effect of establishing religion through a federally funded program. *Parents' Ass'n of P.S. 16 v. Quinones*, 803 F.2d 1235 (2d Cir.1986).

This case involved the same sect. Parents of handicapped children who lived in a Hasidic Jewish community in New York requested in 1984 that their local school district furnish special education and related services at the Hasidic community. Both the parents and their handicapped children adhered to the practices of Hasidism which generally requires the separation of males and females. Male and female students in the community attended separate private Hasidic schools.

After providing some services during the 1984-85 school year at one of the Hasidic schools, the school district determined that it could furnish special education and related services to the community's handicapped students only in the public schools, together with public school students. This decision was based upon a New York state law which provided that "[p]upils enrolled in nonpublic schools for whom services are provided . . . shall receive such services in regular classes of the public school and shall not be provided such services separately from pupils regularly attending the public schools." The district's Committee on the Handicapped recommended a public school special education program for each handicapped Hasidic child after conducting individualized evaluations. The parents refused to allow their children to attend the public school programs, employed private tutors and sought administrative review of the individual public school placements.

The school district sought a judicial declaration that it was only required to furnish special education services to the Hasidic children in regular public school classes along with public school students. A trial court, however, ordered the district to provide the Hasidic children with special education and related services in a "mobile or other appropriate site not physically or educationally identified with but reasonably accessible to the [Hasidic] children." The school district appealed.

On appeal, a New York appellate court considered the school district's argument that the trial court's order violated the Establishment Clause of the First Amendment. The court determined that although the trial court's order reflected the clearly secular purpose of providing special education and related services to school children, it violated the Establishment Clause because it had the primary effect of advancing religion. The court pointed out that the "mobile or other appropriate site" that the trial court had ordered to be provided for use in the Hasidic community was necessary "not because of the nature of [the children's] handicaps, but because of their Hasidic faith and socio-cultural background." It found that the creation of a "mobile or other appropriate site" for the Hasidic children posed a "substantial risk that the [school district] will be required to plan and administer its special education curriculum according to the religious requirements of . . . Hasidism." The court ruled in favor of the school district. *Bd. of Educ. v. Wieder*, 522 N.Y.S.2d 878 (A.D.2d Dept.1987).

New Jersey's department of education issued detailed regulations governing private schools which educate handicapped children. The regulations applied only to private schools to which local school boards sent handicapped children in order to satisfy the local board's educational obligations. These private schools were required to submit detailed budgets, establish strict bookkeeping and accounting procedures, submit to annual audits by the state, and most objectionably, a school's profit was limited to 2.5% of its per pupil costs. Several private school associations sued the department seeking to have the regulations declared invalid. They claimed that the regulations were "confiscatory" and had been enacted without proper authority.

The New Jersey Superior Court, Appellate Division, upheld the regulations as within the scope of the department's powers. Especially persuasive to the court was the argument that private schools, by choosing to accept handicapped students on referral from local school boards, should expect to relinquish a degree of privacy and autonomy over their affairs. The 2.5% profit ceiling is a reasonable exercise of department authority over private schools which, said the court, have voluntarily submitted to department control. However, the court left open the possibility that in the future, if a private school were able to show that due to its financial condition the regulations were unreasonable as applied to it, then a waiver of the regulations might be justified. *Council of Private Schools for Children with Special Needs v. Cooperman*, 501 A.2d 575 (N.J.Super.A.D.1985).

A private school in Pennsylvania alleged it was denied due process of law after the Pennsylvania Secretary of Education denied the school's application for status as an approved private school for socially and emotionally disturbed children. A hearing examiner determined that three State Board of Education standards were not met: first, the student interns used in the school classrooms did not provide full-time supportive assistance to the classroom teachers; second, the school lacked an immediately available supervisor or other competent and trained person to handle a student in a period of crisis and to remove that student, if necessary from the classroom; third, the school's behavior management systems did not permit its classroom teachers to control classroom conduct adequately. The school appealed to the Commonwealth Court of Pennsylvania, which affirmed the hearing examiner's decision. The school then appealed to the Supreme Court of Pennsylvania, which found that the evidence was sufficient to support a finding that the school failed to provide adequate staff assistance to classroom teachers. The court concluded that the hearing examiner's findings went to the heart of the Pennsylvania regulatory scheme of insuring that approved private schools were able to provide adequate and necessary training and education to handicapped children. *Wiley House v. Scanlon*, 465 A.2d 995 (Pa.1983).

B. Facilities and Programs

The appropriateness of private school facilities and programs to the particular needs of handicapped students has been a source of dispute between schools and students, schools and parents, and schools and states.

A New York father placed his thirteen-year-old daughter who suffered from anorexia nervosa at the Hedges Treatment Center, a Pennsylvania residential treatment facility. He placed her at Hedges due to several placement delays by a school district's committee on the handicapped (COH). A U.S. district court denied his request for tuition reimbursement because he had failed to exhaust administrative remedies. He then sought an administrative hearing and the hearing officer ordered placement at Hedges. However, the New York Commissioner of Education refused to provide tuition reimbursement because Hedges was approved only for fourteen-year-olds and older. The father appealed to the same U.S. district court. It upheld the placement. The daughter received all of the benefits and rights at Hedges that she would have received at a New York school even though Hedges was not approved for her age.

On appeal before the U.S. Court of Appeals, Third Circuit, the commissioner contended that the district court exceeded its authority by ordering the placement. The court of appeals agreed with the commissioner. EAHCA § 1401(18)(B) required that the daughter receive special education and related services which met the state educational agency standards. Section 1413(a)(4)(B)(ii) of the EAHCA provided that the state determine whether private facilities like Hedges met those standards. Thus, the EAHCA incorporated state educational standards. It was the state of New York's obligation (through the commissioner) to ensure that private facilities met applicable state educational standards. No court or agency could approve a placement at a private facility consistent with the EAHCA unless the commissioner approved the facility prior to the placement. The hearing officer and the district court wrongly placed the daughter at Hedges without the commissioner's approval. The district court decision was reversed and the father was denied reimbursement. *Antkowiak v. Ambach*, 838 F.2d 635 (2d Cir.1988).

Students at a school for the blind in California brought suit against state education officials under the EAHCA and the Rehabilitation Act, challenging a move of the school to a new site. Among the objections to the move were allegations that the new site was an earthquake-prone, dangerous area. The school had been granted permission to open over the protest of the students because some parents objected to the possibility that, if the move was blocked, no special school for the blind would be available. The students sought a preliminary injunction to stop the move and made the seismic safety claims a major focus of their lawsuit. A U.S. district court ordered seismic studies of the site and, finding California's pre-construction seismic safety investigation inadequate, the court granted the students' request for a preliminary injunction.

The state appealed this ruling to the U.S. Court of Appeals, Ninth Circuit, which held that under the prohibition of the Rehabilitation Act against discriminating against the handicapped, California was required to make its school for the blind as safe as other schools and to make such reasonable adjustments as were necessary to make the school as safe as schools for non-handicapped students. To the state's argument that the general anti-discrimination provisions of the Rehabilitation Act cannot be used to make an "end run" around the more specific provisions of the EAHCA, the court said that while the EAHCA is more specific than the Rehabilitation Act as to educational programs, the Rehabilitation Act is more specific as to physical facilities. The court found no conflict between the two Acts.

Finally, because a strong argument could be made that a seismically unsafe school denied the students a "free appropriate education" under the EAHCA, the Court of Appeals held that the district court properly granted the students' request for a preliminary injunction. The district court ruling was affirmed and the superintendent of Public Instruction of California appealed to the U.S. Supreme Court, which held that the question of whether the district court erred in issuing the preliminary injunction was moot; subsequent to the time of the district court's order, and prior to the Supreme Court's ruling, the tests had been completed. *Honig v. Students of California School for the Blind*, 105 S.Ct. 1820 (1985).

The mother of a seriously emotionally disturbed nineteen-year-old brought suit against a Tennessee school district alleging that her son had not been placed in an appropriate facility. A hearing officer had determined that a Tennessee residential school providing psychiatric treatment was the appropriate placement for the boy. The mother, however, wanted him placed in a special school in Texas. She appealed the hearing officer's decision to a federal district court, which held for the school district. The mother then appealed to the U.S. Court of Appeals, Sixth Circuit, which reversed the district court ruling. The Court of Appeals was persuaded by psychiatric testimony which established that the Texas school, which offered long-term treatment and had locked wards, was a better school for the boy. The court rejected the school district's argument that because the Texas school cost $88,000 per year as compared to $55,000 per year for the school chosen by the board, placement at the Tennessee school was warranted. It stated that cost considerations, when devising programs for individual handicapped students, are only relevant when choosing between several options, all of which offer an "appropriate" education. *Clevenger v. Oak Ridge School Board*, 744 F.2d 514 (6th Cir.1984).

The following case involved a dispute between a school for the handicapped and the state of Illinois over the nature of a program offered by the school. The school alleged in federal district court that the Illinois Guardianship and Advocacy Commission (GAC) violated the school's First Amendment right to freedom of speech and its constitutional right to due process of law. The school contended that the GAC's prevailing philosophy with respect to the proper way to handle the education of multiply handicapped and developmentally disabled children conflicted with the school's philosophy, and that the GAC sought to punish the school for the school's nonconformist philosophy and for criticisms of the GAC's philosophy. The school argued that the GAC instituted a harassment campaign under the guise of an investigation of charges the GAC knew were false.

Allegations by the school included the GAC's numerous visits to the school's campus to question students and employees and burdensome document requests, all of which disrupted the school's operation. Further, argued the school, the GAC held a public "hearing" at which it released a number of false charges against the school and its executive director, including charges of understaffing, improper distribution of medication and permitting sexual abuse of its residents. The school claimed that the GAC refused its several requests for advance notice of the nature of the charges, that the school was not given the opportunity to object or respond at the hearing, and that without the school's input, the GAC released its findings and recommendations to the press.

The GAC subsequently recommended that other Illinois agencies and the Illinois legislature take action against the school, including cutting off the school's funding, removing the executive director and revoking the school's licenses. The school claimed that as a result of the GAC's actions and the adverse publicity, it suffered disruption in providing its services, frustration in accomplishing its educational goals and a loss of reputation, enrollment and revenues. The school sought compensatory and punitive damages against the GAC.

The district court held that the school stated a valid First Amendment claim but that its due process claim was not supported by the evidence. The school had failed to prove that merely threatening the revocation of its licenses, which had not actually been revoked, deprived it of its alleged "prospective business advantage" or that the alleged loss of funding from two sources was attributable to the GAC's actions. Thus, the school was allowed to proceed with its First Amendment claims but the due process claims were dismissed.

Concerning its First Amendment claim, the Grove School later argued to the court that by investigating its practices the GAC had actually been seeking to silence the school's advocacy of alternative approaches to education. It contended that the GAC's investigation had been a pretext for harassment and that the GAC knew that the charges leveled against the Grove School were baseless, having been made by individuals who held grudges against the school. As evidence for the school's charge that the GAC had sought to extinguish the school's First Amendment right to advocate nonconformist educational methods, the school cited the following comment made by a GAC member at the public hearing:

> I think one of the most truly disturbing [things] that came through in our investigation was that the Executive Director, who is not a qualified professional in even a related field of education, . . . has demonstrated through his actions that he feels that he is more qualified than professionals to decide what is important and not important for handicapped students to learn. He is running Grove School by his own philosophy according to his own rules and regulations in complete disregard of the law and this is just absolutely appalling.

However, the U.S. district court found it unnecessary to determine whether the GAC had infringed upon the school's rights by investigating it. Because the GAC members were state officials, they could be held liable under § 1983 of the Civil Rights Act only if they had violated "clearly established constitutional rights" possessed by the school. Thus, the question was not whether the First Amendment rights of the school had been violated, but whether the

GAC members had violated constitutional rights which, at the time of the alleged violation, were clearly established. The court held that the school had failed to prove this. It was likely that the GAC had been seeking to deter *conduct*, not speech, which the GAC perceived to be harmful to handicapped students. Thus, the court ruled that the GAC members had not acted in violation of any clearly established constitutional right possessed by the school. The individual GAC members were therefore immune from suit under the Civil Rights Act and the remainder of the lawsuit was dismissed. *Grove School v. Guardianship & Advocacy Comm'n*, 642 F.Supp. 1043 (N.D. Ill.1986).

C. Contracts

Most cases concerning contract disputes involve private schools, which enjoy the unfettered ability to enter into contractual agreements with the parents of handicapped children, or school districts, to provide special education services.

In 1978, the state of New York agreed to pay the tuition costs of a schizophrenic boy who had been placed in a private residential psychiatric hospital which operated an accredited academic high school. Behavioral problems prevented the boy from attending the high school, but he continued to reside at the hospital. His doctors hoped that the behavior problems could be overcome. The boy's parents, after petitioning state officials in vain, sought to compel the state to pay the cost of the boy's residential care at the hospital from the time of his placement, July, 1978, through June, 1983, when the boy turned twenty-one years old. The state argued that as long as the child's behavioral problems prevented him from attending the high school at the institution, he was in effect uneducable and therefore the state had no responsibility for any of his expenses.

The court ruled that once the state placed the boy at the psychiatric hospital, it became obligated to pay the entire expense of the placement. The state could not escape its responsibility for costs of the boy's residential care simply by stating that those costs did not directly address educational problems. As long as the boy could be educated (however little) through a residential placement, the state remained responsible for the cost of that placement. *Vander Malle v. Ambach*, 667 F.Supp. 1015 (S.D.N.Y. 1987).

The Woods Schools (Woods) is an approved Pennsylvania nonprofit corporation which operated a residential private school for exceptional children. In March 1985, an exceptional child from Central Dauphin enrolled at Woods. In August, 1985, Woods requested that Central Dauphin and the child's parents find an alternate placement for the child. In October, 1985, Woods requested that Central Dauphin initiate due process proceedings leading to the child's removal since § 171.18 of the Standards of Approved Private Schools (Standards) provided that "an approved private school may not . . . disenroll a student . . . until notice and the opportunity for a hearing have been given in accordance with Chapter 13 (relative to special education)." Central Dauphin refused and Woods filed a petition with the Commonwealth Court of Pennsylvania stating that Woods was not receiving payment for the full cost of the child's program and that the child was admitted to Woods upon the express condition that Central Dauphin bear the full cost of the child's program.

In ruling for Central Dauphin the court reasoned that it could not yet be determined what Woods' reimbursement would be and therefore it could not adjudicate the cost controversy. Woods emphasized that its primary claim was its inability to initiate due process procedures to disenroll the child. The court observed that § 171.20(a) of the Standards stated that an "approved private school shall operate in accordance with this chapter" and that Woods knew of the Standard's cost restrictions when it agreed to accept the child. Woods was bound by and limited to the steps outlined in administrative agency law in seeking additional reimbursement. Woods was required to continue serving the child until either the parent or school district determined that its program was inadequate. Woods had to pursue a remedy regarding the educational costs and replacement of the child through administrative procedures outlined by the Standards before it could look to the court for any help. *Woods Schools v. Commonwealth Dep't of Educ.*, 514 A.2d 686 (Pa.Cmwlth.1986).

The parents of a handicapped child in Illinois brought suit against a Massachusetts private school, alleging that the school violated the terms of an agreement between the parents and the school. The parents claimed the agreement provided that the school would apply for increased funding from the state of Illinois for their handicapped daughter's placement at the Massachusetts school. The amounts the parents received in assistance from the state of Illinois proved to be insufficient to cover the costs of the child's attendance at the school. The parents also claimed that a school official called the child's mother requesting that the child not return to school for the summer session preceding the 1979-80 school year as well as the following school year. If the parents sent their daughter to the school on a plane there would be no one to meet her at the airport. The child's father negotiated an arrangement with the school whereby the child would be allowed to return for summer session, with the parents paying the full cost of her attendance and the school applying for the funds due from Illinois. When summer session ended, the school received a contract from Illinois for the child's placement for the 1980-81 school year. The school refused to sign the contract, knowing it was not going to get the tuition reimbursement it was due.

The father then wrote a letter to the school requesting that his daughter be allowed to remain there, while the school investigated the possibility of receiving funding from Illinois. The school's investigation revealed that it was not on the Illinois State Board of Education's (ISBE) list of approved schools; thus, even if the school had signed the contract it would not have been paid. New Illinois law would not allow Massachusetts to assess parents the difference between what Illinois would pay and what the Massachusetts school charged. The school then informed the parents that the child would be allowed to remain as a private student only; otherwise she would be requested to leave and not return after Christmas vacation of the 1980-81 school year. The child stayed at the school during Christmas because of a family disruption. Shortly thereafter, the father visited the director of the school, who signed an agreement to apply to Illinois for ISBE eligibility. Eligibility was denied by Illinois. The child remained at the school until March, with no money from any source being offered for the child's placement.

In April the school threatened to return the child to Illinois. The father went to Massachusetts again and obtained a temporary restraining order preventing the school from discharging the child. The father sued the Massachusetts school for failing to apply for Illinois funds. The school sued the father for tuition, room and board. In the parents' lawsuit, a jury awarded the parents $4,000 in compensatory damages, $30,000 for fraud and $50,000 to the wife for intentional infliction of emotional distress resulting from the phone call she received from the school. The school appealed and both lawsuits were consolidated in a U.S. district court in Illinois, which upheld the compensatory damage award but set aside the jury's awards for fraud and emotional distress.

The parents appealed to the U.S. Court of Appeals, Seventh Circuit, which held that the parents were not entitled to damages. The child's father, a medical doctor, had not shown that on the days of his trips to Massachusetts to resolve the problems with the school, that he would otherwise have been in consultation with patients. Thus, the $4,000 damage award, consisting of travel and lodging costs, lost consulting fees and attorney expenses was denied. The court also found that there was no implied contract wherein the parents agreed to pay the complete tuition for the 1979-80 school year. Thus, the parents were not liable for tuition for that year. However, the parents reenrolled their child in the school the following year with the full knowledge that the school was having tuition reimbursement problems with Illinois. Thus, there was an implied contract for the 1980-81 school year for the parents to bear the tuition expenses.

The telephone call to the child's mother regarding the school's request that the child not return to school was not intentional infliction of emotional distress. Under Massachusetts law, only "extreme and outrageous" conduct can give rise to such a claim. Such conduct does not qualify as extreme and outrageous unless it is "beyond all bounds of decency and utterly intolerable in a civilized community." The court found no evidence of fraud as the school merely made a promise to apply for additional funding and, although not always gracious about the circumstances, intended to carry out that promise. *Dr. Franklin Perkins School v. Freeman*, 741 F.2d 1503 (7th Cir.1984).

After a private school brought an action to recover tuition expenses from the mother of a student, the mother counterclaimed against the school for breach of contract, fraudulent/negligent misrepresentation and negligent infliction of emotional distress. The school moved to dismiss the mother's counterclaim for failure to state a claim for which relief could be granted. The mother's counterclaim alleged that the school's agents represented to her that they possessed a specialized faculty that could identify and individually treat children with learning disabilities. She claimed that these representations were fraudulently and/or negligently made, and that, to her detriment, she relied on the representations in entering into her agreement with the school. She also claimed that the school did not provide the stated services and therefore breached their contract. Finally, the mother alleged that psychiatric intervention was necessary because her son received services which proved to be inappropriate and harmful when the school failed to diagnose (or misdiagnosed) his learning disability. This, she claimed, constituted negligent infliction of emotional distress.

The Civil Court of the City of New York granted a portion of the private school's motion and denied part of the motion. The court held that the mother's breach of contract claim, alleging that the school agreed to detect her child's learning deficiencies and to provide the necessary tutorial and guidance services but failed to do so, was permissible. However, the mother could make a claim for fraudulent misrepresentation only if she could show that the school knowingly made the misrepresentations to her. Thus, she could only maintain an action based on intentional misrepresentation, not negligent misrepresentation. Finally, the mother could not recover under her claim for negligent infliction of emotional distress. The court noted that it is well established that physical contact or injury is no longer necessary for such a claim. However, the courts have unanimously held that monetary damages for educational malpractice based on a negligence theory are not recoverable. Therefore, the mother could not sue for alleged mental distress caused by negligence in educational practices. *Village Comm. School v. Adler*, 478 N.Y.S.2d 546 (N.Y.City Civ.Ct.1984).

In a breach of contract case, a private residential facility for the treatment of mentally handicapped adolescent boys located in Milwaukee, Wisconsin, brought suit in Illinois against the Chicago Board of Education and another local suburban school district to recover the value of services rendered to students from the defendant school districts. The dispute arose from the placement with the facility of six high school students. The facility, unfamiliar with Illinois procedures for the payment of tuition to private facilities for handicapped students, accepted the Illinois students into its program before it had received approval from Illinois for its rate structure. Without such approval, the facility was ineligible under Illinois law to receive tuition payments from Illinois school boards. The facility ultimately received the necessary approval and then sought payment of tuition for the entire time the children were at the facility. The school districts, however, refused to pay for any treatment provided prior to the facility's approval for Illinois funds. The facility then filed suit, seeking recovery for breach of contract.

A lower court held that the facts were not sufficient to prove the existence of an express or implied contract since the districts had not agreed to assume responsibility for the tuition for services provided prior to Illinois approval of the facility, nor did the districts have authority to enter into such agreements. The case was appealed to the Appellate Court of Illinois, which affirmed the lower court.

The appellate court rejected an argument made by the facility that a statute involved here was not applicable. Said the court, "the statute on its face clearly prohibits the placement of Illinois students in a nonapproved institution," such as the one involved here. The facility also argued that, under federal law, the school districts had a duty to provide handicapped children with a free education and that, therefore, the Illinois School Code could not be construed to prohibit the school districts from contracting with the facility. The court dismissed this argument by stating that a private education facility, such as the one involved here, lacks standing to assert the rights of handicapped children to a free education. The facility, therefore, could not rely on the students' rights under federal law to advance its contract claim. *Juneau Academy v. Chicago Bd. of Educ.*, 461 N.E.2d 597 (Ill.App.1st Dist.1984).

IV. TRAINING PERSONNEL UNDER THE EAHCA

Section 1431 of the EAHCA provides grants to colleges and state agencies to facilitate training of personnel for the education of handicapped. Whether this "training" provision also applies to parents is an issue which has been presented before the courts.

The parents of a handicapped student in Ohio attacked the quality of education their son was receiving. They asserted that the EAHCA obligated school districts to provide in-service training to parents of handicapped students. They also claimed that the Act required the school district to include summer classes and continuous occupational therapy in their child's curriculum. They requested and received a hearing but were unsuccessful in reversing the district's denial of the services. The Ohio State Board of Education affirmed the hearing officer's determination and the parents appealed to a U.S. district court, which affirmed the hearing officer's decision but directed the school district to provide the student with one hour of extracurricular activities each week. Both the parents and the school board appealed. The U.S. Court of Appeals, Sixth Circuit, affirmed the district court ruling, saying that the EAHCA did not obligate school districts to provide in-service training to parents of handicapped students. The court also affirmed the district court's denial of summer classes and continuous occupational therapy. These programs, the court found, were not necessary to permit the child to benefit from his instruction. Finally, the court reversed the district court decision to include a nonacademic extracurricular activity once per week, saying that the EAHCA did not require that states maximize the potential of handicapped children commensurate with the opportunity provided to other children. Accordingly, the district court holding was affirmed in part and reversed in part. *Rettig v. Kent City School Dist.*, 720 F.2d 463 (6th Cir.1983).

A U.S. district court in Texas, however, held that the parents of a handicapped child were entitled to training in behavioral techniques to handle their autistic and possibly mentally retarded daughter. *Stacey G. v. Pasadena School District*, 547 F.Supp. 61 (S.D.Tex.1982).

V. GIFTED PROGRAMS

In Pennsylvania a student who had scored 121 on an I.Q. test sued her school district in U.S. district court claiming that her exclusion from a gifted student program violated her rights under the EAHCA. Pennsylvania law provides as follows:

> Persons shall be assigned to a program for the gifted when they have an IQ of 130 or higher. A limited number of persons with IQ scores lower than 130 *may* be admitted to gifted programs when other educational criteria in the profile of the person strongly indicates gifted ability. (22 Pa. Admin. Code § 341.1)

In addressing the student's arguments, the district court held that although Pennsylvania law extended the same due process guarantees to gifted students as it did to handicapped students, the student was not entitled to the procedural protections of the EAHCA as a matter of federal law. The court also rejected the student's claim that she had been denied due process of law under the Fourteenth Amendment. It reasoned that because she had not achieved an I.Q. score of 130 or higher, the student had no "property interest" in being admitted to the gifted student program. Although under Pennsylvania law a student with a I.Q. score of less than 130 "may" be admitted to a gifted student program, this did not mean that such a student was entitled to admittance. Also, the court rejected the argument that the student's equal protection rights had been violated by the school district. It observed that because there is no fundamental right to an education under the U.S. Constitution, Pennsylvania's I.Q. regulations were only required to be "rationally related" to some legitimate state purpose. Accordingly, the district court ruled in favr of the school district. *Student Roe v. Commonwealth*, 638 F.Supp. 929 (E.D.Pa.1986).

A "placement lottery" was recently upheld by a New York appeals court. In this case a school district established a talented and gifted (TAG) program for its elementary school students. Although it identified 109 children as being gifted, it established a full-time TAG program with space available for only 27 students. The school district then used the lottery method to determine which of the 109 children would be admitted to the full-time TAG program. Consequently, the parents of a gifted child (one of the original 109) whose name was not chosen sued the school district, contending that the lottery was an arbitrary and capricious method of selection. The New York Supreme Court, Appellate Division, rejected this contention due to the fact that there is no constitutional right to a "gifted or talented" education. The parents' attempt to analogize their case to one in which a lottery was employed to select children for a handicapped student program was rejected by the court. The lottery method was upheld as a valid, reasonable way for the school district to solve its space limitation problem. *Bennett v. City School Dist.*, 497 N.Y.S.2d 72 (A.D.2d Dept.1985).

In the 1982-83 school year, a Pennsylvania school district organized a special program for gifted elementary students. The program was for public and nonpublic students and provided instruction one-half day per week in one of the district's public school buildings. Nonpublic school students were transported to the public schools by the school district. In the 1983-84 school year, the district reorganized its gifted student program. Instruction was offered in each public school and teachers traveled to each school on scheduled days, which eliminated the need for any student transportation. The parents of the nonpublic school students filed a lawsuit in the Commonwealth Court of Pennsylvania arguing that their children's right to a special education was violated. The Pennsylvania Department of Education investigated and found that the district was in violation of state law and directed the district to provide midday transportation to the nonpublic school students. Both the school district and the Department sought a court decision determining what their respective obligations were in providing midday transportation for the nonpublic school students.

The court stated that the issue was whether the district had an obligation to provide midday transportation to the nonpublic school students. The school district contended that its only transportation obligation to the gifted students arose out of a state statute which required school districts to provide identical transportation services to public and nonpublic school students. The Department argued that a different, more specific statute was controlling. The court observed that when a general provision in a statute is in conflict with a special provision in the same or other statute, the special provisions prevail, and the two will be construed, if possible, so that effect may be given to both statutes.

The court agreed with the Department that the controlling provision for the transportation of exceptional students was the more specific section of the code. The court said that the statute applied to the nonpublic elementary school gifted students since they were exceptional children and were regularly enrolled in an approved "special class" operated by the school district. The school district was required to furnish free transportation to the exceptional students enrolled in the nonpublic schools. *Woodland Hills School Dist. v. Commonwealth*, 516 A.2d 875 (Pa.Cmwlth.1986).

CHAPTER SEVEN
HANDICAP DISCRIMINATION

Page

The Rehabilitation Act of 1973 prohibits discrimination against the handicapped in programs receiving federal financial assistance. Under the Act, no otherwise qualified handicapped individual is to be excluded from employment, programs or services to which he or she is entitled. Additionally, claims for alleged discrimination are sometimes brought under the Equal Protection Clause of the U.S. Constitution, which also prohibits discrimination by guaranteeing that laws will be applied equally to all citizens.

I. DUTY NOT TO DISCRIMINATE AGAINST THE HANDICAPPED

The duty not to discriminate against handicapped individuals may arise by statute, and/or may be concomitant with the receipt of federal funding. Where a state's asserted interest in discriminating against the handicapped is outweighed by the liberty interests of the handicapped, the state must affirmatively act to eliminate the source of discrimination, or, in other cases, must refrain from acting when doing so would promote unfair discrimination.

A. Students, Patients and Other Individuals

The U.S. Supreme Court ruled recently that mental retardation is not a "suspect classification" calling for heightened protection under the U.S. Constitution. This case arose when the operator of a proposed group home for mentally handicapped individuals was denied a building-use permit by the city council of Cleburne, Texas. The city council determined that the group home would be classified as a "hospital for the feebleminded" under the zoning laws and proceeded to deny a permit to the group home. The operator sued the city in federal court, claiming that the council's action unlawfully discriminated against mentally retarded citizens in violation of the Equal Protection Clause of the U.S. Constitution.

The Supreme Court, while ordering that the group home be granted a permit, held that government regulations regarding mentally retarded individuals are not to be subjected to rigorous judicial analysis as are classifications based on race, alienage or sex. The Equal Protection Clause, held the Court, does not afford the same protection to handicapped citizens as it does to minorities. Although in this case the group home won its building-use permit, the Supreme Court's holding limited the scope of the Equal Protection Clause to cases involving irrational, unfounded or arbitrary action against the handicapped. *City of Cleburne, Texas v. Cleburne Living Center*, 105 S.Ct. 3249, 473 U.S. 432 (1985).

A New Hampshire father alleged that his daughter, a handicapped child, was not receiving a free appropriate education. He was granted an administrative due process hearing by the state. Dissatisfied with the results of the hearing, he sued the New Hampshire State Board of Education in U.S. district court. After the state refused to provide him with a free written transcript of the administrative hearing, he brought a separate lawsuit against it in the same court. The court ruled that the state did not have to provide a free written transcript of the hearing so he appealed to the U.S. Court of Appeals, First Circuit.

The court of appeals observed that, although a written transcript of the hearing would be more helpful than a recording for purposes of a lawsuit under the EAHCA, § 1415(d)(3) of the EAHCA only granted the right to receive either a written *or* electronic verbatim record of the hearing. Since the state had provided an electronic verbatim record of the administrative due process hearing, it had fulfilled its responsibility. The father's claim that because he could not afford the $3,000 for a written transcript, his due process rights had been violated, was rejected by the court of appeals. It concluded that the administrative due process hearing itself satisfied the father's basic due process rights.

The father also contended that the failure to provide a transcript violated his rights under the Equal Protection Clause. He claimed that the refusal to provide the transcript was the result of unconstitutional discrimination based upon either his daughter's handicap or his lack of wealth. The court of appeals did not accept the first argument since the father had failed to show that the EAHCA provision infringed upon the rights of any "suspect class." [A "suspect class" is a group of persons who are afforded special protection under the Equal Protection Clause (e.g. racial minorities).] It observed that the U.S. Supreme Court has held in *City of Cleburne v. Cleburne Living Center*, 473 U.S. 432 (1985), that handicapped persons are not a suspect class. Thus, legislative classifications based upon handicaps will not be given rigorous examination by the courts. Further, the court of appeals held that a classification based upon indigence received closer examination only if indigents were "completely unable to pay for some desired benefit [which results in] an absolute deprivation of a meaningful opportunity to enjoy that benefit." Here, the alleged classification based upon wealth only made recourse to the courts more difficult rather than impossible. The district court's decision was upheld. *Edward B. v. Paul*, 814 F.2d 52 (1st Cir.1987).

Pennsylvania's Public School Code provided that children who were removed from their parents' home by court order and placed in foster homes outside of the school district in which their parents resided (non-resident foster children) could be denied special education by the school district in which they were placed if no appropriate special education program existed within the district. Children placed in institutions or in homes which did not receive compensation for accepting the children could not be denied special education on these grounds.

Two handicapped children were placed in foster homes outside their parents' school districts. Their school districts of placement refused to provide the children with special education because it could not be provided within the districts. The children filed a class action lawsuit to challenge the disparate treatment of handicapped children who live in foster homes and those placed in institutions or in private homes which did not receive funds.

A U.S. district court noted that the Equal Protection Clause of the Fourteenth Amendment to the U.S. Constitution guarantees that similarly situated persons receive similar treatment. Differently situated persons may be treated differently as long as the classification thereby established is adequately tailored to serve an important governmental objective. The court declared that foster children were a "sensitive class" because they constituted a "discreet group of persons who, in the vast majority of cases, lack responsibility for and control over their status, and the power to change it, but who may, nevertheless, because of their status, be precluded from attending school in a non-resident district." The state, therefore, had to prove that the disparate treatment of non-resident foster children was "substantially related to the achievement of important governmental objectives."

The court determined that the disparate treatment of foster children was unconstitutional because foster children were not situated differently from other children with respect to the purpose of the Code provision. The state argued that the provision furthered the state's interest in providing public education with administrative and economic efficiency. Although this was a valid governmental objective, the court declared that the disparate treatment of foster children was not substantially related to its achievement. The court declared the code provision unconstitutional. It ordered that the children be provided public education services in the school districts in which their foster families resided. *Nancy M. v. Scanlon*, 666 F.Supp. 723 (E.D.Pa.1987).

A Kansas school district used a 3′ x 5′ "time-out" room for in-school suspensions of a handicapped student. The student had a history of truancy, violent behavior and wilful disobedience of school rules. The student was placed in the time-out room when he was disruptive so he could regain his composure and to prevent him from disturbing other students. He was to engage in classroom work while in the time-out room. The student sued the school district in a U.S. district court. He alleged that use of the time-out room violated his due process rights under the Fourteenth Amendment to the U.S. Constitution. He also claimed that use of the time-out room violated the Eighth Amendment's prohibition against cruel and inhumane punishment. The school district argued that the student's fundamental contention was that it had violated the EAHCA's change-in-placement provision. Therefore, the student's claim should fail because he had not exhausted his administrative remedies under the EAHCA.

The court held for the student concerning the exhaustion of remedies argument. The use of the time-out room was not an activity the EAHCA was intended to prevent. Therefore, the EAHCA was not the exclusive avenue through which the student could bring his lawsuit. The student could sue alleging deprivation of his constitutional rights under § 1983 of the Civil Rights Act.

The court also concluded that the use of the time-out room did not constitute cruel and inhumane punishment. The Supreme Court has held that the

Eighth Amendment protection against such punishment should not be extended to lawsuits brought by public school students.

The court held for the school district regarding the student's due process claim. The student was not deprived of his constitutional interest in education when he was placed in the time-out room. In fact, the use of the time-out room ensured that the student would not be deprived of his right to a public education when he was suspended because it kept him in school during that time. The student was not deprived of due process because he was placed in the time-out room only after three documented disciplinary violations. He was given sufficient prior notice of the reason for placement in the time-out room. The school sent written notice to his parents when use of the time-out room was contemplated. His parents were notified about time-out room use in conferences with school officials. The school district was not liable for violating the student's constitutional rights. *Hayes v. Unified School Dist. No. 377*, 669 F.Supp. 1519 (D.Kan.1987).

Six years after a handicapped individual was denied admission to a California nursing school, a federal appeals court ruled that she was entitled to damages for unlawful discrimination. The prospective student suffered from Crohn's Disease, an inflammatory bowel disorder which causes loss of weight, nausea, vomiting and other complications. She had been accepted to the Los Angeles County Medical Center School of Nursing in April, 1979, and had attended an orientation session. Two days before classes were to begin she was told that due to an unacceptable physical examination, she was being denied admission to the school. She filed suit in federal district court under the Rehabilitation Act, seeking an order that the school be compelled to accept her.

After twice being denied relief by the district court, the case came before the U.S. Court of Appeals, Ninth Circuit. The appeals court found that the woman was a handicapped individual within the meaning of the Rehabilitation Act, and noted that the school's physician had recommended that her application for admission be rejected because, in his opinion, it would be "too stressful" for her to study at the school. The court stated that "[i]t is precisely this type of general assumption about a handicapped person's ability that [the Act] was designed to avoid." Finding that the woman had been denied admission solely on the basis of her handicap, the court remanded the case to the district court with instructions to award her monetary damages and attorney's fees. *Kling v. County of Los Angeles*, 769 F.2d 532 (9th Cir.1985).

An Illinois case resulted in a ruling that a handicapped student may not sue the U.S. Secretary of Education. Here, a graduate student pursuing an MBA at Chicago's Roosevelt University failed to inform university officials that he was handicapped, and did not tell them that he was learning disabled. Instead, the university thought that he was recovering from a serious illness. In view of the student's "illness," the university allowed him to continue in its MBA program even though he had received his third "C," which usually results in academic dismissal. Eventually, the student was unable to meet the MBA program's requirements. He attempted to bring suit under the Rehabilitation Act directly against the U.S. Secretary of Education, seeking damages due to the secretary's refusal to review his claim that the university had discriminated against him on the basis of his handicap.

The federal district court observed that the student had never informed the university that he was handicapped by a learning disability. Unquestionably, he had no claim against the university since the Rehabilitation Act imposes no duty upon institutions which are unaware of a person's handicap, said the court, and this no doubt explained why he had attempted to sue the secretary instead. The student's lawsuit was thus dismissed by the court, which stated: "There is no doubt that a recipient or applicant of federal funds has a cause of action against the Secretary under Section 603 [of the Rehabilitation Act]. There is also no doubt that a beneficiary in [the handicapped student's] position has a private right of action against the recipient institution. But no private cause of action exists under Section 504 [of the Act] for a beneficiary against the Secretary." The student's complaint against the secretary was dismissed and he appealed to the U.S. Court of Appeals, Seventh Circuit.

The question before the court was whether the student could force the secretary to review his case or force the secretary to cut off the university's federal funding. The court held that "a request for damages against administrative adjudicators is not supported by any statute. . . . A request for damages against the Secretary of Education, who personally played no role in the administrative adjudication, also is not provided by any other statute." The court concluded that a private person has no legal interest in public enforcement of matters such as the termination of federal funding. The student had to be content with his own remedies against the university. The lower court's ruling that the student could not maintain a lawsuit against the secretary of education was upheld. *Salvador v. Bennett*, 800 F.2d 97 (7th Cir.1986).

As a result of reports of patient abuse at the Pennhurst State Hospital, a Pennsylvania institution for the severely mentally retarded, a state police officer was assigned to become an undercover aide at the hospital. Several hospital employees were later indicted by a federal grand jury and a male aide was convicted of violating the right of severely retarded persons to personal security, a federal crime. The evidence showed that the aide frequently "punched, kicked, kneed, or shoved" patients for no reason and that he frequently flicked cigarette butts on the floor where he hoped that more severely retarded patients would ingest them. The U.S. Court of Appeals, Third Circuit, upheld his conviction. The aide had knowingly deprived the patients of their federally protected right to personal security while acting under the authority of state law. *United States v. Dise*, 763 F.2d 586 (3d Cir.1985).

In a Texas case, the parents of a mentally handicapped child, who was enrolled in a private school, contacted a public school district regarding a possible public school placement for their child. A meeting was held a year later at which the parents were not present and of which they had no knowledge. At the meeting, it was decided that the child should be placed in an EMR class in the public schools. When the parents were finally contacted they rejected the recommendation, saying that their son was not mentally retarded. The parents continued private school placement for their child.

Approximately two years later the school district started a public awareness "blitz" to reach handicapped children not then receiving a free appropriate public education. A year after they became aware of this "child find" program, the parents once again contacted the school district for a possible public school placement. The child was eventually enrolled in a public school program and the parents sought reimbursement for their private school tuition expenses in a U.S. district court.

The court held that the school district had been under an affirmative duty to determine what special services would be needed for the child and then to provide those services. In failing to do so, the school district had discriminated against the child in violation of section 504 of the Rehabilitation Act. The parents were not entitled to damages under the EAHCA but were entitled to private school tuition reimbursement under the Rehabilitation Act. However, the court found that the parents were not entitled to tuition reimbursement subsequent to the time they became aware of the "child find" program. *David H. v. Spring Branch Indep. School Dist.*, 569 F.Supp. 1324 (S.D.Tex.1983).

A group of mentally retarded children in Virginia brought suit against the Virginia Commissioner of the Department of Welfare, and other state officials, seeking injunctive relief enjoining the defendants from maintaining them in an institution or state hospital. The children claimed that these placements were made in lieu of providing them with an appropriate education and services in a foster home or other community-based facility in their home communities. A U.S. district court held that the children had a valid claim under the Developmentally Disabled Assistance and Bill of Rights Act, the EAHCA and the Rehabilitation Act. These statutes afford personal civil rights to beneficiaries under the statutes, which were intended to promote equal treatment of and equal opportunity to the beneficiaries. The defendants' motion for summary judgment on the ground that the children had failed to state a valid claim was denied. *Medley v. Ginsberg*, 492 F.Supp. 1294 (S.D.W.Va.1980).

A group of mentally retarded children brought suit against the Board of Education of the City of New York challenging a proposed plan to segregate within the public schools those retarded children who were carriers of hepatitis B virus. The board argued that the plan was valid because it was formulated pursuant to New York City health department guidelines. A U.S. district court held in favor of the children, saying that the health department guidelines were more "akin to general statements of policy than mandatory prescriptions." Thus, the guidelines would not be afforded "presumptive validity." The plan was also flawed because it violated the Rehabilitation Act and the EAHCA. The New York Board of Education had not shown that the hepatitis B carriers had actually engaged in unhygienic contacts. The court noted that the segregation plan would violate the EAHCA in that the children would not be educated in the "least restrictive environment." Finally, despite the fact that there were over one million school children in New York City's public school system, no group other than the mentally retarded students was tested for hepatitis B. This violated the children's equal protection rights under the U.S. Constitution. This decision was affirmed by the U.S. Court of Appeals, Second Circuit. *New York State Ass'n for Retarded Children v. Carey*, 612 F.2d 644 (2d Cir.1979).

In New Hampshire an unsuccessful discrimination claim was brought by the mother of a disabled child in U.S. district court, alleging discrimination under the federal Rehabilitation Act. She alleged that the New Hampshire Medical Assistance Program (NHMAP) unlawfully discriminated against her son solely on the basis of his handicap. The NHMAP provides medical assistance under the medical needs program only to persons under eighteen years of age who are blind, she pointed out, while denying benefits to persons under eighteen years of age who are handicapped by any other disability. The state moved to dismiss the action for failure to state a claim upon which relief could be granted and the motion was granted.

The court stated that the state's refusal to expand the eligibility requirements for medical assistance to include the plaintiff in this case was not so unreasonable and arbitrary as to constitute unlawful discrimination. It was noted that the plaintiffs did not allege that New Hampshire's exclusion of sight-disabled children from medical assistance was motivated by an animus against handicapped individuals. In fact, the statutory history revealed that the exclusion was based on congressional authorization designed to encourage continued state participation in the Medicaid program, through limitation of the state's financial commitment. In the absence of any statutory or regulatory requirement identifying as discriminatory the refusal to undertake affirmative action by extending additional services to the handicapped, the court held that it was not at liberty to fashion its own affirmative action requirements. Thus, in spite of the plaintiff's obvious need for medical assistance and the compelling nature of his request for medical assistance equal to that afforded other disabled persons under the NHMAP, the court determined it should not overrule the judgment of state of New Hampshire and Congress on this matter of social policy. *Duquette v. Dupuis*, 582 F.Supp. 1365 (D.N.H.1984).

A group of students and would-be students at the University of Texas at Austin sought declaratory and injunctive relief in federal district court requiring the university to make its shuttle buses accessible to wheelchairs. The plaintiffs were all confined to wheelchairs and, therefore, handicapped individuals under the Rehabilitation Act of 1973. They were required to pay a mandatory student services fee each semester, which was used in part to pay for the operation of the shuttle bus system. However, they could not use the system because the buses were not accessible to wheelchairs. They contended that the university's failure to provide them with accessible shuttle service limited their ability to fully participate in academic and extracurricular programs, and that this failure was in violation of federal law. They also contended that the failure to accommodate wheelchairs was a breach of their contract with the university to provide them with bus transportation in exchange for student service fees.

The district court disagreed with these contentions. It held that the shuttle bus system was not a program receiving federal financial assistance for purposes of the Rehabilitation Act and therefore was not subject to the requirements of the Act, that the university had no obligation under the Equal Protection Clause of the Fourteenth Amendment to make major expenditures of funds required to make the shuttle bus system accessible to wheelchairs, and that the university had not "contracted" to provide shuttle bus service to mobility-impaired students on the basis of statements made in the university general information booklet. The students' request for declaratory and injunctive relief was therefore denied. *Ferris v. Univ. of Texas at Austin*, 558 F.Supp. 536 (W.D.Tex.1983).

B. Teachers

Teachers and other school employees are also protected by the Rehabilitation Act against discrimination on the basis of handicap.

The U.S. Supreme Court ruled that tuberculosis is a handicap under § 504 of the Rehabilitation Act. The Act defines a handicapped individual as "any person who (i) has a physical or mental impairment which substantially limits one or more of such person's major life activities, (ii) has a record of such impairment or (iii) is regarded as having such an impairment." It defines "physical impairment" as disorders affecting, among other things, the respiratory system and defines "major life activities" as "functions such as caring for one's self . . . and working."

The case involved a Florida elementary school teacher who was discharged because of the continued recurrence of tuberculosis. The teacher sued the school board under § 504 but a U.S. district court dismissed her claims. However, the U.S. Court of Appeals, Eleventh Circuit, reversed the district court's decision and the school board appealed to the U.S. Supreme Court.

The Supreme Court ruled that tuberculosis was a handicap under § 504 because it affected the respiratory system and affected her ability to work (a major life activity). The school board contended that in defining a handicapped individual under § 504, the contagious effects of a disease can be distinguished from the disease's physical effects. However, the Court reasoned that the teacher's contagion and her physical impairment both resulted from the same condition: tuberculosis. It would be unfair to allow an employer to distinguish between a disease's potential effect on others and its effect on the afflicted employee in order to justify discriminatory treatment. Allowing discrimination based on the contagious effects of a physical impairment would be inconsistent with the underlying purpose of § 504. According to the Court, that purpose is to ensure that handicapped persons are not denied jobs because of prejudice or ignorance. It noted that society's myths and fears about disability and disease are as handicapping as the physical impairment, and concluded that contagion cannot remove a person from § 504 coverage. It remanded the case to the district court to determine whether the teacher was "otherwise qualified" for her job and whether the school board could reasonably accommodate her as an employee. *School Bd. of Nassau County v. Arline*, 107 S.Ct. 1123 (1987).

A teacher of hearing-impaired children was relegated to an administrative position when the school district discovered that he had AIDS. The teacher sued the school board asserting that it had violated his rights under the Rehabilitation Act of 1973 by removing him from the classroom. The teacher's request for a preliminary injunction which would have allowed him to teach until the court could hold a trial and issue a ruling was denied by a U.S.

district court. The U.S. Court of Appeals, Ninth Circuit, reversed and issued the preliminary injunction. The court of appeals has now issued a decision which sets out the reasons for the issuance of the preliminary injunction.

The court noted that to acquire the preliminary injunction the teacher had to demonstrate a combination of probable success at trial and a possibility of irreparable injury. Under the Rehabilitation Act the teacher could not be dismissed because of his handicapping condition (AIDS) if he was otherwise qualified to teach. The court then applied a test devised by the U.S. Supreme Court in *School Board of Nassau County v. Arline*. The test provided that "[a] person who poses a significant risk of communicating an infectious disease to others in the workplace will not be otherwise qualified for his or her job if reasonable accommodations will not eliminate that risk." The court then pointed out the district court's finding that transmission of AIDS was unlikely to occur in the classroom. The court held that the teacher was otherwise qualified for his position because his presence in the classroom would not pose "a significant risk of communicating an infectious disease to others." This finding meant that the teacher would probably succeed at trial.

The court then noted that although the teacher's salary was not reduced when he was transferred to the administrative position, the transfer removed him from a job for which he had developed special skills and from which he derived "tremendous personal satisfaction and joy." The administrative position, on the other hand, involved no student contact and did not utilize the teacher's skills, training or experience. The court also observed that the teacher's ability to work would surely be affected in time by AIDS which has proved fatal in all reported cases. The court concluded that any delay in returning the teacher to the classroom caused an irretrievable loss of the teacher's productive time. This established the possibility of irreparable injury if the preliminary injunction was not awarded.

Because the teacher had shown 1) that he would probably succeed at trial, and 2) that the denial of a preliminary injunction in his favor could cause him irreparable injury the court awarded the preliminary injunction. The teacher was returned to the classroom. *Chalk v. U.S. District Court*, 840 F.2d 701 (9th Cir.1988).

An applicant for a special education teaching position in Iowa sued a local school district under both the federal Rehabilitation Act and Iowa law, alleging that the district refused to hire him due to his physical disability. The teacher, a resident of Vermont, suffered from several severe handicaps, but was able to walk without assistance and to lift children and drive. The teacher applied to the Iowa school district for a job and was scheduled for an interview in Iowa, at his own expense, with possible reimbursement if he were hired. After arranging the interview, the teacher became concerned that he had not disclosed his handicaps. Because of his limited financial resources, he did not wish to fly to Iowa, only to be rejected because of his handicaps. He called the school district and explained his handicaps. He was told that the job involved transporting children which, in turn, required a bus driver's permit that the teacher probably could not get because of his handicaps. The district suggested that a trip to Iowa would probably be futile. The teacher then sued in U.S. district court, which found in his favor.

The court stated that the test of proof for a discrimination claim under the Rehabilitation Act is: 1) that the plaintiff is a handicapped individual under the terms of the statute; 2) that the plaintiff is otherwise qualified to participate in the program or activity at issue; 3) that the plaintiff was excluded from the program or activity solely by reason of her or his handicap; and 4) that the program or activity receives federal financial assistance. There was no dispute that the plaintiff was a "handicapped individual" within the meaning of the Rehabilitation Act, the court had little difficulty in finding that the plaintiff was "otherwise qualified" for the position because of his superior credentials. The court also found that the plaintiff had satisfied the third and fourth prongs of the test in that the district was a recipient of federal financial assistance, including funds received pursuant to the EAHCA and that, with a minimum of accommodation, the school district could have arranged an alternative situation whereby the teacher would not have had to transport children. The court awarded the teacher $1,000 damages for mental anguish, and $5,150 for loss of earnings. *Fitzgerald v. Green Valley Educ. Agency*, 589 F.Supp. 1130 (S.D.Iowa 1984).

In 1979, the Council for the Hearing Impaired of Long Island and others brought suit in U.S. district court against the Commissioner of Education of the State of New York, and several federal officials, alleging that the offering of lower salaries at educational institutions for handicapped students was unlawful. Specifically, the plaintiffs contended that because teaching salaries at these institutions were lower than those found in other schools, there existed a relatively high staff turnover rate which had an adverse impact on handicapped students' educations. The plaintiffs charged that this violated the EAHCA, § 504 of the Rehabilitation Act, section 1983 of the Civil Rights Act, and the First and Ninth Amendments to the U.S. Constitution.

On a motion for summary judgment, the district court dismissed the claim that a high staff turnover rate was violative of the EAHCA, noting that nothing in the EAHCA requires that the education of handicapped children be "equal" to that of other children. All that is required is that handicapped children be provided with an "educational benefit." Also dismissed were the plaintiff's claims under the First and Ninth Amendments, since education is not guaranteed by the U.S. Constitution. However, the plaintiffs were allowed to proceed with their claims under the Rehabilitation Act and the Civil Rights Act, insofar as they alleged that the state of New York had unlawfully discriminated between handicapped and nonhandicapped children in the provision of educational services. The district court then proceeded to admonish the plaintiffs for failing to diligently prosecute their case, stating that they "have been content to file repetitive motions with this Court without developing the factual bases necessary to support their claims." The court stated that unless the plaintiffs brought new evidence establishing their claims, the case would be dismissed for lack of prosecution. *Council for the Hearing Impaired v. Ambach*, 610 F.Supp. 1051 (E.D.N.Y.1985).

II. RACIAL DISCRIMINATION IN PLACEMENT PROGRAMS

The de facto overrepresentation of minority students in special education programs, or underrepresentation of such students in gifted programs is insufficient to prove racial discrimination in placement programs. A plaintiff must prove that the alleged overrepresentation or underrepresentation is the result of purposeful discriminatory intention.

In 1976, a desegregation order made busing mandatory in Dallas, Texas. Despite the order, minority scores on national achievement tests remained low, and the Dallas area school districts wanted to improve minority education scores. However, they were ordered by the federal district court not to disturb the present levels of desegregation in the schools brought about by the 1976 order because the court deemed the levels acceptable. Three South Dallas Education Centers for remedial learning were then developed for minorities by the school districts and were approved by the U.S. district court and Court of Appeals as complying with the desegregation order.

The school districts made another proposal for four remedial education centers for West Dallas minority students. Students in the fourth through sixth grades who were currently being bused would attend a center in their own attendance zone. The centers would have a teacher-pupil ratio of 1:18 rather than the required 1:27. Although salaries would be higher, requirements for teachers in the centers would be more stringent. In order to avoid disruptions due to "pull outs" for special lessons and tutoring, students would attend the school for extended hours. In addition, enhanced programs in special fields such as science were also planned.

Opponents of the proposed centers questioned the progress that the school districts claimed to have made in the existing South Dallas Centers, contending that the methodology used to tabulate improvements among the students attending the centers was flawed. However, the district court approved the West Dallas plan in spite of the opponents' objections. The court determined that providing remedial learning did more to prevent segregation than busing because it improved the quality of minority education. Furthermore, stated the court, the centers were the best educational opportunity available to the students. The proposal for the remedial education centers was therefore approved. *Tasby v. Wright*, 630 F.Supp. 597 (N.D.Tex.1986).

The Georgia chapter of the NAACP commenced a class action lawsuit in U.S. district court on behalf of all black children in the state, claiming that the Georgia State Board of Education and a number of local school districts were assigning black students to programs for the educable mentally retarded in a racially discriminatory manner. The NAACP produced uncontroverted statistical evidence that a disproportionately high number of black students had been taken out of regular classrooms and placed in EMR programs. Depending on the school district, this was done on the basis of state I.Q. tests, the Metropolitan Achievement Test, the Development Indicators for the Assessment of Learning Tests, the MacMillan Placement Test, as well as other familiar evaluation devices and procedures. The NAACP made two basic allegations: 1) the use of these placement methods was intended to produce intraschool racial segregation, and 2) black children were assigned to the EMR programs in a discriminatory manner. Thus, the essence of the plaintiff's lawsuit was that since a disproportionately large number of black children were assigned to EMR programs, racial segregation had been the inevitable result. The methods of assignment to the programs, as well as the programs themselves, were alleged to be in violation of the U.S. Constitution, the Civil Rights Act and the Rehabilitation Act. The district court ruled against the plaintiffs on all counts and an appeal was taken to the U.S. Court of Appeals, Eleventh Circuit.

The appellate court held that ability grouping *per se*, and placement of black students in special education programs, did not violate federal law "even when it results in racial disparity in a school district's classrooms." The problem, said the court of appeals, stemmed from past racial segregation. Georgia's black children had previously been confined to grossly inferior "black" schools, receiving substandard public educations. When integration took place, "lack of [prior] educational quality would predictably cause [black] students from the inferior system to immediately be resegregated" within special education classes. The court of appeals had previously struck down this practice, holding that a newly-integrated school district may not use ability groupings if the result is racial segregation.

However, in the present case none of the black children had ever attended racially segregated public schools; all of Georgia's public schools had been integrated since the early 1970's. Therefore, the black children in this case could not claim that they had been placed in special education classes due to their past attendance at substandard schools. Past segregation had not caused them to be assigned to special education classes. Indeed, the court found that "'family background' and 'hard work,' rather than race, had the most powerful and consistent relationship to scholastic success." Accordingly, the court declared that the grouping of students on the basis of ability or achievement was permissible, even if the impact of such ability grouping was not racially neutral, as long as the school district had operated a nonsegregated school system "for a period of at least several years."

The NAACP also argued that "ability grouping exacerbates, rather than relieves, the problem of disproportionately lower achievement by black students." This argument was dismissed by the court, which found that ability grouping was educationally sound and "permits more resources to be routed to lower achieving students in the form of lower pupil-teacher ratios and additional instructional materials." Although nearly all of the district court's rulings against the NAACP were affirmed, the court of appeals remanded the case to the district court for a hearing on whether the NAACP was entitled to relief under the Rehabilitation Act for the school district's misinterpretation of state I.Q. regulations. *Georgia State Conference of Branches of NAACP v. State of Georgia*, 775 F.2d 1403 (11th Cir.1985).

Black parents in Maryland sought to reopen a school desegregation case which had been decided in 1972. The parents, who had been plaintiffs in the earlier case, now alleged that the school district was not in compliance with the 1972 desegregation order. The parents claimed that the district was intentionally discriminating on racial grounds in the area of special education. They claimed that statistical evidence showed that racial imbalances existed in the district's special education and talented and gifted education programs.

The same U.S. district court held that despite the statistical overrepresentation of blacks in special education programs, the procedures followed by the school system in placing children in special education programs did not discriminate against black children. The district utilized a checklist which included physical, emotional and academic evaluations and from which, once a handicapping condition was verified, it formulated an individualized education program. If parents objected to the proposed IEP or any part of the process of identification, diagnosis or formulation of an IEP, they were afforded administrative hearings as required by the Education for All Handicapped Children Act. The court also upheld the district's use of the California Achievement Test and the Cognitive Abilities Test for admission into the district's gifted student program. It also found that there had been a constant effort on the part of the district's staff to include greater numbers of black children in the gifted program. Accordingly, it concluded that the district had not intentionally discriminated against black children in the area of special education.

The case was appealed to the U.S. Court of Appeals, Fourth Circuit, which partially upheld the district court. The lower court had properly noted that usually, where numerical racial disparities exist in special programs, it is presumed that such disparities are the result of "chance" and not illegal racial discrimination. However, the rule is different in school districts that have a past history of racial segregation. The appeals court held that in such districts, the burden of proof is on the district to show that the disparities in the number of minority youths assigned to special and gifted programs is not the result of racial discrimination. Because the Maryland school district in this case had, in the past, operated a racially segregated school system, the Court of Appeals remanded the case to the lower court with instructions to force the school district to meet its higher standard of proof in determining whether the placement of students in special programs was discriminatory. *Vaughs v. Bd. of Educ. of Prince George's County*, 758 F.2d 983 (4th Cir.1985).

APPENDIX A

THE EDUCATION FOR ALL HANDICAPPED CHILDREN ACT OF 1975

AS AMÉNDED THROUGH MAY, 1988

[The EAHCA is reproduced here in its entirety, fully compiled, as amended by Congress through May, 1988. No separate section on amendments is included in this volume because all amendments have been placed in the appropriate location in the statutory text, and any repealed sections have been deleted from the text. The Handicapped Children's Protection Act of 1986 appears in § 1415(e)(4) and § 1415(f). The major provisions of the Education of the Handicapped Act Amendments of 1986 appear in §§ 1408, 1411, 1413, 1418, 1419, 1433, and 1471-85. The statutory text provided here is completely updated and allows for handy, one-stop referencing of the EAHCA.]

CHAPTER 33—EDUCATION OF THE HANDICAPPED

SUBCHAPTER I—GENERAL PROVISIONS

Sec.

1400. Congressional statements and declarations.
 (a) Short title.
 (b) Findings.
 (c) Purpose.

1401. Definitions.

1402. Office of Special Education Programs.
 (a) Establishment; purposes.
 (b) Deputy Assistant Secretary: selection and supervision, compensation; Associate Deputy Assistant Secretary and minimum number of assistants: establishment, compensation.

1403. Repealed.

1404. Acquisition of equipment and construction of necessary facilities.
 (a) Authorization for use of funds.
 (b) Recovery of payments under certain conditions.

1405. Employment of handicapped individuals.

1406. Removal of architectural barriers.
 (a) Grants.
 (b) Authorization of appropriations.

1407. Regulation requirements.
 (a) Minimum period for comment before effective date.
 (b) Lessening of procedural or substantive protections as in effect on July 20, 1983, prohibited.
 (c) Transmission to Advisory Committee.

1408. Eligibility for financial assistance.

SUBCHAPTER II—ASSISTANCE FOR EDUCATION OF ALL HANDICAPPED CHILDREN

1411. Entitlements and allocations.
 (a) Formula for determining maximum State entitlement.
 (b) Distribution and use of grant funds by States for fiscal year ending September 30, 1978.
 (c) Distribution and use of grant funds by States for fiscal years ending September 30, 1979, and thereafter.
 (d) Allocation of funds within States to local educational agencies and intermediate educational units.
 (e) Territories and possessions.
 (f) Indian reservations.
 (g) Reductions or increases.

1412. Eligibility requirements.

SUBCHAPTER III—CENTERS AND SERVICES TO MEET SPECIAL NEEDS OF THE HANDICAPPED

SUBCHAPTER IV—TRAINING PERSONNEL FOR THE EDUCATION OF THE HANDICAPPED

SUBCHAPTER V— RESEARCH IN THE EDUCATION OF THE HANDICAPPED

SUBCHAPTER VI—INSTRUCTIONAL MEDIA FOR THE HANDICAPPED

SUBCHAPTER VII—SPECIAL PROGRAMS FOR CHILDREN WITH SPECIFIC LEARNING DISABILITIES

SUBCHAPTER VIII—HANDICAPPED INFANTS AND TODDLERS [NEW]

SUBCHAPTER I—GENERAL PROVISIONS

§ 1400. Congressional statements and declarations

(a) Short title

This chapter may be cited as the "Education of the Handicapped Act".

(b) Findings

The Congress finds that—

(1) there are more than eight million handicapped children in the United States today;

(2) the special educational needs of such children are not being fully met;

(3) more than half of the handicapped children in the United States do not receive appropriate educational services which would enable them to have full equality of opportunity;

(4) one million of the handicapped children in the United States are excluded entirely from the public school system and will not go through the educational process with their peers;

(5) there are many handicapped children throughout the United States participating in regular school programs whose handicaps prevent them from having a successful educational experience because their handicaps are undetected;

(6) because of the lack of adequate services within the public school system, families are often forced to find services outside the public school system, often at great distance from their residence and at their own expense;

(7) developments in the training of teachers and in diagnostic and instructional procedures and methods have advanced to the point that, given appropriate funding, State and local educational agencies can and will provide effective special education and related services to meet the needs of handicapped children;

(8) State and local educational agencies have a responsibility to provide education for all handicapped children, but present financial resources are inadequate to meet the special educational needs of handicapped children; and

(9) it is in the national interest that the Federal Government assist State and local efforts to provide programs to meet the educational needs of handicapped children in order to assure equal protection of the law.

(c) Purpose

It is the purpose of this chapter to assure that all handicapped children have available to them, within the time periods specified in section 1412(2)(B) of this title, a free appropriate public education which emphasizes special education and related services designed to meet their unique needs, to assure that the rights of handicapped children and their parents or guardians are protected, to assist States and localities to provide for the education of all handicapped children, and to assess and assure the effectiveness of efforts to educate handicapped children.

§ 1401. Definitions

(a) As used in this chapter—

(1) The term "handicapped children" means mentally retarded, hard of hearing, deaf, speech or language impaired, visually handicapped, seriously emotionally disturbed, orthopedically impaired, or other health impaired children, or children with specific learning disabilities, who by reason thereof require special education and related services.

(2) Repealed. Pub. L. 98-199, § 2(2), Dec. 2, 1983, 97 Stat. 1357.

(3) The term "Advisory Committee" means the National Advisory Committee on the Education of Handicapped Children.

(4) The term "construction", except where otherwise specified, means (A) erection of new or expansion of existing structures, and the acquisition and installation of equipment therefor; or (B) acquisition of existing structures not owned by any agency or institution making application for assistance under this chapter; or (C) remodeling or alteration (including the acquisition, installation, modernization, or replacement of equipment) of existing structures; or (D) acquisition of land in connection with activities in clauses (A), (B), and (C); or (E) a combination of any two or more of the foregoing.

(5) The term "equipment" includes machinery, utilities, and built-in equipment and any necessary enclosures or structures to house them, and includes all other items necessary for the functioning of a particular facility as a facility for the provision of educational services, including items such as instructional equipment and necessary furniture, printed, published, and audio-visual instructional materials, telecommunications, sensory, and other technological aids and devices, and books, periodicals, documents, and other related materials.

(6) The term "State" means any of the several States, the District of Columbia, the Commonwealth of Puerto Rico, the Virgin Islands, Guam, American Samoa, the Northern Mariana Islands, or the Trust Territory of the Pacific Islands.

(7) The term "State educational agency" means the State board of education or other agency or officer primarily responsible for the State supervision of public elementary and secondary schools, or, if there is no such officer or agency, an officer or agency designated by the Governor or by State law.

(8) The term "local educational agency" means a public board of education or other public authority legally constituted within a State for either administrative control or direction of, or to perform a service function for, public elementary or secondary schools in a city, county, township, school district, or other political subdivision of a State, or such combination of school districts or counties as are recognized in a State as an administrative agency for its public elementary or secondary schools. Such term also includes any other public institution or agency having administrative control and direction of a public elementary or secondary school.

(9) The term "elementary school" means a day or residential school which provides elementary education, as determined under State law.

(10) The term "secondary school" means a day or residential school which provides secondary education, as determined under State law, except that it does not include any education provided beyond grade 12.

(11) The term "institution of higher education" means an educational institution in any State which—

(A) admits as regular students only individuals having a certificate of graduation from a high school, or the recognized equivalent of such a certificate;

(B) is legally authorized within such State to provide a program of education beyond high school;

(C) provides an educational program for which it awards a bachelor's degree, or provides not less than a two-year program which is acceptable for full credit toward such a degree, or offers a two-year program in engineering, mathematics, or the physical or biological sciences which is designed to prepare the student to work as a technician and at a semiprofessional level in engineering, scientific, or other technological fields which require the understanding and application of basic engineering, scientific, or mathematical principles or knowledge;

(D) is a public or other nonprofit institution; and

(E) is accredited by a nationally recognized accrediting agency or association listed by the Secretary pursuant to this paragraph or, if not so accredited, is an institution whose credits are accepted, on transfer, by not less than three institutions which are so accredited, for credit on the same basis as if transferred from an institution so accredited: *Provided, however,* That in the case of an institution offering a two-year program in engineering, mathematics, or the physical or biological sciences which is designed to prepare the student to work as a technician and at a semiprofessional level in engineering, scientific, or technological fields which require the understanding and application of basic engineering, scientific, or mathematical principles or knowledge, if the Secretary determines that there is no nationally recognized accrediting agency or association qualified to accredit such institutions, he shall appoint an advisory committee, composed of persons specially qualified to evaluate training provided by such institutions, which shall prescribe the standards of content, scope, and quality which must be met in order to qualify such institutions to participate under this Act and shall also determine whether particular institutions meet such standards. For the purposes of this paragraph the Secretary shall publish a list of nationally recognized accrediting agencies or associations which he determines to be reliable authority as to the quality of education or training offered; and

(F) The term includes community colleges receiving funding from the Secretary of the Interior under Public Law 95-471.

(12) The term "nonprofit" as applied to a school, agency, organization, or institution means a school, agency, organization, or institution owned and operated by one or more non-profit corporations or associations no part of the net earnings of which inures, or may lawfully inure, to the benefit of any private shareholder or individual.

(13) The term "research and related purposes" means research, research training (including the payment of stipends and allowances), surveys, or

demonstrations in the field of education of handicapped children, or the dissemination of information derived therefrom, including (but without limitation) experimental schools.

(14) The term "Secretary" means the Secretary of Education.

(15) The term "children with specific learning disabilities" means those children who have a disorder in one or more of the basic psychological processes involved in understanding or in using language, spoken or written, which disorder may manifest itself in imperfect ability to listen, think, speak, read, write, spell, or do mathematical calculations. Such disorders include such conditions as perceptual handicaps, brain injury, minimal brain dysfunction, dyslexia, and developmental aphasia. Such term does not include children who have learning problems which are primarily the result of visual, hearing, or motor handicaps, of mental retardation, of emotional disturbance, or of environmental, cultural, or economic disadvantage.

(16) The term "special education" means specially designed instruction, at no cost to parents or guardians, to meet the unique needs of a handicapped child, including classroom instruction, instruction in physical education, home instruction, and instruction in hospitals and institutions.

(17) The term "related services" means transportation, and such developmental, corrective, and other supportive services (including speech pathology and audiology, psychological services, physical and occupational therapy, recreation, and medical and counseling services, except that such medical services shall be for diagnostic and evaluation purposes only) as may be required to assist a handicapped child to benefit from special education, and includes the early identification and assessment of handicapping conditions in children.

(18) The term "free appropriate public education" means special education and related services which (A) have been provided at public expense, under public supervision and direction, and without charge, (B) meet the standards of the State educational agency, (C) include an appropriate preschool, elementary, or secondary school education in the State involved, and (D) are provided in conformity with the individualized education program required under section 1414(a)(5) of this title.

(19) The term "individualized education program" means a written statement for each handicapped child developed in any meeting by a representative of the local educational agency or an intermediate educational unit who shall be qualified to provide, or supervise the provision of, specially designed instruction to meet the unique needs of handicapped children, the teacher, the parents or guardian of such child, and, whenever appropriate, such child, which statement shall include (A) a statement of the present levels of educational performance of such child, (B) a statement of annual goals, including short-term instructional objectives, (C) a statement of the specific educational services to be provided to such child, and the extent to which such child will be able to participate in regular educational programs, (D) the projected date for initiation and anticipated duration of such services, and (E) appropriate objective criteria and evaluation procedures and schedules for determining, on at least an annual basis, whether instructional objectives are being achieved.

(20) The term "excess costs" means those costs which are in excess of the average annual per student expenditure in a local educational agency during the preceding school year for an elementary or secondary school student, as

may be appropriate, and which shall be computed after deducting (A) amounts received under this subchapter or under title I [20 U.S.C. 2701 et seq.] or title VII [20 U.S.C. 3221 et seq.] of the Elementary and Secondary Education Act of 1965, and (B) any State or local funds expended for programs which would qualify for assistance under this subchapter or under such titles.

(21) The term "native language" has the meaning given that term by section 703(a)(2) of the Bilingual Education Act [20 U.S.C. 3223(a)(2)].

(22) The term "intermediate educational unit" means any public authority, other than a local educational agency, which is under the general supervision of a State educational agency, which is established by State law for the purpose of providing free public education on a regional basis, and which provides special education and related services to handicapped children within that State.

(23)(A) The term "public or private nonprofit agency or organization" includes an Indian tribe.

(B) The terms "Indian", "American Indian", and "Indian American" mean an individual who is a member of an Indian tribe.

(C) The term "Indian tribe" means any Federal or State Indian tribe, band, rancheria, pueblo, colony, or community, including any Alaskan native village or regional village corporation (as defined in or established under the Alaska Native Claims Settlement Act).

(b) For purposes of subchapter III of this chapter, "handicapped youth" means any handicapped child (as defined in subsection (a) (1) of this section) who

(1) is twelve years of age or older; or

(2) is enrolled in the seventh or higher grade in school.

§ 1402. Office of Special Education Programs

(a) Administration and execution of programs and activities

There shall be, within the Office of Special Education and Rehabilitation Services in the Department of Education, an Office of Special Education Programs which shall be the principal agency in the Department for administering and carrying out this and other programs and activities concerning the education and training of the handicapped.

(b) Deputy Assistant Secretary: selection and supervision, General Schedule and Senior Executive Service status; Associate Deputy Assistant Secretary and minimum assistantships: establishment, General Schedule status

(1) The office established under subsection (a) of this section shall be headed by a Deputy Assistant Secretary who shall be selected by the Secretary and shall report directly to the Assistant Secretary for Special Education and Rehabilitative Services. The position of Deputy Assistant Secretary shall be in grade GS-18 of the General Schedule under section 5104 of Title 5 and shall be a Senior Executive Service position for the purposes of section 3132(a)(2) of such Title.

(2) In addition to such Deputy Assistant Secretary, there shall be established in such office not less than six positions for persons to assist the Dep-

uty Assistant Secretary, including the position of the Associate Deputy Assistant Secretary. Each such position shall be in grade GS-15 of the General Schedule under section 5104 of Title 5.

§ 1403. Repealed.

§ 1404. Acquisition of equipment and construction of necessary facilities

(a) Authorization for use of funds

In the case of any program authorized by this chapter, if the Secretary determines that such program will be improved by permitting the funds authorized for such program to be used for the acquisition of equipment and the construction of necessary facilities, he may authorize the use of such funds for such purposes.

(b) Recovery of payments under certain conditions

If within twenty years after the completion of any construction (except minor remodeling or alteration) for which funds have been paid pursuant to a grant or contract under this chapter the facility constructed ceases to be used for the purposes for which it was constructed, the United States, unless the Secretary determines that there is good cause for releasing the recipient of the funds from its obligation, shall be entitled to recover from the applicant or other owner of the facility an amount which bears the same ratio to the then value of the facility as the amount of such Federal funds bore to the cost of the portion of the facility financed with such funds. Such value shall be determined by agreement of the parties or by action brought in the United States district court for the district in which the facility is situated.

§ 1405. Employment of handicapped individuals

The Secretary shall assure that each recipient of assistance under this chapter shall make positive efforts to employ and advance in employment qualified handicapped individuals in programs assisted under this chapter.

§ 1406. Grants for removal of architectural barriers; authorization of appropriations

(a) The Secretary is authorized to make grants and to enter into cooperative agreements with the Secretary of the Interior and with State educational agencies to assist such agencies in making grants to local educational agencies or intermediate educational units to pay part or all of the cost of altering existing buildings and equipment in accordance with standards promulgated under the Act approved August 12, 1968 (Public Law 90-480), relating to architectural barriers.

(b) For the purposes of carrying out the provisions of this section, there are authorized to be appropriated such sums as may be necessary.

§ 1407. Regulation requirements

(a) Minimum period for comment before effective date

For purposes of complying with section 1232(b) of this title with respect to regulations promulgated under subchapter II of this chapter, the thirty-day period under such section shall be ninety days.

(b) Lessening of procedural or substantive protections as in effect on July 20, 1983, prohibited

The Secretary may not implement, or publish in final form, any regulation prescribed pursuant to this chapter which would procedurally or substantively lessen the protections provided to handicapped children under this chapter, as embodied in regulations in effect on July 20, 1983 (particularly as such protections relate to parental consent to initial evaluation or initial placement in special education, least restrictive environment, related services, timelines,[1] attendance of evaluation personnel at IEP meetings, or qualifications of personnel), except to the extent that such regulation reflects the clear and unequivocal intent of the Congress in legislation.

(c) Transmission to Advisory Committee

The Secretary shall transmit a copy of any regulations promulgated under this chapter to the National Advisory Committee on the Education of the Handicapped[2] concurrently with publication in the Federal Register.

§ 1408. Eligibility for financial assistance

Effective for fiscal years for which the Secretary may make grants under section 1419(b)(1) of this title, no State or local educational agency or intermediate educational unit or other public institution or agency may receive a grant under subchapters III through VII of this chapter which relate exclusively to programs, projects, and activities pertaining to children aged three to five, inclusive, unless the State is eligible to receive a grant under section 1419(b)(1) of this title.

---

[1]Reproduced as enacted. Probably should be "timeliness."

[2]Reproduced as enacted. Probably should be "of Handicapped Children and Youth."

SUBCHAPTER II—ASSISTANCE FOR EDUCATION OF ALL HANDICAPPED CHILDREN

§ 1411. Entitlements and allocations

(a) Formula for determining maximum State entitlement

(1) Except as provided in paragraph (3) and in section 1419 of this title, the maximum amount of the grant to which a State is entitled under this subchapter for any fiscal year shall be equal to—

(A) the number of handicapped children aged 3-5, inclusive, in a State who are receiving special education and related services as determined under paragraph (3) if the State is eligible for a grant under section 1419 of this title and the number of handicapped children aged 6-21, inclusive, in a State who are receiving special education and related services as so determined;

multiplied by—

(B)(i) 5 per centum, for the fiscal year ending September 30, 1978, of the average per pupil expenditure in public elementary and secondary schools in the United States;

(ii) 10 per centum, for the fiscal year ending September 30, 1979, of the average per pupil expenditure in public elementary and secondary schools in the United States;

(iii) 20 per centum, for the fiscal year ending September 30, 1980, of the average per pupil expenditure in public elementary and secondary schools in the United States;

(iv) 30 per centum, for the fiscal year ending September 30, 1981, of the average per pupil expenditure in public elementary and secondary schools in the United States; and

(v) 40 per centum, for the fiscal year ending September 30, 1982, and for each fiscal year thereafter, of the average per pupil expenditure in public elementary and secondary schools in the United States:

except that no State shall receive an amount which is less than the amount which such State received under this subchapter for the fiscal year ending September 30, 1977.

(2) For the purpose of this subsection and subsection (b) through subsection (e) of this section, the term "State" does not include Guam, American Samoa, the Virgin Islands, the Northern Mariana Islands, and the Trust Territory of the Pacific Islands.

(3) The number of handicapped children receiving special education and related services in any fiscal year shall be equal to number of such children receiving special education and related services on December 1 of the fiscal year preceding the fiscal year for which the determination is made.

(4) For purposes of paragraph (1)(B), the term "average per pupil expenditure" in the United States, means the aggregate current expenditures, during the second fiscal year preceding the fiscal year for which the computation is made (or, if satisfactory data for such year are not available at the time of computation, then during the most recent preceding fiscal year for which satisfactory data are available) of all local educational agencies in the United States (which, for purposes of this subsection, means the fifty States and the

District of Columbia), as the case may be, plus any direct expenditures by the State for operation of such agencies (without regard to the source of funds from which either of such expenditures are made), divided by the aggregate number of children in average daily attendance to whom such agencies provided free public education during such preceding year.

(5)(A) In determining the allotment of each State under paragraph (1), the Secretary may not count—

(i) handicapped children aged three to seventeen, inclusive, in such State under paragraph (1)(A) to the extent the number of such children is greater than 12 percent of the number of all children aged three to seventeen, inclusive, in such State and the State serves all handicapped children aged three to five, inclusive, in the State pursuant to State law or practice or the order of any court,

(ii) handicapped children aged five to seventeen, inclusive, in such State under paragraph (1)(A) to the extent the number of such children is greater than 12 percent of the number of all children aged five to seventeen, inclusive, in such State and the State does not serve all handicapped children aged three to five, inclusive, in the State pursuant to State law or practice on the order of any court; and

(iii) handicapped children who are counted under section 2731 of this title.

(B) For purposes of subparagraph (A), the number of children aged five to seventeen inclusive, in any State shall be determined by the Secretary on the basis of the most recent satisfactory data available to him.

(b) Distribution and use of grant funds by States for fiscal year ending September 30, 1978

(1) Of the funds received under subsection (a) of this section by any State for the fiscal year ending September 30, 1978—

(A) 50 per centum of such funds may be used by such State in accordance with the provisions of paragraph (2); and

(B) 50 per centum of such funds shall be distributed by such State pursuant to subsection (d) of this section to local educational agencies and intermediate educational units in such State, for use in accordance with the priorities established under section 1412(3) of this title.

(2) Of the funds which any State may use under paragraph (1)(A)—

(A) an amount which is equal to the greater of—

(i) 5 per centum of the total amount of funds received under this subchapter by such State; or

(ii) $200,000;

may be used by such State for administrative costs related to carrying out sections 1412 and 1413 of this title;

(B) the remainder shall be used by such State to provide support services and direct services, in accordance with the priorities established under section 1412(3) of this title.

(c) Distribution and use of grant funds by States for fiscal years ending September 30, 1979, and thereafter

(1) Of the funds received under subsection (a) of this section by any State for the fiscal year ending September 30, 1979, and for each fiscal year thereafter—

(A) 25 per centum of such funds may be used by such State in accordance with the provisions of paragraph (2); and

(B) except as provided in paragraph (4), 75 per centum of such funds shall be distributed by such State pursuant to subsection (d) of this section to local educational agencies and intermediate educational units in such State, for use in accordance with priorities established under section 1412(3) of this title.

(2)(A) Subject to the provisions of subparagraph (B), of the funds which any State may use under paragraph (1)(A)—

(i) an amount which is equal to the greater of—

(I) 5 per centum of the total amount of funds received under this subchapter by such State; or

(II) $350,000;

may be used by such State for administrative costs related to carrying out the provisions of sections 1412 and 1413 of this title; and

(ii) the part remaining after use in accordance with clause (i) shall be used by the State (I) to provide support services and direct services in accordance with the priorities established under section 1412(3) of this title, and (II) for the administrative costs of monitoring and complaint investigation but only to the extent that such costs exceed the costs of administration incurred during fiscal year 1985.

(B) The amount expended by any State from the funds available to such State under paragraph (1)(A) in any fiscal year for the provisions of support services or for the provision of direct services shall be matched on a program basis by such State, from funds other than Federal funds, for the provision of support services or for the provision of direct services for the fiscal year involved.

(3) The provisions of section 1413(a)(9) of this title shall not apply with respect to amounts available for use by any State under paragraph (2).

(4)(A) No funds shall be distributed by any State under this subsection in any fiscal year to any local educational agency or intermediate educational unit in such State if—

(i) such local educational agency or intermediate educational unit is entitled, under subsection (d) of this section, to less than $7,500 for such fiscal year; or

(ii) such local educational agency or intermediate educational unit has not submitted an application for such funds which meets the requirements of section 1414 of this title.

(B) Whenever the provisions of subparagraph (A) apply, the State involved shall use such funds to assure the provision of a free appropriate education to handicapped children residing in the area served by such local educational agency or such intermediate educational unit. The provisions of paragraph (2)(B) shall not apply to the use of such funds.

(d) Allocation of funds within States to local educational agencies and intermediate educational units

From the total amount of funds available to local educational agencies and intermediate educational units in any State under subsection (b)(1)(B) or subsection (c)(1)(B) of this section, as the case may be, each local educational agency or intermediate educational unit shall be entitled to an amount which bears the same ratio to the total amount available under subsection (b)(1)(B) or subsection (c)(1)(B) of this section, as the case may be, as the number of handicapped children aged three to twenty-one, inclusive, receiving special education and related services in such local educational agency or intermediate educational unit bears to the aggregate number of handicapped children aged three to twenty-one, inclusive, receiving special education and related services in all local educational agencies and intermediate educational units which apply to the State educational agency involved for funds under this subchapter.

(e) Territories and possessions

(1) The jurisdictions to which this subsection applies are Guam, American Samoa, the Virgin Islands, the Northern Mariana Islands, and the Trust Territory of the Pacific Islands.

(2) Each jurisdiction to which this subsection applies shall be entitled to a grant for the purposes set forth in section 1400(c) of this title in an amount equal to an amount determined by the Secretary in accordance with criteria based on respective needs, except that the aggregate of the amount to which such jurisdictions are so entitled for any fiscal year shall not exceed an amount equal to 1 per centum of the aggregate of the amounts available to all States under this subchapter for that fiscal year. If the aggregate of the amounts, determined by the Secretary pursuant to the preceding sentence, to be so needed for any fiscal year exceeds an amount equal to such 1 per centum limitation, the entitlement of each such jurisdiction shall be reduced proportionately until such aggregate does not exceed such 1 per centum limitation.

(3) The amount expended for administration by each jurisdiction under this subsection shall not exceed 5 per centum of the amount allotted to such jurisdiction for any fiscal year, or $35,000, whichever is greater.

(f) Indian reservations

(1) The Secretary shall make payments to the Secretary of the Interior according to the need for assistance for the education of handicapped children on reservations serviced by elementary and secondary schools operated for Indian children by the Department of the Interior. The amount of such payment for any fiscal year shall be 1.25 percent of the aggregate amounts available to all States under this section for that fiscal year.

(2) The Secretary of the Interior may receive an allotment under paragraph (1) only after submitting to the Secretary an application which—

(A) meets the applicable requirements of sections 1412, 1413, and 1414(a) of this title,

(B) includes satisfactory assurance that all handicapped children aged 3 to 5, inclusive receive a free appropriate public education by or before the 1987-1988 school year,

(C) includes an assurance that there are public hearings, adequate notice of such hearings, and an opportunity for comment afforded to members of tribes, tribal governing bodies, and designated local school boards before adoption of the policies, programs, and procedures required under sections 1412, 1413, and 1414(a) of this title, and

(D) is approved by the Secretary.

Section 1416 of this title shall apply to any such application.

(g) Reductions or increases

(1) If the sums appropriated under subsection (h) of this section for any fiscal year for making payments to States under subsection (a) of this section are not sufficient to pay in full the total amounts which all States are entitled to receive under subsection (a) of this section for such fiscal year, the maximum amounts which all States are entitled to receive under subsection (a) of this section for such fiscal year shall be ratably reduced. In case additional funds become available for making such payments for any fiscal year during which the preceding sentence is applicable, such reduced amounts shall be increased on the same basis as they were reduced.

(2) In the case of any fiscal year in which the maximum amounts for which States are eligible have been reduced under the first sentence of paragraph (1), and in which additional funds have not been made avalable to pay in full the total of such maximum amounts under the last sentence of such paragraph, the State educational agency shall fix dates before which each local educational agency or intermediate educational unit shall report to the State educational agency on the amount of funds available to the local educational agency or intermediate educational unit, under the provisions of subsection (d) of this section, which it estimates that it will expend in accordance with the provisions of this section. The amounts so available to any local educational agency or intermediate educational unit, or any amount which would be available to any other local educational agency or intermediate educational unit if it were to submit a program meeting the requirements of this subchapter, which the State educational agency determines will not be used for the period of its availability, shall be available for allocation to those local educational agencies or intermediate educational units, in the manner provided by this section, which the State educational agency determines will need and be able to use additional funds to carry out approved programs.

(h) Authorization of appropriations.

For grants under subsection (a) of this section there are authorized to be appropriated such sums as may be necessary.

§ 1412. Eligibility requirements

In order to qualify for assistance under this subchapter in any fiscal year, a State shall demonstrate to the Secretary that the following conditions are met:

(1) The State has in effect a policy that assures all handicapped children the right to a free appropriate public education.

(2) The State has developed a plan pursuant to section 1413(b) of this title in effect prior to November 29, 1975, and submitted not later than August 21, 1975, which will be amended so as to comply with the provisions of this paragraph. Each such amended plan shall set forth in detail the policies and procedures which the State will undertake or has undertaken in order to assure that—

(A) there is established (i) a goal of providing full educational opportunity to all handicapped children, (ii) a detailed timetable for accomplishing such a goal, and (iii) a description of the kind and number of facilities, personnel, and services necessary throughout the State to meet such a goal;

(B) a free appropriate public education will be available for all handicapped children between the ages of three and eighteen within the State not later than September 1, 1978, and for all handicapped children between the ages of three and twenty-one within the State not later than September 1, 1980, except that, with respect to handicapped children aged three to five and aged eighteen to twenty-one, inclusive, the requirements of this clause shall not be applied in any State if the application of such requirements would be inconsistent with State law or practice, or the order of any court, respecting public education within such age groups in the State;

(C) all children residing in the State who are handicapped, regardless of the severity of their handicap, and who are in need of special education and related services are identified, located, and evaluated, and that a practical method is developed and implemented to determine which children are currently receiving needed special education and related services and which children are not currently receiving needed special education and related services;

(D) policies and procedures are established in accordance with detailed criteria prescribed under section 417(c) of this title; and

(E) the amendment to the plan submitted by the State required by this section shall be available to parents, guardians, and other members of the general public at least thirty days prior to the date of submission of the amendment to the Secretary.

(3) The State has established priorities for providing a free appropriate public education to all handicapped children, which priorities shall meet the timetables set forth in clause (B) of paragraph (2) of this section, first with respect to handicapped children who are not receiving an education, and second with respect to handicapped children, within each disability, with the most severe handicaps who are receiving an inadequate education, and has made adequate progress in meeting the timetables set forth in clause (B) of paragraph (2) of this section.

(4) Each local educational agency in the State will maintain records of the individualized education program for each handicapped child, and such program shall be established, reviewed, and revised as provided in section 1414(a)(5) of this title.

(5) The State has established (A) procedural safeguards as required by section 1415 of this title, (B) procedures to assure that, to the maximum extent appropriate, handicapped children, including children in public or private institutions or other care facilities, are educated with children who are not handicapped, and that special classes, separate schooling, or other re-

moval of handicapped children from the regular educational environment occurs only when the nature or severity of the handicap is such that education in regular classes with the use of supplementary aids and services cannot be achieved satisfactorily, and (C) procedures to assure that testing and evaluation materials and procedures utilized for the purposes of evaluation and placement of handicapped children will be selected and administered so as not to be racially or culturally discriminatory. Such materials or procedures shall be provided and administered in the child's native language or mode of communication, unless it clearly is not feasible to do so, and no single procedure shall be the sole criterion for determining an appropriate educational program for a child.

(6) The State educational agency shall be responsible for assuring that the requirements of this subchapter are carried out and that all educational programs for handicapped children within the State, including all such programs administered by any other State or local agency, will be under the general supervision of the persons responsible for educational programs for handicapped children in the State educational agency and shall meet education standards of the State educational agency. This paragraph shall not be construed to limit the responsibility of agencies other than educational agencies in a State from providing or paying for some or all of the costs of a free appropriate public education to be provided handicapped children in the State.

(7) The State shall assure that (A) in carrying out the requirements of this section procedures are established for consultation with individuals involved in or concerned with the education of handicapped children, including handicapped individuals and parents or guardians of handicapped children, and (B) there are public hearings, adequate notice of such hearings, and an opportunity for comment available to the general public prior to adoption of the policies, programs, and procedures required pursuant to the provisions of this section and section 1413 of this title.

§ 1413. State plans

(a) Requisite features

Any State meeting the eligibility requirements set forth in section 1412 of this title and desiring to participate in the program under this subchapter shall submit to the Secretary, through its State educational agency, a State plan at such time, in such manner, and containing or accompanied by such information, as he deems necessary. Each such plan shall—

(1) set forth policies and procedures designed to assure that funds paid to the State under this subchapter will be expended in accordance with the provisions of this subchapter, with particular attention given to the provisions of sections 1411(b), 1411(c), 1411(d), 1412(2), and 1412(3) of this title;

(2) provide that programs and procedures will be established to assure that funds received by the State or any of its political subdivisions under any other Federal program, including section 241c-1 of this title, section 844a(b)(8) of this title or its successor authority, and section 1262(a)(4)(B) of this title, under which there is specific authority for the provision of assistance for the education of handicapped children, will be utilized by the State,

or any of its political subdivisions, only in a manner consistent with the goal of providing a free appropriate public education for all handicapped children, except that nothing in this clause shall be construed to limit the specific requirements of the laws governing such Federal programs;

(3) set forth, consistent with the purposes of this chapter, a description of programs and procedures for (A) the development and implementation of a comprehensive system of personnel development which shall include the inservice training of general and special educational instructional and support personnel, detailed procedures to assure that all personnel necessary to carry out the purposes of this chapter are appropriately and adequately prepared and trained, and effective procedures for acquiring and disseminating to teachers and administrators of programs for handicapped children significant information derived from educational research, demonstration, and similar projects, and (B) adopting, where appropriate, promising educational practices and materials development through such projects;

(4) set forth policies and procedures to assure—

(A) that, to the extent consistent with the number and location of handicapped children in the State who are enrolled in private elementary and secondary schools, provision is made for the participation of such children in the program assisted or carried out under this subchapter by providing for such children special education and related services; and

(B) that (i) handicapped children in private schools and facilities will be provided special education and related services (in conformance with an individualized educational program as required by this subchapter) at no cost to their parents or guardian, if such children are placed in or referred to such schools or facilities by the State or appropriate local educational agency as the means of carrying out the requirements of this subchapter or any other applicable law requiring the provision of special education and related services to all handicapped children within such State, and (ii) in all such instances the State educational agency shall determine whether such schools and facilities meet standards that apply to State and local educational agencies and that children so served have all the rights they would have if served by such agencies;

(5) set forth policies and procedures which assure that the State shall seek to recover any funds made available under this subchapter for services to any child who is determined to be erroneously classified as eligible to be counted under section 1411(a) or 1411(d) of this title;

(6) provide satisfactory assurance that the control of funds provided under this subchapter, and title to property derived therefrom, shall be in a public agency for the uses and purposes provided in this subchapter, and that a public agency will administer such funds and property;

(7) provide for (A) making such reports in such form and containing such information as the Secretary may require to carry out his functions under this subchapter, and (B) keeping such records and affording such access thereto as the Secretary may find necessary to assure the correctness and verification of such reports and proper disbursement of Federal funds under this subchapter;

(8) provide procedures to assure that final action with respect to any application submitted by a local educational agency or an intermediate educational unit shall not be taken without first affording the local educational agency or intermediate educational unit involved reasonable notice and op-

portunity for a hearing;

(9) provide satisfactory assurance that Federal funds made available under this subchapter (A) will not be commingled with State funds, and (B) will be so used as to supplement and increase the level of Federal, State, and local funds (including funds that are not under the direct control of State or local educational agencies) expended for special education and related services provided to handicapped children under this subchapter and in no case to supplant such Federal, State, and local funds, except that, where the State provides clear and convincing evidence that all handicapped children have available to them a free appropriate public education, the Secretary may waive in part the requirement of this clause if he concurs with the evidence provided by the State;

(10) provide, consistent with procedures prescribed pursuant to section 1417(a)(2) of this title, satisfactory assurance that such fiscal control and fund accounting procedures will be adopted as may be necessary to assure proper disbursement of, and accounting for, Federal funds paid under this subchapter to the State, including any such funds paid by the State to local educational agencies and intermediate educational units;

(11) provide for procedures for evaluation at least annually of the effectiveness of programs in meeting the educational needs of handicapped children (including evaluation of individualized education programs), in accordance with such criteria that the Secretary shall prescribe pursuant to section 1417 of this title;

(12) provide that the State has an advisory panel, appointed by the Governor or any other official authorized under State law to make such appointments, composed of individuals involved in or concerned with the education of handicapped children, including handicapped individuals, teachers, parents or guardians of handicapped children, State and local education officials, and administrators of programs for handicapped children, which (A) advises the State educational agency of unmet needs within the State in the education of handicapped children, (B) comments publicly on any rules or regulations proposed for issuance by the State regarding the education of handicapped children and the procedures for distribution of funds under this subchapter, and (C) assists the State in developing and reporting such data and evaluations as may assist the Secretary in the performance of his responsibilities under section 1418 of this title;

(13) set forth policies and procedures for developing and implementing interagency agreements between the State educational agency and other appropriate State and local agencies to (A) define the financial responsibility of each agency for providing handicapped children and youth with free appropriate public education, and (B) resolve interagency disputes, including procedures under which local educational agencies may initiate proceedings under the agreement in order to secure reimbursement from other agencies or otherwise implement the provisions of the agreement.[1]

(14) policies and procedures relating to the establishment and maintenance of standards to ensure that personnel necessary to carry out the purposes of this subchapter are appropriately and adequately prepared and trained, including—

---

[1]Reproduced as enacted. Probably should be ";".

(A) the establishment and maintenance of standards which are consistent with any State approved or recognized certification, licensing, registration, or other comparable requirements which apply to the area in which he or she is providing special education or related services, and

(B) to the extent such standards are not based on the highest requirements in the State applicable to a specific profession or discipline, the steps the State is taking to require the retraining or hiring of personnel that meet appropriate professional requirements in the State.

(b) Additional assurances

Whenever a State educational agency provides free appropriate public education for handicapped children, or provides direct services to such children, such State educational agency shall include, as part of the State plan required by subsection (a) of this section, such additional assurances not specified in such subsection (a) of this section as are contained in section 1414(a) of this title, except that funds available for the provision of such education or services may be expended without regard to the provisions relating to excess costs in section 1414(a) of this title.

(c) Notice and hearing prior to disapproval of plan

The Secretary shall approve any State plan and any modification thereof which—

(1) is submitted by a State eligible in accordance with section 1412 of this title; and

(2) meets the requirements of subsection (a) and subsection (b) of this section.

The Secretary shall disapprove any State plan which does not meet the requirements of the preceding sentence, but shall not finally disapprove a State plan except after reasonable notice and opportunity for a hearing to the State.

(d) Participation of handicapped children in private schools; payment of Federal amount; determinations of Secretary: notice and hearing; judicial review: jurisdiction of court of appeals, petition, record, conclusiveness of findings, remand, review by Supreme Court

(1) If, on December 2, 1983, a State educational agency is prohibited by law from providing for the participation in special programs of handicapped children enrolled in private elementary and secondary schools as required by subsection (a)(4) of this section, the Secretary shall waive such requirement, and shall arrange for the provision of services to such children through arrangements which shall be subject to the requirements of subsection (a)(4) of this section.

(2)(A) When the Secretary arranges for services pursuant to this subsection, the Secretary, after consultation with the appropriate public and private school officials, shall pay to the provider of such services an amount per child which may not exceed the Federal amount provided per child under this subchapter to all handicapped children enrolled in the State for services for the fiscal year preceding the fiscal year for which the determination is made.

(B) Pending final resolution of any investigation or complaint that could result in a determination under this subsection, the Secretary may withhold from the allocation of the affected State educational agency the amount the Secretary estimates would be necessary to pay the cost of such services.

(C) Any determination by the Secretary under this section shall continue in effect until the Secretary determines that there will no longer be any failure or inability on the part of the State educational agency to meet the requirements of subsection (a)(4) of this section.

(3)(A) The Secretary shall not take any final action under this subsection until the State educational agency affected by such action has had an opportunity, for at least 45 days after receiving written notice thereof, to submit written objections and to appear before the Secretary or his designee to show cause why such action should not be taken.

(B) If a State educational agency is dissatisfied with the Secretary's final action after a proceeding under subparagraph (A) of this paragraph, it may, within 60 days after notice of such action, file with the United States court of appeals for the circuit in which such state is located a petition for review of that action. A copy of the petition shall be forthwith transmitted by the clerk of the court to the Secretary. The Secretary thereupon shall file in the court the record of the proceedings on which he based his action, as provided in section 2112 of title 28.

(C) The findings of fact by the Secretary, if supported by substantial evidence, shall be conclusive; but the court, for good cause shown, may remand the case to the Secretary to take further evidence, and the Secretary may thereupon make new or modified findings of fact and may modify his previous action, and shall file in the court the record of the further proceedings. Such new or modified findings of fact shall likewise be conclusive if supported by substantial evidence.

(D) Upon the filing of a petition under subparagraph (B), the court shall have jurisdiction to affirm the action of the Secretary or to set it aside, in whole or in part. The judgment of the court shall be subject to review by the Supreme Court of the United States upon certiorari or certification as provided in section 1254 of title 28.

(e) Reduction of medical and other assistance or alteration of eligibility under social security provisions prohibited.

This chapter shall not be construed to permit a State to reduce medical and other assistance available or to alter eligibility under titles V and XIX of the Social Security Act with respect to the provision of a free appropriate public education for handicapped children within the State; and [2]

§ 1414. Application

(a) Requisite features

[2]Reproduced as enacted.

A local educational agency or an intermediate educational unit which desires to receive payments under section 1411(d) of this title for any fiscal year shall submit an application to the appropriate State educational agency. Such application shall—

(1) provide satisfactory assurance that payments under this subchapter will be used for excess costs directly attributable to programs which—

(A) provide that all children residing within the jurisdiction of the local educational agency or the intermediate educational unit who are handicapped, regardless of the severity of their handicap, and are in need of special education and related services will be identified, located, and evaluated, and provide for the inclusion of a practical method of determining which children are currently receiving needed special education and related services and which children are not currently receiving such education and services;

(B) establish policies and procedures in accordance with detailed criteria prescribed under section 1417(c) of this title;

(C) establish a goal of providing full educational opportunities to all handicapped children, including—

(i) procedures for the implementation and use of the comprehensive system of personnel development established by the State educational agency under section 1413(a)(3) of this title;

(ii) the provision of, and the establishment of priorities for providing, a free appropriate public education to all handicapped children, first with respect to handicapped children who are not receiving an education, and second with respect to handicapped children, within each disability, with the most severe handicaps who are receiving an inadequate education;

(iii) the participation and consultation of the parents or guardian of such children; and

(iv) to the maximum extent practicable and consistent with the provisions of section 1412(5)(B) of this title, the provision of special services to enable such children to participate in regular educational programs;

(D) establish a detailed timetable for accomplishing the goal described in subclause (C); and

(E) provide a description of the kind and number of facilities, personnel, and services necessary to meet the goal described in subclause (C);

(2) provide satisfactory assurance that (A) the control of funds provided under this subchapter, and title to property derived from such funds, shall be in a public agency for the uses and purposes provided in this subchapter, and that a public agency will administer such funds and property, (B) Federal funds expended by local educational agencies and intermediate educational units for programs under this subchapter (i) shall be used to pay only the excess costs directly attributable to the education of handicapped children, and (ii) shall be used to supplement and, to the extent practicable, increase the level of State and local funds expended for the education of handicapped children, and in no case to supplant such State and local funds, and (C) State and local funds will be used in the jurisdiction of the local educational agency or intermediate educational unit to provide services in program areas which, taken as a whole, are at least comparable to services being provided in areas of such jurisdiction which are not receiving funds under this subchapter;

(3)(A) provide for furnishing such information (which, in the case of reports relating to performance, is in accordance with specific performance criteria related to program objectives), as may be necessary to enable the State educational agency to perform its duties under this subchapter, including information relating to the educational achievement of handicapped children participating in programs carried out under this subchapter; and

(B) provide for keeping such records, and provide for affording such access to such records, as the State educational agency may find necessary to assure the correctness and verification of such information furnished under subclause (A);

(4) provide for making the application and all pertinent documents related to such application available to parents, guardians, and other members of the general public, and provide that all evaluations and reports required under clause (3) shall be public information;

(5) provide assurances that the local educational agency or intermediate educational unit will establish, or revise, whichever is appropriate, an individualized education program for each handicapped child at the beginning of each school year and will then review and, if appropriate revise, its provisions periodically, but not less than annually;

(6) provide satisfactory assurance that policies and programs established and administered by the local educational agency or intermediate educational unit shall be consistent with the provisions of paragraph (1) through paragraph (7) of section 1412 and section 1413(a) of this title; and

(7) provide satisfactory assurance that the local educational agency or intermediate educational unit will establish and maintain procedural safeguards in accordance with the provisions of sections 1412(5)(B), 1412(5)(C), and 1415 of this title.

(b) Approval by State educational agencies of applications submitted by local educational agencies or intermediate educational units; notice and hearing

(1) A State educational agency shall approve any application submitted by a local educational agency or an intermediate educational unit under subsection (a) of this section if the State educational agency determines that such application meets the requirements of subsection (a) of this section, except that no such application may be approved until the State plan submitted by such State educational agency under subsection (a) of this section is approved by the Secretary under section 1413(c) of this title. A State educational agency shall disapprove any application submitted by a local educational agency or an intermediate educational unit under subsection (a) of this section if the State educational agency determines that such application does not meet the requirements of subsection (a) of this section.

(2)(A) Whenever a State educational agency, after reasonable notice and opportunity for a hearing, finds that a local educational agency or an intermediate educational unit, in the administration of an application approved by the State educational agency under paragraph (1), has failed to comply with any requirement set forth in such application, the State educational agency, after giving appropriate notice to the local educational agency or the intermediate educational unit, shall—

(i) make no further payments to such local educational agency or such intermediate educational unit under section 1420 of this title until the State educational agency is satisfied that there is no longer any failure to comply with the requirement involved; or

(ii) take such finding into account in its review of any application made by such local educational agency or such intermediate educational unit under subsection (a) of this section.

(B) The provisions of the last sentence of section 1416(a) of this title shall apply to any local educational agency or any intermediate educational unit receiving any notification from a State educational agency under this paragraph.

(3) In carrying out its functions under paragraph (1), each State educational agency shall consider any decision made pursuant to a hearing held under section 1415 of this title which is adverse to the local educational agency or intermediate educational unit involved in such decision.

(c) Consolidated applications

(1) A State educational agency may, for purposes of the consideration and approval of applications under this section, require local educational agencies to submit a consolidated application for payments if such State educational agency determines that any individual application submitted by any such local educational agency will be disapproved because such local educational agency is ineligible to receive payments because of the application of section 1411(c)(4)(A)(i) of this title or such local educational agency would be unable to establish and maintain programs of sufficient size and scope to effectively meet the educational needs of handicapped children.

(2)(A) In any case in which a consolidated application of local educational agencies is approved by a State educational agency under paragraph (1), the payments which such local educational agencies may receive shall be equal to the sum of payments to which each such local educational agency would be entitled under section 1411(d) of this title if an individual application of any such local educational agency had been approved.

(B) The State educational agency shall prescribe rules and regulations with respect to consolidated applications submitted under this subsection which are consistent with the provisions of paragraph (1) through paragraph (7) of section 1412 and section 1413(a) of this title and which provide participating local educational agencies with joint responsibilities for implementing programs receiving payments under this subchapter.

(C) In any case in which an intermediate educational unit is required pursuant to State law to carry out the provisions of this subchapter, the joint responsibilities given to local educational agencies under subparagraph (B) shall not apply to the administration and disbursement of any payments received by such intermediate educational unit. Such responsibilities shall be carried out exclusively by such intermediate educational unit.

(d) Special education and related services provided directly by State educational agencies: regional or State centers

Whenever a State educational agency determines that a local educational agency—

(1) is unable or unwilling to establish and maintain programs of free

appropriate public education which meet the requirements established in subsection (a) of this section;

(2) is unable or unwilling to be consolidated with other local educational agencies in order to establish and maintain such programs; or

(3) has one or more handicapped children who can best be served by a regional or State center designed to meet the needs of such children;

the State educational agency shall use the payments which would have been available to such local educational agency to provide special education and related services directly to handicapped children residing in the area served by such local educational agency. The State educational agency may provide such education and services in such manner, and at such locations (including regional or State centers), as it considers appropriate, except that the manner in which such education and services are provided shall be consistent with the requirements of this subchapter.

(e) Reallocation of funds

Whenever a State educational agency determines that a local educational agency is adequately providing a free appropriate public education to all handicapped children residing in the area served by such agency with State and local funds otherwise available to such agency, the State educational agency may reallocate funds (or such portion of those funds as may not be required to provide such education and services) made available to such agency, pursuant to section 1411(d) of this title, to such other local educational agencies within the State as are not adequately providing special education and related services to all handicapped children residing in the areas served by such other local educational agencies.

(f) Programs using State or local funds

Notwithstanding the provisions of subsection (a)(2)(B)(ii) of this section, any local educational agency which is required to carry out any program for the education of handicapped children pursuant to a State law shall be entitled to receive payments under section 1411(d) of this title for use in carrying out such program, except that such payments may not be used to reduce the level of expenditures for such program made by such local educational agency from State or local funds below the level of such expenditures for the fiscal year prior to the fiscal year for which such local educational agency seeks such payments.

§ 1415. Procedural safeguards

(a) Establishment and maintenance

Any State educational agency, any local educational agency, and any intermediate educational unit which receives assistance under this subchapter shall establish and maintain procedures in accordance with subsection (b) through subsection (e) of this section to assure that handicapped children and their parents or guardians are guaranteed procedural safeguards with respect to the provision of free appropriate public education by such agencies and units.

(b) Required procedures; hearing

(1) The procedures required by this section shall include, but shall not be limited to—

(A) an opportunity for the parents or guardian of a handicapped child to examine all relevant records with respect to the identification, evaluation, and educational placement of the child, and the provision of a free appropriate public education to such child, and to obtain an independent educational evaluation of the child;

(B) procedures to protect the rights of the child whenever the parents or guardian of the child are not known, unavailable, or the child is a ward of the State, including the assignment of an individual (who shall not be an employee of the State educational agency, local educational agency, or intermediate educational unit involved in the education or care of the child) to act as a surrogate for the parents or guardian;

(C) written prior notice to the parents or guardian of the child whenever such agency or unit—

(i) proposes to initiate or change, or

(ii) refuses to initiate or change,

the identification, evaluation, or educational placement of the child or the provision of a free appropriate public education to the child;

(D) procedures designed to assure that the notice required by clause (C) fully inform the parents or guardian, in the parents' or guardian's native language, unless it clearly is not feasible to do so, of all procedures available pursuant to this section; and

(E) an opportunity to present complaints with respect to any matter relating to the identification, evaluation, or educational placement of the child, or the provision of a free appropriate public education to such child.

(2) Whenever a complaint has been received under paragraph (1) of this subsection, the parents or guardian shall have an opportunity for an impartial due process hearing which shall be conducted by the State educational agency or by the local educational agency or intermediate educational unit, as determined by State law or by the State educational agency. No hearing conducted pursuant to the requirements of this paragraph shall be conducted by an employee of such agency or unit involved in the education or care of the child.

(c) Review of local decision by State education agency

If the hearing required in paragraph (2) of subsection (b) of this section is conducted by a local educational agency or an intermediate educational unit, any party aggrieved by the findings and decision rendered in such a hearing may appeal to the State educational agency which shall conduct an impartial review of such hearing. The officer conducting such review shall make an independent decision upon completion of such review.

(d) Enumeration of rights accorded parties to hearings

Any party to any hearing conducted pursuant to subsections (b) and (c) of this section shall be accorded (1) the right to be accompanied and advised by counsel and by individuals with special knowledge or training with respect to the problems of handicapped children, (2) the right to present evidence and confront, cross-examine, and compel the attendance of witnesses, (3) the right to a written or electronic verbatim record of such hearing, and (4) the right to written findings of fact and decisions (which findings and decisions shall also be transmitted to the advisory panel established pursuant to section 1413(a)(12) of this title).

(e) Civil action; jurisdiction; attorney fees

(1) A decision made in a hearing conducted pursuant to paragraph (2) of subsection (b) of this section shall be final, except that any party involved in such hearing may appeal such decision under the provisions of subsection (c) and paragraph (2) of this subsection. A decision made under subsection (c) of this section shall be final, except that any party may bring an action under paragraph (2) of this subsection.

(2) Any party aggrieved by the findings and decision made under subsection (b) of this section who does not have the right to an appeal under subsection (c) of this section, and any party aggrieved by the findings and decision under subsection (c) of this section, shall have the right to bring a civil action with respect to the complaint presented pursuant to this section, which action may be brought in any State court of competent jurisdiction or in a district court of the United States without regard to the amount in controversy. In any action brought under this paragraph the court shall receive the records of the administrative proceedings, shall hear additional evidence at the request of a party, and, basing its decision of the preponderance of the evidence, shall grant such relief as the court determines is appropriate.

(3) During the pendency of any proceedings conducted pursuant to this section, unless the State or local educational agency and the parents or guardian otherwise agree, the child shall remain in the then current educational placement of such child, or, if applying for initial admission to a public school, shall, with the consent of the parents or guardian, be placed in the public school program until all such proceedings have been completed.

(4)(A) The district courts of the United States shall have jurisdiction of actions brought under this subsection without regard to the amount in controversy.

(B) In any action or proceeding brought under this subsection, the court, in its discretion, may award reasonable attorneys' fees as part of the costs to the parents or guardian of a handicapped child or youth who is the prevailing party.

(C) For the purpose of this subsection, fees awarded under this subsection shall be based on rates prevailing in the community in which the action or proceeding arose for the kind and quality of services furnished. No bonus or multiplier may be used in calculating the fees awarded under this subsection.

(D) No award of attorneys' fees and related costs may be made in any action or proceeding under this subsection for services performed subsequent to the time of a written offer of settlement to a parent or guardian, if—

(i) the offer is made within the time prescribed by Rule 68 of the Federal Rules of Civil Procedure or, in the case of an administrative proceeding, at any time more than ten days before the proceeding begins;

(ii) the offer is not accepted within ten days; and

(iii) the court or administrative officer finds that the relief finally obtained by the parents or guardian is not more favorable to the parents or guardian than the offer of settlement.

(E) Notwithstanding the provisions of subparagraph (D), an award of attorneys' fees and related costs may be made to a parent or guardian who is the prevailing party and who was substantially justified in rejecting the settlement offer.

(F) Whenever the court finds that—

(i) the parent or guardian, during the course of the action or proceeding, unreasonably protracted the final resolution of the controversy;

(ii) the amount of the attorneys' fees otherwise authorized to be awarded unreasonably exceeds the hourly rate prevailing in the community for similar services by attorneys of reasonably comparable skill, experience, and reputation; or

(iii) the time spent and legal services furnished were excessive considering the nature of the action or proceeding,

the court shall reduce, accordingly, the amount of the attorneys' fees awarded under this subsection.

(G) The provisions of subparagraph (F) shall not apply in any action or proceeding if the court finds that the State or local educational agency unreasonably protracted the final resolution of the action or proceeding or there was a violation of this section.

(f) Effect on other laws

Nothing in this chapter shall be construed to restrict or limit the rights, procedures, and remedies available under the Constitution, title V of the Rehabilitation Act of 1973 [29 U.S.C.A. § 790 et seq.], or other Federal statutes protecting the rights of handicapped children and youth, except that before the filing of a civil action under such laws seeking relief that is also available under this subchapter, the procedures under subsections (b)(2) and (c) of this section shall be exhausted to the same extent as would be required had the action been brought under this subchapter.

Effective Date of 1986 Amendment. Section 5 of the HCPA, Pub.L. 99-372, provided that: "The amendment made by section 2 [amending 20 U.S.C. § 1415(e)(4)] shall apply with respect to actions or proceedings brought under section 615(e) of the Education of the Handicapped Act 20 U.S.C. § 1415(e) after July 3, 1984, and actions or proceedings brought prior to July 4, 1984, under such section which were pending on July 4, 1984."

§ 1416. Withholding of payments

(a) Failure to comply with this subchapter; limitations; public notice

Whenever the Secretary, after reasonable notice and opportunity for hearing to the State educational agency involved (and to any local educational agency or intermediate educational unit affected by any failure described in clause (2)), finds—

(1) that there has been a failure to comply substantially with any provision of section 1412 or section 1413 of this title, or

(2) that in the administration of the State plan there is a failure to comply with any provision of this subchapter or with any requirements set forth in the application of a local educational agency or intermediate educational unit approved by the State educational agency pursuant to the State plan,

the Secretary (A) shall, after notifying the State educational agency, withhold any further payments to the State under this subchapter, and (B) may, after notifying the State educational agency, withhold further payments to the State under the Federal programs specified in section 1413(a)(2) of this title within his jurisdiction, to the extent that funds under such programs are available for the provision of assistance for the education of handicapped children. If the Secretary withholds further payments under clause (A) or clause (B) he may determine that such withholding will be limited to programs or projects under the State plan, or portions thereof, affected by the failure, or that the State educational agency shall not make further payments under this subchapter to specified local educational agencies or intermediate educational units affected by the failure. Until the Secretary is satisfied that there is no longer any failure to comply with the provisions of this subchapter, as specified in clause (1) or clause (2), no further payments shall be made to the State under this subchapter or under the Federal programs specified in section 1413(a)(2) of this title within his jurisdiction to the extent that funds under such programs are available for the provision of assistance for the education of handicapped children, or payments by the State educational agency under this subchapter shall be limited to local educational agencies and intermediate educational units whose actions did not cause or were not involved in the failure, as the case may be. Any State educational agency, local educational agency, or intermediate educational unit in receipt of a notice pursuant to the first sentence of this subsection shall, by means of a public notice, take such measures as may be necessary to bring the pendency of an action pursuant to this subsection to the attention of the public within the jurisdiction of such agency or unit.

(b) Judicial review

(1) If any State is dissatisfied with the Secretary's final action with respect to its State plan submitted under section 1413 of this title, such State may, within sixty days after notice of such action, file with the United States court of appeals for the circuit in which such State is located a petition for review of that action. A copy of the petition shall be forthwith transmitted by the clerk of the court to the Secretary. The Secretary thereupon shall file in the court the record of the proceedings on which he based his action, as provided in section 2112 of title 28.

(2) The findings of fact by the Secretary, if supported by substantial evidence, shall be conclusive; but the court, for good cause shown, may remand the case to the Secretary to take further evidence, and the Secretary may thereupon make new or modified findings of fact that may modify his previous action, and shall file in the court the record of the further proceed-

ings. Such new or modified findings of fact shall likewise be conclusive if supported by substantial evidence.

(3) Upon the filing of such petition, the court shall have jurisdiction to affirm the action of the Secretary or to set it aside, in whole or in part. The judgment of the court shall be subject to review by the Supreme Court of the United States upon certiorari or certification as provided in section 1254 of title 28.

§ 1417. Administration

(a) Duties of Secretary

(1) In carrying out his duties under this subchapter, the Secretary shall

(A) cooperate with, and furnish all technical assistance necessary, directly or by grant or contract, to the States in matters relating to the education of handicapped children and the execution of the provisions of this subchapter;

(B) provide such short-term training programs and institutes as are necessary;

(C) disseminate information, and otherwise promote the education of all handicapped children within the States; and

(D) assure that each State shall, within one year after November 29, 1975, provide certification of the actual number of handicapped children receiving special education and related services in such State.

(2) As soon as practicable after November 29, 1975, the Secretary shall, by regulation, prescribe a uniform financial report to be utilized by State educational agencies in submitting State plans under this subchapter in order to assure equity among the States.

(b) Rules and regulations

In carrying out the provisions of this subchapter, the Secretary shall issue, not later than January 1, 1977, amend, and revoke such rules and regulations as may be necessary. No other less formal method of implementing such provisions is authorized.

(c) Protection of rights and privacy of parents and students

The Secretary shall take appropriate action, in accordance with the provisions of section 1232g of this title, to assure the protection of the confidentiality of any personally identifiable data, information, and records collected or maintained by the Secretary and by State and local educational agencies pursuant to the provisions of this subchapter.

(d) Hiring of qualified personnel

The Secretary is authorized to hire qualified personnel necessary to conduct data collection and evaluation activities required by subsections (b), (c) and (d) of section 1418 of this title and to carry out his duties under subsection (a)(1) of this section without regard to the provisions of title 5 relating to appointments in the competitive service and without regard to chapter 51 and subchapter III of chapter 53 of such title relating to classification and general schedule pay rates except that no more than twenty such personnel shall be employed at any time.

§ 1418. Evaluation

(a) Duties of Secretary

The Secretary shall directly or by grant, contract, or cooperative agreement, collect data and conduct studies, investigations, and evaluations—

(1) to assess progress in the implementation of this chapter, the impact, and the effectiveness of State and local efforts by the Secretary of Interior to provide free appropriate public education to all handicapped children and youth and early intervention services to handicapped infants and toddlers, and

(2) to provide—

(A) Congress with information relevant to policymaking, and

(B) Federal, State, and local agencies and the Secretary of Interior with information relevant to program management, administration, and effectiveness with respect to such education and early intervention services.

(b) Collection of data on education of handicapped infants, toddlers, children and youth; additional information

In carrying out subsection (a) of this section, the Secretary, on at least an annual basis, shall obtain data concerning programs and projects assisted under this chapter and under other Federal laws relating to handicapped infants, toddlers, children, and youth, and such additional information, from State and local educational agencies, the Secretary of Interior, and other appropriate sources, as is necessary for the implementation of this chapter including—

(1) the number of handicapped infants, toddlers, children, and youth in each State receiving a free appropriate public education or early intervention services (A) in age groups 0-2 and 3-5, and (B) in age groups 6-11, 12-17, and 18-21 by disability category,

(2) the number of handicapped children and youth in each State who are participating in regular educational programs (consistent with the requirements of sections 1412(5)(B) of this title and 1414(a)(1)(C)(iv) of this title) by disability category, and the number of handicapped children and youth in separate classes, separate schools or facilities, or public or private residential facilities, or who have been otherwise removed from the regular education environment,

(3) the number of handicapped children and youth exiting the education system each year through program completion or otherwise (A) in age group 3-5, and (B) in age groups 6-11, 12-17, and 18-21 by disability category and anticipated services for the next year,

(4) the amount of Federal, State, and local funds expended in each State specifically for special education and related services and for early

intervention services (which may be based upon a sampling of data from State agencies including State and local educational agencies),

(5) the number and type of personnel that are employed in the provision of special education and related services to handicapped children and youth and early intervention services to handicapped infants and toddlers by disability category served, and the estimated number and type of additional personnel by disability category needed to adequately carry out the policy established by this chapter, and

(6) a description of the special education and related services and early intervention services needed to fully implement this chapter throughout each State, including estimates of the number of handicapped infants and toddlers in the 0-2 age group and estimates of the number of handicapped children and youth (A) in age group 3-5 and (B) in age groups 6-11, 12-17, and 18-21 and by disability category.

(c) Evaluation studies by grant, contract, or cooperative agreement

The Secretary shall, by grant, contract, or cooperative agreement, provide for evaluation studies to determine the impact of this chapter. Each such evaluation shall include recommendations for improvement of the programs under this chapter. The Secretary shall, not later than July 1 of each year, submit to the appropriate committees of each House of the Congress and publish in the Federal Register proposed evaluation priorities for review and comment.

(d) Cooperative agreements with State educational agencies

(1) The Secretary may enter into cooperative agreements with State educational agencies and other State agencies to carry out studies to assess the impact and effectiveness of programs assisted under this chapter.

(2) An agreement under paragraph (1) shall—

(A) provide for the payment of not to exceed 60 percent of the total cost of studies conducted by a participating State agency to assess the impact and effectiveness of programs assisted under this chapter, and

(B) be developed in consultation with the State Advisory Panel established under this chapter, the local educational agencies, and others involved in or concerned with the education of handicapped children and youth and the provision of early intervention services to handicapped infants and toddlers.

(3) The Secretary shall provide technical assistance to participating State agencies in the implementation of the study design, analysis, and reporting procedures.

(4) In addition, the Secretary shall disseminate information from such studies to State agencies, regional resources centers, and clearinghouses established by this chapter, and, as appropriate, to others involved in, or concerned with, the education of handicapped children and youth and the provision of early intervention services to handicapped infants and toddlers.

(e) Specifically mandated studies

(1) At least one study shall be a longitudinal study of a sample of handicapped students, encompassing the full range of handicapping conditions, examining their educational progress while in special education and their occupational, educational, and independent living status after graduating from secondary school or otherwise leaving special education.

(2) At least one study shall focus on obtaining and compiling current information available, through State educational agencies and local educational agencies and other service providers, regarding State and local expenditures for educational services for handicapped students (including special education and related services) and shall gather information needed in order to calculate a range of per pupil expenditures by handicapping condition.

(f) Annual report

(1) Not later than 120 days after the close of each fiscal year, the Secretary shall publish and disseminate an annual report on the progress being made toward the provision of a free appropriate public education to all handicapped children and youth and early intervention services for handicapped infants and toddlers. The annual report shall be transmitted to the appropriate committees of each House of Congress and published and disseminated in sufficient quantities to the education community at large and to other interested parties.

(2) The Secretary shall include in each annual report under paragraph (1)—

(A) a compilation and analysis of data gathered under subsection (b) of this section.

(B) an index and summary of each evaluation activity and results of studies conducted under subsection (c) of this section,

(C) a description of findings and determinations resulting from monitoring reviews of State implementation of this subchapter,

(D) an analysis and evaluation of the participation of handicapped children and youth in vocational education programs and services,

(E) an analysis and evaluation of the effectiveness of procedures undertaken by each State educational agency, local educational agency, and intermediate educational unit to ensure that handicapped children and youth receive special education and related services in the least restrictive environment commensurate with their needs and to improve programs of instruction for handicapped children and youth in day or residential facilities, and

(F) any recommendation for change in the provisions of this chapter or any other Federal law providing support for the education of handicapped children and youth.

(3) In the annual report under paragraph (1) for fiscal year 1985 which is published in 1986 and for every third year thereafter, the Secretary shall include in the annual report—

(A) an index of all current projects funded under subchapters III through VII of this chapter, and

(B) data reported under sections 1421, 1422, 1423, 1426, 1434, 1441, and 1461 of this title.

(4) In the annual report under paragraph (1) for fiscal year 1988 which is published in 1989, the Secretary shall include special sections addressing the provision of a free appropriate public education to handicapped infants, toddlers, children, and youth in rural areas and to handicapped migrants, handicapped Indians (particularly programs operated under section 1411(f) of this title) handicapped Native Hawaiian, and other native Pacific basin children and youth, handicapped infants, toddlers, children and youth of limited English proficiency.

(5) Beginning in 1986, in consultation with the National Council for the Handicapped and the Bureau of Indian Affairs Advisory Committee for Exceptional Children, a description of the status of early intervention services for handicapped infants and toddlers from birth through age two, inclusive, and special education and related services to handicapped children from 3 through 5 years of age (including those receiving services through Head Start, Developmental Disabilities Programs, Crippled Children's Services, Mental Health/Mental Retardation Agency, and State child-development centers and private agencies under contract with local schools).

(g) Authorization of appropriations

There are authorized to be appropriated $3,800,000 for fiscal year 1987, $4,000,000 for fiscal year 1988, and $4,200,000 for fiscal year 1989 to carry out this section.

§ 1419. Pre-school grants

(a) Grants for fiscal years 1987 through 1989; amount of grants

(1) For fiscal years 1987 through 1989 (or fiscal year 1990 if the Secretary makes a grant under this paragraph for such fiscal year) the Secretary shall make a grant to any State which—

(A) has met the eligibility requirements of section 1412 of this title,

(B) has a State plan approved under section 1413 of this title, and

(C) provides special education and related services to handicapped children aged three to five, inclusive.

(2)(A) For fiscal year 1987 the amount of a grant to a State under paragraph (1) may not exceed—

(i) $300 per handicapped child aged three to five, inclusive, who received special education and related services in such State as determined under section 1411(a)(3) of this section, or

(ii) if the amount appropriated under subsection (e) of this section exceeds the product of $300 and the total number of handicapped children aged three to five, inclusive, who received special education and related services as determined under section 1411(a)(3) of this title—

(I) $300 per handicapped child aged three to five, inclusive, who received special education and related services in such State as determined under section 1411(a)(3) of this title, plus

(II) an amount equal to the portion of the appropriation available after allocating funds to all States under subclause (I) (the excess appropriation) divided by the estimated increase, from the preceding fiscal year, in the number of handicapped children aged three to five, inclusive, who will be receiving special education and related services in all States multiplied by the estimated number of such children in such State.

(B) For fiscal year 1988, funds shall be distributed in accordance with clause (i) or (ii) of paragraph (2)(A), except that the amount specified therein shall be $400 instead of $300.

(C) For fiscal year 1989, funds shall be distributed in accordance with clause (i) or (ii) of paragraph (2)(A), except that the amount specified therein shall be $500 instead of $300.

(D) If the Secretary makes a grant under paragraph (1) for fiscal year 1990, the amount of a grant to a State under such paragraph may not exceed $1,000 per handicapped child aged three to five, inclusive, who received special education and related services in such State as determined under section 1411(a)(3) of this title.

(E) If the actual number of additional children served in a fiscal year differs from the estimate made under clause (ii)(II) of the applicable subparagraph, subparagraph (A)(ii)(II), the Secretary shall adjust (upwards or downwards) a State's allotment in the subsequent fiscal year.

(F)(i) The amount of a grant under subparagraph (A), (B), or (C) to any State for a fiscal year may not exceed $3,800 per estimated handicapped child aged three to five, inclusive, who will be receiving or handicapped child, age three to five, inclusive, who is receiving special education and related services in such State.

(ii) If the amount appropriated under subsection (e) of this section for any fiscal year exceeds the amount of grants which may be made to the States for such fiscal year, the excess amount appropriated shall remain available for obligation under this section for 2 succeeding fiscal years.

(3) To receive a grant under paragraph (1) a State shall make an application to the Secretary at such time, in such manner, and containing or accompanied by such information as the Secretary may reasonably require.

(b) Grants for fiscal year 1990 and thereafter; amount of grants

(1) For fiscal year 1990 (or fiscal year 1991 if required by paragraph (2)) and fiscal years thereafter the Secretary shall make a grant to any State which—

(A) has met the eligibility requirements of section 1412 of this title, and

(B) has a State plan approved under section 1413 of this title which includes policies and procedures that assure the availability under the State law and practice of such State of a free appropriate public education for all handicapped children aged three to five, inclusive.

The Secretary may make a grant under paragraph (1) only for fiscal year 1990 and fiscal years thereafter, except that if—

(A) the aggregate amount that was appropriated under subsection (e) of this section for fiscal years 1987, 1988, and 1989 was less than $656,000,000, and

(B) the amount appropriated for fiscal year 1990 under subsection (e) of this section is less than $306,000,000,

the Secretary may not make a grant under paragraph (1) until fiscal year 1991 and shall make a grant under subsection (a)(1) of this section for fiscal year 1990.

(3) The amount of any grant to any State under paragraph (1) for any fiscal year may not exceed $1,000 for each handicapped child in such State aged three to five, inclusive.

(4) To receive a grant under paragraph (1) a State shall make an application to the Secretary at such time, in such manner, and containing or accompanied by such information as the Secretary may reasonably require.

(c) Distribution by State of received funds

(1) For fiscal year 1987, a State which receives a grant under subsection (a)(1) of this section shall—

(A) distribute at least 70 percent of such grant to local educational agencies and intermediate educational units in such State in accordance with paragraph (3), except that in applying such section only handicapped children aged three to five, inclusive, shall be considered,

(B) use not more than 25 percent of such grant for the planning and development of a comprehensive delivery system for which a grant could have been made under section 1423(b) of this title in effect through fiscal year 1987 and for direct and support services for handicapped children, and

(C) use not more than 5 percent of such grant for administrative expenses related to the grant.

(2) For fiscal years beginning after fiscal year 1987, a State which receives a grant under subsection (a)(1) of this section or (b)(1) of this section shall—

(A) distribute at least 75 percent of such grant to local educational agencies and intermediate educational units in such State in accordance with paragraph (3), except that in applying such section only handicapped children aged three to five, inclusive, shall be considered.

(B) use not more than 20 percent of such grant for the planning and development of a comprehensive delivery system for which a grant could have been made under section 1423(b) of this title in effect through fiscal year 1987 and for direct and support services for handicapped children, and

(C) use not more than 5 percent of such grant for administrative expenses related to the grant.

(3) From the amount of funds available to local educational agencies and intermediate educational units in any State under this section, each local educational agency or intermediate educational unit shall be entitled to—

(A) an amount which bears the same ratio to the amount available under subsection (a)(2)(A)(i) of this title or subsection (a)(2)(A)(ii)(I) of this title, as the case may be, as the number of handicapped children aged three to five, inclusive, who received special education and related services as determined under section 1411(a)(3) of this title in such local educational agency or intermediate educational unit bears to the aggregate number of handicapped children aged three to five, inclusive, who received special education and related services in all local educational agencies and intermediate educational units in the State entitled to funds under this section, and

(B) to the extent funds are available under subsection (a)(2)(A)(ii)(II) of this section, an amount which bears the same ratio to the amount available under subsection (a)(2)(A)(ii)(II) of this section as the estimated number of additional handicapped children aged three to five, inclusive, who will be receiving special education and related services in such local educational agency or intermediate educational unit bears to the aggregate number of handicapped children aged three to five, inclusive, who will be receiving special education and related services in all local educational agencies and intermediate educational units in the State entitled to funds under this section.

(d) Insufficiency of appropriated amounts; reduction of maximum amounts receivable by States

If the sums appropriated under subsection (e) of this section for any fiscal year for making payments to States under subsection (a)(1) of this section or (b)(1) are not sufficient to pay in full the maximum amounts which all States may receive under such subsection for such fiscal year, the maximum amounts which all States may receive under such subsection for such fiscal year shall be ratably reduced by first ratably reducing amounts computed under the excess appropriation provision of subsection (a)(2)(A)(ii)(II) of this section. If additional funds become available for making such payments for any fiscal year during which the preceding sentence is applicable, the reduced maximum amounts shall be increased on the same basis as they were reduced.

(e) Authorization of appropriations

For grants under subsections (a)(1) of this section and (b)(1) of this section there are authorized to be appropriated such sums as may be necessary.

§ 1420. Payments

(a) Payments to States; distribution by States to local educational agencies and intermediate educational units

The Secretary shall make payments to each State in amounts which the State educational agency of such State is eligible to receive under this subchapter. Any State educational agency receiving payments under this subsection shall distribute payments to the local educational agencies and intermediate educational units of such State in amounts which such agencies and units are eligible to receive under this subchapter after the State educational agency has approved applications of such agencies or units for payments in accordance with section 1414(b) of this title.

(b) Advances, reimbursements, and installments

Payments under this subchapter may be made in advance or by way of reimbursement and in such installments as the Secretary may determine necessary.

SUBCHAPTER III—CENTERS AND SERVICES TO MEET SPECIAL NEEDS OF THE HANDICAPPED

§ 1421. Regional resource centers

(a) Establishment; functions

The Secretary may make grants to, or enter into contracts or cooperative agreements with, institutions of higher education, public agencies, private nonprofit organizations, State educational agencies, or combinations of such agencies or institutions (which combinations may include one or more local educational agencies) within particular regions of the United States, to pay all or part of the cost of the establishment and operation of regional resource centers. Each regional resource center shall provide consultation, technical assistance, and training to State educational agencies and through such State educational agencies to local educational agencies and to other appropriate State agencies providing early intervention services. The services provided by a regional resource center shall be consistent with the priority needs identified by the States served by the center and the findings of the Secretary in monitoring reports prepared by the Secretary under section 1417 of this title. Each regional resource center established or operated under this section shall—

(1) assist in identifying and solving persistent problems in providing quality special education and related services for handicapped children and youth and early intervention services to handicapped infants and toddlers and their families,

(2) assist in developing, identifying, and replicating successful programs and practices which will improve special education and related services to handicapped children and youth and their families and early intervention services to handicapped infants and toddlers and their families,

(3) gather and disseminate information to all State educational agencies within the region and coordinate activities with other centers assisted under this subsection and other relevant projects conducted by the Department of Education.

(4) assist in the improvement of information dissemination to and training activities for professionals and parents of handicapped infants, toddlers, children, and youth, and

(5) provide information to and training for agencies, institutions, and organizations, regarding techniques and approaches for submitting applications for grants, contracts, and cooperative agreements under this subchapter and subchapters IV through VII.

(b) Considerations governing approval of application

In determining whether to approve an application for a project under subsection (a) of this section, the Secretary shall consider the need for such a center in the region to be served by the applicant and the capability of the applicant to fulfill the responsibilities under subsection (a) of this section.

(c) Annual report; summary of information

Each regional resource center shall report a summary of materials produced or developed and the summaries reported shall be included in the annual report to Congress required under section 1418 of this title.

(d) Coordination technical assistance center; establishment; duties

The Secretary may establish one coordinating technical assistance center focusing on national priorities established by the Secretary to assist the regional resource centers in the delivery of technical assistance, consistent with such national priorities.

(e) Amounts available for coordination technical assistance center

Before using funds made available in any fiscal year to carry out this section for purposes of subsection (d) of this section, not less than the amount made available for this section in the previous fiscal year shall be made available for regional resource centers under subsection (a) of this section and in no case shall more than $500,000 be made available for the center under subsection (d) of this section.

§ 1422. Services for deaf-blind children and youth

(a) Grant and contract authority; types and scope of programs; governing considerations

(1) The Secretary is authorized to make grants to, or to enter into cooperative agreements or contracts with, public or nonprofit private agencies, institutions, or organizations to assist State educational agencies to—

(A) assure deaf-blind children and youth provision of special education and related services as well as vocational and transitional services; and

(B) make available to deaf-blind youth upon attaining the year of twenty-two, programs and services to facilitate their transition from educational to other services.

(2) A grant, cooperative agreement, or contract pursuant to paragraph (1)(A) may be made only for programs providing (A) technical assistance to agencies, institutions, or organizations providing educational services to deaf-blind children or youth; (B) preservice or inservice training to paraprofessionals, professionals, or related services personnel preparing to serve, or serving, deaf-blind children or youth; (C) replication of successful innovative approaches to providing educational or related services to deaf-blind children and youth; and (D) facilitation of parental involvement in the education of their deaf-blind children and youth. Such programs may include—

(i) the diagnosis and educational evaluation of children and youth at risk of being certified deaf-blind;

(ii) programs of adjustment, education, and orientation for deaf-blind children and youth; and

(iii) consultative, counseling, and training services for the families of deaf-blind children and youth.

(3) A grant, cooperative agreement, or contract pursuant to paragraph (1)(B) may be made only for programs providing (A) technical assistance to agencies, institutions, and organizations serving, or proposing to serve, deaf-blind individuals who have attained age twenty-two years; (B) training or inservice training to paraprofessionals or professionals serving, or preparing to serve, such individuals; and (C) assistance in the development or replication of successful innovative approaches to providing rehabilitative, semi-supervised, or independent living programs.

(4) In carrying out this subsection, the Secretary shall take into consideration the need for a center for deaf-blind children and youth in light of the general availability and quality of existing services for such children and youth in the part of the country involved.

(b) Contract authority for regional programs of technical assistance

The Secretary is also authorized to enter into a limited number of cooperative agreements or contracts to establish and support regional programs for the provision of technical assistance in the education of deaf-blind children and youth.

(c) Annual report to Secretary; examination of numbers and services and revision of numbers; annual report to Congress: summary of data

(1) Programs supported under this section shall report annually to the Secretary on (A) the numbers of deaf-blind children and youth served by age, severity, and nature of deaf-blindness; (B) the number of paraprofessionals, professionals, and family members directly served by each activity; and (C) the types of services provided.

(2) The Secretary shall examine the number of deaf-blind children and youth (A) reported under subparagraph (c)(1)(A) and by the States; (B) served by the programs under subchapter II of this chapter and subpart 2 of part B, title I, of the Elementary and Secondary Education Act of 1965 [20 U.S.C. 2771 et seq.] (as modified by chapter 1 of the Education Consolidation and Improvement Act of 1981 [20 U.S.C. 3801 et seq.]); and (C) the Deaf-Blind Registry of each State. The Secretary shall revise the count of deaf-blind children and youth to reflect the most accurate count.

(3) The Secretary shall summarize these data for submission in the annual report required under section 1418 of this title.

(d) Dissemination of materials and information concerning working practices

The Secretary shall disseminate materials and information concerning effective practices in working with deaf-blind children and youth.

(e) Extended school year demonstration programs

The Secretary is authorized to make grants to, or enter into contracts or cooperative agreements with, public or nonprofit private agencies, institutions, or organizations for the development and operation of extended school year demonstration programs for severely handicapped children and youth, including deaf-blind children and youth.

(f) Grants for purposes under other parts of this chapter

The Secretary may make grants to, or enter into contracts or cooperative agreements with, the entities under section 1424(a) of this title for the purposes in such section.

§ 1423. Experimental, demonstration, and outreach preschool and intervention programs for handicapped children

(a) Contracts, grants and cooperative agreements; purpose; community coordination programs; national dispersion in urban and rural areas; Federal share; non-Federal contributions; arrangements with Indian tribes

(1) The Secretary may arrange by contract, grant, or cooperative agreement with appropriate public and private nonprofit organizations, for the development and operation of experimental, demonstration, and outreach preschool and early intervention programs for handicapped children which the Secretary determines show promise of promoting a comprehensive and strengthened approach to the special problems of such children. Such programs shall include activities and services designed to (1) facilitate the intellectual, emotional, physical, mental, social, speech, language development, and self-help skills of such children, (2) encourage the participation of the parents of such children in the development and operation of any such program, and (3) acquaint the community to be served by any such program with the problems and potentialities of such children, (4) offer training about exemplary models and practices to State and local personnel who provide services to handicapped children from birth through eight, and (5) support the adaption of exemplary models and practices in States and local communities.

(2) Programs authorized by paragraph (1) shall be coordinated with similar programs in the schools operated or supported by State or local educational agencies of the community to be served and with similar programs operated by other public agencies in such community.

(3) As much as is feasible, programs assisted under paragraph (1) shall be geographically dispersed throughout the Nation in urban as well as rural areas.

(4)(A) Except as provided in subparagraph (B), no arrangement under paragraph (1) shall provide for the payment of more than 90 percent of the total annual costs of development, operation, and evaluation of any program. Non-Federal contributions may be in cash or in kind, fairly evaluated, including plant, equipment, and services.

(B) The Secretary may waive the requirement of subparagraph (A) in the case of an arrangement entered into under paragraph (1) with governing bodies of Indian tribes located on Federal or State reservations and with consortia of such bodies.

(b) Technical assistance development programs

The Secretary shall arrange by contract, grant, or cooperative agreement with appropriate public agencies and private nonprofit organizations for the establishment of a technical assistance development system to assist entities operating experimental, demonstration, and outreach programs and to assist State agencies to expand and improve services provided to handicapped children.

(c) Early childhood research institutes

The Secretary shall arrange by contract, grant, or cooperative agreement with appropriate public agencies and private nonprofit organizations for the establishment of early childhood research institutes to carry on sustained research to generate and disseminate new information on preschool and early intervention for handicapped children and their families.

(d) Grants or contracts with organizations to identify needs of handicapped children and for training of personnel

The Secretary may make grants to, enter into contracts or cooperative agreements under this section with, such organizations or institutions, as are determined by the Secretary to be appropriate, for research to identify and meet the full range of special needs of handicapped children and for training of personnel for programs specifically designed for handicapped children.

(e) Notice in Federal Register of intent to accept application for grants, contracts, etc.

At least one year before the termination of a grant, contract, or cooperative agreement made or entered into under subsections (b) and (c) of this section, the Secretary shall publish in the Federal Register a notice of intent to accept application for such a grant, contract, or cooperative agreement contingent on the appropriation of sufficient funds by Congress.

(f) "Handicapped children" defined

For purposes of this section the term "handicapped children" includes children from birth through eight years of age.

§ 1424. Research, innovation, training, and dissemination activities in connection with model centers and services for the handicapped

(a) Grant and contract authority

The Secretary may make grants to, or enter into contracts or cooperative agreements with, such organizations or institutions, as are determined by the Secretary to be appropriate, to address the needs of severely handicapped children and youth, for—

(1) research to identify and meet the full range of special needs of such handicapped children and youth,

(2) the development or demonstration of new, or improvements in, existing, methods, approaches, or techniques which would contribute to the adjustment and education of such handicapped children and youth,

(3) training of personnel for programs specifically designed for such children, and

(4) dissemination of materials and information about practices found effective in working with such children and youth.

(b) Coordination of activities with similar activities under other parts of this chapter

In making grants and contracts under subsection (a) of this section, the Secretary shall ensure that the activities funded under such grants and contracts will be coordinated with similar activities funded from grants and contracts under other sections of this chapter.

(c) National geographic dispersion of programs in urban and rural areas

To the extent feasible, programs, authorized by subsection (a) of this section shall be geographically dispersed throughout the nation in urban and rural areas.

§ 1424a. Postsecondary and other specially designed model programs

(a) Grants and contract authority; development, operation, and dissemination of postsecondary, vocational, technical, continuing, or adult education programs; priority of programs; notice in Federal Register of intent to accept application for grant or contract; national geographic dispersion in urban and rural areas; availability of sums for regional centers

(1) The Secretary may make grants to, or enter into contracts with, State educational agencies, institutions of higher education, junior and community colleges, vocational and technical institutions, and other appropriate nonprofit educational agencies for the development, operation, and dissemination of specially designed model programs of postsecondary, vocational, technical, continuing, or adult education for handicapped individuals.

(2) In making grants or contracts on a competitive basis under paragraph (1), the Secretary shall give priority consideration to 4 regional centers for the deaf and to model programs for individuals with handicapping conditions other than deafness—

(A) for developing and adapting programs of postsecondary, vocational, technical, continuing, or adult education to meet the special needs of handicapped individuals, and

(B) for programs that coordinate, facilitate, and encourage education of handicapped individuals with their nonhandicapped peers.

(3) Persons operating programs for handicapped persons under a grant or contract under paragraph (1) must coordinate their efforts with and dis-

seminate information about their activities to the clearinghouse on postsecondary programs established under section 1433(b) of this title.

(4) At least one year before the termination of a grant or contract with any of the 4 regional centers for the deaf, the Secretary shall publish in the Federal Register a notice of intent to accept application for such grant or contract, contingent on the appropriation of sufficient funds by Congress.

(5) To the extent feasible, programs authorized by paragraph (1) shall be geographically dispensed throughout the nation in urban and rural areas.

(6) Of the sums made available for programs under paragraph (1), not less than $2,000,000 shall first be available for the 4 regional centers for the deaf.

(b) "Handicapped individuals" defined

For the purposes of subsection (a) of this section the term "handicapped individuals" means individuals who are mentally retarded, hard of hearing, deaf, speech or language impaired, visually handicapped, seriously emotionally disturbed, orthopedically impaired, other health impaired individuals, or individuals with specific learning disabilities who by reason thereof require special education and related services.

§ 1425. Secondary education and transitional services for handicapped youth

(a) Grant and contract authority; statement of purposes; national geographic dispersion in urban and rural areas

The Secretary may make grants to, or enter into contracts with, institutions of higher education, State educational agencies, local educational agencies, or other appropriate public and private nonprofit institutions or agencies (including the State job training coordinating councils and service delivery area administrative entities established under the Job Training Partnership Act (Public Law 97-300) [29 U.S.C.A. § 1501 et seq.]) to—

(1) strengthen and coordinate special education and related services for handicapped youth currently in school or who recently left school to assist them in the transition to postsecondary education, vocational training, competitive employment (including supported employment), continuing education, or adult services,

(2) stimulate the improvement and development of programs for secondary special education, and

(3) stimulate the improvement of the vocational and life skills of handicapped students to enable them to be better prepared for transition to adult life and services.

To the extent feasible, such programs shall be geographically dispersed through the Nation in urban and rural areas.

(b) Description of specific projects

Projects assisted under subsection (a) of this section may include—

(1) developing strategies and techniques for transition to independent living, vocational training, vocational rehabilitation, postsecondary edu-

cation, and competitive employment (including supported employment) for handicapped youth,

(2) establishing demonstration models for services, programs, and individualized education programs, which emphasize vocational training, transitional services, and placement for handicapped youth,

(3) conducting demographic studies which provide information on the numbers, age levels, types of handicapping conditions, and services required for handicapped youth in need of transitional programs,

(4) specially designed vocational programs to increase the potential for competitive employment for handicapped youth,

(5) research and development projects for exemplary service delivery models and the replication and dissemination of successful models,

(6) initiating cooperative models between educational agencies and adult service agencies, including vocational rehabilitation, mental health, mental retardation, public employment, and employers, which facilitate the planning and developing of transitional services for handicapped youth to postsecondary education, vocational training, employment, continuing education, and adult services,

(7) developing appropriate procedures for evaluating vocational training, placement, and transitional services for handicapped youth,

(8) conducting studies whch provide information on the numbers, age levels, types of handicapping conditions and reasons why handicapped youth drop out of school,

(9) developing special education curriculum and instructional techniques that will improve handicapped students' acquisition of the skills necessary for transition to adult life and services, and

(10) specifically designed physical education and therapeutic recreation programs to increase the potential of handicapped youths for community participation.

(c) Coordination of non-educational-agency applicant with State educational agency

For purposes of paragraphs (1) and (2) of subsection (b) of this section, if an applicant is not an educational agency, such applicant shall coordinate with the State educational agency.

(d) Applications for assistance; contents

Applications for assistance under subsection (a) of this section other than for the purpose of conducting studies or evaluations shall—

(1) describe the procedures to be used for disseminating relevant findings and data to regional resource centers, clearinghouses, and other interested persons, agencies, or organizations,

(2) describe the procedures that will be used for coordinating services among agencies for which handicapped youth are or will be eligible, and

(3) to the extent appropriate, provide for the direct participation of handicapped students and the parents of handicapped students in the planning, development, and implementation of such projects.

(e) Development or demonstration of new or improvement in methods, approaches, or techniques

The Secretary is authorized to make grants to, or to enter into contracts or cooperative agreements with, such organizations or institutions as are determined by the Secretary to be appropriate for the development or demonstration of new or improvements in existing methods, approaches, or techniques which will contribute to the adjustment and education of handicapped children and youth and the dissemination of materials and information concerning practices found effective in working with such children and youth.

(f) Coordination of educational programs with vocational rehabilitation projects

The Secretary, as appropriate, shall coordinate programs described under subsection (a) of this section with projects developed under section 777a of Title 29.

§ 1426. Program evaluations; submittal of analyses to Congressional committees

The Secretary shall conduct, either directly or by contract, a thorough and continuing evaluation of the effectiveness of each program assisted under this subchapter. Results of the evaluations shall be analyzed and submitted to the appropriate committees of each House of Congress together with the annual reports under section 1418 of this title.

§ 1427. Authorization of appropriations

(a) There are authorized to be appropriated to carry out section 1421 of this title, $6,700,000 for fiscal year 1987, $7,100,000 for fiscal year 1988, and $7,500,000 for fiscal year 1989.

(b) There are authorized to be appropriated to carry out section 1422 of this title, $15,900,000 for fiscal year 1987, $16,800,000 for fiscal year 1988, and $17,800,000 for fiscal year 1989.

(c) There are authorized to be appropriated to carry out section 1423 of this title, $24,470,000 for fiscal year 1987, $25,870,000 for fiscal year 1988, and $27,410,000 for fiscal year 1989.

(d) There are authorized to be appropriated to carry out section 1424 of this title, $5,300,000 for fiscal year 1987, $5,600,000 for fiscal year 1988, and $5,900,000 for fiscal year 1989.

(e) There are authorized to be appropriated to carry out section 1424a of this title, $5,900,000 for fiscal year 1987, $6,200,000 for fiscal year 1988, and $6,600,000 for fiscal year 1989.

(f) There are authorized to be appropriated to carry out section 1425 of this title, $7,300,000 for fiscal year 1987, $7,700,000 for fiscal year 1988, and $8,100,000 for fiscal year 1989.

SUBCHAPTER IV—TRAINING PERSONNEL FOR THE EDUCATION OF THE HANDICAPPED

§ 1431. Grants for personnel training

(a) Careers in special education; personnel standards; training-study and fellowships-traineeships costs; contract authority for areas of personnel shortages

(1) The Secretary may make grants, which may include scholarships with necessary stipends and allowances, to institutions of higher education (including the university-affiliated facilities program under the Rehabilitation Act of 1973 and satellite network of the developmental disabilities program) and other appropriate nonprofit agencies to assist them in training personnel for careers in special education and early intervention, including—

(A) special education teaching, including speech-language pathology and audiology, and adaptive physical education,

(B) related services to handicapped children and youth in educational settings,

(C) special education supervision and administration,

(D) special education research, and

(E) training of special education personnel and other personnel providing special services and pre-school and early intervention services for handicapped children.

(2)(A) In making grants under paragraph (1), the Secretary shall base the determination of such grants on information relating to the present and projected need for the personnel to be trained based on identified State, regional, or national shortages, and the capacity of the institution or agency to train qualified personnel, and other information considered appropriate by the Secretary.

(B) The Secretary shall ensure that grants are only made under paragraph (1) to applicant agencies and institutions that meet State and professionally recognized standards for the preparation of special education and related services personnel unless the grant is for the purpose of assisting the applicant agency of institution to meet such standards.

(3) Grants under paragraph (1) may be used by institutions to assist in covering the cost of courses of training or study for such personnel and for establishing and maintaining fellowships or traineeships with such stipends and allowances as may be determined by the Secretary.

(4) The Secretary in carrying out paragraph (1) may reserve a sum not to exceed 5 percent of the amount available for paragraph (1) in each fiscal year for contracts to prepare personnel in areas where shortages exist when a response to that need has not been adequately addressed by the grant process.

(b) Special projects for preservice training, regular educators, and inservice training of special education personnel.

The Secretary may make grants to institutions of higher education and other appropriate nonprofit agencies to conduct special projects to develop and demonstrate new approaches (including the application of new technology) for the preservice training purposes set forth in subsection (a) of this section for regular educators, for the training of teachers to work in community and school settings with handicapped secondary school students, and for the inservice training of special education personnel, including classroom aides, related services personnel, and regular education personnel who serve handicapped children and personnel providing early intervention services.

(c) Parent training and information programs

(1) The Secretary may make grants through a separate competition to private nonprofit organizations for the purpose of providing training and information to parents of handicapped children and persons who work with parents to enable such individuals to participate more effectively with professionals in meeting the educational needs of handicapped children. Such grants shall be designed to meet the unique training and information needs of parents of handicapped children living in the area to be served by the grant, particularly those who are members of groups that have been traditionally underrepresented.

(2) In order to receive a grant under paragraph (1) a private nonprofit organization shall—

(A) be governed by a board of directors on which a majority of the members are parents of handicapped children and which includes members who are professionals in the field of special education and related services who serve handicapped children and youth, or if the nonprofit private organization does not have such a board, such organization shall have a membership which represents the interests of individuals with handicapping conditions, and shall establish a special governing committee on which a majority of the members are parents of handicapped children and which includes members who are professionals in the fields of special education and related services, to operate the training and information program under paragraph (1),

(B) serve the parents of children with the full range of handicapping conditions under such grant program, and

(C) demonstrate the capacity and expertise to conduct effectively the training and information activities for which a grant may be made under paragraph (1).

(3) The board of directors or special governing committee of a private nonprofit organization receiving a grant under paragraph (1) shall meet at least once in each calendar quarter to review the parent training and information activities for which the grant is made, and each such committee shall advise the governing board directly of its views and recommendations. Whenever a private nonprofit organization requests the renewal of a grant under paragraph (1) for a fiscal year, the board of directors or the special governing committee shall submit to the Secretary a written review of the parent training and information program conducted by that private nonprofit organization during the preceding fiscal year.

(4) The Secretary shall ensure that grants under paragraph (1) will—

(A) be distributed geographically to the greatest extent possible throughout all the States and give priority to grants which involve unserved areas, and

(B) be targeted to parents of handicapped children in both urban and rural areas or on a State or regional basis.

(5) Parent training and information programs assisted under paragraph (1) shall assist parents to—

(A) better understand the nature and needs of the handicapping conditions of children,

(B) provide followup support for handicapped children's educational programs,

(C) communicate more effectively with special and regular educators, administrators, related services personnel, and other relevant professionals,

(D) participate in educational decisionmaking processes including the development of a handicapped child's individualized educational program,

(E) obtain information about the programs, services, and resources available to handicapped children and the degree to which the programs, services and resources are appropriate, and

(F) understand the provisions for the education of handicapped children as specified under subchapter II of this chapter.

(6) Parent training and information programs may, at a grant recipients discretion, include State or local educational personnel where such participation will further an objective of the program assisted by the grant.

(7) Each private nonprofit organization operating a program receiving a grant under paragraph (1) shall consult with appropriate agencies which serve or assist handicapped children and youth and are located in the jurisdictions served by the program.

(8) The Secretary shall provide technical assistance, by grant or contract, for establishing, developing, and coordinating parent training and information programs.

§ 1432. Grants to State educational agencies and institutions for traineeships

The Secretary shall make grants to each State educational agency and may make grants to institutions of higher education to assist in establishing and maintaining preservice and inservice programs to prepare personnel to meet the needs of handicapped infants, toddlers, children, and youth or supervisors of such persons, consistent with the personnel needs identified in the State's comprehensive system of personnel development under section 1413 of this title.

§ 1433. Clearinghouses

(a) National clearinghouse on education of handicapped; establishment; other support projects; statement of objectives

The Secretary is authorized to make a grant to or enter into a contract with a public agency or a nonprofit private organization or institution for a national clearinghouse on the education of the handicapped and to make grants or contracts with a public agency or a nonprofit private organization or institution for other support projects which may be deemed necessary by the Secretary to disseminate information and provide technical assistance on a national basis to parents, professionals, and other interested parties concerning—

(1) programs relating to the education of the handicapped under this chapter and other Federal laws, and

(2) participation in such programs, including referral of individuals to appropriate national, State, and local agencies and organizations for further assistance.

(b) National clearinghouse on postsecondary education for handicapped; establishment; statement of purpose

In addition to the clearinghouse established under subsection (a) of this section, the Secretary shall make a grant or enter into a contract for a national clearinhouse on postsecondary education for handicapped individuals for the purpose of providing information on available services and programs in postsecondary education for the handicapped.

(c) National clearinghouse to encourage careers and employment in fields relating to education of the handicapped

The Secretary shall make a grant or enter into a contract for a national clearinghouse designed to encourage students to seek careers and professional personnel to seek employment in the various fields relating to the education of handicapped children and youth through the following:

(1) Collection and dissemination of information on current and future national, regional, and State needs for special education and related services personnel.

(2) Dissemination to high school counselors and others concerning current career opportunities in special education, location of programs, and various forms of financial assistance (such as scholarships, stipends, and allowances).

(3) Identification of training programs available around the country.

(4) Establishment of a network among local and State educational agencies and institutions of higher education concerning the supply of graduates and available openings.

(5) Technical assistance to institutions seeking to meet State and professionally recognized standards.

(d) Considerations governing awards; limitation of contracts with profitmaking organizations

(1) In awarding the grants and contracts under this section, the Secretary shall give particular attention to any demonstrated experience at the national level relevant to performance of the functions established in this section, and ability to conduct such projects, communicate with the intended consumers of information, and maintain the necessary communication with other agencies and organizations.

(2) The Secretary is authorized to make contracts with profitmaking organizations under this section only when necessary for materials or media access.

§ 1434. Reports to the Secretary

(a) Not more than sixty days after the end of any fiscal year, each recipient of a grant or contract under this subchapter during such fiscal year shall prepare and submit a report to the Secretary. Each such report shall be in such form and detail as the Secretary determines to be appropriate, and shall include—

(1) the number of individuals trained under the grant or contract, by category of training and level of training; and

(2) the number of individuals trained under the grant or contract receiving degrees and certification, by category and level of training.

(b) A summary of the data required by this section shall be included in the annual report of the Secretary under section 1418 of this title.

§ 1435. Authorization of appropriations

(a) Subchapter IV, personnel recruitment, and opportunities for handicapped programs

There are authorized to be appropriated to carry out this subchapter (other than section 1433 of this title) $70,400,000 for fiscal year 1987, $74,500,000 for fiscal year 1988, and $79,000,000 for fiscal year 1989. There are authorized to be appropriated to carry out section 1433 of this title, $1,200,000 for fiscal year 1987, $1,900,000 for fiscal year 1988, and $2,000,000 for fiscal year 1989.

(b) Personnel training for careers in special education and early intervention

Of the funds appropriated pursuant to subsection (a) of this section for any fiscal year, the Secretary shall reserve not less than 65 per centum for activities described in subparagraphs (A) through (E) of section 1431(a)(1) of this section.

(c) Parent training and information programs

Of the funds appropriated under subsection (a) of this section for any fiscal year, the Secretary shall reserve 10 percent for activities under section 1431(c) of this title.

§ 1436. Omitted

SUBCHAPTER V—RESEARCH IN THE EDUCATION OF THE HANDICAPPED

§ 1441. Research and demonstration projects in education of handicapped children

(a) Grant and contract authority; statement of objectives; description of specific activities

The Secretary may make grants to, or enter into contracts or cooperative agreements with, State and local educational agencies, institutions of higher education, and other public agencies and nonprofit private organizations for research and related activities to assist special education personnel, related services personnel, early intervention personnel, and other appropriate persons, including parents, in improving the special education and related services and early intervention services for handicapped infants, toddlers, children, and youth, and to conduct research, surveys, or demonstrations relating to the provision of services to handicapped infants, toddlers, children, and youth. Research and related activities shall be designed to increase knowledge and understanding of handicapped conditions, and teaching, learning, and education-related developmental practices and services for handicapped infants, toddlers, children and youth. Research and related activities assisted under this section shall include the following:

(1) The development of new and improved techniques and devices for teaching handicapped infants, toddlers, children and youth.

(2) The development of curricula which meet the unique educational and developmental needs of handicapped infants, toddlers, children and youth.

(3) The application of new technologies and knowledge for the purpose of improving the instruction of handicapped infants, toddlers, children and youth.

(4) The development of program models and exemplary practices in areas of special education and early intervention.

(5) The dissemination of information on research and related activities conducted under this subchapter to regional resource centers and interested individuals and organizations.

(6) The development of instruments, including tests, inventories, and scales for measuring progress of handicapped infants, toddlers, children and youth across a number of developmental domains.

(b) Qualifications of applicant

In carrying out subsection (a) of this section, the Secretary shall consider the special education or early intervention experience of applicants under such subsection.

(c) Publication of research priorities in Federal Register

The Secretary shall publish proposed research priorities in the Federal Register every 2 years, not later than July 1, and shall allow a period of 60 days for public comments and suggestions. After analyzing and considering the public comments, the Secretary shall publish final research priorities in the Federal Register not later than 30 days after the close of the comment period.

(d) Reports of research projects; index of research projects for annual report; availability to interested parties

The Secretary shall provide an index (including the title of each research project and the name and address of the researching organization) of all research projects conducted in the prior fiscal year in the annual report described under section 1418 of this title. The Secretary shall make reports of research projects available to the education community at large and to other interested parties.

(e) Coordination of related research priorities; information respecting research priorities to Federal entities

The Secretary shall coordinate the research priorities established under subsection (c) of this section with research priorities established by the National Institute of Handicapped Research and shall provide information concerning research priorities established under such subsection to the National Council on the Handicapped, and to the Bureau of Indian Affairs Advisor Committee for Exceptional Children.

§ 1442. Research and demonstration projects in physical education and recreation for handicapped children

The Secretary is authorized to make grants to States, State or local educational agencies, institutions of higher education, and other public or nonprofit private educational or research agencies and organizations, and to make contracts with States, State or local educational agencies, institutions of higher education, and other public or private educational or research agencies and organizations, for research and related purposes relating to physical education or recreation for handicapped children, and to conduct research, surveys, or demonstrations relating to physical education or recreation for handicapped children.

§ 1443. Panels of experts

(a) Convention; composition

The Secretary shall convene, in accordance with subsection (b) of this section, panels of experts who are competent to evaluate proposals for projects under subchapters III through VII of this chapter. The panels shall be composed of—

(1) individuals from the field of special education for the handicapped and other relevant disciplines who have significant expertise and

experience in the content areas and age levels addressed in the proposals, and

(2) handicapped individuals and parents of handicapped individuals when appropriate.

(b) Funding requests for which panel required to be convened; membership; expenses and fees

(1) The Secretary shall convene panels under subsection (a) of this section for any application which includes a total funding request exceeding $60,000 and may convene or otherwise appoint panels for applications which include funding requests that are less than such amount.

(2) Such panels shall include a majority of non-Federal members. Such non-Federal members shall be provided travel and per diem not to exceed the rate provided to other educational consultants used by the Department and shall be provided consultant fees at such a rate.

(c) Use of funds available under other parts of this chapter for payment of expenses and fees

The Secretary may use funds available under subchapters III to VII of this chapter to pay expenses and fees of non-Federal members under subsection (b) of this section.

§ 1444. Authorization of appropriations

For purposes of carrying out this subchapter, there are authorized to be appropriated $18,000,000 for fiscal year 1987, $19,000,000 for fiscal year 1988, and $20,100,000 for fiscal year 1989.

SUBCHAPTER VI—INSTRUCTIONAL MEDIA FOR THE HANDICAPPED

§ 1451. Congressional statement of purposes

(a)[1] The purposes of this subchapter are to promote—

(1) the general welfare of deaf persons by (A) bringing to such persons understanding and appreciation of those films which play such an important part in the general and cultural advancement of hearing persons, (B) providing through these films enriched educational and cultural experiences through which deaf persons can be brought into better touch with the realities of their environment, and (C) providing a wholesome and rewarding experience which deaf persons may share together; and

(2) the educational advancement of handicapped persons by (A) carrying on research in the use of educational media for the handicapped, (B) producing and distributing educational media for the use of handicapped persons, their parents, their actual or potential employers, and other persons directly involved in work for the advancement of the handicapped, and (C) training persons in the use of educational media for the instruction of the handicapped.

§ 1452. Captioned films and educational media for handicapped persons

(a) Establishment of loan service

The Secretary shall establish a loan service of captioned films and educational media for the purpose of making such materials available, in accordance with regulations, in the United States for nonprofit purposes to handicapped persons, parents of handicapped persons, and other persons directly involved in activities for the advancement of the handicapped, including for the purpose of addressing problems of illiteracy among the handicapped.

(b) Authority of Secretary

The Secretary is authorized to—

(1) acquire films (or rights thereto) and other educational media by purchase, lease, or gift;

(2) acquire by lease or purchased[2] equipment necessary to the administration of this subchapter;

(3) provide, by grant or contract, for the captioning of films;

(4) provide, by grant or contract, for the distribution of captioned films and other educational media and equipment through State schools for the handicapped, public libraries, and such other agencies as the Secretary may deem appropriate to serve as local or regional centers for such distribution;

---

[1]Reproduced as in original. Enacted with no subsec. (b).

[2]Reproduced as in original.

(5) provide, by grant or contract, for the conduct of research in the use of educational and training films and other educational media for the handicapped, for the production and distribution of educational and training films and other educational media for the handicapped and the training of persons in the use of such films and media, including the payment to those persons of such stipends (including allowances for travel and other expenses of such persons and their dependents) as he may determine, which shall be consistent with prevailing practices under comparable federally supported programs;

(6) utilize the facilities and services of other governmental agencies; and

(7) accept gifts, contributions, and voluntary and uncompensated services of individuals and organizations, and

(8) provide by grant or contract for educational media and materials for the deaf.

(c) Cooperative agreements with National Theatre of the Deaf, Inc.

The Secretary may make grants to or enter into contracts or cooperative agreements with the National Theatre of the Deaf, Inc. for the purpose of providing theatrical experiences to—

(1) enrich the lives of deaf children and adults,

(2) increase public awareness and understanding of deafness and of the artistic and intellectual achievements of deaf people, and

(3) promote the integration of hearing and deaf people through shared cultural experiences.

§ 1453. Repealed.

§ 1454. Authorization of appropriations

For the purposes of carrying out this subchapter, there are authorized to be appropriate $15,000,000 for fiscal year 1987, $15,750,000 for fiscal year 1988, and $16,540,000 for fiscal year 1989.

SUBCHAPTER VII—TECHNOLOGY, EDUCATIONAL MEDIA, AND MATERIALS FOR THE HANDICAPPED

§ 1461. Authority of Secretary; purpose of projects or centers

The Secretary may make grants or enter into contracts or cooperative agreements with institutions of higher education, State and local educational agencies, or other appropriate agencies and organizations for the purpose of advancing the use of new technology, media, and materials in the education of handicapped students and the provision of early intervention to handicapped infants and toddlers. In carrying out this subsection, the Secretary may fund projects or centers for the purposes of—

(1) determining how technology, media, and materials are being used in the education of the handicapped and how they can be used more effectively,

(2) designing and adapting new technology, media, and materials to improve the education of handicapped students,

(3) assisting the public and private sectors in the development and marketing of new technology, media, and materials for the education of the handicapped, and

(4) disseminating information on the availability and use of new technology, media, and materials for the education of the handicapped.

§ 1462. Authorization of appropriations

For the purposes of carrying out this subchapter, there are authorized to be appropriated $10,000,000 for fiscal year 1987, $10,500,000 for fiscal year 1988, and $11,025,000 for fiscal year 1989.

SUBCHAPTER VIII—HANDICAPPED INFANTS AND TODDLERS [NEW]

§ 1471. Findings and policy

(a) Findings

The Congress finds that there is an urgent and substantial need—

(1) to enhance the development of handicapped infants and toddlers and to minimize their potential for developmental delay,

(2) to reduce the educational costs to our society, including our Nation's schools, by minimizing the need for special education and related services after handicapped infants and toddlers reach school age,

(3) to minimize the likelihood of institutionalization of handicapped individuals and maximize the potential for their independent living in society, and

(4) to enhance the capacity of families to meet the special needs of their infants and toddlers with handicaps.

(b) Policy

It is therefore the policy of the United States to provide financial assistance to States—

(1) to develop and implement a statewide, comprehensive, coordinated, multidisciplinary, interagency program of early intervention services for handicapped infants and toddlers and their families,

(2) to facilitate the coordination of payment for early intervention services from Federal, State, local, and private sources (including public and private insurance coverage), and

(3) to enhance its capacity to provide quality early intervention services and expand and improve existing early intervention services being provided to handicapped infants, toddlers, and their families.

§ 1472. Definitions

As used in this subchapter—

(1) The term "handicapped infants and toddlers" means individuals from birth to age 2, inclusive, who need early intervention services because they—

(A) are experiencing developmental delays, as measured by appropriate diagnostic instruments and procedures in one or more of the following areas: Cognitive development, physical development, language and speech development, psychosocial development, or self-help skills, or

(B) have a diagnosed physical or mental condition which has a high probability of resulting in developmental delay.

Such term may also include, at a State's discretion, individuals from birth to age 2, inclusive, who are at risk of having substantial developmental delays if early intervention services are not provided.

(2) "Early intervention services" are developmental services which—

(A) are provided under public supervision,

(B) are provided at no cost except where Federal or State law provides for a system of payments by families, including a schedule of sliding fees,

(C) are designed to meet a handicapped infant's or toddler's developmental need in any one or more of the following areas:

(i) physical development,

(ii) cognitive development,

(iii) language and speech development,

(iv) psycho-social development, or

(v) self-help skills,

(D) meet the standards of the State, including the requirements of this part,

(E) include—

(i) family training, counseling, and home visits,

(ii) special instruction,

(iii) speech pathology and audiology,

(iv) occupational therapy,

(v) physical therapy,

(vi) psychological services,

(vii) case management services,

(viii) medical services only for diagnostic or evaluation purposes,

(ix) early identification, screening and assessment services, and

(x) health services necessary to enable the infant or toddler to benefit from the other early intervention services,

(F) are provided by qualified personnel, including—

(i) special educators,

(ii) speech and language pathologists and audiologists,

(iii) occupational therapists,

(iv) physical therapists,

(v) psychologists,

(vi) social workers,

(vii) nurses, and

(viii) nutritionists, and

(G) are provided in conformity with an individualized family service plan adopted in accordance with section 1477 of this title.

(3) The term "developmental delay" has the meaning given such term by a State under section 1476(b)(1) of this title.

(4) The term "Council" means the State Interagency Coordinating Council established under section 1482 of this title.

§ 1473. General authority

The Secretary shall, in accordance with this subchapter, make grants to States (from their allocations under section 1484 of this title) to assist each State to develop a statewide, comprehensive, coordinated, multidisciplinary, interagency system to provide early intervention services for handicapped infants and toddlers and their families.

§ 1474. General eligibility

In order to be eligible for a grant under section 1473 of this title for any fiscal year, a State shall demonstrate to the Secretary (in its application under section 1478 of this title) that the State has established a State Interagency Coordinating Council which meets the requirements of section 1482 of this title.

§ 1475. Continuing eligibility

(a) First two years

In order to be eligible for a grant under section 1473 of this title for the first or second year of a State's participation under this subchapter, a State shall include in its application under section 1478 of this title for that year assurances that funds received under section 1473 of this title shall be used to assist the State to plan, develop, and implement the statewide system required by section 1476 of this title.

(b) Third and fourth year

(1) In order to be eligible for a grant under section 1473 of this title for the third or fourth year of a State's participation under this subchapter, a State shall include in its application under section 1478 of this title for that year information and assurances demonstrating to the satisfaction of the Secretary that—

(A) the State has adopted a policy which incorporates all of the components of a statewide system in accordance with section 1476 of this title or obtained a waiver from the Secretary under paragraph (2).

(B) funds shall be used to plan, develop, and implement the statewide system required by section 1476 of this title, and

(C) such statewide system will be in effect no later than the beginning of the fourth year of the State's participation under section 1473 of this title, except that with respect to section 1476(b)(4) of this title, a State need only conduct multidisciplinary assessments, develop individualized family service plans, and make available case management services.

(2) Notwithstanding paragraph (1), the Secretary may permit a State to continue to receive assistance under section 1473 of this title during such third year even if the State has not adopted the policy required by paragraph (1)(A) before receiving assistance if the State demonstrates in its application—

(A) that the State has made a good faith effort to adopt such a policy,

(B) the reasons why it was unable to meet the timeline and the steps remaining before such a policy will be adopted, and

(C) an assurance that the policy will be adopted to go into effect before the fourth year of such assistance.

(c) Fifth and succeeding years

In order to be eligible for a grant under section 1473 of this title for a fifth and any succeeding year of a State's participation under this subchapter, a State shall include in its application under section 1478 of this title for that year information and assurances demonstrating to the satisfaction of the Secretary that the State has in effect the statewide system required by section 1476 of this title and a description of services to be provided under section 1476(b)(2) of this title.

(d) Exception

Notwithstanding subsections (a) and (b) of this section, a State which has in effect a State law, enacted before September 1, 1986, that requires the provision of free appropriate public education to handicapped children from birth through age 2, inclusive, shall be eligible for a grant under section 1473 of this title for the first through fourth years of a State's participation under this subchapter.

§ 1476. Requirements for statewide system

(a) In general

A statewide system of coordinate, comprehensive, multidisciplinary, interagency programs providing appropriate early intervention services to all handicapped infants and toddlers and their families shall include the minimum components under subsection (b) of this section.

(b) Minimum components

The statewide system required by subsection (a) of this section shall include, at a minimum—

(1) a definition of the term "developmentally delayed" that will be used by the State in carrying out programs under this subchapter,

(2) timetables for ensuring that appropriate early intervention services will be available to all handicapped infants and toddlers in the State before the beginning of the fifth year of a State's participation under this subchapter,

(3) a timely, comprehensive, multidisciplinary evaluation of the functioning of each handicapped infant and toddler in the State and the needs of the families to appropriately assist in the development of the handicapped infant or toddler,

(4) for each handicapped infant and toddler in the State, an individualized family service plan in accordance with section 1477 of this title, including case management services in accordance with such service plan,

(5) a comprehensive child find system, consistent with subchapter II of this chapter, including a system for making referrals to service providers that includes timelines and provides for the participation by primary referral sources,

(6) a public awareness program focusing on early identification of handicapped infants and toddlers,

(7) a central directory which includes early intervention services, resources, and experts available in the State and research and demonstration projects being conducted in the State,

(8) a comprehensive system of personnel development,

(9) a single line of responsibility in a lead agency designated or established by the Governor for carrying out—

(A) the general administration, supervision, and monitoring of programs and activities receiving assistance under section 1473 of this title to ensure compliance with this subchapter,

(B) the identification and coordination of all available resources within the State from Federal, State, local and private sources,

(C) the assignment of financial responsibility to the appropriate agency,

(D) the development of procedures to ensure that services are provided to handicapped infants and toddlers and their families in a timely manner pending the resolution of any disputes among public agencies or service providers,

(E) the resolution of intra- and interagency disputes, and

(F) the entry into formal interagency agreements that define the financial responsibility of each agency for paying for early intervention services (consistent with State law) and procedures for resolving disputes and that include all additional components necessary to ensure meaningful cooperation and coordination.

(10) a policy pertaining to the contracting or making of other arrangements with service providers to provide early intervention services in the State, consistent with the provisions of this subchapter, including the contents of the application used and the conditions of the contract or other arrangements,

(11) a procedure for securing timely reimbursement of funds used under this subchapter in accordance with section 1481(a) of this title,

(12) procedural safeguards with respect to programs under this subchapter as required by section 1480 of this title, and

(13) policies and procedures relating to the establishment and maintenance of standards to ensure that personnel necessary to carry out this subchapter are appropriately and adequately prepared and trained, including—

(A) the establishment and maintenance of standards which are consistent with any State approved or recognized certification, licensing, registration, or other comparable requirements which apply to the area in which such personnel are providing early intervention services, and

(B) to the extent such standards are not based on the highest requirements in the State applicable to a specific profession or discipline, the steps the State is taking to require the retraining or hiring of personnel that meet appropriate professional requirements in the State, and

(14) a system for compiling data on the numbers of handicapped infants and toddlers and their families in the State in need of appropriate early intervention services (which may be based on a sampling of data), the numbers of such infants and toddlers and their families served, the types of services provided (which may be based on a sampling of data), and other information required by the Secretary.

§ 1477. Individualized family service plan

(a) Assessment and program development

Each handicapped infant or toddler and the infant or toddler's family shall receive—

(1) a multidisciplinary assessment of unique needs and the identification of services appropriate to meet such needs, and

(2) a written individualized family service plan developed by a multidisciplinary team, including the parent or guardian, as required by subsection (d) of this section.

(b) Periodic review

The individualized family service plan shall be evaluated once a year and the family shall be provided a review of the plan at 6 month-intervals (or more often where appropriate based on infant and toddler and family needs).

(c) Promptness after assessment

The individualized family service plan shall be developed within a reasonable time after the assessment required by subsection (a)(1) of this section is completed. With the parent's consent, early intervention services may commence prior to the completion of such assessment.

(d) Contents of plan

The individualized family service plan shall be in writing and contain—

(1) a statement of the infant's or toddler's present levels of physical development, cognitive development, language and speech development, psycho-social development, and self-help skills, based on acceptable objective criteria,

(2) a statement of the family's strengths and needs relating to enhancing the development of the family's handicapped infant or toddler,

(3) a statement of the major outcomes expected to be achieved for the infant and toddler and the family, and the criteria, procedures, and timelines used to determine the degree to which progress toward achieving the outcomes are being made and whether modifications or revisions of the outcomes or services are necessary,

(4) a statement of specific early intervention services necessary to meet the unique needs of the infant or toddler and the family, including the frequency, intensity, and the method of delivering services,

(5) the projected dates for initiation of services and the anticipated duration of such services,

(6) the name of the case manager from the profession most immediately relevant to the infant's and toddler's or family's needs who will be responsible for the implementation of the plan and coordination with other agencies and persons, and

(7) the steps to be taken supporting the transition of the handicapped

toddler to services provided under subchapter II of this chapter to the extent such services are considered appropriate.

§ 1478. State application and assurances

(a) Application

Any State desiring to receive a grant under section 1473 of this title for any year shall submit an application to the Secretary at such time and in such manner as the Secretary may reasonably require by regulation. Such an application shall contain—

(1) a designation of the lead agency in the State that will be responsible for the administration of funds provided under section 1473 of this title,

(2) information demonstrating eligibility of the State under section 1474 of this title,

(3) the information or assurances required to demonstrate eligibility of the State for the particular year of participation under section 1475 of this title, and

(4)(A) information demonstrating that the State has provided (i) public hearings, (ii) adequate notice of such hearings, and (iii) an opportunity for comment to the general public before the submission of such application and before the adoption by the State of the policies described in such application, and (B) a summary of the public comments and the State's responses,

(5) a description of the uses for which funds will be expended in accordance with this subchapter and for the fifth and succeeding fiscal years a description of the services to be provided,

(6) a description of the procedure used to ensure an equitable distribution of resources made available under this subchapter among all geographic areas within the State, and

(7) such other information and assurances as the Secretary may reasonably require by regulation.

(b) Statement of assurances

Any State desiring to receive a grant under section 1473 of this title shall file with the Secretary a statement at such time and in such manner as the Secretary may reasonably require by regulation. Such statement shall—

(1) assure that funds paid to the State under section 1473 of this title will be expended in accordance with this subchapter,

(2) contain assurances that the State will comply with the requirements of section 1481 of this title,

(3) provide satisfactory assurance that the control of funds provided under section 1473 of this title, and title to property derived therefrom, shall be in a public agency for the uses and purposes provided in this subchapter and that a public agency will administer such funds and property,

(4) provide for (A) making such reports in such form and containing such information as the Secretary may require to carry out the Secretary's

functions under this subchapter, and (B) keeping such records and affording such access thereto as the Secretary may find necessary to assure the correctness and verification of such reports and proper disbursement of Federal funds under this subchapter,

(5) provide satisfactory assurance that Federal funds made available under section 1473(A) of this title will not be commingled with State funds, and (B) will be so used as to supplement and increase the level of State and local funds expended for handicapped infants and toddlers and their families and in no case to supplant such State and local funds.

(6) provide satisfactory assurance that such fiscal control and fund accounting procedures will be adopted as may be necessary to assure proper disbursement of, and accounting for, Federal funds paid under section 1473 of this title to the State, and

(7) such other information and assurances as the Secretary may reasonably require by regulation.

(c) Approval of application and assurances required

No State may receive a grant under section 1473 of this title unless the Secretary has approved the application and statement of assurances of that State. The Secretary shall not disapprove such an application or statement of assurances unless the Secretary determines, after notice and opportunity for a hearing, that the application or statement of assurances fails to comply with the requirements of this section.

§ 1479. Use of funds

In addition to using funds provided under section 1473 of this title to plan, develop, and implement the statewide system required by section 1476 of this title, a State may use such funds—

(1) for direct services for handicapped infants and toddlers that are not otherwise provided from other public or private sources, and

(2) to expand and improve on services for handicapped infants and toddlers that are otherwise available.

§ 1480. Procedural safeguards

The procedural safeguards required to be included in a statewide system under section 1476(b)(12) of this title shall provide, at a minimum, the following:

(1) The timely administrative resolution of complaints by parents. Any party aggrieved by the findings and decision regarding an administrative complaint shall have the right to bring a civil action with respect to the complaint, which action may be brought in any State court of competent jurisdiction or in a district court of the United States without regard to the amount in controversy. In any action brought under this paragraph, the court shall receive the records of the administrative proceedings, shall hear additional evidence at the request of a party, and, basing its decision on

the preponderance of the evidence, shall grant such relief as the court determines is appropriate.

(2) The right to confidentiality of personally identifiable information.

(3) The opportunity for parents and a guardian to examine records relating to assessment, screening, eligibility determinations, and the development and implementation of the individualized family service plan.

(4) Procedures to protect the rights of the handicapped infant and toddlers whenever the parents or guardian of the child are not known or unavailable or the child is a ward of the State, including the assignment of an individual (who shall not be an employee of the State agency providing services) to act as a surrogate for the parents or guardian.

(5) Written prior notice to the parents or guardian of the handicapped infant or toddler whenever the State agency or service provider proposes to initiate or change or refuses to initiate or change the identification, evaluation, placement, or the provision of appropriate early intervention services to the handicapped infant or toddler.

(6) Procedures designed to assure that the notice required by paragraph (5) fully informs the parents or guardian, in the parents' or guardian's native language, unless it clearly is not feasible to do so, of all procedures available pursuant to this section.

(7) During the pendency of any proceeding or action involving a complaint, unless the State agency and the parents or guardian otherwise agree, the child shall continue to receive the appropriate early intervention services currently being provided or if applying for initial services shall receive the services not in dispute.

§ 1481. Payor of last resort

(a) Nonsubstitution

Funds provided under section 1473 of this title may not be used to satisfy a financial commitment for services which would have been paid for from another public or private source but for the enactment of this subchapter, except that whenever considered necessary to prevent the delay in the receipt of appropriate early intervention services by the infant or toddler or family in a timely fashion, funds provided under section 1473 of this title may be used to pay the provider of services pending reimbursement from the agency which has ultimate responsibility for the payment.

(b) Reduction of other benefits

Nothing in this subchapter shall be construed to permit the State to reduce medical or other assistance available or to alter eligibility under title V of the Social Security Act (relating to maternal and child health) or title XIX of the Social Security Act (relating to medicaid for handicapped infants and toddlers) within the State.

§ 1482. State Interagency Coordinating Council

(a) Establishment

(1) Any State which desires to receive financial assistance under section 1473 of this title shall establish a State Interagency Coordinating Council composed of 15 members.

(2) The Council and the chairperson of the Council shall be appointed by the Governor. In making appointments to the Council, the Governor shall ensure that the membership of the Council reasonably represents the population of the State.

(b) Composition

The council shall be composed of—

(1) at least 3 parents of handicapped infants or toddlers or handicapped children aged 3 through 6, inclusive,

(2) at least 3 public or private providers of early intervention services,

(3) at least one representative from the State legislature,

(4) at least one person involved in personnel preparation, and

(5) other members representing each of the appropriate agencies involved in the provision of or payment for early intervention services to handicapped infants and toddlers and their families and others selected by the Governor.

(c) Meetings

The Council shall meet at least quarterly and in such places as it deems necessary. The meetings shall be publicly announced, and, to the extent appropriate, open and accessible to the general public.

(d) Management authority

Subject to the approval of the Governor, the Council may prepare and approve a budget using funds under this subchapter to hire staff, and obtain other services of such professional, technical, and clerical personnel as may be necessary to carry out its functions under this subchapter.

(e) Functions of Council

The Council shall—

(1) advise and assist the lead agency designated or established under section 1476(b)(9) of this title in the performance of the responsibilities set out in such section, particularly the identification of the sources of fiscal and other support for services for early intervention programs, assignment of financial responsibility to the appropriate agency, and the promotion of the interagency agreements,

(2) advise and assist the lead agency in the preparation of applications and amendments thereto, and

(3) prepare and submit an annual report to the Governor and to the Secretary on the status of early intervention programs for handicapped infants and toddlers and their families operated within the State.

(f) Conflict of interest

No member of the Council shall cast a vote on any matter which would provide direct financial benefit to that member or otherwise give the appearance of a conflict of interest under State law.

(g) Use of existing Councils

To the extent that a State has established a Council before September 1, 1986, that is comparable to the Council described in this section, such Council shall be considered to be in compliance with this section. Within 4 years after the date the State accepts funds under section 1473 of this title, such State shall establish a council that complies in full with this section.

§ 1483. Federal administration

Sections 1416, 1417 and 1420 of this title shall, to the extent not inconsistent with this subchapter, apply to the program authorized by this subchapter, except that—

(1) any reference to a State educational agency shall be deemed to a reference to the State agency established or designated under section 1476(b)(9) of this section,

(2) any reference to the education of handicapped children and the education of all handicapped children and the provision of free public education to all handicapped children shall be deemed to be a reference to the provision of services to handicapped infants and toddlers in accordance with this subchapter, and

(3) any reference to local educational agencies and intermediate educational agencies shall be deemed to be a reference to local service providers under this subchapter.

§ 1484. Allocation of funds

(a) Territories and insular possessions

From the sums appropriated to carry out this subchapter for any fiscal year, the Secretary may reserve 1 percent for payments to Guam, American Samoa, the Virgin Islands, the Republic of the Marshall Islands, the Federated States of Micronesia, the Republic of Palau, and the Commonwealth of Northern Mariana Islands in accordance with their respective needs.

(b) Secretary of Interior for assistance to Indians

(1) The Secretary shall make payments to the Secretary of the Interior according to the need for such assistance for the provision of early interven-

tion services to handicapped infants and toddlers and their families on reservations serviced by the elementary and secondary schools operated for Indians by the Department of the Interior. The amount of such payment for any fiscal year shall be 1.25 percent of the aggregate of the amount available to all States under this subchapter for that fiscal year.

(2) The Secretary of the Interior may receive an allotment under paragraph (1) only after submitting to the Secretary an application which meets the requirements of section 1478 of this title and which is approved by the Secretary. Section 1416 of this title shall apply to any such application.

(c) States

(1) For each of the fiscal years 1987 through 1991 from the funds remaining after the reservation and payments under subsections (a) and (b) of this section, the Secretary shall allot to each State an amount which bears the same ratio to the amount of such remainder as the number of infants and toddlers in the State bears to the number of infants and toddlers in all States, except that no State shall receive less than 0.5 percent of such remainder.

(2) For the purpose of paragraph (1)—

(A) the terms "infants" and "toddlers" mean children from birth to age 2, inclusive, and

(B) the term "State'' does not include the jurisdictions described in subsection (a) of this section.

(d) Election by State not to receive allotment

If any State elects not to receive it allotment under subsection (c)(1) of this section, the Secretary shall reallot, among the remaining States, amounts from such State in accordance with such subsection.

§ 1485. Authorization of appropriations

There are authorized to be appropriated to carry out this subchapter $50,000,000 for fiscal year 1987, $75,000,000 for fiscal year 1988, and such sums as may be necessary for each of the 3 succeeding fiscal years.

APPENDIX B

FEDERAL REGULATIONS

[The most important federal regulations affecting the education of handicapped children, Parts 300 and 104 of Title 34 of the Code of Federal Regulations, have been reproduced here in their entirety as promulgated by the U.S. Department of Education.]

PART 300—ASSISTANCE TO STATES FOR EDUCATION OF HANDICAPPED CHILDREN

Subpart A—General

PURPOSE, APPLICABILITY, AND GENERAL PROVISIONS REGULATIONS

Subpart B—State Annual Program Plans and Local Applications

ANNUAL PROGRAM PLANS—GENERAL

ANNUAL PROGRAM PLANS—CONTENTS

LOCAL EDUCATIONAL AGENCY APPLICATIONS—GENERAL

LOCAL EDUCATIONAL AGENCY APPLICATIONS—CONTENTS

AUTHORITY: 20 U.S.C. 1411-1420, unless otherwise noted.

SOURCE: 42 FR 42476, Aug. 23, 1977, unless otherwise noted. Redesignated at 45 FR 77368, Nov. 21, 1980.

Subpart A—General

PURPOSE, APPLICABILITY, AND GENERAL PROVISIONS REGULATIONS

§ 300.1 Purpose.

The purpose of this part is:

(a) To insure that all handicapped children have available to them a free appropriate public education which includes special education and related services to meet their unique needs,

(b) To insure that the rights of handicapped children and their parents are protected,

(c) To assist States and localities to provide for the education of all handicapped children, and

(d) To assess and insure the effectiveness of efforts to educate those children.

(Authority: 20 U.S.C. 1401 Note)

§ 300.2 Applicability to State, local, and private agencies.

(a) *States.* This part applies to each State which receives payments under Part B of the Education of the Handicapped Act.

(b) *Public agencies within the State.* The annual program plan is submitted by the State educational agency on behalf of the State as a whole. Therefore, the provisions of this part apply to all political subdivisions of the State that are involved in the education of handicapped children. These would include:

(1) The State educational agency, (2) local educational agencies and intermediate educational units, (3) other State agencies and schools (such as Departments of Mental Health and Welfare and State schools for the deaf or blind), and (4) State correctional facilities.

(c) *Private schools and facilities.* Each public agency in the State is responsible for insuring that the rights and protections under this part are given to children referred to or placed in private schools and facilities by that public agency.

(See §§ 300.400-300.403)

(Authority: 20 U.S.C. 1412(1), (6); 1413(a); 1413(a)(4)(B))

Comment. The requirements of this part are binding on each public agency that has direct or delegated authority to provide special education and related services in a State that receives funds under Part B of the Act, regardless of whether that agency is receiving funds under Part B.

§ 300.3 Regulations that apply to assistance to States for education of handicapped children.

(a) *Regulations.* The following regulations apply to this program of Assistance to States for Education of Handicapped Children.

(1) The Education Department General Administrative Regulations (EDGAR) in 34 CFR Part 76 (State-Administered Programs) and Part 77 (Definitions).

(2) The regulations in this Part 300.

(b) *How to use regulations; how to apply for funds.* The "Introduction to Regulations of the Department" at the beginning of EDGAR includes general information to assist in—

(1) Using regulations that apply to Department programs; and

(2) Applying for assistance under a Department program.

(Authority: 20 U.S.C. 1221e-3(a)(1))

DEFINITIONS

Comment. Definitions of terms that are used throughout these regulations are included in this subpart. Other terms are defined in the specific subparts in which they are used. Below is a list of those terms and the specific sections and subparts in which they are defined:

Consent (§ 300.500 of Subpart E)
Destruction (§ 300.560 of Subpart E)
Direct services (§ 300.370(b)(1) of Subpart C)
Evaluation (§ 300.500 of Subpart E)

First priority children (§ 300.320(a) of Subpart C)
Independent educational evaluation (§ 300.503 of Subpart E)
Individualized education program (§ 300.340 of Subpart C)
Participating agency (§ 300.560 of Subpart E)
Personally identifiable (§ 300.500 of Subpart E)
Private school handicapped children (§ 300.450 of Subpart D)
Public expense (§ 300.503 of Subpart E)
Second priority children (§ 300.320(b) of Subpart C)
Special definition of "State" (§ 300.700 of Subpart G)
Support services (§ 300.370(b)(2) of Subpart C)

[42 FR 42476, Aug. 23, 1977, as amended at 45 FR 22531, Apr. 3, 1980. Redesignated at 45 FR 77368, Nov. 21, 1980]

§ 300.4 Free appropriate public education.

As used in this part, the term "free appropriate public education" means special education and related services which:

(a) Are provided at public expense, under public supervision and direction, and without charge.

(b) Meet the standards of the State educational agency, including the requirements of this part,

(c) Include preschool, elementary school, or secondary school education in the State involved, and

(d) Are provided in conformity with an individualized education program which meets the requirements under §§ 300.340-300.349 of Subpart C.

(Authority: 20 U.S.C. 1401(18))

§ 300.5 Handicapped children.

(a) As used in this part, the term "handicapped children" means those children evaluated in accordance with §§ 300.530-300.534 as being mentally retarded, hard of hearing, deaf, speech impaired, visually handicapped, seriously emotionally disturbed, orthopedically impaired, other health impaired, deaf-blind, multi-handicapped, or as having specific learning disabilities, who because of those impairments need special education and related services.

(b) The terms used in this definition are defined as follows:

(1) "Deaf" means a hearing impairment which is so severe that the child is impaired in processing linguistic information through hearing, with or without amplification, which adversely affects educational performance.

(2) "Deaf-blind" means concomitant hearing and visual impairments, the combination of which causes such severe communication and other developmental and educational problems that they cannot be accommodated in special education programs solely for deaf or blind children.

(3) "Hard of Hearing" means a hearing impairment, whether permanent or fluctuating, which adversely affects a child's educational performance but which is not included under the definition of "deaf" in this section.

(4) "Mentally retarded" means significantly subaverage general intellectual functioning existing concurrently with deficits in adaptive behavior and manifested during the developmental period, which adversely affects a child's educational performance.

(5) "Multihandicapped" means concomitant impairments (such as mentally retarded—blind, mentally retarded-orthopedically impaired, etc.), the combination of which causes such severe educational problems that they cannot be accommodated in special education programs solely for one of the impairments. The term does not include deaf-blind children.

(6) "Orthopedically impaired" means a severe orthopedic impairment which adversely affects a child's educational performance. The term includes impairments caused by congenital anomaly (e.g., clubfoot, absence of some member, etc.), impairments caused by disease (e.g. poliomyelitis, bone tuberculosis, etc.), and impairments from other causes (e.g., cerebral palsy, amputations, and fractures or burns which cause contractures).

(7) "Other health impaired" means (i) having an autistic condition which is manifested by severe communication and other developmental and educational problems; or (ii) having limited strength, vitality or alertness, due to chronic or acute health problems such as a heart condition, tuberculosis, rhematic fever, nephritis, asthma, sickle cell anemia, hemophilia, epilepsy, lead poisoning, leukemia, or diabe-

tes, which adversely affects a child's educational performance.

(8) "Seriously emotionally disturbed" is defined as follows:

(i) The term means a condition exhibiting one or more of the following characteristics over a long period of time and to a marked degree, which adversely affects educational performance:

(A) An inability to learn which cannot be explained by intellectual, sensory, or health factors;

(B) An inability to build or maintain satisfactory interpersonal relationships with peers and teachers;

(C) Inappropriate types of behavior or feelings under normal circumstances;

(D) A general pervasive mood of unhappiness or depression; or

(E) A tendency to develop physical symptoms or fears associated with personal or school problems.

(ii) The term includes children who are schizophrenic. The term does not include children who are socially maladjusted, unless it is determined that they are seriously emotionally disturbed.

(9) "Specific learning disability" means a disorder in one or more of the basic psychological processes involved in understanding or in using language, spoken or written, which may manifest itself in an imperfect ability to listen, think, speak, read, write, spell, or to do mathematical calculations. The term includes such conditions as perceptual handicaps, brain injury, minimal brain disfunction, dyslexia, and developmental aphasia. The term does not include children who have learning problems which are primarily the result of visual, hearing, or motor handicaps, of mental retardation of emotional disturbance or of environmental, cultural, or economic disadvantage.

(10) "Speech impaired" means a communication disorder such as stuttering, impaired articulation, a language impairment, or a voice impairment, which adversely affects a child's educational performance.

(11) "Visually handicapped" means a visual impairment which, even with correction, adversely affects a child's educational performance. The term includes both partially seeing and blind children.

(Authority: 20 U.S.C. 1401(1), (15))

[42 FR 42476, Aug. 23, 1977, as amended at 42 FR 65083, Dec. 29, 1977. Redesignated at 45 FR 77368, Nov. 21, 1980, and further amended at 46 FR 3866, Jan. 16, 1981]

§ 300.6 Include.

As used in this part, the term "include" means that the items named are not all of the possible items that are covered, whether like or unlike the ones named.

(Authority: 20 U.S.C. 1417(b))

§ 300.7 Intermediate educational unit.

As used in this part, the term "intermediate educational unit" means any public authority, other than a local educational agency, which:

(a) Is under the general supervision of a State educational agency;

(b) Is established by State law for the purpose of providing free public education on a regional basis; and

(c) Provides special education and related services to handicapped children within that State.

(Authority: 20 U.S.C. 1401 (22))

§ 300.8 Local educational agency.

(a) [Reserved]

(b) For the purposes of this part, the term "local educational agency" also includes intermediate educational units.

(Authority: 20 U.S.C. 1401 (8))

[42 FR 42476, Aug. 23, 1977, as amended at 45 FR 22531, Apr. 3, 1980. Redesignated at 45 FR 77368, Nov. 21, 1980]

§ 300.9 Native language.

As used in this part, the term "native language" has the meaning given that term by section 703(a)(2) of the Bilingual Education Act, which provides as follows:

> The term "native language", when used with reference to a person of limited English-speaking ability, means the language normally used by that person, or in the case of a child, the language normally used by the parents of the child.

(Authority: 20 U.S.C. 880b-1(a)(2); 1401(21))

Comment. Section 602(21) of the Education of the Handicapped Act states that the term "native language" has the same meaning as the definition from the Bilingual Education Act. (The term is used in the prior notice and evaluation sections under § 300.505(b)(2) and § 300.532(a)(1) of Subpart E.) In using the term, the Act does not prevent the following means of communication:

(1) In all direct contact with a child (including evaluation of the child), communication would be in the language normally used by the child and not that of the parents, if there is a difference between the two.

(2) If a person is deaf or blind, or has no written language, the mode of communication would be that normally used by the person (such as sign language, braille, or oral communication).

§ 300.10 Parent.

As used in this part, the term "parent" means a parent, a guardian, a person acting as a parent of a child, or a surrogate parent who has been appointed in accordance with § 300.514. The term does not include the State if the child is a ward of the State.

(Authority: 20 U.S.C. 1415)

Comment. The term "parent" is defined to include persons acting in the place of a parent, such as a grandmother or stepparent with whom a child lives, as well as persons who are legally responsible for a child's welfare.

§ 300.11 Public agency.

As used in this part, the term "public agency" includes the State educational agency, local educational agencies, intermediate educational units, and any other political subdivision of the State which are responsible for providing education to handicapped children.

(Authority: 20 U.S.C. 1412(2)(B); 1412(6); 1413(a))

§ 300.12 Qualified.

As used in this part, the term "qualified" means that a person has met State educational agency approved or recognized certification, licensing, registration, or other comparable requirements which apply to the area in which he or she is providing special education or related services.

(Authority: 20 U.S.C. 1417(b))

§ 300.13 Related services.

(a) As used in this part, the term "related services" means transportation and such developmental, corrective, and other supportive services as are required to assist a handicapped child to benefit from special education, and includes speech pathology and audiology, psychological services, physical and occupational therapy, recreation, early identification and assessment of disabilities in children, counseling services, and medical services for diagnostic or evaluation purposes. The term also includes school health services, social work services in schools, and parent counseling and training.

(b) The terms used in this definition are defined as follows:

(1) "Audiology" includes:

(i) Identification of children with hearing loss;

(ii) Determination of the range, nature, and degree of hearing loss, including referral for medical or other professional attention for the habilitation of hearing;

(iii) Provision of habilitative activities, such as language habilitation, auditory training, speech reading (lip-reading), hearing evaluation, and speech conservation;

(iv) Creation and administration of programs for prevention of hearing loss;

(v) Counseling and guidance of pupils, parents, and teachers regarding hearing loss; and

(vi) Determination of the child's need for group and individual amplification, selecting and fitting an appropriate aid, and evaluating the effectiveness of amplification.

(2) "Counseling services" means services provided by qualified social workers, psychologists, guidance counselors, or other qualified personnel.

(3) "Early identification" means the implementation of a formal plan for identifying a disability as early as possible in a child's life.

(4) "Medical services" means services provided by a licensed physician to determine a child's medically related handicapping condition which results in the child's need for special education and related services.

(5) "Occupational therapy" includes:

(i) Improving, developing or restoring functions impaired or lost through illness, injury, or deprivation;

(ii) Improving ability to perform tasks for independent functioning when functions are impaired or lost; and

(iii) Preventing, through early intervention, initial or further impairment or loss of function.

(6) "Parent counseling and training" means assisting parents in understanding the special needs of their child and providing parents with information about child development.

(7) "Physical therapy" means services provided by a qualified physical therapist.

(8) "Psychological services" include:

(i) Administering psychological and educational tests, and other assessment procedures;

(ii) Interpreting assessment results;

(iii) Obtaining, integrating, and interpreting information about child behavior and conditions relating to learning.

(iv) Consulting with other staff members in planning school programs to meet the special needs of children as indicated by psychological tests, interviews, and behavioral evaluations; and

(v) Planning and managing a program of psychological services, including psychological counseling for children and parents.

(9) "Recreation" includes:

(i) Assessment of leisure function;

(ii) Therapeutic recreation services;

(iii) Recreation programs in schools and community agencies; and

(iv) Leisure education.

(10) "School health services" means services provided by a qualified school nurse or other qualified person.

(11) "Social work services in schools" include:

(i) Preparing a social or developmental history on a handicapped child;

(ii) Group and individual counseling with the child and family;

(iii) Working with those problems in a child's living situation (home, school, and community) that affect the child's adjustment in school; and

(iv) Mobilizing school and community resources to enable the child to receive maximum benefit from his or her educational program.

(12) "Speech pathology" includes:

(i) Identification of children with speech or language disorders;

(ii) Diagnosis and appraisal of specific speech or languge disorders;

(iii) Referral for medical or other professional attention necessary for the habilitation of speech or language disorders;

(iv) Provisions of speech and language services for the habilitation or prevention of communicative disorders; and

(v) Counseling and guidance of parents, children, and teachers regarding speech and language disorders.

(13) "Transportation" includes:

(i) Travel to and from school and between schools,

(ii) Travel in and around school buildings, and

(iii) Specialized equipment (such as special or adapted buses, lifts, and ramps), if required to provide special transportation for a handicapped child.

(Authority: 20 U.S.C. 1401 (17))

Comment. With respect to related services, the Senate Report states:

The Committee bill provides a definition of "related services," making clear that all such related services may not be required for each individual child and that such term includes early identification and assessment of handicapping conditions and the provision of services to minimize the effects of such conditions.

(Senate Report No. 94-168, p. 12 (1975))

The list of related services is not exhaustive and may include other developmental, corrective, or supportive services (such as artistic and cultural programs, and art, music, and dance therapy), if they are required to assist a handicapped child to benefit from special education.

There are certain kinds of services which might be provided by persons from varying professional backgrounds and with a variety of operational titles, depending upon requirements in individual States. For example, counseling services might be provided by social workers, psychologists, or guidance counselors; and psychological testing might be done by qualified psychological examiners, psychometrists, or psychologists, depending upon State standards.

Each related service defined under this part may include appropriate administrative and supervisory activities that are necessary for program planning, management, and evaluation.

§ 300.14 Special education.

(a) (1) As used in this part, the term "special education" means specially designed instruction, at no cost to the parent, to meet the unique needs of a handicapped child, including classroom instruction, instruction in physical education, home instruction, and instruction in hospitals and institutions.

(2) The term includes speech pathology, or any other related service, if the service consists of specially designed instruction, at no cost to the parents, to meet the unique needs of a handicapped child, and is considered "special education" rather than a "related service" under State standards.

(3) The term also includes vocational education if it consists of specially designed instruction, at no cost to the parents, to meet the unique needs of a handicapped child.

(b) The terms in this definition are defined as follows:

(1) "At no cost" means that all specially designed instruction is provided without charge, but does not preclude incidental fees which are normally charged to non-handicapped students or their parents as a part of the regular education program.

(2) "Physical education" is defined as follows:

(i) The term means the development of:

(A) Physical and motor fitness;

(B) Fundamental motor skills and patterns; and

(C) Skills in aquatics, dance, and individual and group games and sports (including intramural and lifetime sports).

(ii) The term includes special physical education, adapted physical education, movement education, and motor development.

(Authority: 20 U.S.C. 1401 (16))

(3) "Vocational education" means organized educational programs which are directly related to the preparation of individuals for paid or unpaid employment, or for additional preparation for a career requiring other than a baccalaureate or advanced degree.

(Authority: 20 U.S.C. 1401 (16))

Comment. (1) The definition of "special education" is a particularly important one under these regulations, since a child is not handicapped unless he or she needs special education. (See the definition of "handicapped children" in § 300.5.) The definition of "related services" (§ 300.13) also depends on this definition, since a related service must be necessary for a child to benefit from special education. Therefore, if a child does not need special education, there can be no "related services," and the child (because not "handicapped") is not covered under the Act.

(2) The above definition of vocational education is taken from the Vocational Education Act of 1963, as amended by Pub. L. 94-482. Under that Act, "vocational education" includes industrial arts and consumer and homemaking education programs.

Subpart B—State Annual Program Plans and Local Applications

Annual Program Plans—General

§ 300.110 Condition of assistance.

In order to receive funds under Part B of the Act for any fiscal year, a State must submit an annual program plan to the Secretary through its State educational agency.

(Authority: 20 U.S.C. 1232c(b), 1412, 1413)

§ 300.111 Contents of plan.

Each annual program plan must contain the provisions required in this subpart.

(Authority: 20 U.S.C. 1412, 1413, 1232c(b))

Annual Program Plans—Contents

§ 300.121 Right to a free appropriate public education.

(a) Each annual program plan must include information which shows that the State has in effect a policy which insures that all handicapped children have the right to a free appropriate public education within the age ranges and timelines under § 300.122.

(b) The information must include a copy of each State statute, court order, State Attorney General opinion, and other State document that shows the source of the policy.

(c) The information must show that the policy:

(1) Applies to all public agencies in the State;

(2) Applies to all handicapped children;

(3) Implements the priorities established under § 300.127(a)(1) of this subpart; and

(4) Establishes timeliness for implementing the policy, in accordance with § 300.122.

(Authority: 20 U.S.C. 1412(1)(2)(B), (6); 1413(a)(3))

§ 300.122 Timeliness and ages for free appropriate public education.

(a) *General.* Each annual program plan must include in detail the policies and procedures which the State will undertake or has undertaken in order to insure that a free appropriate public education is available for all handicapped children aged three through eighteen within the State not later than September 1, 1978, and for all handicapped children aged three through twenty-one within the State not later than September 1, 1980.

(b) *Documents relating to timeliness.* Each annual program plan must include a copy of each statute, court order, attorney general decision, an other State document which demonstrates that the State has established timelines in accordance with paragraph (a) of this secton.

(c) *Exception.* The requirement in paragraph (a) of this section does not apply to a State with respect to handicapped children aged three, four, five, eighteen, nineteen, twenty, or twenty-one to the extent that the requirement would be inconsistent with State law or practice, or the order of any court, respecting public education for one or more of those age groups in the State.

(d) *Documents relating to exceptions.* Each annual program plan must:

(1) Describe in detail the extent to which the exception in paragraph (c) of this section applies to the State, and

(2) Include a copy of each State law, court order, and other document which provides a basis for the exception.

(Authority: 20 U.S.C. 1412(2)(B))

§ 300.123 Full educational opportunity goal.

Each annual program plan must include in detail the policies and procedures which the State will undertake, or has undertaken, in order to insure that the State has a goal of providing full educational opportunity to all handicapped children aged birth through twenty-one.

(Authority: 20 U.S.C. 1412(2)(A))

§ 300.124 Full educational opportunity goal—data requirement.

Beginning with school year 1978–1979, each annual program plan must contain the following information:

(a) The estimated number of handicapped children who need special education and related services.

(b) For the current school year:

(1) The number of handicapped children aged birth through two, who are receiving special education and related services; and

(2) The number of handicapped children:

(i) Who are receiving a free appropriate public education,

(ii) Who need, but are not receiving a free appropriate public education,

(iii) Who are enrolled in public private institutions who are receiving a free appropriate public education, and

(iv) Who are enrolled in public and private institutions and are not receiving a free appropriate public education.

(c) The estimated numbers of handicapped children who are expected to receive special education and related services during the next school year.

(d) A description of the basis used to determine the data required under this section.

(e) The data required by paragraphs (a), (b), and (c) of this section must be provided:

(1) For each disability category (except for children aged birth through two), and

(2) For each of the following age ranges: birth through two, three through five, six through seventeen, and eighteen through twenty-one.

(Authority: 20 U.S.C. 1412(2)(A))

Comment. In Part B of the Act, the term "disability" is used interchangeably with "handicapping condition". For consistency in this regulation, a child with a "disability" means a child with one of the impairments listed in the definition of "handicapped children" in § 300.5, if the child needs special education because of the impairment. In essence, there is a continuum of impairments. When an impairment is of such a nature that the child needs special education, it is referred to as a disability, in these regulations, and the child is a "handicapped" child.

States should note that data required under this section are not to be transmitted to the Secretary in personally identifiable form. Generally, except for such purposes as monitoring and auditing, neither the States nor the Federal Government should have to collect data under this part in personally identifiable form.

§ 300.125 Full educational opportunity goal—timetable.

(a) *General requirement.* Each annual program plan must contain a detailed timetable for accomplishing the goal of providing full educational opportunity for all handicapped children.

(b) *Content of timetable.* (1) The timetable must indicate what percent of the total estimated number of handicapped children the State expects to have full educational opportunity in each succeeding school year.

(2) The data required under this paragraph must be provided:

(i) For each disability category (except for children aged birth through two), and

(ii) For each of the following age ranges: birth through two, three through five, six through seventeen, and eighteen through twenty-one.

(Authority: 20 U.S.C. 1412(2)(A))

§ 300.126 Full educational opportunity goal—facilities, personnel, and services.

(a) *General requirement.* Each annual program plan must include a description of the kind and number of facilities, personnel, and services necessary throughout the State to meet the goal of providing full educational opportunity for all handicapped children. The State educational agency shall include the data required under paragraph (b) of this section and whatever additional data are necessary to meet the requirement.

(b) *Statistical description.* Each annual program plan must include the following data:

(1) The number of additional special class teachers, resource room teachers, and intinerant or consultant teachers needed for each disability category and the number of each of these who are currently employed in the State.

(2) The number of other additional personnel needed, and the number currently employed in the State, including school psychologists, school social workers, occupational therapists, physical therapists, home-hospital teachers, speech-language pathologists, audiologists, teacher aides, vocational education teachers, work study coordinators, physical education teachers, therapeutic recreation specialists, diagnostic personnel, supervisors, and other instructional and non-instructional staff.

(3) The total number of personnel reported under paragraphs (b) (1) and (2) of this section, and the salary costs of those personnel.

(4) The number and kind of facilities needed for handicapped children and the number and kind currently in use in the State, including regular classes serving handicapped children, self-contained classes on a regular school campus, resource rooms, private special education day schools, public special education day schools, private special education residential schools, public special education residential schools, hospital programs, occupational therapy facilities, physical therapy facilities, public sheltered workshops, private sheltered workshops, and other types of facilities.

(5) The total number of transportation units needed for handicapped children, the number of transportation units designed for handicapped children which are in use in the State, and the number of handicapped children who use these units to benefit from special education.

(c) *Data categories.* The data required under paragraph (b) of this section must be provided as follows:

(1) Estimates for serving all handicapped children who require special education and related services,

(2) Current year data, based on the actual numbers of handicapped children receiving special education and related services (as reported under Subpart G), and

(3) Estimates for the next school year.

(d) *Rationale.* Each annual program plan must include a description of the means used to determine the number and salary costs of personnel.

(Authority: 20 U.S.C. 1412(2)(A))

§ 300.127 Priorities.

(a) *General requirement.* Each annual program plan must include information which shows that:

(1) The State has established priorities which meet the requirements under §§ 300.320–300.324 of Subpart C.

(2) The State priorities meet the timelines under § 300.122 of this subpart, and

(3) The State has made progress in meeting those timeliness.

(b) *Child data.* (1) Each annual program plan must show the number of handicapped children known by the State to be in each of the first two priority groups named in § 300.321 of Subpart C:

(i) By disability category, and

(ii) By the age ranges in § 300.124(e)(2) of this subpart.

(c) *Activities and resources.* Each annual program plan must show for each of the first two priority groups:

(1) The programs, services, and activities that are being carried out in the State,

(2) The Federal, State, and local resources that have been committed during the current school year, and

(3) The programs, services, activities, and resources that are to be provided during the next school year.

(Authority: 20 U.S.C. 1412(3))

§ 300.128 Identification, location, and evaluation of handicapped children.

(a) *General requirement.* Each annual program plan must include in detail the policies and procedures which the State will undertake or has undertaken to insure that:

(1) All children who are handicapped, regardless of the severity of their handicap, and who are in need of special education and related services are identified, located, and evaluated; and

(2) A practical method is developed and implemented to determine which children are currently receiving needed special education and related services and which children are not currently receiving needed special education and related services.

(b) *Information.* Each annual program plan must:

(1) Designate the State agency (if other than the State educational agency) responsible for coordinating the planning and implementation of the policies and procedures under paragraph (a) of this section;

(2) Name each agency that participates in the planning and implementation and describe the nature and extent of its participation;

(3) Describe the extent to which:

(i) The activities described in paragraph (a) of this section have been achieved under the current annual program plan, and

(ii) The resources named for these activities in that plan have been used;

(4) Describe each type of activity to be carried out during the next school year, including the role of the agency named under paragraph (b)(1) of this section, timelines for completing those activities, resources that will be used, and expected outcomes;

(5) Describe how the policies and procedures under paragraph (a) of this section will be monitored to insure that the State educational agency obtains:

(i) The number of handicapped children within each disability category that have been identified, located, and evaluated, and

(ii) Information adequate to evaluate the effectiveness of those policies and procedures; and

(6) Describe the method the State uses to determine which children are currently receiving special education and related services and which children are not receiving special education and related services.

(Authority: 20 U.S.C. 1412(2)(C))

Comment. The State is responsible for insuring that all handicapped children are identified, located, and evaluated, including children in all public and private agencies and institutions in the State. Collection and use of data are subject to the confidentiality requirements in §§ 300.560–300.576.

§ 300.129 Confidentiality of personally identifiable information.

(a) Each annual program plan must include in detail the policies and procedures which the State will undertake or has undertaken in order to insure the protection of the confidentiality of any personally identifiable information collected, used, or maintained under this part.

(b) The Secretary shall use the criteria in §§ 300.560–300.576 of Subpart E to evaluate the policies and procedures of the State under paragraph (a) of this section.

(Authority: 20 U.S.C. 1412(2)(D); 1417(c))

Comment. The confidentiality regulations were published in the FEDERAL REGISTER in final form on February 27, 1976 (41 FR 8603–8610), and met the requirements of Part B of the Act, as amended by Pub. L. 94–142. Those regulations are incorporated in §§ 300.560–300.576 of Subpart E.

§ 300.130 Individualized education programs.

(a) Each annual program plan must include information which shows that each public agency in the State maintains records of the individualized education program for each handicapped child, and each public agency establishes, reviews, and revises each program as provided in Subpart C.

(b) Each annual program plan must include:

(1) A copy of each State statute, policy, and standard that regulates the manner in which individualized education programs are developed, implemented, reviewed, and revised, and

(2) The procedures which the State educational agency follows in monitoring and evaluating those programs.

(Authority: 20 U.S.C. 1412(4))

§ 300.131 Procedural safeguards.

Each annual program plan must include procedural safeguards which insure that the requirements in §§ 300.500–300.514 of Subpart E are met.

(Authority: 20 U.S.C. 1412(5)(A))

§ 300.132 Least restrictive environment.

(a) Each annual program plan must include procedures which insure that the requirements in §§ 300.550–300.556 of Subpart E are met.

(b) Each annual program plan must include the following information:

(1) The number of handicapped children in the State, within each disability category, who are participating in regular education programs, consistent with §§ 300.550–300.556 of Subpart E.

(2) The number of handicapped children who are in separate classes or separate school facilities, or who are otherwise removed from the regular education environment.

(Authority: 20 U.S.C. 1412(5)(B))

§ 300.133 Protection in evaluation procedures.

Each annual program plan must include procedures which insure that the requirements in §§ 300.530–300.534 of Subpart E are met.

(Authority: 20 U.S.C. 1412(5)(C))

§ 300.134 Responsibility of State educational agency for all educational programs.

(a) Each annual program plan must include information which shows that the requirements in § 300.600 of Subpart F are met.

(b) The information under paragraph (a) of this section must include a copy of each State statute, State regulation, signed agreement between respective agency officials, and any other document that shows compliance with that paragraph.

(Authority: 20 U.S.C. 1412(6))

§ 300.135 [Reserved]

§ 300.136 Implementation procedures—State educational agency.

Each annual program plan must describe the procedures the State educational agency follows to inform each public agency of its responsibility for insuring effective implementation of procedural safeguards for the handicapped children served by that public agency.

(Authority: 20 U.S.C. 1412(6))

§ 300.137 Procedures for consultation.

Each annual program plan must include an assurance that in carrying out the requirements of section 612 of the Act, procedures are established for consultation with individuals involved in or concerned with the education of handicapped children, including handicapped individuals and parents of handicapped children.

(Authority: 20 U.S.C. 1412(7)(A))

§ 300.138 Other Federal programs.

Each annual program plan must provide that programs and procedures are established to insure that funds received by the State or any public agency in the State under any other Federal program, including section 121 of the Elementary and Secondary Education Act of 1965 (20 U.S.C. 241e-2), section 305(b)(8) of that Act (20 U.S.C. 844a(b)(8)) or Title IV-C of that Act (20 U.S.C. 1831), and section 110(a) of the Vocational Education Act of 1963, under which there is specific authority for assistance for the education of handicapped children, are used by the State, or any public agency in the State, only in a manner consistent with the goal of providing free appropriate public education for all handicapped children, except that nothing in this section limits the specific requirements of the laws governing those Federal programs.

(Authority: 20 U.S.C. 1413(a)(2))

§ 300.139 Comprehensive system of personnel development.

Each annual program plan must include the material required under §§ 300.380-300.387 of Subpart C.

(Authority: 20 U.S.C. 1413(a)(3))

§ 300.140 Private schools.

Each annual program plan must include policies and procedures which insure that the requirements of Subpart D are met.

(Authority: 20 U.S.C. 1413(a)(4))

§ 300.141 Recovery of funds for misclassified children.

Each annual program plan must include policies and procedures which insure that the State seeks to recover any funds provided under Part B of the Act for services to a child who is determined to be erroneously classified as eligible to be counted under section 611 (a) or (d) of the Act.

(Authority: 20 U.S.C. 1413(a)(5))

§ 300.142—300.143 [Reserved]

§ 300.144 Hearing on application.

Each annual program plan must include procedures to insure that the State educational agency does not take any final action with respect to an application submitted by a local educational agency before giving the local educational agency reasonable notice and an opportunity for a hearing.

(Authority: 20 U.S.C. 1413(a)(8))

§ 300.145 Prohibition of commingling.

Each annual program plan must provide assurance satisfactory to the Secretary that funds provided under Part B of the Act are not commingled with State funds.

(Authority: 20 U.S.C. 1413(a)(9))

Comment. This assurance is satisfied by the use of a separate accounting system that includes an "audit trail" of the expenditure of the Part B funds. Separate bank accounts are not required. (See 34 CFR 76, Subpart F (Cash Depositories))

§ 300.146 Annual evaluation.

Each annual program plan must include procedures for evaluation at least annually of the effectivesness of programs in meeting the educational needs of handicapped children, including evaluation of individualized education programs.

(Authority: 20 U.S.C. 1413(a)(11))

§ 300.147 State advisory panel.

Each annual program plan must provide that the requirements of §§ 300.650-300.653 of Subpart F are met.

(Authority: 20 U.S.C. 1413(a)(12))

§ 300.148 Policies and procedures for use of Part B funds.

Each annual program plan must set forth policies and procedures designed to insure that funds paid to the State under Part B of the Act are spent in accordance with the provisions of Part B, with particular attention given to sections 611(b), 611(c), 611(d), 612(2), and 612(3) of the Act.

(Authority: 20 U.S.C. 1413(a)(1))

§ 300.149 Description of use of Part B funds.

(a) *State allocation.* Each annual program plan must include the following information about the State's use of funds under § 300.370 of Subpart C and § 300.620 of Subpart F:

(1) A list of administrative positions, and a description of duties for each person whose salary is paid in whole or in part with those funds.

(2) For each position, the percentage of salary paid with those funds.

(3) A description of each administrative activity the State educational agency will carry out during the next school year with those funds.

(4) A description of each direct service and each support service which the State educational agency will provide during the next school year with those funds, and the activities the State advisory panel will undertake during that period with those funds.

(b) *Local educational agency allocation.* Each annual program plan must include:

(1) An estimate of the number and percent of local educational agencies in the State which will receive an allocation under this part (other than local educational agencies which submit a consolidated application),

(2) An estimate of the number of local educational agencies which will receive an allocation under a consolidated application,

(3) An estimate of the number of consolidated applications and the average number of local educational agencies per application, and

(4) A description of direct services the State educational agency will provide under § 300.360 of Subpart C.

(Authority: 20 U.S.C. 1232c(b)(1)(B)(ii))

§ 300.150 [Reserved]

§ 300.151 Additional information if the State educational agency provides direct services.

If a State educational agency provides free appropriate public education for handicapped children or provides them with direct services, its annual program plan must include the information required under §§ 300.226–300.228, 300.231, and 300.235.

(Authority: 20 U.S.C. 1413(b))

LOCAL EDUCATIONAL AGENCY APPLICATIONS—GENERAL

§ 300.180 Submission of application.

In order to receive payments under Part B of the Act for any fiscal year a local educational agency must submit an application to the State educational agency.

(Authority: 20 U.S.C. 1414(a))

§ 300.181 [Reserved]

§ 300.182 The excess cost requirement.

A local educational agency may only use funds under Part B of the Act for the excess costs of providing special education and related services for handicapped children.

(Authority: 20 U.S.C. 1414 (a)(1), (a)(2)(B)(i))

§ 300.183 Meeting the excess cost requirement.

(a) A local educational agency meets the excess cost requirement if it has on the average spent at least the amount determined under § 300.184 for the education of each of its handicapped children. This amount may not include capital outlay or debt service.

(Authority: 20 U.S.C. 1402(20); 1414(a)(1))

Comment. The excess cost requirement means that the local educational agency must spend a certain minimum amount for the education of its handicapped children before Part B funds are used. This insures that children served with Part B funds have at least the same average amount spent on them, from sources other than Part B, as do the children in the school district taken as a whole.

The minimum amount that must be spent for the education of handicapped children is computed under a statutory formula. Section 300.184 implements this forumula and gives a step-by-step method to determine the minimum amount. Excess costs are those costs of special education and related services which exceed the minimum amount. Therefore, if a local educational agency can show that it has (on the average) spent the minimum amount for the education of each of its handicapped children, it has met the excess cost requirement, and all additional costs are excess costs. Part B funds can then be used to pay for these additional costs, subject to the other requirements of Part B (priorities, etc.). In the "Comment" under § 300.184, there is an example of how the minimum amount is computed.

[42 FR 42476, Aug. 23, 1977, as amended at 45 FR 22531, Apr. 3, 1980. Redesignated at 45 FR 77368, Nov. 21, 1980]

§ 300.184 Excess costs—computation of minimum amount.

The minimum average amount a local educational agency must spend under § 300.183 for the education of each of its handicapped children is computed as follows:

(a) Add all expenditures of the local educational agency in the preceding school year, except capital outlay and debt service:

(1) For elementary school students, if the handicapped child is an elementary school student, or

(2) For secondary school students, if the handicapped child is a secondary school student.

(b) From this amount, subtract the total of the following amounts spent for elementary school students or for secondary school students, as the case may be:

(1) Amounts the agency spent in the preceding school year from funds awarded under Part B of the Act and Titles I and VII of the Elementary and Secondary Education Act of 1965, and

(2) Amounts from State and local funds which the agency spent in the preceding school year for:

(i) Programs for handicapped children,

(ii) Programs to meet the special educational needs of educationally deprived children, and

(iii) Programs of bilingual education for children with limited English-speaking ability.

(c) Divide the result under paragraph (b) of this section by the average number of students enrolled in the agency in the preceding school year:

(1) In its elementary schools, if the handicapped child is an elementary school student, or

(2) In its secondary schools, if the handicapped child is a secondary school student.

(Authority: 20 U.S.C. 1414(a)(1))

Comment. The following is an example of how a local educational agency might compute the average minimum amount it must spend for the education of each of its handicapped children, under § 300.183. This example follows the formula in § 300.184. Under the statute and regulations, the local educational agency must make one computation for handicapped children in its elementary schools and a separate computation for handicapped children in its secondary schools. The computation for handicapped elementary school students would be done as follows:

a. First, the local educational agency must determine its total amount of expenditures for elementary school students from all sources—local, State, and Federal (including Part B)—in the preceding school year. Only capital outlay and debt service are excluded.

Example: A local educational agency spent the following amounts last year for elementary school students (including its handicapped elementary school students):

(1) From local tax funds	$2,750,000
(2) From State funds	7,000,000
(3) From Federal funds	750,000
	10,500,000

Of this total, $500,000 was for capital outlay and debt service relating to the education of elementary school students. This must be subtracted from total expenditures:

	$10,500,000
	—500,000
Total expenditures for elementary school students (less capital outlay and debt service)	= 10,000,000

b. Next, the local educational agency must subtract amounts spent for:

(1) Programs for handicapped children;

(2) Programs to meet the special educaional needs of educationally deprived children; and

(3) Programs of bilingual education for children with limited English-speaking ability.

These are funds which the local edcational agency actually spent, not funds received last year but carried over for the current school year.

Example: The local educational agency spent the following amounts for elementary school students last year:

(1) From funds under Title I of the Elementary and Secondary Education Act of 1965	$300,000
(2) From a special State program for educationally deprived children	200,000
(3) From a grant under Part B	200,000
(4) From State funds for the education of handicapped children	500,000
(5) From a locally-funded program for handicapped children	250,000
(6) From a grant for a bilingual education program under Title VII of the Elementary and Secondary Education Act of 1965	150,000
Total	1,600,000

(A local educational agency would also include any other funds it spent from Federal, State, or local sources for the three basic purposes: Handicapped children, educationally deprived children, and bilingual education for children with limited English-speaking ability.)

This amount is subtracted from the local educational agency's total expenditure for elementary school students computed above:

$$\begin{array}{r} \$10{,}000{,}000 \\ -\ 1{,}600{,}000 \\ \hline 8{,}400{,}000 \end{array}$$

c. The local educational agency next must divide by the average number of students enrolled in the elementary schools of the agency last year (including its handicapped students).

Example: Last year, an average of 7,000 students were enrolled in the agency's elementary schools. This must be divided into the amount computed under the above paragraph:

$8,400,000/7,000 students=$1,200/student

This figure is in the minimum amount the local educational agency must spend (on the average) for the education of each of its handicapped students. Funds under Part B may be used only for costs over and above this minimum. In this example, if the local educational agency has 100 handicapped elementary school students, it must keep records adequate to show that it has spent at least $120,000 for the education of those students (100 students times $1,200/student), not including capital outlay and debt service.

This $120,000 may come from any funds except funds under Part B, subject to any legal requirements that govern the use of those other funds.

If the local educational agency has handicapped secondary school students, it must do the same computation for them. However the amounts used in the computation would be those the local educational agency spent last year for the education of secondary school students, rather than for elementary school students.

§ 300.185 Computation of excess costs—consolidated application.

The minimum average amount under § 300.183 where two or more local educational agencies submit a consolidated application, is the average of the combined minimum average amounts determined under § 300.184 in those agencies for elementary or secondary school students, as the case may be.

(Authority: 20 U.S.C. 1414(a)(1))

§ 300.186 Excess costs—limitation on use of Part B funds.

(a) The excess cost requirement prevents a local educational agency from using funds provided under Part B of the Act to pay for all of the costs directly attributable to the education of a handicapped child, subject to paragraph (b) of this section.

(b) The excess cost requirement does not prevent a local educational agency from using Part B funds to pay for all of the costs directly attributable to the education of a handicapped child in any of the age ranges three, four, five, eighteen, nineteen, twenty, or twenty-one, if no local or State funds are available for non-handicapped children in that age range. However, the local educational agency must comply with the non-supplanting and other requirements of this part in providing the education and services.

(Authority: 20 U.S.C. 1402(20); 1414(a)(1))

§ 300.190 Consolidated applications.

(a) [Reserved]

(b) *Required applications.* A State educational agency may require local educational agencies to submit a consolidated application for payments under Part B of the Act if the State educational agency determines that an individual application submitted by a local educational agency will be disapproved because:

(1) The agency's entitlement is less than the $7,500 minimum required by section 611(c)(4)(A)(i) of the Act (§ 300.360(a)(1) of Subpart C); or

(2) The agency is unable to establish and maintain programs of sufficient size and scope to effectively meet the educational needs of handicapped children.

(c) *Size and scope of program.* The State educational agency shall establish standards and procedures for determinations under paragraph (b)(2) of this section.

(Authority: 20 U.S.C. 1414(c)(1))

[42 FR 42476, Aug. 23, 1977, as amended at 45 FR 22531, Apr. 3, 1980. Redesignated at 45 FR 77368, Nov. 21, 1980]

§ 300.191 [Reserved]

§ 300.192 State regulation of consolidated applications.

(a) The State educational agency shall issue regulations with respect to consolidated applications submitted under this part.

(b) The State educational agency's regulations must:

(1) Be consistent with section 612 (1)-(7) and section 613(a) of the Act, and

(2) Provide participating local educational agencies with joint responsibilities for implementing programs receiving payments under this part.

(Authority: 20 U.S.C. 1414(c)(2)(B))

(c) If an intermediate educational unit is required under State law to carry out this part, the joint responsibilities given to local educational agencies under paragraph (b)(2) of this section do not apply to the administration and disbursement of any payments received by the intermediate educational unit. Those administrative responsibilities must be carried out exclusively by the intermediate educational unit.

(Authority: 20 U.S.C. 1414(c)(2)(C))

§ 300.193 State educational agency approval; disapproval.

(a)-(b) [Reserved]

(c) In carrying out its functions under this section, each State educational agency shall consider any decision resulting from a hearing under §§ 300.506-300.513 of Subpart E which is adverse to the local educational agency involved in the decision.

(Authority: 20 U.S.C. 1414(b)(3))

[42 FR 42476, Aug. 23, 1977, as amended at 45 FR 22531, Apr. 3, 1980. Redesignated at 45 FR 77368, Nov. 21, 1980]

§ 300.194 Withholding.

(a) If a State educational agency, after giving reasonable notice and an opportunity for a hearing to a local educational agency, decides that the local educational agency in the administration of an application approved by the State educational agency has failed to comply with any requirement in the application, the State educational agency, after giving notice to the local educational agency, shall:

(1) Make no further payments to the local educational agency until the State educational agency is satisfied that there is no longer any failure to comply with the requirement; or

(2) Consider its decision in its review of any application made by the local educational agency under § 300.180;

(3) Or both.

(b) Any local educational agency receiving a notice from a State educational agency under paragraph (a) of this section is subject to the public notice provision in § 300.592.

(Authority: 20 U.S.C. 1414(b)(2))

LOCAL EDUCATIONAL AGENCY APPLICATIONS—CONTENTS

§ 300.220 Child identification.

Each application must include procedures which insure that all children residing within the jurisdiction of the local educational agency who are handicapped, regardless of the severity of their handicap, and who are in need of special education and related services are identified, located, and evaluated, including a practical method of determining which children

73-111 O—86——2

are currently receiving needed special education and related services and which children are not currently receiving needed special education and related services.

(Authority: 20 U.S.C. 1414(a)(1)(A))

Comment. The local educational agency is responsible for insuring that all handicapped children within its jurisdiction are identified, located, and evaluated, including children in all public and private agencies and institutions within that jurisdiction. Collection and use of data are subject to the confidentiality requirements in §§ 300.560-300.576 of Subpart E.

§ 300.221 Confidentiality of personally identifiable information.

Each application must include policies and procedures which insure that the criteria in §§ 300.560-300.574 of Subpart E are met.

(Authority: 20 U.S.C. 1414(a)(1)(B))

§ 300.222 Full educational opportunitiy goal; timetable.

Each application must: (a) Include a goal of providing full educational opportunity to all handicapped children, aged birth through 21, and

(b) Include a detailed timetable for accomplishing the goal.

(Authority: 20 U.S.C. 1414(a)(1) (C), (D))

§ 300.223 Facilities, personnel, and services.

Each application must provide a description of the kind and number of facilities, personnel, and services necessary to meet the goal in § 300.222.

(Authority: 20 U.S.C. 1414(a)(1)(E))

§ 300.224 Personnel development.

Each application must include procedures for the implementation and use of the comprehensive system of personnel development established by the State educational agency under § 300.140.

(Authority: 20 U.S.C. 1414(a)(1)(C)(i))

§ 300.225 Priorities.

Each application must include priorities which meet the requirements of §§ 300.320-300.324.

(Authority: 20 U.S.C. 1414(a)(1)(C)(ii))

§ 300.226 Parent involvement.

Each application must include procedures to insure that, in meeting the goal under § 300.222, the local educational agency makes provision for participation of and consultation with parents or guardians of handicapped children.

(Authority: 20 U.S.C. 1414(a)(1)(C)(iii))

§ 300.227 Participation in regular education programs.

(a) Each application must include procedures to insure that to the maximum extent practicable, and consistent with §§ 300.550-300.553 of Subpart E, the local educational agency provides special services to enable handicapped children to participate in regular educational programs.

(b) Each application must describe:

(1) The types of alternative placements that are available for handicapped children, and

(2) The number of handicapped children within each disability category who are served in each type of placement.

(Authority: 20 U.S.C. 1414(a)(1)(C)(iv))

§ 300.228 [Reserved]

§ 300.229 Excess cost.

Each application must provide assurance satisfactory to the State educational agency that the local educational agency uses funds provided under Part B of the Act only for costs which exceed the amount computed under § 300.184 and which are directly attributable to the education of handicapped children.

(Authority: 20 U.S.C. 1414(a)(2)(B))

§ 300.230 Nonsupplanting.

(a) Each application must provide assurance satisfactory to the State educational agency that the local educational agency uses funds provided under Part B of the Act to supplement and, to the extent practicable, increase the level of State and local funds expended for the education of handicapped children, and in no case to supplant those State and local funds.

(b) To meet the requirement in paragraph (a) of this section:

(1) The total amount or average per capita amount of State and local school funds budgeted by the local educational agency for expenditures in the current fiscal year for the education of handicapped children must be at least equal to the total amount or average per capita amount of State and local school funds actually expended for the education of handicapped children in the most recent preceding fiscal year for which the information is available. Allowance may be made for:

(i) Decreases in enrollment of handicapped children; and

(ii) Unusually large amounts of funds expended for such long-term purposes as the acquisition of equipment and the construction of school facilities; and

(2) The local educational agency must not use Part B funds to displace State or local funds for any particular cost.

(Authority: 20 U.S.C. 1414(a)(2)(B))

Comment. Under statutes such as Title I of the Elementary and Secondary Education Act of 1965, as amended, the requirement is to not supplant funds that "would" have been expended if the Federal funds were not available. The requirement under Part B, however, is to not supplant funds which have been "expended." This use of the past tense suggests that the funds referred to are those which the State or local agency actually spent at some time before the use of the Part B funds. Therefore, in judging compliance with this requirement, the Secretary looks to see if Part B funds are used for any costs which were previously paid for with State or local funds.

The nonsupplanting requirement prohibits a local educational agency from supplanting State and local funds with Part B funds on either an aggregate basis or for a given expenditure. This means that if an LEA spent $100,000 for special education in FY 1977, it must budget at least $100,000 in FY 1978, unless one of the conditions in § 300.230(b)(1) applies.

Whether a local educational agency supplants with respect to a particular cost would depend on the circumstances of the expenditure. For example, if a teacher's salary has been switched from local funding to Part B funding, this would appear to be supplanting. However, if that teacher was taking over a different position (such as a resource room teacher, for example), it would not be supplanting. Moreover, it might be important to consider whether the particular action of a local educational agency led to an increase in services for handicapped children over that which previously existed. The intent of the requirement is to insure that Part B funds are used to increase State and local efforts and are not used to take their place. Compliance would be judged with this aim in mind. The supplanting requirement is not intended to inhibit better services to handicapped children.

§ 300.231 Comparable services.

(a) Each application must provide assurance satisfactory to the State educational agency that the local educational agency meets the requirements of this section.

(b) A local educational agency may not use funds under Part B of the Act to provide services to handicapped children unless the agency uses State and local funds to provide services to those children which, taken as a whole, are at least comparable to services provided to other handicapped children in that local educational agency.

(c) Each local educational agency shall maintain records which show that the agency meets the requirement in paragraph (b) of this section.

(Authority: 20 U.S.C. 1414(a)(2)(C))

Comment. Under the "comparability" requirement, if State and local funds are used to provide certain services, those services must be provided with State and local funds to all handicapped children in the local educational agency who need them. Part B funds may then be used to supplement existing services, or to provide additional services to meet special needs. This, of course, is subject to the other requirements of the Act, including the priorities under §§ 300.320-300.324.

§§ 300.232—300.234 [Reserved]

§ 300.235 Individualized education program.

Each application must include procedures to assure that the local educational agency complies with §§ 300.340-300.349 of Subpart C.

(Authority: 20 U.S.C. 1414(a)(5))

§ 300.236 [Reserved]

§ 300.237 Procedural safeguards.

Each application must provide assurance satisfactory to the State educational agency that the local educational agency has procedural safeguards which meet the requirements of §§ 300.500–300.514 of Subpart E.

(Authority: 20 U.S.C. 1414(a)(7))

§ 300.238 Use of Part B funds.

Each application must describe how the local educational agency will use the funds under Part B of the Act during the next school year.

(Authority: 20 U.S.C. 1414(a))

§ 300.239 [Reserved]

§ 300.240 Other requirements.

Each local application must include additional procedures and information which the State educational agency may require in order to meet the State annual program plan requirements under §§ 300.120–300.151.

(Authority: 20 U.S.C. 1414(a)(6))

APPLICATION FROM SECRETARY OF INTERIOR

§ 300.260 Submission of annual application; approval.

In order to receive payments under this part, the Secretary of Interior shall submit an annual application which:

(a) Meets applicable requirements of section 614(a) of the Act;

(b) Includes monitoring procedures which are consistent with § 300.601; and

(c) Includes other material as agreed to by the Secretary and the Secretary of Interior.

(Authority: 20 U.S.C. 1411(f))

§ 300.261 Public participation.

In the development of the application for the Department of Interior, the Secretary of Interior shall provide for public participation consistent with §§ 300.280–300.284.

(Authority: 20 U.S.C. 1411(f))

§ 300.262 Use of Part B funds.

(a) The Department of the Interior may use five percent of its payment in any fiscal year, or $350,000, whichever is greater, for administrative costs in carrying out the provisions of this part.

(b) The remainder of the payments to the Secretary of the Interior in any fiscal year must be used in accordance with the priorities under §§ 300.320–300.324 of Subpart C.

(Authority: 20 U.S.C. 1411(f))

[42 FR 42476, Aug. 23, 1977. Redesignated at 45 FR 77368, Nov. 21, 1980 and amended at 51 FR 19311, May 28, 1986]

EFFECTIVE DATE NOTE: In § 300.262, paragraph (a) was revised at 51 FR 19311, May 28, 1986, effective July 23, 1986. For the convenience of the reader, the superseded text is set forth below.

§ 300.262 Use of Part B funds.

(a) The Department of Interior may use five percent of its payments in any fiscal year, or $200,000, whichever is greater, for administrative costs in carrying out the provisions of this part.

* * * * *

§ 300.263 Applicable regulations.

The Secretary of the Interior shall comply with the requirements under Subparts C, E, and F.

(Authority: 20 U.S.C. 1411(f)(2))

PUBLIC PARTICIPATION

§ 300.280 Public hearings before adopting an annual program plan.

(a) Prior to its adoption of an annual program plan, the State educational agency shall:

(1) Make the plan available to the general public,

(2) Hold public hearings, and

(3) Provide an opportunity for comment by the general public on the plan.

(Authority: 20 U.S.C. 1412(7))

§ 300.281 Notice.

(a) The State educational agency shall provide notice to the general public of the public hearings.

(b) The notice must be in sufficient detail to inform the public about:

(1) The purpose and scope of the annual program plan and its relation to Part B of the Education of the Handicapped Act,

(2) The availability of the annual program plan,

(3) The date, time, and location of each public hearing,

(4) The procedures for submitting written comments about the plan, and

(5) The timetable for developing the final plan and submitting it to the Secretary for approval.

(c) The notice must be published or announced:

(1) In newspapers or other media, or both, with circulation adequate to notify the general public about the hearings, and

(2) Enough in advance of the date of the hearings to afford interested parties throughout the State a reasonable opportunity to participate.

(Authority: 20 U.S.C. 1412(7))

§ 300.282 Opportunity to participate; comment period.

(a) The State educational agency shall conduct the public hearings at times and places that afford interested parties throughout the State a reasonable opportunity to participate.

(b) The plan must be available for comment for a period of at least 30 days following the date of the notice under § 300.281.

(Authority: 20 U.S.C. 1412(7))

§ 300.283 Review of public comments before adopting plan.

Before adopting its annual program plan, the State educational agency shall:

(a) Review and consider all public comments, and

(b) Make any necessary modifications in the plan.

(Authority: 20 U.S.C. 1412(7))

§ 300.284 Publication and availability of approved plan.

After the Secretary approves an annual program plan, the State educational agency shall give notice in newspapers or other media, or both, that the plan is approved. The notice must name places throughout the State where the plan is available for access by any interested person.

(Authority: 20 U.S.C. 1412(7))

Subpart C—Services

Free Appropriate Public Education

§ 300.300 Timeliness for free appropriate public education.

(a) *General.* Each State shall insure that free appropriate public education is available to all handicapped children aged three through eighteen within the State not later than September 1, 1978, and to all handicapped children aged three through twenty-one within the State not later than September 1, 1980.

(b) *Age ranges 3-5 and 18-21.* This paragraph provides rules for applying the requirement in paragraph (a) of this section to handicapped children aged three, four, five, eighteen, nineteen, twenty, and twenty-one:

(1) If State law or a court order requires the State to provide education for handicapped children in any disability category in any of these age groups, the State must make a free appropriate public education available to all handicapped children of the same age who have that disability.

(2) If a public agency provides education to non-handicapped children in any of these age groups, it must make a free appropriate public education available to at least a proportionate number of handicapped children of the same age.

(3) If a public agency provides education to 50 percent or more of its handicapped children in any disability category in any of these age groups, it must make a free appropriate public education available to all of its handicapped children of the same age who have that disability.

(4) If a public agency provides education to a handicapped child in any of these age groups, it must make a free appropriate public education available to that child and provide that child and his or her parents all of the rights under Part B of the Act and this part.

(5) A State is not required to make a free appropriate public education

available to a handicapped child in one of these age groups if:

(i) State law expressly prohibits, or does not authorize, the expenditure of public funds to provide education to nonhandicapped children in that age group; or

(ii) The requirement is inconsistent with a court order which governs the provision of free public education to handicapped children in that State.

(Authority: 20 U.S.C. 1412(2)(B); Sen. Rept. No. 94-168 p. 19 (1975))

Comment. 1. The requirement to make free appropriate public education available applies to all handicapped children within the State who are in the age ranges required under § 300.300 and who need special education and related services. This includes handicapped children already in school and children with less severe handicaps, who are not covered under the priorities under § 300.321.

2. In order to be in compliance with § 300.300, each State must insure that the requirement to identify, locate, and evaluate all handicapped children is fully implemented by public agencies throughout the State. This means that before September 1, 1978, every child who has been referred or is on a waiting list for evaluation (including children in school as well as those not receiving an education) must be evaluated in accordance with §§ 300.530-300.533 of Subpart E. If, as a result of the evaluation, it is determined that a child needs special education and related services, an individualized education program must be developed for the child by September 1, 1978, and all other applicable requirements of this part must be met.

3. The requirement to identify, locate, and evaluate handicapped children (commonly referred to as the "child find system") was enacted on August 21, 1974, under Pub. L. 93-380. While each State needed time to establish and implement its child find system, the four year period between August 21, 1974, and September 1, 1978, is considered to be sufficient to insure that the system is fully operational and effective on a State-wide basis.

Under the statute, the age range for the child find requirement (0-21) is greater than the mandated age range for providing free appropriate public education (FAPE). One reason for the broader age requirement under "child find" is to enable States to be aware of and plan for younger children who will require special education and related services. It also ties in with the full educational opportunity goal requirement, which has the same age range as child find. Moreover, while a State is not required to provide "FAPE" to handicapped children below the age ranges mandated under § 300.300, the State may, at its discretion, extend services to those children, subject to the requirements on priorities under §§ 300.320-300.324.

§ 300.301 Free appropriate public education—methods and payments.

(a) Each State may use whatever State, local, Federal, and private sources of support are available in the State to meet the requirements of this part. For example, when it is necessary to place a handicapped child in a residential facility, a State could use joint agreements between the agencies involved for sharing the cost of that placement.

(b) Nothing in this part relieves an insurer or similar third party from an otherwise valid obligation to provide or to pay for services provided to a handicapped child.

(Authority: 20 U.S.C. 1401 (18); 1412(2)(B))

§ 300.302 Residential placement.

If placement in a public or private residential program is necessary to provide special education and related services to a handicapped child, the program, including non-medical care and room and board, must be at no cost to the parents of the child.

(Authority: 20 U.S.C. 1412(2)(B); 1413(a)(4)(B))

Comment. This requirement applies to placements which are made by public agencies for educational purposes, and includes placements in State-operated schools for the handicapped, such as a State school for the deaf or blind.

§ 300.303 Proper functioning of hearing aids.

Each public agency shall insure that the hearing aids worn by deaf and hard of hearing children in school are functioning properly.

(Authority: 20 U.S.C. 1412(2)(B))

Comment. The report of the House of Representatives on the 1978 appropriation bill includes the following statement regarding hearing aids:

In its report on the 1976 appropriation bill the Committee expressed concern about the condition of hearing aids worn by children in public schools. A study done at the Committee's direction by the Bureau of Education for the Handicapped reveals that up to one-third of the hearing aids are malfunctioning. Obviously, the Committee expects the Office of Education will ensure that hearing impaired school children are receiving adequate professional assessment, follow-up and services.

(Authority: House Report No. 95-381, p. 67 (1977))

§ 300.304 Full educational opportunity goal.

(a) Each State educational agency shall insure that each public agency establishes and implements a goal of providing full educational opportunity to all handicapped children in the area served by the public agency.

(b) Subject to the priority requirements under §§ 300.320-300.324, a State or local educational agency may use Part B funds to provide facilities, personnel, and services necessary to meet the full educational opportunity goal.

(Authority: 20 U.S.C. 1412(2)(A); 1414(a)(1)(C))

Comment. In meeting the full educational opportunity goal, the Congress also encouraged local educational agencies to include artistic and cultural activities in programs supported under this part, subject to the priority requirements under §§ 300.320-300.324. This point is addressed in the following statements from the Senate Report on Pub. L. 94-142:

The use of the arts as a teaching tool for the handicapped has long been recognized as a viable, effective way not only of teaching special skills, but also of reaching youngsters who had otherwise been unteachable. The Committee envisions that programs under this bill could well include an arts component and, indeed, urges that local educational agencies include the arts in programs for the handicapped funded under this Act. Such a program could cover both appreciation of the arts by the handicapped youngsters, and the utilization of the arts as a teaching tool per se.

Museum settings have often been another effective tool in the teaching of handicapped children. For example, the Brooklyn Museum has been a leader in developing exhibits utilizing the heightened tactile sensory skill of the blind. therefore, in light of the national policy concerning the use of museums in federally supported education programs enunciated in the Education Amendments of 1974, the Committee also urges local educational agencies to include museums in programs for the handicapped funded under this Act.

(Authority: Senate Report No. 94-168, p. 13 (1975))

§ 300.305 Program options.

Each public agency shall take steps to insure that its handicapped children have available to them the variety of educational programs and services available to non-handicapped children in the area served by the agency, including art, music, industrial arts, consumer and homemaking education, and vocational education.

(Authority: 20 U.S.C. 1412(2)(A); 1414(a)(1)(C))

Comment. The above list of program options is not exhaustive, and could include any program or activity in which nonhandicapped students participate. Moreover, vocational education programs must be specially designed if necessary to enable a handicapped student to benefits fully from those programs; and the set-aside funds under the Vocational Education Act of 1963, as amended by Pub. L. 94-482, may be used for this purpose. Part B funds may also be used, subject to the priority requirements under §§ 300.320-300.324.

§ 300.306 Nonacademic services.

(a) Each public agency shall take steps to provide nonacademic and extracurricular services and activities in such manner as is necessary to afford handicapped children an equal opportunity for participation in those services and activities.

(b) Nonacademic and extracurricular services and activities may include counseling services, athletics, transportation, health services, recreational activities, special interest groups or clubs sponsored by the public agency, referrals to agencies which provide assistance to handicapped persons, and employment of students, including both employment by the public agency and assistance in making outside employment available.

(Authority: 20 U.S.C. 1412(2)(A); 1414(a)(1)(C))

§ 300.307 Physical education.

(a) *General.* Physical education services, specially designed if necessary, must be made available to every handicapped child receiving a free appropriate public education.

(b) *Regular physical education.* Each handicapped child must be afforded the opportunity to participate in the regular physical education program available to non-handicapped children unless:

(1) The child is enrolled full time in a separate facility; or

(2) The child needs specially designed physical education, as prescribed in the child's individualized education program.

(c) *Special physical education.* If specially designed physical education is prescribed in a child's individualized education program, the public agency responsible for the education of that child shall provide the services directly, or make arrangements for it to be provided through other public or private programs.

(d) *Education in separate facilities.* The public agency responsible for the education of a handicapped child who is enrolled in a separate facility shall insure that the child receives appropriate physical education services in compliance with paragraphs (a) and (c) of this section.

(Authority: 20 U.S.C. 1401(16); 1412(5)(B); 1414(a)(6))

Comment. The Report of the House of Representatives on Pub. L. 94–142 includes the following statement regarding physical education:

Special education as set forth in the Committee bill includes instruction in physical education, which is provided as a matter of course to all non-handicapped children enrolled in public elementary and secondary schools. The Committee is concerned that although these services are available to and required of all children in our school systems, they are often viewed as a luxury for handicapped children.

* * * * *

The Committee expects the Commissioner of Education to take whatever action is necessary to assure that physical education services are available to all handicapped children, and has specifically included physical education within the definition of special education to make clear that the Committee expects such services, specially designed where necessary, to be provided as an integral part of the educational program of every handicapped child.

(Authority: House Report No. 94–332, p. 9 (1975))

PRIORITIES IN THE USE OF PART B FUNDS

§ 300.320 Definitions of "first priority children" and "second priority children."

For the purposes of §§ 300.321–300.324, the term:

(a) "First priority children" means handicapped children who:

(1) Are in an age group for which the State must make available free appropriate public education under § 300.300; and

(2) Are not receiving any education.

(b) "Second priority children" means handicapped children, within each disability, with the most severe handicaps who are receiving an inadequate education.

(Authority: 20 U.S.C. 1412(3))

Comment. After September 1, 1978, there should be no second priority children, since States must insure, as a condition of receiving Part B funds or fiscal year 1979, that all handicapped children will have available a free appropriate public education by that date.

NOTE: The term "free appropriate public education," as defined in § 300.4 of Subpart A, means "special education and related services which * * * are provided in conformity with an individualized education program * * *."

New "First priority children" will continue to be found by the State after September 1, 1978 through on-going efforts to identify, locate, and evaluate all handicapped children.

§ 300.321 Priorities.

(a) Each State and local educational agency shall use funds provided under Part B or the Act in the following order of priorities:

(1) To provide free appropriate public education to first priority children, including the identification, location, and evaluation of first priority children.

(2) To provide free appropriate public education to second priority children, including the identification, location, and evaluation of second priority children.

(3) To meet the other requirements in this part.

(b) The requirements of paragraph (a) of this section do not apply to funds which the State uses for administration under § 300.620.

(Authority: 20 U.S.C. 1411 (b)(1)(B), (b)(2)(B), (c)(1)(B), (c)(2)(A)(ii))

(c) State and local educational agencies may not use funds under Part B of the Act for preservice training.

(Authority: 20 U.S.C. 1413(a)(3); Senate Report No. 94-168, p. 34 (1975))

Comment. Note that a State educational agency as well as local educational agencies must use Part B funds (except the portion used for State administration) for the priorities. A State may have to set aside a portion of its Part B allotment to be able to serve newly identified first priority children.

After September 1, 1978, Part B funds may be used:

(1) To continue supporting child identification, location, and evaluation activities;

(2) To provide free appropriate public education to newly identified first priority children;

(3) To meet the full educational opportunities goal required under § 300.304, including employing additional personnel and providing inservice training, in order to increase the level, intensity and quality of services provided to individual handicapped children; and

(4) To meet the other requirements of Part B.

§ 300.322 First priority children—school year 1977-1978.

(a) In school year 1977-1978, if a major component of a first priority child's proposed educational program is not available (for example, there is no qualified teacher), the public agency responsible for the child's education shall:

(1) Provide an interim program of services for the child; and

(2) Develop an individualized education program for full implementation no later than September 1, 1978.

(b) A local educational agency may use Part B funds for training or other support services in school year 1977-1978 only if all of its first priority children have available to them at least an interim program of services.

(c) A State educational agency may use Part B funds for training or other support services in school year 1977-1978 only if all first priority children in the State have available to them at least an interim program of services.

(Authority: 20 U.S.C. 1411 (b), (c))

Comment. This provision is intended to make it clear that a State or local educational agency may not delay placing a previously unserved (first priority) child until it has, for example, implemented an inservice training program. The child must be placed. After the child is in at least an interim program, the State or local educational agency may use Part B funds for training or other support services needed to provide that child with a free appropriate public education.

§ 300.323 Services to other children.

If a State or a local educational agency is providing free appropriate public education to all of its first priority children, that State or agency may use funds provided under Part B of the Act:

(a) To provide free appropriate public education to handicapped children who are not receiving any education and who are in the age groups not covered under § 300.300 in that State; or

(b) To provide free appropriate public education to second priority children; or

(c) Both.

(Authority: 20 U.S.C. 1411 (b)(1)(B), (b)(2)(B), (c)(2)(A)(ii))

§ 300.324 Application of local educational agency to use funds for the second priority.

A local educational agency may use funds provided under Part B of the Act for second priority children, if it provides assurance satisfactory to the State educational agency in its application (or an amendment to its application):

(a) That all first priority children have a free appropriate public education available to them;

(b) That the local educational agency has a system for the identification, location, and evaluation of handicapped children, as described in its application; and

(c) That whenever a first priority child is identified, located, and evaluated, the local educational agency makes available a free appropriate public education to the child.

(Authority: 20 U.S.C. 1411 (b)(1)(B), (c)(1)(B); 1414(a)(1)(C)(ii))

INDIVIDUALIZED EDUCATION PROGRAMS

§ 300.340 Definition.

As used in this part, the term "individualized education program" means a written statement for a handicapped child that is developed and implemented in accordance with §§ 300.341-300.349.

(Authority: 20 U.S.C. 1401(19))

§ 300.341 State educational agency responsibility.

(a) *Public agencies.* The State educational agency shall insure that each public agency develops and implements an individualized education program for each of its handicapped children.

(b) *Private schools and facilities.* The State educational agency shall insure that an individualized education program is developed and implemented for each handicapped child who:

(1) Is placed in or referred to a private school or facility by a public agency; or

(2) Is enrolled in a parochial or other private school and receives special education or related services from a public agency.

(Authority: 20 U.S.C. 1412 (4), (6); 1413(a)(4))

Comment. This section applies to all public agencies, including other State agencies (e.g., departments of mental health and welfare), which provide special education to a handicapped child either directly, by contract or through other arrangements. Thus, if a State welfare agency contracts with a private school or facility to provide special education to a handicapped child, that agency would be responsible for insuring that an individualized education program is developed for the child.

§ 300.342 When individualized education programs must be in effect.

(a) On October 1, 1977, and at the beginning of each school year thereafter, each public agency shall have in effect an individualized education program for every handicapped child who is receiving special education from that agency.

(b) An individualized education program must:

(1) Be in effect before special education and related services are provided to a child; and

(2) Be implemented as soon as possible following the meetings under § 300.343.

(Authority: 20 U.S.C. 1412 (2)(B), (4), (6); 1414(a)(5); Pub. L. 94-142, Sec. 8(c) (1975))

Comment. Under paragraph (b)(2), it is expected that a handicapped child's individualized education program (IEP) will be implemented immediately following the meetings under § 300.343. An exception to this would be (1) when the meetings occur during the summer or a vacation period, or (2) where there are circumstances which require a short delay (e.g., working out transportation arrangements). However, there can be no undue delay in providing special education and related services to the child.

§ 300.343 Meetings.

(a) *General.* Each public agency is responsible for initiating and conducting meetings for the purpose of developing, reviewing, and revising a handicapped child's individualized education program.

(b) *Handicapped children currently served.* If the public agency has determined that a handicapped child will receive special education during school year 1977-1978, a meeting must be held early enough to insure that an individualized education program is developed by October 1, 1977.

(c) *Other handicapped children.* For a handicapped child who is not included under paragraph (b) of this action, a meeting must be held within thirty calendar days of a determination that the child needs special education and related services.

(d) *Review.* Each public agency shall initiate and conduct meetings to periodically review each child's individualized education program and if appropriate revise its provisions. A meeting must be held for this purpose at least once a year.

(Authority: 20 U.S.C. 1412(2)(B), (4), (6); 1414(a)(5))

Comment. The dates on which agencies must have individualized education programs (IEPs) in effect are specified in

§ 300.342 (October 1, 1977, and the beginning of each school year thereafter). However, except for new handicapped children (i.e., those evaluated and determined to need special education after October 1, 1977), the timing of meetings to develop, review, and revise IEPs is left to the discretion of each agency.

In order to have IEPs in effect by the dates in § 300.342, agencies could hold meetings at the end of the school year or during the summer preceding those dates. In meeting the October 1, 1977 timeline, meetings could be conducted up through the October 1 date. Thereafter, meetings may be held any time throughout the year, as long as IEPs are in effect at the beginning of each school year.

The statute requires agencies to hold a meeting at least once each year in order to review, and if appropriate revise, each child's IEP. The timing of those meetings could be on the anniversary date of the last IEP meeting on the child, but this is left to the discretion of the agency.

§ 300.344 Participants in meetings.

(a) *General.* The public agency shall insure that each meeting includes the following participants:

(1) A representative of the public agency, other than the child's teacher, who is qualified to provide, or supervise the provision of, special education.

(2) The child's teacher.

(3) One or both of the child's parents, subject to § 300.345.

(4) The child, where appropriate.

(5) Other individuals at the discretion of the parent or agency.

(b) *Evaluation personnel.* For a handicapped child who has been evaluated for the first time, the public agency shall insure:

(1) That a member of the evaluation team participates in the meeting; or

(2) That the representative of the public agency, the child's teacher, or some other person is present at the meeting, who is knowledgeable about the evaluation procedures used with the child and is familiar with the results of the evaluation.

(Authority: 20 U.S.C. 1401(19); 1412 (2)(B), (4), (6); 1414(a)(5))

Comment. 1. In deciding which teacher will participate in meetings on a child's individualized education program, the agency may wish to consider the following possibilities:

(a) For a handicapped child who is receiving special education, the "teacher" could be the child's special education teacher. If the child's handicap is a speech impairment, the "teacher" could be the speech-language pathologist.

(b) For a handicapped child who is being considered for placement in special education, the "teacher" could be the child's regular teacher, or a teacher qualified to provide education in the type of program in which the child may be placed, or both.

(c) If the child is not in school or has more than one teacher, the agency may designate which teacher will participate in the meeting.

2. Either the teacher or the agency representative should be qualified in the area of the child's suspected disability.

3. For a child whose primary handicap is a speech impairment, the evaluation personnel participating under paragraph (b)(1) of this section would normally be the speech-language pathologist.

§ 300.345 Parent participation.

(a) Each public agency shall take steps to insure that one or both of the parents of the handicapped child are present at each meeting or are afforded the opportunity to participate, including:

(1) Notifying parents of the meeting early enough to insure that they will have an opportunity to attend; and

(2) Scheduling the meeting at a mutually agreed on time and place.

(b) The notice under paragraph (a)(1) of this section must indicate the purpose, time, and location of the meeting, and who will be in attendance.

(c) If neither parent can attend, the public agency shall use other methods to insure parent participation, including individual or conference telephone calls.

(d) A meeting may be conducted without a parent in attendance if the public agency is unable to convince the parents that they should attend. In this case the public agency must have a record of its attempts to arrange a mutually agreed on time and place such as:

(1) Detailed records of telephone calls made or attempted and the results of those calls.

(2) Copies of correspondence sent to the parents and any responses received, and

(3) Detailed records of visits made to the parent's home or place of employment and the results of those visits.

(e) The public agency shall take whatever action is necessary to insure that the parent understands the proceedings at a meeting, including arranging for an interpreter for parents who are deaf or whose native language is other than English.

(f) The public agency shall give the parent, on request, a copy of the individualized education program.

(Authority: 20 U.S.C. 1401(19); 1412 (2)(B), (4), (6); 1414(a)(5))

Comment. The notice in paragraph (a) could also inform parents that they may bring other people to the meeting. As indicated in paragraph (c), the procedure used to notify parents (whether oral or written or both) is left to the discretion of the agency, but the agency must keep a record of its efforts to contact parents.

§ 300.346 Content of individualized education program.

The individualized education program for each child must include:

(a) A statement of the child's present levels of educational performance;

(b) A statement of annual goals, including short term instructional objectives;

(c) A statement of the specific special education and related services to be provided to the child, and the extent to which the child will be able to participate in regular educational programs;

(d) The projected dates for initiation of services and the anticipated duration of the services; and

(e) Appropriate objective criteria and evaluation procedures and schedules for determining, on at least an annual basis, whether the short term instructional objectives are being achieved.

(Authority: 20 U.S.C. 1401(19); 1412 (2)(B), (4), (6); 1414(a)(5); Senate Report No. 94-168, p. 11 (1975))

§ 300.347 Private school placements.

(a) *Developing individualized education programs.* (1) Before a public agency places a handicapped child in, or refers a child to, a private school or facility, the agency shall initiate and conduct a meeting to develop an individualized education program for the child in accordance with § 300.343.

(2) The agency shall insure that a representative of the private school facility attends the meeting. If the representative cannot attend, the agency shall use other methods to insure participation by the private school or facility, including individual or conference telephone calls.

(3) The public agency shall also develop an individualized educational program for each handicapped child who was placed in a private school or facility by the agency before the effective date of these regulations.

(b) *Reviewing and revising individualized education programs.* (1) After a handicapped child enters a private school or facility, any meetings to review and revise the child's individualized education program may be initiated and conducted by the private school or facility at the discretion of the public agency.

(2) If the private school or facility initiates and conducts these meetings, the public agency shall insure that the parents and an agency representative:

(i) Are involved in any decision about the child's individualized education program; and

(ii) Agree to any proposed changes in the program before those changes are implemented.

(c) *Responsibility.* Even if a private school or facility implements a child's individualized education program, responsibility for compliance with this part remains with the public agency and the State educational agency.

(Authority: 20 U.S.C. 1413(a)(4)(B))

§ 300.348 Handicapped children in parochial or other private schools.

If a handicapped child is enrolled in a parochial or other private school and receives special education or related services from a public agency, the public agency shall:

(a) Initiate and conduct meetings to develop, review, and revise an individualized education program for the child, in accordance with § 300.343; and

(b) Insure that a representative of the parochial or other private school attends each meeting. If the representative cannot attend, the agency shall use other methods to insure participation by the private school, including individual or conference telephone calls.

(Authority: 20 U.S.C. 1413(a)(4)(A))

§ 300.349 Individualized education program—accountability.

Each public agency must provide special education and related services to a handicapped child in accordance with an individualized education program. However, Part B of the Act does not require that any agency, teacher, or other person be held accountable if a child does not achieve the growth projected in the annual goals and objectives.

(Authority: 20 U.S.C. 1412(2)(B); 1414(a) (5), (6); Cong. Rec. at H7152 (daily ed., July 21, 1975))

Comment. This section is intended to relieve concerns that the individualized education program constitutes a guarantee by the public agency and the teacher that a child will progress at a specified rate. However, this section does not relieve agencies and teachers from making good faith efforts to assist the child in achieving the objectives and goals listed in the individualized education program. Further, the section does not limit a parent's right to complain and ask for revisions of the child's program, or to invoke due process procedures, if the parent feels that these efforts are not being made.

Direct Service by the State Educational Agency

§ 300.360 Use of local educational agency allocation for direct services.

(a) A State educational agency may not distribute funds to a local educational agency, and shall use those funds to insure the provision of a free appropriate public education to handicapped children residing in the area served by the local educational agency, if the local educational agency, in any fiscal year:

(1) Is entitled to less than $7,500 for that fiscal year (beginning with fiscal year 1979);

(2) Does not submit an application that meets the requirements of §§ 300.220–300.240;

(3) Is unable or unwilling to establish and maintain programs of free appropriate public education;

(4) Is unable or unwilling to be consolidated with other local educational agencies in order to establish and maintain those programs; or

(5) Has one or more handicapped children who can best be served by a regional or State center designed to meet the needs of those children.

(b) In meeting the requirements of paragraph (a) of this section, the State educational agency may provide special education and related services directly, by contract, or through other arrangements.

(c) The excess cost requirements under §§ 300.182–300.186 do not apply to the State educational agency.

(Authority: 20 U.S.C. 1411(c)(4); 1413(b); 1414(d))

Comment. Section 300.360 is a combination of three provisions in the statute (Sections 611(c)(4), 613(b), and 614(d)). This section focuses mainly on the State's administration and use of local entitlements under Part B.

The State educational agency, as a recipient of Part B funds is responsible for insuring that all public agencies in the State comply with the provisions of the Act, regardless of whether they receive Part B funds. If a local educational agency elects not to apply for its Part B entitlement, the State would be required to use those funds to insure that a free appropriate public education (FAPE) is made available to children residing in the area served by that local agency. However, if the local entitlement is not sufficient for this purpose, additional State or local funds would have to be expended in order to insure that "FAPE" and the other requirements of the Act are met.

Moreover, if the local educational agency is the recipient of any other Federal funds, it would have to be in compliance with Subpart D of the regulations for section 504 of the Rehabilitation Act of 1973 (34 CFR Part 104). It should be noted that the term "FAPE" has different meanings under Part B and section 504. For Example, under Part B, "FAPE" is a statutory term which requires special education and related services to be provided in accordance with an individualized education program (IEP). However, under section 504, each recipient must provide an education which includes services that are "designed to meet individual educational needs of handicapped persons as adequately as the needs of nonhandicapped persons are met * * *" Those regulations state that implementation of an IEP, in accordance with Part B, is one means of meeting the "FAPE" requirement.

§ 300.361 Nature and location of services.

The State educational agency may provide special education and related services under § 300.360(a) in the manner and at the location it considers appropriate. However, the manner in which the education and services are provided must be consistent with the requirements of this part (including the least restrictive environment provisions in §§ 300.550–300.556 of Subpart E).

(Authority: 20 U.S.C. 1414(d))

§ 300.370 Use of State educational agency allocation for direct and support services.

(a) The State shall use the portion of its allocation it does not use for administration to provide support services and direct services in accordance with the priority requirements under §§ 300.320–300.324.

(b) For the purposes of paragraph (a) of this section:

(1) "Direct services" means services provided to a handicapped child by the State directly, by contract, or through other arrangements.

(2) "Support services" includes implementing the comprehensive system of personnel development under §§ 300.380–300.388, recruitment and training of hearing officers and surrogate parents, and public information and parent training activities relating to a free appropriate public education for handicapped children.

(Authority: 20 U.S.C. 1411(b)(2), (c)(2))

§ 300.371 State matching.

Beginning with the period July 1, 1978–June 30, 1979, and for each following year, the funds that a State uses for direct and support services under § 300.370 must be matched on a program basis by the State from funds other than Federal funds. This requirement does not apply to funds that the State uses under § 300.360.

(Authority: 20 U.S.C. 1411(c)(2)(B), (c)(4)(B))

Comment. The requirement in § 300.371 would be satisfied if the State can document that the amount of State funds expended for each major program area (e.g., the comprehensive system of personnel development) is at least equal to the expenditure of Federal funds in that program area.

§ 300.372 Applicability of nonsupplanting requirement.

Beginning with funds appropriated for Fiscal Year 1979 and for each following Fiscal Year, the requirement in section 613(a)(9) of the Act, which prohibits supplanting with Federal funds, does not apply to funds that the State uses from its allocation under § 300.706(a) of Subpart G for administration, direct services, or support services.

(Authority: 20 U.S.C. 1411(c)(3))

Comprehensive System of Personnel Development

§ 300.380 Scope of system.

Each annual program plan must include a description of programs and procedures for the development and implementation of a comprehensive system of personnel development which includes:

(a) The inservice training of general and special educational instructional, related services, and support personnel;

(b) Procedures to insure that all personnel necessary to carry out the purposes of the Act are qualified (as defined in § 300.12 of Subpart A) and that activities sufficient to carry out this personnel development plan are scheduled; and

(c) Effective procedures for acquiring and disseminating to teachers and administrators of programs for handicapped children significant information derived from educational research, demonstration, and similar projects, and for adopting, where appropriate, promising educational practices and materials developed through those projects.

(Authority: 20 U.S.C. 1413(a)(3))

§ 300.381 Participation of other agencies and institutions.

(a) The State educational agency must insure that all public and private institutions of higher education, and other agencies and organizations (including representatives of handicapped, parent, and other advocacy organizations) in the state which have an interest in the preparation of personnel for the education of handicapped children, have an opportunity to participate fully in the development, review, and annual updating of the comprehensive system of personnel development.

(b) The annual program plan must describe the nature and extent of participation under paragraph (a) of this section and must describe responsibilities of the State educational agency, local educational agencies, public and private institutions of higher education, and other agencies:

(1) With respect to the comprehensive system as a whole, and

(2) With respect to the personnel development plan under § 300.383.

(Authority: 20 U.S.C. 1412(7)(A); 1413(a)(3))

§ 300.382 Inservice training.

(a) As used in this section, "inservice training" means any training other than that received by an individual in a full-time program which leads to a degree.

(b) Each annual program plan must provide that the State educational agency:

(1) Conducts an annual needs assessment to determine if a sufficient number of qualified personnel are available in the State; and

(2) Initiates inservice personnel development programs based on the assessed needs of State-wide significance related to the implementation of the Act.

(c) Each annual program plan must include the results of the needs assessment under paragraph (b)(1) of this section, broken out by need for new personnel and need for retrained personnel.

(d) The State educational agency may enter into contracts with institutions of higher education, local educational agencies or other agencies, institutions, or organizations (which may include parent, handicapped, or other advocacy organizations), to carry out:

(1) Experimental or innovative personnel development programs;

(2) Development or modification of instructional materials; and

(3) Dissemination of significant information derived from educational research and demonstration projects.

(e) Each annual program plan must provide that the State educational agency insures that ongoing inservice training programs are available to all personnel who are engaged in the education of handicapped children, and that these programs include:

(1) The use of incentives which insure participation by teachers (such as released time, payment for participation, options for academic credit, salary step credit, certification renewal, or updating professional skills);

(2) The involvement of local staff; and

(3) The use of innovative practices which have been found to be effective.

(f) Each annual program plan must:

(1) Describe the process used in determining the inservice training needs of personnel engaged in the education of handicapped children;

(2) Identify the areas in which training is needed (such as individualized education programs, non-discriminatory testing, least restrictive environment, procedural safeguards, and surrogate parents);

(3) Specify the groups requiring training (such as special teachers, regular teachers, administrators, psychologists, speech-language pathologists, audiologists, physical education teachers, therapeutic recreation specialists, physical therapists, occupational therapists, medical personnel, parents, volunteers, hearing officers, and surrogate parents);

(4) Describe the content and nature of training for each area under paragraph (f)(2) of this section;

(5) Describe how the training will be provided in terms of (i) geographical scope (such as Statewide, regional, or local), and (ii) staff training source (such as college and university staffs, State and local educational agency personnel, and non-agency personnel);

(6) *Specify*: (i) The funding sources to be used, and

(ii) The time frame for providing it; and

(7) Specify procedures for effective evaluation of the extent to which program objectives are met.

(Authority: 20 U.S.C. 1413(a)(3))

§ 300.383 Personnel development plan.

Each annual program plan must: (a) Include a personnel development plan which provides a structure for personnel planning and focuses on preservice and inservice education needs;

(b) Describe the results of the needs assessment under § 300.382(b)(1) with respect to identifying needed areas of training, and assigning priorities to those areas; and

(c) Identify the target populations for personnel development, including general education and special education instructional and administrative personnel, support personnel, and other personnel (such as paraprofessionals, parents, surrogate parents, and volunteers).

(Authority: 20 U.S.C. 1413(a)(3))

§ 300.384 Dissemination.

(a) Each annual program plan must include a description of the State's procedures for acquiring, reviewing, and disseminating to general and special educational instructional and support personnel, administrators of programs for handicapped children, and other interested agencies and organizations (including parent, handicapped, and other advocacy organizations) significant information and promising practices derived from educational research, demonstration, and other projects.

(b) Dissemination includes:

(1) Making those personnel, administrators, agencies, and organizations aware of the information and practices;

(2) Training designed to enable the establishment of innovative programs and practices targeted on identified local needs; and

(3) Use of instructional materials and other media for personnel development and instructional programming.

(Authority: 20 U.S.C. 1413(a)(3))

§ 300.385 Adoption of educational practices.

(a) Each annual program plan must provide for a statewide system designed to adopt, where appropriate, promising educational practices and materials proven effective through research and demonstration.

(b) Each annual program plan must provide for thorough reassessment of educational practices used in the State.

(c) Each annual program plan must provide for the identification of State, local, and regional resources (human and material) which will assist in meeting the State's personnel preparation needs.

(Authority: 20 U.S.C. 1413(a)(3))

§ 300.386 [Reserved]

§ 300.387 Technical assistance to local educational agencies.

Each annual program plan must include a description of technical assistance that the State educational agency gives to local educational agencies in their implementation of the State's comprehensive system of personnel development.

(Authority: 20 U.S.C. 1413(a)(3))

Subpart D—Private Schools

Handicapped Children in Private Schools Placed or Referred by Public Agencies

§ 300.400 Applicability of §§ 300.401–300.403.

Sections 300.401–300.403 apply only to handicapped children who are or have been placed in or referred to a private school or facility by a public agency as a means of providing special education and related services.

(Authority: 20 U.S.C. 1413(a)(4)(B))

§ 300.401 Responsibility of State educational agency.

Each State educational agency shall insure that a handicapped child who is placed in or referred to a private school or facility by a public agency:

(a) Is provided special education and related services:

(1) In conformance with an individualized education program which meets the requirements under §§ 300.340-300.349 of Subpart C;

(2) At no cost to the parents; and

(3) At a school or facility which meets the standards that apply to State and local educational agencies (including the requirements in this part); and

(b) Has all of the rights of a handicapped child who is served by a public agency.

(Authority: 20 U.S.C. 1413(a)(4)(B))

§ 300.402 Implementation by State educational agency.

In implementing § 300.401, the State educational agency shall:

(a) Monitor compliance through procedures such as written reports, on-site visits, and parent questionnaires;

(b) Disseminate copies of applicable standards to each private school and facility to which a public agency has referred or placed a handicapped child; and

(c) Provide an opportunity for those private schools and facilities to participate in the development and revision of State standards which apply to them.

(Authority: 20 U.S.C. 1413(a)(4)(B))

§ 300.403 Placement of children by parents.

(a) If a handicapped child has available a free appropriate public education and the parents choose to place the child in a private school or facility, the public agency is not required by this part to pay for the child's education at the private school or facility. However, the public agency shall make services available to the child as provided under §§ 300.450-300.460.

(b) Disagreements between a parent and a public agency regarding the availability of a program appropriate for the child, and the question of financial responsibility, are subject to the due process procedures under §§ 300.500-300.514 of Subpart E.

(Authority: 20 U.S.C. 1412(2)(B); 1415)

HANDICAPPED CHILDREN IN PRIVATE SCHOOLS NOT PLACED OR REFERRED BY PUBLIC AGENCIES

§ 300.450 Definition of "private school handicapped children."

As used in this part, "private school handicapped children" means handicapped children enrolled in private schools or facilities other than handicapped children covered under §§ 300.400—300.402.

(Authority: 20 U.S.C. 1413(a)(4)(A))

[49 FR 48526, Dec. 12, 1984]

§ 300.451 State educational agency responsibility.

The State educational agency shall insure that—

(a) To the extent consistent with their number and location in the State, provision is made for the participation of private school handicapped children in the program assisted or carried out under this part by providing them with special education and related services; and

(b) The requirements in 34 CFR 76.651-76.663 of EDGAR are met.

(Authority: 20 U.S.C. 1413(a)(4)(A))

[45 FR 22531, Apr. 3, 1980. Redesignated at 45 FR 77368, Nov. 21, 1980]

§ 300.452 Local educational agency responsibility.

(a) Each local educational agency shall provide special education and related services designed to meet the needs of private school handicapped children residing in the jurisdiction of the agency.

(Authority: Sec. 1413(a)(4)(A); 1414(a)(6))

[42 FR 42476, Aug. 23, 1977, as amended at 45 FR 22531, Apr. 3, 1980. Redesignated at 45 FR 77368, Nov. 21, 1980]

PROCEDURES FOR BY-PASS

§ 300.480 By-pass—general.

(a) The Secretary implements a by-pass if a State educational agency is, and was on December 2, 1983, prohibited by law from providing for the participation of private school handicapped children in the program assisted or carried out under this part, as required by section 613(a)(4)(A) of the Act and by §§ 300.451-300.452.

(b) The Secretary waives the requirement of section 613(a)(4)(A) of the Act and of §§ 300.451-300.452 if the Secretary implements a by-pass.

(Authority: 20 U.S.C. 1413(d)(1))

[49 FR 48526, Dec. 12, 1984]

§ 300.481 Provisions for services under a by-pass.

(a) Before implementing a by-pass, the Secretary consults with appropriate public and private school officials, including State educational agency officials, in the affected State to consider matters such as—

(1) The prohibition imposed by State law which results in the need for a by-pass;

(2) The scope and nature of the services required by private school handicapped children in the State, and the number of children to be served under the by-pass; and

(3) The establishment of policies and procedures to ensure that private school handicapped children receive services consistent with the requirements of section 613(a)(4)(A) of the Act, §§ 300.451-300.452, and 34 CFR 76.651-76.662.

(b) After determining that a by-pass is required, the Secretary arranges for the provision of services to private school handicapped children in the State in a manner consistent with the requirements of section 613(a)(4)(A) of the Act and §§ 300.451—300.452 by providing services through one or more agreements with appropriate parties.

(c) For any fiscal year in which a by-pass is implemented, the Secretary determines the maximum amount to be paid to the providers of services by multiplying—

(1) A per child amount, which may not exceed the amount per child provided by the Secretary under this part for all handicapped children in the State for the preceding fiscal year; by

(2) The number of private school handicapped children (as defined by §§ 300.5(a) and 300.450) in the State, as determined by the Secretary on the basis of the most recent satisfactory data available, which may include an estimate of the number of those handicapped children.

(d) The Secretary deducts from the State's allocation under this part the amount the Secretary determines is necessary to implement a by-pass and pays that amount to the provider of services. The Secretary may withhold this amount from the State's allocation pending final resolution of any investigation or complaint that could result in a determination that a by-pass must be implemented.

(Authority: 20 U.S.C. 1413(d)(2))

[49 FR 48526, Dec. 12, 1984]

Due Process Procedures

Source: Sections 300.482 through 300.486 appear at 49 FR 48526, Dec. 12, 1984, unless otherwise noted.

§ 300.482 Notice of intent to implement a by-pass.

(a) Before taking any final action to implement a by-pass, the Secretary provides the affected State educational agency with written notice.

(b) In the written notice, the Secretary—

(1) States the reasons for the proposed by-pass in sufficient detail to allow the State educational agency to respond;

(2) Advises the State educational agency that it has a specific period of time (at least 45 days) from receipt of the written notice to submit written objections to the proposed by-pass and that it may request in writing the opportunity for a hearing to show cause why a by-pass should not be implemented.

(c) The Secretary sends the notice to the State educational agency by certified mail with return receipt requested.

(Authority: 20 U.S.C. 1413(d)(3)(A))

§ 300.483 Request to show cause.

A State educational agency seeking an opportunity to show cause why a by-pass should not be implemented shall submit a written request for a show cause hearing to the Secretary.

(Authority: 20 U.S.C. 1413(d)(3)(A))

§ 300.484 Show cause hearing.

(a) If a show cause hearing is requested, the Secretary—

(1) Notifies the State educational agency and other appropriate public and private school officials of the time and place for the hearing; and

(2) Designates a person to conduct the show cause hearing. The designee must not have had any responsibility for the matter brought for a hearing.

(b) At the show cause hearing, the designee considers matters such as—

(1) The necessity for implementing a by-pass;

(2) Possible factual errors in the written notice of intent to implement a by-pass; and

(3) The objections raised by public and private school representatives.

(c) The designee may regulate the course of the proceedings and the conduct of parties during the pendency of the proceedings. The designee takes all steps necessary to conduct a fair and impartial proceeding, to avoid delay, and to maintain order, including procedures such as those established in 34 CFR 78.61(a), *Authority and Responsibilities of Panels.*

(d) The designee may interpret applicable statutes and regulations, but may not waive them or rule on their validity.

(e) The designee arranges for the preparation, retention, and, if appropriate, dissemination of the record of the hearing.

(Authority: 20 U.S.C. 1413(d)(3)(A))

§ 300.485 Decision.

(a) The designee who conducts the show cause hearing—

(1) Issues a written decision which includes a statement of findings; and

(2) Submits a copy of the decision to the Secretary and sends a copy to each party by certified mail with return receipt requested.

(b) Each party may submit comments and recommendations on the designee's decision to the Secretary within 15 days of the date the party receives the designee's decision.

(c) The Secretary adopts, reverses, or modifies the designee's decision and notifies the State educational agency of the Secretary's final action. That notice is sent by certified mail with return receipt requested.

(Authority: 20 U.S.C. 1413(d)(3)(A))

§ 300.486 Judicial review.

If dissatisfied with the Secretary's final action, the State educational agency may, within 60 days after notice of that action, file a petition for review with the United States court of appeals for the circuit in which the State is located. The procedures for judicial review are described in section 613(d)(3)(B)—(D) of the Act.

(Authority: 20 U.S.C. 1413(d)(3)(B)—(D)))

Subpart E—Procedural Safeguards

Due Process Procedures for Parents and Children

§ 300.500 Definitions of "consent", "evaluation", and "personally identifiable".

As used in this part: "Consent" means that:

(a) The parent has been fully informed of all information relevant to the activity for which consent is sought, in his or her native language, or other mode of communication;

(b) The parent understands and agrees in writing to the carrying out of the activity for which his or her consent is sought, and the consent describes that activity and lists the records (if any) which will be released and to whom; and

(c) The parent understands that the granting of consent is voluntary on the part of the parent and may be revoked at any time.,

"Evaluation" means procedures used in accordance with §§ 300.530-300.534 to determine whether a child is handicapped and the nature and extent of the special education and related services that the child needs. The term means procedures used selectively with an individual child and does not include basic tests administered to or procedures used with all children in a school, grade, or class.

"Personally identifiable" means that information includes:

(a) The name of the child, the child's parent, or other family member;

(b) The address of the child;

(c) A personal identifier, such as the child's social security number or student number; or

(d) A list of personal characteristics or other information which would make it possible to identify the child with reasonable certainty.

(Authority: 20 U.S.C. 1415, 1417(c))

§ 300.501 General responsibility of public agencies.

Each State educational agency shall insure that each public agency establishes and implements procedural safeguards which meet the requirements of §§ 300.500–300.514.

(Authority: 20 U.S.C. 1415(a))

§ 300.502 Opportunity to examine records.

The parents of a handicapped child shall be afforded, in accordance with the procedures in §§ 300.562–300.569 an opportunity to inspect and review all education records with respect to:

(a) The identification, evaluation, and educational placement of the child, and

(b) The provision of a free appropriate public education to the child.

(Authority: 20 U.S.C. 1415(b)(1)(A))

§ 300.503 Independent educational evaluation.

(a) *General.* (1) The parents of a handicapped child have the right under this part to obtain an independent educational evaluation of the child, subject to paragraphs (b) through (e) of this section.

(2) Each public agency shall provide to parents, on request, information about where an independent educational evaluation may be obtained.

(3) For the purposes of this part:

(i) "Independent educational evaluation" means an evaluation conducted by a qualified examiner who is not employed by the public agency responsible for the education of the child in question.

(ii) "Public expense" means that the public agency either pays for the full cost of the evaluation or insures that the evaluation is otherwise provided at no cost to the parent, consistent with § 300.301 of Subpart C.

(b) *Parent right to evaluation at public expense.* A parent has the right to an independent educational evaluation at public expense if the parent disagrees with an evaluation obtained by the public agency. However, the public agency may initiate a hearing under § 300.506 of this subpart to show that its evaluation is appropriate. If the final decision is that the evaluation is appropriate, the parent still has the right to an independent educational evaluation, but not at public expense.

(c) *Parent initiated evaluations.* If the parent obtains an independent educational evaluation at private expense, the results of the evaluation:

(1) Must be considered by the public agency in any decision made with respect to the provision of a free appropriate public education to the child, and

(2) May be presented as evidence at a hearing under this subpart regarding that child.

(d) *Requests for evaluations by hearing officers.* If a hearing officer requests an independent educational evaluation as part of a hearing, the cost of the evaluation must be at public expense.

(e) *Agency criteria.* Whenever an independent evaluation is at public expense, the criteria under which the evaluation is obtained, including the location of the evaluation and the qualifications of the examiner, must be the same as the criteria which the public agency uses when it initiates an evaluation.

(Authority: 20 U.S.C. 1415(b)(1)(A))

§ 300.504 Prior notice; parent consent.

(a) *Notice.* Written notice which meets the requirements under § 300.505 must be given to the parents of a handicapped child a reasonable time before the public agency:

(1) Proposes to initiate or change the identification, evaluation, or educational placement of the child or the provision of a free appropriate public education to the child, or

(2) Refuses to initiate or change the identification, evaluation, or educational placement of the child or the

provision of a free appropriate public education to the child.

(b) *Consent.* (1) Parental consent must be obtained before:

(i) Conducting a preplacement evaluation; and

(ii) Initial placement of a handicapped child in a program providing special education and related services.

(2) Except for preplacement evaluation and initial placement, consent may not be required as a condition of any benefit to the parent or child.

(c) *Procedures where parent refuses consent.* (1) Where State law requires parental consent before a handicapped child is evaluated or initially provided special education and related services, State procedures govern the public agency in overriding a parent's refusal to consent.

(2) (i) Where there is no State law requiring consent before a handicapped child is evaluated or initially provided special education and related services, the public agency may use the hearing procedures in §§ 300.506–300.508 to determine if the child may be evaluated or initially provided special education and related services without parental consent.

(ii) If the hearing officer upholds the agency, the agency may evaluate or initially provide special education and related services to the child without the parent's consent, subject to the parent's rights under §§ 300.510–300.513.

(Authority: 20 U.S.C. 1415(b)(1)(C), (D))

Comment. 1. Any changes in a child's special education program, after the initial placement, are not subject to parental consent under Part B, but are subject to the prior notice requirement in paragraph (a) and the individualized education program requirements in Subpart C.

2. Paragraph (c) means that where State law requires parental consent before evaluation or before special education and related services are initially provided, and the parent refuses (or otherwise withholds) consent, State procedures, such as obtaining a court order authorizing the public agency to conduct the evaluation or provide the education and related services, must be followed.

If, however, there is no legal requirement for consent outside of these regulations, the public agency may use the due process procedures under this subpart to obtain a decision to allow the evaluation or services without parental consent. The agency must notify the parent of its actions, and the parent has appeal rights as well as rights at the hearing itself.

§ 300.505 Content of notice.

(a) The notice under § 300.504 must include:

(1) A full explanation of all of the procedural safeguards available to the parents under Subpart E;

(2) A description of the action proposed or refused by the agency, an explanation of why the agency proposes or refuses to take the action, and a description of any options the agency considered and the reasons why those options were rejected;

(3) A description of each evaluation procedure, test, record, or report the agency uses as a basis for the proposal or refusal; and

(4) A description of any other factors which are relevant to the agency's proposal or refusal.

(b) The notice must be:

(1) Written in language understandable to the general public, and

(2) Provided in the native language of the parent or other mode of communication used by the parent, unless it is clearly not feasible to do so.

(c) If the native language or other mode of communication of the parent is not a written language, the State or local educational agency shall take steps to insure:

(1) That the notice is translated orally or by other means to the parent in his or her native language or other mode of communication;

(2) That the parent understands the content of the notice, and

(3) That there is written evidence that the requirements in paragraphs (c) (1) and (2) of this section have been met.

(Authority: 20 U.S.C. 1415(b)(1)(D))

§ 300.506 Impartial due process hearing.

(a) A parent or a public educational agency may initiate a hearing on any of the matters described in § 300.504(a) (1) and (2).

(b) The hearing must be conducted by the State educational agency or the public agency directly responsible for the education of the child, as determined under State statute, State regulation, or a written policy of the State educational agency.

(c) The public agency shall inform the parent of any free or low-cost legal and other relevant services available in the area if:

(1) The parent requests the information; or

(2) The parent or the agency initiates a hearing under this section.

(Authority: 20 U.S.C. 1416(b)(2))

Comment: Many States have pointed to the success of using mediation as an intervening step prior to conducting a formal due process hearing. Although the process of mediation is not required by the statute or these regulations, an agency may wish to suggest mediation in disputes concerning the identification, evaluation, and educational placement of handicapped children, and the provision of a free appropriate public education to those children. Mediations have been conducted by members of State educational agencies or local educational agency personnel who were not previously involved in the particular case. In many cases, mediation leads to resolution of differences between parents and agencies without the development of an adversarial relationship and with minimal emotional stress. However, mediation may not be used to deny or delay a parent's rights under this subpart.

§ 300.507 Impartial hearing officer.

(a) A hearing may not be conducted:

(1) By a person who is an employee of a public agency which is involved in the education or care of the child, or

(2) By any person having a personal or professional interest which would conflict with his or her objectivity in the hearing.

(b) A person who otherwise qualifies to conduct a hearing under paragraph (a) of this section is not an employee of the agency solely because he or she is paid by the agency to serve as a hearing officer.

(c) Each public agency shall keep a list of the persons who serve as hearing officers. The list must include a statement of the qualifications of each of those persons.

(Authority: 20 U.S.C. 1414(b)(2))

§ 300.508 Hearing rights.

(a) Any party to a hearing has the right to:

(1) Be accompanied and advised by counsel and by individuals with special knowledge or training with respect to the problems of handicapped children;

(2) Present evidence and confront, cross-examine, and compel the attendance of witnesses;

(3) Prohibit the introduction of any evidence at the hearing that has not been disclosed to that party at least five days before the hearing;

(4) Obtain a written or electronic verbatim record of the hearing;

(5) Obtain written findings of fact and decisions. (The public agency shall transmit those findings and decisions, after deleting any personally identifiable information, to the State advisory panel established under Subpart F).

(b) Parents involved in hearings must be given the right to:

(1) Have the child who is the subject of the hearing present; and

(2) Open the hearing to the public.

(Authority: 20 U.S.C. 1415(d))

§ 300.509 Hearing decision; appeal.

A decision made in a hearing conducted under this subpart is final, unless a party to the hearing appeals the decision under § 300.510 or § 300.511.

(Authority: 20 U.S.C. 1415(c))

§ 300.510 Administrative appeal; impartial review.

(a) If the hearing is conducted by a public agency other than the State educational agency, any party aggrieved by the findings and decision in the hearing may appeal to the State educational agency.

(b) If there is an appeal, the State educational agency shall conduct an impartial review of the hearing. The official conducting the review shall:

(1) Examine the entire hearing record;

(2) Insure that the procedures at the hearing were consistent with the requirements of due process;

(3) Seek additional evidence if necessary. If a hearing is held to receive additional evidence, the rights in § 300.508 apply;

(4) Afford the parties an opportunity for oral or written argument, or both, at the discretion of the reviewing official;

(5) Make an independent decision on completion of the review; and

(6) Give a copy of written findings and the decision to the parties.

(c) The decision made by the reviewing official is final, unless a party brings a civil action under § 300.512.

(Authority: 20 U.S.C. 1415 (c), (d); H. Rep. No. 94-664, at p. 49 (1975))

Comment. 1. The State educational agency may conduct its review either directly or through another State agency acting on its behalf. However, the State educational agency remains responsible for the final decision on review.

2. All parties have the right to continue to be represented by counsel at the State administrative review level, whether or not the reviewing official determines that a further hearing is necessary. If the reviewing official decides to hold a hearing to receive additional evidence, the other rights in § 300.508, relating to hearings, also apply.

§ 300.511 Civil action.

Any party aggrieved by the findings and decision made in a hearing who does not have the right to appeal under § 300.510 of this subpart, and any party aggrieved by the decision of a reviewing officer under § 300.510 has the right to bring a civil action under section 615(e)(2) of the Act.

(Authority: 20 U.S.C. 1415)

§ 300.512 Timeliness and convenience of hearings and reviews.

(a) The public agency shall insure that not later than 45 days after the receipt of a request for a hearing:

(1) A final decision is reached in the hearing; and

(2) A copy of the decision is mailed to each of the parties.

(b) The State educational agency shall insure that not later than 30 days after the receipt of a request for a review:

(1) A final decision is reached in the review; and

(2) A copy of the decision is mailed to each of the parties.

(c) A hearing or reviewing officer may grant specific extensions of time beyond the periods set out in paragraphs (a) and (b) of this section at the request of either party.

(d) Each hearing and each review involving oral arguments must be conducted at a time and place which is reasonably convenient to the parents and child involved.

(Authority: 20 U.S.C. 1415)

§ 300.513 Child's status during proceedings.

(a) During the pendency of any administrative or judicial proceeding regarding a complaint, unless the public agency and the parents of the child agree otherwise, the child involved in the complaint must remain in his or her present educational placement.

(b) If the complaint involves an application for initial admission to public school, the child, with the consent of the parents, must be placed in the public school program until the completion of all the proceedings.

(Authority: 20 U.S.C. 1415(e)(3))

Comment. Section 300.513 does not permit a child's placement to be chaged during a complaint proceeding, unless the parents and agency agree otherwise. While the placement may not be changed, this does not preclude the agency from using its normal procedures for dealing with children who are endangering themselves or others.

§ 300.514 Surrogate parents.

(a) *General.* Each public agency shall insure that the rights of a child are protected when:

(1) No parent (as defined in § 300.10) can be identified;

(2) The public agency, after reasonable efforts, cannot discover the whereabouts of a parent; or

(3) The child is a ward of the State under the laws of that State.

(b) *Duty of public agency.* The duty of a public agency under paragraph (a) of this section includes the assignment of an individual to act as a surrogate for the parents. This must include a method (1) for determining whether a child needs a surrogate parent, and (2) for assigning a surrogate parent to the child.

(c) *Criteria for selection of surrogates.* (1) The public agency may select a surrogate parent in any way permitted under State law.

(2) Public agencies shall insure that a person selected as a surrogate:

(i) Has no interest that conflicts with the interest of the child he or she represents; and

(ii) Has knowledge and skills, that insure adequate representation of the child.

(d) *Non-employee requirement; compensation.* (1) A person assigned as a surrogate may not be an employee of a public agency which is involved in the education or care of the child.

(2) A person who otherwise qualifies to be a surrogate parent under paragraphs (c) and (d)(1) of this section, is not an employee of the agency solely because he or she is paid by the agency to serve as a surrogate parent.

(e) *Responsibilities.* The surrogate parent may represent the child in all matters relating to:

(1) The identification, evaluation, and educational placement of the child, and

(2) The provision of a free appropriate public education to the child.

(Authority: 20 U.S.C. 1415(b)(1)(B))

PROTECTION IN EVALUATION PROCEDURES

§ 300.530 General.

(a) Each State educational agency shall insure that each public agency establishes and implements procedures which meet the requirements of §§ 300.530–300.534.

(b) Testing and evaluation materials and procedures used for the purposes of evaluation and placement of handicapped children must be selected and administered so as not to be racially or culturally discriminatory.

(Authority: 20 U.S.C. 1412(5)(C))

§ 300.531 Preplacement evaluation.

Before any action is taken with respect to the initial placement of a handicapped child in a special education program, a full and individual evaluation of the child's educational needs must be conducted in accordance with the requirements of § 300.532.

(Authority: 20 U.S.C. 1412(5)(C))

§ 300.532 Evaluation procedures.

State and local educational agencies shall insure, at a minimum, that:

(a) Tests and other evaluation materials:

(1) Are provided and administered in the child's native language or other mode of communication, unless it is clearly not feasible to do so;

(2) Have been validated for the specific purpose for which they are used; and

(3) Are administered by trained personnel in conformance with the instructions provided by their producer;

(b) Tests and other evaluation materials include those tailored to assess specific areas of educational need and not merely those which are designed to provide a single general intelligence quotient;

(c) Tests are selected and administered so as best to ensure that when a test is administered to a child with impaired sensory, manual, or speaking skills, the test results accurately reflect the child's aptitude or achievement level or whatever other factors the test purports to measure, rather than reflecting the child's impaired sensory, manual, or speaking skills (except where those skills are the factors which the test purports to measure);

(d) No single procedure is used as the sole criterion for determining an appropriate educational program for a child; and

(e) The evaluation is made by a multidisciplinary team or group of persons, including at least one teacher or other specialist with knowledge in the area of suspected disability.

(f) The child is assessed in all areas related to the suspected disability, including, where appropriate, health, vision, hearing, social and emotional status, general intelligence, academic performance, communicative status, and motor abilities.

(Authority: 20 U.S.C. 1412(5)(C))

Comment. Children who have a speech impairment as their primary handicap may not need a complete battery of assessments (e.g., psychological, physical, or adaptive behavior). However, a qualified speech-language pathologist would (1) evaluate each speech impaired child using procedures that are appropriate for the diagnosis and appraisal of speech and language disorders, and (2) where necessary, make referrals for additional assessments needed to make an appropriate placement decision.

§ 300.533 Placement procedures.

(a) In interpreting evaluation data and in making placement decisions, each public agency shall:

(1) Draw upon information from a variety of sources, including aptitude and achievement tests, teacher recommendations, physical condition, social or cultural background, and adaptive behavior;

(2) Insure that information obtained from all of these sources is documented and carefully considered;

(3) Insure that the placement decision is made by a group of persons, including persons knowledgeable about the child, the meaning of the evaluation data, and the placement options; and

(4) Insure that the placement decision is made in conformity with the least restrictive environment rules in §§ 300.550–300.554.

(b) If a determination is made that a child is handicapped and needs special education and related services, an individualized education program must be developed for the child in accordance with §§ 300.340–300.349 of Subpart C.

(Authority: 20 U.S.C. 1412(5)(C); 1414(a)(5))

Comment. Paragraph (a)(1) includes a list of examples of sources that may be used by a public agency in making placement decisions. The agency would not have to use all the sources in every instance. The point of the requirement is to insure that more than one source is used in interpreting evaluation data and in making placement decisions. For example, while all of the named sources would have to be used for a child whose suspected disability is mental retardation, they would not be necessary for certain other handicapped children, such as a child who has a severe articulation disorder as his primary handicap. For such a child, the speech-language pathologist, in complying with the multisource requirement, might use (1) a standardized test of articulation, and (2) observation of the child's articulation behavior in conversational speech.

§ 300.534 Reevaluation.

Each State and local educational agency shall insure:

(a) That each handicapped child's individualized education program is reviewed in accordance with §§ 300.340–300.349 of Subpart C, and

(b) That an evaluation of the child, based on procedures which meet the requirements under § 300.532, is conducted every three years or more frequently if conditions warrant or if the child's parent or teacher requests an evaluation.

(Authority: 20 U.S.C. 1412(5)(c))

Additional Procedures for Evaluating Specific Learning Disabilities

§ 300.540 Additional team members.

In evaluating a child suspected of having a specific learning disability, in addition to the requirements of § 300.532, each public agency shall include on the multidisciplinary evaluation team:

(a) (1) The child's regular teacher; or

(2) If the child does not have a regular teacher, a regular classroom teacher qualified to teach a child of his or her age; or

(3) For a child of less than school age, an individual qualified by the State educational agency to teach a child of his or her age; and

(b) At least one person qualified to conduct individual diagnostic examinations of children, such as a school psychologist, speech-language pathologist, or remedial reading teacher.

(Authority: 20 U.S.C. 1411 note)

[42 FR 65083, Dec. 29, 1977. Redesignated at 45 FR 77368, Nov. 21, 1980]

§ 300.541 Criteria for determining the existence of a specific learning disability.

(a) A team may determine that a child has a specific learning disability if:

(1) The child does not achieve commensurate with his or her age and ability levels in one or more of the areas listed in paragraph (a)(2) of this section, when provided with learning experiences appropriate for the child's age and ability levels; and

(2) The team finds that a child has a severe discrepancy between achieve-

ment and intellectual ability in one or more of the following areas:

(i) Oral expression;

(ii) Listening comprehension;

(iii) Written expression;

(iv) Basic reading skill;

(v) Reading comprehension;

(vi) Mathematics calculation; or

(vii) Mathematics reasoning.

(b) The team may not identify a child as having a specific learning disability if the severe discrepancy between ability and achievement is primarily the result of:

(1) A visual, hearing, or motor handicap;

(2) Mental retardation;

(3) Emotional disturbance; or

(4) Environmental, cultural or economic disadvantage.

(Authority: 20 U.S.C. 1411 note)

[42 FR 65083, Dec. 29, 1977. Redesignated at 45 FR 77368, Nov. 21, 1980]

§ 300.542 Observation.

(a) At least one team member other than the child's regular teacher shall observe the child's academic performance in the regular classroom setting.

(b) In the case of a child of less than school age or out of school, a team member shall observe the child in an environment appropriate for a child of that age.

(Authority: 20 U.S.C. 1411 note)

[42 FR 65083, Dec. 29, 1977. Redesignated at 45 FR 77368, Nov. 21, 1980]

§ 300.543 Written report.

(a) The team shall prepare a written report of the results of the evaluation.

(b) The report must include a statement of:

(1) Whether the child has a specific learning disability;

(2) The basis for making the determination;

(3) The relevant behavior noted during the observation of the child;

(4) The relationship of that behavior to the child's academic functioning;

(5) The educationally relevant medical findings, if any;

(6) Whether there is a severe discrepancy between achievement and ability which is not correctable without special education and related services; and

(7) The determination of the team concerning the effects of environmental, cultural, or economic disadvantage.

(c) Each team member shall certify in writing whether the report reflects his or her conclusion. If it does not reflect his or her conclusion, the team member must submit a separage statement presenting his or her conclusions.

(Authority: 20 U.S.C. 1411 note)

[42 FR 65083, Dec. 29, 1977. Redesignated at 45 FR 77368, Nov. 21, 1980]

LEAST RESTRICTIVE ENVIRONMENT

§ 300.550 General.

(a) Each State educational agency shall insure that each public agency establishes and implements procedures which meet the requirements of §§ 300.550–300.556.

(b) Each public agency shall insure:

(1) That to the maximum extent appropriate, handicapped children, including children in public or private institutions or other care facilities, are educated with children who are not handicapped, and

(2) That special classes, separate schooling or other removal of handicapped children from the regular educational environment occurs only when the nature or severity of the handicap is such that education in regular classes with the use of supplementary aids and services cannot be achieved satisfactorily.

(Authority: 20 U.S.C. 1412(5)(B); 1414(a)(1)(C)(iv))

§ 300.551 Continuum of alternative placements.

(a) Each public agency shall insure that a continuum of alternative placements is available to meet the needs of handicapped children for special education and related services.

(b) The continuum required under paragraph (a) of this section must:

(1) Include the alternative placements listed in the definition of special education under § 300.13 of Subpart A (instruction in regular classes, special classes, special schools, home instruction, and instruction in hospitals and institutions), and

(2) Make provision for supplementary services (such as resource room or itinerant instruction) to be provided in conjunction with regular class placement.

(Authority: 20 U.S.C. 1412(5)(B))

§ 300.552 Placements.

Each public agency shall insure that:

(a) Each handicapped child's educational placement: (1) Is determined at least annually,

(2) Is based on his or her individualized education program, and

(3) Is as close as possible to the child's home;

(b) The various alternative placements included under § 300.551 are available to the extent necessary to implement the individualized education program for each handicapped child;

(c) Unless a handicapped child's individualized education program requires some other arrangement, the child is educated in the school which he or she would attend if not handicapped; and

(d) In selecting the least restrictive environment, consideration is given to any potential harmful effect on the child or on the quality of services which he or she needs.

(Authority: 20 U.S.C. 1412(5)(B))

Comment. Section 300.552 includes some of the main factors which must be considered in determining the extent to which a handicapped child can be educated with children who are not handicapped. The overriding rule in this section is that placement decisions must be made on an individual basis. The section also requires each agency to have various alternative placements available in order to insure that each handicapped child receives an education which is appropriate to his or her individual needs.

The analysis of the regulations for Section 504 of the Rehabilitation Act of 1973 (34 CFR Part 104—Appendix, Paragraph 24) includes several points regarding educational placements of handicapped children which are pertinent to this section:

1. With respect to determining proper placements, the analysis states: "* * * it should be stressed that, where a handicapped child is so disruptive in a regular classroom that the education of other students is significantly impaired, the needs of the handicapped child cannot be met in that environment. Therefore regular placement would not be appropriate to his or her needs * * *."

2. With respect to placing a handicapped child in an alternate setting, the analysis states that among the factors to be considered in placing a child is the need to place the child as close to home as possible. Recipients are required to take this factor into account in making placement decisions. The parent's right to challenge the placement of their child extends not only to placement in special classes or separate schools, but also to placement in a distant school, particularly in a residential program. An equally appropriate education program may exist closer to home; and this issue may be raised by the parent under the due process provisions of this subpart.

§ 300.553 Nonacademic settings.

In providing or arranging for the provision of nonacademic and extracurricular services and activities, including meals, recess periods, and the services and activities set forth in § 300.306 of Subpart C, each public agency shall insure that each handicapped child participates with nonhandicapped children in those services and activities to the maximum extent appropriate to the needs of that child.

(Authority: 20 U.S.C. 1412(5)(B))

Comment. Section 300.553 is taken from a new requirement in the final regulations for Section 504 of the Rehabilitation Act of 1973. With respect to this requirement, the analysis of the Section 504 Regulations includes the following statement: "[A new paragraph] specifies that handicapped children must also be provided nonacademic services in as integrated a setting as possible. This requirement is especially important for children whose educational needs necessitate their being solely with other handicapped children during most of each day. To the maximum extent appropriate, children in residential settings are also to be provided opportunities for participation with other children." (34 CFR Part 104—Appendix, Paragraph 24.)

§ 300.554 Children in public or private institutions.

Each State educational agency shall make arrangements with public and private institutions (such as a memorandum of agreement or special implementation procedures) as may be necessary to insure that § 300.550 is effectively implemented.

(Authority: 20 U.S.C. 1412(5)(B))

Comment. Under section 612(5)(B) of the statute, the requirement to educate handicapped children with nonhandicapped children also applies to children in public and private institutions or other care facilities. Each State educational agency must insure that each applicable agency and institution in the State implements this requirement. Regardless of other reasons for institutional placement, no child in an institution who is capable of education in a regular public school setting may be denied access to an education in that setting.

§ 300.555 Technical assistance and training activities.

Each State educational agency shall carry out activities to insure that teachers and administrators in all public agencies:

(a) Are fully informed about their responsibilities for implementing § 300.550, and

(b) Are provided with technical assistance and training necessary to assist them in this effort.

(Authority: 20 U.S.C. 1412(5)(B))

§ 300.556 Monitoring activities.

(a) The State educational agency shall carry out activities to insure that § 300.550 is implemented by each public agency.

(b) If there is evidence that a public agency makes placements that are inconsistent with § 300.550 of this subpart, the State educational agency:

(1) Shall review the public agency's justification for its actions, and

(2) Shall assist in planning and implementing any necessary corrective action.

(Authority: 20 U.S.C. 1412(5)(B))

CONFIDENTIALITY OF INFORMATION

§ 300.560 Definitions.

As used in this subpart:

"Destruction" means physical destruction or removal of personal identifiers from information so that the information is no longer personally identifiable.

"Education records" means the type of records covered under the definition of "education records" in Part 99 of this title (the regulations implementing the Family Educational Rights and Privacy Act of 1974).

"Participating agency" means any agency or institution which collects, maintains, or uses personally identifiable information, or from which information is obtained, under this part.

(Authority: 20 U.S.C. 1412(2)(D); 1417(c))

§ 300.561 Notice to parents.

(a) The State educational agency shall give notice which is adequate to fully inform parents about the requirements under § 300.128 of Subpart B, including:

(1) A description of the extent to which the notice is given in the native languages of the various population groups in the State;

(2) A description of the children on whom personally identifiable information is maintained, the types of information sought, the methods the State intends to use in gathering the information (including the sources from whom information is gathered), and the uses to be made of the information;

(3) A summary of the policies and procedures which participating agencies must follow regarding storage, disclosure to third parties, retention, and destruction of personally identifiable information; and

(4) A description of all of the rights of parents and children regarding this information, including the rights under section 438 of the General Education Provisions Act and Part 99 of this title (the Family Educational Rights and Privacy Act of 1974, and implementing regulations).

(b) Before any major identification, location, or evaluation activity, the notice must be published or announced in newspapers or other media, or both, with circulation adequate to notify parents throughout the State of the activity.

(Authority: 20 U.S.C. 1412(2)(D); 1417(c))

§ 300.562 Access rights.

(a) Each participating agency shall permit parents to inspect and review any education records relating to their children which are collected, maintained, or used by the agency under this part. The agency shall comply with a request without unnecessary delay and before any meeting regarding an individualized education program or hearing relating to the identification, evaluation, or placement of the child, and in no case more than 45 days after the request has been made.

(b) The right to inspect and review education records under this section includes:

(1) The right to a response from the participating agency to reasonable requests for explanations and interpretations of the records;

(2) The right to request that the agency provide copies of the records containing the information if failure to provide those copies would effectively prevent the parent from exercising the right to inspect and review the records; and

(3) The right to have a representative of the parent inspect and review the records.

(c) An agency may presume that the parent has authority to inspect and review records relating to his or her child unless the agency has been advised that the parent does not have the authority under applicable State law governing such matters as guardianship, separation, and divorce.

(Authority: 20 U.S.C. 1412(2)(D); 1417(c))

§ 300.563 Record of access.

Each participating agency shall keep a record of parties obtaining access to education records collected, maintained, or used under this part (except access by parents and authorized employees of the participating agency), including the name of the party, the date access was given, and the purpose for which the party is authorized to use the records.

(Authority: 20 U.S.C. 1412(2)(D); 1417(c))

§ 300.564 Records on more than one child.

If any education record includes information on more than one child, the parents of those children shall have the right to inspect and review only the information relating to their child or to be informed of that specific information.

(Authority: 20 U.S.C. 1412(2)(D); 1417(c))

§ 300.565 List of types and locations of information.

Each participating agency shall provide parents on request a list of the types and locations of education records collected, maintained, or used by the agency.

(Authority: 20 U.S.C. 1412(2)(D); 1417(c))

§ 300.566 Fees.

(a) A participating education agency may charge a fee for copies of records which are made for parents under this part if the fee does not effectively prevent the parents from exercising their right to inspect and review those records.

(b) A participating agency may not charge a fee to search for or to retrieve information under this part.

(Authority: 20 U.S.C. 1412(2)(D); 1417(c))

§ 300.567 Amendment of records at parent's request.

(a) A parent who believes that information in education records collected, maintained, or used under this part is inaccurate or misleading or violates the privacy or other rights of the child, may request the participating agency which maintains the information to amend the information.

(b) The agency shall decide whether to amend the information in accordance with the request within a reasonable period of time of receipt of the request.

(c) If the agency decides to refuse to amend the information in accordance with the request it shall inform the parent of the refusal, and advise the parent of the right to a hearing under § 300.568.

(Authority: 20 U.S.C. 1412(2)(D); 1417(c))

§ 300.568 Opportunity for a hearing.

The agency shall, on request, provide an opportunity for a hearing to challenge information in education records to insure that it is not inaccurate, misleading, or otherwise in violation of the privacy or other rights of the child.

(Authority: 20 U.S.C. 1412(2)(D); 1417(c))

§ 300.569 Result of hearing.

(a) If, as a result of the hearing, the agency decides that the information is inaccurate, misleading or otherwise in violation of the privacy or other rights of the child, it shall amend the information accordingly and so inform the parent in writing.

(b) If, as a result of the hearing, the agency decides that the information is not inaccurate, misleading, or otherwise in violation of the privacy of other rights of the child, it shall inform the parent of the right to place in the records it maintains on the child a statement commenting on the information or setting forth any reasons for disagreeing with the decision of the agency.

(c) Any explanation placed in the records of the child under this section must:

(1) Be maintained by the agency as part of the records of the child as long as the record or contested portion is maintained by the agency; and

(2) If the records of the child or the contested portion is disclosed by the agency to any party, the explanation must also be disclosed to the party.

(Authority: 20 U.S.C. 1412(2)(D); 1417(c))

§ 300.570 Hearing procedures.

A hearing held under § 300.568 of this subpart must be conducted according to the procedures under § 99.22 of this title.

(Authority: 20 U.S.C. 1412(2)(D); 1417(c))

§ 300.571 Consent.

(a) Parental consent must be obtained before personally identifiable information is:

(1) Disclosed to anyone other than officials of participating agencies collecting or using the information under this part, subject to paragraph (b) of this section; or

(2) Used for any purpose other than meeting a requirement under this part.

(b) An educational agency or institution subject to Part 99 of this title may not release information from education records to participating agencies without parental consent unless authorized to do so under Part 99 of this title.

(c) The State educational agency shall include policies and procedures in its annual program plan which are used in the event that a parent refuses to provide consent under this section.

(Authority: 20 U.S.C. 1412(2)(D); 1417(c))

§ 300.572 Safeguards.

(a) Each participating agency shall protect the confidentiality of personally identifiable information at collection, storage, disclosure, and destruction stages.

(b) One official at each participating agency shall assume responsibility for insuring the confidentiality of any personally identifiable information.

(c) All persons collecting or using personally identifiable information must receive training or instruction regarding the State's policies and procedures under § 300.129 of Subpart B and Part 99 of this title.

(d) Each participating agency shall maintain, for public inspection, a current listing of the names and positions of those employees within the agency who may have access to personally identifiable information.

(Authority: 20 U.S.C. 1412(2)(D); 1417(c))

§ 300.573 Destruction of information.

(a) The public agency shall inform parents when personally identifiable information collected, maintained, or used under this part is no longer needed to provide educational services to the child.

(b) The information must be destroyed at the request of the parents. However, a permanent record of a student's name, address, and phone number, his or her grades, attendance record, classes attended, grade level completed, and year completed may be maintained without time limitation.

(Authority: 20 U.S.C. 1412(2)(D); 1417(c))

Comment. Under § 300.573, the personally identifiable information on a handicapped child may be retained permanently unless the parents request that it be destroyed. Destruction of records is the best protection against improper and unauthorized disclosure. However, the records may be needed for other purposes. In informing parents about their rights under this section, the agency should remind them that the records may be needed by the child or the parents for social security benefits or other purposes. If the parents request that the information be destroyed, the agency may retain the information in paragraph (b).

§ 300.574 Children's rights.

The State educational agency shall include policies and procedures in its annual program plan regarding the extent to which children are afforded rights of privacy similar to those afforded to parents, taking into consideration the age of the child and type or severity of disability.

(Authority: 20 U.S.C. 1412(2)(D); 1417(c))

Comment. Note that under the regulations for the Family Educational Rights and Privacy Act (45 CFR 99.4(a)), the rights of parents regarding education records are transferred to the student at age 18.

§ 300.575 Enforcement.

The State educational agency shall describe in its annual program plan the policies and procedures, including sanctions, which the State uses to insure that its policies and procedures are followed and that the requirements of the Act and the regulations in this part are met.

(Authority: 20 U.S.C. 1412(2)(D); 1417(c))

§ 300.576 Department.

If the Department or its authorized representatives collect any personally identifiable information regarding handicapped children which is not subject to 5 U.S.C. 552a (The Privacy Act of 1974), the Secretary shall apply the requirements of 5 U.S.C. section 552a (b) (1)-(2), (4)-(11); (c); (d); (e)(1); (2); (3)(A), (B), and (D), (5)-(10); (h); (m); and (n), and the regulations implementing those provisions in Part 5b of this title.

(Authority: 20 U.S.C. 1412(2)(D); 1417(c))

DEPARTMENT PROCEDURES

300.580 Opportunity for a hearing.

The Secretary gives a State educational agency reasonable notice and an opportunity for a hearing before taking any of the following actions:

(a) Disapproval of a State's annual program plan under § 300.113 of Subpart B.

(b) Withholding payments from a State under § 300.590 or under section 434(c) of the General Education Provisions Act.

(c) Waiving the requirement under § 300.589 of this subpart regarding supplementing and supplanting with funds provided under Part B of the Act.

(Authority: 20 U.S.C. 1232(c); 1413(a)(9)(b); 1413(c); 1416)

EFFECTIVE DATE NOTE: Section 300.580 was removed and reserved at 51 FR 17905, May 15, 1986, effective July 23, 1986.

§ 300.581 Disapproval of a State plan.

Before disapproving a State plan, the Secretary gives the State educational agency written notice and an opportunity for a hearing.

(Authority: 20 U.S.C. 1413(c))

[51 FR 17905, May 15, 1986]

EFFECTIVE DATE NOTE: Section 300.581 was added at 51 FR 17905, May 15, 1986, effective July 23, 1986.

§ 300.582 Content of notice.

(a) In the written notice, the Secretary—

(1) States the basis on which the Secretary proposes to disapprove the State plan;

(2) May describe possible options for resolving the issues;

(3) Advises the State educational agency that it may request a hearing and that the request for a hearing must be made not later than 30 calendar days after it receives the notice of proposed disapproval; and

(4) Provides information about the procedures followed for a hearing.

(b) The Secretary sends the written notice to the State educational agency by certified mail with return receipt requested.

(Authority: 20 U.S.C. 1413(c))

[51 FR 17905, May 15, 1986]

EFFECTIVE DATE NOTE: Section 300.582 was added at 51 FR 17905, May 15, 1986, effective July 23, 1986.

§ 300.583 Hearing official or panel.

(a) If the State educational agency requests a hearing, the Secretary designates one or more individuals, either from the Department or elsewhere, not responsible for or connected with the administration of the program under this part, to conduct a hearing.

(b) If more than one individual is designated, the Secretary designates one of those individuals as the Chief Hearing Official of the Hearing Panel. If one individual is designated, that individual is the Hearing Official.

(c) If the State has an appeal pending with the Education Appeal Board on a matter arising out of the same State plan, or on the same issue arising from a prior plan, the State may contest the disapproval of its plan before the Education Appeal Board in accordance with 34 CFR Part 78.

(Authority: 20 U.S.C. 1413(c))

[51 FR 17905, May 15, 1986]

EFFECTIVE DATE NOTE: Section 300.583 was added at 51 FR 17905, May 15, 1986, effective July 23, 1986.

§ 300.584 Hearing procedures.

(a) As used in §§ 300.581—300.586 the term "party" or "parties" means the following:

(1) A State educational agency that requests a hearing regarding the proposed disapproval of its State plan under this part.

(2) The Department of Education official who administers the program of financial assistance under this part.

(3) A person, group or agency with an interest in and having relevant information about the case who has applied for and been granted leave to intervene by the Hearing Official or Panel.

(b) Within 15 calendar days after receiving a request for a hearing, the Secretary designates a Hearing Official or Panel and notifies the parties.

(c) The Hearing Official or Panel may regulate the course of proceedings and the conduct of the parties during the proceedings. The Hearing Official or Panel takes all steps necessary to conduct a fair and impartial proceeding, to avoid delay, and to maintain order, including the following:

(1) The Hearing Official or Panel may hold conferences or other types of appropriate proceedings to clarify, simplify, or define the issues or to consider other matters that may aid in the disposition of the case.

(2) The Hearing Official or Panel may schedule a prehearing conference of the Hearing Official or Panel and parties.

(3) Any party may request the Hearing Official or Panel to schedule a prehearing or other conference. The Hearing Official or Panel decides whether a conference is necessary and notifies all parties.

(4) At a prehearing or other conference, the Hearing Official or Panel and the parties may consider subjects such as—

(i) Narrowing and clarifying issues;

(ii) Assisting the parties in reaching agreements and stipulations;

(iii) Clarifying the positions of the parties;

(iv) Determining whether an evidentiary hearing or oral argument should be held;

(v) Setting dates for—

(A) The exchange of written documents;

(B) The receipt of comments from the parties on the need for oral argument or evidentiary hearing;

(C) Further proceedings before the Hearing Official or Panel (including an evidentiary hearing or oral argument, if either is scheduled);

(D) Requesting the names of witnesses each party wishes to present at an evidentiary hearing and estimation of time for each presentation; or

(E) Completion of the review and the initial decision of the Hearing Official or Panel.

(5) A prehearing or other conference held under paragraph (b)(4) of this section may be conducted by telephone conference call.

(6) At a prehearing or other conference, the parties shall be prepared to discuss the subjects listed in paragraph (b)(4) of this section.

(7) Following a prehearing or other conference the Hearing Official or Panel may issue a written statement describing the issues raised, the action taken, and the stipulations and agreements reached by the parties.

(d) The Hearing Official or Panel may require parties to state their positions and to provide all or part of the evidence in writing.

(e) The Hearing Official or Panel may require parties to present testimony through affidavits and to conduct cross-examination through interrogatories.

(f) The Hearing Official or Panel may direct the parties to exchange relevant documents or information and lists of witnesses, and to send copies to the Hearing Official or Panel.

(g) The Hearing Official or Panel may receive, rule on, exclude, or limit evidence at any stage of the proceedings.

(h) The Hearing Official or Panel may rule on motions and other issues at any stage of the proceedings.

(i) The Hearing Official or Panel may examine witnesses.

(j) The Hearing Official or Panel may set reasonable time limits for submission of written documents.

(k) The Hearing Official or Panel may refuse to consider documents or other submissions if they are not submitted in a timely manner unless good cause is shown.

(l) The Hearing Official or Panel may interpret applicable statutes and regulations but may not waive them or rule on their validity.

(m)(1) The parties shall present their positions through briefs and the submission of other documents and may request an oral argument or evidentiary hearing. The Hearing Official or Panel shall determine whether an oral argument or an evidentiary hearing is needed to clarify the positions of the parties.

(2) The Hearing Official or Panel gives each party an opportunity to be represented by counsel.

(n) If the Hearing Official or Panel determines that an evidentiary hearing would materially assist the resolution of the matter, the Hearing Official or Panel gives each party, in addition to the opportunity to be represented by counsel—

(1) An opportunity to present witnesses on the party's behalf; and

(2) An opportunity to cross-examine witnesses either orally or with written questions.

(o) The Hearing Official or Panel accepts any evidence that it finds is relevant and material to the proceedings and is not unduly repetitious.

(p)(1) The Hearing Official or Panel—

(i) Arranges for the preparation of a transcript of each hearing;

(ii) Retains the original transcript as part of the record of the hearing; and

(iii) Provides one copy of the transcript to each party.

(2) Additional copies of the transcript are available on request and with payment of the reproduction fee.

(q) Each party shall file with the Hearing Official or Panel all written motions, briefs, and other documents and shall at the same time provide a copy to the other parties to the proceedings.

(Authority: 20 U.S.C. 1413(c))

[51 FR 17905, May 15, 1986]

EFFECTIVE DATE NOTE: Section 300.584 was added at 51 FR 17905, May 15, 1986, effective July 23, 1986.

§ 300.585 Initial decision; final decision.

(a) The Hearing Official or Panel prepares an initial written decision which addresses each of the points in the notice sent by the Secretary to the State educational agency under § 300.582.

(b) The initial decision of a Panel is made by a majority of Panel members.

(c) The Hearing Official or Panel mails by certified mail with return receipt requested a copy of the initial decision to each party (or to the party's counsel) and to the Secretary, with a notice stating that each party has an opportunity to submit written comments regarding the decision to the Secretary.

(d) Each party may file comments and recommendations on the initial decision with the Hearing Official or Panel within 15 calendar days of the date the party receives the Panel's decision.

(e) The Hearing Official or Panel sends a copy of a party's initial comments and recommendations to the other parties by certified mail with return receipt requested. Each party may file responsive comments and recommendations with the Hearing Official or Panel within seven calendar days of the date the party receives the initial comments and recommendations.

(f) The Hearing Official or Panel forwards the parties' initial and responsive comments on the initial deci-

73-111 O—86——3

sion to the Secretary who reviews the initial decision and issues a final decision.

(g) The initial decision of the Hearing Official or Panel becomes the final decision of the Secretary unless, within 25 calendar days after the end of the time for receipt of written comments, the Secretary informs the Hearing Official or Panel and the parties to a hearing in writing that the decision is being further reviewed for possible modification.

(h) The Secretary may reject or modify the initial decision of the Hearing Official or Panel if the Secretary finds that it is clearly erroneous.

(i) The Secretary conducts the review based on the initial decision, the written record, the Hearing Official's or Panel's proceedings, and written comments. The Secretary may remand the matter for further proceedings.

(j) The Secretary issues the final decision within 30 calendar days after notifying the Hearing Official or Panel that the initial decision is being further reviewed.

[51 FR 17906, May 15, 1986]

EFFECTIVE DATE NOTE: Section 300.585 was added at 51 FR 17906, May 15, 1986, effective July 23, 1986.

§ 300.586 Judicial review.

If a State is dissatisfied with the Secretary's final action with respect to its State plan, the State may, within 60 calendar days after notice of that action, file a petition for review with the United States court of appeals for the circuit in which the State is located.

(Authority: 20 U.S.C. 1416(b)(1))

[51 FR 17906, May 15, 1986]

EFFECTIVE DATE NOTE: Section 300.586 was added at 51 FR 17906, May 15, 1986, effective July 23, 1986.

§§ 300.587—300.588 [Reserved]

§ 300.589 Waiver of requirement regarding supplementing and supplanting with Part B funds.

(a) Under sections 613(a)(9)(B) and 614(a)(2)(B)(ii) of the Act, State and local educational agencies must insure that Federal funds provided under Part B of the Act are used to supplement the level of State and local funds expended for the education of handicapped children, and in no case to supplant those State and local funds. Beginning with funds appropriated for fiscal year 1979 and for each following fiscal year, the nonsupplanting requirement only applies to funds allocated to local educational agencies. (See § 300.372.)

(b) If the State provides clear and convincing evidence that all handicapped children have available to them a free appropriate public education, the Secretary may waive in part the requirement under sections 613(a)(9)(B) and 614(a)(2)(B)(ii) of the Act if the Secretary concurs with the evidence provided by the State.

(c) If a State wishes to request a waiver, it must inform the Secretary in writing. The Secretary then provides the State with a finance and membership report form which provides the basis for the request.

(d) In its request for a waiver, the State shall include the results of a special study made by the State to obtain evidence of the availability of a free appropriate public education to all handicapped children. The special study must include statements by a representative sample of organizations which deal with handicapped children, and parents and teachers of handicapped children, relating to the following areas:

(1) The adequacy and comprehensiveness of the State's system for locating, identifying, and evaluating handicapped children, and

(2) The cost to parents, if any, for education for children enrolled in public and private day schools, and in public and private residential schools and institutions, and

(3) The adequacy of the State's due process procedures.

(e) In its request for a waiver, the State shall include finance data relating to the availability of a free appropriate public education for all handicapped children, including:

(1) The total current expenditures for regular education programs and special education programs by function and by source of funds (State, local, and Federal) for the previous school year, and

(2) The full-time equivalent membership of students enrolled in regular programs and in special programs in the previous school year.

(f) The Secretary considers the information which the State provides under paragraphs (d) and (e) of this section, along with any additional information he may request, or obtain through on-site reviews of the State's education programs and records, to determine if all children have available to them a free appropriate public education, and if so, the extent of the waiver.

(g) The State may request a hearing with regard to any final action by the Secretary under this section.

(Authority: 20 U.S.C. 1411(c)(3); 1413(a)(9)(B))

[42 FR 42476, Aug. 23, 1977. Redesignated at 45 FR 77368, Nov. 21, 1980 and amended at 51 FR 17906, May 15, 1986]

EFFECTIVE DATE NOTE: Section 300.589(g) was revised at 51 FR 17906, May 15, 1986, effective July 23, 1986. For the convenience of the reader, the superseded text is set forth below.

§ 300.589 Waiver of requirement regarding supplementing and supplanting with Part B funds.

* * * * *

(g) The State may request a hearing under §§ 300.580—300.583 with regard to any final action by the Secretary under this section.

Subpart F—State Administration

STATE EDUCATIONAL AGENCY RESPONSIBILITIES: GENERAL

§ 300.600 Responsibility for all educational programs.

(a) The State educational agency is responsible for insuring;

(1) That the requirements of this part are carried out; and

(2) That each educational program for handicapped children administered within the State, including each program administered by any other public agency:

(i) Is under the general supervision of the persons responsible for educational programs for handicapped children in the State educational agency, and

(ii) Meets education standards of the State educational agency (including the requirements of this part).

(b) The State must comply with paragraph (a) of this section through State statute, State regulation, signed agreement between respective agency officials, or other documents.

(Authority: 20 U.S.C. 1412(6))

Comment. The requirement in § 300.600(a) is taken essentially verbatim from section 612(6) of the statute and reflects the desire of the Congress for a central point of responsibility and accountability in the education of handicapped children within each State. With respect to State educational agency responsibility, the Senate Report on Pub. L. 94-142 includes the following statements:

This provision is included specifically to assure a single line of responsibility with regard to the education of handicapped children, and to assure that in the implementation of all provisions of this Act and in carrying out the right to education for handicapped children, the State educational agency shall be the responsible agency * * *.

Without this requirement, there is an abdication of responsibility for the education of handicapped children. Presently, in many States, responsibility is divided, depending upon the age of the handicapped child, sources of funding, and type of services delivered. While the Committee understands that different agencies may, in fact, deliver services, the responsibility must remain in a central agency overseeing the education of handicapped children, so that failure to deliver services or the violation of the rights of handicapped children is squarely the responsibility of one agency. (Senate Report No. 94-168, p. 24 (1975))

In meeting the requirements of this section, there are a number of acceptable options which may be adopted, including the following:

(1) Written agreements are developed between respective State agencies concerning State educational agency standards and monitoring. These agreements are binding on the local or regional counterparts of each State agency.

(2) The Governor's Office issues an administrative directive establishing the State educational agency responsibility.

(3) State law, regulation, or policy designates the State educational agency as responsible for establishing standards for all educational programs for the handicapped, and includes responsibility for monitoring.

(4) State law mandates that the State educational agency is responsible for all educational programs.

USE OF FUNDS

§ 300.620 Federal funds for State administration.

A State may use five percent of the total State allotment in any fiscal year under Part B of the Act, or $350,000, whichever is greater, for administrative costs related to carrying out sections 612 and 613 of the Act. However, this amount cannot be greater than twenty-five percent of the State's total allotment for the fiscal year under Part B of the Act.

(Authority: 20 U.S.C. 1411 (b), (c))

[51 FR 19311, May 28, 1986]

EFFECTIVE DATE NOTE: Section 300.620 was revised at 51 FR 19311, May 28, 1986, effective July 23, 1986. For the convenience of the reader, the superseded text is set forth below.

§ 300.620 Federal funds for State administration.

A State may use five percent of the total State allotment in any fiscal year under Part B of the Act, or $200,000, whichever is greater, for administrative costs related to carrying out sections 612 and 613 of the Act. However, this amount cannot be greater than the amount which the State may use under § 300.704 or § 300.705, as the case may be.

(Authority: 20 U.S.C. 1411 (b), (c))

§ 300.621 Allowable costs.

(a) The State educational agency may use funds under § 300.620 of this subpart for:

(1) Administration of the annual program plan and for planning at the State level, including planning, or assisting in the planning, of programs or projects for the education of handicapped children;

(2) Approval, supervision, monitoring, and evaluation of the effectiveness of local programs and projects for the education of handicapped children;

(3) Technical assistance to local educational agencies with respect to the requirements of this part;

(4) Leadership services for the program supervision and management of special education activities for handicapped children; and

(5) Other State leadership activities and consultative services.

(b) The State educational agency shall use the remainder of its funds under § 300.620 in accordance with § 300.370 of Subpart C.

(Authority: 20 U.S.C. 1411 (b), (c))

STATE ADVISORY PANEL

§ 300.650 Establishment.

(a) Each State shall establish, in accordance with the provisions of this subpart, a State advisory panel on the education of handicapped children.

(b) The advisory panel must be appointed by the Governor or any other official authorized under State law to make those appointments.

(c) If a State has an existing advisory panel that can perform the functions in § 300.652, the State may modify the existing panel so that it fulfills all of the requirements of this subpart, instead of establishing a new advisory panel.

(Authority: 20 U.S.C. 1413(a)(12))

§ 300.651 Membership.

(a) The membership of the State advisory panel must be composed of persons involved in or concerned with the education of handicapped children. The membership must include at least one person representative of each of the following groups:

(1) Handicapped individuals.

(2) Teachers of handicapped children.

(3) Parents of handicapped children.

(4) State and local educational officials.

(5) Special education program administrators.

(b) The State may expand the advisory panel to include additional persons in the groups listed in paragraph (a) of this section and representatives of other groups not listed.

(Authority: 20 U.S.C. 1413(a)(12))

Comment. The membership of the State advisory panel, as listed in paragraphs (a) (1)-(5), is required in section 613(a)(12) of the Act. As indicated in paragraph (b), the composition of the panel and the number of members may be expanded at the discretion of the State. In adding to the membership, consideration could be given to having:

(1) An appropriate balance between professional groups and consumers (i.e., parents, advocates, and handicapped individuals);

(2) Broad representation within the consumer-advocate groups, to insure that the interests and points of view of various parents, advocates and handicapped individuals are appropriately represented;

(3) Broad representation within professional groups (e.g., (a) regular education personnel, (b) special educators, including teachers, teacher trainers, and administrators, who can properly represent various dimensions in the education of handicapped children, and (c) appropriate related services personnel); and

(4) Representatives from other State advisory panels (such as vocational education).

If a State elects to maintain a small advisory panel (e.g., 10-15 members), the panel itself could take steps to insure that it (1) consults with and receives inputs from various consumer and special interest professional groups, and (2) establishes committees for particular short-term purposes composed of representatives from those input groups.

§ 300.652 Advisory panel functions.

The State advisory panel shall:

(a) Advise the State educational agency of unmet needs within the State in the education of handicapped children;

(b) Comment publicly on the State annual program plan and rules or regulations proposed for issuance by the State regarding the education of handicapped children and the procedures for distribution of funds under this part; and

(c) Assist the State in developing and reporting such information and evaluations as may assist the Secretary in the performance of his responsibilities under section 618.

(Authority: 20 U.S.C. 1413(a)(12))

§ 300.653 Advisory panel procedures.

(a) The advisory panel shall meet as often as necessary to conduct its business.

(b) By July 1 of each year, the advisory panel shall submit an annual report of panel activities and suggestions to the State educational agency. This report must be made available to the public in a manner consistent with other public reporting requirements under this part.

(c) Official minutes must be kept on all panel meetings and shall be made available to the public on request.

(d) All advisory panel meetings and agenda items must be publicly announced prior to the meeting, and meetings must be open to the public.

(e) Interpreters and other necessary services must be provided at panel meetings for panel members or participants. The State may pay for these services from funds under § 300.620.

(f) The advisory panel shall serve without compensation but the State must reimburse the panel for reasonable and necessary expenses for attending meetings and performing duties. The State may use funds under § 300.620 for this purpose.

(Authority: 20 U.S.C. 1413(a)(12))

Subpart G—Allocation of Funds; Reports

Allocations

§ 300.700 Special definition of the term State.

For the purposes of § 300.701, § 300.702, and §§ 300.704-300.708, the term "State" does not include Guam, American Samoa, the Virgin Islands, and the Trust Territory of the Pacific Islands.

(Authority: 20 U.S.C. 1411(a)(2))

§ 300.701 State entitlement; formula.

(a) The maximum amount of the grant to which a State is entitled under section 611 of the Act in any fiscal year is equal to the number of handicapped children aged three through 21 in the State who are receiving special education and related services, multiplied by the applicable percentage, under paragraph (b) of this section, of the average per pupil expenditure in public elementary and secondary schools in the United States.

(b) For the purposes of the formula in paragraph (a) of this section, the applicable percentage of the average per pupil expenditure in public elementary and secondary schools in the United States for each fiscal year is:

(1) 1978—5 percent,

(2) 1979—10 percent,

(3) 1980—20 percent,

(4) 1981—30 percent, and

(5) 1982, and for each fiscal year after 1982, 40 percent.

(Authority: 20 U.S.C. 1411(a)(1))

(c) For the purposes of this section, the average per pupil expenditure in public elementary and secondary schools in the United States, means the aggregate expenditures during the second fiscal year preceding the fiscal year for which the computation is made (or if satisfactory data for that year are not available at the time of computation, then during the most recent preceding fiscal year for which satisfactory data are available) of all local educational agencies in the United States (which, for the purpose of this section, means the fifty States and the District of Columbia), plus any direct expenditures by the State for operation of those agencies (without regard to the source of funds from which either of those expenditures are made), divided by the aggregate number of children in average daily attendance to whom those agencies provided free public education during that preceding year.

(Authority: 20 U.S.C. 1411(a)(4))

§ 300.702 Limitations and exclusions.

(a) In determining the amount of a grant under § 300.701 of this subpart, the Secretary may not count:

(1) Handicapped children in a State to the extent that the number of those children is greater than 12 percent of the number of all children aged five through 17 in the State; and

(2) [Reserved]

(3) Handicapped children who are counted under section 121 of the Elementary and Secondary Education Act of 1965.

(b) For the purposes of paragraph (a) of this section, the number of children aged five through 17 in any State shall be determined by the Secretary on the basis of the most recent satisfactory data available to him.

(Authority: 20 U.S.C. 1411(a)(5))

[42 FR 42476, Aug. 23, 1977, as amended at 42 FR 65083, Dec. 29, 1977. Redesignated at 45 FR 77368, Nov. 21, 1980]

§ 300.703 Ratable reductions.

(a) *General.* If the sums appropriated for any fiscal year for making payments to States under section 611 of the Act are not sufficient to pay in full the total amounts to which all States are entitled to receive for that fiscal year, the maximum amount which all States are entitled to receive for that fiscal year shall be ratably reduced. In case additional funds become available for making payments for any fiscal year during which the preceding sentence is applicable, those reduced amounts shall be increased on the same basis they were reduced.

(Authority: 20 U.S.C. 1411(g)(1))

(b) *Reporting dates for local educational agencies and reallocations.* (1) In any fiscal year in which the State entitlements have been ratably reduced, and in which additional funds have not been made available to pay in full the total of the amounts under paragraph (a) of this section, the State educational agency shall fix dates before which each local educational agency shall report to the State the amount of funds available to it under this part which it estimates it will expend.

(2) The amounts available under paragraph (a)(1) of this section, or any amount which would be available to any other local educational agency if it were to submit an application meeting the requirements of this part, which the State educational agency determines will not be used for the period of its availability, shall be available for allocation to those local educational agencies, in the manner provided in § 300.707, which the State educational agency determines will need and be able to use additional funds to carry out approved programs.

(Authority: 20 U.S.C. 1411(g)(2))

§ 300.704 Hold harmless provision.

No State shall receive less than the amount it received under Part B of the Act for fiscal year 1977.

(Authority: 20 U.S.C. 1411(a)(1))

§ 300.705 Allocation for State in which bypass is implemented for private school handicapped children.

In determining the allocation under §§ 300.700–300.703 of a State in which the Secretary will implement a by-pass for private school handicapped children under §§ 300.451–300.486, the Secretary includes in the State's child count—

(a) For the first year of a by-pass, the actual or estimated number of private school handicapped children (as defined in §§ 300.5(a) and 300.450 in the State, as of the preceding December 1; and

(b) For succeeding years of a by-pass, the number of private school handicapped children who received special education and related services under the by-pass in the preceding year.

(Authority: 20 U.S.C. 1411(a)(1)(A), 1411(a)(3), 1413(d))

[49 FR 48526, Dec. 12, 1984]

§ 300.706 Within-State distribution: Fiscal year 1979 and after.

Of the funds received under § 300.701 by any State for fiscal year 1979, and for each fiscal year after fiscal year 1979:

(a) 25 percent may be used by the State in accordance with § 300.620 of Subpart F and § 300.370 of Subpart C, and

(b) 75 percent shall be distributed to the local educational agencies in the State in accordance with § 300.707.

(Authority: 20 U.S.C. 1411(c)(1))

§ 300.707 Local educational agency entitlements; formula.

From the total amount of funds available to all local educational agencies, each local educational agency is entitled to an amount which bears the same ratio to the total amount as the number of handicapped children aged three through 21 in that agency who are receiving special education and related services bears to the aggregate number of handicapped children aged three through 21 receiving special education and related services in all local educational agencies which apply to the State educational agency for funds under Part B of the Act.

(Authority: 20 U.S.C. 1411(d))

§ 300.708 Reallocation of local educational agency funds.

If a State educational agency determines that a local educational agency is adequately providing a free appropriate public education to all handicapped children residing in the area served by the local agency with State and local funds otherwise available to the local agency, the State educational agency may reallocate funds (or portions of those funds which are not required to provide special education and related services) made available to the local agency under § 300.707, to other local educational agencies within the State which are not adequately providing special education and related services to all handicapped children residing in the areas served by the other local educational agencies.

(Authority: 20 U.S.C. 1414(e))

§ 300.709 Payments to Secretary of Interior.

(a) The Secretary is authorized to make payments to the Secretary of the Interior according to the need for that assistance for the education of handicapped children on reservations serviced by elementary and secondary schools operated for Indian children by the Department of the Interior.

(b) The amount of those payments for any fiscal year shall not exceed one percent of the aggregate amounts available to all States for that fiscal year under Part B of the Act.

(Authority: 20 U.S.C. 1411(f)(1))

§ 300.710 Entitlements to jurisdictions.

(a) The jurisdictions to which this section applies are Guam, American Samoa, the Virgin Islands, and the Trust Territory of the Pacific Islands.

(b) Each jurisdiction under paragraph (a) of this section is entitled to a grant for the purposes set forth in section 601(c) of the Act. The amount to which those jurisdictions are so entitled for any fiscal year shall not exceed an amount equal to 1 percent of the aggregate of the amounts available to all States under this part for that fiscal year. Funds appropriated for those jurisdictions shall be allocated proportionately among them on the basis of the number of children aged three through twenty-one in each jurisdiction. However, no jurisdiction shall receive less than $150,000, and other allocations shall be ratably reduced if necessary to insure that each jurisdiction receives at least that amount.

(c) The amount expended for administration by each jurisdiction under this section shall not exceed 5 percent of the amount allotted to the jurisdiction for any fiscal year, or $35,000, whichever is greater.

(Authority: 20 U.S.C. 1411(e))

Reports

§ 300.750 Annual report of children served—report requirement.

(a) The State educational agency shall report to the Secretary no later than February 1 of each year the number of handicapped children aged three through 21 residing in the State who are receiving special education and related services.

(Authority: 20 U.S.C. 1411(a)(3))

(b) The State educational agency shall submit the report on forms provided by the Secretary.

(Authority: 20 U.S.C. 1411(a)(3))

Comment. It is very important to understand that this report and the requirements that relate to it are solely for allocation purposes. The population of children the State may count for allocation purposes may differ from the population of children to whom the State must make available a free appropriate public education. For example, while section 611(a)(5) of the Act limits the number of children who may be counted for allocation purposes to 12 percent of the general school population aged five through seventeen, a State might find that 14 percent (or some other percentage) of its children are handicapped. In that case, the State must make free appropriate public education available to all of those handicapped children.

[42 FR 42476, Aug. 23, 1977, as amended at 45 FR 7551, Feb. 4, 1980. Redesignated at 45 FR 77368, Nov. 21, 1980]

§ 300.751 Annual report of children served—information required in the report.

(a) In its report, the State educational agency shall include a table which shows:

(1) The number of handicapped children receiving special education and related services on December 1 of that school year;

(2) The number of those handicapped children within each disability category, as defined in the definition of "handicapped children" in § 300.5 of Subpart A; and

(3) The number of those handicapped children aged three through twenty-one for each year of age (three, four, five, etc.). For fiscal year 1985, a State educational agency that does not currently collect information in this manner may report the number of those handicapped children within each of the following age groups:

(i) Three through five.

(ii) Six through eleven.

(iii) Twelve through seventeen.

(iv) Eighteen through twenty-one.

(b) For the purpose of this part, a child's age is the child's actual age on the date of the child count: December 1.

(c) The State educational agency may not report a child under more than one disability category.

(d) If a handicapped child has more than one disability, the State educational agency shall report that child in accordance with the following procedure:

(1) A child who is both deaf and blind must be reported as "deaf-blind."

(2) A child who has more than one disability (other than a deaf-blind child) must be reported as "multihandicapped."

(The information collection requirements contained in paragraphs (a)(3) and (b) were approved by the Office of Management and Budget under control number 1820-0043)

(Authority: 20 U.S.C. 1411(a)(3); 1411(a)(5)(A)(ii); 1418(b))

[42 FR 42476, Aug. 23, 1977, as amended at 45 FR 7551, Feb. 4, 1980. Redesignated at 45

FR 77368, Nov. 21, 1980; 49 FR 48525, Dec. 12, 1984]

§ 300.752 Annual report of children served—certification.

The State educational agency shall include in its report a certification signed by an authorized official of the agency that the information provided is an accurate and unduplicated count of handicapped children receiving special education and related services on the dates in question.

(Authority: 20 U.S.C. 1411(a)(3); 1417(b))

§ 300.753 Annual report of children served—criteria for counting children.

(a) The State educational agency may include handicapped children in its report who are enrolled in a school or program which is operated or supported by a public agency, and which either:

(1) Provides them with both special education and related services; or

(2) Provides them only with special education if they do not need related services to assist them in benefitting from that special education.

(b) The State educational agency may not include handicapped children in its report who:

(1) Are not enrolled in a school or program operated or supported by a public agency;

(2) Are not provided special education that meets State standards;

(3) Are not provided with a related service that they need to assist them in benefitting from special education;

(4) Are counted by a State agency under section 121 of the Elementary and Secondary Education Act of 1965, as amended; or

(5) Are receiving special education funded solely by the Federal Government. However, the State may count children covered under § 300.186(b) of Subpart B.

(Authority: 20 U.S.C. 1411(a)(3); 1417(b))

Comment. 1. Under paragraph (a), the State may count handicapped children in a Head Start or other preschool program operated or supported by a public agency if those children are provided special education that meets State standards.

2. "Special education," by statutory definition, must be at no cost to parents. As of September 1, 1978, under the free appropriate public education requirement, both special education and related services must be at no cost to parents.

There may be some situations, however, where a child receives special education from a public source at no cost, but whose parents pay for the basic or regular education. This child may be counted. The Department expects that there would only be limited situations where special education would be clearly separate from regular education—generally, where speech therapy is the only special education required by the child. For example, the child might be in a regular program in a parochial or other private school but receiving speech therapy in a program funded by the local educational agency. Allowing these children to be counted will provide incentives (in addition to complying with the legal requirement in section 613(a)(4)(A) of the Act regarding private schools) to public agencies to provide services to children in private schools, since funds are generated in part on the basis of the number of children provided special education and related services. Agencies should understand, however, that where a handicapped child is placed in or referred to a public or private school for educational purposes, special education includes the entire educational program provided to the child. In that case, parents may not be charged for any part of the child's education.

A State may not count Indian children on or near reservations and children on military facilities if it provides them no special education. If a State or local educational agency is responsible for serving these children, and does provide them special education and related services, they may be counted.

§ 300.754 Annual report of children served—other responsibilities of the State educational agency.

In addition to meeting the other requirements in this subpart, the State educational agency shall:

(a) Establish procedures to be used by local educational agencies and other educational institutions in counting the number of handicapped children receiving special education and related services;

(b) Set dates by which those agencies and institutions must report to the State educational agency to insure that the State complies with § 300.750(a);

(c) Obtain certification from each agency and institution that an unduplicated and accurate count has been made;

(d) Aggregate the data from the count obtained from each agency and institution, and prepare the reports required under this subpart; and

(e) Insure that documentation is maintained which enables the State and the Secretary to audit the accuracy of the count.

(Authority: 20 U.S.C. 1411(a)(3); 1417(b))

Comment. States should note that the data required in the annual report of children served are not to be transmitted to the Secretary in personally identifiable form. States are encouraged to collect these data in non-personally identifiable form.

PART 104—NONDISCRIMINATION ON THE BASIS OF HANDICAP IN PROGRAMS AND ACTIVITIES RECEIVING OR BENEFITING FROM FEDERAL FINANCIAL ASSISTANCE

AUTHORITY: Sec. 504, Rehabilitation Act of 1973, Pub. L. 93-112, 87 Stat. 394 (29 U.S.C. 794); sec. 111(a), Rehabilitation Act Amendments of 1974, Pub. L. 93-516, 88 Stat. 1619 (29 U.S.C. 706); sec. 606, Education of the Handicapped Act (20 U.S.C. 1405), as amended by Pub. L. 94-142, 89 Stat. 795.

Subpart A—General Provisions

§ 104.1 Purpose.

The purpose of this part is to effectuate section 504 of the Rehabilitation Act of 1973, which is designed to eliminate discrimination on the basis of handicap in any program or activity receiving Federal financial assistance.

§ 104.2 Application.

This part applies to each recipient of Federal financial assistance from the Department of Education and to each program or activity that receives or benefits from such assistance.

§ 104.3 Definitions.

As used in this part, the term:

(a) "The Act" means the Rehabilitation Act of 1973, Pub. L. 93-112, as amended by the Rehabilitation Act Amendments of 1974, Pub. L. 93-516, 29 U.S.C. 794.

(b) "Section 504" means section 504 of the Act.

(c) "Education of the Handicapped Act" means that statute as amended by the Education for all Handicapped Children Act of 1975, Pub. L. 94-142, 20 U.S.C. 1401 et seq.

(d) "Department" means the Department of Education.

(e) "Assistant Secretary" means the Assistant Secretary for Civil Rights of the Department of Education.

(f) "Recipient" means any state or its political subdivision, any instrumentality of a state or its political subdivision, any public or private agency, institution, organization, or other entity, or any person to which Federal financial assistance is extended directly or through another recipient, including any successor, assignee, or transferee of a recipient, but excluding the ultimate beneficiary of the assistance.

(g) "Applicant for assistance" means one who submits an application, request, or plan required to be approved by a Department official or by a recipient as a condition to becoming a recipient.

(h) "Federal financial assistance" means any grant, loan, contract (other than a procurement contract or a contract of insurance or guaranty), or any other arrangement by which the Department provides or otherwise makes available assistance in the form of:

(1) Funds;

(2) Services of Federal personnel; or

(3) Real and personal property or any interest in or use of such property, including:

(i) Transfers or leases of such property for less than fair market value or for reduced consideration; and

(ii) Proceeds from a subsequent transfer or lease of such property if the Federal share of its fair market value is not returned to the Federal Government.

(i) "Facility" means all or any portion of buildings, structures, equipment, roads, walks, parking lots, or other real or personal property or interest in such property.

(j) "Handicapped person." (1) "Handicapped persons" means any person who (i) has a physical or mental impairment which substantially limits one or more major life activities, (ii) has a record of such an impairment, or (iii) is regarded as having such an impairment.

(2) As used in paragraph (j)(1) of this section, the phrase:

(i) "Physical or mental impairment" means (A) any physiological disorder or condition, cosmetic disfigurement, or anatomical loss affecting one or more of the following body systems: neurological; musculoskeletal; special sense organs; respiratory, including speech organs; cardiovascular; reproductive, digestive, genito-urinary; hemic and lymphatic; skin; and endocrine; or (B) any mental or psychological disorder, such as mental retardation, organic brain syndrome, emotional or mental illness, and specific learning disabilities.

(ii) "Major life activities" means functions such as caring for one's self, performing manual tasks, walking, seeing, hearing, speaking, breathing, learning, and working.

(iii) "Has a record of such an impairment" means has a history of, or has been misclassified as having, a mental or physical impairment that substantially limits one or more major life activities.

(iv) "Is regarded as having an impairment" means (A) has a physical or mental impairment that does not substantially limit major life activities but that is treated by a recipient as constituting such a limitation; (B) has a physical or mental impairment that substantially limits major life activities only as a result of the attitudes of others toward such impairment; or (C) has none of the impairments defined in paragraph (j)(2)(i) of this section but is treated by a recipient as having such an impairment.

(k) "Qualified handicapped person" means:

(1) With respect to employment, a handicapped person who, with reasonable accommodation, can perform the essential functions of the job in question;

(2) With respect to public preschool elementary, secondary, or adult educational services, a handicappped person (i) of an age during which nonhandicapped persons are provided such services, (ii) of any age during which it is mandatory under state law to provide such services to handicapped persons, or (iii) to whom a state is required to provide a free appropriate public education under section 612 of the Education of the Handicapped Act; and

(3) With respect to postsecondary and vocational education services, a handicapped person who meets the academic and technical standards requisite to admission or participation in the recipient's education program or activity;

(4) With respect to other services, a handicapped person who meets the es-

sential eligibility requirements for the receipt of such services.

(l) "Handicap" means any condition or characteristic that renders a person a handicapped person as defined in paragraph (j) of this section.

§ 104.4 Discrimination prohibited.

(a) *General.* No qualified handicapped person shall, on the basis of handicap, be excluded from participation in, be denied the benefits of, or otherwise be subjected to discrimination under any program or activitiy which receives or benefits from Federal financial assistance.

(b) *Discriminatory actions prohibited.* (1) A recipient, in providing any aid, benefit, or service, may not, directly or through contractual, licensing, or other arrangements, on the basis of handicap:

(i) Deny a qualified handicapped person the opportunity to participate in or benefit from the aid, benefit, or service;

(ii) Afford a qualified handicapped person an opportunity to participate in or benefit from the aid, benefit, or service that is not equal to that afforded others;

(iii) Provide a qualified handicapped person with an aid, benefit, or service that is not as effective as that provided to others;

(iv) Provide different or separate aid, benefits, or services to handicapped persons or to any class of handicapped persons unless such action is necessary to provide qualified handicapped persons with aid, benefits, or services that are as effective as those provided to others;

(v) Aid or perpetuate discrimination against a qualified handicapped person by providing significant assistance to an agency, organization, or person that discriminates on the basis of handicap in providing any aid, benefit, or service to beneficiaries of the recipients program;

(vi) Deny a qualified handicapped person the opportunity to participate as a member of planning or advisory boards; or

(vii) Otherwise limit a qualified handicapped person in the enjoyment of any right, privilege, advantage, or opportunity enjoyed by others receiving an aid, benefit, or service.

(2) For purposes of this part, aids, benefits, and services, to be equally effective, are not required to produce the identical result or level of achievement for handicapped and nonhandicapped persons, but must afford handicapped persons equal opportunity to obtain the same result, to gain the same benefit, or to reach the same level of achievement, in the most integrated setting appropriate to the person's needs.

(3) Despite the existence of separate or different programs or activities provided in accordance with this part, a recipient may not deny a qualified handicapped person the opportunity to participate in such programs or activities that are not separate or different.

(4) A recipient may not, directly or through contractual or other arrangements, utilize criteria or methods of administration (i) that have the effect of subjecting qualified handicapped persons to discrimination on the basis of handicap, (ii) that have the purpose or effect of defeating or substantially impairing accomplishment of the objectives of the recipient's program with respect to handicapped persons, or (iii) that perpetuate the discrimination of another recipient if both recipients are subject to common administrative control or are agencies of the same State.

(5) In determining the site or location of a facility, an applicant for assistance or a recipient may not make selections (i) that have the effect of excluding handicapped persons from, denying them the benefits of, or otherwise subjecting them to discrimination under any program or activity that receives or benefits from Federal financial assistance or (ii) that have the purpose or effect of defeating or substantially impairing the accomplishment of the objectives of the program or activity with respect to handicapped persons.

(6) As used in this section, the aid, benefit, or service provided under a program or activity receiving or benefiting from Federal financial assistance includes any aid, benefit, or service provided in or through a facility

that has been constructed, expanded, altered, leased or rented, or otherwise acquired, in whole or in part, with Federal financial assistance.

(c) *Programs limited by Federal law.* The exclusion of nonhandicapped persons from the benefits of a program limited by Federal statute or executive order to handicapped persons or the exclusion of a specific class of handicapped persons from a program limited by Federal statute or executive order to a different class of handicapped persons is not prohibited by this part.

§ 104.5 Assurances required.

(a) *Assurances.* An applicant for Federal financial assistance for a program or activity to which this part applies shall submit an assurance, on a form specified by the Assistant Secretary, that the program will be operated in compliance with this part. An applicant may incorporate these assurances by reference in subsequent applications to the Department.

(b) *Duration of obligation.* (1) In the case of Federal financial assistance extended in the form of real property or to provide real property or structures on the property, the assurance will obligate the recipient or, in the case of a subsequent transfer, the transferee, for the period during which the real property or structures are used for the purpose for which Federal financial assistance is extended or for another purpose involving the provision of similar services or benefits.

(2) In the case of Federal financial assistance extended to provide personal property, the assurance will obligate the recipient for the period during which it retains ownership or possession of the property.

(3) In all other cases the assurance will obligate the recipient for the period during which Federal financial assistance is extended.

(c) *Covenants.* (1) Where Federal financial assistance is provided in the form of real property or interest in the property from the Department, the instrument effecting or recording this transfer shall contain a covenant running with the land to assure nondiscrimination for the period during which the real property is used for a purpose for which the Federal financial assistance is extended or for another purpose involving the provision of similar services or benefits.

(2) Where no transfer of property is involved but property is purchased or improved with Federal financial assistance, the recipient shall agree to include the covenant described in paragraph (b)(2) of this section in the instrument effecting or recording any subsequent transfer of the property.

(3) Where Federal financial assistance is provided in the form of real property or interest in the property from the Department, the covenant shall also include a condition coupled with a right to be reserved by the Department to revert title to the property in the event of a breach of the covenant. If a transferee of real property proposes to mortgage or otherwise encumber the real property as security for financing construction of new, or improvement of existing, facilities on the property for the purposes for which the property was transferred, the Assistant Secretary may, upon request of the transferee and if necessary to accomplish such financing and upon such conditions as he or she deems appropriate, agree to forbear the exercise of such right to revert title for so long as the lien of such mortgage or other encumbrance remains effective.

§ 104.6 Remedial action, voluntary action, and self-evaluation.

(a) *Remedial action.* (1) If the Assistant Secretary finds that a recipient has discriminated against persons on the basis of handicap in violation of section 504 or this part, the recipient shall take such remedial action as the Assistant Secretary deems necessary to overcome the effects of the discrimination.

(2) Where a recipient is found to have discriminated against persons on the basis of handicap in violation of section 504 or this part and where another recipient exercises control over the recipient that has discriminated, the Assistant Secretary, where appropriate, may require either or both recipients to take remedial action.

(3) The Assistant Secretary may, where necessary to overcome the effects of discrimination in violation of section 504 or this part, require a recipient to take remedial action (i) with respect to handicapped persons who are no longer participants in the recipient's program but who were participants in the program when such discrimination occurred or (ii) with respect to handicapped persons who would have been participants in the program had the discrimination not occurred.

(b) *Voluntary action.* A recipient may take steps, in addition to any action that is required by this part, to overcome the effects of conditions that resulted in limited participation in the recipient's program or activity by qualified handicapped persons.

(c) *Self-evaluation.* (1) A recipient shall, within one year of the effective date of this part:

(i) Evaluate, with the assistance of interested persons, including handicapped persons or organizations representing handicapped persons, its current policies and practices and the effects thereof that do not or may not meet the requirements of this part;

(ii) Modify, after consultation with interested persons, including handicapped persons or organizations representing handicapped persons, any policies and practices that do not meet the requirements of this part; and

(iii) Take, after consultation with interested persons, including handicapped persons or organizations representing handicapped persons, appropriate remedial steps to eliminate the effects of any discrimination that resulted from adherence to these policies and practices.

(2) A recipient that employs fifteen or more persons shall, for at least three years following completion of the evaluation required under paragraph (c)(1) of this section, maintain on file, make available for public inspection, and provide to the Assistant Secretary upon request: (i) A list of the interested persons consulted (ii) a description of areas examined and any problems identified, and (iii) a description of any modifications made and of any remedial steps taken.

§ 104.7 Designation of responsible employee and adoption of grievance procedures.

(a) *Designation of responsible employee.* A recipient that employs fifteen or more persons shall designate at least one person to coordinate its efforts to comply with this part.

(b) *Adoption of grievance procedures.* A recipient that employs fifteen or more persons shall adopt grievance procedures that incorporate appropriate due process standards and that provide for the prompt and equitable resolution of complaints alleging any action prohibited by this part. Such procedures need not be established with respect to complaints from applicants for employment or from applicants for admission to postsecondary educational institutions.

§ 104.8 Notice.

(a) A recipient that employs fifteen or more persons shall take appropriate initial and continuing steps to notify participants, beneficiaries, applicants, and employees, including those with impaired vision or hearing, and unions or professional organizations holding collective bargaining or professional agreements with the recipient that it does not discriminate on the basis of handicap in violation of section 504 and this part. The notification shall state, where appropriate, that the recipient does not discriminate in admission or access to, or treatment or employment in, its programs and activities. The notification shall also include an identification of the responsible employee designated pursuant to § 104.7(a). A recipient shall make the initial notification required by this paragraph within 90 days of the effective date of this part. Methods of initial and continuing notification may include the posting of notices, publication in newspapers and magazines, placement of notices in recipients' publication, and distribution of memoranda or other written communications.

(b) If a recipient publishes or uses recruitment materials or publications containing general information that it makes available to participants, beneficiaries, applicants, or employees, it shall include in those materials or publications a statement of the policy described in paragraph (a) of this section. A recipient may meet the requirement of this paragraph either by including appropriate inserts in existing materials and publications or by revising and reprinting the materials and publications.

§ 104.9 Administrative requirements for small recipients.

The Assistant Secretary may require any recipient with fewer than fifteen employees, or any class of such recipients, to comply with §§ 104.7 and 104.8, in whole or in part, when the Assistant Secretary finds a violation of this part or finds that such compliance will not significantly impair the ability of the recipient or class of recipients to provide benefits or services.

§ 104.10 Effect of state or local law or other requirements and effect of employment opportunities.

(a) The obligation to comply with this part is not obviated or alleviated by the existence of any state or local law or other requirement that, on the basis of handicap, imposes prohibitions or limits upon the eligibility of qualified handicapped persons to receive services or to practice any occupation or profession.

(b) The obligation to comply with this part is not obviated or alleviated because employment opportunities in any occupation or profession are or may be more limited for handicapped persons than for nonhandicapped persons.

Subpart B—Employment Practices

§ 104.11 Discrimination prohibited.

(a) *General.* (1) No qualified handicapped person shall, on the basis of handicap, be subjected to discrimination in employment under any program or activity to which this part applies.

(2) A recipient that receives assistance under the Education of the Handicapped Act shall take positive steps to employ and advance in employment qualified handicapped persons in programs assisted under that Act.

(3) A recipient shall make all decisions concerning employment under any program or activity to which this part applies in a manner which ensures that discrimination on the basis of handicap does not occur and may not limit, segregate, or classify applicants or employees in any way that adversely affects their opportunities or status because of handicap.

(4) A recipient may not participate in a contractual or other relationship that has the effect of subjecting qualified handicapped applicants or employees to discrimination prohibited by this subpart. The relationships referred to in this paragraph include relationships with employment and referral agencies, with labor unions, with organizations providing or administering fringe benefits to employees of the recipient, and with organizations providing training and apprenticeship programs.

(b) *Specific activities.* The provisions of this subpart apply to:

(1) Recruitment, advertising, and the processing of applications for employment;

(2) Hiring, upgrading, promotion, award of tenure, demotion, transfer, layoff, termination, right of return from layoff and rehiring;

(3) Rates of pay or any other form of compensation and changes in compensation;

(4) Job assignments, job classifications, organizational structures, position descriptions, lines of progression, and seniority lists;

(5) Leaves of absense, sick leave, or any other leave;

(6) Fringe benefits available by virtue of employment, whether or not administered by the recipient;

(7) Selection and financial support for training, including apprenticeship, professional meetings, conferences, and other related activities, and selection for leaves of absence to pursue training;

(8) Employer sponsored activities, including social or recreational programs; and

(9) Any other term, condition, or privilege of employment.

(c) A recipient's obligation to comply with this subpart is not affected by any inconsistent term of any collective bargaining agreement to which it is a party.

§ 104.12 Reasonable accommodation.

(a) A recipient shall make reasonable accommodation to the known physical or mental limitations of an otherwise qualified handicapped applicant or employee unless the recipient can demonstrate that the accommodation would impose an undue hardship on the operation of its program.

(b) Reasonable accommodation may include: (1) Making facilities used by employees readily accessible to and usable by handicapped persons, and (2) job restructuring, part-time or modified work schedules, acquisition or modification of equipment or devices, the provision of readers or interpreters, and other similar actions.

(c) In determining pursuant to paragraph (a) of this section whether an accommodation would impose an undue hardship on the operation of a recipient's program, factors to be considered include:

(1) The overall size of the recipient's program with respect to number of employees, number and type of facilities, and size of budget;

(2) The type of the recipient's operation, including the composition and structure of the recipient's workforce; and

(3) The nature and cost of the accommodation needed.

(d) A recipient may not deny any employment opportunity to a qualified handicapped employee or applicant if the basis for the denial is the need to make reasonable accommodation to the physical or mental limitations of the employee or applicant.

§ 104.13 Employment criteria.

(a) A recipient may not make use of any employment test or other selection criterion that screens out or tends to screen out handicapped persons or any class of handicapped persons unless: (1) The test score or other selection criterion, as used by the recipient, is shown to be job-related for the position in question, and (2) alternative job-related tests or criteria that do not screen out or tend to screen out as many handicapped persons are not shown by the Director to be available.

(b) A recipient shall select and administer tests concerning employment so as best to ensure that, when administered to an applicant or employee who has a handicap that impairs sensory, manual, or speaking skills, the test results accurately reflect the applicant's or employee's job skills, aptitude, or whatever other factor the test purports to measure, rather than reflecting the applicant's or employee's impaired sensory, manual, or speaking skills (except where those skills are the factors that the test purports to measure).

§ 104.14 Preemployment inquiries.

(a) Except as provided in paragraphs (b) and (c) of this section, a recipient may not conduct a preemployment medical examination or may not make preemployment inquiry of an applicant as to whether the applicant is a handicapped person or as to the nature or severity of a handicap. A recipient may, however, make preemployment inquiry into an applicant's ability to perform job-related functions.

(b) When a recipient is taking remedial action to correct the effects of past discrimination pursuant to § 104.6 (a), when a recipient is taking voluntary action to overcome the effects of conditions that resulted in limited participation in its federally assisted program or activity pursuant to § 104.6(b), or when a recipient is taking affirmative action pursuant to section 503 of the Act, the recipient may invite applicants for employment to indicate whether and to what extent they are handicapped, *Provided,* That:

(1) The recipient states clearly on any written questionnaire used for this purpose or makes clear orally if no written questionnaire is used that the information requested is intended for use solely in connection with its remedial action obligations or its voluntary or affirmative action efforts; and

(2) The recipient states clearly that the information is being requested on a voluntary basis, that it will be kept confidential as provided in paragraph

(d) of this section, that refusal to provide it will not subject the applicant or employee to any adverse treatment, and that it will be used only in accordance with this part.

(c) Nothing in this section shall prohibit a recipient from conditioning an offer of employment on the results of a medical examination conducted prior to the employee's entrance on duty, *Provided*, That: (1) All entering employees are subjected to such an examination regardless of handicap, and (2) the results of such an examination are used only in accordance with the requirements of this part.

(d) Information obtained in accordance with this section as to the medical condition or history of the applicant shall be collected and maintained on separate forms that shall be accorded confidentiality as medical records, except that:

(1) Supervisors and managers may be informed regarding restrictions on the work or duties of handicapped persons and regarding necessary accommodations;

(2) First aid and safety personnel may be informed, where appropriate, if the condition might require emergency treatment; and

(3) Government officials investigating compliance with the Act shall be provided relevant information upon request.

Subpart C—Program Accessibility

§ 104.21 Discrimination prohibited.

No qualified handicapped person shall, because a recipient's facilities are inaccessible to or unusable by handicapped persons, be denied the benefits of, be excluded from participation in, or otherwise be subjected to discrimination under any program or activity to which this part applies.

§ 104.22 Existing facilities.

(a) *Program accessibility.* A recipient shall operate each program or activity to which this part applies so that the program or activity, when viewed in its entirety, is readily accessible to handicapped persons. This paragraph does not require a recipient to make each of its existing facilities or every part of a facility accessible to and usable by handicapped persons.

(b) *Methods.* A recipient may comply with the requirements of paragraph (a) of this section through such means as redesign of equipment, reassignment of classes or other services to accessible buildings, assignment of aides to beneficiaries, home visits, delivery of health, welfare, or other social services at alternate accessible sites, alteration of existing facilities and construction of new facilities in conformance with the requirements of § 104.23, or any other methods that result in making its program or activity accessible to handicapped persons. A recipient is not required to make structural changes in existing facilities where other methods are effective in achieving compliance with paragraph (a) of this section. In choosing among available methods for meeting the requirement of paragraph (a) of this section, a recipient shall give priority to those methods that offer programs and activities to handicapped persons in the most integrated setting appropriate.

(c) *Small health, welfare, or other social service providers.* If a recipient with fewer than fifteen employees that provides health, welfare, or other social services finds, after consultation with a handicapped person seeking its services, that there is no method of complying with paragraph (a) of this section other than making a significant alteration in its existing facilities, the recipient may, as an alternative, refer the handicapped person to other providers of those services that are accessible.

(d) *Time period.* A recipient shall comply with the requirement of paragraph (a) of this section within sixty days of the effective date of this part except that where structural changes in facilities are necessary, such changes shall be made within three years of the effective date of this part, but in any event as expeditiously as possible.

(e) *Transition plan.* In the event that structural changes to facilities are necessary to meet the requirement of paragraph (a) of this section, a recipient shall develop, within six months of the effective date of this part, a transition plan setting forth the steps necessary to complete such changes. The plan shall be developed with the assistance of interested persons, including handicapped persons or organizations representing handicapped persons. A copy of the transition plan shall be made available for public inspection. The plan shall, at a minimum:

(1) Identify physical obstacles in the recipient's facilities that limit the accessibility of its program or activity to handicappped persons;

(2) Describe in detail the methods that will be used to make the facilities accessible;

(3) Specify the schedule for taking the steps necessary to achieve full program accessibility and, if the time period of the transition plan is longer than one year, identify the steps of that will be taken during each year of the transition period; and

(4) Indicate the person responsible for implementation of the plan.

(f) *Notice.* The recipient shall adopt and implement procedures to ensure that interested persons, including persons with impaired vision or hearing, can obtain information as to the existence and location of services, activities, and facilities that are accessible to and usuable by handicapped persons.

§ 104.23 New construction.

(a) *Design and construction.* Each facility or part of a facility constructed by, on behalf of, or for the use of a recipient shall be designed and constructed in such manner that the facility or part of the facility is readily accessible to and usable by handicapped persons, if the construction was commenced after the effective date of this part.

(b) *Alteration.* Each facility or part of a facility which is altered by, on behalf of, or for the use of a recipient after the effective date of this part in a manner that affects or could affect the usability of the facility or part of the facility shall, to the maximum extent feasible, be altered in such manner that the altered portion of the facility is readily accessible to and usable by handicapped persons.

(c) *American National Standards Institute accessibility standards.* Design, construction, or alteration of facilities in conformance with the "American National Standard Specifications for Making Buildings and Facilities Accessible to, and Usable by, the Physically Handicapped," published by the American National Standards Institute, Inc. (ANSI A117.1-1961 (R1971)), which is incorporated by reference in this part, shall constitute compliance with paragraphs (a) and (b) of this section. Departures from particular requirements of those standards by the use of other methods shall be permitted when it is clearly evident that equivalent access to the facility or part of the facility is thereby provided. Incorporation by reference provisions approved by the Director of the Federal Register, May 27, 1975. Incorporated documents are on file at the Office of the Federal Register. Copies of the standards are obtainable from American National Standards Institute, Inc., 1430 Broadway, New York, N.Y. 10018.

[45 FR 30936, May 9, 1980; 45 FR 37426, June 3, 1980]

Subpart D—Preschool, Elementary, and Secondary Education

§ 104.31 Application of this subpart.

Subpart D applies to preschool, elementary, secondary, and adult education programs and activities that receive or benefit from Federal financial assistance and to recipients that operate, or that receive or benefit from Federal financial assistance for the operation of, such programs or activities.

§ 104.32 Location and notification.

A recipient that operates a public elementary or secondary education program shall annually:

(a) Undertake to identify and locate every qualified handicapped person residing in the recipient's jurisdiction who is not receiving a public education; and

(b) Take appropriate steps to notify handicapped persons and their parents or guardians of the recipient's duty under this subpart.

§ 104.33 Free appropriate public education.

(a) *General.* A recipient that operates a public elementary or secondary education program shall provide a free appropriate public education to each qualified handicapped person who is in the recipient's jurisdiction, regardless of the nature or severity of the person's handicap.

(b) *Appropriate education.* (1) For the purpose of this subpart, the provision of an appropriate education is the provision of regular or special education and related aids and services that (i) are designed to meet individual educational needs of handicapped persons as adequately as the needs of nonhandicapped persons are met and (ii) are based upon adherence to procedures that satisfy the requirements of §§ 104.34, 104.35, and 104.36.

(2) Implementation of an individualized education program developed in accordance with the Education of the Handicapped Act is one means of meeting the standard established in paragraph (b)(1)(i) of this section.

(3) A recipient may place a handicapped person in or refer such person to a program other than the one that it operates as its means of carrying out the requirements of this subpart. If so, the recipient remains responsible for ensuring that the requirements of this subpart are met with respect to any handicapped person so placed or referred.

(c) *Free education*—(1) *General.* For the purpose of this section, the provision of a free education is the provision of educational and related services without cost to the handicapped person or to his or her parents or guardian, except for those fees that are imposed on non-handicapped persons or their parents or guardian. It may consist either of the provision of free services or, if a recipient places a handicapped person in or refers such person to a program not operated by the recipient as its means of carrying out the requirements of this subpart, of payment for the costs of the program. Funds available from any public or private agency may be used to meet the requirements of this subpart. Nothing in this section shall be construed to relieve an insurer or similar third party from an otherwise valid obligation to provide or pay for services provided to a handicapped person.

(2) *Transportation.* If a recipient places a handicapped person in or refers such person to a program not operated by the recipient as its means of carrying out the requirements of this subpart, the recipient shall ensure that adequate transportation to and from the program is provided at no greater cost than would be incurred by the person or his or her parents or guardian if the person were placed in the program operated by the recipient.

(3) *Residential placement.* If placement in a public or private residential program is necessary to provide a free appropriate public education to a handicapped person because of his or her handicap, the program, including non-medical care and room and board, shall be provided at no cost to the person or his or her parents or guardian.

(4) *Placement of handicapped persons by parents.* If a recipient has made available, in conformance with the requirements of this section and § 104.34, a free appropriate public education to a handicapped person and the person's parents or guardian choose to place the person in a private school, the recipient is not required to pay for the person's education in the private school. Disagreements between a parent or guardian and a recipient regarding whether the recipient has made such a program available or otherwise regarding the question of financial responsibility are subject to the due process procedures of § 104.36.

(d) *Compliance.* A recipient may not exclude any qualified handicapped person from a public elementary or secondary education after the effective date of this part. A recipient that is not, on the effective date of this regulation, in full compliance with the other requirements of the preceding paragraphs of this section shall meet such requirements at the earliest practicable time and in no event later than September 1, 1978.

§ 104.34 Educational setting.

(a) *Academic setting.* A recipient to which this subpart applies shall educate, or shall provide for the education of, each qualified handicapped person in its jurisdiction with persons who are not handicapped to the maximum extent appropriate to the needs of the handicapped person. A recipient shall place a handicapped person in the regular educational environment operated by the recipient unless it is demonstrated by the recipient that the education of the person in the regular environment with the use of supplementary aids and services cannot be achieved satisfactorily. Whenever a recipient places a person in a setting other than the regular educational environment pursuant to this paragraph, it shall take into account the proximity of the alternate setting to the person's home.

(b) *Nonacademic settings.* In providing or arranging for the provision of nonacademic and extracurricular services and activities, including meals, recess periods, and the services and activities set forth in § 104.37(a)(2), a recipient shall ensure that handicapped persons participate with nonhandicapped persons in such activities and services to the maximum extent appropriate to the needs of the handicapped person in question.

(c) *Comparable facilities.* If a recipient, in compliance with paragraph (a) of this section, operates a facility that is identifiable as being for handicapped persons, the recipient shall ensure that the facility and the services and activities provided therein are comparable to the other facilities, services, and activities of the recipient.

§ 104.35 Evaluation and placement.

(a) *Preplacement evaluation.* A recipient that operates a public elementary or secondary education program shall conduct an evaluation in accordance with the requirements of paragraph (b) of this section of any person who, because of handicap, needs or is belived to need special education or related services before taking any action with respect to the initial placement of the person in a regular or special education program and any subsequent significant change in placement.

(b) *Evaluation procedures.* A recipient to which this subpart applies shall establish standards and procedures for the evaluation and placement of persons who, because of handicap, need or are believed to need special education or related services which ensure that:

(1) Tests and other evaluation materials have been validated for the specific purpose for which they are used and are administered by trained personnel in conformance with the instructions provided by their producer;

(2) Tests and other evaluation materials include those tailored to assess specific areas of educational need and not merely those which are designed to provide a single general intelligence quotient; and

(3) Tests are selected and administered so as best to ensure that, when a test is administered to a student with impaired sensory, manual, or speaking skills, the test results accurately reflect the student's aptitude or achievement level or whatever other factor the test purports to measure, rather than reflecting the student's impaired sensory, manual, or speaking skills (except where those skills are the factors that the test purports to measure).

(c) *Placement procedures.* In interpreting evaluation data and in making placement decisions, a recipient shall (1) draw upon information from a variety of sources, including aptitude and achievement tests, teacher recommendations, physical condition, social or cultural background, and adaptive behavior, (2) establish procedures to ensure that information obtained from all such sources is documented and carefully considered, (3) ensure that the placement decision is made by a group of persons, including persons knowledgeable about the child, the meaning of the evaluation data, and the placement options, and (4) ensure that the placement decision is made in conformity with § 104.34.

(d) *Reevaluation.* A recipient to which this section applies shall establish procedures, in accordance with paragraph (b) of this section, for periodic reevaluation of students who have been provided special education and related services. A reevaluation procedure consistent with the Education for the Handicapped Act is one means of meeting this requirement.

§ 104.36 Procedural safeguards.

A recipient that operates a public elementary or secondary education program shall establish and implement, with respect to actions regarding the identification, evaluation, or educational placement of persons who, because of handicap, need or are believed to need special instruction or related services, a system of procedural safeguards that includes notice, an opportunity for the parents or guardian of the person to examine relevant records, an impartial hearing with opportunity for participation by the person's parents or guardian and representation by counsel, and a review procedure. Compliance with the procedural safeguards of section 615 of the Education of the Handicapped Act is one means of meeting this requirement.

§ 104.37 Nonacademic services.

(a) *General.* (1) A recipient to which this subpart applies shall provide nonacademic and extracurricular services and activities in such manner as is necessary to afford handicapped students an equal opportunity for participation in such services and activities.

(2) Nonacademic and extracurricular services and activities may include counseling services, physical recreational athletics, transportation, health services, recreational activities, special interest groups or clubs sponsored by the recipients, referrals to agencies which provide assistance to handicapped persons, and employment of students, including both employment by the recipient and assistance in making available outside employment.

(b) *Counseling services.* A recipient to which this subpart applies that provides personal, academic, or vocational counseling, guidance, or placement services to its students shall provide these services without discrimination on the basis of handicap. The recipient shall ensure that qualified handicapped students are not counseled toward more restrictive career objectives than are nonhandicapped students with similar interests and abilities.

(c) *Physical education and athletics.* (1) In providing physical education courses and athletics and similar programs and activities to any of its students, a recipient to which this subpart applies may not discriminate on the basis of handicap. A recipient that offers physical education courses or that operates or sponsors interscholastic, club, or intramural athletics shall provide to qualified handicapped students an equal opportunity for participation in these activities.

(2) A recipient may offer to handicapped students physical education and athletic activities that are separate or different from those offered to nonhandicapped students only if separation or differentiation is consistent with the requirements of § 104.34 and only if no qualified handicapped student is denied the opportunity to compete for teams or to participate in courses that are not separate or different.

§ 104.38 Preschool and adult education programs.

A recipient to which this subpart applies that operates a preschool education or day care program or activity or an adult education program or activity may not, on the basis of handicap, exclude qualified handicapped persons from the program or activity and shall take into account the needs of such persons in determining the aid, benefits, or services to be provided under the program or activity.

§ 104.39 Private education programs.

(a) A recipient that operates a private elementary or secondary education program may not, on the basis of handicap, exclude a qualified handicapped person from such program if the person can, with minor adjustments, be provided an appropriate education, as defined in § 104.33(b)(1), within the recipient's program.

(b) A recipient to which this section applies may not charge more for the provision of an appropriate education to handicapped persons than to nonhandicapped persons except to the extent that any additional charge is justified by a substantial increase in cost to the recipient.

(c) A recipient to which this section applies that operates special education programs shall operate such programs in accordance with the provisions of §§ 104.35 and 104.36. Each recipient to which this section applies is subject to the provisions of §§ 104.34, 104.37, and 104.38.

Subpart E—Postsecondary Education

§ 104.41 Application of this subpart.

Subpart E applies to postsecondary education programs and activities, including postsecondary vocational education programs and activities, that receive or benefit from Federal financial assistance and to recipients that operate, or that receive or benefit from Federal financial assistance for the operation of, such programs or activities.

§ 104.42 Admissions and recruitment.

(a) *General.* Qualified handicapped persons may not, on the basis of handicap, be denied admission or be subjected to discrimination in admission or recruitment by a recipient to which this subpart applies.

(b) *Admissions.* In administering its admission policies, a recipient to which this subpart applies:

(1) May not apply limitations upon the number or proportion of handicapped persons who may be admitted;

(2) May not make use of any test or criterion for admission that has a disproportionate, adverse effect on handicapped persons or any class of handicapped persons unless (i) the test or criterion, as used by the recipient, has been validated as a predictor of success in the education program or activity in question and (ii) alternate tests or criteria that have a less disproportionate, adverse effect are not shown by the Assistant Secretary to be available.

(3) Shall assure itself that (i) admissions tests are selected and administered so as best to ensure that, when a test is administered to an applicant who has a handicap that impairs sensory, manual, or speaking skills, the test results accurately reflect the applicant's aptitude or achievement level or whatever other factor the test purports to measure, rather than reflecting the applicant's impaired sensory, manual, or speaking skills (except where those skills are the factors that the test purports to measure); (ii) admissions tests that are designed for persons with impaired sensory, manual, or speaking skills are offered as often and in as timely a manner as are other admissions tests; and (iii) admissions tests are administered in facilities that, on the whole, are accessible to handicapped persons; and

(4) Except as provided in paragraph (c) of this section, may not make preadmission inquiry as to whether an applicant for admission is a handicapped person but, after admission, may make inquiries on a confidential basis as to handicaps that may require accommodation.

(c) *Preadmission inquiry exception.* When a recipient is taking remedial action to correct the effects of past discrimination pursuant to § 104.6(a) or when a recipient is taking voluntary action to overcome the effects of conditions that resulted in limited participation in its federally assisted program or activity pursuant to § 104.6(b), the recipient may invite applicants for admission to indicate whether and to what extent they are handicapped, *Provided,* That:

(1) The recipient states clearly on any written questionnaire used for this purpose or makes clear orally if no written questionnaire is used that the information requested is intended for use solely in connection with its remedial action obligations or its voluntary action efforts; and

(2) The recipient states clearly that the information is being requested on a voluntary basis, that it will be kept confidential, that refusal to provide it will not subject the applicant to any adverse treatment, and that it will be used only in accordance with this part.

(d) *Validity studies.* For the purpose of paragraph (b)(2) of this section, a recipient may base prediction equations on first year grades, but shall conduct periodic validity studies against the criterion of overall success in the education program or activity in question in order to monitor the general validity of the test scores.

§ 104.43 Treatment of students; general.

(a) No qualified handicapped student shall, on the basis of handicap, be excluded from participation in, be denied the benefits of, or otherwise be subjected to discrimination under any academic, research, occupational training, housing, health insurance, counseling, financial aid, physical education, athletics, recreation, transportation, other extracurricular, or other postsecondary education program or activity to which this subpart applies.

(b) A recipient to which this subpart applies that considers participation by students in education programs or activities not operated wholly by the recipient as part of, or equivalent to, and education program or activity operated by the recipient shall assure itself that the other education program or activity, as a whole, provides an equal opportunity for the participation of qualified handicapped persons.

(c) A recipient to which this subpart applies may not, on the basis of handicap, exclude any qualified handicapped student from any course, course of study, or other part of its education program or activity.

(d) A recipient to which this subpart applies shall operate its programs and activities in the most integrated setting appropriate.

§ 104.44 Academic adjustments.

(a) *Academic requirements.* A recipient to which this subpart applies shall make such modifications to its academic requirements as are necessary to ensure that such requirements do not discriminate or have the effect of discriminating, on the basis of handicap, against a qualified handicapped applicant or student. Academic requirements that the recipient can demonstrate are essential to the program of instruction being pursued by such student or to any directly related licensing requirement will not be regarded as discriminatory within the meaning of this section. Modifications may include changes in the length of time permitted for the completion of degree requirements, substitution of specific courses required for the completion of degree requirements, and adaptation of the manner in which specific courses are conducted.

(b) *Other rules.* A recipient to which this subpart applies may not impose upon handicapped students other rules, such as the prohibition of tape recorders in classrooms or of dog guides in campus buildings, that have the effect of limiting the participation of handicapped students in the recipient's education program or activity.

(c) *Course examinations.* In its course examinations or other procedures for evaluating students' academic achievement in its program, a recipient to which this subpart applies shall provide such methods for evaluating the achievement of students who have a handicap that impairs sensory, manual, or speaking skills as will best ensure that the results of the evaluation represents the student's achievement in the course, rather than reflecting the student's impaired sensory, manual, or speaking skills (except where such skills are the factors that the test purports to measure).

(d) *Auxiliary aids.* (1) A recipient to which this subpart applies shall take such steps as are necessary to ensure that no handicapped student is denied the benefits of, excluded from participation in, or otherwise subjected to discrimination under the education program or activity operated by the recipient because of the absence of educational auxiliary aids for students with impaired sensory, manual, or speaking skills.

(2) Auxiliary aids may include taped texts, interpreters or other effective methods of making orally delivered materials available to students with hearing impairments, readers in libraries for students with visual impairments, classroom equipment adapted for use by students with manual impairments, and other similar services and actions. Recipients need not provide attendants, individually prescribed devices, readers for personal use or study, or other devices or services of a personal nature.

§ 104.45 Housing.

(a) *Housing provided by the recipient.* A recipient that provides housing to its nonhandicapped students shall provide comparable, convenient, and accessible housing to handicapped students at the same cost as to others. At the end of the transition period provided for in Subpart C, such housing shall be available in sufficient quantity and variety so that the scope of handicapped students' choice of living accommodations is, as a whole, comparable to that of nonhandicapped students.

(b) *Other housing.* A recipient that assists any agency, organization, or person in making housing available to any of its students shall take such action as may be necessary to assure itself that such housing is, as a whole, made available in a manner that does not result in discrimination on the basis of handicap.

§ 104.46 Financial and employment assistance to students.

(a) *Provision of financial assistance.* (1) In providing financial assistance to qualified handicapped persons, a recipient to which this subpart applies may not (i), on the basis of handicap, provide less assistance than is provided to nonhandicapped persons, limit eligibility for assistance, or otherwise discriminate or (ii) assist any entity or person that provides assistance to any of the recipient's students in a manner that discriminates against qualified handicapped persons on the basis of handicap.

(2) A recipient may administer or assist in the administration of scholarships, fellowships, or other forms of financial assistance established under wills, trusts, bequests, or similar legal instruments that require awards to be made on the basis of factors that discriminate or have the effect of discriminating on the basis of handicap only if the overall effect of the award of scholarships, fellowships, and other forms of financial assistance is not discriminatory on the basis of handicap.

(b) *Assistance in making available outside employment.* A recipient that assists any agency, organization, or person in providing employment opportunities to any of its students shall assure itself that such employment opportunities, as a whole, are made available in a manner that would not violate Subpart B if they were provided by the recipient.

(c) *Employment of students by recipients.* A recipient that employs any of its students may not do so in a manner that violates Subpart B.

§ 104.47 Nonacademic services.

(a) *Physical education and athletics.* (1) In providing physical education courses and athletics and similar programs and activities to any of its students, a recipient to which this subpart applies may not disacriminate on the basis of handicap. A recipient that offers physical education courses or that operates or sponsors intercollegiate, club, or intramural athletics shall provide to qualified handicapped students an equal opportunity for participation in these activities.

(2) A recipient may offer to handicapped students physical education and athletic activities that are separate or different only if separation or differentiation is consistent with the requirements of § 104.43(d) and only if no qualified handicapped student is denied the opportunity to compete for teams or to participate in courses that are not separate or different.

(b) *Counseling and placement services.* A recipient to which this subpart applies that provides personal, academic, or vocational counseling, guidance, or placement services to its students shall provide these services without discrimination on the basis of handicap. The recipient shall ensure that qualified handicapped students are not counseled toward more restrictive career objectives than are nonhandicapped students with similar interests and abilities. This requirement does not preclude a recipient from providing factual information about licensing and certification requirements that may present obstacles to handicapped persons in their pursuit of particular careers.

(c) *Social organizations.* A recipient that provides significant assistance to fraternities, sororities, or similar organizations shall assure itself that the membership practices of such organizations do not permit discrimination otherwise prohibited by this subpart.

Subpart F—Health, Welfare, and Social Services

§ 104.51 Application of this subpart.

Subpart F applies to health, welfare, and other social service programs and activities that receive or benefit from Federal financial assistance and to recipients that operate, or that receive or benefit from Federal financial assistance for the operation of, such programs or activities.

§ 104.52 Health, welfare, and other social services.

(a) *General.* In providing health, welfare, or other social services or benefits, a recipient may not, on the basis of handicap:

(1) Deny a qualified handicapped person these benefits or services;

(2) Afford a qualified handicapped person an opportunity to receive benefits or services that is not equal to that offered nonhandicapped persons;

(3) Provide a qualified handicapped person with benefits or services that are not as effective (as defined in § 104.4(b)) as the benefits or services provided to others;

(4) Provide benefits or services in a manner that limits or has the effect of limiting the participation of qualified handicapped persons; or

(5) Provide different or separate benefits or services to handicapped persons except where necessary to provide qualified handicapped persons with benefits and services that are as effective as those provided to others.

(b) *Notice.* A recipient that provides notice concerning benefits or services or written material concerning waivers of rights or consent to treatment shall take such steps as are necessary to ensure that qualified handicapped persons, including those with impaired sensory or speaking skills, are not denied effective notice because of their handicap.

(c) *Emergency treatment for the hearing impaired.* A recipient hospital that provides health services or benefits shall establish a procedure for effective communication with persons with impaired hearing for the purpose of providing emergency health care.

(d) *Auxiliary aids.* (1) A recipient to which this subpart applies that employs fifteen or more persons shall provide appropriate auxiliary aids to persons with impaired sensory, manual, or speaking skills, where necessary to afford such persons an equal opportunity to benefit from the service in question.

(2) The Assistant Secretary may require recipients with fewer than fifteen employees to provide auxiliary aids where the provision of aids would not significantly impair the ability of the recipient to provide its benefits or services.

(3) For the purpose of this paragraph, auxiliary aids may include brailled and taped material, interpreters, and other aids for persons with impaired hearing or vision.

§ 104.53 Drug and alcohol addicts.

A recipient to which this subpart applies that operates a general hospital or outpatient facility may not discriminate in admission or treatment against a drug or alcohol abuser or alcoholic who is suffering from a medical condition, because of the person's drug or alcohol abuse or alcoholism.

§ 104.54 Education of institutionalized persons.

A recipient to which this subpart applies and that operates or supervises a program or activity for persons who are institutionalized because of handicap shall ensure that each qualified handicapped person, as defined in § 104.3(k)(2), in its program or activity is provided an appropriate education, as defined in § 104.33(b). Nothing in this section shall be interpreted as altering in any way the obligations of recipients under Subpart D.

Subpart G—Procedures

§ 104.61 Procedures.

The procedural provisions applicable to title VI of the Civil Rights Act of 1964 apply to this part. These procedures are found in §§ 100.6–100.10 and Part 101 of this title.

APPENDIX C

U.S. SUPREME COURT CASES

*It should be noted that the Handicapped Children's Protection Act of 1986 overturned much of this decision. See chapters one and four; see also Appendix A, § 1415(e)(4) and § 1415(f).

Board of Education v. Rowley

U.S. Supreme Court, 458 U.S. 176, 102 S.Ct. 3034 (1982).

Syllabus*

The Education for All Handicapped Children Act of 1975 (Act) provides federal money to assist state and local agencies in educating handicapped children. To qualify for federal assistance, a State must demonstrate (through a detailed plan submitted for federal approval) that it has in effect a policy that assures all handicapped children the right to a "free appropriate public education," which must be tailored to the unique needs of the handicapped child by means of an "individualized educational program" (IEP). The IEP must be prepared (and reviewed at least annually) by school officials with participation by the child's parents or guardian. The Act also requires that a participating State provide specified administrative procedures by which the child's parents or guardian may challenge any change in the evaluation and education of the child. Any party aggrieved by the state administrative decisions is authorized to bring a civil action in either a state court or a federal district court. Respondents—a child with only minimal residual hearing who had been furnished by school authorities with a special hearing aid for use in the classroom and who was to receive additional instruction from tutors, and the child's parents—filed suit in Federal District Court to review New York administrative proceedings that had upheld the school administrators' denial of the parents' request that the child also be provided a qualified sign-language interpreter in all of her academic classes. Entering judgment for respondents, the District Court found that although the child performed better than the average child in her class and was advancing easily from grade to grade, she was not performing as well academically as she would without her handicap. Because of this disparity between the child's achievement and her potential, the court held that she was not receiving a "free appropriate public education," which the court defined as "an opportunity to achieve [her] full potential commensurate with the opportunity provided to other children." The Court of Appeals affirmed.

Held:

1. The Act's requirement of a "free appropriate public education" is satisfied when the State provides personalized instruction with sufficient support services to permit the handicapped child to benefit educationally from that instruction. Such instruction and services must be provided at public expense, must meet the State's educational standards, must approximate grade levels used in the State's regular education, and must comport with the child's IEP, as formulated in accordance with the Act's requirements. If the child is being educated in regular classrooms, as here, the IEP should be reasonably calculated to enable the child to achieve passing marks and advance from grade to grade.

(a) This interpretation is supported by the definitions contained in the Act, as well as by other provisions imposing procedural requirements and setting forth statutory findings and priorities for States to follow in extending educational services to handicapped children. The Act's language contains no express substantive standard prescribing the level of education to be accorded handicapped children.

*The syllabus constitutes no part of the opinion of the Court but has been prepared by the Reporter of Decisions for the convenience of the reader.

(b) The Act's legislative history shows that Congress sought to make public education available to handicapped children, but did not intend to impose upon the States any greater substantive educational standard than is necessary to make such access to public education meaningful. The Act's intent was more to open the door of public education to handicapped children by means of specialized educational services than to guarantee any particular substantive level of education once inside.

(c) While Congress sought to provide assistance to the States in carrying out their constitutional responsibilities to provide equal protection of the laws, it did not intend to achieve strict equality of opportunity or services for handicapped and nonhandicapped children, but rather sought primarily to identify and evaluate handicapped children, and to provide them with access to a free public education. The Act does not require a State to maximize the potential of each handicapped child commensurate with the opportunity provided nonhandicapped children.

2. In suits brought under the Act's judicial-review provisions, a court must first determine whether the State has complied with the statutory procedures, and must then determine whether the individualized program developed through such procedures is reasonably calculated to enable the child to receive educational benefits. If these requirements are met, the State has complied with the obligations imposed by Congress and the courts can require no more.

(a) Although the judicial-review provisions do not limit courts to ensuring that States have complied with the Act's procedural requirements, the Act's emphasis on procedural safeguards demonstrates the legislative conviction that adequate compliance with prescribed procedures will in most cases assure much, if not all, of what Congress wished in the way of substantive content in an IEP.

(b) The courts must be careful to avoid imposing their view of preferable educational methods upon the States. Once a court determines that the Act's requirements have been met, questions of methodology are for resolution by the States.

3. Entrusting a child's education to state and local agencies does not leave the child without protection. As demonstrated by this case, parents and guardians will not lack ardor in seeking to ensure that handicapped children receive all of the benefits to which they are entitled by the Act.

4. The Act does not require the provision of a sign-language interpreter here. Neither of the courts below found that there had been a failure to comply with the Act's procedures, and the findings of neither court will support a conclusion that the child's educational program failed to comply with the substantive requirements of the Act.

632 F. 2d 945, reversed and remanded.

REHNQUIST, J., delivered the opinion of the Court, in which BURGER, C.J., and POWELL, STEVENS, and O'CONNOR, JJ., joined. BLACKMUN, J., filed an opinion concurring in the judgment. WHITE, J., filed a dissenting opinion, in which BRENNAN and MARSHALL, JJ., joined.

JUSTICE REHNQUIST delivered the opinion of the Court.

This case presents a question of statutory interpretation. Petitioners contend that the Court of Appeals and the District Court misconstrued the requirements imposed by Congress upon States which receive federal funds under the Education for All Handicapped Children Act. We agree and reverse the judgement of the Court of Appeals.

I

The Education for All Handicapped Children Act of 1975 (Act), 20 U.S.C. § 1401 *et seq.,* provides federal money to assist state and local agencies in educating handicapped children, and conditions such funding upon a State's compliance with extensive goals and procedures. The Act represents an ambitious federal effort to promote the education of handicapped children, and was passed in response to Congress' perception that a majority of handicapped children in the United States "were either totally excluded from schools or [were] sitting idly in regular classrooms awaiting the time when they were old enough to 'drop out.' " H.R. Rep. No. 94-332, p. 2 (1975). The Act's evolution and major provisions shed light on the question of statutory interpretation which is at the heart of this case.

Congress first addressed the problem of educating the handicapped in 1966 when it amended the Elementary and Secondary Education Act of 1965 to establish a grant program "for the purpose of assisting the States in the initiation, expansion, and improvement of programs and projects . . . for the education of handicapped children." Pub. L. No. 89-750, § 161, 80 Stat. 1204 (1966). That program was repealed in 1970 by the Education for the Handicapped Act, Pub. L No. 91-230, 84 Stat. 175, Part B of which established a grant program similar in purpose to the repealed legislation. Neither the 1966 nor the 1970 legislation contained specific guidelines for state use of the grant money; both were aimed primarily at stimulating the States to develop educational resources and to train personnel for educating the handicapped.[1]

Dissatisfied with the progress being made under these earlier enactments, and spurred by two district court decisions holding that handicapped children should be given access to a public education,[2] Congress in 1974 greatly increased federal funding for education of the handicapped and for the first time required recipient States to adopt "a goal of providing full educational opportunities to all handicapped children." Pub. L. 93-380, 88 Stat. 579, 583 (1974) (the 1974 statute).

The 1974 statute was recognized as an interim measure only, adopted "in order to give the Congress an additional year in which to study what if any additional Federal assistance [was] required to enable the States to meet the needs of handicapped children." H.R. Rep. No. 94-332, *supra,* p. 4. The ensuing year of study produced the Education for All Handicapped Children Act of 1975.

In order to qualify for federal financial assistance under the Act, a State must demonstrate that it "has in effect a policy that assures all handicapped children the right to a free appropriate public education." 20 U. S. C. § 1412(1). That policy must be reflected in a state plan submitted to and

---

[1]See S. Rep. No. 94-168, p. 5 (1975); H.R. Rep. No. 94-332, pp. 2-3 (1975).

[2]Two cases, *Mills v. Board of Education of the District of Columbia,* 348 F. Supp. 866 (DC 1972), and *Pennsylvania Association for Retarded Children v. Commonwealth of Pennsylvania,* 334 F. Supp. 1257 (1971); 343 F. Supp. 279 (ED Pa 1972), were later identified as the most prominent of the cases contributing to Congress' enactment of the Act and the statutes which preceded it. H.R. Rep. No. 94-332, *supra,* at 3-4. Both decisions are discussed in Part III of this opinion, *infra.*

approved by the Commissioner of Education,[3] § 1413, which describes in detail the goals, programs, and timetables under which the State intends to educate handicapped children within its borders. §§ 1412, 1413. States receiving money under the Act must provide education to the handicapped by priority, first "to handicapped children who are not receiving an education" and second "to handicapped children . . . with the most severe handicaps who are receiving an inadequate education," § 1412(3), and "to the maximum extent appropriate" must educate handicapped children "with children who are not handicapped." § 1412(5).[4] The Act broadly defines "handicapped children" to include "mentally retarded, hard of hearing, deaf, speech impaired, visually handicapped, seriously emotionally disturbed, orthopedically impaired, [and] other health impaired children, [and] children with specific learning disabilities." § 1401(1).[5]

The "free appropriate public education" required by the Act is tailored to the unique needs of the handicapped child by means of an "individualized educational program" (IEP) § 1401(18). The IEP, which is prepared at a meeting between a qualified representative of the local educational agency, the child's teacher, the child's parents or guardian, and, where appropriate, the child, consists of a written document containing

> "(A) a statement of the present levels of educational performance of the child, (B) a statement of annual goals, including short-term instructional objectives, (C) a statement of the specific educational services to be provided to such child, and the extent to which such child will be able to participate in regular educational programs, (D) the projected date for initiation and anticipated duration of such service, and (E) appropriate objective criteria and evaluation procedures and schedules for determining, on at least an annual basis, whether instructional objectives are being achieved." § 1401(19).

Local or regional educational agencies must review, and where appropriate revise, each child's IEP at least annually. § 1404(a)(5). See also §§ 1413(a)(11), 1414(a)(5).

In addition to the state plan and the IEP already described, the Act imposes extensive procedural requirements upon States receiving federal funds under its provisions. Parents or guardians of handicapped children

---

[3]All functions of the Commissioner of Education, formerly an officer in the Department of Health, Education, and Welfare, were transferred to the Secretary of Education in 1979 when Congress passed the Department of Education Organization Act, 20 U. S. C. § 3401 *et seq.* See 20 U. S. C. § 3441(a)(1).

[4]Despite this preference for "mainstreaming" handicapped children—educating them with nonhandicapped children—Congress recognized that regular classrooms simply would not be a suitable setting for the education of many handicapped children. The Act expressly acknowledges that "the nature or severity of the handicap [may be] such that education in regular classes with the use of supplementary aids and services cannot be achieved satisfactorily." § 1412(5). The Act thus provides for the education of some handicapped children in separate classes or institutional settings. See *ibid.;* § 1413(a)(4).

[5]In addition to covering a wide variety of handicapping conditions, the Act requires special educational services for children "regardless of the severity of their handicap." §§ 1412(2)(C), 1414(a)(1)(A).

must be notified of any proposed change in "the identification, evaluation, or educational placement of the child or the provision of a free appropriate public education to the child," and must be permitted to bring a complaint about "any matter relating to" such evaluation and education. § 1415(b)(1)(D) and (E).[6] Complaints brought by parents or guardians must be resolved at "an impartial due process hearing," and appeal to the State educational agency must be provided if the initial hearing is held at the local or regional level. § 1415(b)(2) and (c).[7]

Thereafter, "[a]ny party aggrieved by the findings and decisions" of the state administrative hearing has "the right to bring a civil action with respect to the complaint . . . in any State court of competent jurisdiction or in a district court of the United States without regard to the amount in controversy." § 1415(e)(2).

Thus, although the Act leaves to the States the primary responsibility for developing and executing educational programs for handicapped children, it imposes significant requirements to be followed in the discharge of that responsibility. Compliance is assured by provisions permitting the withholding of federal funds upon determination that a participating state or local agency has failed to satisfy the requirements of the Act, §§ 1414(b)(2)(A), 1416, and by the provision for judicial review. At present, all States except New Mexico receive federal funds under the portions of the Act at issue today. Brief for the United States as *Amicus Curiae* 2, n. 2.

II

This case arose in connection with the education of Amy Rowley, a deaf student at the Furnace Woods School in the Hendrick Hudson Central School District, Peekskill, New York. Amy has minimal residual hearing and is an excellent lipreader. During the year before she began attending Furnace

[6]The requirements that parents be permitted to file complaints regarding their child's education, and be present when the child's IEP is formulated, represent only two examples of Congress' effort to maximize parental involvement in the education of each handicapped child. In addition, the Act requires that parents be permitted "to examine all relevant records with respect to the identification, evaluation, and educational placement of the child, and . . . to obtain an independent educational evaluation of the child." § 1415(b)(1)(A). See also §§ 1412(4), 1414(a)(4). State educational policies and the state plan submitted to the Commissioner of Education must be formulated in "consultation with individuals involved in or concerned with the education of handicapped children, including handicapped individuals and parents or guardians of handicapped children." § 1412(7). See also § 1412(2)(E). Local agencies, which receive funds under the Act by applying to the state agency, must submit applications which assure that they have developed procedures for "the participation and consultation of the parents or guardian[s] of [handicapped] children" in local educational programs, § 1414(a)(1)(C)(iii), and the application itself, along with "all pertinent documents related to such application," must be made "available to parents, guardians, and other members of the general public." § 1414(a)(4).

[7]"Any party" to a state or local administrative hearing must "be accorded (1) the right to be accompanied and advised by counsel and by individuals with special knowledge or training with respect to the problems of handicapped children, (2) the right to present evidence and confront, cross examine, and compel the attendance of witnesses, (3) the right to a written or electronic verbatim record of such hearing, and (4) the right to written findings of fact and decision." § 1415(d).

Woods, a meeting between her parents and school administrators resulted in a decision to place her in a regular kindergarten class in order to determine what supplemental services would be necessary to her education. Several members of the school administration prepared for Amy's arrival by attending a course in sign-language interpretation, and a teletype machine was installed in the principal's office to facilitate communication with her parents who are also deaf. At the end of the trial period it was determined that Amy should remain in the kindergarten class, but that she should be provided with an FM hearing aid which would amplify words spoken into a wireless receiver by the teacher or fellow students during certain classroom activities. Amy successfully completed her kindergarten year.

As required by the Act, an IEP was prepared for Amy during the fall of her first-grade year. The IEP provided that Amy should be educated in a regular classroom at Furnace Woods, should continue to use the FM hearing aid, and should receive instruction from a tutor for the deaf for one hour each day and from a speech therapist for three hours each week. The Rowleys agreed with the IEP but insisted that Amy also be provided a qualified sign-language interpreter in all of her academic classes. Such an interpreter had been placed in Amy's kindergarten class for a two-week experimental period, but the interpreter had reported that Amy did not need his services at that time. The school administrators likewise concluded that Amy did not need such an interpreter in her first-grade classroom. They reached this conclusion after consulting the school district's Committee on the Handicapped, which had received expert evidence from Amy's parents on the importance of a sign-language interpreter, received testimony from Amy's teacher and other persons familiar with her academic and social progress, and visited a class for the deaf.

When their request for an interpreter was denied, the Rowleys demanded and received a hearing before an independent examiner. After receiving evidence from both sides, the examiner agreed with the administrators' determination that an interpreter was not necessary because "Amy was achieving educationally, academically, and socially" without such assistance. App. to Pet. for Cert. F-22. The examiner's decision was affirmed on appeal by the New York Commissioner of Education on the basis of substantial evidence in the record. *Id.,* at E-4. Pursuant to the Act's provision for judicial review, the Rowleys then brought an action in the United States District Court for the Southern District of New York, claiming that the administrators' denial of the sign-language interpreter constituted a denial of the "free appropriate public education" guaranteed by the Act.

The District Court found that Amy "is a remarkably well-adjusted child" who interacts and communicates well with her classmates and has "developed an extraordinary rapport" with her teachers. 483 F. Supp. 528, 531. It also found that "she performs better than the average child in her class and is advancing easily from grade to grade," *id.* at 534, but "that she understands considerably less of what goes on in class than she would if she were not deaf" and thus "is not learning as much, or performing as well academically, as she would without her handicap," *id.,* at 532. This disparity between Amy's achievement and her potential led the court to decide that she was not receiving a "free appropriate public education," which the court defined as "an opportunity to achieve [her] full potential commensurate with the opportunity provided to other children." *Id.*, at 534. According to the

District Court, such a standard "requires that the potential of the handicapped child be measured and compared to his or her performance, and that the remaining differential or 'shortfall' be compared to the shortfall experienced by non-handicapped children." *Ibid.* The District Court's definition arose from its assumption that the responsibility for "giv[ing] content to the requirement of an 'appropriate education' " had "been left entirely to the federal courts and the hearing officers." *Id.,* at 533.[8]

A divided panel of the United States Court of Appeals for the Second Circuit affirmed. The Court of Appeals "agree[d] with the [D]istrict [C]ourt's conclusions of law," and held that its "findings of fact [were] not clearly erroneous." 632 F. 2d 945, 947 (1980).

We granted certiorari to review the lower courts' interpretation of the Act. 454 U.S. 961 (1981). Such review requires us to consider two questions: What is meant by the Act's requirement of a "free appropriate public education?" And what is the role of state and federal courts in exercising the review granted by § 1415 of the Act? We consider these questions separately.[9]

III

A

This is the first case in which this Court has been called upon to interpret any provision of the Act. As noted previously, the District Court and the Court of Appeals concluded that "[t]he Act itself does not define 'appropriate education,'" 483 F. Supp., at 533, but leaves "to the courts and the hearing officers" the responsibility of "giv[ing] content to the requirement of an appropriate education." *Ibid.* See also 632 F. 2d, at 947. Petitioners contend that the definition of the phrase "free appropriate public education" used by the courts below overlooks the definition of that phrase actually found in the Act. Respondents agree that the Act defines "free appropriate public education," but contend that the statutory definition is not "functional" and thus "offers judges no guidance in their consideration of controversies involving the 'identification, evaluation, or educational placement of

[8]For reasons that are not revealed in the record, the District Court concluded that "[t]he Act itself does not define 'appropriate education.'" 483 F. Supp., at 533. In fact, the Act expressly defines the phrase "free appropriate public education," see § 1401(18), to which the District Court was referring. See 483 F. Supp., at 533. After overlooking the statutory definition, the District Court sought guidance not from regulations interpreting the Act, but from regulations promulgated under Section 504 of the Rehabilitation Act. See 483 F. Supp., at 533, citing 45 CFR § 84.33(b).

[9]The IEP which respondents challenged in the District Court was created for the 1978-1979 school year. Petitioners contend that the District Court erred in reviewing that IEP after the school year had ended and before the school administrators were able to develop another IEP for subsequent years. We disagree. Judicial review invariably takes more than nine months to complete, not to mention the time consumed during the preceding state administrative hearings. The District Court thus correctly ruled that it retained jurisdiction to grant relief because the alleged deficiencies in the IEP were capable of repetition as to the parties before it yet evading review. *Rowley* v. *The Board of Education of the Hendrick Hudson Central School District,* 483 F. Supp. 536, 538 (1980). See *Murphy* v. *Hunt,* 455 U.S. 478, 482 (1982); *Weinstein* v. *Bradford,* 423 U.S. 147, 149 (1975).

the child or the provision of a free appropriate public education.' " Brief for Respondents 28. The United States, appearing as *amicus curiae* on behalf of respondents, states that "[a]lthough the Act includes definitions of 'free appropriate public education' and other related terms, the statutory definitions do not adequately explain what is meant by 'appropriate.' " Brief for United States as *Amicus Curiae* 13.

We are loath to conclude that Congress failed to offer any assistance in defining the meaning of the principal substantive phrase used in the Act. It is beyond dispute that, contrary to the conclusions of the courts below, the Act does expressly define "free appropriate public education":

> "The term 'free appropriate public education' means *special education* and *related services* which (A) have been provided at public expense, under public supervision and direction, and without charge, (B) meet the standards of the State educational agency, (C) include an appropriate preschool, elementary, or secondary school education in the State involved, and (D) are provided in conformity with the individualized education program required under section 1414(a)(5) of this title." § 1401(18) (emphasis added).

"Special education," as referred to in this definition, means "specially designed instruction, at no cost to parents or guardians, to meet the unique needs of a handicapped child, including classroom instruction, instruction in physical education, home instruction, and instruction in hospitals and institutions." § 1401(16). "Related services" are defined as "transportation, and such developmental, corrective, and other supportive services . . . as may be required to assist a handicapped child to benefit from special education." § 1401(17).[10]

Like many statutory definitions, this one tends toward the cryptic rather than the comprehensive, but that is scarcely a reason for abandoning the quest for legislative intent. Whether or not the definition is a "functional" one as respondents contend it is not, it is the principal tool which Congress has given us for parsing the critical phrase of the Act. We think more must be made of it than either respondents or the United States seems willing to admit.

According to the definitions contained in the Act, a "free appropriate public education" consists of educational instruction specially designed to meet the unique needs of the handicapped child, supported by such services as are necessary to permit the child "to benefit" from the instruction. Almost as a checklist for adequacy under the Act, the definition also requires that such instruction and services be provided at public expense and under public supervision, meet the State's educational standards, approximate the grade levels used in the State's regular education, and comport with the child's IEP. Thus, if personalized instruction is being provided with sufficient supportive services to permit the child to benefit from the instruction, and the other items on the definitional checklist are satisfied, the child is receiving a "free appropriate public education" as defined by the Act.

---

[10]Examples of "related services" identified in the Act are "speech pathology and audiology, psychological services, physical and occupational therapy, recreation, and medical and counseling services, except that such medical services shall be for diagnostic and evaluation purposes only" § 1401(17).

Other portions of the statute also shed light upon congressional intent. Congress found that of the roughly eight million handicapped children in the United States at the time of enactment, one million were "excluded entirely from the public school system" and more than half were receiving an inappropriate education. Note to § 1401. In addition, as mentioned in Part I, the Act requires States to extend educational services first to those children who are receiving no education and second to those children who are receiving an "inadequate education." § 1412(3). When these express statutory findings and priorities are read together with the Act's extensive procedural requirements and its definition of "free appropriate public education," the face of the statute evinces a congressional intent to bring previously excluded handicapped children into the public education systems of the States and to require the States to adopt *procedures* which would result in individualized consideration of and instruction for each child.

Noticeably absent from the language of the statute is any substantive standard prescribing the level of education to be accorded handicapped children. Certainly the language of the statute contains no requirement like the one imposed by the lower courts—that States maximize the potential of handicapped children "commensurate with the opportunity provided to other children." 483 F. Supp., at 534. That standard was expounded by the District Court without reference to the statutory definitions or even to the legislative history of the Act. Although we find the statutory definition of "free appropriate public education" to be helpful in our interpretation of the Act, there remains the question of whether the legislative history indicates a congressional intent that such education meet some additional substantive standard. For an answer, we turn to that history.[11]

---

[11]The dissent, finding that "the standard of the courts below seems . . . to reflect the congressional purpose" of the Act, *post*, concludes that our answer to this question "is not a satisfactory one." *Id.* Presumably, the dissent also agrees with the District Court's conclusion that "it has been left entirely to the courts and the hearing officers to give content to the requirement of an 'appropriate education.'" 483 F. Supp., at 533. It thus seems that the dissent would give the courts carte blanche to impose upon the States whatever burden their various judgments indicate should be imposed. Indeed, the dissent clearly characterizes the requirement of an "appropriate education" as open-ended, noting that "if there are limits not evident from the face of the statute on what may be considered an 'appropriate education,' they must be found in the purpose of the statute or its legislative history." *Post.* Not only are we unable to find any suggestion from the face of the statute that the requirement of an "appropriate private education" was to be limitless, but we also view the dissent's approach as contrary to the fundamental proposition that Congress, when exercising its spending power, can impose no burden upon the States unless it does so unambiguously. See *infra.*

No one can doubt that this would have been an easier case if Congress had seen fit to provide a more comprehensive statutory definition of the phrase "free appropriate public education." But Congress did not do so, and "our problem is to construe what Congress has written. After all, Congress expresses its purpose by words. It is for us to ascertain—neither to add nor to subtract, neither to delete nor to distort." *62 Cases of Jam* v. *United States,* 340 U.S. 593, 596 (1951). We would be less than faithful to our obligation to construe what Congress has written if in this case we were to disregard the statutory language and legislative history of the Act by concluding that Congress had imposed upon the States a burden of unspecified proportions and weight, to be revealed only through case by case adjudication in the courts.

B

(i)

As suggested in Part I, federal support for education of the handicapped is a fairly recent development. Before passage of the Act some States had passed laws to improve the educational services afforded handicapped children,[12] but many of these children were excluded completely from any form of public education or were left to fend for themselves in classrooms designed for education of their nonhandicapped peers. The House Report begins by emphasizing this exclusion and misplacement, noting that millions of handicapped children "were either totally excluded from schools or [were] sitting idly in regular classrooms awaiting the time when they were old enough to 'drop out.' " H.R. Rep. No. 94-332, *supra,* at 2. See also S. Rep. No. 94-168, p. 8 (1975). One of the Act's two principal sponsors in the Senate urged its passage in similar terms:

> "While much progress has been made in the last few years, we can take no solace in the progress until all handicapped children are, in fact, receiving an education. The most recent statistics provided by the Bureau of Education for the Handicapped estimate that . . . 1.75 million handicapped children do not receive any educational services, and 2.5 million handicapped children are not receiving an appropriate education." 121 Cong. Rec. 19486 (1975) (remarks of Sen. Williams).

This concern, stressed repeatedly throughout the legislative history,[13] confirms the impression conveyed by the language of the statute: By passing the Act, Congress sought primarily to make public education available to handicapped children. But in seeking to provide such access to public education, Congress did not impose upon the States any greater substantive educational standard than would be necessary to make such access meaningful. Indeed, Congress expressly "recognize[d] that in many instances the process of providing special education and related services to handicapped children is not guaranteed to produce any particular outcome." S. Rep. No. 94-168, *supra,* at 11. Thus, the intent of the Act was more to open the door of public education to handicapped children on appropriate terms than to guarantee any particular level of education once inside.

Both the House and the Senate reports attribute the impetus for the Act and its predecessors to two federal court judgments rendered in 1971 and 1972. As the Senate Report states, passage of the Act "followed a series of landmark court cases establishing in law the right to education for all handi-

---

[12]See H.R. Rep. No. 94-332, *supra,* at 10; Note, The Education of All Handicapped Children Act of 1975, Mich. J. L. Ref. 110, 119 (1976).

[13]See, e.g., 121 Cong. Rec. 19494 (1975) (remarks of Sen. Javits) ("all too often, our handicapped citizens have been denied the opportunity to receive an adequate education"); 121 Cong. Rec. 19502 (1975) (remarks of Sen. Cranston) (million of handicapped "children are largely excluded from educational opportunities that we give to our other children"); 121 Cong. rec. 23708 (1975) (remarks of Rep. Mink) ("handicapped children . . . are denied access to public schools because of a lack of trained personnel").

capped children." S. Rep. No. 94-168, *supra,* at 6.[14] The first case, *Pennsylvania Association for Retarded Children* v. *Commonwealth of Pennsylvania (PARC),* 334 F. Supp. 1257 (1971), 343 F. Supp. 279 (ED Pa 1972), was a suit on behalf of retarded children challenging the constitutionality of a Pennsylvania statute which acted to exclude them from public education and training. The case ended in a consent decree which enjoined the State from "deny[ing] to any mentally retarded child *access* to a free public program of education and training." 334 F. Supp., at 1258 (emphasis added).

PARC was followed by *Mills* v. *Board of Education of the District of Columbia,* 348 F. Supp. 866 (DC 1972), a case in which the plaintiff handicapped children had been excluded from the District of Columbia public schools. The court's judgment, quoted at page 6 of the Senate Report on the Act, provided

> "[t]hat no [handicapped] child eligible for a publicly supported education in the District of Columbia public schools shall be *excluded* from a regular school assignment by a rule, policy, or practice of the Board of Education of the District of Columbia or its agents unless such child is provided (a) *adequate* alternative educational services suited to the child's needs, which may include special education or tuition grants, and (b) a constitutionally adequate prior hearing and periodic review of the child's status, progress, and the *adequacy* of any educational alternative." 348 F. Supp., at 878 (emphasis added).

Mills and *PARC* both held that handicapped children must be given access to an adequate, publicly supported education. Neither case purports to require any particular substantive level of education.[15] Rather, like the language of the Act, the cases set forth extensive procedures to be followed in formulating personalized educational programs for handicapped children.

---

[14]Similarly, the Senate Report states that it was an "[i]ncreased awareness of the educational needs of handicapped children and landmark court decisions establishing the right to education for handicapped children [that] pointed to the necessity of an expanded federal role." S. Rep. No. 94-168, *supra,* at 5. See also H.R. Rep. No. 94-332, *supra,* at 2-3.

[15]The only substantive standard which can be implied from these cases comports with the standard implicit in the Act. *PARC* states that each child must receive "access to a free public program of education and training *appropriate to his learning capacities,"* 334 F. Supp., at 1258, and that further state action is required when it appears that "the needs of the mentally retarded child are not being *adequately* served," *id.,* at 1266. (Emphasis added.) *Mills* also speaks in terms of "adequate" educational services, 348 F. Supp., at 878, and sets a realistic standard of providing *some* educational services to each child when every need cannot be met.

"If sufficient funds are not available to finance all of the services and programs that are needed and desirable in the system then the available funds must be expended equitably in such a manner that no child is entirely excluded from a publicly supported education consistent with his needs and ability to benefit therefrom. The inadequacies of the District of Columbia Public School System whether occasioned by insufficient funding or administrative inefficiency, certainly cannot be permitted to bear more heavily on the 'exceptional' or handicapped child than on the normal child." *Id.,* at 876.

See 348 F. Supp., at 878-883; 334 F. Supp., at 1258-1267.[16] The fact that both *PARC* and *Mills* are discussed at length in the legislative reports[17] suggests that the principles which they established are the principles which, to a significant extent, guided the drafters of the Act. Indeed, immediately after discussing these cases the Senate Report describes the 1974 statute as having "incorporated the major principles of the right to education cases." S. Rep. No. 94-168, *supra,* at 8. Those principles in turn became the basis of the Act, which itself was designed to effectuate the purposes of the 1974 statute. H.R. Rep. No. 94-332, *supra,* at 5.[18]

That the Act imposes no clear obligation upon recipient States beyond the requirement that handicapped children receive some form of specialized education is perhaps best demonstrated by the fact the Congress, in explaining the need for the Act, equated an "appropriate education" to the receipt of some specialized educational services. The Senate Report states: [T]he most recent statistics provided by the Bureau of Education for the Handicapped estimate that of the more than 8 million children . . . with handicapping conditions requiring special education and related services, only 3.9 million such children are receiving an appropriate education." S. Rep. No.

---

[16]Like the Act, *PARC* required the State to "identify, locate, [and] evaluate" handicapped children 334 F. Supp., at 1267, to create for each child an individual educational program, *id.,* at 1265, and to hold a hearing "on any change in educational assignment," *id.,* 1266. *Mills* also required the preparation of an individual educational program for each child. In addition, *Mills* permitted the child's parents to inspect records relevant to the child's education, to obtain an independent educational evaluation of the child, to object to the IEP and receive a hearing before an independent hearing officer, to be represented by counsel at the hearing, and to have the right confront and cross-examine adverse witnesses, all of which are also permitted by the Act. 348 F. Supp., at 879-881. Like the Act, *Mills* also required that the education of handicapped children be conducted pursuant to an overall plan prepared by the District of Columbia, and established a policy of educating handicapped children with nonhandicapped children whenever possible. *Ibid.*

[17]*See S. Rep. No. 94-168, supra,* at 6-7; H.R. Rep. No. 94-332, *supra,* at 3-4.

[18]The 1974 statute "incorporated the major principles of the right to education cases," by "add[ing] important new provisions to the Education of the Handicapped Act which require the States to: establish a goal of providing full educational opportunities to all handicapped children; provide procedures for insuring that handicapped children and their parents or guardians are guaranteed procedural safeguards in decisions regarding identification, evaluation, and education placement of handicapped children; establish procedures to insure that, to the maximum extent appropriate, handicapped children . . . are educated with children who are not handicapped; . . . and establish procedures to insure that testing and evaluation materials and procedures utilized for the purposes of classification and placement of handicapped children will be selected and administered so as not to be racially or culturally discriminatory," S. Rep. No. 94-168, *supra,* at 8.

The House Report explains that the Act simply incorporated these purposes of the 1974 statute: the Act intended "primarily to amend . . . the Education of the Handicapped Act in order to provide permanent authorization and a comprehensive mechanism which will insure that those provisions enacted during the 93rd Congress [the 1974 statute] will result in maximum benefits for handicapped children and their families." H.R. Rep. No. 94-332, *supra,* at 5. Thus, the 1974 statute's purpose of providing handicapped children *access* to a public education became the purpose of the Act.

94-168, *supra,* at 8.[19] This statement, which reveals Congress' view that 3.9 million handicapped children were "receiving an appropriate education" in 1975, is followed immediately in the Senate Report by a table showing that 3.9 million handicapped children were "served" in 1975 and a slightly larger number were "unserved." A similar statement and table appear in the House Report. H.R. Rep. No. 94-332, *supra,* at 11-12.

It is evident from the legislative history that the characterization of handicapped children as "served" referred to children who were receiving some form of specialized educational services from the States, and that the characterization of children as "unserved" referred to those who were receiving no specialized educational services. For example, a letter sent to the United State Commissioner of Education by the House Committee on Education and Labor, signed by two key sponsors of the Act in the House, asked the Commissioner to identify the number of handicapped "children served" in each State. The letter asked for statistics on the number of children "being served" in various types of "special education program[s]" and the number of children who were not "receiving education services." Hearings on S. 6 before the Subcommittee on the Handicapped of the Senate Committee on Labor and Public Welfare, 94th Cong., 1st Sess., 205-207 (1975). Similarly, Senator Randolph, one of the Act's principal sponsors in the Senate, noted that roughly one-half of the handicapped children in the United States "are receiving special educational services." *Id.,* at 1.[20] By characterizing the 3.9

[19]These statistics appear repeatedly throughout the legislative history of the Act, demonstrating a virtual consensus among legislators that 3.9 million handicapped children were receiving and appropriate education in 1975. See, e.g., 121 Cong. Rec. 19486 (1975) (remarks of Sen. Williams); 121 Cong. Rec. 19504 (1975) (remarks of Sen. Schweicker); 121 Cong. Rec. 23702 (1975) (remarks of Rep. Madden); 121 Cong. Rec. 23702 (1975) (remarks of Rep. Brademas); 121 Cong. Rec. 23709 (1975) (remarks of Rep. Minish); 121 Cong. Rec. 37024 (1975) (remarks of Rep. Brademas); 121 Cong. Rec. 37027 (1975) (remarks of Rep. Gude); 121 Cong. Rec. 37417 (1975) (remarks of Sen. Javits); 121 Cong., Rec. 37420 (1975) (remarks of Sen. Hathaway).

[20]Senator Randolph stated: "only 55 percent of the school-aged handicapped children and 22 percent of the pre-school-aged handicapped children are receiving special educational services." Hearings on S. 6 before the Subcommittee on the Handicapped of the Senate Committee on Labor and Public Welfare, 94th Cong., 1st Sess., 1 (1975). Although the figures differ slightly in various parts of the legislative history, the general thrust of congressional calculations was that roughly one-half of the handicapped children in the United States were not receiving specialized educational services, and thus were not "served." See, e.g., 121 Cong. Rec. 19494 (1975) (remarks of Sen. Javits) ("only 50 percent of the Nation's handicapped children received proper education services"); 121 Cong. Rec. 19504 (1975) (remark of Sen. Humphrey) ("[a]lmost 3 million handicapped children, while in school, receive none of the special services that they require in order to make education a meaningful experience"); 121 Cong. Rec. 23706 (1975) (remarks of Rep. Quie) ("only 55 percent [of handicapped children] were receiving a public education"); 121 Cong. Rec. 233709 (1975) (remarks of Rep. Biaggi) ("[o]ver 3 million [handicapped] children in this country are receiving either below par education or none at all").

Statements similar to those appearing in the text, which equate "served" as it appears in the Senate Report to "receiving special educational services," appear throughout the legislative history. See, e.g. 121 Cong. Rec. 19492 (1975) (remarks of Sen. Williams); 121 Cong. Rec. 19494 (1975) (remarks of Sen. Javits); 121 Cong. Rec. 19496 (1975) (remarks of Sen. Stone); 121 Cong. Rec. 19504-19505 (1975) (remarks of Sen. Humphrey); 121 Cong. Rec. 23703 (1975) (remarks of Rep. Brademas); Hearings million handicapped children who were "served" as children who were "receiving an appropriate education," the Senate and House reports unmistakably disclose Congress' perception of the type of education required by the Act: an "appropriate education" is provided when personalized educational services are provided.[21]

(ii)

Respondents contend that "the goal of the Act is to provide each handicapped child with an equal educational opportunity." Brief for Respondents 35. We think, however, that the requirement that a State provide specialized educational services to handicapped children generates no additional requirement that the services so provided be sufficient to maximize each child's potential "commensurate with the opportunity provided other children." Respondents and the United States correctly note that Congress sought "to provide assistance to the States in carrying out their responsibilities under . . . the Constitution of the United States to provide equal protection of the laws." S. Rep. No. 94-168, *supra,* at 13.[22] But we do not think that such

on H.R. 7217 before the Subcommittee on Select Education of the Committee on Education and Labor of the House of Representatives, 94th Cong., 1st Sess., 91, 150, 153 (1975); Hearings on H.R. 4199 before the Select Subcommittee on Education of the Committee on Education and Labor of the House of Representatives, 93rd Cong., 1st Sess., 130, 139 (1973). See also 45 CFR § 121a.343(b) (1980).

[21]In seeking to read more into the Act than its language or legislative history will permit, the United States focuses upon the word "appropriate," arguing that "the statutory definitions do not adequately explain what [it means]." Brief for the United States as *Amicus Curiae* 13. Whatever Congress meant by an "appropriate" education, it is clear that it did not mean a potential-maximizing education.

The term as used in reference to education the handicapped appears to have originated in the *PARC* decision, where the District Court required that handicapped children be provided with "education and training appropriate to [their] learning capacities." 334 F. Supp., at 1258. The word appears again in the *Mills* decision, The district Court at one point referring to the need for "an appropriate educational program," 348 F. Supp., at 879, and at another point speaking of a "suitable publicly-supported education," *id.,* at 878. Both cases also refer to the need for an "adequate" education. See 334 F. Supp., at 1266; 348 F. Supp., at 878.

The use of "appropriate" in the language of the Act, although by no means definitive, suggests that Congress used the word as much to describe the settings in which handicapped children should be educated as to prescribe the substantive content or supportive services of their education. For example, § 1412(5) requires that handicapped children be educated in classrooms with nonhandicapped children "to the maximum extent appropriate." Similarly, § 1401(19) provides that, "whenever appropriate," handicapped children should attend and participate in the meeting at which their IEP is drafted. In addition, the definition of "free appropriate public education" itself states that instruction given handicapped children should be at an "appropriate preschool, elementary, or secondary school" level. § 1401(18)(C). The Act's use of the word "appropriate" thus seems to reflect Congress' recognition that some settings simply are not suitable environments for the participation of some handicapped children. At the very least, these statutory uses of the word refute the contention that Congress used "appropriate" as a term of art which concisely expresses the standard found by the lower courts.

[22]See also 121 Cong. Rec. 19492(1975) (remarks of Sen. Williams); 121 Cong. Rec. 19504 (1975) (remarks of Sen. Humphrey).

statements imply a congressional intent to achieve strict equality of opportunity or services.

The educational opportunities provided by our public school systems undoubtedly differ from student to student, depending upon a myriad of factors that might affect a particular student's ability to assimilate information presented in the classroom. The requirement that States provide "equal" educational opportunities would thus seem to present an entirely unworkable standard requiring impossible measurements and comparisons. Similarly, furnishing handicapped children with only such services as are available to nonhandicapped children would in all probability fall short of the statutory requirement of "free appropriate public education;" to require, on the other hand, the furnishing of every special service necessary to maximize each handicapped child's potential is, we think, further than Congress intended to go. Thus to speak in terms of "equal" services in one instance gives less than what is required by the Act and in another instance more. The theme of the Act is "free appropriate public education," a phrase which is too complex to be captured by the word "equal" whether one is speaking of opportunities or services.

The legislative conception of the requirements of equal protection was undoubtedly informed by the two district court decisions referred to above. But cases such as *Mills* and *PARC* held simply that handicapped children may not be excluded entirely from public education. In *Mills,* the District Court said:

> "If sufficient funds are not available to finance all of the services and programs that are needed and desirable in the system then the available funds must be expended equitably in such a manner that no child is entirely excluded from a publicly supported education consistent with his needs and ability to benefit therefrom." 348 F. Supp., at 876

The *PARC* Court used similar language, saying "[i]t is the commonwealth's obligation to place each mentally retarded child in a free, public program of education and training appropriate to the child's capacity. . . ." 334 F. Supp., at 1260. The right of access to free public education enunciated by these cases is significantly regardless of capacity. To the extent that Congress might have looked further than these cases which are mentioned in the legislative history, at the time of enactment of the Act this Court had held at least twice that the Equal Protection Clause of the Fourteenth Amendment does not require States to expend equal financial resources on the education of each child. *San Antonio School District* v. *Rodriguez,* 411 U. S. 1 (1975); *McInnis* v. *Shapiro,* 293 F. Supp. 327 (ND Ill. 1968), *aff'd sub nom, McInnis* v. *Ogilvie,* 394 U. S. 322 (1969).

In explaining the need for federal legislation, the House Report noted that "no congressional legislation, has required a precise guarantee for handicapped children, i.e. a basic floor of opportunity that would bring into compliance all school districts with the constitutional right of equal protection with respect to handicapped children." H.R. Rep. No. 94-332, *supra,* at 14. Assuming that the Act was designed to fill the need identified in the House Report—that is, to provide a "basic floor of opportunity" consistent with equal protection—neither the Act nor its history persuasively demonstrate that Congress thought that equal protection required anything more than equal access. Therefore, Congress' desire to provide specialized educational services, even in furtherance of ''equality,'' cannot be read as imposing any particular substantive educational standard upon the States.

The District Court and the Court of Appeals thus erred when they held that the Act requires New York to maximize the potential of each handicapped child commensurate with the opportunity provided nonhandicapped children. Desirable though that goal might be, it is not the standard that Congress imposed upon States which receive funding under the Act. Rather, Congress sought primarily to identify and evaluate handicapped children, and to provide them with access to a free public education.

(iii)

Implicit in the congressional purpose of providing access to a "free appropriate public education'' is the requirement that the education to which *access* is provided be sufficient to confer some educational benefit upon the handicapped child. It would do little good for Congress to spend millions of dollars in providing access to a public education only to have the handicapped child receive no benefit from that education. The statutory definition of "free appropriate public education," in addition to requiring that States provide each child with "specially designed instruction," expressly requires the provision of "such . . . supportive services . . . as may be required to assist a handicapped child to *benefit* from special education. § 1401(17) (emphasis added). We therefore conclude that the "basic floor of opportunity" provided by the Act consists of access to specialized instruction and related services which are individually designed to provide educational benefit to the handicapped child.[23]

[23]This view is supported by the congressional intention, frequently expressed in the legislative history, that handicapped children be enabled to achieve a reasonable degree of self sufficiency. After referring to statistics showing that many handicapped children were excluded from public education, the Senate Report states:

''The long range implications of these statistics are that public agencies and taxpayers will spend billions of dollars over the lifetimes of these individuals to maintain such persons as dependents and in a minimally acceptable lifestyle. With proper education services, many would be able to become productive citizens, contributing to society instead of being forced to remain burdens. Others, through such services, would increase their independence, thus reducing their dependence on society.'' S. Rep. No. 94-168, *supra,* at 9. See also H.R. Rep. No. 94-332, *supra,* at 11.

Similarly, one of the principal Senate sponsors of the Act stated that ''providing appropriate educational services now means that many of these individuals will be able to become a contributing part of our society, and they will not have to depend on subsistence payments from public funds.'' 121 Cong. Rec. 19492 (1975) (remarks of Sen. Williams). See also 121 Cong. Rec. 25541 (1975) (remarks of Rep. Harkin); 121 Cong. Rec. 37024-37025 (1975) (remarks of Rep. Brademas); 121 Cong. Rec. 37027 (1975) (remarks of Rep. Gude); 121 Cong. Rec. 37410 (1975) (remarks of Sen. Randolph); 121 Cong. Rec. 37416 (1975) (Remarks of Sen. Williams).

The desire to provide handicapped children with an attainable degree of personal independence obviously anticipated that state educational programs would confer educational benefits upon such children. But at the same time, the goal of achieving some degree of self sufficiency in most cases is a good deal more modest than the potential-maximizing goal adopted by the lower courts.

Despite its frequent mention, we cannot conclude, as did the dissent in the Court of

The determination of when handicapped children are receiving sufficient educational benefits to satisfy the requirements of the Act presents a more difficult problem. The Act requires participating States to educate a wide spectrum of handicapped children, from the marginally hearing-impaired to the profoundly retarded and palsied. It is clear that the benefits obtainable by children at one end of the spectrum will differ dramatically from those obtained by children at the other end, with infinite variations in between. One child may have little difficulty competing successfully in an academic setting with nonhandicapped children while another child may encounter great difficulty in acquiring even the most basic of self-maintenance skills. We do not attempt today to establish any one test for determining the adequacy of educational benefits conferred upon all children covered by the Act. Because in this case we are presented with a handicapped child who is receiving substantial specialized instruction and related services, and who is performing above average in the regular classrooms of a public school system, we confine our analysis to that situation.

The Act requires participating States to educate handicapped children with nonhandicapped children whenever possible.[24] When that "mainstreaming" preference of the Act has been met and a child is being educated in the regular classrooms of a public school system, the system itself monitors the educational progress of the child. Regular examinations are administered, grades are awarded, and yearly advancement to higher grade levels is permitted for those children who attain an adequate knowledge of the course material. The grading and advancement system thus constitutes an important factor in determining educational benefit. Children who graduate from our public school systems are considered by our society to have been "educated" at least to the grade level they have completed, and access to an "education" for handicapped children is precisely what Congress sought to provide in the Act.[25]

Appeals, the self sufficiency was itself the substantive standard which Congress imposed upon the States. Because many mildly handicapped children will achieve self sufficiency without state assistance while personal independence for the severely handicapped may be an unreachable goal, "self sufficiency" as a substantive standard is at once an inadequate protection and an overly demanding requirement. We thus view these references in the legislative history as evidence of Congress' intention that the services provided handicapped children be educationally beneficial, whatever the nature of severity of their handicap.

[24]Section 1412(5) of the Act requires that participating States establish "procedures to assure that, to the maximum extent appropriate, handicapped children, including children in public or private institutions or other care facilities, are educated with children who are not handicapped, and that special classes, separate schooling, or other removal of handicapped children from the regular educational environment occurs only when the nature of severity of the handicap is such that education in regular classes with the use of supplementary aids and services cannot be achieved satisfactorily."

[25]We do not hold today that every handicapped child who is advancing from grade to grade in a regular public school system is automatically receiving a "free appropriate public education." In this case, however, we find Amy's academic progress, when considered with the special services and professional consideration accorded by the Furnace Woods school administrators, to be dispositive.

C

When the language of the Act and its legislative history are considered together, the requirements imposed by Congress become tolerably clear. Insofar as a State is required to provide a handicapped child with a "free appropriate public education," we hold that it satisfies this requirement by providing personalized instruction with sufficient support services to permit the child to benefit educationally from that instruction. Such instruction and services must be provided at public expense, must meet the State's educational standards, must approximate the grade levels used in the State's regular education, and must comport with the child's IEP. In addition, the IEP, and therefore the personalized instruction, should be formulated in accordance with the requirements of the Act and, if the child is being educated in the regular classrooms of the public education system, should be reasonably calculated to enable the child to achieve passing marks and advance from grade to grade.[26]

IV

A

As mentioned in Part I, the Act permits "[a]ny party aggrieved by the findings and decision" of the state administrative hearings "to bring a civil action" in "any State court of competent jurisdiction or in a district court of the United States without regard to the amount in controversy." § 1415(e)(2). The complaint, and therefore the civil action, may concern "any matter relating to the identification, evaluation, or educational placement of the child, or the provision of a free appropriate public education to such child." § 1415(b)(1)(E). In reviewing the complaint, the Act provides that a court

---

[26]In defending the decisions of the District Court and the Court of Appeals, respondents and the United States rely upon isolated statements in the legislative history concerning the achievement of maximum potential, see H.R. Rep. No. 94-332, *supra*, at 13, as support for their contention that Congress intended to impose greater substantive requirements than we have found. These statements, however, are too thin a reed on which to base an interpretation of the Act which disregards both its language and the balance of its legislative history. "Passing references and isolated phrases are not controlling when analyzing a legislative history." *Department of State* v. *The Washington Post Co.,* 456 U.S. 595 (1982)

Moreover, even were we to agree that these statements evince a congressional intent to maximize each child's potential, we could not hold that Congress had successfully imposed that burden upon the States.

"[L]egislation enacted pursuant to the spending power is much in the nature of a contract: in return for federal funds, the States agree to comply with federally imposed conditions. The legitimacy of Congress' power to legislate under the spending power thus rests on whether the State voluntarily and knowingly accepts the terms of the 'contract.' . . . Accordingly, if Congress intends to impose a condition on the grant of federal moneys, it must do so unambiguously." *Pennhurst State School* v. *Halderman,* 451 U.S. 1, 17(1981).

As already demonstrated, the Act and its history impose no requirements on the States like those imposed by the District Court and the Court of Appeals. *A fortiori* Congress has not done so unambiguously, as required in the valid exercise of its spending power.

"shall receive the record of the [state] administrative proceeding, shall hear additional evidence at the request of a party, and, basing its decision on the preponderance of the evidence, shall grant such relief as the court determines is appropriate." § 1415(e)(2).

The parties disagree sharply over the meaning of these provisions, petitioners contending that courts are given only limited authority to review for state compliance with the Act's procedural requirements and no power to review the substance of the state program, and respondents contending that the Act requires courts to exercise *de novo* review over state educational decisions and policies. We find petitioners' contention unpersuasive, for Congress expressly rejected provisions that would have so severely restricted the role of reviewing courts. In substituting the current language of the statute for language that would have made state administrative findings conclusive if supported by substantial evidence, The Conference Committee explained that courts were to make "independent decision[s] based on a preponderance of the evidence." S. Cong. Rec. 37416 (1975) (remarks of Sen. Williams).

But although we find that this grant of authority is broader than claimed by petitioners, we think the fact that it is found in § 1415 of the Act, which is entitled "Procedural Safeguards," is not without significance. When the elaborate and highly specific procedural safeguards embodied in § 1415 are contrasted with the general and somewhat imprecise substantive admonitions contained in the Act, we think that the importance Congress attached to these procedural safeguards cannot be gainsaid. It seems to us no exaggeration to say that Congress placed every bit as much emphasis upon compliance with procedures giving parents and guardians a large measure of participation at every stage of the administrative process, see, e. g. § 1415(a)-(d), as it did upon the measurement of the resulting IEP against a substantive standard. We think that the Congressional emphasis upon full participation of concerned parties throughout the development of the IEP, as well as the requirements that state and local plans be submitted to the Commissioner for approval, demonstrate the legislative conviction that adequate compliance with the procedures prescribed would in most cases assure much if not all of what Congress wished in the way of substantive content in an IEP.

Thus the provision that a reviewing court base its decision on the "preponderance of the evidence" is by no means an invitation to the courts to substitute their own notions of sound educational policy for those of the school authorities which they review. The very importance which Congress has attached to compliance with certain procedures in the preparation of an IEP would be frustrated if a court were permitted simply to set state decisions at nought. The fact that § 1415(e) requires that the reviewing court "receive the records of the [state] administrative proceedings" carries with it the implied requirement that due weight shall be given to these proceedings. And we find nothing in the Act to suggest that merely because Congress was rather sketchy in establishing substantive requirements, as opposed to procedural requirements of the preparation of an IEP, it intended that reviewing courts should have a free hand to impose substantive standards of review which cannot be derived from the Act itself. In short, the statutory authorization to grant "such relief as the court determines is appropriate" cannot be read without reference to the obligations, largely procedural in nature, which are imposed upon recipient States by Congress.

Therefore, a court's inquiry in suits brought under § 1415(e)(2) is twofold. First, has the State complied with the procedures set forth in the Act?[27] And second, is the individualized educational program developed through the Act's procedures reasonably calculated to enable the child to receive educational benefits?[28] If these requirements are met, the State has complied with the obligations imposed by Congress and the Courts can require no more.

B

In assuring that the requirements of the Act have been met, courts must be careful to avoid imposing their view of preferable educational methods upon the States.[29] The primary responsibility for formulating the education to be accorded a handicapped child, and for choosing the educational method most suitable to the child's needs, was left by the Act to state and local educational agencies in cooperation with the parents or guardian of the child. The Act expressly charges States with the responsibility of "acquiring and disseminating to teachers and administrators of programs for handicapped children significant information derived from educational research, demonstration, and similar projects, and [of] adopting, where appropriate, promising educational practices and materials." § 1413(a)(3). In the face of such a clear statutory directive, it seems highly unlikely that Congress intended courts to overturn a State's choice of appropriate educational theories in a proceeding conducted pursuant to § 1415(e)(2).[30]

We previously have cautioned that courts lack the "specialized knowledge and experience" necessary to resolve "persistent and difficult questions of educational policy." *San Antonio School District* v. *Rodriguez,* 411 U. S. 1, 42 (1973). We think that Congress shared that view when it passed the Act. As already demonstrated, Congress' intention was not that the Act displace the primacy of States in the field of education, but that States receive funds to assist them in extending their educational systems to the handicapped.

---

[27]This inquiry will require a court not only to satisfy itself that the State has adopted the state plan, policies, and assurances required by the Act, but also to determine that the State has created an IEP for the child in question which conforms with the requirements of § 1401(19).

[28]When the handicapped child is being educated in the regular classrooms of a public school system, the achievement of passing marks and advancement from grade to grade will be one important factor in determining educational benefit. See Part III, *supra.*.

[29]In this case, for example, both the state hearing officer and the District Court were presented with evidence as to the best method for educating the deaf, a question long debated among scholars. See Large, Special Problems of the Deaf Under the Education for All Handicapped Children Act of 1975, 58 Washington U. L. Q. 213,229 (1980). The District Court accepted the testimony of respondents' experts that there was "a trend supported by studies showing the greater degree of success of students brought up in deaf households using [the method of communication used by the Rowleys]." 483 F. Supp., at 535.

[30]It is clear that Congress was aware of the States' traditional role in the formulation and execution of educational policy. "Historically, the States have had the primary responsibility for the education of children at the elementary and secondary level." 121 Cong. Rec. 19498 (1975) (remarks of Sen. Dole). See also *Epperson* v. *Arkansas,* 393 U. S. 97, 104 (1968) ("[b]y and large, public education in our Nation is committed to the control of state and local authorities").

Therefore, once a court determines that the requirements of the Act have been met, questions of methodology are for resolution by the States.

V

Entrusting a child's education to state and local agencies does not leave the child without protection. Congress sought to protect individual children by providing for parental involvement in the development of State plans and policies, *supra,* at 4-5 and n. 6, and in formulation of the child's individual educational program. As the Senate Report states:

> "The Committee recognizes that in many instances the process of providing special education and related services to handicapped children is not guaranteed to produce any particular outcome. By changing the language [of the provision relating to individualized educational programs] to emphasize the process of parent and child involvement and to provide a written record of reasonable expectations, the Committee intends to clarify that such individualized planning conferences are a way to provide parent involvement and protection to assure that appropriate services are provided to a handicapped child." S. Rep. No. 94-168, *supra,* at 11-12. See also S. Conf. Rep. No. 94-445, p. 30 (1975); 45 CFR § 121a.345 (1980).

As this very case demonstrates, parents and guardians will not lack ardor in seeking to ensure that handicapped children receive all of the benefits to which they are entitled by the Act.[31]

VI

Applying these principles to the facts of this case, we conclude that the Court of Appeals erred in affirming the decision of the District Court. Neither the District Court nor the Court of Appeals found that petitioners had failed to comply with the procedures of the Act, and the findings of neither court would support a conclusion that Amy's educational program failed to comply with the substantive requirements of the Act. On the contrary, the District Court found that the "evidence firmly establishes that Amy is receiving an 'adequate' education, since she performs better than the average child

[31]In addition to providing for extensive parental involvement in the formulation of state and local policies, as well as the preparation of individual educational programs, the Act ensures that States will receive the advice of experts in the field of educating handicapped children. As a condition for receiving federal funds under the Act, States must create "an advisory panel, appointed by the Governor or any other official authorized under State law to make such appointments, composed of individuals involved in or concerned with the education of handicapped children, including handicapped individuals, teachers, parents or guardians of handicapped children, State and local education officials, and administrators of programs for handicapped children, which (A) advises that State educational agency of unmet needs within the State in the education of handicapped children, [and] (B) comments publicly on any rules or regulations proposed for issuance by the State regarding the education of handicapped children." § 1413(a)(12).

in her class and is advancing easily from grade to grade." 483 F. Supp., at 534. In light of this finding, and of the fact that Amy was receiving personalized instruction and related services calculated by the Furnace Woods school administrators to meet her educational needs, the lower courts should not have concluded that the Act requires the provision of a sign-language interpreter. Accordingly, the decision of the Court of Appeals is reversed and the case is remanded for further proceedings consistent with this opinion.[32]

So ordered.

JUSTICE BLACKMUN, concurring in the judgment.

Although I reach the same result as the court does today, I read the legislative history and goals of the Education for All Handicapped Children Act differently. Congress unambiguously stated that it intended to "take a more active role under its responsibility for equal protection of the laws to guarantee that handicapped children are provided *equal educational opportunity.*" S. Rep. No 94-168, p. 9(1975) (emphasis added). See also 20 U.S.C. § 1412(2)(A)(i) (requiring States to establish plans with the "goal of providing full educational opportunity to all handicapped children").

As I have observed before, "[i]t seems plain to me that Congress, in enacting [this statute], intended to do more than merely set out politically self-serving but essentially meaningless language about what the [handicapped] deserve at the hands of state . . . authorities." *Pennhurst State School* v. *Halderman,* 451 U.S. 1, 32(1981) (opinion concurring in part and concurring in the judgment). The clarity of the legislative intent convinces me that the relevant question here is not, as the Court says, whether Amy Rowley's individualized education program was "reasonably calculated to enable [her] to receive additional benefits," *ante*, measured in part by whether or not she "achieve[s] passing marks and advances[s] from grade to grade," *ante*. Rather, the question is whether Amy's program, *viewed as a whole*, offered her an opportunity to understand and participate in the classroom that was substantially equal to that given her nonhandicapped classmates. This is a standard predicated on equal educational opportunity and equal access to the educational process, rather than upon Amy's achievement of any particular educational outcome.

In answering this question, I believe that the District Court and the Court of Appeals should have given greater deference than they did to the findings of the School District's impartial hearing officer and the State's Commissioner of Education, both of whom sustained petitioner's refusal to add a sign-language interpreter to Amy's individualized education program. Cf. 20 U.S.C. § 1415(e)(2) (requiring reviewing court to "receive the records of the administrative proceeding" before granting relief). I would suggest further that those courts focused too narrowly on the presence or absence of a particular service—a sign-language interpreter—rather than on the total package of services furnished to Amy by the School Board.

---

[32]Because the District Court declined to reach respondents' contention that petitioners had failed to comply with the Act's procedural requirements in developing Amy's IEP, 483 F. Supp., at 533, n. 8, the case must be remanded for further proceedings consistent with this opinion.

As the Court demonstrates, *ante*, petitioner Board has provided Amy Rowley considerably more than "a teacher with a loud voice." See *post*, (dissenting opinion). By concentrating on whether Amy was "learning as much, or performing as well academically, as she would without her handicap," 483 F Supp. 528, 532 (SDNY 1980), the District Court and the Court of Appeals paid too little attention to whether, on the entire record, respondent's individualized education program offered her an educational opportunity substantially equal to that provided her nonhandicapped classmates. Because I believe that standard has been satisfied here, I agree that the judgment of the Court of Appeals should be reversed.

JUSTICE WHITE, with whom JUSTICE BRENNAN and JUSTICE MARSHALL join, dissenting.

In order to reach its result in this case, the majority opinion contradicts itself, the language of the statute, and the legislative history. Both the majority's standard for a "free appropriate education" and its standard for judicial review disregard congressional intent.

I

The majority first turns its attention to the meaning of a "free appropriate public education." The Act provides:

> "The term 'free appropriate public education' means special education and related services which (A) have been provided at public expense, under public supervision and direction, and without charge, (B) meet the standards of the State educational agency, (C) include an appropriate preschool, elementary, or secondary school education in the State involved, and (D) are provided in conformity with the individualized education program required under section 1414(a)(5) of this title." 20 U.S.C. 1401(18).

The majority reads this statutory language as establishing a congressional intent limited to bringing "previously excluded handicapped children into the public education systems of the States and requiring the States to adopt *procedures* which would result in individualized consideration of and instruction for each child." *Ante*. In its attempt to constrict the definition of "appropriate" and the thrust of the Act, the majority opinion states, "Noticeably absent from the language of the statute is any substantive standard prescribing the level of education to be accorded handicapped children. Certainly the language of the statute contains no requirement like the one imposed by the lower courts—that States maximize the potential of handicapped children commensurate with opportunity provided to other children." *Ante*, quoting 483 F. Supp. at 534.

I agree that the language of the Act does not contain a substantive standard beyond requiring that the education offered must be "appropriate." However, if there are limits not evident from the face of the statute on what may be considered an "appropriate education," they must be found in the purpose of the statute or its legislative history. The Act itself announces it will provide a "*full* educational opportunity to all handicapped children." 20

U.S.C. § 1412(2)(A) (emphasis added). This goal is repeated throughout the legislative history, in statements too frequent to be "passing references and isolated phrases."[1] *Ante*, quoting *Department of State* v. *Washington Post Co.*, 456 U.S. 596 (1982). These statements elucidate the meaning of "appropriate." According to the Senate Report, for example, the Act does "guarantee that handicapped children are provided *equal* educational opportunity." S. Rep. No. 94-168, at 9 (1975) (emphasis added). This promise appears throughout the legislative history. See 121 Cong. Rec. 19482-19483 (1975) (remarks of Sen. Randolph); *id.,* at 19504 (Sen. Humphrey); *id.,* at 19505 (Sen. Beall); *id.,* at 23704 (Rep. Brademas); *id.,* at 25538 (Rep. Cornell); *id.,* at 25540 (Rep. Grassley); *id.,* at 37025 (Rep. Perkins); *id.,* at 37030 (Rep. Mink); *id.,* at 37412 (Sen. Taft); *id.,* at 37413 (Sen. Williams); *id.,* at 37418-37419 (Sen. Cranston); *id.,* at 37419-37420 (Sen. Beall). Indeed, at times the purpose of the Act was described as tailoring each handicapped child's educational plan to enable the child "to achieve his or her maximum potential." H.R. Rep. No. 94-332, 94th Cong. 1st Sess. 13, 19 (1975), see 121 Cong. Rec. 23709 (1975). Sen. Stafford, one of the sponsors of the Act, declared, "We can all agree that the education [given a handicapped child] should be equivalent, at least, to the one those children who are not handicapped receive." 121 Cong. Rec. 19483 (1975). The legislative history thus directly supports the conclusion that the Act intends to give handicapped children an educational opportunity commensurate with that given other children.

The majority opinion announces a different substantive standard, that "Congress did not impose upon the States any greater substantive standard than would be necessary to make such access meaningful." *Ante*. While "meaningful" is no more enlightening than "appropriate," the Court purports to clarify itself. Because Amy was provided with *some* specialized instruction from which she obtained *some*benefit and because she passed from grade to grade, she was receiving a meaningful and therefore appropriate education.[2]

---

[1]The Court's opinion relies heavily on the statement, which occurs throughout the legislative history, that, at the time of enactment, one million of the roughly eight million handicapped children in the United States were excluded entirely from the public school system and more than half were receiving an inappropriate education. See, e.g., *ante*. But this statement was often linked to statements urging equal educational opportunity. See e.g., 121 Cong. Rec. 19502 (remarks of Sen. Cranston); *id.* at 23702 (remarks of Rep. Brademas). That is, Congress wanted not only to bring handicapped children into the schoolhouse, but also to benefit them once they had entered.

[2]As further support for its conclusion, the majority opinion turns to *Pennsylvania Association for Retarded Children* v. *Commonwealth of Pennsylvania* (PARC), 334 F. Supp. 1257 (1971), 343 F. Supp. 279 (ED Pa. 1972) and *Mills* v. *Board of Education of the District of Columbia,* 348 F. Supp. 866 (DDC 1972). That these decisions served as an impetus for the Act does not, however, establish them as the limits of the Act. In any case, the very language that the majority quotes from *Mills, ante*, sets a standard not of *some* education, but of educational opportunity equal to that of non-handicapped children.

Indeed, *Mills*, relying on decisions since called into question by this Court's opinion in *San Antonio School District* v. *Rodriguez,* 411 U.S. 1 (1973), states,

"In *Hobson* v. *Hansen* [269 F. Supp. 401 (DDC),] Judge Wright found that denying poor public school children educational opportunity equal to that available to

This falls far short of what the Act intended. The Act details as specifically as possible the kind of specialized education each handicapped child must receive. It would apparently satisfy the Court's standard of "access to specialized instruction and related services which are individually designed to provide educational benefit to the handicapped child," *ante*, for a deaf child such as Amy to be given a teacher with a loud voice, for she would benefit from the service. The Act requires more. It defines "special education" to mean "specifically designed instruction, at no cost to parents or guardians, to *meet the unique needs* of a handicapped child. . . ." § 1401(16) (emphasis added).[3] Providing a teacher with a loud voice would not meet Amy's needs and would not satisfy the Act. The basic floor of opportunity is instead, as the courts below recognized, intended to eliminate the effects of the handicap, at least to the extent that the child will be given an equal opportunity to learn if that is reasonably possible. Amy Rowley, without a sign language interpreter, comprehends less than half of what is said in the classroom—less than half of what normal children comprehend. This is hardly an equal opportunity to learn, even if Amy makes passing grades.

Despite its reliance on the use of "appropriate" in the definition of the Act, the majority opinion speculates that "Congress used the word as much to describe the settings in which the children should be educated as to prescribe the substantive content or supportive services of their education." *Ante*. Of course, the word "appropriate" can be applied in many ways; at times in the Act, Congress used it to recommend mainstreaming handicapped children; at other points, it used the word to refer to the content of the individualized education. The issue before us is what standard the word "appropriate" incorporates when it is used to modify "education." The answer given by the Court is not a satisfactory one.

II

The Court's discussion of the standard for judicial review is as flawed as its discussion of a "free appropriate public education." According to the Court, a court can ask only whether the State has "complied with the procedures set forth in the Act" and whether the individualized education program is "reasonably calculated to enable the child to receive educational benefit." *Ante*. Both the language of the Act and the legislative history, however, demonstrate that Congress intended the courts to conduct a far more searching inquiry.

The majority assigns major significance to the review provision's being found in a section entitled "Procedural Safeguards." But where else would a

---

more affluent public school children was violative of the Due Process Clause of the Fifth Amendment. *A fortiori,* the defendants' conduct here, denying plaintiffs and their class not just an equal publicly supported education but all publicly supported education while providing such education to other children, is violative of the Due Process Clause." 348 F. Supp., at 875.

Whatever the effect of *Rodriguez* on the validity of this reasoning, the statement exposes the majority's mischaracterization of the opinion and thus of the assumptions of the legislature that passed the act.

[3] "Related services" are "transportation, and such developmental, corrective, and other supportive services . . . as may be required to assist a handicapped child to benefit from special education." § 1401(17).

provision for judicial review belong? The majority does acknowledge that the current language, specifying that a court "shall receive the record of the administrative proceeding, shall hear additional evidence at the request of a party, and basing its decision on the preponderance of the evidence, shall grant such relief as the court determines is appropriate," § 1415(e)(2), was substituted at Conference for language that would have restricted the role of the reviewing court much more sharply. It is clear enough to me that Congress decided to reduce substantially judicial deference to state administrative decisions.

The legislative history shows that judicial review is not limited to procedural matters and that the state educational agencies are given first, but not final, responsibility for the content of a handicapped child's education. The Conference Committee directs courts to make an "independent decision." S. Conf. Rep. No. 94-455, at 50. The deliberate change in the review provision is an unusually clear indication the Congress intended courts to undertake substantive review instead of relying on the conclusions of the state agency.

On the floor of the Senate, Senator Williams, the chief sponsor of the bill, committee chairman, and floor manager responsible for the legislation in the Senate, emphasized the breadth of the review provisions at both the administrative and judicial levels:

> "Any parent or guardian may present a complaint concerning *any matter* regarding the identification, evaluation, or educational placement of the child or the provision of a free appropriate public education to such a child. In this regard, Mr. President, I would like to stress that the language referring to 'free appropriate education' has been adopted to make clear that a complaint may involve matters such as questions respecting a child's individualized education program, questions of whether special education and related services are being provided without charge to the parents or guardians, questions relating to whether the services provided a child meet the standards of the State education agency, or *any other question* within the scope of the definition of 'free appropriate public education.' In addition, it should be clear that a parent or guardian may present a complaint alleging that a State or local education agency has refused to provide services to which a child may be entitled or alleging that the State or local educational agency has erroneously classified a child as a handicapped child when, in fact, that child is not a handicapped child." 121 Cong. Rec. 37415 (emphasis added).

There is no doubt that the state agency itself must make substantive decisions. The legislative history reveals that the courts are to consider, *de novo,* the same issues. Senator Williams explicitly stated that the civil action permitted under the Act encompasses all matters related to the original complaint. *Id.,* at 37416.

Thus, the Court's limitations on judicial review have no support in either the language of the Act or the legislative history. Congress did not envision that inquiry would end if a showing is made that the child is receiving passing marks and is advancing from grade to grade. Instead, it intended to permit a full and searching inquiry into any aspect of a handicapped child's education. The Court's standard, for example, would not permit a challenge to part of the IEP; the legislative history demonstrates beyond doubt that Congress intended such challenges to be possible, even if the plan as developed is reasonably calculated to give the child some benefits.

Parents can challenge the IEP for failing to supply the special education and related services needed by the individual handicapped child. That is what Rowleys did. As the Government observes, "courts called upon to review the content of an IEP, in accordance with 20 U.S.C. § 1415(e) inevitably are required to make a judgment on the basis of the evidence presented, concerning whether the educational methods proposed by the local school district are 'appropriate' for the handicapped child involved." Brief for United States as *Amicus Curiae* 13. The courts below, as they were required by the Act, did precisely that.

Under the judicial review provisions of the Act, neither the District Court nor the Court of Appeals was bound by the state's construction of what an "appropriate'' education means in general or by what the state authorities considered to be an appropriate education for Amy Rowley. Because the standard of the courts below seems to me to reflect the congressional purpose and because their factual findings are not clearly erroneous, I respectfully dissent.

Smith v. Robinson

U.S. Supreme Court, 468 U.S. 992, 104 S.Ct. 3457 (1984).

Syllabus*

When the Superintendent of Schools in Cumberland, R. I., informed petitioner parents of petitioner child, who suffers from cerebral palsy, that the School Committee no longer would fund the child's placement in a special education program, the parents, in addition to appealing the Superintendent's decision to the School Committee and thereafter through the state administrative process, filed an action in Federal District Court against the School Committee and, subsequently, against certain state school officials. They asserted, at various points in the proceedings, claims for declaratory and injunctive relief based on state law, on the Education of the Handicapped Act (EHA), on § 504 of the Rehabilitation Act of 1973, and, with respect to certain federal constitutional claims, on 42 U. S. C. § 1983. The District Court held that the child was entitled, as a matter of state law, to a free appropriate special education paid for by the School Committee, and that it was therefore unnecessary and improper to reach petitioners' federal statutory and constitutional claims. By agreement between the parties, the court awarded attorney's fees against the School Committee. Petitioners then requested attorney's fees against the state defendants. The District Court held that petitioners were entitled to such fees for the hours spent in the state administrative process both before and after the date the state defendants were named as parties, reasoning that because petitioners were required to exhaust their EHA remedies before asserting their § 1983 and § 504 claims, they were entitled to fees for those procedures. The Court of Appeals reversed, holding that since the action and relief granted fell within the reach of the EHA, which establishes a comprehensive federal-state scheme for the provision of special education to handicapped children but does not provide for attorney's fees, the District Court had to look to 42 U. S. C. § 1988 and § 505 of the Rehabilitation Act for such fees. The Court of Appeals concluded that even if the unaddressed § 1983 claims were substantial enough to support federal jurisdiction so as generally to warrant an award of attorney's fees, nevertheless, given the comprehensiveness of the EHA, Congress could not have intended its omission of attorney's fees relief in that statute to be rectified by recourse to § 1988. The court disposed of the Rehabilitation Act basis for attorney's fees for similar reasons.

Held:

1. Petitioners were not entitled to attorney's fees under § 1988.

(a) The fact that petitioners prevailed on their initial claim that the School Committee violated due process by refusing to grant petitioners a full hearing before terminating funding of petitioner child's special education program does not by itself entitle petitioners to attorney's fees for the subsequent administrative and judicial proceedings. That due process claim was entirely separate from the claims made in the subsequent proceedings, and was not sufficiently related to petitioners' ultimate success to support an award of fees for the entire proceeding.

(b) As to petitioners' claim that the child was being discriminated against on the basis of his handicapped condition, in violation of the Equal Protection Clause of the Fourteenth Amendment, it is apparent that Congress intended the

*The syllabus constitutes no part of the opinion of the Court but has been prepared by the Reporter of Decisions for the convenience of the reader.

EHA to be the exclusive avenue through which such a claim can be pursued. The EHA is a comprehensive scheme to aid the States in complying with their constitutional obligations to provide public education for the handicapped. Allowing a plaintiff to circumvent the EHA's administrative remedies by relying on § 1983 as a remedy for a substantial equal protection claim would be inconsistent with that scheme.

(c) Even if petitioners' due process challenge to the partiality of the state hearing officer who reviewed the School Committee's decision might be maintained as an independent challenge, petitioners are not entitled to attorney's fees for such claim. That claim had no bearing on the substantive claim on which petitioners prevailed, that the School Board, as a matter of state and federal law, was required to pay for petitioner child's education. Where petitioners presented different claims for different relief, based on different facts and legal theories, and prevailed only on a nonfee claim, they are not entitled to a fee award simply because the other claim was a constitutional claim that could be asserted through § 1983.

2. Nor were petitioners entitled to attorney's fees under § 505 of the Rehabilitation Act. Congress struck a careful balance in the EHA between clarifying and making enforceable the rights of handicapped children to a free appropriate public education and endeavoring to relieve the financial burden imposed on the agencies responsible to guarantee those rights. It could not have intended a handicapped child to upset that balance by relying on § 504 for otherwise unavailable damages or for an award of attorney's fees. Where, as here, whatever remedy might be provided under § 504—which prevents discrimination on the basis of a handicap in any program receiving federal financial assistance—is provided with more clarity and precision under the EHA, a plaintiff may not circumvent or enlarge on the remedies available under the EHA by resort to § 504.

703 F. 2d 4, affirmed.

BLACKMUN, J., delivered the opinion of the Court, in which BURGER, C. J., and WHITE, POWELL, REHNQUIST, and O'CONNOR, JJ., joined. BRENNAN, J., filed a dissenting opinion, in which MARSHALL and STEVENS, JJ., joined.

JUSTICE BLACKMUN delivered the opinion of the Court.

This case presents questions regarding the award of attorney's fees in a proceeding to secure a "free appropriate public education" for a handicapped child. At various stages in the proceeding, petitioners asserted claims for relief based on state law, on the Education of the Handicapped Act (EHA), 84 Stat. 175, as amended, 20 U. S. C. §§ 1400 *et seq.*, on § 504 of the Rehabilitation Act of 1973, 87 Stat. 394, as amended, 29 U. S. C. § 794, and on the Due Process and Equal Protection Clauses of the Fourteenth Amendment to the United States Constitution. The United States Court of Appeals for the First Circuit concluded that because the proceeding, in essence, was one to enforce the provisions of the EHA, a statute that does not provide for the payment of attorney's fees, petitioners were not entitled to such fees. *Smith* v. *Cumberland School Committee*, 703 F. 2d 4 (1983). Petitioners insist that this Court's decision in *Maher* v. *Gagne*, 448 U. S. 122 (1980), compels a different conclusion.

I

The procedural history of the case is complicated, but it is significant to the resolution of the issues. Petitioner Thomas F. Smith, III (Tommy), suffers from cerebral palsy and a variety of physical and emotional handicaps. When this proceeding began in November 1976, Tommy was 8 years old. In the preceding December, the Cumberland School Committee had agreed to place Tommy in a day program at Emma Pendleton Bradley Hospital in East Providence, R. I., and Tommy began attending that program. In November 1976, however, the Superintendent of Schools informed Tommy's parents, who are the other petitioners here, that the School Committee no longer would fund Tommy's placement because, as it construed Rhode Island law, the responsibility for educating an emotionally disturbed child lay with the State's Divison of Mental Health, Retardation and Hospitals [MHRH]. App. 25-26.

Petitioners took an appeal from the decision of the Superintendent to the School Committee. In addition, petitioners filed a complaint under 42 U. S. C. § 1983 in the United States District Court for the District of Rhode Island against the members of the School Committee, asserting that due process required that the Committee comply with "Article IX—Procedural Safeguards" of the Regulations adopted by the State Board of Regents regarding Education of Handicapped Children [Regulations][1] and that Tommy's placement in his program be continued pending appeal of the Superintendent's decision.

In orders issued in December 1976 and January 1977, the District Court entered a temporary restraining order and then a preliminary injunction. The court agreed with petitioners that the Regulations required the School Committee to continue Tommy in his placement at Bradley Hospital pending appeal of the Superintendent's decision. The School Committee's failure to follow the Regulations, the court concluded, would constitute a deprivation of due process.

On May 10, 1978, petitioners filed a First Amended Complaint. App. 49. By that time, petitioners had completed the state administrative process. They had appealed the Superintendent's decision to the School Committee and then to the State Commissioner of Education, who delegated responsibility for conducting a hearing to an Associate Commissioner of Education.

[1]In November 1976, Rhode Island, through its Board of Regents for Education, was in the process of promulgating new regulations concerning the education of handicapped children. The old regulations, approved in 1963, had been issued by the State Department of Education and were entitled "Regulations—Education of Handicapped Children." Most of the new Regulations became effective October 1, 1977. Article IX of Section One, however, was made effective June 14, 1976. See Section One, Art. XII.

The Regulations were promulgated pursuant to R. I. Gen. Laws § 16-24-2 (1981). The immediately preceding section, § 16-24-1, sets out the duty of the local school committee to provide, for a child, "who is either mentally retarded or physically or emotionally handicapped to such an extent that normal educational growth and development is prevented," such type of special education "that will best satisfy the need of the handicapped child, as recommended and approved by the board of regents for education in accordance with its regulations." Section 16-24-1 has its origin in 1952 R. I. Pub. Laws, ch. 2905, § 1, and was in effect in November 1976.

Petitioners had moved that the Associate Commissioner recuse himself from conducting the review of the School Committee's decision, since he was an employee of the State Educational Agency and therefore not an impartial hearing officer. The Associate Commissioner denied the motion to recuse.

All the state officers agreed that, under R. I. Gen. Laws, Tit. 40, ch. 7 (1977), the responsibility for educating Tommy lay with MHRH.[2] The Associate Commissioner acknowledged petitioners' argument that since § 40.1-7-8 would require them to pay a portion of the cost of services provided to Tommy,[3] the statute conflicted with the EHA, but concluded that the problem was not within his jurisdiction to resolve.

In their First Amended Complaint, petitioners added as defendants the Commissioner of Education, the Associate Commissioner of Education, the Board of Regents for Education, and the Director of MHRH. They also specifically relied for the first time on the EHA, noting that at all times mentioned in the complaint, the State of Rhode Island had submitted a plan for state-administered programs of special education and related services and had received federal funds pursuant to the EHA.[4]

In the First Count of their Amended Complaint, petitioners challenged the fact that both the hearing before the School Committee and the hearing before the Associate Commissioner were conducted before examiners who were employees of the local or state education agency. They sought a declaratory judgment that the procedural safeguards contained in Article IX of the Regulations did not comply with the Due Process Clause of the Fourteenth Amendment or with the requirements of the EHA, 20 U. S. C. § 1415, and its accompanying regulations. They also sought an injunction prohibiting the Commissioner and Associate Commissioner from conducting any more hearings in review of decisions of the Rhode Island local education agencies (LEAs) unless and until the Board of Regents adopted regulations that con-

---

[2]Under § 40.1-7-3, enacted by 1971 R. I. Pub. Laws, ch. 89, art. 1, § 1, MHRH is charged "with the responsibility to promote the development of specialized services for the care and treatment of emotionally disturbed children and to cooperate to this end with all reputable agencies of a public or private character serving such children . . ."

[3]Section 40.1-7-8 provides: "The parents of children in the program, depending upon their resources, shall be obligated to participate in the costs of the care and treatment of their children in accordance with regulations to be promulgated by the director."

[4]The 1975 Amendment to the EHA, on which petitioners rely, became effective October 1, 1977. Prior to that date, the federal requirements governing States which, like Rhode Island, submitted state plans and received federal money for the education of handicapped children were found in the Education of the Handicapped Act, 84 Stat. 175, as amended in 1974, 88 Stat. 579. The obligations imposed on a State by that Act were to expend federal money on programs designed to benefit handicapped children. From August 1974 to September 30, 1977, the Act also required that parents be given minimal due process protections when the State proposed to change the educational placement of the child. 88 Stat. 582. The state hearing process in this case began on January 20, 1977, with a hearing before the School Committee. By the time petitioners' appeal progressed to the Associate Commissioner of Education on November 2, 1977, the 1975 Act was in effect. Unless otherwise indicated, future references to the "EHA" refer to the 1975 amendments to that Act.

formed to the requirements of § 1415 and its regulations. Finally, they sought reasonable attorney's fees and costs.

In the Second Count of their Amended Complaint, petitioners challenged the substance of the Associate Commissioner's decision. In their view, the decision violated Tommy's rights "under federal and state law to have his LEA provide a free, appropriate educational placement without regard to whether or not said placement can be made within the local school system." App. 61. They sought both a declaratory judgment that the School Committee, not MHRH, was responsible for providing Tommy a free appropriate education, and an injunction requiring the School Committee to provide Tommy such an education. They also asked for reasonable attorney's fees and costs.

On December 22, 1978, the District Court issued an opinion acknowledging confusion over whether, as a matter of state law, the School Committee or MHRH was responsible for funding and providing the necessary services for Tommy. App. 108. The court also noted that if the Associate Commissioner were correct that Tommy's education was governed by § 40.1-7, the state scheme would appear to be in conflict with the requirements of the EHA, since § 40.1-7 may require parental contribution and may not require MHRH to provide education at all if it would cause the Department to incur a deficit. At the request of the state defendants, the District Court certified to the Supreme Court of Rhode Island the state law questions whether the school committee was required to provide special education for a resident handicapped student if the local educational programs were inadequate, and whether the cost of such programs was the responsibility of the local school committee or of the MHRH.

On May 29, 1979, the District Court granted partial summary judgment for the defendants on petitioners' claim that they were denied due process by the requirement of the Regulations that they submit their dispute to the School Committee and by the Associate State Commissioner's refusal to recuse himself. The court noted that the School Committee's members were not "employees" of the local education agency, but elected officials, and determined that the provision of the EHA directing that no hearing shall be conducted by an employee of an agency or unit involved in the education or care of the child does not apply to hearings conducted by the state education agency.

On June 3, 1980, the Rhode Island Supreme Court issued an opinion answering the certified questions. *Smith* v. *Cumberland School Committee*, —— R. I. ——, 415 A. 2d 168. Noting the responsibility of the Board of Regents for Education to comply with the requirements of the EHA, the court determined that the primary obligation of financing a handicapped child's special education lay with the local School Committee. Whatever obligation § 40.1-7 imposes on MHRH to provide educational services is limited and complements, rather than supplants, the obligations of School Committees under § 16.24-1.

Petitioners thereafter filed their Second Amended and Supplemental Complaint. App. 152. In it they added to Count II claims for relief under the Equal Protection Clause of the Fourteenth Amendment and under § 504 of the Rehabilitation Act of 1973, as amended, 29 U. S. C. § 794. They also requested attorney's fees under 42 U. S. C. § 1988 and what was then 31 U. S. C. § 1244(e) (1976 ed.).[5]

On January 12, 1981, the District Court issued an order declaring petitioners' rights, entering a permanent injunction against the School Committee defendants, and approving an award of attorney's fees against those defendants. App. 172. The court ordered the School Committee to pay the full cost of Tommy's attendance at Harmony Hill School, Tommy's then-current placement. By agreement between petitioners and the School Committee and without prejudice to petitioners' claims against the other defendants, the court awarded attorney's fees in the amount of $8,000, pursuant to 42 U. S. C. § 1988 and the then 31 U. S. C. § 1244 (e).

On June 4, 1981, the District Court issued two orders, this time addressed to petitioners' claims against the state defendants. In the first order, App. 177, the court denied the state defendants' motion to dismiss. In the second order, *id.*, at 189, the court declared that Tommy is entitled to a free appropriate special education paid for by the Cumberland School Committee. The court noted that since Tommy was entitled to the relief he sought as a matter of state law, it was unnecessary and improper for the court to go further and reach petitioners' federal statutory and constitutional claims. Petitioners were given 14 days to move for an award of fees.

The Court of Appeals for the First Circuit affirmed in an unpublished *per curiam* opinion filed on January 11, 1982. It concluded that the Commissioner was not immune from injunctive relief and that petitioners' challenge to the District Court's award of summary judgment to respondents on their due process challenge was moot.

Petitioners requested fees and costs against the state defendants. *Id.*, at 195. On April 30, 1982, the District Court ruled orally that petitioners were entitled to fees and costs in the amount of $32,109 for the hours spent in the state administrative process both before and after the state defendants were named as parties to the federal litigation. App. to Pet. for Cert. A31-A58. Relying on *New York Gaslight Club, Inc.* v. *Carey*, 447 U. S. 54 (1980), and its own opinion in *Turillo* v. *Tyson*, 535 F. Supp. 577 (R. I. 1982), the court reasoned that because petitioners were required to exhaust their EHA remedies before bringing their § 1983 and § 504 claims, they were entitled to fees for those procedures. The court agreed with respondents that petitioners were not entitled to compensation for hours spent challenging the use of employees as hearing officers. No fees were awarded for hours spent obtaining the preliminary injunctive relief, as petitioners already had been compensated for that work by the school committee defendants. Finally, the court rejected the defendants' argument that fees should not be allowed because this was an action under the EHA, which does not provide for fees. In the court's view,

[5]By the time of the filing of petitioners' Second Amended Complaint on September 16, 1980, attorney's fees were available directly under the Rehabilitation Act. See Rehabilitation, Comprehensive Services, and Developmental Disabilities Amendments of 1978, § 120, 92 Stat. 2982, 29 U. S. C. § 794a. Instead of relying on that statute, however, petitioners relied on 31 U. S. C. § 1244(e) (1976 ed.) (now replaced by 31 U. S. C. § 6721(c)(2)), a statute that authorized a civil action to enforce § 504 of the Rehabilitation Act against any State or local government receiving federal funds under the State and Local Fiscal Assistance Act of 1972, 86 Stat. 919, as amended by the State and Local Fiscal Assistance Amendments of 1976, 90 Stat. 2341. Section § 1244(e) authorized an award of attorney's fees to a "prevailing party."

respondents had given insufficient weight to the fact that petitioners had alleged equal protection and § 1983 claims as well as the EHA claim. The court added that it found the equal protection claim petitioners included in their second amended complaint to be colorable and nonfrivolous. Petitioners thus were entitled to fees for prevailing in an action to enforce their § 1983 claim.

The Court of Appeals reversed. *Smith* v. *Cumberland School Committee*, 703 F. 2d 4 (CA1 1983). The court first noted that, under what is labelled the "American Rule," attorney's fees are available as a general matter only when statutory authority so provides. *Alyeska Pipeline Co.* v. *Wilderness Society*, 421 U. S. 240 (1975). Here the action and relief granted in this case fell within the reach of the EHA, a federal statute that establishes a comprehensive federal-state scheme for the provision of special education to handicapped children, but that does not provide for attorney's fees.[6] For fees, the District Court had to look to § 1988 and § 505 of the Rehabilitation Act.

As to the § 1988 claim, the court acknowledged the general rule that when the claim upon which a plaintiff actually prevails is accompanied by a "substantial," though undecided, § 1983 claim arising from the same nucleus of facts, a fee award is appropriate. *Maher* v. *Gagne*, 448 U. S. 122, 130-131 (1980). Here, petitioners' § 1983 claims arguably were at least substantial enough to support federal jurisdiction. *Ibid.* Even if the § 1983 claims were substantial, however, the Court of Appeals concluded that, given the comprehensiveness of the EHA, Congress could not have intended its omission of attorney's fees relief to be rectified by recourse to § 1988.

The Court of Appeals drew support for its conclusion from this Court's decision in *Middlesex County Sewage Auth.* v. *National Sea Clammers Assn.*, 453 U. S. 1 (1981). There the Court held that where Congress had provided comprehensive enforcement mechanisms for protection of a federal right and those mechanisms did not include a private right of action, a litigant could not obtain a private right of action by asserting his claim under § 1983. The Court of Appeals recognized that *Sea Clammers* might not logically preclude a § 1983 action for violation of the EHA, since the EHA expressly recognizes a private right of action, but it does support the more general proposition that when a statute creates a comprehensive remedial scheme, intentional "omissions" from that scheme should not be supplanted by the remedial apparatus of § 1983. In the view of the Court of Appeals, the fact that the § 1983 claims alleged here were based on independent constitutional violations rather than violations of the EHA was immaterial. The constitution claims alleged—a denial of due process and a denial of a free appropriate public education because of handicap—are factually identical to

[6]The District Court purported to award relief on the basis of state law. In light of the decision in *Pennhurst State School and Hospital* v. *Halderman*, 465 U. S. 89 (1984), that was improper. The propriety of the injunctive relief, however, is not at issue here. We think the Court of Appeals was correct in treating the relief as essentially awarded under the EHA, since petitioners had challenged the State Commissioner's construction of state law on the basis of their rights under the EHA, and since the question of state law on which petitioners prevailed was certified by the District Court in an effort to avoid a Supremacy Clause conflict with the EHA. It is clear that the EHA creates a right, enforceable in federal court, to the free appropriate public education required by the statute. *Board of Education* v. *Rowley*, 458 U. S. 176 (1982); 20 U. S. C. § 1415(e)(2).

the EHA claims. If a litigant could obtain fees simply by an incantation of § 1983, fees would become available in almost every case.[7]

The court disposed of the Rehabilitation Act basis for fees in a similar fashion. Even if Congress did not specifically intend to pre-empt § 504 claims with the EHA, the EHA's comprehensive remedial scheme entails a rejection of fee-shifting that properly limits the fees provision of the more general Rehabilitation Act.

Because of confusion in the circuits over the proper interplay among the various statutory and constitutional bases for relief in cases of this nature, and over the effect of that interplay on the provision of attorney's fees,[8] we granted certiorari, 464 U. S. 932 (1983).

II

Petitioners insist that the Court of Appeals simply ignored the guidance of this Court in *Mayer* v. *Gagne, supra*, that a prevailing party who asserts substantial but unaddressed constitutional claims is entitled to attorney's fees under 42 U. S. C. § 1988. They urge that the reliance of the Court of Appeals on *Sea Clammers* was misplaced. *Sea Clammers* had to do only with an effort to enlarge a statutory remedy by asserting a claim based on that statute under the "and laws" provision of § 1983.[9] In this case, petitioners made no effort to enlarge the remedies available under the EHA by asserting their claim through the "and laws" provision of § 1983. They presented separate constitutional claims, properly cognizable under § 1983. Since the claim on which they prevailed and their constitutional claims arose out of a "common nucleus of operative fact," *Mayer* v. *Gagne*, 448 U. S., at 132, n. 15, quoting

---

[7]The Court of Appeals added that it did not intend to indicate that the EHA in any way limits the scope of a handicapped child's constitutional rights. Claims not covered by the EHA should still be cognizable under § 1983, with fees available for such actions. The court noted, for instance, that to the extent petitioners' securing of a preliminary injunction fell outside any relief available under the EHA, attorney's fees might be appropriate for that relief. Because the award of fees against the School Committee for work done in obtaining the preliminary injunction was not challenged on appeal, the court had no occasion to decide the issue.

[8]See, *e. g., Quackenbush* v. *Johnson City School District*, 716 F. 2d 141 (CA2 1983) (§ 1983 remedy, including damages, available for claim that plaintiff was denied access to EHA procedures); *Department of Education* v. *Katherine D.*, 727 F. 2d 809 (CA 9 1983) (EHA precludes reliance on § 1983 or § 504); *Robert M.* v. *Benton*, 671 F. 2d 1104 (CA8 1982) (fees available under § 1988 because plaintiff made colorable due process as well as EHA challenges to use of state agency employee as hearing officer); *Hymes* v. *Harnett County Board of Education*, 664 F. 2d 410 (CA4 1981) (claims made under the EHA, § 504 and § 1983; fees available for due process relief not available under the EHA); *Anderson* v. *Thompson*, 658 F. 2d 1205 (CA7 1981) (EHA claim not assertable under § 1983; attorney's fees therefore not available).

[9]42 U. S. C. § 1983 provides a remedy for a deprivation, under color of state law, "of any rights, privileges, or immunities secured by the Constitution *and laws*" (emphasis added). In *Maine* v. *Thiboutot*, 448 U. S. 1 (1980), the Court held that § 1983 authorizes suits to redress violations by state officials of rights created by federal statutes as well as by the Federal Constitution and that fees are available under § 1988 for such statutory violations.

Sea Clammers excluded from the reach of *Thiboutot* cases in which Congress specifically foreclosed a remedy under § 1983. 453 U. S., at 19.

H. R. Rep. No. 94-1558, p. 4, n. 7 (1976), and since the constitutional claims were found by the District Court and assumed by the Court of Appeals to be substantial, petitioners urge that they are entitled to fees under § 1988. In addition, petitioners presented a substantial claim under § 504 of the Rehabilitation Act. Since § 505 of that Act authorizes attorney's fees in the same manner as does § 1988 and in fact incorporates the legislative history of § 1988, see 124 Cong. Rec. 30346 (1978) (remarks of Sen. Cranston), the reasoning of *Maher* applies to claims based on § 504. Petitioners therefore, it is claimed, are entitled to fees for substantial, though unaddressed, § 504 claims.

Respondents counter that petitioners simply are attempting to circumvent the lack of a provision for attorney's fees in the EHA by resorting to the pleading trick of adding surplus constitutional claims and similar claims under § 504 of the Rehabilitation Act. Whatever Congress' intent was in authorizing fees for substantial, unaddressed claims based on § 1988 or § 505, it could not have been to allow plaintiffs to receive an award of attorney's fees in a situation where Congress has made clear its intent that fees not be available.

Resolution of this dispute requires us to explore congressional intent, both in authorizing fees for substantial unaddressed constitutional claims and in setting out the elaborate substantive and procedural requirements of the EHA, with no indication that attorney's fees are available in an action to enforce those requirements. We turn first to petitioners' claim that they were entitled to fees under 42 U. S. C. § 1988 because they asserted substantial constitutional claims.

III

As the legislative history illustrates and as this Court has recognized, § 1988 is a broad grant of authority to courts to award attorney's fees to plaintiffs seeking to vindicate federal constitutional and statutory rights. *Maine* v. *Thiboutot*, 448 U. S. 1, 9 (1980); *Maher* v. *Gagne, supra; Hutto* v. *Finney*, 437 U. S. 678, 694 (1978); S. Rep. No. 94-1011, p. 4 (1976) (a prevailing plaintiff "'should ordinarily recover an attorney's fee unless special circumstances would render such an award unjust,'" quoting *Newman* v. *Piggie Park Enterprises, Inc.*, 390 U. S. 400, 402 (1968). Congress did not intend to have that authority extinguished by the fact that the case was settled or resolved on a nonconstitutional ground. *Maher* v. *Gagne*, 448 U. S., at 132. As the Court also has recognized, however, the authority to award fees in a case where the plaintiff prevails on substantial constitutional claims is not without qualification. Due regard must be paid, not only to the fact that a plaintiff "prevailed," but also to the relationship between the claims on which effort was expended and the ultimate relief obtained. *Hensley* v. *Eckerhart,* 461 U. S. 424 (1983); *Blum* v. *Stenson*, 465 U. S. 886 (1984). Thus, for example, fees are not properly awarded for work done on a claim on which a plaintiff did not prevail and which involved distinctly different facts and legal theories from the claims on the basis of which relief was awarded. *Hensley* v. *Eckerhart*, 461 U. S., at 434-435, 440. Although, in most cases, there is no clear line between hours of work that contributed to a plaintiff's success and those that did not, district courts remain charged with the responsibility, imposed by Congress, of evaluating the award requested in light of the relationship between particular claims for which work is done and the plaintiff's success. *Id.*, at 436-437.

A similar analysis is appropriate in a case like this, where the prevailing plaintiffs rely on substantial, unaddressed constitutional claims as the basis for an award of attorney's fees. The fact that constitutional claims are made does not render automatic an award of fees for the entire proceeding. Congress' purpose in authorizing a fee award for an unaddressed constitutional claim was to avoid penalizing a litigant for the fact that courts are properly reluctant to resolve constitutional questions if a nonconstitutional claim is dispositive. H. R. Rep. No. 94-1558, p. 4, n. 7. That purpose does not alter the requirement that a claim for which fees are awarded be reasonably related to the plaintiff's ultimate success. It simply authorizes a district court to assume that the plaintiff has prevailed on his fee-generating claim and to award fees appropriate to that success.[10]

In light of the requirement that a claim for which fees are awarded be reasonably related to the plaintiff's ultimate success, it is clear that plaintiffs may not rely simply on the fact that substantial fee-generating claims were made during the course of the litigation. Closer examination of the nature of the claims and the relationship between those claims and petitioners' ultimate success is required.

Besides making a claim under the EHA, petitioners asserted at two different points in the proceedings that procedures employed by state officials denied them due process. They also claimed that Tommy was being discriminated against on the basis of his handicapping condition, in violation of the Equal Protection Clause of the Fourteenth Amendment.

A

The first due process claim may be disposed of briefly. Petitioners challenged the refusal of the School Board to grant them a full hearing before terminating Tommy's funding. Petitioners were awarded fees against the School Board for their efforts in obtaining an injunction to prevent that due process deprivation. The award was not challenged on appeal and we therefore assume that it was proper.

The fact that petitioners prevailed on their initial due process claim, however, by itself does not entitle them to fees for the subsequent administrative and judicial proceedings. The due process claim that entitled petitioners to an order maintaining Tommy's placement throughout the course of the subsequent proceedings is entirely separate from the claims petitioners made in those proceedings. Nor were those proceedings necessitated by the School Board's failings. Even if the School Board had complied with state regulations and had guaranteed Tommy's continued placement pending adminis-

[10]The legislative history also makes clear that the fact that a plaintiff has prevailed on one of two or more alternative bases for relief does not prevent an award of fees for the unaddressed claims, as long as those claims are reasonably related to the plaintiff's ultimate success. See S. Rep. No. 94-1011, p. 6 (1976), citing *Davis* v. *County of Los Angeles*, 8 EPD ¶9444 (CD Cal. 1974). See also *Hensley* v. *Eckerhart*, 461 U. S. 424, at 435. The same rule should apply when an unaddressed constitutional claim provides an alternative, but reasonably related, basis for the plaintiff's ultimate relief.

trative review of its decision, petitioners still would have had to avail themselves of the administrative process in order to obtain the permanent relief they wanted—an interpretation of state law that placed on the School Board the obligation to pay for Tommy's education. Petitioners' initial due process claim is not sufficiently related to their ultimate success to support an award of fees for the entire proceeding. We turn, therefore, to petitioners' other § 1983 claims.

As petitioners emphasize, their § 1983 claims were not based on alleged violations of the EHA,[11] but on independent claims of constitutional deprivations. As the Court of Appeals recognized, however, petitioners' constitutional claims, a denial of due process and a denial of a free appropriate public education as guaranteed by the Equal Protection Clause, are virtually identical to their EHA claims.[12] The question to be asked, therefore, is whether Congress intended that the EHA be the exclusive avenue through which a plaintiff may assert those claims.

B

We have little difficulty concluding that Congress intended the EHA to be the exclusive avenue through which a plaintiff may assert an equal protection claim to a publicly financed special education. The EHA is a comprehensive scheme set up by Congress to aid the States in complying with their constitutional obligations to provide public education for handicapped children. Both the provisions of the statute and its legislative history indicate that Congress intended handicapped children with constitutional claims to a free appropriate public education to pursue those claims through the carefully tailored administrative and judicial mechanism set out in the statute.

In the statement of findings with which the EHA begins, Congress noted that there were more than 8,000,000 handicapped children in the country, the special education needs of most of whom were not being fully met. 20 U. S. C. §§ 1400(b)(1), (2), and (3). Congress also recognized that in a series of "landmark court cases," the right to an equal education opportunity for handicapped children had been established. S. Rep. No. 94-168, p. 6 (1975). See also *id.*, at 13 ("It is the intent of the Committee to establish and protect the right to education for all handicapped children and to provide assistance to the States in carrying out their responsibilities under State law and the Constitution of the United States to provide equal protection of the laws"). The EHA was an attempt to relieve the fiscal burden placed on States and

[11]Courts generally agree that the EHA may not be claimed as the basis for a § 1983 action. See, *e. g., Quackenbush* v. *Johnson City School District, supra; Department of Education* v. *Katherine D., supra; Anderson* v. *Thompson, supra.*

[12]The timing of the filing of petitioners' second amended complaint, after the Supreme Court of Rhode Island had ruled that petitioners were entitled to the relief they sought, reveals that the equal protection claim added nothing to petitioners' claims under the EHA and provides an alternative basis for denying attorney's fees on the basis of that claim. There is, of course, nothing wrong with seeking relief on the basis of certain statutes because those statutes provide for attorney's fees, or with amending a complaint to include claims that provide for attorney's fees. But where it is clear that the claims that provide for attorney's fees had nothing to do with a plaintiff's success, *Hensley* v. *Eckerhart, supra,* requires that fees not be awarded on the basis of those claims.

localities by their responsibility to provide education for all handicapped children. 20 U. S. C. §§ 1400(b)(8) and (9). At the same time, however, Congress made clear that the EHA is not simply a funding statute. The responsibility for providing the required education remains on the States. S. Rep. No. 94-168, at 22. And the Act establishes an enforceable substantive right to a free appropriate public education. See *Board of Education* v. *Rowley*, 458 U. S. 176 (1982). See also 121 Cong. Rec. 37417 (1975) (statement of Sen. Schweiker: "It can no longer be the policy of the Government to merely establish an unenforceable goal requiring all children to be in school. [The bill] takes positive necessary steps to insure that the rights of children and their families are protected").[13] Finally, the Act establishes an elaborate procedural mechanism to protect the rights of handicapped children. The procedures not only ensure that hearings conducted by the State are fair and adequate. They also effect Congress' intent that each child's individual educational needs be worked out through a process that begins on the local level and includes ongoing parental involvement, detailed procedural safeguards, and a right to judicial review. §§ 1412(4), 1414(a)(5), 1415. See also S. Rep. No. 94-168, at 11-12 (emphasizing the role of parental involvement in assuring that appropriate services are provided to a handicapped child); *id.*, at p. 22; Board of Education v. *Rowley*, 458 U. S., at 208-209.

In light of the comprehensive nature of the procedures and guarantees set out in the EHA and Congress' express efforts to place on local and state educational agencies the primary responsibility for developing a plan to accommodate the needs of each individual handicapped child, we find it difficult to believe that Congress also meant to leave undisturbed the ability of a handicapped child to go directly to court with an equal protection claim to a free appropriate public education.[14] Not only would such a result render su-

---

[13]Prior to 1975, federal provisions for the education of handicapped children were contained in the Education of the Handicapped Act, passed in 1970, 84 Stat. 175, and amended in 1974, 88 Stat. 579 (current version at 20 U. S. C. § 1400 *et seq.*). The Act then provided for grants to States to facilitate the development of programs for the education of handicapped children. § 611(a). The only requirements imposed on the States were that they use federal funds on programs designed to meet the special education needs of handicapped children, § 613(a), and that parents or guardians be guaranteed minimum procedural safeguards, including prior notice and an opportunity to be heard when a State proposed to change the educational placement of the child. § 614(d). See n. 4, *supra*.

[14]The District Court in this case relied on similar reasoning—that Congress could not have meant for a plaintiff to be able to circumvent the EHA administrative process—and concluded that a handicapped child asserting an equal protection claim to public education was required to exhaust his administrative remedies before making his § 1983 claim. See *Turillo* v. *Tyson*, 535 F. Supp. 577, 583 (R. I. 1982), cited in the District Court's oral decision of April 30, 1982, App. to Pet. for Cert. A40. Because exhaustion was required, the court, relying on *New York Gaslight Club, Inc.* v. *Carey*, 447 U. S. 54 (1980), concluded that attorney's fees were appropriate under § 1988 for work performed in the state administrative process.

The difference between *Carey* and this case is that in *Carey*, the statute that authorized fees, Title VII, also required a plaintiff to pursue available state administrative remedies. In contrast, nothing in § 1983 requires that a plaintiff exhaust his administrative remedies before bringing a § 1983 suit. See *Patsy* v. *Florida Board of Regents*, 457 U. S. 496 (1982). If § 1983 stood as an independent avenue of relief for petitioners, then they could go straight to court to assert it.

perfluous most of the detailed procedural protections outlined in the statute, but, more important, it would run counter to Congress' view that the needs of handicapped children are best accommodated by having the parents and the local education agency work together to formulate an individualized plan for each handicapped child's education. No federal district court presented with a constitutional claim to a public education can duplicate that process.

We do not lightly conclude that Congress intended to preclude reliance on § 1983 as a remedy for a substantial equal protection claim. Since 1871, when it was passed by Congress, § 1983 has stood as an independent safeguard against deprivations of federal constitutional and statutory rights. See *Patsy* v. *Florida Board of Regents*, 457 U. S. 496 (1982); *Mitchum* v. *Foster*, 407 U. S. 225, 242 (1972); *Monroe* v. *Pape*, 365 U. S. 167, 183 (1961). Nevertheless, § 1983 is a statutory remedy and Congress retains the authority to repeal it or replace it with an alternative remedy.[15] The crucial consideration is what Congress intended. See *Brown* v. *GSA*, 425 U. S. 820, 825-829 (1976); *Johnson* v. *Railway Express Agency*, 421 U. S. 454, 459 (1975); *Adickes* v. *S. H. Kress & Co.*, 398 U. S. 144, 151, n. 5 (1970).

In this case, we think Congress' intent is clear. Allowing a plaintiff to circumvent the EHA administrative remedies would be inconsistent with Congress' carefully tailored scheme. The legislative history gives no indication that Congress intended such a result.[16] Rather, it indicates that Congress perceived the EHA as the most effective vehicle for protecting the constitutional right of a handicapped child to a public education. We conclude, there-

---

[15]There is no issue here of Congress' ability to preclude the federal courts from granting a remedy for a constitutional deprivation. Even if Congress repealed all statutory remedies for constitutional violations, the power of federal courts to grant the relief necessary to protect against constitutional deprivations or to remedy the wrong done is presumed to be available in cases within their jurisdiction. See *Bell* v. *Hood*, 327 U. S. 678, 684 (1946); *Bivens* v. *Six Unknown Fed. Narcotics Agents*, 403 U. S. 388, 396 (1971); *id.*, at 400-406 (Harlan, J., concurring in judgment).

[16]Petitioners insist that regardless of the wisdom of requiring resort to available EHA remedies before a handicapped child may seek judicial review, Congress specifically indicated that it did not intend to limit the judicial remedies otherwise available to a handicapped child. If that were true, we would agree with petitioners that Congress' intent is controlling and that a § 1983 remedy remained availabe to them. See *Johnson* v. *Railway Express Agency*, 421 U. S. 454, 459 (1975). The sentence in the legislative history on which petitioners rely, however, is not the clear expression of congressional intent petitioners would like it to be.

The sentence on which petitioners rely is included in the Committee Report of the Senate's version of the EHA. S. Rep. No. 94-168, pp. 27-28 (1975). The Senate bill included a requirement, not in the Conference bill, see Senate Conference Report No. 94-455, pp. 39-40 (1975), that the States set up an entity for ensuring compliance with the EHA. The compliance entity would be authorized, *inter alia*, to receive complaints regarding alleged violations of the Act. The Committee added that it did "not intend the existence of such an entity to limit the right of individuals to seek redress of grievances through other avenues, such as bringing civil action in Federal or State courts to protect and enforce the rights of handicapped children under applicable law." S. Rep. No. 94-168, p. 26 (1975). In the context in which the statement was made, it appears to establish nothing more than that handicapped children retain a right to judicial review of their individual cases. It does not establish that they can choose whether to avail themselves of the EHA process or go straight to court with an equal protection claim.

fore, that where the EHA is available to a handicapped child asserting a right to a free appropriate public education, based either on the EHA or on the Equal Protection Clause of the Fourteenth Amendment, the EHA is the exclusive avenue through which the child and his parents or guardian can pursue their claim.

C

Petitioners also made a due process challenge to the partiality of the state hearing officer. The question whether this claim will support an award of attorney's fees has two aspects—whether the procedural safeguards set out in the EHA manifest Congress' intent to preclude resort to § 1983 on a due process challenge and, if not, whether petitioners are entitled to attorney's fees for their due process claim. We find it unnecessary to resolve the first question, because we are satisfied that even if an independent due process challenge may be maintained, petitioners are not entitled to attorney's fees for their particular claim.[17]

Petitioners' plea for injunctive relief was not made until after the administrative proceedings had ended. They did not seek an order requiring the Commissioner of Education to grant them a new hearing, but only a declaratory judgment that the state regulations did not comply with the requirements

---

[17]We note that the issue is not the same as that presented by a substantive equal protection claim to a free appropriate public education. The EHA does set out specific procedural safeguards that must be guaranteed by a State seeking funds under the Act. See 20 U. S. C. § 1415. And although some courts have concluded that the EHA does not authorize injunctive relief to remedy procedural deficiencies, see, *e. g., Hymes* v. *Harnett County Board of Education*, 664 F. 2d 410 (CA4 1981), other courts have construed the district courts' authority under § 1415(e)(2) to grant "appropriate relief" as including the authority to grant injunctive relief, either after an unsuccessful and allegedly unfair administrative proceeding, or prior to exhaustion of the state remedies if pursuing those remedies would be futile or inadequate. See, *e. g., Robert M.* v. *Benton*, 622 F. 2d 370 (CA8 1980); *Monahan* v. *Nebraska*, 491 F. Supp. 1074 (Neb. 1980), aff'd in part and vacated in part, 645 F. 2d 592 (CA8 1981); *Howard S.* v. *Friendwood Independent School District*, 454 F. Supp. 634 (SD Tex. 1978); *Armstrong* v. *Kline*, 476 F. Supp. 583, 601-602 (ED Pa. 1979), remanded on other grounds *sub nom. Battle* v. *Pennsylvania*, 629 F. 2d 269 (CA3 1980), cert. denied, 452 U. S. 968 (1981); *North* v. *District of Columbia Board of Education*, 471 F. Supp. 136 (D. C. 1979). See also 121 Cong. Rec. 37416 (1975) (remarks of Sen. Williams) ("exhaustion of the administrative procedures established under this part should not be required for any individual complainant filing a judicial action in cases where such exhaustion would be futile either as a legal or practical matter").

On the other hand, unlike an independent equal protection claim, maintenance of an independent due process challenge to state procedures would not be inconsistent with the EHA's comprehensive scheme. Under either the EHA or § 1983, a plaintiff would be entitled to bypass the administrative process by obtaining injunctive relief only on a showing that irreparable harm otherwise would result. See *Monahan* v. *Nebraska*, 645 F. 2d 592, 598-599 (CA8 1981). And, while Congress apparently has determined that local and state agencies should not be burdened with attorney's fees to litigants who succeed, through resort to the procedures outlined in the EHA, in requiring those agencies to provide free schooling, there is no indication that agencies should be exempt from a fee award where plaintiffs have had to resort to judicial relief to force the agencies to provide them the process they were constitutionally due.

of due process and the EHA, and an injunction prohibiting the Commissioner from conducting further hearings under those regulations. App. 59-60. That due process claim and the substantive claim on which petitioners ultimately prevailed involved entirely separate legal theories and, more important, would have warranted entirely different relief. According to their complaint, petitioners did not even seek relief for themselves on the due process claim, but sought only to protect the rights of others coming after them in the administrative process. The efforts petitioners subsequently expended in the judicial process addressed only the substantive question as to which agency, as a matter of state and federal law, was required to pay for Tommy's education. Whether or not the state procedures accorded petitioners the process they were due had no bearing on that substantive question.

We conclude that where, as here, petitioners have presented distinctly different claims for different relief, based on different facts and legal theories, and have prevailed only on a non-fee claim, they are not entitled to a fee award simply because the other claim was a constitutional claim that could be asserted through § 1983. We note that a contrary conclusion would mean that every EHA plaintiff who seeks judicial review after an adverse agency determination could ensure a fee award for successful judicial efforts simply by including in his substantive challenge a claim that the administrative process was unfair. If the court ignored the due process claim but granted substantive relief, the due process claim could be considered a substantial unaddressed constitutional claim and the plaintiff would be entitled to fees.[18] It is unlikely that Congress intended such a result.

IV

We turn, finally, to petitioners' claim that they were entitled to fees under § 505 of the Rehabilitation Act, because they asserted a substantial claim for relief under § 504 of that Act.

Much of our analysis of petitioners' equal protection claim is applicable here. The EHA is a comprehensive scheme designed by Congress as the most effective way to protect the right of a handicapped child to a free appropriate public education. We concluded above that in enacting the EHA, Congress was aware of, and intended to accommodate, the claims of handicapped children that the Equal Protection Clause required that they be ensured access to public education. We also concluded that Congress did not intend to have the EHA scheme circumvented by resort to the more general provisions of § 1983. We reach the same conclusion regarding petitioners' § 504 claim. The relationship between the EHA and § 504, however, requires a slightly different analysis from that required by petitioners' equal protection claim.

Section 504 and the EHA are different substantive statutes. While the

[18]Even if the court denied the due process claim, as here, it is arguable that the plaintiff would be entitled to have an appellate court determine whether the district court was correct in its ruling on the due process claim. In this case, the District Court ruled against petitioners on their due process claim and the Court of Appeals determined, on appeal from the District Court's award of substantive relief, that the issue was moot. Nevertheless, in considering the propriety of the District Court's award of fees, the Court of Appeals recognized that the due process claim was at least substantial enough to support federal jurisdiction. 703 F. 2d, at 7.

EHA guarantees a right to a free appropriate public education, § 504 simply prevents discrimination on the basis of handicap. But while the EHA is limited to handicapped children seeking access to public education, § 504 protects handicapped persons of all ages from discrimination in a variety of programs and activities receiving federal financial assistance.

Because both statutes are built around fundamental notions of equal access to state programs and facilities, their substantive requirements, as applied to the right of a handicapped child to a public education, have been interpreted to be strikingly similar. In regulations promulgated pursuant to § 504, the Secretary of Education[19] has interpreted § 504 as requiring a recipient of federal funds that operates a public elementary or secondary education program to provide a free appropriate public education to each qualified handicapped person in the recipient's jurisdiction. 34 CFR § 104.33(a) (1983).[20] The requirement extends to the provision of a public or private residential placement if necessary to provide a free appropriate public education. § 104.33(c)(3). The regulations also require that the recipient implement procedural safeguards, including notice, an opportunity for the parents or guardian to examine relevant records, an impartial hearing with opportunity for participation by the parents or guardian and representation by counsel, and a review procedure. § 104.36. The Secretary declined to require the exact EHA procedures, because those procedures might be inappropriate for some recipients not subject to the EHA, see 34 CFR, subtitle B, ch. 1, App. A, p. 371, but indicated that compliance with EHA procedures would satisfy § 104.36.

On the other hand, although both statutes begin with an equal protection premise that handicapped children must be given access to public education, it does not follow that the affirmative requirements imposed by the two statutes are the same. The significant difference between the two, as applied to special education claims, is that the substantive and procedural rights assumed to be guaranteed by both statutes are specifically required only by the EHA.

Section 504, 29 U. S. C. § 794, provides, in pertinent part, that:

"No otherwise qualified handicapped individual in the United States, . . . shall, solely by reason of his handicap, be excluded from the participation in, be denied the benefits of, or be subjected to discrimination under any program or activity receiving Federal financial assistance . . ."

In *Southeastern Community College* v. *Davis*, 442 U. S. 397 (1979), the Court emphasized that § 504 does not require affirmative action on behalf of handicapped persons, but only the absence of discrimination against those

[19]The regulations were promulgated by the Secretary of Health, Education, and Welfare (HEW). 42 Fed. Reg. 22676 (1977). The functions of the Secretary of HEW under the Rehabilitation Act and under the EHA were transferred in 1979 to the Secretary of Education under the Department of Education Organization Act, § 301(a), 93 Stat. 677, 20 U. S. C. § 3441(a).

[20]Regulations under § 504 and the EHA were being formulated at the same time. The § 504 regulations were effective June 3, 1977. 42 Fed. Reg., at 22676. The EHA regulations were effective October 1, 1977. *Id.*, at 42474. The Secretary of HEW and the Commissioner of Education emphasized the coordination of effort behind the two sets of regulations and the Department's intent that the § 504 regulations be consistent with the requirements of the EHA. See 41 Fed. Reg. 56967 (1976); 42 Fed. Reg., at 22677.

persons. 442 U. S., at 411-412. In light of *Davis*, courts construing § 504 as applied to the educational needs of handicapped children have expressed confusion about the extent to which § 504 requires special services necessary to make public education accessible to handicapped children.[21]

In the EHA, on the other hand, Congress specified the affirmative obligations imposed on States to ensure that equal access to a public education is not an empty guarantee, but offers some benefit to a handicapped child. Thus, the statute specifically requires "such . . . supportive services . . . as may be required to assist a handicapped child to benefit from special education," see *Board of Education* v. *Rowley*, 458 U. S., at 200, including, if the public facilities are inadequate for the needs of the child, "instruction in hospitals and institutions." 20 U. S. C. §§ 1401(16) and (17).

We need not decide the extent of the guarantee of a free appropriate public education Congress intended to impose under § 504. We note the uncertainty regarding the reach of § 504 to emphasize that it is only in the EHA that Congress specified the rights and remedies available to a handicapped child seeking access to public education. Even assuming that the reach of § 504 is coextensive with that of the EHA, there is no doubt that the remedies, rights, and procedures Congress set out in the EHA are the ones it intended to apply to a handicapped child's claim to a free appropriate public education. We are satisfied that Congress did not intend a handicapped child to be able to circumvent the requirements or supplement the remedies of the EHA by resort to the general antidiscrimination provision of § 504.

There is no suggestion that § 504 adds anything to petitioners' substantive right to a free appropriate public education.[22] The only elements added by § 504 are the possibility of circumventing EHA administrative procedures and going straight to court with a § 504 claim,[23] the possibility of a damages

---

[21]Courts generally have upheld the § 504 regulations on the grounds that they do not require extensive modification of existing programs and that States and localities generally provide nonhandicapped children with educational services appropriate to their needs. See *Phipps* v. *New Hanover County Board of Education*, 551 F. Supp. 732 (ED N. C. 1982). But see *Colin K.* v. *Schmidt*, 715 F. 2d 1, 9 (CA1 1983) (in light of *Davis*, requirement that a school system provide a private residential placement could not be imposed under § 504).

[22]Of course, if a State provided services beyond those required by the EHA, but discriminatorily denied those services to a handicapped child, § 504 would remain available to the child as an avenue of relief. In view of the substantial overlap between the two statutes and Congress' intent that efforts to accommodate educational needs be made first on the local level, the presumption in a case involving a claim arguably with the EHA should be that the plaintiff is required to exhaust EHA remedies, unless doing so would be futile.

[23]Lower courts appear to agree, however, that unless doing so would be futile, EHA administrative remedies must be exhausted before a § 504 claim for the same relief available under the EHA may be brought. See, *e. g., Riley* v. *Ambach*, 668 F. 2d 635 (CA2 1981); *Phipps* v. *New Hanover County Board of Education, supra; Harris* v. *Campbell*, 472 F. Supp. 51 (ED Va. 1979); *H. R.* v. *Hornbeck*, 524 F. Supp. 215 (Md. 1981).

award in cases where no such award is available under the EHA,[24] and attorney's fees. As discussed above, Congress' intent to place on local and state educational agencies the responsibility for determining the most appropriate educational plan for a handicapped child is clear. To the extent § 504 otherwise would allow a plaintiff to circumvent that state procedure, we are satisfied that the remedy conflicts with Congress' intent in the EHA.

Congress did not explain the absence of a provision for a damages remedy and attorney's fees in the EHA. Several references in the statute itself and in its legislative history, however, indicate that the omissions were in response to Congress' awareness of the financial burden already imposed on States by the responsibility of providing education for handicapped children. As noted above, one of the stated purposes of the statute was to relieve this financial burden. See 20 U. S. C. §§ 1400(b)(8) and (9). Discussions of the EHA by its proponents reflect Congress' intent to "make every resource, or as much as possible, available to the direct activities and the direct programs that are going to benefit the handicapped." 121 Cong. Rec. 19501 (1975) (remarks of Sen. Dole). See also *id.*, at 37025 (procedural safeguards designed to further the congressional goal of ensuring full educational opportunity without overburdening the local school districts and state educational agencies) (remarks of Rep. Perkins); S. Rep. No. 94-168, p. 81 (minority views cognizant of financial burdens on localities). The Act appears to represent Congress' judgment that the best way to ensure a free appropriate public education for handicapped children is to clarify and make enforceable the rights of those children while at the same time endeavoring to relieve the financial burden imposed on the agencies responsible to guarantee those rights. Where § 504 adds nothing to the substantive rights of a handicapped child, we cannot believe that Congress intended to have the careful balance struck in the EHA upset by reliance on § 504 for otherwise unavailable damages or for an award of attorney's fees.

We emphasize the narrowness of our holding. We do not address a situation where the EHA is not available or where § 504 guarantees substantive rights greater than those available under the EHA. We hold only that where, as here, whatever remedy might be provided under § 504 is provided with more clarity and precision under the EHA, a plaintiff may not circumvent or enlarge on the remedies available under the EHA by resort to § 504.

In light of our conclusion that § 504 was not available to petitioners as an alternative basis for the relief they sought, we need not decide whether, as petitioners urge, § 505 authorizes attorney's fees for substantial, unaddressed § 504 claims or whether a Rehabilitation Act claim is entitled only to a "determination on the . . . claim for the purpose of awarding counsel fees." H. R. Rep. No. 94-1558, p. 4, n. 7 (1976).

---

[24]There is some confusion among the circuits as to the availability of a damages remedy under § 504 and under the EHA. Without expressing an opinion on the matter, we note that courts generally agree that damages are available under § 504, but are available under the EHA only in exceptional circumstances. See, *e. g., Miener* v. *Missouri*, 673 F. 2d 969, 978 (CA8 1982), cert. denied, 459 U. S. 909 (1983); *Anderson* v. *Thompson*, 658 F. 2d 1205 (CA7 1981); *Monahan* v. *Nebraska*, 491 F. Supp., at 1094; *Hurry* v. *Jones*, 560 F. Supp. 500 (R. I. 1983); *Gregg B.* v. *Board of Education*, 535 F. Supp. 1333, 1339-1340 (ED N. Y. 1982).

V

The judgment of the Court of Appeals is affirmed.

It is so ordered.

JUSTICE BRENNAN, with whom JUSTICE MARSHALL and JUSTICE STEVENS join, dissenting.

In this case we are called upon to analyze the interaction among five statutory provisions: § 1 of the Civil Rights Act of 1871, as amended, 42 U. S. C. § 1983; § 2 of the Civil Rights Attorney's Fees Awards Act of 1976, 42 U. S. C. § 1988; § 504 of the Rehabilitation Act of 1973, as amended, 29 U. S. C. § 794; § 505(b) of the Rehabilitation Act, 29 U. S. C. § 794a(b); and § 615(e)(2) of the Education of the Handicapped Act (EHA or Act), as added, 89 Stat. 789, 20 U. S. C. § 1415(e)(2).

Section 1983 provides:

> "Every person who, under color of any statute, ordinance, regulation, custom, or usage, of any State or Territory, subjects, or causes to be subjected, any citizen of the United States or other person within the jurisdiction thereof to the deprivation of *any rights, privileges, or immunities secured by the Constitution* and laws, shall be liable to the party injured in an action at law, suit in equity, or other proper proceeding for redress." (Emphasis added).

And § 1988 provides that the prevailing party in an action prosecuted under § 1983 may be awarded reasonable attorney's fees. Similarly, §§ 504 and 505(b) of the Rehabilitation Act provide a cause of action and attorney's fees, respectively, to an individual who, "solely by reason of his handicap," has been "excluded from the participation in, . . . denied the benefits of, . . . [or] subjected to discrimination under any program or activity receiving Federal financial assistance." Finally, § 615(e)(2) of the EHA authorizes judicial review of the States' provision of "free appropriate public education'' to handicapped children. Unlike 42 U. S. C. § 1983 and § 504 of the Rehabilitation Act, however, § 615(e)(2) has no counterpart in the EHA authorizing the award of attorney's fees to prevailing parties.

Petitioners challenge Rhode Island's discriminatory failure to afford Thomas F. Smith III access to certain educational programs made available to other handicapped children. As the Court recognizes, *ante*, this challenge states a meritorious claim under the EHA and a substantial claim under the Equal Protection Clause of the Fourteenth Amendment. In addition, petitioners' claim appears to fall squarely within the terms of § 504 of the Rehabilitation Act. Consequently, if §§ 504 and 1983 are available as bases for petitioners' action, petitioners are entitled to recover reasonable attorney's fees under § 1988 and, at a minimum, to be given an opportunity to establish the meritoriousness of their § 504 claim. *Maher* v. *Gagne*, 448 U. S. 122 (1980); H. R. Rep. No. 94-1558, p. 4, n. 7 (1976); Brief for Petitioners 61-62,

n. 26 (legislative history establishes that § 505(b) incorporates standards governing § 1988).[1]

To determine whether § 504 or § 1983 is available, each provision must be read together with the EHA.[2] As the Court demonstrates, in enacting the EHA, Congress surely intended that individuals with claims covered by that Act would pursue relief through the administrative channels that the Act established before seeking redress in court. See *ante*. It would make little sense for Congress to have established such a detailed and comprehensive administrative system and yet allow individuals to bypass the system, at their option, by bringing suits directly to the courts under either § 504 or § 1983. To that extent, therefore, the statutes before us are in conflict with one another. Accordingly, our guide must be the familiar principle of statutory construction that conflicting statutes should be interpreted so as to give effect to each but to allow a later-enacted, more specific statute to amend an earlier, more general statute only to the extent of the repugnancy between the two statutes. *Watt* v. *Alaska* , 451 U. S. 259, 267 (1981); *Radzanower* v. *Touche Ross & Co.*, 426 U. S. 148, 153 (1976); *Morton* v. *Mancari*, 417 U. S. 535, 551 (1974). We must, therefore, construe the statutory provisions at issue here so as to promote the congressional intent underlying the EHA, which was enacted after §§ 504 and 1983 and which is addressed specifically to the problems facing handicapped school children. At the same time, however, we must preserve those aspects of §§ 504 and 1983 that are not in irreconcilable conflict with the EHA.

The natural resolution of the conflict between the EHA, on the one hand, and §§ 504 and 1983, on the other, is to require a plaintiff with a claim covered by the EHA to pursue relief through the administrative channels established by that Act before seeking redress in the courts under § 504 or § 1983. Under this resolution, the integrity of the EHA is preserved entirely, and yet §§ 504 and 1983 are also preserved to the extent that they do not undermine the EHA. Although the primary function of §§ 504 and 1983 is to provide direct access to the courts for certain types of claims, these provi-

[1]The Court holds that petitioners may not recover any fees for this lawsuit. That result is wrong, I believe, without regard to whether § 505(b) requires an unlitigated § 504 claim to be meritorious or merely "substantial." Even if petitioners must establish the meritoriousness, and not just the substantiality, of the unlitigated § 504 claim, affirmance of the Court of Appeals' judgment would be improper, for petitioners have been given no opportunity to establish that their § 504 claim has merit and because petitioners are entitled to fees under § 1988. Since I think petitioners are entitled to fees under § 1988, and since even my dissent from the Court's holding on § 505(b) does not depend on whether the substantiality standard applies to unlitigated § 504 claims, I do not address that question.

I also need not consider what effect petitioners' due process claim against respondents, *ante*, may have on petitioners' entitlement to fees. I dissent from the Court's holding because I believe that petitioners are entitled to fees under § 1988 and may be entitled to fees under § 505(b) of the Rehabilitation Act. Petitioners' due process claim might have a bearing on the amount of fees they should recover, but it does not deprive petitioners of all entitlement to a fee award.

[2]Some claims covered by the EHA are also grounded in the Constitution and hence could be pursued under § 1983. Others are nonconstitutional claims cognizable under § 504. Still others are nonconstitutional claims cognizable only under the EHA. This case is concerned only with claims that have as a substantive basis both the EHA and either the Constitution or § 504.

sions also operate, as this case demonstrates, to identify those types of causes of action for which Congress has authorized the award of attorney's fees to prevailing parties. Significantly, this function does not in any way conflict with the goals or operation of the EHA. There is no basis, therefore, for concluding that either § 504 or § 1983 is unavailable for this limited purpose.

The Court, however, has responded to the conflict among these statutes by restricting the applicability of §§ 504 and 1983 far more than is necessary to resolve their inconsistency. Indeed, the Court holds that both §§ 504 and 1983 are wholly unavailable to individuals seeking to secure their rights to a free appropriate public education, despite the fact that the terms and intent of Congress in enacting each of these provisions unquestionably extend to many of those claims. As a result, the Court finds that attorney's fees, which would otherwise be available to those individuals under §§ 505(b) and 1988, are now unavailable. Yet the Court recognizes that there is absolutely no indication in the language of the EHA or in the Act's legislative history that Congress meant to effect such a repeal, let alone any indication that Congress specifically intended to bar the recovery of attorney's fees for parties that prevail in this type of action. The Court's rationale for effectively repealing §§ 504, 505(b), 1983, and 1988 to the extent that they cover petitioners' claim is that the comprehensiveness and detail with which the EHA addresses the problem of providing schooling to handicapped children implies that Congress intended to repeal all other remedies that overlap with the EHA, even if they do not conflict with the EHA.[3]

Repeals by implication, however, are strongly disfavored. *St. Martin Lutheran Church* v. *South Dakota*, 451 U. S. 772, 788 (1981); *Morton* v. *Mancari, supra*, at 550; *Posadas* v. *National City Bank*, 296 U. S. 497, 503 (1936). And, as stated above, they are tolerated only to the extent necessary to resolve clear repugnancy between statutes. *Radzanower* v. *Touche Ross & Co. supra*, at 154; *Posadas* v. *National City Bank, supra*, at 503. The function that §§ 504 and 1983 perform of identifying those claims for which attorney's fees are authorized under §§ 505(b) and 1988 is not repugnant to the EHA. The Court therefore has erred in concluding that petitioners cannot obtain attorney's fees.

In cases like this, it is particularly important that the Court exercise restraint in concluding that one act of Congress implicitly repeals another, not only to avoid misconstruction of the law effecting the putative repeal, but also to preserve the intent of later Congresses that have already enacted laws that are dependent on the continued applicability of the law whose implicit repeal is in question. By failing to exercise such restraint here, and hence concluding that the EHA implicitly repealed, in part, §§ 504 and 1983, the Court has not only misconstrued the congressional intent underlying the EHA, it has also frustrated Congress' intent in enacting §§ 505(b) and 1988—each of which was enacted after the EHA and premised on a view of §§ 504 and 1983 that was significantly more expansive than that offered by the

---

[3]The Court at one point seems to indicate that Congress actually considered the question of withholding attorney's fees from prevailing parties in actions covered by the EHA. *Ante*. But at the time the EHA was enacted, neither § 505(b) of the Rehabilitation Act nor § 1988 had yet been enacted. In that context, congressional silence on the question of attorney's fees can only be interpreted to indicate that Congress did not consider the matter. Thus, this claim is particularly unpersuasive and, in fact, does not appear to constitute a significant basis of the Court's decision.

Court today. Although in enacting the EHA, Congress was silent with respect to the continued availability of §§ 504 and 1983 for claims that could be brought directly under the EHA, there can be no doubt that, at the time §§ 505(b) and 1988 were passed, Congress believed that the EHA had not eliminated these alternative remedies. Congressional understanding at these later points certainly sheds light on Congress' earlier intent in enacting the EHA, but perhaps more importantly, it demonstrates the extent to which the Court's finding of an implicit repeal has undermined the congressional intent behind the enactment of §§ 505(b) and 1988.

The Department of Health, Education, and Welfare (HEW) promulgated regulations under § 504 of the Rehabilitation Act *after* the EHA was passed. Those regulations contained a lengthy subpart governing the provision of education to the handicapped stating: "A recipient that operates a public elementary or secondary education program shall provide a free appropriate public education to each qualified handicapped person who is in the recipient's jurisdiction, regardless of the nature or severity of the person's handicap." 42 Fed. Reg. 22676, 22682 (1977). Thus, the department charged with enforcing the Rehabilitation Act and the EHA did not understand the latter to repeal the former with respect to handicapped education.[4] And, of course, the interpretation of the Act by the agency responsible for its enforcement is entitled to great deference. *Griggs* v. *Duke Power Co.*, 401 U. S. 424, 434 (1971). Furthermore, Congress was very much aware of HEW's interpretation of the two acts. During oversight hearings on the Rehabilitation Act, held after the enactment of the EHA, representatives of HEW testified that the agency had recently promulgated regulations under § 504 and that those regulations addressed discrimination in the provision of education to handicapped children.[5] Hearings on Implementation of Section 504, Rehabilitation Act of 1973, before the Subcommittee on Select Education of the House Committee on Education and Labor, 95th Cong., 1st Sess., 296-297 (1977) (statement of David Tatel, Director, Office for Civil Rights, Department of Health, Education, and Welfare);[6] Hearings on the Rehabilitation of the Handicapped Programs, 1976, before the Subcommittee on the Handicapped of the Senate Committee on Labor and Public Welfare, 94th Cong., 2d Sess., 1498, 1499, 1508, 1539-1546 (1976) (statement of Martin H. Gerry, Director, Office for Civil Rights, Department of Health, Education, and Welfare). No

---

[4]As the Court notes, *ante*, the regulations promulgated under § 504 and the EHA were closely coordinated with one another. See 42 Fed. Reg. 22677 (1977).

[5]In addition, testimony was generally taken on the success of § 504 as applied to discrimination against handicapped children in the provision of publicly funded education. See, *e. g.* Hearings on Implementation of Section 504, Rehabilitation Act of 1973, before the Subcommittee on Select Education of the House Committee on Education and Labor, 95th Cong., 1st Sess., 263-265 (1977). (statement of Daniel Yohalem, Children's Defense Fund), 278-285 (statement of Edward E. Corbett, Jr., Maryland School for the Deaf).

[6]Mr. Tatel's testimony included the following:

"With regard to preschool, elementary, and secondary education institutions, the regulations require:

"—annual identification and location of unserved handicapped children;

"—free appropriate public education to each qualified handicapped child regardless of the nature or severity of the handicap (including coverage of nonmedical care,

member of the House or Senate committee raised any question regarding § 504's continued coverage of discrimination in education after the passage of the EHA.

Indeed, the Senate Report accompanying the bill that included § 505(b) of the Rehabilitation Act explicitly referred to, and approved, the regulations promulgated under § 504. The Report then went on to address the need for attorney's fees, referring to the rights that § 504 extended to handicapped individuals generally and intimating no exception for handicapped children seeking education. S. Rept. No. 95-890, p. 19-20.

Similarly, the House Report stated:

> "[t]he proposed amendment is not in any way unique. At present there are at least 90 separate attorney's fees provisions to promote enforcement of over 90 different Federal laws. In fact, disabled individuals are one of the very few minority groups in this country who have not been authorized by the Congress to seek attorney's fees. The amendment proposes to correct this omission and thereby assist handicapped individuals in securing the legal protection guaranteed them under title V of the Act. H. R. Rep. No. 95-1149, p. 21 (1978).

Neither the terms nor the logic of this statement admits of the possibility that Congress intended to exclude from the coverage of § 505(b) the claims of handicapped children seeking a free appropriate public education.

Finally, although Congress, in enacting § 1988, did not specifically refer to the applicability of § 1983 to constitutional claims by handicapped children seeking education, it clearly intended to authorize attorney's fees in all cases involving the deprivation of civil rights. Adopted in response to this Court's decision in *Alyeska Pipeline Service Co.* v. *Wilderness Society*, 421 U. S. 240 (1975), § 1988 was intended to close "anomalous gaps in our civil rights laws whereby awards of fees are . . . unavailable." S. Rep. No. 94-1011, p. 4 (1976). The Senate Report thus stated:

> "In many cases arising under our civil rights laws, the citizen who must sue to enforce the law has little or no money with which to hire a lawyer. If private citizens are to be able to assert their civil rights, and if those who violate the Nation's fundamental laws are not to proceed with impunity, then citizens must have the opportunity to recover what it costs them to vindicate these rights in court.
>
> * * *
>
> "'Not to award counsel fees in cases such as this would be tantamount to repealing the Act itself by frustrating its basic purpose. ***

---

room and board where residential placement required);

"—education of handicapped students to maximum extent possible;

"—comparability of facilities (including services and activities provided therein) identifiable as being for handicapped persons;

"—evaluation requirements to insure proper classification and placement of handicapped children and procedural safeguards;

"—equal opportunity for participation of handicapped students in non-academic and extracurricular services and activities." *Id.*, at 296 (statement of David Tatel, Director, Office of Civil Rights, Department of Health, Education, and Welfare).

> Without counsel fees the grant of Federal jurisdiction is but an empty gesture ***. *Hall* v. *Cole*, 412 U. S. 1 (1973), quoting 462 F. 2d 777, 780-81 (2d Cir. 1972).'
>
> "The remedy of attorneys' fees has always been recognized as particularly appropriate in the civil rights area, and civil rights and attorneys' fees have always been closely interwoven." *Id.*, at 2-3.

It would be anomalous, to say the least, for Congress to have passed a provision as broad as § 1988, and to provide an equally broad explanation, and yet to leave a "gap" in its own coverage of the constitutional claims of handicapped children seeking a free appropriate public education.[7] See also H. R. Rep. No. 94-1558, pp. 4-5 (1976).

In sum, the Court's conclusion that the EHA repealed the availability of §§ 504 and 1983 to individuals seeking a free appropriate public education runs counter to well-established principles of statutory interpretation. It finds no support in the terms or legislative history of the EHA. And, most importantly, it undermines the intent of Congress in enacting both §§ 505(b) and 1988. Had this case arisen prior to the enactment of §§ 505(b) and 1988, Congress could have taken account of the Court's expansive interpretation of the EHA. Presumably, it would have either clarified the applicability of §§ 504 and 1983 to claims for a free appropriate public education, or it would have extended the coverage of §§ 505(b) and 1988 to certain claims brought under the EHA. But with today's decision coming as it does after Congress has spoken on the subject of attorney's fees, Congress will now have to take the time to revisit the matter. And until it does, the handicapped children of this country whose difficulties are compounded by discrimination and by other deprivations of constitutional rights will have to pay the costs. It is at best ironic that the Court has managed to impose this burden on handicapped children in the course of interpreting a statute wholly intended to promote the educational rights of those children.

---

[7]Moreover, Congress was fully aware of the possibility that the same claim in the civil rights area might have duplicative statutory remedies. For instance, one of the "gaps" that Congress sought to close in enacting § 1988 was the possibility that an individual could bring an employment discrimination suit under Title VII of the 1964 Civil Rights Act and receive attorney's fees, although another individual bringing the same suit under 42 U. S. C. § 1981 could not recover attorney's fees. S. Rep. No. 94-1011, p. 4 (1976). Congress' response to this situation was to ensure that attorney's fees would be available under either provision.

Irving Independent School District v. Tatro

U.S. Supreme Court, 468 U.S. 883, 104 S.Ct. 3371 (1984).

Syllabus*

Respondents' 8-year-old daughter was born with a defect known as spina bifida. As a result she suffers from orthopedic and speech impairments and a neurogenic bladder, which prevents her from emptying her bladder voluntarily. Consequently, she must be catheterized every three or four hours to avoid injury to her kidneys. To accomplish this, a procedure known as clean intermittent catheterization (CIC) was prescribed. This is a simple procedure that can be performed in a few minutes by a layperson with less than an hour's training. Since petitioner School District received federal funding under the Education of the Handicapped Act it was required to provide the child with "a free appropriate public education," which is defined in the Act to include "related services," which are defined in turn to include "supportive services (including . . . medical . . . services except that such medical services shall be for diagnostic and evaluation purposes only) as may be required to assist a handicapped child to benefit from special education." Pursuant to the Act, petitioner developed an individualized education program for the child, but the program made no provision for school personnel to administer CIC. After unsuccessfully pursuing administrative remedies to secure CIC services for the child during school hours, respondents brought an action against petitioner and others in Federal District Court, seeking injunctive relief, damages, and attorney's fees. Respondents invoked the Education of the Handicapped Act, arguing that CIC is one of the included "related services" under the statutory definition, and also invoked § 504 of the Rehabilitation Act of 1973, which forbids a person, by reason of a handicap, to be "excluded from the participation in, be denied the benefits of, or be subjected to discrimination under" any program receiving federal aid. After its initial denial of relief was reversed by the Court of Appeals, the District Court, on remand, held that CIC was a "related service" under the Education of the Handicapped Act, ordered that the child's education program be modified to include provision of CIC during school hours, and awarded compensatory damages against petitioner. The court further held that respondents had proved a violation of § 504 of the Rehabilitation Act, and awarded attorney's fees to respondents under § 505 of that Act. The Court of Appeals affirmed.

Held:

1. CIC is a "related service" under the Education of the Handicapped Act.

(a) CIC services qualify as a "supportive servic[e] . . . required to assist a handicapped child to benefit from special education," within the meaning of the Act. Without CIC services available during the school day, respondents' child cannot attend school and thereby "benefit from special education." Such services are no less related to the effort to educate than are services that enable a child to reach, enter, or exit a school.

(b) The provision of CIC is not subject to exclusion as a "medical service." The Department of Education regulations, which are entitled to deference, define "related services" for handicapped children to include "school health services," which are defined in turn as "services provided by a qualified school nurse or other qualified person," and define "medical services" as "ser-

*The syllabus constitutes no part of the opinion of the Court but has been prepared by the Reporter of Decisions for the convenience of the reader.

vices provided by a licensed physician." This definition of "medical services" is a reasonable interpretation of congressional intent to exclude physician's services as such and to impose an obligation to provide school nursing services.

2. Section 504 of the Rehabilitation Act is inapplicable when relief is available under the Education of the Handicapped Act to remedy a denial of educational service, *Smith* v. *Robinson, post*, p. ——, and therefore respondents are not entitled to any relief under § 504, including recovery of attorney's fees.

703 F. 2d 823, affirmed in part and reversed in part.

BURGER, C.J., delivered the opinion of the Court, in which WHITE, BLACKMUN, POWELL, REHNQUIST, and O'CONNOR, JJ., joined, and in all but Part III of which BRENNAN, MARSHALL, and STEVENS, JJ., joined. BRENNAN, J., filed an opinion concurring in part and dissenting in part, in which MARSHALL, J., joined. STEVENS, J., filed an opinion concurring in part and dissenting in part.

CHIEF JUSTICE BURGER delivered the opinion of the Court.

We granted certiorari to determine whether the Education of the Handicapped Act or the Rehabilitation Act of 1973 requires a school district to provide a handicapped child with clean intermittent catheterization during school hours.

I

Amber Tatro is an 8-year-old girl born with a defect known as spina bifida. As a result she suffers from orthopedic and speech impairments and a neurogenic bladder, which prevents her from emptying her bladder voluntarily. Consequently, she must be catheterized every three or four hours to avoid injury to her kidneys. In accordance with accepted medical practice, clean intermittent catheterization (CIC), a procedure involving the insertion of a catheter into the urethra to drain the bladder, has been prescribed. The procedure is a simple one that can be performed in a few minutes by a layperson with less than an hour's training. Amber's parents, babysitter, and teenage brother are all qualified to administer CIC, and Amber soon will be able to perform this procedure herself.

In 1979 petitioner Irving Independent School District agreed to provide special education for Amber, who was then three and one-half years old. In consultation with her parents, who are respondents here, petitioner developed an individualized education program for Amber under the requirements of the Education of the Handicapped Act, 84 Stat. 175, as amended significantly by the Education for All Handicapped Children Act of 1975, 89 Stat. 773, 20 U. S. C. §§ 1401(19), 1414(a)(5). The individualized education program provided that Amber would attend early childhood development classes and receive special services such as physical and occupational therapy. That program, however, made no provision for school personnel to administer CIC.

Respondents unsuccessfully pursued administrative remedies to secure

CIC services for Amber during school hours.[1] In October 1979 respondents brought the present action in District Court against petitioner, the State Board of Education, and others. See § 1415(e)(2). They sought an injunction ordering petitioner to provide Amber with CIC and sought damages and attorney's fees. First, respondents invoked the Education of the Handicapped Act. Because Texas received funding under that statute, petitioner was required to provide Amber with a "free appropriate public education," §§1412(1), 1414(a)(1)(C)(ii), which is defined to include "related services," § 1401(18). Respondents argued that CIC is one such "related service."[2] Second, respondents invoked § 504 of the Rehabilitation Act of 1973, 87 Stat. 394, as amended, 29 U. S. C. § 794, which forbids an individual, by reason of a handicap, to be "excluded from the participation in, be denied the benefits of, or be subjected to discrimination under" any program receiving federal aid.

The District Court denied respondents' request for a preliminary injunction. *Tatro* v. *Texas*, 481 F. Supp. 1224 (ND Tex. 1979). That court concluded that CIC was not a "related service" under the Education of the Handicapped Act because it did not serve a need arising from the effort to educate. It also held that § 504 of the Rehabilitation Act did not require "the setting up of governmental health care for people seeking to participate" in federally funded programs. *Id.*, at 1229.

The Court of Appeals reversed. *Tatro* v. *Texas*, 625 F. 2d 557 (CA5 1980) (*Tatro I*). First, it held that CIC was a "related service" under the Education of the Handicapped Act, 20 U. S. C. § 1401(17), because without the procedure Amber could not attend classes and benefit from special education. Second, it held that petitioner's refusal to provide CIC effectively excluded her from a federally funded educational program in violation of § 504 of the Rehabilitation Act. The Court of Appeals remanded for the District Court to develop a factual record and apply these legal principles.

On remand petitioner stressed the Education of the Handicapped Act's explicit provision that "medical services" could qualify as "related services" only when they served the purpose of diagnosis or evaluation. See n. 2, *supra*. The District Court held that under Texas law a nurse or other qualified person may administer CIC without engaging in the unauthorized practice of medicine, provided that a doctor prescribes and supervises the procedure. The District Court then held that, because a doctor was not needed to administer CIC, provision of the procedure was not a "medical service" for purposes of the Education of the Handicapped Act. Finding CIC to be a "related service" under that Act, the District Court ordered petitioner and the State Board of Education to modify Amber's individualized education program to include provision of CIC during school hours. It also awarded

[1]The Education of the Handicapped Act's procedures for administrative hearings are set out in 20 U. S. C. § 1415. In this case a hearing officer ruled that the Education of the Handicapped Act did require the school to provide CIC, and the Texas Commissioner of Education adopted the hearing officer's decision. The State Board of Education reversed, holding that the Act did not require petitioner to provide CIC.

[2]As discussed more fully later, the Education of the Handicapped Act defines "related services" to include "supportive services (including . . . medical and counseling services, except that such medical services shall be for diagnostic and evaluation purposes only) as may be required to assist a handicapped child to benefit from special education." 20 U. S. C. § 1401(17).

compensatory damages against petitioner.[3] *Tatro* v. *Texas*, 516 F. Supp. 968 (ND Tex. 1981).

On the authority of *Tatro I*, the District Court then held that respondents had proved a violation of § 504 of the Rehabilitation Act. Although the District Court did not rely on this holding to authorize any greater injunctive or compensatory relief, it did invoke the holding to award attorney's fees against petitioner and the State Board of Education.[4] 516 F. Supp., at 968; App. to Pet. for Cert. 55a-63a. The Rehabilitation Act, unlike the Education of the Handicapped Act, authorizes prevailing parties to recover attorney's fees. See 29 U. S. C. § 794a.

The Court of Appeals affirmed. *Tatro* v. *Texas*, 703 F. 2d 823 (CA5 1983) *(Tatro II)*. That court accepted the District Court's conclusion that state law permitted qualified persons to administer CIC without the physical presence of a doctor, and it affirmed the award of relief under the Education of the Handicapped Act. In affirming the award of attorney's fees based on a finding of liability under the Rehabilitation Act, the Court of Appeals held that no change of circumstances since *Tatro I* justified a different result.

We granted certiorari, 464 U. S. 1007 (1983), and we affirm in part and reverse in part.

II

This case poses two separate issues. The first is whether the Education of the Handicapped Act requires petitioner to provide CIC services to Amber. The second is whether § 504 of the Rehabilitation Act creates such an obligation. We first turn to the claim presented under the Education of the Handicapped Act.

States receiving funds under the Act are obliged to satisfy certain conditions. A primary condition is that the state implement a policy "that assures all handicapped children the right to a free appropriate public education." 20 U. S. C. § 1412(1). Each educational agency applying to a state for funding must provide assurances in turn that its program aims to provide "a free appropriate public education to all handicapped children." § 1414(a)(1)(C)(ii).

A "free appropriate public education" is explicitly defined as "special education and related services." § 1401(18).[5] The term "special education" means

---

[3]The District Court dismissed the claims against all defendants other than petitioner and the State Board, though it retained the members of the State Board "in their official capacities for the purpose of injunctive relief." 516 F. Supp., at 972-974.

[4]The District Court held that § 505 of the Rehabilitation Act, 29 U. S. C. § 794a, which authorizes attorney's fees as a part of a prevailing party's costs, abrogated the State Board's immunity under the Eleventh Amendment. See App. to Pet. for Cert. 56a-60a. The State Board did not petition for certiorari, and the Eleventh Amendment issue is not before us.

[5]Specifically, the "special education and related services" must

"(A) have been provided at public expense, under public supervision and direction, and without charge, (B) meet the standards of the State educational agency, (C) include an appropriate preschool, elementary, or secondary school education in the State involved, and (D) [be] provided in conformity with the individualized education program required under section 1414(a)(5) of this title." § 1401(18).

"specially designed instruction, at no cost to parents or guardians, to meet the unique needs of a handicapped child, including classroom instruction, instruction in physical education, home instruction, and instruction in hospitals and institutions." § 1401(16).

"Related service" are defined as

"transportation, and such developmental, corrective, and other *supportive services (including* speech pathology and audiology, psychological services, physical and occupational therapy, recreation, and *medical* and counseling *services, except that such medical services shall be for diagnostic and evaluation purposes only) as may be required to assist a handicapped child to benefit from special education*, and includes the early identification and assessment of handicapping conditions in children." § 1401(17)(emphasis added).

The issue in this case is whether CIC is a "related service" that petitioner is obliged to provide to Amber. We must answer two questions: first, whether CIC is a "supportive servic[e] . . . required to assist a handicapped child to benefit from special education"; and second, whether CIC is excluded from this definition as a "medical servic[e]" serving purposes other than diagnosis or evaluation.

A

The Court of Appeals was clearly correct in holding that CIC is a "supportive servic[e] . . . required to assist a handicapped child to benefit from special education."[6] It is clear on this record that, without having CIC services available during the school day, Amber cannot attend school and thereby "benefit from special education." CIC services therefore fall squarely within the definition of a "supportive service"[7]

As we have stated before, "Congress sought primarily to make public education available to handicapped children" and "to make such access

[6]Petitioner claims that courts deciding cases arising under the Education of the Handicapped Act are limited to inquiring whether a school district has followed the requirements of the state plan and has followed the Acts's procedural requirements. However, we held in *Board of Education of Hendrick Hudson Central School District* v. *Rowley*, 458 U. S. 176, 206, n. 27 (1982), that a court is required "not only to satisfy itself that the State has adopted the state plan, policies, and assurances required by the Act, but also to determine that the State has created an [individualized education plan] for the child in question which conforms with the requirements of § 1401(19) [defining such plans]." Judicial review is equally appropriate in this case, which presents the legal question of a school's substantive obligation under the "related services" requirement of § 1401(197).

[7]The Department of Education has agreed with this reasoning in an interpretive ruling that specifically found CIC to be a "related service." 46 Fed. Reg. 4912 (1981). Accord *Tokarcik* v. *Forest Hills School District*, 665 F. 2d 443 (CA3 1981), cert. denied *sub nom. Scanlon* v. *Tokarcik*, 458 U. S. 1121 (1982). The Secretary twice postponed temporarily the effective date of this interpretive ruling, see 46 Fed. Reg. 12495 (1981); *id.* at 18975, and later postponed it indefinitely, *id.* at 25614. But the Department presently does view CIC services as an allowable cost under Part B of the Act. *Ibid.*

meaningful." *Board of Education of Hendrick Hudson Central School District* v. *Rowley*, 458 U. S. 176, 192 (1982). A service that enables a handicapped child to remain at school during the day is an important means of providing the child with the meaningful access to education that Congress envisioned. The Act makes specific provision for services, like transportation, for example, that do no more than enable a child to be physically present in class, see 20 U. S. C. § 1401(17); and the Act specifically authorizes grants for schools to alter buildings and equipment to make them accessible to the handicapped, § 1406; see S. Rep, No. 94-168, p. 38 (1975); 121 Cong. Rec. 19483-19484 (1975) (remarks of Sen. Stafford). Services like CIC that permit a child to remain at school during the day are no less related to the effort to educate than are services that enable the child to reach, enter, or exit the school.

We hold that CIC services in this case qualify as a "supportive servic[e] . . . required to assist a handicapped child to benefit from special education."[8]

B

We also agree with the Court of Appeals that provision of CIC is not a "medical servic[e]," which a school is required to provide only for purposes of diagnosis or evaluation. See 20 U. S. C. § 1401(17). We begin with the regulations of the Department of Education, which are entitled to deference.[9] See, *e. g., Blum* v. *Bacon*, 457 U. S. 132, 141 (1982). The regulations define "related services" for handicapped children to include "school health services," 34 CFR § 300.13(a)(1983), which are defined in turn as "services provided by a qualified school nurse or other qualified person," § 300.13(b)(10). "Medical services" are defined as "services provided by a licensed physician." § 300.13(b)(4).[10] Thus, the Secretary has determined that the services of a school nurse otherwise qualifying as a "related service" are not subject to exclusion as a "medical service," but that the services of a physician are excludable as such.

[8]The obligation to provide special education and related services is expressly phrased as a "conditio[n]" for a state to receive funds under the Act. See 20 U. S. C. § 1412; see also S. Rep. No. 94-168, p. 16 (1975). This refutes petitioner's contention that the Act did not "impos[e] an obligation on the States to spend state money to fund certain rights as a condition of receiving federal moneys" but "spoke merely in precatory terms," *Pennhurst State School and Hospital* v. *Halderman*, 451 U. S. 1, 18 (1981).

[9]The Secretary of Education is empowered to issue such regulations as may be necessary to carry out the provisions of the Act. 20 U. S. C. § 1417(b). This function was initially vested in the Commissioner of Education of the Department of Health, Education, and Welfare, who promulgated the regulations in question. This function was transferred to the Secretary of Education when Congress created that position, see Department of Education Organization Act. §§ 301(a)(1), (2)(H), 93 Stat. 677, 20 U. S. C. §§ 3441(a)(1), (2)(H).

[10]The regulations actually define only those "medical services" that *are* owed to handicapped children: "services provided by a licensed physician to determine a child's medically related handicapping condition which results in the child's need for special education and related services." 34 CFR § 300.13(b)(4) (1983). Presumably this means that "medical services" *not* owed under the statute are those "services by a licensed physician" that serve other purposes.

This definition of "medical services" is a reasonable interpretation of congressional intent. Although Congress devoted little discussion to the "medical services" exclusion, the Secretary could reasonably have concluded that it was designed to spare schools from an obligation to provide a service that might well prove unduly expensive and beyond the range of their competence.[11] From this understanding of congressional purpose, the Secretary could reasonably have concluded that Congress intended to impose the obligation to provide school nursing services.

Congress plainly required schools to hire various specially trained personnel to help handicapped children, such as "trained occupational therapists, speech therapists, psychologists, social workers and other appropriately trained personnel." S. Rep. No. 94-168, *supra*, at 33. School nurses have long been a part of the educational system, and the Secretary could therefore reasonably conclude that school nursing services are not the sort of burden that Congress intended to exclude as a "medical service." By limiting the "medical services" exclusion to the services of a physician or hospital, both far more expensive, the Secretary has given a permissible construction to the provision.

Petitioner's contrary interpretation of the "medical services" exclusion is unconvincing. In petitioner's view, CIC is a "medical service," even though it may be provided by a nurse or trained layperson; that conclusion rests on its reading of Texas law that confines CIC to uses in accordance with a physician's prescription and under a physician's ultimate supervision. Aside from conflicting with the Secretary's reasonable interpretation of congressional intent, however, such a rule would be anomalous. Nurses in petitioner's school district are authorized to dispense oral medications and administer emergency injections in accordance with a physician's prescription. This kind of service for nonhandicapped children is difficult to distinguish from the provision of CIC to the handicapped.[12] It would be strange indeed if Congress, in attempting to extend special services to handicapped children, were unwilling to guarantee them services of a kind that are routinely provided to the nonhandicapped.

To keep in perspective the obligation to provide services that relate to both the health and educational needs of handicapped students, we note several limitations that should minimize the burden petitioner fears. First, to be entitled to related services, a child must be handicapped so as to require

[11] Children with serious medical needs are still entitled to an education. For example, the Act specifically includes instruction in hospitals and at home within the definition of "special education." See 20 U. S. C. § 1401(16).

[12] Petitioner attempts to distinguish the administration of prescription drugs from the administration of CIC on the ground that Texas law expressly limits the liability of school personnel performing the former, see Tex. Educ. Code Ann. § 21.914(c) (Supp. 1984), but not the latter. This distinction, however, bears no relation to whether CIC is a "related service." The introduction of handicapped children into a school creates numerous new possibilities for injury and liability. Many of these risks are more serious than that posed by CIC, which the courts below found is a safe procedure even when performed by a 9-year-old girl. Congress assumed that states receiving the generous grants under the Act were up to the job of managing these new risks. Whether petitioner decides to purchase more liability insurance or to persuade the state to extend the limitation on liability, the risks posed by CIC should not prove to be a large burden.

special education. See 20 U. S. C. § 1401(1); 34 CFR § 300.5 (1983). In the absence of a handicap that requires special education, the need for what otherwise might qualify as a related service does not create an obligation under the Act. See 34 CFR § 300.14, Comment (1) (1983).

Second, only those services necessary to aid a handicapped child to benefit from special education must be provided, regardless how easily a school nurse or layperson could furnish them. For example, if a particular medication or treatment may appropriately be administered to a handicapped child other than during the school day, a school is not required to provide nursing services to administer it.

Third, the regulations state that school nursing services must be provided only if they can be performed by a nurse or other qualified person, not if they must be performed by a physician. See 34 CFR §§/300.13(a), (b)(4), (b)(10) (1983). It bears mentioning that here not even the services of a nurse are required; as is conceded, a layperson with minimal training is qualified to provide CIC. See also, *e. g., Department of Education of Hawaii* v. *Katherine D.*, 727 F. 2d 809 (CA9 1983).

Finally, we note that respondents are not asking petitioner to provide *equipment* that Amber needs for CIC. Tr. of Oral Arg. 18-19. They seek only the *services* of a qualified person at the school.

We conclude that provision of CIC to Amber is not subject to exclusion as a "medical service," and we affirm the Court of Appeals' holding that CIC is a "related service" under the Education of the Handicapped Act.[13]

III

Respondents sought relief not only under the Education of the Handicapped Act but under § 504 of the Rehabilitation Act as well. After finding petitioner liable to provide CIC under the former, the District Court proceeded to hold that petitioner was similarly liable under § 504 and that respondents were therefore entitled to attorney's fees under § 505 of the Rehabilitation Act, 29 U. S. C. § 794a. We hold today, in *Smith* v. *Robinson,* 468 U. S. 992 (1984), that § 504 is inapplicable when relief is available under the Education of the Handicapped Act to remedy a denial of educational services. Respondents are therefore not entitled to relief under § 504, and we reverse the Court of Appeals' holding that respondents are entitled to recover attorney's fees. In all other respects, the judgment of the Court of Appeals is affirmed.

It is so ordered.

[13]We need not address respondents' claim that CIC, in addition to being a "related service," is a "supplementary ai[d] and servic[e]" that petitioner must provide to enable Amber to attend classes with nonhandicapped students under the Act's "mainstreaming" directive. See 20 U. S. C. § 1412(5)(B). Respondents have not sought an order prohibiting petitioner from educating Amber with handicapped children alone. Indeed, any request for such an order might not present a live controversy. Amber's present individualized education program provides for regular public school classes with nonhandicapped children. And petitioner has admitted that it would be far more costly to pay for Amber's instruction and CIC services at a private school, or to arrange for home tutoring, than to provide CIC at the regular public school placement provided in her current individualized education program. Tr. of Oral Arg. 12.

JUSTICE BRENNAN, with whom JUSTICE MARSHALL joins, concurring in part and dissenting in part.

I join all but Part III of the Court's opinion. For the reasons stated in my dissenting opinion in *Smith* v. *Robinson, post*, at 992, I would affirm the award of attorney's fees to the respondents.

JUSTICE STEVENS, concurring in part and dissenting in part.

The petition for certiorari did not challenge the award of attorney's fees. It contested only the award of relief on the merits to respondents. Inasmuch as the judgment on the merits is supported by the Court's interpretation of the Education of the Handicapped Act, there is no need to express any opinion concerning the Rehabilitation Act of 1973.* Accordingly, while I join Parts I and II of the Court's opinion, I do not join Part III.

---

*The "Statement of the Questions Presented" in the petition for certiorari reads as follows:

"1. Whether 'medical treatment' such as clean intermittent catheterization is a 'related service' required under the Education for All Handicapped Children Act and, therefore, required to be provided to the minor respondent.

"2. Is a public school required to provide and perform the medical treatment prescribed by the physician of a handicapped child by the Education of All Handicapped Children Act or the Rehabilitation Act of 1973?

"3. Whether the Fifth Circuit Court of Appeals misconstrued the opinions of this Court in *Southeastern Community College, Pennhurst State School & Hospital* v. *Halderman*, and *State Board of Education* v. *Rowley.*" Pet. for Cert. i.

Because the Court does not hold that the Court of Appeals answered any of these questions incorrectly, it is not justified in reversing in part the judgment of that court.

JUSTICE MARSHALL, with whom JUSTICE BRENNAN joins, concurring in part and dissenting in part.

"3. Whether the Fifth Circuit Court of Appeals correctly applied the opinions of this Court in *Southeastern Community College v. Davis*, 442 U.S. 397 (1979) and *Pennhurst State School and Hospital v. Halderman*, 451 U.S. 1 (1981)?

"4. [illegible]"

Burlington School Committee v. Department of Education of Massachusetts

U.S. Supreme Court, 471 U.S. 359, 105 S.Ct. 1996 (1985).

Syllabus*

The Education of the Handicapped Act requires participating state and local educational agencies to assure that handicapped children and their parents are guaranteed procedural safeguards with respect to the provision of free appropriate public education for such children. These procedures include the parents' right to participate in the development of an "individualized education program" (IEP) for the child and to challenge in administrative and court proceedings a proposed IEP with which they disagree. With respect to judicial review, the Act in 20 U. S. C. § 1415(e)(2) authorizes the reviewing court to "grant such relief as the court determines is appropriate." Section 1415(e)(3) provides that during the pendency of any review proceedings, unless the state or local educational agency and the parents otherwise agree, "the child shall remain in the then current educational placement of such child." Respondent father of a handicapped child rejected petitioner town's proposed IEP for the 1979-1980 school year calling for placement of the child in a certain public school, and sought review by respondent Massachusetts Department of Education's Bureau of Special Education Appeals (BSEA). Meanwhile, the father, at his own expense, enrolled the child in a state-approved private school for special education. The BSEA thereafter decided that the town's proposed IEP was inappropriate and that the private school was better suited for the child's educational needs, and ordered the town to pay the child's expenses at the private school for the 1979-1980 school year. The town then sought review in Federal District Court. Ultimately, after the town in the meantime had agreed to pay for the child's private-school placement for the 1980-1981 school year but refused to reimburse the father for the 1979-1980 school year as ordered by the BSEA, the court overturned the BSEA's decision, holding that the appropriate 1979-1980 placement was the one proposed in the IEP and that the town was not responsible for the costs at the private school for the 1979-1980 through 1981-1982 school years. The Court of Appeals, remanding, held that the father's unilateral change of the child's placement during the pendency of the administrative proceedings would not be a bar to reimbursement if such change were held to be appropriate.

Held:

1. The grant of authority to a reviewing court under § 1415(e)(2) includes the power to order school authorities to reimburse parents for their expenditures on private special education for a child if the court ultimately determines that such placement, rather than a proposed IEP, is proper under the Act. The ordinary meaning of the language in § 1415(e)(2) directing the court to "grant such relief as [it] determines is appropriate" confers broad discretion on the court. To deny such reimbursement would mean that the child's right to a free appropriate public education, the parents' right to participate fully in developing a proper IEP, and all of the procedural safeguards of the Act would be less than complete.

---

*The syllabus constitutes no part of the opinion of the Court but has been prepared by the Reporter of Decisions for the convenience of the reader.

2. A parental violation of § 1415(e)(3) by changing the "then current educational placement" of their child during the pendency of proceedings to review a challenged proposed IEP does not constitute a waiver of the parents' right to reimbursement for expenses of the private placement. Otherwise, the parents would be forced to leave the child in what may turn out to be an inappropriate educational placement or to obtain the appropriate placement only by sacrificing any claim for reimbursement. But if the courts ultimately determine that the proposed IEP was appropriate, the parents would be barred from obtaining reimbursement for any interim period in which their child's placement violated § 1415(e)(3).

736 F. 2d 773, affirmed.

REHNQUIST, J., delivered the opinion for a unanimous Court.

JUSTICE REHNQUIST delivered the opinion of the Court.

The Education of the Handicapped Act (Act), 84 Stat. 175, as amended, 20 U. S. C. § 1401 *et seq.*, requires participating state and local educational agencies "to assure that handicapped children and their parents or guardians are guaranteed procedural safeguards with respect to the provision of free appropriate public education" to such handicapped children. § 1415(a). These procedures include the right of the parents to participate in the development of an "individualized education program" (IEP) for the child and to challenge in administrative and court proceedings a proposed IEP with which they disagree. §§ 1401(19), 1415(b),(d),(e). Where as in the present case review of a contested IEP takes years to run its course—years critical to the child's development—important practical questions arise concerning interim placement of the child and financial responsibility for that placement. This case requires us to address some of those questions.

Michael Panico, the son of respondent Robert Panico, was a first grader in the public school system of petitioner Town of Burlington, Massachusetts, when he began experiencing serious difficulties in school. It later became evident that he had "specific learning disabilities" and thus was "handicapped" within the meaning of the Act, 20 U. S. C. § 1401(1). This entitled him to receive at public expense specially designed instruction to meet his unique needs, as well as related transportation. §§ 1401(16), 1401(17). The negotiations and other proceedings between the Town and the Panicos, thus far spanning more than 8 years, are too involved to relate in full detail; the following are the parts relevant to the issues on which we granted certiorari.

In the spring of 1979, Michael attended the third grade of the Memorial School, a public school in Burlington, Mass., under an IEP calling for individual tutoring by a reading specialist for one hour a day and individual and group counselling. Michael's continued poor performance and the fact that Memorial School encompassed only grades K through 3 led to much discussion between his parents and Town school officials about his difficulties and his future schooling. Apparently the course of these discussions did not run smoothly; the upshot was that the Panicos and the Town agreed that Michael was generally of above average to superior intelligence, but had special educational needs calling for a placement in a school other than Memorial. They disagreed over the source and exact nature of Michael's learning difficulties, the Town believing the source to be emotional and the parents believing it to be neurological.

In late June, the Town presented the Panicos with a proposed IEP for Michael for the 1979-1980 academic year. It called for placing Michael in a highly structured class of six children with special academic and social needs, located at another Town public school, the Pine Glen School. On July 3, Michael's father rejected the proposed IEP and sought review under § 1415(b)(2) by respondent Massachusetts Department of Education's Bureau of Special Education Appeals (BSEA). A hearing was initially scheduled for August 8, but was apparently postponed in favor of a mediation session on August 17. The mediation efforts proved unsuccessful.

Meanwhile the Panicos received the results of the latest expert evaluation of Michael by specialists at Massachusetts General Hospital, who opined that Michael's "emotional difficulties are secondary to a rather severe learning disorder characterized by perceptual difficulties" and recommended "a highly specialized setting for children with learning handicaps . . . such as the Carroll School," a state approved private school for special education located in Lincoln, Mass. App. 26, 31. Believing that the Town's proposed placement of Michael at the Pine Glen school was inappropriate in light of Michael's needs, Mr. Panico enrolled Michael in the Carroll School in mid-August at his own expense, and Michael started there in September.

The BSEA held several hearings during the fall of 1979, and in January 1980 the hearing officer decided that the Town's proposed placement at the Pine Glen School was inappropriate and that the Carroll School was "the least restrictive adequate program within the record" for Michael's educational needs. The hearing officer ordered the Town to pay for Michael's tuition and transportation to the Carroll School for the 1979-1980 school year, including reimbursing the Panicos for their expenditures on these items for the school year to date.

The Town sought judicial review of the State's administrative decision in the United States District Court for the District of Massachusetts pursuant to 20 U. S. C. § 1415(e)(2) and a parallel state statute, naming Mr. Panico and the State Department of Education as defendants. In November 1980, the District Court granted summary judgment against the Town on the state-law claim under a "substantial evidence" standard of review, entering a final judgment on this claim under Federal Rule of Civil Procedure 54(b). The Court also set the federal claim for future trial. The Court of Appeals vacated the judgment on the state-law claim, holding that review under the state statute was pre-empted by § 1415(e)(2), which establishes a "preponderance of the evidence" standard of review and which permits the reviewing court to hear additional evidence.

In the meantime, the Town had refused to comply with the BSEA order, the District Court had denied a stay of that order, and the Panicos and the State had moved for preliminary injunctive relief. The State also had threatened outside of the judicial proceedings to freeze all of the Town's special education assistance unless it complied with the BSEA order. Apparently in response to this threat, the Town agreed in February 1981 to pay for Michael's Carroll School placement and related transportation for the 1980-1981 term, none of which had yet been paid, and to continue paying for these expenses until the case was decided. But the Town persisted in refusing to reimburse Mr. Panico for the expenses of the 1979-1980 school year. When the Court of Appeals disposed of the state claim, it also held that under this status quo none of the parties could show irreparable injury and thus none was entitled to a preliminary injunction. The court reasoned that the Town had not shown that Mr. Panico would not be able to repay the tuition and related costs borne by the Town if he ultimately lost on the merits, and Mr. Panico had not shown that he would be irreparably harmed if not reimbursed immediately for past payments which might ultimately be determined to be the Town's responsibility.

On remand, the District Court entered an extensive pretrial order on the Town's federal claim. In denying the Town summary judgment, it ruled that 20 U. S. C. § 1415(e)(3) did not bar reimbursement despite the Town's insistence that the Panicos violated that provision by changing Michael's placement to the Carroll School during the pendency of the administrative proceedings. The court reasoned that § 1415(e)(3) concerned the physical placement of the child and not the right to tuition reimbursement or to procedural review of a contested IEP. The court also dealt with the problem that no IEP had been developed for the 1980-1981 or 1981-1982 school years. It held that its power under § 1415(e)(A) to grant "appropriate" relief upon reviewing the contested IEP for the 1979-1980 school year included the power to grant relief for subsequent school years despite the lack of IEPs for those years. In this connection, however, the court interpreted the statute to place the burden of proof on the Town to upset the BSEA decision that the IEP was inappropriate for 1979-1980 and on the Panicos and the State to show that the relief for subsequent terms was appropriate.

After a 4-day trial, the District Court in August 1982 overturned the BSEA decision, holding that the appropriate 1979-1980 placement for Michael was the one proposed by the town in the IEP and that the parents had failed to show that this placement would not also have been appropriate for subsequent years. Accordingly, the court concluded that the Town was "not responsible for the cost of Michael's education at the Carroll School for the academic years 1979-80 through 1981-82."

In contesting the Town's proposed form of judgment embodying the court's conclusion, Mr. Panico argued that, despite finally losing on the merits of the IEP in August 1982, he should be reimbursed for his expenditures in 1979-1980, that the Town should finish paying for the recently completed 1981-1982 term, and that he should not be required to reimburse the Town for its payments to date, apparently because the school terms in question fell within the pendency of the administrative and judicial review contemplated by § 1415(e)(2). The case was transferred to another District Judge and consolidated with two other cases to resolve similar issues concerning the reimbursement for expenditures during the pendency of review proceedings.

In a decision on the consolidated case, the court rejected Mr. Panico's argument that the Carroll School was the "current educational placement" during the pendency of the review proceedings and thus that under § 1415(e)(3) the Town was obligated to maintain that placement. *Doe* v. *Anrig*, 561 F. Supp. 121 (1983). The court reasoned that the Panicos' unilateral action in placing Michael at the Carroll School without the Town's consent could not "confer thereon the imprimatur of continued placement," *id.*, at 129, n. 5, even though strictly speaking there was no actual placement in effect during the summer of 1979 because all parties agreed Michael was finished with the Memorial School and the Town itself proposed in the IEP to transfer him to a new school in the fall.

The District Court next rejected an argument, apparently grounded at least in part on a state regulation, that the Panicos were entitled to rely on the BSEA decision upholding their placement contrary to the IEP, regardless of whether that decision were ultimately reversed by a court. With respect to the payments made by the Town after the BSEA decision, under the State's threat to cut off funding, the court criticized the State for resorting to extra-judicial pressure to enforce a decision subject to further review. Because this "was not a case where the town was legally obliged under section 1415(e)(3) to continue payments preserving the status quo," the State's coercion could not be viewed as "the basis for a final decision on liability" and it could only be "regarded as other than wrongful . . . on the assumption that the payments were to be returned if the order was ultimately reversed." *Id.*, at 130. The court entered a judgment ordering the Panicos to reimburse the Town for its payments for Michael's Carroll placement and related transportation in 1980-1981 and 1981-1982. The Panicos appealed.

In a broad opinion, most of which we do not review, the Court of Appeals for the First Circuit remanded the case a second time. 736 F. 2d 773 (1984). The court ruled, among other things, that the District Court erred in conducting a full trial *de novo*, that it gave insufficient weight to the BSEA findings, and that in other respects it did not properly evaluate the IEP. The court also considered several questions about the availability of reimbursement for interim placement. The Town argued that § 1415(e)(3) bars the Panicos from any reimbursement relief, even if on remand they were to prevail on the merits of the IEP, because of their unilateral change of Michael's placement during the pendency of the § 1415(e)(2) proceedings. The court held that such unilateral parental change of placement would not be "a bar to reimbursement of the parents if their actions are held to be appropriate at final judgment." *Id.*, at 799. In dictum the court suggested, however, that a lack of parental consultation with the Town or "attempt to achieve a negotiated compromise and agreement on a private placement," as contemplated by the Act, "may be taken into account in a district court's computation of an award of equitable reimbursement." *Ibid.* To guide the District Court on remand, the court stated that "whether to order reimbursement, and at what amount, is a question determined by balancing the equities." *Id.*, at 801. The court also held that the Panicos' reliance on the BSEA decision would estop the Town from obtaining reimbursement "for the period of reliance and requires that where parents have paid the bill for the period, they must be reimbursed." *Ibid.*

The Town filed a petition for a writ of certoriari in this Court challenging the decision of the Court of Appeals on numerous issues, including the scope of judicial review of the administrative decision and the relevance to the merits of an IEP of violations by local school authorities of the Act's procedural requirements. We granted certiorari, 469 U. S. — (1984), only to consider the following two issues: whether the potential relief available under § 1415(e)(2) includes reimbursement to parents for private school tuition and related expenses, and whether § 1415(e)(3) bars such reimbursement to parents who reject a proposed IEP and place a child in a private school without the consent of local school authorities. We express no opinion on any of the many other views stated by the Court of Appeals.

Congress stated the purpose of the Act in these words:

> "to assure that all handicapped children have available to them . . . a free appropriate public education which emphasizes special education and related services designed to meet their unique needs [and] to assure that the rights of handicapped children and their parents or guardians are protected." 20 U. S. C. § 1400(c).

The Act defines a "free appropriate public education" to mean:

> "special education and related services which (A) have been provided at public expense, under public supervision and direction, and without charge, (B) meet the standards of the State educational agency, (C) include an appropriate preschool, elementary, or secondary school education in the State involved, and (D) are provided in conformity with [an] individualized education program." 20 U. S. C. § 1401(18).

To accomplish this ambitious objective, the Act provides federal money to state and local educational agencies that undertake to implement the substantive and procedural requirements of the Act. See *Hendrick Hudson District Bd. of Education* v. *Rowley*, 458 U. S. 176, 179-184 (1982).

The *modus operandi* of the Act is the already mentioned "individualized educational program." The IEP is in brief a comprehensive statement of the educational needs of a handicapped child and the specially designed instruction and related services to be employed to meet those needs. § 1401(19). The IEP is to be developed jointly by a school official qualified in special education, the child's teacher, the parents or guardian, and, where appropriate, the child. In several places, the Act emphasizes the participation of the parents in developing the child's educational program and assessing its effectiveness. See §§ 1400(c), 1401(19), 1412(7), 1415(b)(1)(A), (C), (D), (E), and 1415(b)(2); 34 CFR § 300.345 (1984).

Apparently recognizing that this cooperative approach would not always produce a consensus between the school officials and the parents, and that in any disputes the school officials would have a natural advantage, Congress incorporated an elaborate set of what it labeled "procedural safeguards" to insure the full participation of the parents and proper resolution of substantive disagreements. Section 1415(b) entitles the parents "to examine all relevant records with respect to the identification, evaluation, and educational placement of the child," to obtain an independent educational evaluation of the child, to notice of any decision to initiate or change the identification, evaluation, or educational placement of the child, and to present complaints with respect to any of the above. The parents are further entitled to "an impartial due process hearing," which in the instant case was the BSEA hearing, to resolve their complaints.

The Act also provides for judicial review in state or federal court to "[a]ny party aggrieved by the findings and decision" made after the due process hearing. The Act confers on the reviewing court the following authority:

> "[T]he court shall receive the records of the administrative proceedings, shall hear additional evidence at the request of a party, and, bas-

> ing its decision of the preponderance of the evidence, shall grant such relief as the court determines is appropriate." § 1415(e)(2).

The first question on which we granted certiorari requires us to decide whether this grant of authority includes the power to order school authorities to reimburse parents for their expenditures on private special education for a child if the court ultimately determines that such placement, rather than a proposed IEP, is proper under the Act.

We conclude that the Act authorizes such reimbursement. The statute directs the court to "grant such relief as [it] determines is appropriate." The ordinary meaning of these words confers broad discretion on the court. The type of relief is not further specified, except that it must be "appropriate." Absent other reference, the only possible interpretation is that the relief is to be "appropriate" in light of the purpose of the Act. As already noted, this is principally to provide handicapped children with "a free appropriate public education which emphasizes special education and related services designed to meet their unique needs." The Act contemplates that such education will be provided where possible in regular public schools, with the child participating as much as possible in the same activities as nonhandicapped children, but the Act also provides for placement in private schools at public expense where this is not possible. See § 1412(5); 34 CFR §§ 300.132, 300.227, 300.307(b), 300.347 (1984). In a case where a court determines that a private placement desired by the parents was proper under the Act and that an IEP calling for placement in a public school was inappropriate, it seems clear beyond cavil that "appropriate" relief would include a prospective injunction directing the school officials to develop and implement at public expense an IEP placing the child in a private school.

If the administrative and judicial review under the Act could be completed in a matter of weeks, rather than years, it would be difficult to imagine a case in which such prospective injunctive relief would not be sufficient. As this case so vividly demonstrates, however, the review process is ponderous. A final judicial decision on the merits of an IEP will in most instances come a year or more after the school term covered by that IEP has passed. In the meantime, the parents who disagree with the proposed IEP are faced with a choice: go along with the IEP to the detriment of their child if it turns out to be inappropriate or pay for what they consider to be the appropriate placement. If they choose the latter course, which conscientious parents who have adequate means and who are reasonably confident of their assessment normally would, it would be an empty victory to have a court tell them several years later that they were right but that these expenditures could not in a proper case be reimbursed by the school officials. If that were the case, the child's right to a *free* appropriate public education, the parents' right to participate fully in developing a proper IEP, and all of the procedural safeguards would be less than complete. Because Congress undoubtedly did not intend this result, we are confident that by empowering the court to grant "appropriate" relief Congress meant to include retroactive reimbursement to parents as an available remedy in a proper case.

In this Court, the Town repeatedly characterizes reimbursement as "damages," but that simply is not the case. Reimbursement merely requires the Town to belatedly pay expenses that it should have paid all along and would have borne in the first instance had it developed a proper IEP. Such a *post-hoc* determination of financial responsibility was contemplated in the legislative history:

> "If a parent contends that he or she has been forced, at that parent's own expense, to seek private schooling for the child because an appropriate program does not exist within the local educational agency responsible for the child's education and the local educational agency disagrees, that disagreement and *the question of who remains financially responsible* is a matter to which the due process procedures established under [the predecessor to § 1415] appl[y]." S. Rep. No. 94-168, p. 32 (1975) (emphasis added).

See 34 CFR § 300.403(b)(1984) (disagreements and question of financial responsibility subject to the due process procedures).

Regardless of the availability of reimbursement as a form of relief in a proper case, the Town maintains that the Panicos have waived any right they otherwise might have to reimbursement because they violated § 1415(e)(3), which provides:

> "During the pendency of any proceedings conducted pursuant to [§ 1415], unless the State or local educational agency and the parents or guardian otherwise agree, the child shall remain in the then current educational placement of such child. . . ."

We need not resolve the academic question of what Michael's "then current placement" was in the summer of 1979, when both the Town and the parents had agreed that a new school was in order. For the purposes of our decision, we assume that the Pine Glen School, proposed in the IEP, was Michael's current placement and, therefore, that the Panicos did "change" his placement after they had rejected the IEP and had set the administrative review in motion. In so doing, the Panicos contravened the conditional command of § 1415(e)(3) that "the child shall remain in the then current educational placement."

As an initial matter, we note that the section calls for agreement by *either* the *State or* the *local educational agency.* The BSEA's decision in favor of the Panicos and the Carroll School placement would seem to constitute agreement by the State to the change of placement. The decision was issued in January 1980, so from then on the Panicos were no longer in violation of § 1415(e)(3). This conclusion, however, does not entirely resolve the instant dispute because the Panicos are also seeking reimbursement for Michael's expenses during the fall of 1979, prior to the State's concurrence in the Carroll School placement.

We do not agree with the Town that a parental violation of § 1415(e)(3) constitutes a waiver of reimbursement. The provision says nothing about financial responsibility, waiver, or parental right to reimbursement at the conclusion of judicial proceedings. Moreover, if the provision is interpreted to cut off parental rights to reimbursement, the principal purpose of the Act will in many cases be defeated in the same way as if reimbursement were never available. As in this case, parents will often notice a child's learning difficulties while the child is in a regular public school program. If the school officials disagree with the need for special education of the adequacy of the public school's program to meet the child's needs, it is unlikely they will agree to an interim private school placement while the review process runs its course. Thus, under the Town's reading of § 1415(e)(3), the parents are forced to leave the child in what may turn out to be an inappropriate educational placement or to obtain the appropriate placement only by sacrificing any claim for reimbursement. The Act was intended to give handicapped children both an appropriate education and a free one; it should not be interpreted to defeat one or the other of those objectives.

The legislative history supports this interpretation, favoring a proper interim placement pending the resolution of disagreements over the IEP:

> "The conferees are cognizant that an impartial due process hearing may be required to assure that the rights of the child have been completely protected. We did feel, however, that the placement, or change of placement should not be unnecessarily delayed while long and tedious administrative appeals were being exhausted. Thus the conference adopted a flexible approach to try to meet the needs of both the child and the State." 121 Cong. Rec. 37412 (1975) (Sen. Stafford).

We think at least one purpose of § 1415(e)(3) was to prevent school officials from removing a child from the regular public school classroom over the parents' objection pending completion of the review proceedings. As we observed in *Rowley*, 458 U. S., at 192, the impetus for the Act came from two federal court decisions, *Pennsylvania Assn. for Retarded Children* v. *Commonwealth*, 334 F. Supp. 1257 (ED Pa. 1971), and 343 F. Supp. 279 (1972), and *Mills* v. *Board of Education of District of Columbia*, 348 F. Supp. 866 (DC 1972), which arose from the efforts of parents of handicapped children to prevent the exclusion or expulsion of their children from the public schools. Congress was concerned about the apparently widespread practice of relegating handicapped children to private institutions or warehousing them in special classes. See § 1400(4); 34 CFR § 300.347(a) (1984). We also note that § 1415(e)(3) is located in a section detailing procedural safeguards which are largely for the benefit of the parents and the child.

This is not to say that § 1415(e)(3) has no effect on parents. While we doubt that this provision would authorize a court to order parents to leave their child in a particular placement, we think it operates in such a way that parents who unilaterally change their child's placement during the pendency of review proceedings, without the consent of state or local school officials, do so at their own financial risk. If the courts ultimately determine that the IEP proposed by the school officials was appropriate, the parents would be barred from obtaining reimbursement for any interim period in which their child's placement violated § 1415(e)(3). This conclusion is supported by the agency's interpretation of the Act's application to private placements by the parents:

> "(a) If a handicapped child has available a free appropriate public education and the parents choose to place the child in a private school or facility, the public agency is not required by this part to pay for the child's education at the private school or facility. . . .
>
> "(b) Disagreements between a parent and a public agency regarding the availability of a program appropriate for the child, and the

question of financial responsibility, are subject to the due process procedures under [§ 1415]." 34 CFR § 300.403 (1984).

We thus resolve the questions on which we granted certiorari; because the case is here in an interlocutory posture, we do not consider the estoppel ruling below or the specific equitable factors identified by the Court of Appeals for granting relief. We do think that the court was correct in concluding that "such relief as the court determines is appropriate," within the meaning of § 1415(e)(2), means that equitable considerations are relevant in fashioning relief.

The judgment of the Court of Appeals is

Affirmed.

Honig, California Superintendent of Public Instruction v. Doe

U.S. Supreme Court, 108 S.Ct. 592 (1988).

Syllabus*

In order to assure that States receiving federal financial assistance will provide a "free appropriate public education" for all disabled children, including those with serious emotional disturbances, the Education of the Handicapped Act (EHA or Act) establishes a comprehensive system of procedural safeguards designed to provide meaningful parental participation in all aspects of a child's educational placement, including an opportunity for an impartial due process hearing with respect to any complaints such parents have concerning their child's placement, and the right to seek administrative review of any decisions they think inappropriate. If that review proves unsatisfactory, either the parents or the local educational agency may file a civil action in any state or federal court for "appropriate" relief. 20 U. S. C. § 1415(e)(2). The Act's "stay-put" provision directs that a disabled child "shall remain in [his or her] then current educational placement" pending completion of any review proceedings, unless the parents and state or local educational agencies otherwise agree. § 1415(e)(3). Respondents Doe and Smith, who were emotionally disturbed students, were suspended indefinitely for violent and disruptive conduct related to their disabilities, pending the completion of expulsion proceedings by the San Francisco Unified School District (SFUSD). After unsuccessfully protesting the action against him, Doe filed a suit in Federal District Court, in which Smith intervened, alleging that the suspension and proposed expulsion violated the EHA, and seeking injunctive relief against SFUSD officials and petitioner, the State Superintendent of Public Instruction. The court entered summary judgment for respondents on their EHA claims and issued a permanent injunction. The Court of Appeals affirmed with slight modifications.

Held:

1. The case is moot as to respondent Doe, who is now 24 years old, since the Act limits eligibility to disabled children between the ages of 3 and 21. However, the case is justiciable with respect to respondent Smith, who continues to be eligible for EHA educational services since he is currently only 20 and has not yet completed high school. This Court has jurisdiction since there is a reasonable likelihood that Smith will again suffer the deprivation of EHA-mandated rights that gave rise to this suit. Given the evidence that he is unable to conform his conduct to socially acceptable norms, and the absence of any suggestion that he has overcome his behavioral problems, it is reasonable to expect that he will again engage in aggressive and disruptive classroom misconduct. Moreover, it is unreasonable to suppose that any future educational placement will so perfectly suit his emotional and academic needs that further disruptions on his part are improbable. If Smith does repeat the objectionable conduct, it is likely that he will again be subjected to the same type of unilateral school action in any California school district in which he is enrolled, in light of the lack of a statewide policy governing local school responses to disability-related misconduct, and petitioner's insistence that all local school district retain residual authority to exclude disabled children for dangerous conduct. In light of the

*The syllabus constitutes no part of the opinion of the Court but has been prepared by the Reporter of Decisions for the convenience of the reader.

ponderousness of review procedures under the Act, and the fact that an aggrieved student will often be finished with school or otherwise ineligible for EHA protections by the time review can be had in this Court, the conduct Smith complained of is "capable of repetition, yet evading review." Thus his EHA claims are not moot.

2. The "stay-put" provision prohibits state or local school authorities from unilaterally excluding disabled children from the classroom for dangerous or disruptive conduct growing out of their disabilities during the pendency of review proceedings. Section 1415(e)(3) is unequivocal in its mandate that "the child *shall* remain in the then current educational placement" (emphasis added), and demonstrates a congressional intent to strip school of the *unilateral* authority they had traditionally employed to exclude disabled students, particularly emotionally disturbed students, from school. This Court will not rewrite the statute to infer a "dangerousness" exception on the basis of obviousness or congressional inadvertence, since, in drafting the statute, Congress devoted close attention to *Mills* v. *Board of Education of District of Columbia*, 348 F. Supp. 866, and *Pennsylvania Assn. for Retarded Children* v. *Pennsylvania*, 334 F. Supp. 1257, and 343 F. Supp. 279, thereby establishing that the omission of an emergency exception for dangerous students was intentional. However, Congress did not leave school administrators powerless to deal with such students, since implementing regulations allow the use of normal, nonplacement-changing procedures, including temporary suspensions for up to 10 schooldays for students posing an immediate threat to others' safety, while the Act allows for interim placements where parents and school officials are able to agree, and authorizes officials to file a § 1415(e)(2) suit for "appropriate" injunctive relief where such an agreement cannot be reached. In such a suit, § 1415(e)(3) effectively creates a presumption in favor of the child's current educational placement which school officials can rebut only by showing that maintaining the current placement is substantially likely to result in injury to the student or to others. Here, the District Court properly balanced respondents' interests under the Act against the state and local school officials' safety interest, and both lower courts properly construed and applied § 1415(e)(3), except insofar as the Court of Appeals held that a suspension exceeding 10 schooldays does not constitute a prohibited change in placement. The Court of Appeals' judgment is modified to that extent.

3. Insofar as the Court of Appeals' judgment affirmed the District Court's order directing the State to provide services directly to a disabled child where the local agency has failed to do so, that judgment is affirmed by an equally divided Court.

793 F. 2d 1470, affirmed.

BRENNAN, J., delivered the opinion of the Court as to holdings number 1 and 2 above, in which REHNQUIST, C. J., and WHITE, MARSHALL, BLACKMUN, and STEVENS, JJ., joined. REHNQUIST, C. J., filed a concurring opinion. SCALIA, J., filed a dissenting opinion, in which O'CONNOR, J., joined.

JUSTICE BRENNAN delivered the opinion of the Court.

As a condition of federal financial assistance, the Education of the Handicapped Act requires States to ensure a "free appropriate public education" for all disabled children within their jurisdictions. In aid of this goal, the Act establishes a comprehensive system of procedural safeguards designed to ensure parental participation in decisions concerning the education of their disabled children and to provide administrative and judicial review of any decisions with which those parents disagree. Among these safeguards is the so-called "stay-put" provision, which directs that a disabled child "shall remain in [his or her] then current educational placement" pending completion of any review proceedings, unless the parents and state or local educational agencies otherwise agree. 20 U. S. C. § 1415(e)(3). Today we must decide whether, in the face of this statutory proscription, state or local school authorities may nevertheless unilaterally exclude disabled children from the classroom for dangerous or disruptive conduct growing out of their disabilities. In addition, we are called upon to decide whether a district court may, in the exercise of its equitable powers, order a State to provide educational services directly to a disabled child when the local agency fails to do so.

I

In the Education of the Handicapped Act (EHA or the Act), 84 Stat. 175, as amended, 20 U. S. C. § 1400 *et seq.*, Congress sought "to assure that all handicapped children have available to them . . . a free appropriate public education which emphasizes special education and related services designed to meet their unique needs, [and] to assure that the rights of handicapped children and their parents or guardians are protected." § 1400(c). When the law was passed in 1975, Congress had before it ample evidence that such legislative assurances were sorely needed: 21 years after this Court declared education to be "perhaps the most important function of state and local governments," *Brown* v. *Board of Education*, 347 U. S. 483 (1954), Congressional studies revealed that better than half of the Nation's eight million disabled children were not receiving appropriate educational services. § 1400(b)(3). Indeed, one out of every eight of these children was excluded from the public school system altogether, § 1400(b)(4); many others were simply "warehoused" in special classes or were neglectfully shepherded through the system until they were old enough to drop out. See H. R. Rep. No. 94-332, p. 2 (1975). Among the most poorly served of disabled students were emotionally disturbed children: Congressional statistics revealed that for the school year immediately preceding passage of the Act, the educational needs of 82 percent of all children with emotional disabilities went unmet. See S. Rep. No. 94-168, p. 8 (1975) (hereinafter S. Rep.).

Although these educational failings resulted in part from funding constraints, Congress recognized that the problem reflected more than a lack of financial resources at the state and local levels. Two federal-court decisions, which the Senate Report characterized as "landmark," see *id.*, at 6, demonstrated that many disabled children were excluded pursuant to state statutes or local rules and policies, typically without any consultation with, or even notice to, their parents. See *Mills* v. *Board of Education of District of Columbia*, 348 F. Supp. 866 (DC 1972); *Pennsylvania Assn. for Retarded Children* v. *Pennsylvania*, 334 F. Supp. 1257 (ED Pa. 1971), and 343 F. Supp. 279 (1972) (*PARC*). Indeed, by the time of the EHA's enactment, parents had brought legal challenges to similar exclusionary practices in 27 other states. See S. Rep., at 6.

In responding to these problems, Congress did not content itself with passage of a simple funding statute. Rather, the EHA confers upon disabled students an enforceable substantive right to public education in participating States, see *Board of Education of Hendrick Hudson Central School Dist.* v. *Rowley*, 458 U. S. 176 (1982),[1] and conditions federal financial assistance upon a State's compliance with the substantive and procedural goals of the Act. Accordingly, States seeking to qualify for federal funds must develop policies assuring all disabled children the "right to a free appropriate public education," and must file with the Secretary of Education formal plans mapping out in detail the programs, procedures and timetables under which they will effectuate these policies. 20 U. S. C. §§ 1412(1), 1413(a). Such plans must assure that, "to the maximum extent appropriate," States will "mainstream" disabled children, *i. e.*, that they will educate them with children who are not disabled, and that they will segregate or otherwise remove such children from the regular classroom setting "only when the nature or severity of the handicap is such that education in regular classes . . . cannot be achieved satisfactorily." § 1412(5).

The primary vehicle for implementing these congressional goals is the "individualized educational program" (IEP), which the EHA mandates for each disabled child. Prepared at meetings between a representative of the local school district, the child's teacher, the parents or guardians, and, whenever appropriate, the disabled child, the IEP sets out the child's present educational performance, establishes annual and short-term objectives for improvements in that performance, and describes the specially designed instruction and services that will enable the child to meet those objectives. § 1410(19). The IEP must be reviewed and, where necessary, revised at least once a year in order to ensure that local agencies tailor the statutorily required "free appropriate public education" to each child's unique needs. § 1414(a)(5).

Envisioning the IEP as the centerpiece of the statute's education delivery system for disabled children, and aware that schools had all too often denied such children appropriate educations without in any way consulting their parents, Congress repeatedly emphasized throughout the Act the importance and indeed the necessity of parental participation in both the development of the IEP and any subsequent assessments of its effectiveness. See §§ 1400(c), 1401(19), 1412(7), 1415(b)(1)(A), (C), (D), (E), and 1415(b)(2). Accordingly,

---

[1] Congress' earlier efforts to ensure that disabled students received adequate public education had failed in part because the measures it adopted were largely hortatory. In the 1966 amendments to the Elementary and Secondary Education Act of 1965, Congress established a grant program "for the purpose of assisting the States in the initiation, expansion, and improvement of programs and projects . . . for the education of handicapped children." Pub. L. 89-750, § 161, 80 Stat. 1204. It repealed that program four years later and replaced it with the original version of the Education of the Handicapped Act, Pub. L. 91-230, 84 Stat. 175, Part B of which contained a similar grant program. Neither statute, however, provided specific guidance as to how States were to use the funds, nor did they condition the availability of the grants on compliance with any procedural or substantive safeguards. In amending the EHA to its present form, Congress rejected its earlier policy of "merely establish[ing] an unenforceable goal requiring all children to be in school." 121 Cong. Rec. 37417 (1975) (remarks of Sen. Schweiker). Today, all 50 states and the District of Columbia receive funding assistance under the EHA. U. S. Dept. of Education, Ninth Annual Report to Congress on Implementation of Education of the Handicapped Act (1987).

the Act establishes various procedural safeguards that guarantee parents both an opportunity for meaningful input into all decisions affecting their child's education and the right to seek review of any decisions they think inappropriate. These safeguards include the right to examine all relevant records pertaining to the identification, evaluation and educational placement of their child; prior written notice whenever the responsible educational agency proposes (or refuses) to change the child's placement or program; an opportunity to present complaints concerning any aspect of the local agency's provision of a free appropriate public education; and an opportunity for "an impartial due process hearing" with respect to any such complaints. § 1415(b)(1), (2).

At the conclusion of any such hearing, both the parents and the local educational agency may seek further administrative review and, where that proves unsatisfactory, may file a civil action in any state or federal court. § 1415(c), (e)(2). In addition to reviewing the administrative record, courts are empowered to take additional evidence at the request of either party and to "grant such relief as [they] determine[] is appropriate." § 1415(e)(2). The "stay-put" provision at issue in this case governs the placement of a child while these often lengthy review procedures run their course. It directs that:

> "During the pendency of any proceedings conducted pursuant to [§ 1415], unless the State or local educational agency and the parents or guardian otherwise agree, the child shall remain in the then current educational placement of such child . . . ." § 1415(e)(3).

The present dispute grows out of the efforts of certain officials of the San Francisco Unified School District (SFUSD) to expel two emotionally disturbed children from school indefinitely for violent and disruptive conduct related to their disabilities. In November 1980, respondent John Doe assaulted another student at the Louise Lombard School, a developmental center for disabled children. Doe's April 1980 IEP identified him as a socially and physically awkward 17 year old who experienced considerable difficulty controlling his impulses and anger. Among the goals set out in his IEP was "[i]mprovement in [his] ability to relate to [his] peers [and to] cope with frustrating situations without resorting to aggressive acts." App. 17. Frustrating situations, however, were an unfortunately prominent feature of Doe's school career: physical abnormalities, speech difficulties, and poor grooming habits had made him the target of teasing and ridicule as early as the first grade, *id.*, at 23; his 1980 IEP reflected his continuing difficulties with peers, noting that his social skills had deteriorated and that he could tolerate only minor frustration before exploding. *Id.*, at 15-16.

On November 6, 1980, Doe responded to the taunts of a fellow student in precisely the explosive manner anticipated by his IEP: he choked the student with sufficient force to leave abrasions on the child's neck, and kicked out a school window while being escorted to the principal's office afterwards. *Id.*, at 208. Doe admitted his misconduct and the school subsequently suspended him for five days. Thereafter, his principal referred the matter to the SFUSD Student Placement Committee (SPC or Committee) with the recommendation that Doe be expelled. On the day the suspension was to end, the SPC notified Doe's mother that it was proposing to exclude her child permanently from SFUSD and was therefore extending his suspension until such time as the expulsion proceedings were completed.[2] The Committee further advised her that she was entitled to attend the November 25 hearing at which it planned to discuss the proposed expulsion.

After unsuccessfully protesting these actions by letter, Doe brought this suit against a host of local school officials and the state superintendent of public education. Alleging that the suspension and proposed expulsion violated the EHA, he sought a temporary restraining order cancelling the SPC hearing and requiring school officials to convene an IEP meeting. The District Judge granted the requested injunctive relief and further ordered defendants to provide home tutoring for Doe on an interim basis; shortly thereafter, she issued a preliminary injunction directing defendants to return Doe to his then current educational placement at Louise Lombard School pending completion of the IEP review process. Doe re-entered school on December 15, 5½ weeks, and 24 school days, after his initial suspension.

Respondent Jack Smith was identified as an emotionally disturbed child by the time he entered the second grade in 1976. School records prepared that year indicated that he was unable "to control verbal or physical outburst[s]" and exhibited a "[s]evere disturbance in relationships with peers and adults." *Id.*, at 123. Further evaluations subsequently revealed that he had been physically and emotionally abused as an infant and young child and that, despite above average intelligence, he experienced academic and social difficulties as a result of extreme hyperactivity and low self-esteem. *Id.*, at 136, 139, 155, 176. Of particular concern was Smith's propensity for verbal hostility; one evaluator noted that the child reacted to stress by "attempt[ing] to cover his feelings of low self worth through aggressive behavior[,] . . . primarily verbal provocations." *Id.*, at 136.

Based on these evaluations, SFUSD placed Smith in a learning center for emotionally disturbed children. His grandparents, however, believed that his needs would be better served in the public school setting and, in September 1979, the school district acceded to their requests and enrolled him at A. P. Giannini Middle School. His February 1980 IEP recommended placement in a Learning Disability Group, stressing the need for close supervision and a highly structured environment. *Id.*, at 111. Like earlier evaluations, the February 1980 IEP noted that Smith was easily distracted, impulsive, and anxious; it therefore proposed a half-day schedule and suggested that the placement be undertaken on a trial basis. *Id.*, at 112, 115.

At the beginning of the next school year, Smith was assigned to a full-day program; almost immediately thereafter he began misbehaving. School officials met twice with his grandparents in October 1980 to discuss returning him to a half-day program; although the grandparents agreed to the reduction, they apparently were never apprised of their right to challenge the decision through EHA procedures. The school officials also warned them that if

---

[2]California law at the time empowered school principals to suspend students for no more than five consecutive school days, Cal. Educ. Code Ann. § 48903(a) (West 1978), but permitted school districts seeking to expel a suspended student to "extend the suspension until such time as [expulsion proceedings were completed]; provided, that [it] has determined that the presence of the pupil at the school or in an alternative school placement would cause a danger to persons or property or a threat of disrupting the instructional process." § 48903(h). The State subsequently amended the law to permit school districts to impose longer initial periods of suspension. See n. 3, *infra*.

the child continued his disruptive behavior—which included stealing, extorting money from fellow students, and making sexual comments to female classmates—they would seek to expel him. On November 14, they made good on this threat, suspending Smith for five days after he made further lewd comments. His principal referred the matter to the SPC, which recommended exclusion from SFUSD. As it did in John Doe's case, the Committee scheduled a hearing and extended the suspension indefinitely pending a final disposition in the matter. On November 28, Smith's counsel protested these actions on grounds essentially identical to those raised by Doe, and the SPC agreed to cancel the hearing and to return Smith to a half-day program at A. P. Giannini or to provide home tutoring. Smith's grandparents chose the latter option and the school began home instruction on December 10; on January 6, 1981, an IEP team convened to discuss alternative placements.

After learning of Doe's action, Smith sought and obtained leave to intervene in the suit. The District Court subsequently entered summary judgment in favor of respondents on their EHA claims and issued a permanent injunction. In a series of decisions, the District Judge found that the proposed expulsions and indefinite suspensions of respondents for conduct attributable to their disabilities deprived them of their congressionally mandated right to a free appropriate public education, as well as their right to have that education provided in accordance with the procedures set out in the EHA. The District Judge therefore permanently enjoined the school district from taking any disciplinary action other than a two- or five-day suspension against any disabled child for disability-related misconduct, or from effecting any other change in the educational placement of any such child without parental consent pending completion of any EHA proceedings. In addition, the judge barred the State from authorizing unilateral placement changes and directed it to establish an EHA compliance-monitoring system or, alternatively, to enact guidelines governing local school responses to disability-related misconduct. Finally, the judge ordered the State to provide services directly to disabled children when, in any individual case, the State determined that the local educational agency was unable or unwilling to do so.

On appeal, the Court of Appeals for the Ninth Circuit affirmed the orders with slight modifications. *Doe* v. *Maher*, 793 F. 2d 1470 (1986). Agreeing with the District Court that an indefinite suspension in aid of expulsion constitutes a prohibited "change in placement" under § 1415(e)(3), the Court of Appeals held that the stay-put provision admitted of no "dangerousness" exception and that the statute therefore rendered invalid those provisions of the California Education Code permitting the indefinite suspension or expulsion of disabled children for misconduct arising out of their disabilities. The court concluded, however, that fixed suspensions of up to 30 school days did not fall within the reach of § 1415(e)(3), and therefore upheld recent amendments to the state education code authorizing such suspensions.[3] Lastly, the court affirmed that portion of the injunction requiring the State

---

[3]In 1983, the State amended its Education Code to permit school districts to impose initial suspensions of 20, and in certain circumstances, 30 school days. Cal. Educ. Code Ann. §§ 48912(a), 48903 (West Supp. 1988). The legislature did not alter the indefinite suspension authority which the SPC exercised in this case, but simply incorporated the earlier provision into a new section. See § 48911(g).

to provide services directly to a disabled child when the local educational agency fails to do so.

Petitioner Bill Honig, California Superintendent of Public Instruction,[4] sought review in this Court, claiming that the Court of Appeals' construction of the stay-put provision conflicted with that of several other courts of appeals which had recognized a dangerousness exception, compare *Doe* v. *Maher*, 793 F. 2d 1470 (1986) (case below), with *Jackson* v. *Franklin County School Board*, 765 F. 2d 535, 538 (CA5 1985); *Victoria L.* v. *District School Bd. of Lee County, Fla.*, 741 F. 2d 369, 374 (CA11 1984); *S-1* v. *Turlington*, 635 F. 2d 342, 348, n. 9 (CA5), cert. denied, 454 U. S. 1030 (1981), and that the direct services ruling placed an intolerable burden on the State. We granted certiorari to resolve these questions, 479 U. S. —— (1987), and now affirm.

II

At the outset, we address the suggestion, raised for the first time during oral argument, that this case is moot.[5] Under Article III of the Constitution this Court may only adjudicate actual, ongoing controversies. *Nebraska Press Assn* v. *Stuart*, 427 U. S. 539, 546 (1976); *Preiser* v. *Newkirk*, 422 U. S. 395, 401 (1975). That the dispute between the parties was very much alive when suit was filed, or at the time the Court of Appeals rendered its judgment, cannot substitute for the actual case or controversy that an exercise of this Court's jurisdiction requires. *Steffel* v. *Thompson*, 415 U. S. 452, 459 n. 10 (1974); *Roe* v. *Wade*, 410 U. S. 113, 125 (1973). In the present case, we have jurisdiction if there is a reasonable likelihood that respondents will again suffer the deprivation of EHA-mandated rights that gave rise to this suit. We believe that, at least with respect to respondent Smith, such a possibility does in fact exist and that the case therefore remains justiciable.

Respondent John Doe is now 24 years old and, accordingly, is no longer entitled to the protections and benefits of the EHA, which limits eligibility to disabled children between the ages of three and 21. See 20 U. S. C. § 1412(2)(B). It is clear, therefore, that whatever rights to state educational services he may yet have as a ward of the State, see Tr. of Oral Arg. 23, 26, the Act would not govern the State's provision of those services, and thus the case is moot as to him. Respondent Jack Smith, however, is currently 20 and has not yet completed high school. Although at present he is not faced with any proposed expulsion or suspension proceedings, and indeed no longer even resides within the SFUSD, he remains a resident of California and is entitled to a "free appropriate public education" within that State. His claims under the EHA, therefore, are not moot if the conduct he originally complained of is "'capable of repetition, yet evading review.'" *Murphy* v. *Hunt*, 455 U. S. 478, 482 (1982). Given Smith's continued eligibility for edu-

---

[4]At the time respondent Doe initiated this suit, Wilson Riles was the California Superintendent of Public Instruction. Petitioner Honig succeeded him in office.

[5]We note that both petitioner and respondents believe that this case presents a live controversy. See Tr. of Oral Arg. 6, 27-31. Only the United States, appearing as *amicus curiae*, urges that the case is presently nonjusticiable. *Id.*, at 21.

cational services under the EHA,[6] the nature of his disability, and petitioner's insistence that all local school districts retain residual authority to exclude disabled children for dangerous conduct, we have little difficulty concluding that there is a "reasonable expectation," *ibid.*, that Smith would once again be subjected to a unilateral "change in placement" for conduct growing out of his disabilities were it not for the state-wide injunctive relief issued below.

Our cases reveal that, for purposes of assessing the likelihood that state authorities will re-inflict a given injury, we generally have been unwilling to assume that the party seeking relief will repeat the type of misconduct that would once again place him or her at risk of that injury. See *Los Angeles* v. *Lyons*, 461 U. S. 95, 105-106 (1983) (no threat that party seeking injunction

[6]Notwithstanding respondent's undisputed right to a free appropriate public education in California, JUSTICE SCALIA argues in dissent that there is no "demonstrated probability" that Smith will actually avail himself of that right because his counsel was unable to state affirmatively during oral argument that her client would seek to re-enter the state school system. See *post*, at 2. We believe the dissent overstates the stringency of the "capable of repetition" test. Although JUSTICE SCALIA equates "reasonable expectation" with "demonstrated probability," the very case he cites for this proposition described these standards in the disjunctive, see *Murphy* v. *Hunt*, 455 U. S., at 482 ("[T]here must be a 'reasonable expectation' *or* a 'demonstrated probability' that the same controversy will recur" (emphasis added)), and in numerous cases decided both before and since *Hunt* we have found controversies capable of repetition based on expectations that, while reasonable, were hardly demonstrably probable. See *e. g.*, *Burlington Northern R. Co.* v. *Maintenance of Way Employees*, 481 U. S. ——, ——, n. 4 (1987) (parties "reasonably likely" to find themselves in future disputes over collective bargaining agreement); *California Coastal Comm'n* v. *Granite Rock Co.*, 480 U. S. ——, —— (1987) (O'CONNOR, J.) ("likely" that respondent would again submit mining plans that would trigger contested state permit requirement); *Press-Enterprise Co* v. *Superior Court of Cal., Riverside County*, 478 U. S. 1, 6 (1986) ("It can reasonably be assumed" that newspaper publisher will be subjected to similar closure order in the future); *Globe Newspaper Co.*v. *Superior Court of Norfolk County*, 457 U. S. 596, 603 (1982) (same); *United States Parole Comm'n* v. *Geraghty*, 445 U. S. 388, 398 (1980) (case not moot where litigant "faces some likelihood of becoming involved in same controversy in the future") (dicta). Our concern in these cases, as in all others involving potentially moot claims, was whether the controversy was *capable* of repetition and not, as the dissent seems to insist, whether the claimant had demonstrated that a recurrence of the dispute was more probable than not. Regardless, then, of whether respondent has established with mathematical precision the likelihood that he will enroll in public school during the next two years, we think there is at the very least a reasonable expectation that he will exercise his rights under the EHA. In this regard, we believe respondent's actions over the course of the last seven years speak louder than his counsel's momentary equivocation during oral argument. Since 1980, he has sought to vindicate his right to an appropriate public education that is not only free of charge, but free from the threat that school officials will unilaterally change his placement or exclude him from class altogether. As a disabled young man, he has as at least as great a need of a high school education and diploma as any of his peers, and his counsel advises us that he is awaiting the outcome of this case to decide whether to pursue his degree. Tr. Oral Arg. 23-24. Under these circumstances, we think it not only counterintuitive but unreasonable to assume that respondent will forgo the exercise of a right that he has for so long sought to defend. Certainly we have as much reason to expect that respondent will re-enter the California school system as we had to assume that Jane Roe would again both have an unwanted pregnancy and wish to exercise her right to an abortion. See *Roe* v. *Wade*, 410 U. S. 113, 125 (1973).

barring police use of chokeholds would be stopped again for traffic violation or other offense, or would resist arrest if stopped); *Hunt* v. *Murphy*, *supra*, at 484 (no reason to believe that party challenging denial of pretrial bail "will once again be in a position to demand bail"); *O'Shea* v. *Littleton*, 414 U. S. 488, 497 (1974) (unlikely that parties challenging discriminatory bond-setting, sentencing, and jury-fee practices would again violate valid criminal laws). No such reluctance, however, is warranted here. It is respondent Smith's very inability to conform his conduct to socially acceptable norms that renders him "handicapped" within the meaning of the EHA. See 20 U. S. C. § 1401(1); 34 CFR § 300.5(b)(8) (1987). As noted above, the record is replete with evidence that Smith is unable to govern his aggressive, impulsive behavior—indeed, his notice of suspension acknowledged that "Jack's actions seem beyond his control." App. 152. In the absence of any suggestion that respondent has overcome his earlier difficulties, it is certainly reasonable to expect, based on his prior history of behavioral problems, that he will again engage in classroom misconduct. Nor is it reasonable to suppose that Smith's future educational placement will so perfectly suit his emotional and academic needs that further disruptions on his part are improbable. Although JUSTICE SCALIA suggests in his dissent, *post*, that school officials are unlikely to place Smith in a setting where they cannot control his misbehavior, any efforts to ensure such total control must be tempered by the school system's statutory obligations to provide respondent with a free appropriate public education in "the least restrictive environment," 34 CFR § 300.552(d) (1987); to educate him, "to the maximum extent appropriate," with children who are not disabled, 20 U. S. C. § 1412(5); and to consult with his parents or guardians, and presumably with respondent himself, before choosing a placement. §§ 1401(19), 1415(b). Indeed, it is only by ignoring these mandates, as well as Congress' unquestioned desire to wrest from school officials their former unilateral authority to determine the placement of emotionally disturbed children, see *infra*, that the dissent can so readily assume that respondent's future placement will satisfactorily prevent any further dangerous conduct on his part. Overarching these statutory obligations, moreover, is the inescapable fact that the preparation of an IEP, like any other effort at predicting human behavior, is an inexact science at best. Given the unique circumstances and context of this case, therefore, we think it reasonable to expect that respondent will again engage in the type of misconduct that precipitated this suit.

We think it equally probable that, should he do so, respondent will again be subjected to the same unilateral school action for which he initially sought relief. In this regard, it matters not that Smith no longer resides within the SFUSD. While the actions of SFUSD officials first gave rise to this litigation, the District Judge expressly found that the lack of a state policy governing local school responses to disability-related misconduct had let to, and would continue to result in, EHA violations, and she therefore enjoined the state defendant from authorizing, among other things, unilateral placement changes. App. 247-248. She of course also issued injunctions directed at the local defendants, but they did not seek review of those orders in this Court. Only petitioner, the State Superintendent of Public Instruction, has invoked our jurisdiction, and he now urges us to hold that local school districts retain unilateral authority under the EHA to suspend or otherwise remove disabled children for dangerous conduct. Given these representations, we have every reason to believe that were it not for the injunction barring petitioner from authorizing such unilateral action, respondent would be faced with a real and substantial threat of such action in any California school district in which he enrolled. Cf. *Los Angeles* v. *Lyons*, *supra*, at 106 (respondent lacked standing to seek injunctive relief because he could not plausibly allege that police officers choked all persons whom they stopped, or that the City "*authorized* police officers to act in such manner" (emphasis added)). Certainly, if the SFUSD's past practice of unilateral exclusions was at odds with state policy and the practice of local school districts generally, petitioner would not now stand before us seeking to defend the right of all local school districts to engage in such aberrant behavior.[7]

We have previously noted that administrative and judicial review under the EHA is often "ponderous," *Burlington School Committee* v. *Massachusetts Dept. of Education*, 471 U. S. 359, 370 (1985), and this case, which has taken seven years to reach us, amply confirms that observation. For obvious reasons, the misconduct of an emotionally disturbed or otherwise disabled child who has not yet reached adolescence typically will not pose such a serious threat to the well-being of other students that school officials can only ensure classroom safety by excluding the child. Yet, the adolescent student improperly disciplined for misconduct that does pose such a threat will often be finished with school or otherwise ineligible for EHA protections by the time review can be had in this Court. Because we believe that respondent Smith has demonstrated both "a sufficient likelihood that he will again be wronged in a similar way," *Los Angeles* v. *Lyons*, 461 U. S., at 111, and that any resulting claim he may have for relief will surely evade our review, we turn to the merits of his case.

III

The language of § 1415(e)(3) is unequivocal. It states plainly that during the pendency of any proceedings initiated under the Act, unless the state or local educational agency and the parents or guardian of a disabled child otherwise agree, "the child *shall* remain in the then current educational placement." § 1415(e)(3) (emphasis added). Faced with this clear directive, petitioner asks us to read a "dangerousness" exception into the stay-put provision on the basis of either of two essentially inconsistent assumptions: first, that Congress thought the residual authority of school officials to exclude dangerous students from the classroom too obvious for comment; or second, that Congress inadvertently failed to provide such authority and this Court must therefore remedy the oversight. Because we cannot accept either premise, we decline petitioner's invitation to re-write the statute.

Petitioner's arguments proceed, he suggests, from a simple, commonsense proposition: Congress could not have intended the stay-put provision

---

[7]Petitioner concedes that the school district "made a number of procedural mistakes in its eagerness to protect other students from Doe and Smith." Reply Brief for Petitioner 6. According to petitioner, however, unilaterally excluding respondents from school was not among them; indeed, petitioner insists that the SFUSD acted properly in removing respondents and urges that the stay-put provision "should not be interpreted to require a school district to maintain such dangerous children with other children." *Id.*, at 6-7).

to be read literally, for such a construction leads to the clearly unintended, and untenable, result that school districts must return violent or dangerous students to school while the often lengthy EHA proceedings run their course. We think it clear, however, that Congress very much meant to strip schools of the *unilateral* authority they had traditionally employed to exclude disabled students, particularly emotionally disturbed students, from school. In so doing, Congress did not leave school administrators powerless to deal with dangerous students; it did, however, deny school officials their former right to "self-help," and directed that in the future the removal of disabled students could be accomplished only with the permission of the parents or, as a last resort, the courts.

As noted above, Congress passed the EHA after finding that school systems across the country had excluded one out of every eight disabled children from classes. In drafting the law, Congress was largely guided by the recent decisions in *Mills* v. *Board of Education of District of Columbia*, 348 F. Supp. 866 (1972), and *PARC*, 343 F. Supp. 279 (1972), both of which involved the exclusion of hard-to-handle disabled students. *Mills* in particular demonstrated the extent to which schools used disciplinary measures to bar children from the classroom. There, school officials had labeled four of the seven minor plaintiffs "behavioral problems," and had excluded them from classes without providing any alternative education to them or any notice to their parents. 348 F. Supp., at 869-870. After finding that this practice was not limited to the named plaintiffs but affected in one way or another an estimated class of 12,000 to 18,000 disabled students, *id.*, at 868-869, 875, the District Court enjoined future exclusions, suspensions, or expulsions "on grounds of discipline." *Id.*, at 880.

Congress attacked such exclusionary practices in a variety of ways. It required participating States to educate *all* disabled children, regardless of the severity of their disabilities, 20 U. S. C. § 1412(2)(C), and included within the definition of "handicapped" those children with serious emotional disturbances. § 1401(1). It further provided for meaningful parental participation in all aspects of a child's educational placement, and barred schools, through the stay-put provision, from changing that placement over the parent's objection until all review proceedings were completed. Recognizing that those proceedings might prove long and tedious, the Act's drafters did not intend § 1415(e)(3) to operate inflexibly, see 121 Cong. Rec. 37412 (1975) (remarks of Sen. Stafford), and they therefore allowed for interim placements where parents and school officials are able to agree on one. Conspicuously absent from § 1415(e)(3), however, is any emergency exception for dangerous students. This absence is all the more telling in light of the injunctive decree issued in *PARC*, which permitted school officials unilaterally to remove students in "'extraordinary circumstances.'" 343 F. Supp., at 301. Given the lack of any similar exception in *Mills*, and the close attention Congress devoted to these "landmark" decisions, see S. Rep., at 6, we can only conclude that the omission was intentional; we are therefore not at liberty to engraft onto the statute an exception Congress chose not to create.

Our conclusion that § 1415(e)(3) means what it says does not leave educators hamstrung. The Department of Education has observed that, "[w]hile the [child's] placement may not be changed [during any complaint proceeding], this does not preclude the agency from using its normal procedures for dealing with children who are endangering themselves or others." Comment following 34 CFR § 300.513 (1987). Such procedures may include the use of study carrels, timeouts, detention, or the restriction of privileges. More drastically, where a student poses an immediate threat to the safety of others, officials may temporarily suspend him or her for up to 10 school days.[8] This authority, which respondent in no way disputes, not only ensures that school administrators can protect the safety of others by promptly removing the most dangerous of students, it also provides a "cooling down" period during which officials can initiate IEP review and seek to persuade the child's parents to agree to an interim placement. And in those cases in which the parents of a truly dangerous child adamantly refuse to permit any change in placement, the 10-day respite gives school officials an opportunity to invoke the aid of the courts under § 1415(e)(2), which empowers courts to grant any appropriate relief.

Petitioner contends, however, that the availability of judicial relief is more illusory than real, because a party seeking review under § 1415(e)(2) must exhaust time-consuming administrative remedies, and because under the Court of Appeals' construction of § 1415(e)(3), courts are as bound by the stay-put provision's "automatic injunction," 793 F. 2d, at 1486, as are schools.[9] It is true that judicial review is normally not available under § 1415(e)(2) until all administrative proceedings are completed, but as we have previously noted, parents may by-pass the administrative process where

[8]The Department of Education has adopted the position first espoused in 1980 by its Office of Civil Rights that a suspension of up to 10 school days does not amount to a "change in placement" prohibited by § 1415(e)(3). U. S. Dept. of Education, Office of Special Education Programs, Policy Letter (Feb. 26, 1987), Ed. for Handicapped L. Rep. 211:437 (1987). The EHA nowhere defines the phrase "change in placement," nor does the statute's structure or legislative history provide any guidance as to how the term applies to fixed suspensions. Given this ambiguity, we defer to the construction adopted by the agency charged with monitoring and enforcing the statute. See *INS* v. *Cardoza-Fonseca*, 480 U. S. ———, ——— (1987). Moreover, the agency's position comports fully with the purposes of the statute: Congress sought to prevent schools from permanently and unilaterally excluding disabled children by means of indefinite suspensions and expulsions; the power to impose fixed suspensions of short duration does not carry the potential for total exclusion that Congress found so objectionable. Indeed, despite its broad injunction, the District Court in *Mills* v. *Board of Education of District of Columbia*, 348 F. Supp. 866 (DC 1972), recognized that school officials could suspend disabled children on a short-term, temporary basis. See *id.*, at 880. Cf. *Goss* v. *Lopez*, 419 U. S. 565, 574-576, (1975) (suspension of 10 school days or more works a sufficient deprivation of property and liberty interests to trigger the protections of the Due Process Clause). Because we believe the agency correctly determined that a suspension in excess of 10 days does constitute a prohibited "change in placement," we conclude that the Court of Appeals erred to the extent it approved suspensions of 20 and 30 days' duration.

[9]Petitioner also notes that in California, schools may not suspend any given student for more than a total of 20, and in certain special circumstances 30, school days in a single year, see Cal. Educ. Code Ann. § 48903 (West Supp. 1988); he argues, therefore, that a school district may not have the option of imposing a 10-day suspension when dealing with an obstreperous child whose previous suspensions for the year total 18 or 19 days. The fact remains, however, that state law does not define the scope of § 1415(e)(3). There may be cases in which a suspension that is otherwise valid under the stay-put provision would violate local law. The effect of such a violation, however, is a question of state law upon which we express no view.

exhaustion would be futile or inadequate. See *Smith* v. *Robinson* 468 U. S. 992, 1014, n. 17 (1984) (citing cases); see also 121 Cong. Rec. 37416 (1975) (remarks of Sen. Williams) ("[E]xhaustion . . . should not be required . . . in cases where such exhaustion would be futile either as a legal or practical matter"). While may of the EHA's procedural safeguards protect the rights of parents and children, schools can and do seek redress through the administrative review process, and we have no reason to believe that Congress meant to require schools alone to exhaust in all cases, no matter how exigent the circumstances. The burden in such cases, of course, rests with the school to demonstrate the futility or inadequacy of administrative review, but nothing in § 1415(e)(2) suggests that schools are completely barred from attempting to make such a showing. Nor do we think that § 1415(e)(3) operates to limit the equitable powers of district courts such that they cannot, in appropriate cases, temporarily enjoin a dangerous disabled child from attending school. As the EHA's legislative history makes clear, one of the evils Congress sought to remedy was the unilateral exclusion of disabled children by *schools*, not courts, and one of the purposes of § 1415(e)(3), therefore, was "to prevent *school* officials from removing a child from the regular public school classroom over the parents' objection pending completion of the review proceedings." *Burlington School Committee* v. *Massachusetts Dept. of Education*, 471 U. S., at 373 (emphasis added). The stay-put provision in no way purports to limit or pre-empt the authority conferred on courts by § 1415(e)(2), see *Doe* v. *Brookline School Committee*, 722 F. 2d 910, 917 (CA1 1983); indeed, it says nothing whatever about judicial power.

In short, then, we believe that school officials are entitled to seek injunctive relief under § 1415(e)(2) in appropriate cases. In any such action, § 1415(e)(3) effectively creates a presumption in favor of the child's current educational placement which school officials can overcome only by showing that maintaining the child in his or her current placement is substantially likely to result in injury either to himself or herself, or to others. In the present case, we are satisfied that the District Court, in enjoining the state and local defendants from indefinitely suspending respondent or otherwise unilaterally altering his then current placement, properly balanced respondent's interest in receiving a free appropriate public education in accordance with the procedures and requirements of the EHA against the interests of the state and local school officials in maintaining a safe learning environment for all their students.[10]

---

[10]We therefore reject the United States' contention that the District Judge abused her discretion in enjoining the local school officials from indefinitely suspending respondent pending completion of the expulsion proceedings. Contrary to the Government's suggestion, the District Judge did not view herself bound to enjoin any and all violations of the stay-put provision, but rather, consistent with the analysis we set out above, weighed the relative harms to the parties and found that the balance tipped decidedly in favor of respondent. App. 222-223. We of course do not sit to review the factual determinations underlying that conclusion. We do note, however, that in balancing the parties' respective interests, the District Judge gave proper consideration to respondent's rights under the EHA. While the Government complains that the District Court indulged an improper presumption of irreparable harm to respondent, we do not believe that school officials can escape the presumptive effect of the stay-put provision simply by violating it and forcing parents to petition for relief. In any suit brought by parents seeking injunctive relief for a violation of § 1415(e)(3), the burden

IV

We believe the courts below properly construed and applied § 1415(e)(3), except insofar as the Court of Appeals held that a suspension in excess of 10 school days does not constitute a "change in placement."[11] We therefore affirm the Court of Appeals' judgment on this issue as modified herein. Because we are equally divided on the question whether a court may order a State to provide services directly to a disabled child where the local agency has failed to do so, we affirm the Court of Appeals' judgment on this issue as well.

Affirmed.

CHIEF JUSTICE REHNQUIST, concurring.

I write separately on the mootness issue in this case to explain why I have joined Part II of the Court's opinion, and why I think reconsideration of our mootness jurisprudence may be in order when dealing with cases decided by this Court.

The present rule in federal cases is that an actual controversy must exist at all stages of appellate review, not merely at the time the complaint is filed. This doctrine was clearly articulated in *United States* v. *Munsingwear*, 340 U. S. 36 (1950), in which Justice Douglas noted that "[t]he established practice of the Court in dealing with a civil case from a court in the federal system which has become moot while on its way here or pending our decision on the merits is to reverse or vacate the judgment below and remand with a direction to dismiss." *Id.*, at 39. The rule has been followed fairly consistently over the last 30 years. See, *e. g.*, *Preiser* v. *Newkirk*, 422 U. S. 395 (1975); *SEC* v. *Medical Committee for Human Rights*, 404 U. S. 403 (1972).

All agree that this case was "very much alive," *ante*, when the action was filed in the District Court, and very probably when the Court of Appeals decided the case. It is supervening events since the decision of the Court of Appeals which have caused the dispute between the majority and the dissent over whether this case is moot. Therefore, all that the Court actually *holds* is that these supervening events do not deprive *this* Court of the authority to hear the case. I agree with that holding, and would go still further in the direction of relaxing the test of mootness where the events giving rise to the claim of mootness have occurred after our decision to grant certiorari or to note probable jurisdiction.

The Court implies in its opinion, and the dissent expressly states, that the mootness doctrine is based upon Art. III of the Constitution. There is no doubt that our recent cases have taken that position. See *Nebraska Press Assn.* v. *Stuart*, 427 U. S. 539, 546 (1976); *Preiser* v. *Newkirk*, *supra*, at 401; *Sibron* v. *New York*, 392 U. S. 40, 57 (1968); *Liner* v. *Jafco, Inc.*, 375 U. S. 301, 306, n. 3 (1964). But it seems very doubtful that the earliest case I have found discussing mootness, *Mills* v. *Green*, 159 U. S. 651 (1895), was premised on constitutional constraints; Justice Gray's opinion in that case nowhere mentions Art. III.

---

rests with the school district to demonstrate that the educational status quo must be altered.

[11] See n. 8, *supra*.

If it were indeed Art. III which—by reason of its requirement of a case or controversy for the exercise of federal judicial power—underlies the mootness doctrine, the "capable of repetition, yet evading review" exception relied upon by the Court in this case would be incomprehensible. Article III extends the judicial power of the United States only to cases and controversies; it does not except from this requirement other lawsuits which are "capable of repetition, yet evading review." If our mootness doctrine were forced upon us by the case or controversy requirement of Art. III itself, we would have no more power to decide lawsuits which are "moot" but which also raise questions which are capable of repetition but evading review than we would to decide cases which are "moot" but raise no such questions.

The exception to mootness for cases which are "capable of repetition, yet evading review," was first stated by this Court in *Southern Pacific Terminal Co.* v. *ICC*, 219 U. S. 498 (1911). There the Court enunciated the exception in the light of obvious pragmatic considerations, with no mention of Art. III as the principle underlying the mootness doctrine:

> "The questions involved in the orders of the Interstate Commerce Commission are usually continuing (as are manifestly those in the case at bar) and their consideration ought not to be, as they might be, defeated, by short term orders, capable of repetition, yet evading review, and at one time the Government and at another time the carriers have their rights determined by the Commission without a chance of redress." *Id.*, at 515.

The exception was explained again in *Moore* v. *Ogilvie*, 394 U. S. 814, 816 (1969):

> "The problem is therefore 'capable of repetition, yet evading review.' The need for its resolution thus reflects a continuing controversy in the federal-state area where our 'one man, one vote' decisions have thrust" (citation omitted).

It is also worth noting that *Moore* v. *Ogilvie* involved a question which had been mooted by an election, just as did *Mills* v. *Green* some 70 years earlier. But at the time of *Mills*, the case originally enunciating the mootness doctrine, there was no thought of any exception for cases which were "capable of repetition, yet evading review."

The logical conclusion to be drawn from these cases, and from the historical development of the principle of mootness, is that while an unwillingness to decide moot cases may be connected to the case or controversy requirement of Art. III, it is an attenuated connection that may be overridden where there are strong reasons to override it. The "capable of repetition, yet evading review" exception is an example. So too is our refusal to dismiss as moot those cases in which the defendant voluntarily ceases, at some advanced stage of the appellate proceedings, whatever activity prompted the plaintiff to seek an injunction. See, *e. g.*, *City of Mesquite* v. *Aladdin's Castle, Inc.*, 455 U. S. 283, 289, n. 10 (1982); *United States* v. *W. T. Grant Co.*, 345 U. S. 629, 632 (1953). I believe that we should adopt an additional exception to our present mootness doctrine for those cases where the events which render the case moot have supervened since our grant of certiorari or noting of probable jurisdiction in the case. Dissents from denial of certiorari in this Court illustrate the proposition that the roughly 150 or 160 cases which we decide each year on the merits are less than the number of cases warranting review by us if we are to remain, as Chief Justice Taft said many years ago, "the last word on every important issue under the Constitution and the statutes of the United States." But these unique resources—the time spent preparing to decide the case by reading briefs, hearing oral argument, and conferring—are squandered in every case in which it becomes apparent after the decisional process is underway that we may not reach the question presented. To me the unique and valuable ability of this Court to decide a case—we are, at present, the only Art. III court which can decide a federal question in such a way as to bind all other courts—is a sufficient reason either to abandon the doctrine of mootness altogether in cases which this Court has decided to review, or at least to relax the doctrine of mootness in such a manner as the dissent accuses the majority of doing here. I would leave the mootness doctrine as established by our cases in full force and effect when applied to the earlier stages of a lawsuit, but I believe that once this Court has undertaken a consideration of a case, an exception to that principle is just as much warranted as where a case is "capable of repetition, yet evading review."

JUSTICE SCALIA, with whom JUSTICE O'CONNOR joins, dissenting.

Without expressing any views on the merits of this case, I respectfully dissent because in my opinion we have no authority to decide it. I think the controversy is moot.

I

The Court correctly acknowledges that we have no power under Art. III of the Constitution to adjudicate a case that no longer presents an actual, ongoing dispute between the named parties. *Ante*, *citing Nebraska Press Assn.* v. *Stuart*, 427 U. S. 359, 546 (1976); *Preiser* v. *Newkirk*, 422 U. S. 395, 401 (1975). Here, there is obviously no present controversy between the parties, since both respondents are no longer in school and therefore no longer subject to a unilateral "change in placement." The Court concedes mootness with respect to respondent John Doe, who is now too old to receive the benefits of the Education of the Handicapped Act (EHA). *Ante*. It concludes, however, that the case is not moot as to respondent Jack Smith, who has two more years of eligibility but is no longer in the public schools, because the controversy is "capable of repetition, yet evading review." *Ante*.

Jurisdiction on the basis that a dispute is "capable of repetition, yet evading review" is limited to the "exceptional situatio[n]," *Los Angeles* v. *Lyons*, 461 U. S. 95, 109 (1983), where the following two circumstances simultaneously occur: "'(1) the challenged action [is] in its duration too short to be fully litigated prior to its cessation or expiration, and (2) there [is] a reasonable expectation that the same complaining party would be subjected to the same action again.'" *Murphy* v. *Hunt*, 455 U. S. 478, 482 (1982) *(per curiam)*, quoting *Weinstein* v. *Bradford*, 423 U. S. 147, 149 (1975) *(per curiam)*. The second of these requirements is not met in this case.

For there to be a "reasonable expectation" that Smith will be subjected to the same action again, that event be a "demonstrated probability." *Murphy* v. *Hunt*, *supra*, at 482, 483; *Weinstein* v. *Bradford*, *supra*, at 149. I am surprised by the Court's contention, fraught with potential for future mischief, that "reasonable expectation" is satisfied by something less than "demonstrated probability." *Ante.* No one expects that to happen which he does not think probable; and his expectation cannot be shown to be reasonable unless the probability is demonstrated. Thus, as the Court notes, our cases recite the two descriptions side by side ("a 'reasonable expectation' or a 'demonstrated probability,'" *Hunt*, *supra*, at 482). The Court asserts, however, that these standards are "described . . . in the disjunctive," *ante*, — evidently believing that the conjunction "or" has no accepted usage except a disjunctive one, *i. e.*, "expressing an alternative, contrast, or opposition," Webster's Third New International Dictionary 651 (1981). In fact, however, the conjunction is often used "to indicate . . . (3) the synonymous, equivalent, or substitutive character of two words or phrases <fell over a precipice [or] cliff> <the off [or] far side> <lessen [or] abate>; (4) correction or greater exactness of phrasing or meaning <these essays, [or] rather rough sketches> <the present king had no children—[or] no legitimate children . . .>." *Id.*, at 1585. It is obvious that in saying "a reasonable expectation or a demonstrated probability" we have used the conjunction in one of the latter, or nondisjunctive, senses. Otherwise (and according to the Court's exegesis), we would have been saying that a controversy is sufficiently likely to recur if *either* a certain degree of probability exists *or* a higher degree of probability exists. That is rather like a statute giving the vote to persons who are "18 or 21." A bare six years ago, the author of today's opinion and one other member of the majority plainly understood "reasonable expectation" and "demonstrated probability" to be synonymous. Cf. *Edgar* v. *MITE Corp.*, 457 U. S. 624, 662, and n. 11 (1982) (MARSHALL, J., dissenting, joined by BRENNAN, J.) (using the two terms here at issue interchangeably, and concluding that the case is moot because "there is no *demonstrated probability* that the State will have occasion to prevent MITE from making a takeover offer for some other corporation") (emphasis added).

The prior holdings cited by the Court in a footnote, *see ante*, offer no support for the novel proposition that less than a probability of recurrence is sufficient to avoid mootness. In *Burlington Northern R. Co.* v. *Maintenance of Way Employees*, —— U. S. ——, ——, n. 4 (1987), we found that the same railroad and union were "reasonably likely" to find themselves in a recurring dispute over the same issue. Similarly, in *California Coastal Comm'n* v. *Granite Rock Co.*, —— U. S. ——, ——, (1987), we found it "likely" that the plaintiff mining company would submit new plans which the State would seek to subject to its coastal permit requirements. See Webster's Third New International Dictionary 1310 (1981) (defining "likely" as "of such a nature or so circumstanced as to make something probable[;] . . . seeming to justify belief or expectation[;] . . . in all probability"). In the cases involving exclusion orders issued to prevent the press from attending criminal trials, we found that "[i]t can reasonably be assumed" that a news organization covering the area in which the defendant court sat will again be subjected to that court's closure rules. *Press-Enterprise Co.* v. *Superior Court of Cal., Riverside County*, —— U. S. ——, ——, (1986); *Globe Newspaper Co.* v. *Superior Court of Norfolk County*, 457 U. S. 596, 603 (1982). In these and other cases, one may quarrel, perhaps, with the accuracy of the Court's probability assessment; but there is no doubt that assessment was regarded as necessary to establish jurisdiction.

In *Roe* v. *Wade*, 410 U. S. 113, 125 (1973), we found that the "human gestation period is so short that the pregnancy will come to term before the usual appellate process is complete," so that "pregnancy litigation seldom will survive much beyond the trial stage, and appellate review will be effectively denied." *Roe*, at least one other abortion case, see *Doe* v. *Bolton*, 410 U. S. 179, 187 (1973), and some of our election law decisions, see *Rosario* v. *Rockefeller*, 410 U. S. 752, 756, n. 5 (1973); *Dunn* v. *Blumstein*, 405 U. S. 330, 333, n. 2 (1972), differ from the body of our mootness jurisprudence *not* in accepting less than a probability that the issue will recur, in a manner evading review, between the same parties; but in dispensing with the same-party requirement entirely, focusing instead upon the great likelihood that the issue will recur *between the defendant and the other member of the public at large* without ever reaching us. Arguably those cases have been limited to their facts, or to the narrow areas of abortion and election rights, by our more recent insistence that, at least in the absence of a class action, the "capable of repetition" doctrine applies only where "there [is] a reasonable expectation that the *same complaining party* would be subjected to the same action again." *Hunt*, 455 U. S., at 482 (emphasis added), quoting *Weinstein*, 423 U. S., at 149; see *Burlington Northern R. Co.*, *supra*, at ——, n. 4; *Illinois Elections Bd.* v. *Socialist Workers Party*, 440 U. S. 173, 187 (1979). If those earlier cases have not been so limited, however, the conditions for their application do not in any event exist here. There is no extraordinary improbability of the present issue's reaching us as a traditionally live controversy. It would have done so in this very case if Smith had not chosen to leave public school. In sum, on any analysis, the proposition the Court asserts in the present case—that probability need not be shown in order to establish the "same-party-recurrence" exception to mootness—is a significant departure from settled law.

II

If our established mode of analysis were followed, the conclusion that a live controversy exists in the present case would require a demonstrated probability that *all* of the following events will occur: (1) Smith will return to public school; (2) he will be placed in an educational setting that is unable to tolerate his dangerous behavior; (3) he will again engage in dangerous behavior; and (4) local school officials will again attempt unilaterally to change his placement and the state defendants will fail to prevent such action. The Court spends considerable time establishing that the last two of these events are likely to recur, but relegates to a footnote its discussion of the first event, upon which all others depend, and only briefly alludes to the second. Neither the facts in the record, nor even the extra-record assurances of counsel, establish a demonstrated probability of either of them.

With respect to whether Smith will return to school, at oral argument Smith's counsel forthrightly conceded that she "cannot represent whether in fact either of these students will ask for further education from the Petitioners." Tr. of Oral Arg. 23. Rather, she observed, respondents would "look to [our decision in this case] to find out what will happen after that." *Id.*, at 23-

24. When pressed, the most counsel would say was that, in her view, the 20-year-old Smith *could* seek to return to public school because he has not graduated, he is handicapped, and he has a right to an education. *Id.*, at 27. I do not perceive the principle that would enable us to leap from the proposition that Smith could reenter public school to the conclusion that it is a demonstrated probability he will do so.

The Court nevertheless concludes that "there is at the very least a reasonable expectation" that Smith will return to school. *Ante*. I cannot possibly dispute that on the basis of the Court's terminology. Once it is accepted that a "reasonable expectation" can exist without a demonstrable probability that the event in question will occur, the phrase has been deprived of all meaning, and the Court can give it whatever application it wishes without fear of effective contradiction. It is worth pointing out, however, how slim are the reeds upon which this conclusion of "reasonable expectation" (whatever that means) rests. The Court bases its determination on three observations from the record and oral argument. First, it notes that Smith has been pressing this lawsuit since 1980. It suffices to observe that the equivalent argument can be made in every case that remains active and pending; we have hitherto avoided equating the existence of a case or controversy with the existence of a lawsuit. Second, the Court observes that Smith has "as great a need of a high school education and diploma as any of his peers." *Ibid.* While this is undoubtedly good advice, it hardly establishes that the 20-year-old Smith is likely to return to high school, much less to public high school. Finally, the Court notes that counsel "advises us that [Smith] is awaiting the outcome of this case to decide whether to pursue his degree." *Ibid.* Not only do I not think this establishes a current case or controversy, I think it a most conclusive indication that no current case or controversy exists. We do not sit to broaden decision-making options, but to adjudicate the lawfulness of acts that have happened or, at most, are about to occur.

The conclusion that the case is moot is reinforced, moreover, when one considers that, even if Smith does return to public school, the controversy will still not recur unless he is again placed in an educational setting that is unable to tolerate his behavior. It seems to me not only not demonstrably probably, but indeed quite unlikely, given what is now known about Smith's behavioral problems, that local school authorities would again place him in an educational setting that could not control his dangerous conduct, causing a suspension that would replicate the legal issues in this suit. The majority dismisses this further contingency by noting that the school authorities have an obligation under the EHA to provide an "appropriate" education in "the least restrictive environment." *Ante*. This means, however, the least restrictive environment appropriate for the particular child. The Court observes that "the preparation of an [individualized educational placement]" is "an inexact science at best," *ante*, thereby implying that the school authorities are likely to get it wrong. Even accepting this assumption, which seems to me contrary to the premises of the Act, I see no reason further to assume that they will get it wrong by making the same mistake they did last time—assigning Smith to too *un*restrictive an environment, from which he will thereafter be suspended—rather than by assigning him to too *restrictive* an environment. The latter, which seems to me more likely than the former (though both combined are much less likely than a correct placement), might produce a lawsuit, but not a lawsuit involving the issues that we have before us here.

III

THE CHIEF JUSTICE joins the majority opinion on the ground, not that this case is not moot, but that where the events giving rise to the mootness have occurred after we have granted certiorari we may disregard them, since mootness is only a prudential doctrine and not part of the "case or controversy" requirement of Art. III. I do not see how that can be. There is no more reason to intuit that mootness is merely a prudential doctrine than to intuit that initial standing is. Both doctrines have equivalently deep roots in the common-law understanding, and hence the constitutional understanding, of what makes a matter appropriate for judicial disposition. See *Flast* v. *Cohen*, 392 U. S. 83, 95 (1968) (describing mootness and standing as various illustrations of the requirement of "justiciability" in Art. III).

THE CHIEF JUSTICE relies upon the fact that an 1895 case discussing mootness, *Mills* v. *Green*, 159 U. S. 651 (1895), makes no mention of the Constitution. But there is little doubt that the Court believed the doctrine called into question the Court's power and not merely its prudence, for (in an opinion by the same Justice who wrote *Mills*) it had said two years earlier:

> "[T]he court is not *empowered* to decide moot questions or abstract propositions, or to declare . . . principles or rules of law which cannot affect the result as to the thing in issue in the case before it. No stipulation of parties or counsel . . . can enlarge the *power*, or affect the duty, of the court in this regard." *California* v. *San Pablo & Tulare R. Co.*, 149 U. S. 308, 314 (1893) (Gray, J.) (emphasis added).

If it seems peculiar to the modern lawyer that our 19th century mootness cases make no explicit mention of Art. III, that is a peculiarity shared with our 19th century, and even our early 20th century, standing cases. As late as 1919, in dismissing a suit for lack of standing we said simply:

> "Considerations of propriety, as well as long-established practice, demand that we refrain from passing upon the constitutionality of an act of Congress unless obliged to do so in the proper performance of our judicial function, when the question is raised by a party whose interests entitle him to raise it." *Blair* v. *United States*, 250 U. S. 273, 279 (1919).

See also, *e. g.*, *Standard Stock Food Co.* v. *Wright*, 225 U. S. 540, 550 (1912); *Southern Ry. Co.* v. *King*, 217 U. S. 524, 534 (1910); *Turpin* v. *Lemon*, 187 U. S. 51, 60-61 (1902); *Tyler* v. *Judges of Court of Registration*, 179 U. S. 405, 409 (1900). The same is also true of our early cases dismissing actions lacking truly adverse parties, that is, collusive actions. See, *e. g.*, *Cleveland* v. *Chamberlain*, 1 Black 419, 425-426 (1862); *Lord* v. *Veazie*, 8 How. 251, 254-256 (1850). The explanation for this ellipsis is that the courts simply chose to refer directly to the traditional, fundamental limitations upon the powers of common-law courts, rather than referring to Art. III which in turn adopts those limitations through terms ("The judicial Power"; "Cases"; "Controversies") that have virtually no meaning except by reference to that tradition. The ultimate circularity, coming back in the end to tradition, is evident in the statement by Justice Field:

> "By cases and controversies are intended the claims of litigants brought before the courts for determination by such regular proceedings as are established by law or custom for the protection or enforcement of rights, or the prevention, redress, or punishment of wrongs. Whenever the claim of a party under the constitution, laws, or treaties of the United States takes such a form that the judicial power is capable of acting upon it, then it has become a case." *In re Pacific R. Commn.*, 32 F. 241, 255 (CCND Cal. 1887).

See also 2 M. Farrand, Records of the Federal Convention of 1787, p. 430 (rev. ed. 1966):

> "Docr. Johnson moved to insert the words 'this Constitution and the' before the word 'laws'
>
> "Mr Madison doubted whether it was not going too far to extend the jurisdiction of the Court generally to cases arising Under the Constitution, & whether it ought not to be limited to cases of a Judiciary Nature. The right of expounding the Constitution in cases not of this nature ought not to be given to that Department.
>
> "The motion of Docr. Johnson was agreed to nem: con: it being generally supposed that the jurisdiction given was constructively limited to cases of a Judiciary nature—"

In sum, I cannot believe that it is only our prudence, and nothing inherent in the understood nature of "The judicial Power," U. S. Const., Art. III, § 1, that restrains us from pronouncing judgment in a case that the parties have settled, or a case involving a nonsurviving claim where the plaintiff has died, or a case where the law has been changed so that the basis of the dispute no longer exists, or a case where conduct sought to be enjoined has ceased and will not recur. Where the conduct has ceased for the time being but there is a demonstrated probability that it *will* recur, a real-life controversy between parties with a personal stake in the outcome continues to exist, and Art. III is no more violated than it is violated by entertaining a declaratory judgment action. But that is the limit of our power. I agree with THE CHIEF JUSTICE to this extent: the "yet evading review" portion of our "capable of repetition yet evading review" test is prudential; whether or not that criterion is met, a justiciable controversy exists. But the probability of recurrence between the same parties is essential to our jurisdiction as a court, and it is that deficiency which the case before us presents.

* * *

It is assuredly frustrating to find that a jurisdictional impediment prevents us from reaching the important merits issues that were the reason for our agreeing to hear this case. But we cannot ignore such impediments for purposes of our appellate review without simultaneously affecting the principles that govern district courts in their assertion or retention of original jurisdiction. We thus do substantial harm to a governmental structure designed to restrict the courts to matters that actually affect the litigants before them.

School Board of Nassau County, Florida v. Arline

U.S. Supreme Court, 107 S.Ct. 1123 (1987).

Syllabus*

Section 504 of the Rehabilitation Act of 1973, 29 U. S. C. § 794, (Act) provides, *inter alia*, that no "otherwise qualified handicapped individual," as defined in 29 U. S. C. § 706(7), shall, solely by reason of his handicap, be excluded from participation in any program receiving federal financial assistance. Section 706(7)(B) defines "handicapped individual" to mean any person who "(i) has a physical . . . impairment which substantially limits one or more of [his] major life activities, (ii) has a record of such an impairment, or (iii) is regarded as having such an impairment." Department of Health and Human Services (HHS) regulations define "physical impairment" to mean, *inter alia*, any physiological disorder affecting the respiratory system, and define "major life activities" to include working. Respondent was hospitalized for tuberculosis in 1957. The disease went into remission for the next 20 years, during which time respondent began teaching elementary school in Florida. In 1977, March 1978, and November 1978, respondent had relapses, after the latter two of which she was suspended with pay for the rest of the school year. At the end of the 1978-1979 school year, petitioners discharged her after a hearing because of the continued recurrence of tuberculosis. After she was denied relief in state administrative proceedings, she brought suit in Federal District Court, alleging a violation of § 504. The District Court held that she was not a "handicapped person" under the Act, but that, even assuming she were, she was not "qualified" to teach elementary school. The Court of Appeals reversed, holding that persons with contagious diseases are within § 504's coverage, and remanded for further findings as to whether respondent was "otherwise qualified" for her job.

Held:

1. A person afflicted with the contagious disease of tuberculosis may be a "handicapped individual" within the meaning of § 504.

(a) Respondent is a "handicapped individual" as defined in § 706(7)(B) and the HHS regulations. Her hospitalization in 1957 for a disease that affected her respiratory system and that substantially limited "one or more of [her] major life activities" establishes that she has a "record of . . . impairment."

(b) The fact that a person with a record of impairment is also contagious does not remove that person from § 504's coverage. To allow an employer to justify discrimination by distinguishing between a disease's contagious effects on others and its physical effects on a patient would be unfair, would be contrary to § 706(7)(B)(iii) and the legislative history, which demonstrate Congress' concern about an impairment's effect on others, and would be inconsistent with § 504's basic purpose to ensure that handicapped individuals are not denied jobs because of the prejudice or ignorance of others. The Act replaces such fearful, reflexive reactions with actions based on reasoned and medically sound judgments as to whether contagious handicapped persons are "otherwise qualified" to do the job.

2. In most cases, in order to determine whether a person handicapped by contagious disease is "otherwise qualified" under § 504, the District Court must conduct an individualized inquiry and make appropriate findings of fact,

*The syllabus constitutes no part of the opinion of the Court but has been prepared by the Reporter of Decisions for the convenience of the reader.

based on reasonable medical judgments given the state of medical knowledge, about (a) the nature of the risk (*e. g.*, how the disease is transmitted), (b) the duration of the risk (how long is the carrier infectious), (c) the severity of the risk (what is the potential harm to third parties), and (d) the probabilities the disease will be transmitted and will cause varying degrees of harm. In making these findings, courts normally should defer to the reasonable medical judgments of public health officials. Courts must then determine, in light of these findings, whether any "reasonable accommodation" can be made by the employer under the established standards for that inquiry.

3. Because the District Court did not make appropriate findings, it is impossible for this Court to determine whether respondent is "otherwise qualified" for the job of elementary school teacher, and the case is remanded for additional findings of fact.

772 F. 2d 759, affirmed.

BRENNAN, J., delivered the opinion of the Court, in which WHITE, MARSHALL, BLACKMUN, POWELL, STEVENS, and O'CONNOR, JJ., joined. REHNQUIST, C. J., filed a dissenting opinion, in which SCALIA, J., joined.

JUSTICE BRENNAN delivered the opinion of the Court.

Section 504 of the Rehabilitation Act of 1973, 87 Stat. 394, as amended, 29 U. S. C. § 794 (Act), prohibits a federally funded state program from discriminating against a handicapped individual solely by reason of his or her handicap. This case presents the questions whether a person afflicted with tuberculosis, a contagious disease, may be considered a "handicapped individual" within the meaning of § 504 of the Act, and, if so, whether such an individual is "otherwise qualified" to teach elementary school.

I

From 1966 until 1979, respondent Gene Arline taught elementary school in Nassau County, Florida. She was discharged in 1979 after suffering a third relapse of tuberculosis within two years. After she was denied relief in state administrative proceedings, she brought suit in federal court, alleging that the School Board's decision to dismiss her because of her tuberculosis violated § 504 of the Act.[1]

A trial was held in the District Court, at which the principal medical evidence was provided by Marianne McEuen, M. D., an assistant director of the Community Tuberculosis Control Service of the Florida Department of Health and Rehabilitative Services. According to the medical records reviewed by Dr. McEuen, Arline was hospitalized for tuberculosis in 1957. App. 11-12. For the next twenty years, Arline's disease was in remission. *Id.*, at 32. Then, in 1977, a culture revealed that tuberculosis was again active in her system; cultures taken in March 1978 and in November 1978 were also positive. *Id.*, at 12.

[1]Respondent also sought relief under 42 U. S. C. § 1983 alleging that the Board denied her due process of law. Both the District Court and the Court of Appeals rejected this argument, and the respondent did not present the issue to this Court.

The superintendent of schools for Nassau County, Craig Marsh, then testified as to the School Board's response to Arline's medical reports. After both her second relapse, in the Spring of 1978, and her third relapse in November 1978, the School Board suspended Arline with pay for the remainder of the school year. *Id.*, at 49-51. At the end of the 1978-1979 school year, the School Board held a hearing, after which it discharged Arline, "not because she had done anything wrong," but because of the "continued reoccurence [sic] of tuberculosis." *Id.*, at 49-52.

In her trial memorandum, Arline argued that it was "not disputed that the [School Board dismissed her] solely on the basis of her illness. Since the illness in this case qualifies the Plaintiff as a 'handicapped person' it is clear that she was dismissed solely as a result of her handicap in violation of Section 504." Record 119. The District Court held, however, that although there was "[n]o question that she suffers a handicap," Arline was nevertheless not "a handicapped person under the terms of that statute." App. to Pet. for Cert. C-2. The court found it "difficult . . . to conceive that Congress intended contagious diseases to be included within the definition of a handicapped person." The court then went on to state that, "even assuming" that a person with a contagious disease could be deemed a handicapped person, Arline was not "qualified" to teach elementary school. *Id.*, at C-2—C-3.

The Court of Appeals reversed, holding that "persons with contagious diseases are within the coverage of section 504," and that Arline's condition "falls . . . neatly within the statutory and regulatory framework" of the Act. 772 F. 2d 759, 764 (CA11 1985). The court remanded the case "for further findings as to whether the risks of infection precluded Mrs. Arline from being 'otherwise qualified' for her job and, if so, whether it was possible to make some reasonable accommodation for her in that teaching position" or in some other position. *Id.*, at 765 (footnote omitted). We granted certiorari, 475 U. S. —— (1986), and now affirm.

II

In enacting and amending the Act, Congress enlisted all programs receiving federal funds in an effort "to share with handicapped Americans the opportunities for an education, transportation, housing, health care, and jobs that other Americans take for granted." 123 Cong. Rec. 13515 (1977) (statement of Sen. Humphrey). To that end, Congress not only increased federal support for vocational rehabilitation, but also addressed the broader problem of discrimination against the handicapped by including § 504, an antidiscrimination provision patterned after Title VI of the Civil Rights of 1964.[2] Section 504 of the Rehabilitation Act reads in pertinent part:

[2]Congress' decision to pattern § 504 after Title VI is evident in the language of the statute, compare 29 U. S. C. § 794 with 42 U. S. C. § 2000d, and in the legislative history of § 504, see, *e. g.*, S. Rep. No. 93-1297, pp. 39-40 (1974); S. Rep. No. 95-890, p. 19 (1978). Cf. tenBroek & Matson, The Disabled and the Law of Welfare, 54 Cal. L. Rev. 809, 814-815 and nn. 21-22 (1966) (discussing theory and evidence that "negative attitudes and practices toward the disabled resemble those commonly attached to 'underprivileged ethnic and religious minority groups' "). The range of programs subject to § 504's prohibition is broader, however, than that covered by Title VI, because § 504 covers employment discrimination even in programs that receive federal aid with a primary objective other than the promotion of employment. See *Consolidated*

> "No otherwise qualified handicapped individual in the United States, as defined in section 706(7) of this title, shall, solely by reason of his handicap, be excluded from participation in, be denied the benefits of, or be subjected to discrimination under any program or activity receiving Federal financial assistance . . . ." 29 U. S. C. § 794.

In 1974 Congress expanded the definition of "handicapped individual" for use in § 504 to read as follows:[3]

> "[A]ny person who (i) has a physical or mental impairment which substantially limits one or more of such person's major life activities, (ii) has a record of such an impairment, or (iii) is regarded as having such an impairment." 29 U. S. C. § 706(7)(B).

The amended definition reflected Congress' concern with protecting the handicapped against discrimination stemming not only from simple prejudice, but from "archaic attitudes and laws" and from "the fact that the American people are simply unfamiliar with and insensitive to the difficulties confront[ing] individuals with handicaps." S. Rep. No. 93-1297, p. 50 (1974). To combat the effects of erroneous but nevertheless prevalent perceptions about the handicapped, Congress expanded the definition of "handicapped individual" so as to preclude discrimination against "[a] person who has a record of, or is regarded as having, an impairment [but who] may at present have no actual incapacity at all." *Southeastern Community College* v. *Davis*, 442 U. S. 397, 405-406, n. 6 (1979).[4]

In determining whether a particular individual is handicapped as defined by the Act, the regulations promulgated by the Department of Health and Human Services are of significant assistance. As we have previously recognized, these regulations were drafted with the oversight and approval of Congress, see *Consolidated Rail Corporation* v. *Darrone*, 465 U. S. 624, 634-635, and nn. 14-16 (1984); they provide "an important source of guidance on the

---

Rail Corporation v. *Darrone*, 465 U. S. 624 (1984); Note, Accommodating the Handicapped: Rehabilitating Section 504 after *Southeastern*, 80 Colum. L. Rev. 171, 174-175 and nn. 21 (1980).

[3]The primary focus of the 1973 Act was to increase federal support for vocational rehabilitation; the Act's original definition of the term "handicapped individual" reflected this focus by including only those whose disability limited their employability, and those who could be expected to benefit from vocational rehabilitation. After reviewing the Department of Health, Education, and Welfare's subsequent attempt to devise regulations to implement the Act, however, Congress concluded that the definition of "handicapped individual," while appropriate for the vocational rehabilitation provisions in Titles I and III of the Act, was too narrow to deal with the range of discriminatory practices in housing, education, and health care programs which stemmed from stereotypical attitudes and ignorance about the handicapped. S. Rep. No. 93-1297, pp. 16, 37-38, 50 (1974).

[4]See *id.*, at 39 ("This subsection includes within the protection of sections 503 and 504 those persons who do not in fact have the condition which they are perceived as having, as well as those persons whose mental or physical condition does not substantially limit their life activities and who thus are not technically within clause (A) in the new definition. Members of both of these groups may be subjected to discrimination on the basis of their being regarded as handicapped"); *id.*, at 37-39, 63-64; see also 120 Cong. Rec. 30531 (1974) (statement of Sen. Cranston).

meaning of § 504." *Alexander* v. *Choate*, 469 U. S. 287, 304, n. 24 (1985). The regulations are particularly significant here because they define two critical terms used in the statutory definition of handicapped individual.[5] "Physical impairment" is defined as follows:

> "[A]ny physiological disorder or condition, cosmetic disfigurement, or anatomical loss affecting one or more of the following body systems: neurological; musculoskeletal; special sense organs; respiratory, including speech organs; cardiovascular; reproductive, digestive, genito-urinary; hemic and lymphatic; skin; and endocrine." 45 CFR § 84.3(j)(2)(i) (1985).

In addition, the regulations define "major life activities" as:

> "functions such as caring for one's self, performing manual tasks, walking, seeing, hearing, speaking, breathing, learning, and working." § 84.3j(2)(ii).

III

Within this statutory and regulatory framework, then, we must consider whether Arline can be considered a handicapped individual. According to the testimony of Dr. McEuen, Arline suffered tuberculosis "in an acute form in such a degree that it affected her respiratory system," and was hospitalized for this condition. App. 11. Arline thus had a physical impairment as that term is defined by the regulations, since she had a "physiological disorder or condition . . . affecting [her] . . . respiratory [system]." 45 CFR § 84.3(j)(2)(i) (1985). This impairment was serious enough to require hospitalization, a fact more than sufficient to establish that one or more of her major life activities were substantially limited by her impairment. Thus, Arline's hospitalization for tuberculosis in 1957 suffices to establish that she has a "record of . . . impairment" within the meaning of 29 U. S. C. § 706(7)(b)(ii), and is therefore a handicapped individual.

Petitioners concede that a contagious disease may constitute a handicapping condition to the extent that it leaves a person with "diminished physical or mental capabilities," Brief for Petitioners 15, and concede that Arline's

---

[5] In an appendix to these regulations, the Department of Health and Human Services explained that it chose not attempt to "set forth a list of specific diseases and conditions that constitute physical or mental impairments because of the difficulty of ensuring the comprehensiveness of any such list." 45 CFR pt. 84, App. A, p. 310 (1985). Nevertheless, the Department went on to state that "such diseases and conditions as orthopedic, visual, speech, and hearing impairments, cerebral palsy, epilepsy, muscular dystrophy, multiple sclerosis, cancer, heart disease, diabetes, mental retardation, [and] emotional illness" would be covered. *Ibid*. The Department also reinforced what a careful reading of the statute makes plain, "that a physical or mental impairment does not constitute a handicap for purposes of section 504 unless its severity is such that it results in a substantial limitation of one or more major life activities." *Ibid*. Although many of the comments on the regulations when first proposed suggested that the definition was unreasonably broad, the Department found that a broad definition, one not limited to so-called "traditional handicaps," is inherent in the statutory definition. *Ibid*.

hospitalization for tuberculosis in 1957 demonstrates that she has a record of a physical impairment, see Tr. of Oral Arg. 52-53. Petitioners maintain, however, Arline's record of impairment is irrelevant in this case, since the School Board dismissed Arline not because of her diminished physical capabilities, but because of the threat that her relapses of tuberculosis posed to the health of others.[6]

We do not agree with petitioners that, in defining a handicapped individual under § 504, the contagious effects of a disease can be meaningfully distinguished from the disease's physical effects on a claimant in a case such as this. Arline's contagiousness and her physical impairment each resulted form the same underlying condition, tuberculosis. It would be unfair to allow an employer to seize upon the distinction between the effects of a disease on others and the effects of a disease on a patient and use that distinction to justify discriminatory treatment.[7]

Nothing in the legislative history of § 504 suggests that Congress intended such a result. That history demonstrates that Congress was as concerned about the effect of an impairment on others as it was about its effect on the individual. Congress extended coverage, in 29 U. S. C. § 706(7)(B)(iii), to those individuals who are simply "regarded as having" a physical or mental impairment.[8] The Senate Report provides as an example of a person who would be covered under this subsection "a person with some kind of visible physical impairment which in fact does not substantially limit that person's functioning." S. Rep. No. 93-1297, p. 64 (1974).[9] Such an impairment might

---

[6]See Brief for Petitioners 15-16 (Act covers conditions that leave individuals with "diminished physical or mental capabilities," but not conditions that could "impair the health of others"); Pet. for Cert. 13-14 ("[T]he concept of a 'handicap' [should be limited] to physical and mental conditions which result in either a real or perceived diminution of an individual's capabilities. . . . [A]n individual suffering from a contagious disease may not necessarily suffer from any physical or mental impairments affecting his ability to perform the job in question. In other words, an employer's reluctance to hire such an individual is not due to any real or perceived inability on the individual's part, but rather because of the employer's reluctance to expose its other employees and its clientele to the threat of infection").

[7]The United States argues that it is possible for a person to be simply a carrier of a disease, that is, to be capable of spreading a disease without having a "physical impairment" or suffering from any other symptoms associated with the disease. The United States contends that this is true in the case of some carriers of the Acquired Immune Deficiency Syndrome (AIDS) virus. From this premise the United States concludes that discrimination solely on the basis of contagiousness is never discrimination on the basis of a handicap. The argument is misplaced in this case, because the handicap here, tuberculosis, gave rise both to a physical impairment *and* to contagiousness. This case does not present, and we therefore do not reach, the questions whether a carrier of a contagious disease such as AIDS could be considered to have a physical impairment, or whether such a person could be considered, solely on the basis of contagiousness, a handicapped person as defined by the Act.

[8]See n. 4, *supra*.

[9]Congress' desire to prohibit discrimination based on the effects a person's handicap may have on others was evident from the inception of the Act. For example, Representative Vanik, whose remarks constitute "a primary signpost on the road toward interpreting the legislative history of § 504," *Alexander* v. *Choate*, 469 U. S. 287, 295-296, and n. 13 (1985), cited as an example of improper handicap discrimination a case in which "a court ruled that a cerebral palsied child, who was not a

not diminish a person's physical or mental capabilities, but could nevertheless substantially limit that person's ability to work as a result of the negative reactions of others to the impairment.[10]

Allowing discrimination based on the contagious effects of a physical impairment would be inconsistent with the basic purpose of § 504, which is to ensure that handicapped individuals are not denied jobs or other benefits because of the prejudiced attitudes or the ignorance of others. By amending the definition of "handicapped individual" to include not only those who are actually physically impaired, but also those who are regarded as impaired and who, as a result, are substantially limited in a major life activity, Congress acknowledged that society's accumulated myths and fears about disability and disease are as handicapping as are the physical limitations that flow from actual impairment.[11] Few aspects of a handicap give rise to the same level of public fear and misapprehension as contagiousness.[12] Even those who suffer or have recovered from such noninfectious diseases as epilepsy or cancer have faced discrimination based on the irrational fear that they might be conta-

---

physical threat and was academically competitive, should be excluded from public school, because his teacher claimed his physical appearance 'produced a nauseating effect' on his classmates." 117 Cong. Rec. 45974 (1971). See also 118 Cong. Rec. 36761 (1972) (remarks of Sen. Mondale) (a woman "crippled by arthritis" was denied a job not because she could not do the work but because "college trustees [thought] 'normal students shouldn't see her.'"); *id.*, at 525 (remarks of Sen. Humphrey); cf. Macgregor, Some Psycho-Social Problems Associated with Facial Deformities, 16 Am. Sociological Rev. 629 (1961).

[10]The Department of Health and Human Services regulations, which include among the conditions illustrative of physical impairments covered by the Act "cosmetic disfigurement," lend further support to Arline's position that the effect of one's impairment on others is as relevant to a determination of whether one is handicapped as is the physical effect of one's handicap on oneself. 45 CFR § 84.3(j)(2)(i)(A) (1985). At oral argument, the Solicitor General took the position that a condition such as cosmetic disfigurement could not substantially limit a major life activity within the meaning of the statute, because the only major life activity that it would affect would be the ability to work. The Solicitor General recognized that "working" was one of the major life activities listed in the regulations, but said that to argue that a condition that impaired *only* the ability to work was a handicapping condition was to make "a totally circular argument which lifts itself by its bootstraps." Tr. or Oral Arg. 15-16. The argument is not circular, however, but direct. Congress plainly intended the Act to cover persons with a physical or mental impairment (whether actual, past, or perceived) that substantially limited one's ability to work. "[T]he primary goal of the Act is to increase employment of the handicapped." *Consolidated Rail Corporation* v. *Darrone*, 465 U. S., 633, at n. 13; see also *id.*, at 632 ("Indeed, enhancing employment of the handicapped was so much the focus of the 1973 legislation that Congress the next year felt it necessary to amend the statute to clarify whether § 504 was intended to prohibit other types of discrimination as well").

[11]S. Rep. No. 93-1297, p. 50 (1974); see n. 4, *supra*. See generally, tenBroek & Matson, 54 Cal. L. Rev., at 814; Strauss, Chronic Illness, in The Sociology of Health and Illness 138, 146-147 (P. Conrad & R. Kern eds.) (1981).

[12]The isolation of the chronically ill and of those perceived to be ill or contagious appears across cultures and centuries, as does the development of complex and often pernicious mythologies about the nature, cause, and transmission of illness. Tuberculosis is no exception. See R. Dubos & J. Dubos, The White Plaque (1952); S. Sontag, Illness as Metaphor (1978).

gious.[13] The Act is carefully structured to replace such reflexive reactions to actual or perceived handicaps with actions based on reasoned and medically sound judgments: the definition of "handicapped individuals" is broad, but only those individuals who are both handicapped *and* otherwise qualified are eligible for relief. The fact that *some* persons who have contagious diseases may pose a serious health threat to others under certain circumstances does not justify excluding from the coverage of the Act *all* persons with actual or perceived contagious diseases. Such exclusion would mean that those accused of being contagious would never have the opportunity to have their condition evaluated in light of medical evidence and a determination made as to whether they were "otherwise qualified." Rather, they would be vulnerable to discrimination on the basis of mythology—precisely the type of injury Congress sought to prevent.[14] We conclude that the fact that a person with a record of a physical impairment is also contagious does not suffice to remove that person from coverage under § 504.[15]

---

[13]Senator Humphrey noted the "irrational fears or prejudice on the part of employers or fellow workers" that make it difficult for former cancer patients to secure employment. 123 Cong. Rec. 13515 (1977). See also Feldman, Wellness and Work, in Psychosocial Stress and Cancer 173-200 (C. Cooper ed. 1984) (documenting job discrimination against recovered cancer patients); S. Sontag, Illness as Metaphor 6 (1978) ("Any disease that is treated as a mystery and acutely enough feared will be felt to be morally, if not literally, contagious. Thus, a surprisingly large number of people with cancer find themselves being shunned by relatives and friends . . . as if cancer, like TB, were an infectious disease"); Dell, Social Dimensions of Epilepsy: Stigma and Response, in Psychopathology in Epilepsy: Social Dimensions 185-210 (S. Whitman & B. Hermann eds. 1986) (reviewing range of discrimination affecting epileptics); Brief for Epilepsy Foundation as *Amicus Curiae* 5-14 ("A review of the history of epilepsy provides a salient example that fear, rather than the handicap itself, is the major impetus for discrimination against persons with handicaps").

[14]Congress reaffirmed this approach in its 1978 amendments to the Act. There, Congress recognized that employers and other grantees might have legitimate reasons not to extend jobs or benefits to drug addicts and alcoholics, but also understood the danger of improper discrimination against such individuals if they were categorically excluded from coverage under the Act. Congress therefore rejected the original House proposal to exclude addicts and alcoholics from the definition of handicapped individual, and instead adopted the Senate proposal excluding only those alcoholics and drug abusers "whose current use of alcohol or drugs prevents such individual from performing the duties of the job in question or whose employment . . . would constitute a direct threat to property or the safety of others." 29 U. S. C. § 706(7)(B). See 124 Cong. Rec. 30322 (1978); Brief for Senator Cranston et al. as *Amici Curiae* 35-36; 43 Op. Atty. Gen. No. 12 (1977).

This approach is also consistent with that taken by courts that have addressed the question whether the Act covers persons suffering from conditions other than contagious diseases that render them a threat to the safety of others. See, *e. g.*, *Strathie* v. *Department of Transportation*, 716 F. 2d 227, 232-234 (CA3 1983); *Doe* v. *New York University*, 666 F. 2d 761, 775 (CA2 1981).

[15]The dissent implies that our holding rests only on our "own sense of fairness and implied support from the Act," *post*, at 1, and that this holding is inconsistent with *Pennhurst State School and Hospital* v. *Halderman*, 451 U. S. 1 (1981). It is evident, however, that our holding is premised on the plain language of the Act, and on the detailed regulations that implement it, neither of which the dissent discusses and both of which support the conclusion that those with a contagious disease such as tuberculosis may be considered "handicapped" under the Act. We also find much support in

IV

The remaining question is whether Arline is otherwise qualified for the job of elementary school teacher. To answer this question in most cases, the District Court will need to conduct an individualized inquiry and make appropriate findings of fact. Such an inquiry is essential if § 504 is to achieve its goal of protecting handicapped individuals from deprivations based on prejudice, stereotypes, or unfounded fear, while giving appropriate weight to such legitimate concerns of grantees as avoiding exposing others to significant health and safety risks.[16] The basic factors to be considered in conducting this inquiry are well established.[17] In the context of the employment of a

---

the legislative history, while the dissent is unable to find any evidence to support its view. Accordingly, the dissent's construction of the Act to exclude those afflicted with a contagious disease is not only arbitrary (and therefore unfair) but unfaithful to basic canons of statutory construction.

Nothing in *Pennhurst* requires such infidelity. The statutory provision at issue there was held to be "simply a general statement of 'findings'" and to express "no more than . . . a congressional preference for certain kinds of treatment." *Id.*, at 19. See *Wright* v. *Roanoke Redevelopment & Housing Auth.*, *ante* at —— (slip op. at 5) ("In *Pennhurst* . . . the statutory provisions were thought to be only statements of 'findings' indicating no more than a congressional preference—at most a 'nudge in the preferred directio[n]'"). The contrast between the congressional preference at issue in *Pennhurst* and the antidiscrimination mandate of § 504 could not be more stark.

Nor is there any reason to think that today's decision will extend the Act beyond manageable bounds. Construing § 504 not to exclude those with contagious diseases will complement rather than complicate state efforts to enforce public health laws. As we state, *infra*, at 14, courts may reasonably be expected normally to defer to the judgments of public health officials in determining whether an individual is otherwise qualified unless those judgments are medically unsupportable. Conforming employment decisions with medically reasonable judgments can hardly be thought to threaten the States' regulation of communicable diseases. Indeed, because the Act requires employers to respond rationally to those handicapped by a contagious disease, the Act will assist local health officials by helping remove an important obstacle to preventing the spread of infectious diseases: the individual's reluctance to report his or her condition. It is not surprising, then, that in their brief as *amici curiae* in support of respondent, the States of California, Maryland, Michigan, Minnesota, New Jersey, New York, and Wisconsin conclude that "inclusion of communicable diseases within the ambit of Section 504 does not reorder the priorities of state regulatory agencies . . . [and] would not alter the balance between state and federal authority." Brief for State of California et al. 30.

[16]A person who poses a significant risk of communicating an infectious disease to others in the workplace will not be otherwise qualified for his or her job if reasonable accommodation will not eliminate that risk. The Act would not require a school board to place a teacher with active, contagious tuberculosis in a classroom with elementary school children. Respondent conceded as much at oral argument. Tr. of Oral Arg. 45.

[17]"An otherwise qualified person is one who is able to meet all of a program's requirements in spite of his handicap." *Southeastern Community College* v. *Davis*, 442 U. S. 397, 406 (1979). In the employment context, an otherwise qualified person is one who can perform "the essential functions" of the job in question. 45 CFR § 84.3(k) (1985). When a handicapped person is not able to perform the essential functions of the job, the court must also consider whether any "reasonable accommodation" by the employer would enable the handicapped person to perform those functions. *Ibid.* Accommodation is not reasonable if it either imposes "undue financial

person handicapped with a contagious disease, we agree with *amicus* American Medical Association that this inquiry should include:

> "[findings of] facts, based on reasonable medical judgments given the state of medical knowledge, about (a) the nature of the risk (how the disease is transmitted), (b) the duration of the risk (how long is the carrier infectious), (c) the severity of the risk (what is the potential harm to third parties) and (d) the probabilities the disease will be transmitted and will cause varying degrees of harm." Brief for American Medical Association as *Amicus Curiae* 19.

In making these findings, courts normally should defer to the reasonable medical judgments of public health officials.[18] The next step in the "otherwise-qualified" inquiry is for the court to evaluate, in light of these medical findings, whether the employer could reasonably accommodate the employee under the established standards for that inquiry. See *supra*, note 17.

Because of the paucity of factual findings by the District Court, we, like the Court of Appeals, are unable at this stage of the proceedings to resolve whether Arline is "otherwise qualified" for her job. The District Court made no findings as to the duration and severity of Arline's condition, nor as to the probability that she would transmit the disease. Nor did the court determine whether Arline was contagious at the time she was discharged, or whether the School Board could have reasonably accommodated her.[19] Accordingly, the resolution of whether Arline was otherwise qualified requires further findings of fact.

V

We hold that a person suffering from the contagious disease of tuberculosis can be a handicapped person within the meaning of the § 504 of the Rehabilitation Act of 1973, and that respondent Arline is such a person. We remand the case to the District Court to determine whether Arline is otherwise qualified for her position. The judgment of the Court of Appeals is

Affirmed.

---

and administrative burdens" on a grantee, *Southeastern Community College* v. *Davis*, *supra*, at 412, or requires "a fundamental alteration in the nature of [the] program" *id.*, at 410. See 45 CFR § 84.12(c) (1985) (listing factors to consider in determining whether accommodation would cause undue hardship); 45 CFR pt. 84, App. A, p. 315 (1985) ("where reasonable accommodation does not overcome the effects of a person's handicap, or where reasonable accommodation causes undue hardship to the employer, failure to hire or promote the handicapped person will not be considered discrimination"); *Davis*, *supra*, at 410-413; *Alexander* v. *Choate*, 469 U. S., at 299-301, and n. 19; *Strathie* v. *Department of Transportation*, *supra*, at 231.

[18] This case does not present, and we do not address, the question whether courts should also defer to the reasonable medical judgments of private physicians on which an employer has relied.

[19] Employers have an affirmative obligation to make a reasonable accommodation for a handicapped employee. Although they are not required to find another job for an employee who is not qualified for the job he or she was doing, they cannot deny an employee alternative employment opportunities reasonably available under the employer's existing policies. See n. 17, *supra*; 45 CFR § 84.12 and App. A, pp. 315-316 (1985).

CHIEF JUSTICE REHNQUIST, with whom JUSTICE SCALIA joins, dissenting.

In *Pennhurst State School and Hospital* v. *Halderman*, 451 U. S. 1 (1981), this Court made clear that, where Congress intends to impose a condition on the grant of federal funds, "it must do so unambiguously." *Id.*, at 17. This principle applies with full force to § 504 of the Rehabilitation Act, which Congress limited in scope to "those who actually 'receive' federal financial assistance." *United States Department of Transportation* v. *Paralyzed Veterans*, 477 U. S. ——, —— (1986). Yet, the Court today ignores this principle, resting its holding on its own sense of fairness and implied support from the Act. *Ante*. Such an approach, I believe, is foreclosed not only by *Pennhurst*, but also by our prior decisions interpreting the Rehabilitation Act.

Our decision in *Pennhurst* was premised on the view that federal legislation imposing obligations only on recipients of federal funds is "much in the nature of a contract." 451 U. S., at 17. See also *Board of Education of Hendrick Hudson Central School District* v. *Rowley*, 458 U. S. 176, 204, n. 26 (1982). As we have stated in the context of the Rehabilitation Act, "'Congress apparently determined it would require . . . grantees to bear the costs of providing employment for the handicapped as a *quid pro quo* for the receipt of federal funds.'" *United States Department of Transportation* v. *Paralyzed Veterans*, *supra*, at ——, quoting *Consolidated Rail Corporation* v. *Darrone*, 465 U. S. 624, 633, n. 13 (1984). The legitimacy of this *quid pro quo* rests on whether recipients of federal funds voluntarily and knowingly accept the terms of the exchange. *Pennhurst*, *supra*, at 17. There can be no knowing acceptance unless Congress speaks "with a clear voice" in identifying the conditions attached to the receipt of funds. 451 U. S., at 17.

The requirement that Congress unambiguously express conditions imposed on federal moneys is particularly compelling in cases such as this where there exists long-standing state and federal regulation of the subject matter. From as early as 1796, Congress has legislated directly in the area of contagious diseases.[1] Congress has also, however, left significant leeway to the States, which have enacted a myriad of public health statutes designed to protect against the introduction and spread of contagious diseases.[2] When faced with such extensive regulation, this Court has declined to read the Rehabilitation Act expansively. See *Bowen* v. *American Hospital Assn.*, 476 U. S. ——, —— (1986); *Alexander* v. *Choate*, 469 U. S. 287, 303, 307 (1985). Absent an expression of intent to the contrary, "Congress . . . 'will

[1]See, *e. g.*, 42 U. S. C. §§ 243, 264; Act of May 27, 1796, ch. 31, 1 Stat. 474; see generally Morgenstern, The Role of the Federal Government in Protecting Citizens from Communicable Diseases, 47 U. Cin. L. Rev. 537 (1978).

[2]The coverage of state statutes regulating contagious diseases is broad, addressing, *inter alia*, reporting requirements, quarantines, denial of marriage licenses based on the presence of certain diseases, compulsory immunization, and certification and medical testing requirements for school employees. See, *e. g.*, Ariz. Rev. Stat. Ann. § 36.621 *et. seq.* (1986) (reporting requirements); Conn. Gen. Stat. §§ 19a-207, 19a-221 (1985) (quarantines); Fla. Stat. §§ 741.051-741.055 (1985) marriage licenses); Mass. Gen. Laws § 71:55B (1984) (certification requirements for school employees); Miss. Code Ann. § 37-7-301(i) (Supp. 1986) (compulsory immunization of school students); W. Va. Code § 16-3-4a (1985) (medical testing).

not be deemed to have significantly changed the federal-state balance.'" *Bowen* v. *American Hospital Assn.*, *supra*, at ——, quoting *United States* v. *Bass*, 404 U. S. 336, 349 (1971).

Applying these principles, I conclude that the Rehabilitation Act cannot be read to support the result reached by the Court. The record in this case leaves no doubt that Arline was discharged because of the contagious nature of tuberculosis, and not because of any diminished physical or mental capabilities resulting from her condition.[3] Thus, in the language of § 504, the central question here is whether discrimination on the basis of contagiousness constitutes discrimination "by reason of . . . handicap." Because the language of the Act, regulations, and legislative history are silent on this issue,[4] the principles outlined above compel the conclusion that contagiousness is not a handicap within the meaning of § 504. It is therefore clear that the protections of the Act do not extend to individuals such as Arline.

In reaching a contrary conclusion, the Court never questions that Arline was discharged because of the threat her condition posed to others. Instead, it posits that the contagious effects of a disease cannot be "meaningfully" distinguished from the disease's effect on a claimant under the Act. *Ante*. To support this position, the Court observes that Congress intended to extend the Act's protections to individuals who have a condition that does not impair their mental and physical capabilities, but limits their major life activities because of the adverse reactions of others. This congressional recognition of a handicap resulting from the reactions of others, we are told, reveals that Congress intended the Rehabilitation Act to regulate discrimination on the basis of contagiousness. *Ante*.

This analysis misses the mark in several respects. To begin with, Congress' recognition that an individual may be handicapped under the Act solely by reason of the reactions of others in no way demonstrates that, for the purposes of interpreting the Act, the reactions of others to the condition cannot be considered separately from the effect of the condition on the claimant. In addition, the Court provides no basis for extending the Act's generalized coverage of individuals suffering discrimination as a result of the reactions of others to coverage of individuals with contagious diseases. Al-

---

[3]In testifying concerning his reasons for recommending Arline's termination, petitioner Craig Marsh, Superintendent of Schools of Nassau County, Florida, stated that "I felt like that for the benefit of the total student population and . . . personnel in Nassau County and the public benefit, that it would be best if—not to continue or offer Mrs. Arline any employment." App. 62. Marsh added:

"I am charged and so is the school board, with the responsibility for the protecting, the safety, health and welfare of students, every student in Nassau County. And the record clearly states that, you know, after all—after the third time that I had knowledge of Mrs. Arline's recurring condition, which was infectious at the time of each reoccurrence, that I felt like it [was] in the best interest of the school system of Nassau County that she be dismissed from the classroom." *Id.*, at 81.

Before Arline's termination, Marsh consulted with Dr. Marianne McEuen, who testified that she recommended the termination because of the threat that Arline's condition posed to the health of the small children with whom Arline was in constant contact. *Id.*, at 12-17.

[4]See, *e. g.*, 29 U. S. C. § 701 *et. seq.*; 45 CFR pt. 84 (1985); H. R. Rep. No. 95-1149 (1978); S. Rep. No. 95-890 (1978); S. Rep. No. 93-1297 (1974); H. R. Rep. No. 93-244 (1973); S. Rep. No. 93-318 (1973).

though citing examples of handicapped individuals described in the regulations and legislative history, the Court points to nothing in these materials suggesting that Congress contemplated that a person with a condition posing a threat to the health of others may be considered handicapped under the Act.[5] Even in an ordinary case of statutory construction, such meager proof of congressional intent would not be determinative. The Court's evidence, therefore, could not possibly provide the basis for "knowing acceptance" by such entities as the Nassau County School Board that their receipt of federal funds is conditioned on Rehabilitation Act regulation of public health issues. *Pennhurst*, 451 U. S., at 17.

In *Alexander* v. *Choate*, 469 U. S., at 299, this Court stated that "[a]ny interpretation of § 504 must . . . be responsive to two powerful but countervailing considerations—the need to give effect to the statutory objectives and the desire to keep § 504 within manageable bounds." The Court has wholly disregarded this admonition here.

---

[5]In fact, two of the examples cited by the Court may be read to support a contrary conclusion. The 1978 amendments to the Rehabilitation Act, cited by the majority, *ante*, specifically exclude from the definition of a handicapped person alcoholics and drug abusers that "constitute a *direct threat* to property or *the safety of others*." 29 U. S. C. § 706(7)(B) (emphasis added). If anything, this exclusion evinces congressional intent to avoid the Act's interference with public health and safety concerns. See Oversight Hearings on Rehabilitation Act of 1973 before the Subcommittee on Select Education of the House Committee on Education and Labor, 95th Cong., 2d Sess., 503 (1978) (statement of Rep. Hyde) ("Congress needs to give thoughtful and wide-ranging consideration to the needs of handicapped persons, balanced against the realities of public safety, economics, and commonsense"). This intent is also present in the statements of Representative Vanik relied on by the Court. See *ante*. Representative Vanik expressed apparent disapproval of a court ruling that "'a cerebral palsied child, *who was not a physical threat* and was academically competitive, should be excluded from public school, because his teacher claimed his physical appearance "produced a nauseating effect" on his classmates.'" *Ante* quoting 117 Cong. Rec. 45974 (1971) (emphasis added).

APPENDIX D

SUBJECT MATTER TABLE OF RECENT LAW REVIEW ARTICLES

AIDS

AIDS and employment discrimination under the Federal Rehabilitation Act of 1973 and Virginia's Rights of Persons with Disabilities Act. 20 U.Rich.L.Rev. 425 (1986).

AIDS as a handicap under the Federal Rehabilitation Act of 1973. 43 Wash. & Lee L.Rev. 1515 (1986).

AIDS: a university's liability for failure to protect its students. 14 J.C.& U.L. 529 (1987).

AIDS: do children with AIDS have a right to attend school? 13 Pepperdine L.Rev. 1041 (1986).

AIDS: does it qualify as a "handicap" under the Rehabilitation Act of 1973? 61 Notre Dame L.Rev. 572 (1986).

AIDS in the classroom: room for reason amidst paranoia. 91 Dick. L.Rev. 1055 (1987).

AIDS quarantine in England and the United States. 10 Hastings Int'l & Comp.L.Rev. 113 (1986).

AIDS-related litigation: the competing interests surrounding discovery of blood donors' identities. 19 Ind.L.Rev. 561 (1986).

Are AIDS victims handicapped? 31 St.Louis U.L.J. 729 (1987).

Closen, Michael L., Susan Marie Connor, Howard L. Kaufman and Mark F. Wojcik. *AIDS: testing democracy—irrational responses to the public health crisis and the need for privacy in serologic testing.* 19 J.Marshall L.Rev. 835 (1986).

Education and administrative law—education of health-impaired children and administrative due process—state Department of Education possesses statutory authority to promulgate administrative rules governing the admission to school of children afflicted with AIDS provided that department affords all parties appropriate procedural due process under those rules. [Bd. of Educ. v. Cooperman, 523 A.2d 655 (1987)] 19 Rutgers L.J. 483 (1988).

Enforcing the rights to a public education for children afflicted with AIDS. 36 Emory L.J. 603 (1987).

Fear and loathing in the classroom: AIDS and public education. 14 J.Legis. 87 (1987).

Harder, Rae A. *A legal guide for the education of legislators facing the inevitable question: AIDS: the problem is real—what do we do?* 13 J.Contemp.L. 121 (1987).

Herman, Donald H.J. *AIDS: malpractice and transmission liability.* 58 U.Colo.L.Rev. 63 (1986-87).

AIDS (continued)

Law, Social Policy and Contagious Disease: a Symposium on Acquired Immune Deficiency Syndrome (AIDS). 14 Hofstra L.Rev. 1 (1986).

Merrit, Deborah Jones. *Communicable disease and constitutional law: controlling AIDS.* 61 N.Y.U.L.Rev. 739 (1986).

Opening the schoolhouse door for children with AIDS: the Education for All Handicapped Children Act. 13 B.C.Envtl.Aff. L.Rev. 583 (1986).

Protecting children with AIDS against arbitrary exclusion from school. 74 Calif.L.Rev. 1373 (1986).

Protecting confidentiality in the effort to control AIDS. 24 Harv.J. on Legis. 315 (1987).

Protection of AIDS victims from employment discrimination under the Rehabilitation Act. 1987 U.Ill.L.Rev. 355.

Public Policy and the AIDS epidemic. 2 J.Contemp. Health L. 169 (1986).

Recent developments: public health and employment issues generated by the AIDS crisis. 25 Washburn L.J. 505 (1986).

Reportability of exposure to the AIDS virus: an equal protection analysis. 7 Cardozo L.Rev. 1103 (1986).

The constitutional implications of mandatory testing for Acquired Immunodeficiency Syndrome—AIDS. 37 Emory L.J. 217 (1988).

The constitutional right of informational privacy: does it protect children suffering from AIDS? 14 Fordham Urb.L.Rev. 927 (1985-86).

The constitutional rights of AIDS carriers. 99 Harv.L.Rev. 1274 (1986).

Undoing a lesson of fear in the classroom: the legal recourse of AIDS-linked children. 135 U.Pa.L.Rev. 193 (1986).

Wasson, Robert P., Jr. *AIDS discrimination under federal, state and local law after Arline.* 15 Fla.St.U.L.Rev. 221 (1987).

You never told me . . . You never asked; tort liability for the sexual transmission of AIDS. 91 Dick.L.Rev. 529 (1986).

Attorney's Fees

Civil rights—attorney's fees award—42 U.S.C. § 1988—the United States Supreme Court has held that an award of attorney's fees under 42 U.S.C. § 1988 is not required to be proportionate to the damages awarded a civil rights plaintiff, thus allowing a fee award seven times the amount of compensatory and punitive damages. [City of Riverside v. Rivera, 106 S.Ct. 2686 (1986)] 26 Duq.L.Rev. 139 (1987).

Dobbs, Dan R. *The market test for attorney fee awards: is the hourly rate test mandatory?* 28 Ariz.L.Rev. 1 (1986).

Education law—the Handicapped Children's Protection Act of 1986: the award of attorney's fees in litigation under the Education of the Handicapped Act. 11 S.Ill.U.L.J. 381 (1987).

Goldberger, David. *First Amendment constraints on the award of attorney's fees against civil rights defendant-intervenors: the dilemma of the innocent volunteer.* 47 Ohio St.L.J. 603 (1986).

Attorney's Fees (continued)

Schreck, Myron. *Attorneys' fees for administrative proceedings under the Education of the Handicapped Act: of Carey, Crest Street and congressional intent.* 60 Temp.L.Q. 599 (1987).

The Supreme Court's interpretation of section 1988 and awards of attorney's fees for work performed in administrative proceedings: a proposal for a result-oriented approach. [North Carolina Dep't of Transp. v. Crest Street Comm. Council, Inc., 107 S.Ct. 336 (1986)] 62 Wash.L.Rev. 889 (1987).

Bilingual Education

Moran, Rachel F. *Bilingual education as a status conflict.* 75 Calif.L.Rev. 321 (1987).

Nelson, F. Howard. *The assessment of English language proficiency: standards for determining participation in transitional language programs.* 15 J.L. & Educ. 83 (1986).

"Official English": federal limits on effort to curtail bilingual service in the states. 100 Harv.L.Rev. 1345 (1987).

Rossell, Christine H. and J. Michael Ross. *The social science evidence on bilingual education.* 15 J.L. & Educ. 385 (1986).

Classification and Identification

AIDS: does it qualify as a "handicap" under the Rehabilitation Act of 1973? 61 Notre Dame L.Rev. 572 (1986).

Bennett, P.E. *The meaning of "mental illness" under the Michigan Mental Health Code.* 4 Cooley L.Rev. 65 (1986).

Reinstitutionalization of the mentally retarded. 32 Wayne L.Rev. 1105 (1986).

The Education for All Handicapped Children Act: the benefits and burdens of mainstreaming capable handicapped children in a regular classroom. 38 Mercer L.Rev. 903 (1987).

What's a handicap anyway? Analyzing handicap claims under the Rehabilitation Act of 1973 and analogous state statutes. 22 Willamette L.Rev. 529 (1986).

Discrimination

Administrative res judicata and section 1983: should the rule of preclusion apply to unreviewed state administrative decisions? 10 Nat'l Black L.J. 73 (1987).

AIDS and employment discrimination under the Federal Rehabilitation Act of 1973 and Virginia's Rights of Persons with Disabilities Act. 20 U.Rich.L.Rev. 425 (1986).

AIDS as a handicap under the Federal Rehabilitation Act of 1973. 43 Wash. & Lee L.Rev. 1515 (1986).

AIDS: do children with AIDS have a right to attend school? 13 Pepperdine L.Rev. 1041 (1986).

An evolutionary step in equal protection analysis. [City of Cleburne v. Cleburne Living Center, 105 S.Ct. 3249 (1985)] 46 Md.L.Rev. 163 (1986).

Bacharach, Robert E. *Section 1983 and an administrative exhaustion requirement.* 40 Okla.L.Rev. 407 (1987).

Chandler, Thomas E. *The end of school busing? School desegregation and the finding of unitary status.* 40 Okla.L.Rev. 519 (1987).

Discrimination (continued)

Civil rights litigation I: developments under section 1983 and Title VII. 1986 Ann.Surv.Am.L. 795.

Civil rights litigation II: developments under section 1988. 1986 Ann.Surv.Am.L. 809.

Civil rights—Massachusetts Civil Rights Act provides remedy for interference with constitutionally secured rights whether or not violations of those rights require state action. [Bell v. Mazza, 394 Mass. 176, 474 N.E.2d 1111 (1985)] 20 Suffolk U.L.Rev. 110 (1986).

Civil rights—statute of limitations—state limitation period for personal injury actions applies to all section 1983 claims. [Wilson v. Garcia, 105 S.Ct. 1938 (1985)] 16 Seton Hall L.Rev. 831 (1986).

Coleman, Jennifer A. *42 U.S.C. section 1988: a congressionally-mandated approach to the construction of section 1983.* 19 Ind. L.Rev. 665 (1986).

Colker, Ruth. *Anti-subordination above all: sex, race and equal protection.* 61 N.Y.U.L.Rev. 1003 (1986).

Constitutional law: although mentally retarded not a quasi-suspect class, denial of special use permit deprived applicants of constitutional right. [City of Cleburne v. Cleburne Living Center, 105 S.Ct. 3249 (1985)] 25 Washburn L.J. 575 (1986).

Constitutional law—equal protection—zoning ordinance excluding home for the mentally retarded fails the rational basis test. [City of Cleburne v. Cleburne Living Center, 105 S.Ct. 3249 (1985)] 8 U.Ark. Little Rock L.J. 721 (1985-86).

Constitutional law—mental health—the mentally handicapped do not constitute a "quasi-suspect" class for purposes of equal protection analysis. [City of Cleburne v. Cleburne Living Center, 105 S.Ct. 3249 (1985)] 62 N.D.L.Rev. 95 (1986).

Constitutional law—mental retardation is not a quasi-suspect classification. 17 St. Mary's L.J. 1053 (1986).

Denial of quasi-suspect status for the mentally retarded and its effect on exclusionary zoning of group homes. [City of Cleburne v. Cleburne Living Center, 105 S.Ct. 3249 (1985)] 17 U.Tol.L.Rev. 1041 (1986).

Employment discrimination against the handicapped: analysis of statutory and constitutional protection in Massachusetts. 21 New Eng.L.Rev. 305 (1985-86).

Employment discrimination: AIDS victims. [Shuttleworth v. Broward County Office of Budget & Management Policy, Daily Lab. Rep. (BNA) No. 242, E-1, 12/17/85] 9 Harv.J.L. & Pub.Pol'y 739 (1986).

Equal protection and the mentally retarded: a denial of quasi-suspect status in . . . [City of Cleburne v. Cleburne Living Center, 105 S.Ct. 3249 (1985)]. 72 Iowa L.Rev. 241 (1986).

Equal protection for the mentally retarded? [City of Cleburne v. Cleburne Living Center, 105 S.Ct. 3249 (1985)] 9 Harv.J.L. & Pub.Pol'y 231 (1986).

Discrimination (continued)

Equal protection—mental retardation is not a quasi-suspect classification requiring heightened judicial scrutiny, but requiring a special use permit for the operation of a group home for the mentally retarded based on irrational prejudices fails even the rational basis test. 36 Drake L.Rev. 201 (1986-87).

Facial discrimination: extending handicap law to employment discrimination on the basis of physical appearance. 100 Harv.L.Rev. 2035 (1987).

Flaccus, Janet A. *Discrimination legislation for the handicapped: much ferment and the erosion of coverage.* 55 U.Cin.L.Rev. 81 (1986).

Getting back on track: challenging racially discriminatory effects of educational tracking. 20 Colum.J.L. & Soc.Probs. 283 (1986).

Grossman, Claudio. *A framework for the examination of states of emergency under the American Convention on Human Rights.* 1 Am.U.J.Int'l L. & Pol'y 35 (1986).

Group homes in Oklahoma: does Jackson v. Williams offer new hope for the mentally retarded? [Jackson v. Williams, 714 P.2d 1017 (1985)] 22 Tulsa L.J. 201 (1986).

Kaufman, Michael J. *Federal and state handicapped discrimination laws: toward an accommodating legal framework.* 18 Loy.U. Chi.L.J. 1119 (1987).

Larson, David D. *What disabilities are protected under the Rehabilitation Act of 1973?* 16 Mem.St.U.L.Rev. 229 (1986).

Mims, William C. *The plight of the handicapped infant: The Federal Response.* 15 U.Balt.L.Rev. 449 (1986).

Minow, Martha. *When difference has its home: group homes for the mentally retarded, equal protection and legal treatment of difference.* 22 Harv.C.R. - C.L.L.Rev. 111 (1987).

Perras, Roichard A. and Walter C. Hunter. *Handicap discrimination in employment: the employer defense of future safety risk.* 6 J.L. & Com. 377 (1986).

Price, Janet R. and Jane R. Stern. *Magnet schools as a strategy for integration and school reform.* 5 Yale L. & Pol'y Rev. 291 (1987).

Program specificity and section 504: making the best of a bad situation. 20 Loy.L.A.L.Rev. 1431 (1987).

Protecting children with AIDS against arbitrary exclusion from school. 74 Calif.L.Rev. 1373 (1986).

Rational basis review under the equal protection clause—a double standard of review. [City of Cleburne v. Cleburne Living Center, 105 S.Ct. 3249 (1985)] 55 Miss.L.J. 329 (1985).

Rational basis with a bite? [City of Cleburne v. Cleburne Living Center, 105 S.Ct. 3249 (1985)] 20 U.S.F.L.Rev. 927 (1986).

Real protection against discrimination for society's new outcasts? [School Bd. of Nassau County v. Arline, 107 S.Ct. 1123 (1987)] 17 Stetson L.Rev. 517 (1988).

Rebell, Michael A. *Structural discrimination and the rights of the disabled.* 74 Geo.L.J. 1435 (1986).

Discrimination (continued)

Rehabilitation Act—Department of Health and Human Services may not interfere in medical treatment decision regarding handicapped infants. [Bowen v. American Hosp. Ass'n, 106 S.Ct. 2101 (1986)] 16 Cum.L.Rev. 607 (1986).

Rothstein, Laura F. *Section 504 of the Rehabilitation Act: emerging issues for colleges and universities.* 13 J.C. & U.L. 229 (1986).

Rubin, Seymour J. *Economic and social human rights and the new international economic order.* 1 Am.U.J. Int'l L. & Pol'y 67 (1986).

Safeguarding equality for the handicapped: compensatory relief under section 504 of the Rehabilitation Act. [Guardians Ass'n v. Civil Service Comm'n, 463 U.S. 582 (1983)] 1986 Duke L.J. 197.

School desegregation and white flight: the unconstitutionality of integration maintenance plans. 1987 U.Chi.Legal F. 389.

Section 504 of the Rehabilitation Act: a re-examination of the civil rights declaration of the handicapped. 21 Suffolk U.L.Rev. 175 (1987).

Section 504 transportation regulations: molding civil rights legislation to meet the reality of economic constraints. 26 Washburn L.J. 558 (1987).

Shedding tiers for the mentally retarded. [City of Cleburne v. Cleburne Living Center, 105 S.Ct. 3249 (1985)] 35 DePaul L.Rev. 485 (1986).

Snelling, Phillip H. *Discrimination against children with special health care needs: Title V Crippled Children's Services programs and section 504 of the Rehabilitation Act of 1973.* 18 Loy.U. Chi.L.J. 995 (1987).

The City of Cleburne v. Cleburne Living Center and the Supreme Court: two minorities move toward acceptance. 63 Den.U.L. Rev. 697 (1986).

The constitutional rights of AIDS carriers. 99 Harv.L.Rev. 1274 (1986).

The mentally retarded and the demise of intermediate scrutiny. [City of Cleburne v. Cleburne Living Center, 105 S.Ct. 3249 (1985)] 20 Val.U.L.Rev. 349 (1986).

Title VII and state courts: divining implicit congressional intent with regard to state court jurisdiction. 28 B.C.L.Rev. 299 (1987).

To infer or not to infer a discriminatory purpose: rethinking equal protection doctrine. 61 N.Y.U.L.Rev. 334 (1986).

Undoing a lesson of fear in the classroom: the legal recourse of AIDS-linked children. 135 U.Pa.L.Rev. 193 (1986).

What's a handicap anyway? Analyzing handicap claims under the Rehabilitation Act of 1973 and analogous state statutes. 22 Willamette L.Rev. 529 (1986).

Education Generally

Asbestos in schools and the economic loss doctrine. 54 U.Chi.L.Rev. 277 (1987).

Education Generally (continued)

Cannon, William B. *Enlightened localism: a narrative account of poverty and education in the Great Society.* [Symposium] 4 Yale L. & Pol'y Rev. 6 (1985).

Cichon, Dennis E. *Educability and education: filling the cracks in service provision responsibility under the Education for All Handicapped Children Act of 1975.* 48 Ohio St.L.J. 1089 (1987).

Devins, Neal. *Centralization in education: why Johnny can't spell bureaucracy.* 75 Calif.L.Rev. 759 (1987).

Dutile, Fernand N. *The law of higher education and the courts: 1986.* 14 J.C. & U.L. 303 (1987).

Educational malpractice: a cause of action in need of a call for action. 22 Val.U.L.Rev. 427 (1988).

Educational malpractice update. 14 Cap.U.L.Rev. 609 (1985).

Education and the Court: the Supreme Court's educational ideology. 40 Vand.L.Rev. 939 (1987).

Goodwin, Robert J. *The Fifth Amendment in public schools: a rationale for its application in investigations and disciplinary proceedings.* 28 Wm. & Mary L.Rev. 683 (1987).

Hill, Kevin D. *Legal conflicts in special education: How competing paradigms in the Education for All Handicapped Children Act create litigation.* 64 U.Det.L.Rev. 129 (1986).

Inequality in Louisiana public school finance: should educational quality depend on a student's school district residency? 60 Tul.L.Rev. 1269 (1986).

Joint ventures: for profit and nonprofit corporations as partners in providing mental health services. 5 Pub.L.F. 201 (1986).

Louisiana Constitution: Article VIII: Education. 46 La.L.Rev. 1137 (1986).

Miller, Laura Ariane. *Head Start: a moving target.* 5 Yale L. & Pol'y Rev. 322 (1987).

Roberts, Robert N. *Public university responses to academic dishonesty.* 15 J.L. & Educ. 369 (1986).

Schwartz, Richard A., Ann L. Majestic and Tamara S. Hatheway. *The Supreme Court and public education: a year in review (Survey).* 18 Urb.Law. 991 (1986).

Szablewicz, James J. and Annette Gibbs. *Colleges' increasing exposure to liability: the new in loco parentis.* 16 J.L. & Educ. 453 (1987).

The evolution of parental rights in education. 16 J.L. & Educ. 339 (1987).

West, Edwin G. *Constitutional judgment on nonpublic school aid: fresh guidelines or new roadblocks?* 35 Emory L.J. 795 (1986).

Employment

AIDS and employment discrimination: should AIDS be considered a handicap? 33 Wayne L.Rev. 1095 (1987).

Education—House Bill 72—teacher competency testing is valid exercise of state legislative police power. [Texas State Teacher's Ass'n v. State, 711 S.W.2d 421 (Tex.App.1986)] 18 St. Mary's L.J. 661 (1986).

Employment (continued)

Employmnent discrimination and AIDS: is AIDS a handicap under section 504 of the Rehabilitation Act? 38 U.Fla.L.Rev. 649 (1986).

Handicapped workers: who should bear the burden of proving job qualifications? 38 Me.L.Rev. 135 (1986).

Ingulli, Elaine D. *Sexual harassment in education.* 18 Rutgers L.J. 281 (1987).

Ludolf, Robert Charles. *Termination of faculty tenure rights due to financial exigency and program discontinuance.* 63 U.Det. L.Rev. 609 (1986).

Tenured faculty and the "uncapped" Age Discrimination in Employment Act. 5 Yale L. & Pol'y Rev. 450 (1987).

The public employee can disagree with the boss—sometimes. [Cox v. Dardanelle Pub. School Dist., 790 F.2d 668 (8th Cir.1986)] 66 Neb.L.Rev. 601 (1987).

Tidwell, James A. *Educator's liability for negative letters of recommendation.* 15 J.L. & Educ. 479 (1986).

Finance

Inequality in Louisiana public school finance: should educational quality depend on a student's school district residency? 60 Tul.L.Rev. 1269 (1986).

First Amendment

An educational perspective on the evolution of Lemon. [Grand Rapids School District v. Ball, 105 S.Ct. 3216 (1985), and Aguilar v. Felton, 105 S.Ct. 3232 (1985)] 1986 B.Y.U.L.Rev. 489.

Bosmajian, Haig. *The judiciary's use of metaphors, metonymies and other tropes to give First Amendment protection to students and teachers.* 15 J.L. & Educ. 439 (1986).

Case comment: the establishment clause and financial aid to students for religious education at private institutions. [Witters v. Washington Dep't of Servs. for the Blind, 106 S.Ct. 748 (1986)] 13 J.C. & U.L. 397 (1987).

Choper, Jesse H. *The establishment clause and aid to parochial schools—an update.* 75 Calif.L.Rev. 5 (1987).

Gibney, Mark P. *State aid to religious-affiliated schools: a political analysis.* 28 Wm. & Mary L.Rev. 119 (1986).

West, Edwin G. *Constitutional judgment on nonpublic school aid: Fresh guidelines or new roadblocks?* 35 Emory L.J. 795 (1986).

Injuries

Henderson, Donald H. *Negligent liability suits emanating from the failure to provide adequate supervision: a critical issue for teachers and school boards.* 16 J.L. & Educ. 435 (1987).

Standard of care, duty & causation in failure to warn actions against mental health professionals. [Peck v. Counseling Service of Addison County, Inc., 499 A.2d 422 (Vt.1985)] 11 Vt.L.Rev. 343 (1986).

The use of closed-circuit television testing in child sexual abuse cases: a Twentieth Century solution to a Twentieth Century problem. 23 San Diego L.Rev. 919 (1986).

Injuries (continued)

The use of videotaped testimony of victims in cases involving child sexual abuse: a constitutional dilemma. 14 Hofstra L.Rev. 291 (1986).

Medical Services

AIDS-related litigation: the competing interests surrounding discovery of blood donors' identities. 19 Ind.L.Rev. 561 (1986).

Baby Doe cases: compromise and moral dilemma. 34 Emory L.J. 545 (1985).

Certificate of need for health care facilities: a time for re-examination. 7 Pace L.Rev. 491 (1987).

Closen, Michael L., Susan Marie Connor, Howard L. Kaufman and Mark F. Wojcik. *AIDS: testing democracy—irrational responses to the public health crisis and the need for privacy in serologic testing.* 19 J.Marshall L.Rev. 835 (1986).

Establishing standards for treating children in mental institutions with psychotropic drugs. 5 Pub.L.F. 215 (1986).

Joint ventures: for profit and nonprofit corporations as partners in providing mental health services. 5 Pub.L.F. 201 (1986).

Law, Social Policy and Contagious Disease: a Symposium on Acquired Immune Deficiency Syndrome (AIDS). 14 Hofstra L.Rev. 1 (1986).

Medical treatment of handicapped infants: who should make the decision? 22 Tul.L.Rev. 259 (1986).

Scott, Elizabeth S. *Sterilization of mentally retarded persons: reproductive rights and family privacy.* 1986 Duke L.J. 806.

Standard of care, duty & causation in failure to warn actions against mental health professionals. [Peck v. Counseling Service of Addison County, Inc., 499 A.2d 422 (Vt.1985)] 11 Vt.L.Rev. 343 (1986).

The best interest standard in court-authorized sterilization of mentally retarded. [In re Debra B., 495 A.2d 781 (Me.1985)] 38 Me.L.Rev. 209 (1987).

The psychotherapist-patient privilege: are patients victims in the investigation of Medicaid fraud? 19 Ind.L.Rev. 831 (1986).

Student Rights

A changing equal protection standard? The Supreme Court's application of a heightened rational basis test in . . . [City of Cleburne v. Cleburne Living Center, 105 S.Ct. 3249, (1985)] 20 Loy. L.A.L.Rev. 921 (1987).

Avery, Charles W. and Robert J. Simpson. *Search and seizure: a risk assessment model for public school officials.* 16 J.L.& Educ. 403 (1987).

Beyond least restrictive alternative: a constitutional right to treatment for mentally disabled persons in the community. 20 Loy. L.A.L.Rev. 1527 (1987).

Compulsory urinalysis of public school students: an unconstitutional search and seizure. 18 Colum.Hum.Rts. L.Rev. 111 (1986-87).

Due process rights in student disciplinary matters. 14 J.C.& U.L. 359 (1987).

Student Rights (continued)

Equal educational opportunity: the visually impaired and Public Law 94-142. [Education for All Handicapped Children Act of 1975] 33 UCLA L.Rev. 549 (1985).

Fleming, Evelyn R. and Donald C. Fleming. *Involvement of minors in special education decision-making.* 16 J.L.& Educ. 389 (1987).

Legal rights of gifted students: special education law at the "other end." 19 Conn.L.Rev. 143 (1986).

Levin, Betsy. *Educating youth for citizenship: the conflict between authority and individual rights in the public school.* 95 Yale L.J. 1647 (1986).

Merritt, Frank S. and Elizabeth E. Hill. *Recent developments in individual rights, health and human resources (Survey).* 18 Urb.Law. 935 (1986).

Perlin, Michael L. *Can mental health professionals predict judicial decisionmaking? Constitutional and tort liability aspects of the right of the institutionalized mentally disabled to refuse treatment: on the cutting edge.* 3 Touro L.Rev. 13 (1986).

Public school drug searches: toward redefining Fourth Amendment "reasonableness" to include individualized suspicion. 14 Fordham Urb.L.Rev. 629 (1986).

Ross, Stephen F. *Legislative enforcement of equal protection.* 72 Minn.L.Rev. 311 (1987).

Searching public schools: T.L.O. and the exclusionary rule. [New Jersey v. T.L.O., 469 U.S. 325 (1985)] 47 Ohio St.L.J. 1099 (1986).

Sheperd, Robert E., Jr. *Legal issues involving children (Survey).* 20 U.Rich.L.Rev. 903 (1986).

State constitutions and statutes as sources of rights for the mentally disabled: the last frontier. 20 Loy.L.A.L.Rev. 1249 (1987).

Sterilization of the mentally disabled in Pennsylvania: three generations without legislative guidance are enough. 92 Dick.L.Rev. 409 (1988).

Student searches: leaving probable cause at the schoolhouse gate. [New Jersey v. T.L.O., 105 S.Ct. 733 (1985)] 15 Stetson L.Rev. 465 (1986).

Suspension and expulsion of handicapped children: an overview in light of . . . [Doe v. Maher, 793 F.2d 1470 (9th Cir.1986)]. 14 W.St.U.L.Rev. 341 (1986).

The Burlington decision: a vehicle to enforce free appropriate public education for the handicapped. [Burlington v. Dep't of Education, 105 S.Ct. 1996 (1985)] 19 Akron L.Rev. 311 (1985).

The duty of California counties to provide mental health care for the indigent and homeless. 25 San Diego L.Rev. 197 (1988).

The role of mental health professionals in child custody resolution. 15 Hofstra L.Rev. 115 (1986).

Suspension and Expulsion

Congress, Smith v. Robinson, *and the myth of attorney representation in special education hearings: is attorney representation desirable?* 37 Syracuse L.Rev. 1161 (1987).

Suspension and Expulsion (continued)

Hartog-Rapp, Fay. *The legal standards for determining the relationship between a child's handicapping condition and misconduct charged in a school disciplinary proceeding.* 1985 S.Ill. U.L.Rev. 243.

Suspension and expulsion of handicapped children: an overview in light of . . . [Doe v. Maher, 793 F.2d 1470 (9th Cir.1986)]. 14 W.St.U.L.Rev. 341 (1986).

INDEX

Use the attached order cards to order your own or extra copies of **HANDICAPPED STUDENTS AND SPECIAL EDUCATION.**

Faculty lounge? Orientation workshops? School library? Your own office? Board members?

Order extra copies of **HANDICAPPED STUDENTS AND SPECIAL EDUCATION** now. The attached cards may be removed from the book for your order.

Please send me _______ copies of **HANDICAPPED STUDENTS AND SPECIAL EDUCATION,** Fifth Edition, at $67.50 per copy. Add $2.50 postage and handling. Total $70.00.

Name ____

Title ____

Address ____

City ______________________ **State** _____ **Zip** __________

Purchase Order Number, if needed ______________________

Send order and check payable to: DATA RESEARCH, INC.,
P.O. BOX 490, ROSEMOUNT, MN 55068

Please send me _______ copies of **HANDICAPPED STUDENTS AND SPECIAL EDUCATION,** Fifth Edition, at $67.50 per copy. Add $2.50 postage and handling. Total $70.00.

Name ____

Title ____

Address ____

City ______________________ **State** _____ **Zip** __________

Purchase Order Number, if needed ______________________

Send order and check payable to: DATA RESEARCH, INC.,
P.O. BOX 490, ROSEMOUNT, MN 55068

OUR GUARANTEE: If you are not satisfied with **HANDICAPPED STUDENTS AND SPECIAL EDUCATION,** for any reason, we'll refund your money.